SHAW & JOYCE

The Florida James Joyce Series

The Florida James Joyce Series
Edited by Bernard Benstock

*The Autobiographical Novel of Co-Consciousness:
Goncharov, Woolf, and Joyce,* by Galya Diment (1994).
Shaw and Joyce: "The Last Word in Stolentelling,"
by Martha Fodaski Black (1995).
Bloom's Old Sweet Song: Essays on Joyce and Music, by Zack Bowen (1995).

SHAW AND JOYCE

"The Last Word in Stolentelling"

Martha Fodaski Black

University Press of Florida
Gainesville/Tallahassee/Tampa/Boca Raton
Pensacola/Orlando/Miami/Jacksonville

Copyright 1995 by the Board of
Regents of the State of Florida
Printed in the United States
of America on acid-free paper
All rights reserved

00 99 98 97 96 95 6 5 4 3 2 1

Library of Congress Cataloging-in-Publication Data

Black, Martha Fodaski.
Shaw and Joyce : "the last word in
stolentelling" / Martha Fodaski Black.
p. cm.—(Florida James Joyce series)
Includes bibliographical references and index.
ISBN 0-8130-1328-3 (alk. paper)
1. Joyce, James, 1882-1941—Knowledge—
Literature. 2. Shaw, Bernard, 1856-1950—
Influence. 3. Influence (Literary, artistic, etc.)
4. Ireland—In literature. I. Title. II. Series.
PR6019.09Z52596 1994
823'.912—dc20   94-27516

The University Press of Florida is the scholarly
publishing agency for the State University System of
Florida, comprised of Florida A & M University,
Florida Atlantic University, Florida International
University, Florida State University, University of
Central Florida, University of Florida, University of
North Florida, University of South Florida, and
University of West Florida.

University Press of Florida
15 Northwest 15th Street
Gainesville, FL 32611

To Nick, Kira, Colin, and Jeremy,
who may one day go on a "photophoric"
pilgrimage through the "funferal"
fictions of Joyce and the "gumpowered"
plays of Shaw,
guided by the "arclight"
of their Matya's book.
And to their "Bopop," sadly waked within the wake.

Contents

Foreword, by Bernard Benstock   ix
Preface   xi
Abbreviations   xv

1. The Case for Joyce's "Piously Forged Palimpsests" of "Lamppost Shawe"   1

2. "Sonny" George and "Sunny" Jim: "Frother" and His "Doblinganger"   24

3. The Devil's Disciple and His Great "Immensipater": *Stephen Hero, A Portrait of the Artist as a Young Man,* and *Exiles*   54
    "Fruting for Firstlings"—"A True Covenanter against the World": *Stephen Hero*   56
    A Portrait of the Artist as a Young Shavian: "O Foenix Culprit!"   70
    Carmen in the Drawing-Room: "Annadominant" "Candidatus" in *Exiles*   88

4. Tripartite *Dubliners:* "Circumcivisizing" the Quintessential Dublin   109
    "Yung and Easily Freudened": Dublin Boys   115
    "Lawanorder on Loveinardor": Dublin's Destructive Ideals   131
    "Our Liffeyside People": Philistines in Dublin   155

5. The Great "*Immensipater*" "Retaled" in Bloom & Co.: *Ulysses*   194
    The Credible Androgyne: "Such is Manowife's Lot To Lose and Win Again"   201
    Irish Nationalism: "The Vilest Bogeyer but Most Attractionable Avatar"   210

Fireworks on the Beach: "Sunny, My Gander, He's Coming to Land Her"   216
Bloom-Shavian Politics: "A London's Alderman . . . Ladled Out by the Waggerful to the Regionals of Pigmyland"   222
Bella Bangs Bloom: "The Morbidization of the Modern Mandaboutwoman Type"   235
Molly as Privatized Life Force: "The Bringer of Pluralities Haloed Be Her Eve"   239
Mother, Son, and Hamlet's Father's Ghost: "Anglers or Angelers Coexistent and Compresent with or without Their Tertium Quid"   249

6. Methuselah at the Wake: "Pelagiarist Penman" and "Grand Precurser"   260

"One to Do and One to Dare, Par by Par, a Peerless Pair"   294
Burrus and Caseous: "Unbeaten Risicide" and "Puir Tyron"   308
"Funferal" Fables: "Grimm Gests of Jacko and Esaup"   324
The Mookse and the Gripes: "Corked Father" and "Dubville Brooder-on-Low"   329
The Ondt and the Gracehoper: "Veripatetic Imago" and "Artaloner"   337
Groundbroken Irishmen and "Anonymoses": The Rann of Persse O'Reilly   347
"Jaunty Jaun": The "Brave Footsore" "Unfrillfrocked Quackfriar"   372
H. C. E.: "Poppypap's a Passport Out"   380
"Anna" and the "Crisscouple . . . Crosscomplimentary" "Jined"   394

A Shaun the Postscript: "A Commodius Vicus of Recirculation"   406

Works Cited   419
Index   428

FOREWORD

Bernard Benstock

Few critics prior to Martha Fodaski Black have tackled the slippery subject of the Shaw-Joyce relationship with much penetration or even enthusiasm. It has always been there, more a subject for casual commentary than an actual problem to be taken too seriously: the influence of the older writer on the younger, thought to be marginal at best; the deferential offhandedness with which the younger treated the older; the passing of two Irish ships in the night with but a bare exchange of signal lights when absolutely necessary. Their similarities were obvious—both were Irish; both were rebellious enough to invoke the image of Lucifer; both were in self-imposed exile from Ireland, uncomfortable with the status quo in their native land but almost as uncomfortable when changes somehow managed to occur. Their differences were insurmountable, mostly in their relations in and attitudes toward literary modernism in the first half of the twentieth century. Both were too cagey to put their signatures to it, but they seem to have made an unwritten agreement to disagree on the basics—political commitment and the functions of art.

Where others have been content with dealing within the confines of such generalities, in her brave and ambitious study of the two famed fictioneers Martha Black has been scrupulously discontent, challenging even the most time-honored premises of the Shaw-Joyce relationship from every conceivable angle. Throughout this fiercely titled *"Last Word in Stolentelling"* Black keeps an eye on both of her subjects, moving them kaleidoscopically around each other and against each other, observing carefully as the sparks fly. She looks behind Joyce's "gentlemanly" pose and through the necessary alliance of the two Irishmen against their common enemies and encourages the reader to consider Joyce's sly shadow boxing with his undisclosed rival as a struggle against his influence as well as an attempt to dissuade his associates from noticing his "stolentelling." Black's study exposes Shem the penman, with his wily stratagems as antagonist of the unwitting Shaw, as Shaun the Post. Although Jim Joyce did not engage in overt combat with the pugnacious propagandist, Black—without any qualms about studied objectivity, providing the evidence is there—over and over makes judgment calls about Joyce's borrowings from the Shavian locker room and his contentions with G. B. S.'s pugilistic persona. In revealing Joyce's piracies and parodies of Shaw, Black serves as a sharp-eyed referee for the sly sparring of the Joycean contender and the heavyweight rival who was, for the most part, unaware that Joyce had engaged him in repeated bouts for the Irish title. As the log of those matches, *"The Last Word in Stolentelling"* may be definitive.

PREFACE

Shaw and Joyce: "The Last Word in Stolentelling" had its inception when Sidney Feshbach asked me to give a lecture on Shaw and Joyce at a combined meeting of the New York Shaw and Joyce societies. The audience at the American Irish Historical Society headquarters on Fifth Avenue was large and enthusiastic. Richard Nickson, president of the Shaw Society, wrote, in thanking me, "Next time we'll get you Felt Forum." I knew that I was onto a connection that was of interest to a lot of literate people. Subsequently, after Sid Feshbach provoked me with skepticism, I began to research and write the book—and to lecture on it in various places: the James Joyce Society at New York's Gotham Book Mart; the Wolfe Institute of CUNY; the South Place Ethical Society on Red Lion Square in London; Joyce conferences in Monaco, Vancouver, Miami, Dublin, and Seville; the International Association for the Study of Anglo-Irish Literature in Leiden; the American Conference for Irish Studies at the University of Tulsa; in New York as keynote speaker for the Irish American Historical Society; at the Central New York Conference on Language and Literature in Cortland, New York; at the American Conference for Irish Studies at West Virginia University.

Joyceans at first resisted the idea of the Joyce-Shaw relationship, but some ended up, like Bernard Benstock, Suzette Henke, and Fritz Senn, encouraging me. Thomas Staley read a brief early version of my work and urged me to turn it into a book. Shavian Stanley Weintraub, who had already discerned some of the links, gave me his imprimatur in the Netherlands. Tea in London with Shaw's biographer Michael Holroyd confirmed my belief that such a study as mine might be a genuine contribution to both Shaw and Joyce studies. Joyceans Jolanta Wawrzycka and Marlena Corcoran selected an essay "excerptirpated" from my chapter on *Ulysses*—"The Great 'Immensipater' 'Retaled' in Bloom & Co."—for publication in their forthcoming essay collection, *Gender in Joyce*. The *Ethical Record* in London published a summary of my lecture at Conway Hall in February 1991. A copy of a lecture given at the Seventh Annual Miami Joyce Birthday Conference in January 1993 was published in the *James Joyce Literary Supplement*. After giving my manuscript a judicious and helpful reading, Terence Brown of Trinity College, Dublin, assured me that the work was "impressive," no doubt controversial, but ultimately convincing.

For their interest in my work, I thank the aforementioned audiences and scholars, but most of all I applaud Richard Dietrich and the late, lamented Bernard Benstock, whose readings of my manuscript were supererogatory and invaluable. Benstock saved me, I hope, from Joycean gaffes, and Dietrich steered me away from Shavian howlers. I also want to express my gratitude to a graduate student whom I met in Vancouver, who already knew that Joyce encoded Shaw as "fish" in the *Wake* (I've misplaced his name. Sorry!); my former colleague Professor Emeritus Charles Sleeth, who stood up at the Woolf Institute to say that my reading of the *Wake* was the first sensible one he'd encountered; my colleague Michael Murphy, who let me convince him; CUNY librarians Bill Gargan and Bill Parise; my graduate student Kathy Dolan, who discovered that Joyce was less sexist than some assume, for he used the gender-neutral *person* in referring to his Dubliners; my students who cheered me on at various lectures and presented me with my first copy of Holroyd's biography of Shaw; my students David Katzman and Dodd Williams, who advised me on the hermetical intricacies of downloading computers (almost as daunting to me as the *Wake* may be to them); Wang Chi Wong and Mike McGetrick of Brooklyn College's Computer Center; my mentor George Peck; R. R. for KP, W. W. for B & B, B. I. for ED, and M. D. for TLC. Finally, I thank my friend and colleague Elayne Feldstein, professor of English at York College, CUNY, who read the manuscript as neither a Shavian nor a Joycean but a highly literate lay reader claiming no expertise in Irish literature and, to my delight, deemed it decidedly readable and credible. I hope that other readers will have her experience with my study of Joyce's relationship to the "Red theatrocrat," the Dublin exile and "puraduxed seer" from "Allkey dallkey" who was the "Grand Precurser" and "Hoary Frother" to Sunny Jim.

Abbreviations

References to the following works will be abbreviated and cited parenthetically in the text:

Joyce

CW	*The Critical Writings of James Joyce,* edited by Ellsworth Mason and Richard Ellmann. New York: Viking, 1959.
D	*Dubliners.* New York: Viking, 1976.
FW	*Finnegans Wake.* New York: Viking, 1959.
JJL	*Letters of James Joyce.* 3 vols. Vol. 1 edited by Stuart Gilbert; vols. 2 and 3 edited by Ellmann. New York: Viking, 1957–66.
JJ1	Ellmann, *James Joyce.* New York: Oxford University Press, 1959.
JJ New	Ellmann, *James Joyce.* New and revised edition. New York: Oxford University Press, 1982.
P	*A Portrait of the Artist as a Young Man.* New York: Viking, 1964.
SH	*Stephen Hero,* edited by John J. Slocum and Herbert Cahoon. New York: New Directions, 1963.
U	*Ulysses,* edited by Hans Gabler et al. New York: Random House, 1986.

Shaw

BM	*Back To Methuselah*. London: Penguin, 1987.
BSL	*Bernard Shaw: Collected Letters*. 3 vols., edited by Dan H. Laurence. New York: Viking, 1985.
CP	*The Complete Prefaces*. London: Hamlyn, 1965.
GBS	Archibald Henderson, *George Bernard Shaw: His Life and Works*. Cincinnati: Steward and Kidd, 1911.
H1	Michael Holroyd, *Bernard Shaw: The Search for Love*. New York: Random House, 1988.
H2	Holroyd, *Bernard Shaw: The Pursuit of Power*. New York: Random House, 1989.
H3	Holroyd, *Bernard Shaw: The Lure of Fantasy*. New York: Random House, 1990.
I&R	*Shaw: Interviews and Recollections*, edited by A. M. Gibbs. Iowa City: University of Iowa Press, 1990.
MC	Henderson, *George Bernard Shaw: Man of the Century*. New York: Appleton-Century-Crofts, 1956.
MCE	*Major Critical Essays*. London: Penguin, 1986.
OTN	*Our Theatre in the Nineties. Collected Works*, vol. 11. New York: William H. Wise, 1932.
Plays	*The Complete Plays*. London: Constable, 1931.
PP	Henderson, *Bernard Shaw: Playboy and Prophet*. New York & London: Appleton, 1932.
PS	*The Portable Shaw*, edited by Stanley Weintraub. New York: Penguin, 1986.
SSS	*Sixteen Self Sketches*. London: Constable, 1949.

CHAPTER

The Case for Joyce's "Piously Forged
Palimpsests" of "Lamppost Shawe"

One

THE SUBTITLE of this study, *"The Last Word in Stolentelling,"* is a phrase borrowed from *Finnegans Wake* (424.35), because my book is about literary borrowings of storyteller James Joyce heretofore unexamined in depth—his "stolen-telling" from George Bernard Shaw. Because there can be no last word on Joyce, this study does not pretend to be the final assessment of his sources, but as one of the latest, it hopes to clear passageways between the writings of Shaw and Joyce and to invite further investigation and reading of both Irishmen. Although I began this investigation in Cartesian doubt, studying the primary evidence brought me to the single assumption upon which my reading of Shaw and Joyce is based—that the connection is real and binding, often linked directly to *Stephen Hero* (1944); subtextually to *A Portrait of the Artist as a Young Man* (1916); dialogically to *Dubliners* (1914), *Exiles* (1918), and *Ulysses* (1922); and often intertextually in the flagrant shamantics of *Finnegans Wake* (1939). Indeed, the penman's artistic development paralleled the playwright's, moving, as Martin Meisel writes of Shaw, from "early realism to late Extravaganza, with remote and fanciful settings, universal concerns, and associations with fairy tale, fable, and parable" (38). Joyce declared his difference, however, by internalizing his late extravaganzas and exploiting their sexual possibilities. Examining Joyce's development in the arc light of Shaw, my study offers the circumstantial and internal evidence in both writers that justifies its thesis.

Because the methods of the two Irishmen appear to be almost antipathetical, my assumption may seem audacious, especially to Joyceans who have studied the artistry and the linguistic and structural complexities of Joyce's fiction without particular consideration of their relationship to their historical and specifically Irish context. Students of Joyce's Irish connections tend, like George Watson, to believe that Shaw, having settled in England (but also having married an Irish heiress), forgot his Irish background (161). Joyce himself detoured his readers from examining his apposition to Shaw by lumping him with Sheridan, Goldsmith, and Wilde as "court jesters to the English" (CW 20). In his preface to *Plays Unpleasant* (1898), Shaw had, in fact, called himself a court jester (171). From the start of his career in London, however, the journalist, as Joyce no doubt knew, persistently addressed Irish issues in essays such as "The Making of the Irish Nation" (1886), "The Tories and Ireland" (1888), "A Crib for Home Rulers" (1888), "The Parnell Forger" (1889), and "Shall Parnell Go?" (1890) (see *The Matter with Ireland*). He never ceased to declare that he was an Irishman. His 1896 review of a performance of Dion Boucicault's *The Colleen Bawn* was entitled "Dear Harp of My Country." Two of his plays—*John Bull's Other Island* (1904) and *O'Flaherty V. C.* (1917)—analyze the Irish situation. He argued vociferously for home rule and set "The Tragedy of an Elderly Gentleman," the fourth play in his "Pentateuch," *Back to Methuselah* (1921), on Galway Bay. In 1912 he declared, "I am pure Dublin" (H2 5). In *The Adventures of the Black Girl in Her Search for God* (1932), the god the black girl finds is a red-headed Irishman. Even when Shaw clowned in front of the English, he let them know that he was performing in the role of the indispensable Irish opposition. Nevertheless, because of his permanent "exile" in England, students of Irish literature have often left him out, just as scholars have omitted him in their considerations of Joyce.

Joyce's rich and complex prose also seems to attract a different sort of reader from the audiences of Shaw. The notorious Joyce styles may have been, in part, a retort to a Shaw challenge, for in the preface to *Man and Superman,* Shaw insisted that, although "effectiveness of assertion is the alpha and omega of style . . . a true original style is never achieved for its own sake: a man will not pay with his whole life and soul to become a mere virtuoso in literature" (CP 165). As proof of Shaw's error, Joyce has become the darling of textual researchers, while interest in Shaw's life and opinions has perhaps overshadowed admiration of his plays, even though they continue to delight theater audiences.

On the basis of the received wisdom, students of Shaw and Joyce may think that the literary world is bifurcated between Shavians and Joyceans and that mating the two Irishmen is like mixing oranges and avocados—or, better still, as Joyce put it in the *Wake,* "orange peelers and green goaters" (522.16–17) (borrowed, it seems, from the Irish ballad, "The Peeler and the Goat"). Shaw's ancestors were admittedly followers of William of Orange, Protestants who defeated the Irish at the Battle of the Boyne in 1690 and (once more) annexed Ireland. An Anglo-Irishman living in England, Shaw took on the job of watchdog of the Irish and gadfly of the English. As he grew older, he may have seemed to Joyce to be a law-and-order man like the members of prime minister Robert Peel's constabulary, called after their founder "bobbies" in England but "peelers" in Ireland. A "green goater," the lapsed Irish Catholic Joyce, from the start castigating himself for the sin of lechery while reveling in it, was green-eyed in his envy of the older Irishman. Not only did Joyce preempt the Orangeman, but he also made the "little green place," Ireland, synonymous with himself. Always interested in the binary opposition of Anglo-Irishman and "native" Celt, however, Joyce recognized in Shaw the Other in his Irish heritage as well as in his literary method.

As avid newspaper reader, Joyce must also have recognized Shaw as a major figure in the popular culture that fascinated him. Shavian pronouncements frequently appeared in the press, on the radio, and in the cinema in early talkie newsreels. Following G. B. S.'s career becomes almost a study of the media, for in Joyce's time Shaw was a public hero, a leprechaun with a forked tongue, perhaps the leading public personality of his age. Highly visible in print and on the stage, he was photographed, caricatured, painted, and sculpted by his peers. His voice became familiar on radio, and when films and television became major dispensers of popular culture, Shaw's hoary-headed image in cap and knickerbockers was enshrined. As Dan Laurence clarifies, "Every word he uttered, every move he made was deemed worthy of mention in every newspaper in the world—except, of course, *The Times* of London" (BSL

1:6). In spite of his own notorious isolation in "silence, exile and cunning," Joyce could not have avoided recognizing his fellow expatriate as his opposite and, at the same time, his equal in ambition, in spite of the differences in their circumstances and styles.

Whereas Shaw's writing is often discursive and digressive and his plays are sometimes interminably talky, Joyce's carefully honed prose is fertile ground for literary archaeologists who delight in delving into the Talmudic intricacies of texts. Shaw's prose does not demand or repay the hermeneutic exegesis under which Joycean texts often deliver up treasure. Despite his persistent attacks on nineteenth-century theater and mores, Shaw's writings are in many respects a carryover from the phallocentric prose of the nineteenth century, aiming to provoke thought and discussion through clarity of expression. Furthermore, his left-of-center ideas were not consonant with the cultural elitism of modernists like Pound and Eliot who supported Joyce's experimental art. Some of the obscurity of *Ulysses* and *Finnegans Wake* probably derives from Joyce's opportunistic need to hide his interest in his fellow Irishman from his avant-garde boosters, for Joyce, whose real sympathies were Shavian, often buried Shaw's ideas in the subtexts of his work. In my digging I kept coming up with shards of Shaw. Hence this book to share my discoveries.

My analysis does not purport to replace any of the judicious Joyce and Shaw scholarship already available, but it opens some of the valves of our attention to Shaw's relevance and presence in Joyce's fiction as a precursor. Central to my thesis is my belief that Joyce's work is always grounded in his life and in the people who were important to him, even if their importance—as in Shaw's case—developed mainly in the life of his imagination. Despite its resistance to closure, Joyce's prose, even in the *Wake,* is not merely self-referential. In full agreement with Camille Paglia on at least one issue, I assume that modern French critics, in their anxiety to insist upon the linguistic independence of literary texts, often overlook or deny the fact that, as Paglia puts it, there is a "person behind a text" (34). My reconstruction of the *Wake* asserts, indeed, that two major persons (among many others of lesser importance) inform the text—Shaw and Joyce himself. In doing some of Finnegan's plumbing work, I hope to put the *Wake* in working order for readers put off by the literary debris that seems to clog its pipes. My work is aimed at contributing to a renewal and *ricorso* in *Wake* studies that will make its structural maze, its humor, and its implications accessible to readers who are not specialists in structuralism, deconstruction, manuscript analysis, or any of the critical *isms*. Therefore, my methods are eclectic. Not dictated by the intention to make Joyce's works serve any single critical theory, my analyses take their cues from the lives and works of the two authors. I also hope to shine Shaw's tarnished halo by indicating his relevance to the acknowledged master of modernist fiction. To highlight the dialogic relationship between the two great fictioneers, I stress the connections between the standard Joyce texts and Shaw's social commentary, criticism, prefaces, and plays.

As Joyce scholarship demonstrates, the consummate craftsman got his ideas from many sources, but *"The Last Word in Stolentelling"* will show that the instigations and corroborations that Joyce found in Shaw were especially cogent support for the younger writer's early protestant revolts against institutions and Irish society. Although Joyce absorbed the climate of his time by osmosis through a particularly thin and sensitive skin (as Shaw did), he avidly read whatever literature supported his inclinations and incorporated and transformed his education, Catholic and otherwise, into his art. As a significant part of Joyce's subversive, unorthodox self-education, Shaw seems to have piqued the younger writer's interest because he too was a Dublin exile, Joyce's opposite as iconoclastic Protestant and polemicist, and a dissatisfied Irishman who had succeeded in his literary ambitions. Only one among a plethora of sources, the insurgent Shaw, who was twenty-six when Joyce was born, qualified uniquely to be the literary father whom Joyce would invent and surpass and with whom, in his literary aspirations, he was consubstantial. But, as Harold Bloom put it in *The Anxiety of Influence,* he "swerved" away from the Great Original to define himself through style.

Except in his undergraduate efforts at University College, Dublin, shortly after reading *The Quintessence of Ibsenism,* Joyce scrupulously rejected Shaw's confrontational style except to parody it. But the germs of Joyce's themes are in the polemics, prefaces, and plays of the famous Fabian. At first attracted to Shaw's insurrections, the expedient Joyce carried on a sub-rosa dialogue with Shaw, provoked by his arguments and—it can be said in defense of Joyce's artistic autonomy—skeptical regarding Shaw's use of literature as propaganda. Nevertheless, in G. B. S.'s apocryphal arguments the younger Dubliner seems to have found many of his own forming attitudes articulated. Shaw prompted the artist to be immoral when it served his creative needs. In response to the question "Who is God?" he asserted that "I am God . . . advancing toward completion" (MC 582); divinity is "a mysterious drive towards greater power over our circumstances and deeper understanding of Nature" (SSS 78). However, it is doubtful that the social activist who located the divine spark in himself ever sat, like the artist god whom Stephen Dedalus imagines, paring his fingernails over his creations. Citing Lucifer, Prometheus, and Siegfried as mythic models for rebellion against patriarchal powers, the "diabolonian" (see CP 744) Shaw disapproved of the assumption that the man is father of the child and avowed that the artist is self-created. He argued that to achieve freedom for the god within, one must repudiate all constricting duties to nation, religion, and family (a "humbug"), "flinging duty and religion, convention and parental authority, to the winds" (MCE 332). In urging daring rebellion as the path to artistic self-realization and scorning self-sacrifice to ideals of fatherhood, family, literary nationalism, repressive religion, and romantic love, Shaw prefigured Joyce.

Stephen Hero (what we have of it) and *A Portrait of the Artist as a Young Man* follow Shaw's prescription for becoming an artist. *Dubliners* illustrates the Shavian paradigm of society based on a majority of spiritually dead philistines blindly obedient to the so-called ideals of its institutions; of "idealists" with vested interests or insubstantial illusions who propound their chosen ideals, although themselves often deluded about them or incapable of realizing them; and of the solitary, budding "realist" who grows by discovering the folly of constraining cultural illusions (see MCE 48–50). In 1896 Shaw announced himself ready "to help in the saving work of reducing the sham Ireland of romance to a heap of unsightly ruins" (PS 114). In 1898 he wrote a magazine article perhaps inspired by pressure from Yeats, who chaired a convention in London to raise a monument for Wolfe Tone—itself a protest against Queen Victoria's 1897 Jubilee visit to Ireland. In the essay Shaw repudiated the romantic nationalism that inspired Yeats to write *Cathleen ni Houlihan* a few years later:

> Only the other day it was proposed to me that I should help to uplift my downtrodden country by assembling with other Irishmen to romance about 1798 [the year of the rebellion led by Wolfe Tone]. I do not take the slightest interest in 1798. Until Irishmen

apply themselves seriously to what the condition of Ireland is to be in 1998 they will get very little patriotism out of
yours sincerely,
G. Bernard Shaw (SSS 47)

Shortly afterward, in "The Day of the Rabblement" (1901), Joyce denounced the "deliberate self-deception" of the Irish Literary Theatre, "shy of presenting Ibsen, Tolstoy or Hauptman" (CW 70). The newly converted Ibsenite, following the party line of the most famous one, G. B. S., criticized the Irish literary movement for surrendering to the "trolls" (CW 71). The messages of *John Bull's Other Island* and later *O'Flaherty V. C.* corroborated and spurred Joyce's response to Irish nationalism, to Yeats's Celtic Twilight movement, and to the Irish. Emulating Shaw's rejection of romantic nationalism in the preface of *John Bull's Other Island,* Joyce satirized Guinness patriots in *Ulysses*. In the same work he adopted Shaw's vocabulary for gender, tested and parodied his ideas regarding androgyny, and borrowed his socialism and ethics in depicting Bloom and Bloom's fantasies. Joyce mined Shaw for theories but, except in *Exiles,* which is influenced by *Candida* in both form and content, diverged from the dramatist in practice. Of course, what he did with the Shavian raw materials makes all of the difference.

Joyce's ambivalent relationship to Ireland matched Shaw's. In 1896 the older Irishman announced that he had gotten out of Ireland "as soon as I possibly could and I cannot say that I have the smallest intention of settling there again" (PS 114). In the preface to *John Bull's Other Island* he advised Irishmen to leave their homeland to pursue their professional goals. To the "quaint . . . Gaelic" movement (CP 457), Shaw preferred cosmopolitan art and internationalist political commitment. He noted in his 1896 review of a production of Boucicault's *The Colleen Bawn* and reiterated in his preface to his first Irish play the Irish "national genius for treachery" (PS 113), which was to become a major Joycean theme. Shaw anticipated Joyce by analyzing the collusion of the Roman Catholic Church in Ireland with the British Empire in keeping Ireland poor and servile.

Although Joyce managed to persuade even a fellow Irishman like Seamus Deane that "he is an author without native predecessors," one who "abjured the possibility of being influenced by any other Irish writer" ("Joyce the Irishman" 41), Joyce's artistic independence derives in part from his need to cover up his indebtedness to Shaw. In addition to urging escape from duty to church and state, G. B. S. impugned education that conserved outmoded values, because it indoctrinated and prejudiced the student. Like the young artist who vividly described a humiliating pandybatting, Shaw opposed corporal punishment in schools and elsewhere. He rejected marriage and supported free love. His literary competition with Shakespeare prefigures Joyce's. The total of Shaw's early attitudes, packaged in his public pronouncements, offered a model that Joyce replicated. Joyce's works indicate that he had only one dispute with Shavian theory—and that important quarrel concerned the aims of art. He veered away from his secret mentor because of his own predilection but also perhaps because of his fear of being discovered as a Shavian disciple. If we can trust his statements regarding his intentions in *Dubliners,* however, at the start of his writing career even his artistic aims paralleled Shaw's: his stories had the didactic purpose of creating "conscience" in his race. Nevertheless, in the area of aesthetics, young Joyce set out from the start to distinguish himself from his unacknowledged preceptor. While its author admits at the outset radical differences in the two Dublin geniuses in method (except in *Exiles* and, in some ways, in *Finnegans Wake*) and in aims (except in *Dubliners*), the book that you are about to read examines Shavian theory as it appears in Joycean praxis.

Both Irishmen were syncretic thinkers who borrowed their ideas from others. But, unlike Joyce, Shaw was among the most honest literary men, the first to admit his sources. Some of G. B. S.'s contemporary mentors, like Samuel Butler and Henri Bergson, were indeed annoyed at the simplifications made by their enthusiastic disciple (see I&R 273–74), but Shaw fearlessly acknowledged their influence. Charged with plagiarism for stealing the plot of *Pygmalion* from Smollett's *Peregrine Pickle,* the playwright wrote, "Like Shakespeare and Molière I take my good things where I find them, giving them a fresh setting, a Shavian philosophy and a modern meaning. I believe it has been remarked that there is nothing new under the sun, and I dare say that Smollett pinched this idea from someone else" (*Bernard Shaw: Selection of His Wit and Wisdom* 234). Joyce, on the other hand, rarely attributed sources, especially if they were living. He obviated the problem by burying his Shavian ideas in his texts and never adverting to Shaw (or any other important contemporary) as an antecedent. Shaw was, nonetheless, the subject of many Joycean remarks, mostly critical and rivalrous, and of many conversations in Paris (Lyons 126). The clever penman was secretive regarding the influence of his literary peers and, in the case of Shaw, he studiously evaded admitting indebtedness, perhaps because the debt was so great and the potential for embarrassment so real, especially with supporters like Pound, who despised Shaw. Priding himself on his originality, he revealed his neoteric adaptations of thinkers long dead, like Aristotle, Aquinas, Bruno, and Vico, and pointed to his use of Homer in *Ulysses* but did not admit indebtedness to strong coevals. Indeed, Joyce informed W. B. Yeats that the poet was too old to be the recipient of his beneficent influence.

Shaw was not, of course, the only contemporary who influenced Joyce, but he is a considerable and overlooked precursor. Because G. B. S., according to Harold Bloom's hostile assessment, "essentially popularized the concepts and images of others" (*Modern Critical Views* 1), the presence of Shavian ideas in Joyce's fiction could have derived from many other sources. As C. E. M. Joad's study of Shaw clarifies, however, because Shaw gave persistent, witty, and iconoclastic arguments for the heterodoxies of the late nineteenth and early twentieth centuries, he was a hero to a generation of young intellectuals rebelling against Victorianism. Even more important, from Joyce's point of view, he was a clever Dublin expatriate who had succeeded by acting out his own subversive dicta. These facts, as well as Joyce's notorious secrecy and his lack of originality in the realm of ideas—despite his revolutionary accomplishments in challenging the linear, phallocentric fictional style—prompted my literary detective work in Shaviana and the texts of the two writers.

In life and in his writing, Joyce tried to lead his admirers astray. When he valued living writers, they were likely to be minor figures like Edouard Dujardin, Italo Svevo, and James Stephens, who were in no way competitors. Drawn irresistibly to everything Irish, Joyce was fascinated by the coincidences that James Stephens's name combined his own first name and that of his alter ego Stephen Dedalus and that (Joyce believed) Stephens was born on the same day as he was, February 2, 1882 (JJ1 605). Joyce had a "complex notion of 'coincidence' as convergence" (Sandulescu 12). Imagine how he must have felt when he realized, as Arland Ussher points out, that he and Shaw were "in fact namesakes. Shaw is the Scottish translation of the Gaelic Seogh (Joyce)"

(24). In 1923 Joyce revealed to Harriet Weaver that he was well aware of the Gaelic transposition of *j* into *sh*. He mentioned in a letter "the odd coincidence of having sent her a picture of an epicene professor of history in an Irish university college seated in a hospice for the dying" and receiving on the same day a Dublin paper with news of the death of an "old schoolfellow" named Sheehy: "More strangely still his name . . . he used to say, was an Irish [Celtic] variant of my own. . . . It is as usual rather uncanny" (JJ1 205). Moreover, a letter to Valery Larbaud (July 28, 1924) underscores Joyce's awareness of "the Irish phonetic system" (JJ1 217).

Furthermore, the coincidences that Joyce's son Giorgio was born on July 27, 1905, a day after Shaw's birthday, and that his daughter Lucia was born on July 26, Shaw's birthday, could not have escaped Joyce. In a letter to Harriet Weaver concerning his superstitious insistence that *Ulysses* be published on his birthday, Joyce admitted the importance of the "coincidence . . . of birthdays" (JJL 1:178). Before Giorgio's birth, Joyce had picked out male and female names for the child whom Nora Barnacle was carrying. The names were those of Shaw and his sister—George and Lucy. He probably believed that Shaw was celebrating his birthday when his children were born, for G. B. S.'s life had become publicly known by the first decade of this century. If in the unlikely event that he was unaware of the date of Shaw's birth and named his son for his dead brother George (as Joyce's biographer Richard Ellmann asserts he did), the coincidence that Giorgio shared his name with G. B. S. was probably fortuitous to Joyce. When he named Lucia (a light-bringer like Luciferian Shaw), he was no doubt fully aware that Shaw's mother's name was Lucinda, for in Dublin she had been a noted amateur mezzo soprano. Shaw's background was publicized in the 1890s when Joyce was coming of age. If he did not know the biographical details regarding the author of *The Quintessence of Ibsenism* (1891), he could have confirmed them in 1911 when Archibald Henderson's first Shaw biography appeared. In any case, coincidences impressed the superstitious Joyce as uncanny, and he liked to make words work overtime. Thus he had many instigations to feel related to Shaw besides being an artist and self-exiled Dubliner whose apostasy was supported by Shavian theory. The initial reasons can be found in Shaw's writings.

The Quintessence of Ibsenism must have been an astonishing epiphany for young Joyce—a prod to and revelation, corroboration, and support of the teenager's insurgent individualism and compelling need to reject duty to the conventional moralities of his dysfunctional family, his repressive religion, and his demoralized country. Readers who may ask whether Joyce read Shaw because he had socialist and artistic leanings or whether he had socialist and artistic leanings because he read Shaw should remember that the impressionable Joyce read *The Quintessence of Ibsenism* while he was still a young student. It put into words the vindication of instinctual rebellions that the adolescent may not have yet articulated. Surely Shaw's pamphlet spurred Joyce's interest in Ibsen, an enthusiasm facilitated by the translations of Shaw's mentor and collaborator, William Archer, with whom Joyce corresponded for three years at the turn of the century when Archer was Shaw's close friend. Although Ellmann credits the young man with studying Dano-Norwegian so that he could read Ibsen in the original, the biographer overlooks Joyce's awareness of Shaw's position as the leading Ibsenite in the English-speaking world—an Ibsenite with the additional appeal of being Irish. Ellmann is, of course, reporting the facts, for from the start Joyce downplayed the importance of Shaw to his life and vocation.

The coverup of his discipleship began early. In his first publication, at age eighteen, a review of Ibsen's *When We Dead Awaken* (1900), Joyce borrowed the epithet "muck-ferreting dog" from *The Quintessence of Ibsenism,* misreading it as applied to Ibsen instead of to his admirer and not attributing his Shavian source, whom he called an "English" critic (CW 48). Actually, the "English" critic was Shaw, who included in *The Quintessence* "Gibberings" extracted by his friend Archer from critical reviews of *Ghosts* (MCE 94). Critics who disapproved of Ibsen were even more critical of his Irish champion. Joyce's cunning practice of "stolentelling" from Shaw began, thus, in his first published essay.

Ellmann reports that in 1904 Joyce was flirting with both socialism and Nietzsche but concludes that "at heart Joyce can scarcely have been a Nietzschean any more than he was a socialist" (JJ1 147). Joyce was neither because he was a covert follower of his fellow Dubliner, whose writing preached to the receptive, impoverished young man the necessity of the redistribution of wealth while also advocating the superman. Shaw's tracts of the 1890s on Ibsen, Wagner, and the high calling of the literary artist, as well as *The Devil's Disciple* (1898), anticipate Joyce's politics and the credo of Stephen Dedalus: "I will not serve" (P 203). G. B. S.'s odd coupling of socialist and superman, debated in

Man and Superman and its preface, was published in 1903 and performed in London in 1905. Like Shaw's, Joyce's first works, as Cixous says, "are polemic, and stake out a lucid and sometimes violent personal opposition to the accepted intellectual solutions" (163).

At the start of his career Joyce considered himself to be a socialist artist: Cixous points out that "he explains this several times and again later in May 1905" while defending his resolve not to marry Nora Barnacle (52). As Bonnie Kime Scott notes, "Edwardian ideologues like George Bernard Shaw and H. G. Wells" had attacked the institution of marriage (172). In the preface to *The Philanderer* (1898), Shaw provided a rationale for Joyce's behavior. The Fabian superman opposed "the grotesque sexual compacts made between men and women under marriage laws which represent . . . an institution which society has outgrown but not modified, and which 'advanced' individuals are therefore forced to evade" (CP 726). The preface to *Man and Superman* calls marriage an "overrated institution" (CP 169). Introduced by a lengthy discussion of matrimony, *Getting Married* (1908) dramatizes the Shavian debate. In telling Nora that his "mind rejects the whole present social order and Christianity—the home, the recognized virtues, classes of life, and religious doctrines" (JJL 2:50), Joyce did not mention that he was summarizing the position of the most outspoken Irish proponent of such politics. Like Shaw before him, Joyce believed that the artist must "free himself from the unfortunate influence" of "the idols of the marketplace . . . that corrupt him from without and within" (CW 185). Joyce had, however, been corrupted within by one of society's ego ideals—the desire to win. In his covert competition with the older Irishman, his pride and his need of the approval of literary elitists who esteemed his originality seem to have prompted him to hide his intellectual indebtedness. My study therefore relies more on the connections between internal evidence in Joyce's work and Shavian theory than on the evidence in Joyce's letters. The works themselves reveal that Joyce's "silence, exile, and cunning" camouflage connections to Shaw. This study uncovers the appropriations.

Joyce's unwitting brother Stanislaus and Joyce himself are the primary culprits in the writer's devious plot to avoid acknowledging Shaw's importance to him. For Joyce, the need for cunning may have arisen when Ezra Pound became his mentor, for Pound scorned the politics and art of Shaw. Eager to get published after years of difficulty with Shaw's publisher, Grant Richards, and with the publisher George Roberts in Dublin, the tyro was no doubt grateful and willing to take support and praise where he found them. But, as Joseph Kelly writes, "Pound deirished Joyce's reputation, and, in the process, stripped his early fiction of its political force" ("Pound's Joyce" 22). His open disdain for Shaw, with whom Joyce secretly identified, must have cautioned the younger Irishman not to defend the older one, even though their agendas, political and artistic, were very much the same when Joyce met the exiled American Imagist bent on making other artists accept his credos. The militant aestheticism of the editor of the *Egoist*, who loudly defended art without social purpose, no doubt influenced Joyce to remain silent about his Shavian enthusiasms and his aim, as Seamus Deane puts it, "to have the effect of a missionary" ("Joyce the Irishman" 41).

Stanislaus's motives for covering up the Shaw factor were different. As Kelly has substantiated, Stanislaus was an unreliable source of information about his brother ("Pound's Joyce"). In the early years, when Stanislaus was James's confidant, Joyce filled the pages of *Stephen Hero*, his first attempt at writing a novel, with Shavian vocabulary and ideas. When Stanislaus reported in *My Brother's Keeper* that James became aware that he had been "deluded by ideals that exacted all his service, 'the big words that make us so unhappy,' as he called them" (53), he apparently did not know that James was taking a Shavian position. Shaw's chapter "Ideals and Idealists" in *The Quintessence of Ibsenism* attacks "self conforming" service to the big words for ideals. In emulation of Shaw, whose early problem plays were written in the 1890s, and of Ibsen, Joyce at first thought drama the highest art form. After *The Sanity of Art* in 1895, Shaw's resounding defense of the artist and a retort to Max Nordau's *Degeneration*, which attacked art for art's sake, the teenager began to think of becoming an artist. After *The Perfect Wagnerite* (1898), Shaw's avant-garde defense of Wagner, Joyce became a Wagner fan. He often wrote to his brother defending socialism, but he did not reveal his interest in G. B. S. Instead he told Stanislaus to kick Shaw's "arse" for him, but detoured Stannie from concluding that he had any special interest in Shaw by including G. K. C. (Chesterson, Shaw's friend) and G. R. (Grant Richards, Shaw's publisher) in the list of arses: "Kick in the arse all round" (JJL 2:203).

By the time Stanislaus wrote *My Brother's Keeper* (1958), he was convinced that James had not been interested in socialism or in Shaw. If Ellmann and Cixous are correct in their descriptions of the relationship between the two brothers, James may not have shared his private enthusiasm with Stanislaus because he did not want his hero-worshipping brother to think that he was a follower instead of a leader, a copier rather than an innovator. Stanislaus's complex view of his older brother was necessarily colored by his enabling relationship to James. For example, in 1909, when James and Giorgio went to Dublin, Stanislaus supported Nora and Lucia at home, as well as father and son in Ireland. When James returned to Trieste, he "had no attention to spare for his brother's mutterings" (JJ1 310). Ellmann's biography often reveals James Joyce's protective cunning regarding what really mattered to him. According to Cixous, as early as 1913 James expelled Stanislaus from his world because he no longer needed him (120). After 1915, because he was interned in Austria as a result of World War I, Stanislaus lost contact with the genius, who was gaining notoriety as a writer. When James became the darling of the avant-garde, Stanislaus, who had always styled himself masochistically as James's rescuer and critic, disdained "the intricacies of *Ulysses,* particularly the technical complications" (JJ1 485). The two brothers met only five times after 1919.

Ellmann concludes that after 1920 the brothers were "never close again" (JJ1 496). Upon reading an early installment of "Work in Progress" in 1924, he reports, Stanislaus called it "nebulous, chaotic . . . unspeakably wearisome" (JJ1 589). Nevertheless, although Stanislaus was out of touch with James's aesthetic and intellectual development after 1915, Ellmann endorses and refocuses as truth many of the puritanical rival brother's views of the genius (see Kelly, "Stanislaus Joyce"). He accepts Stanislaus's statement in *My Brother's Keeper,* backed up by interviews with Stanislaus, that Joyce considered Shaw a bad influence on modern theater. Perhaps revealing more about his own taste than Joyce's, Stanislaus wrote in his memoir that Joyce "found the frank vulgarity of the music hall less offensive than the falsity of most of the legitimate drama of his day: Pinero, Sutro, Phillips . . . and, most of all, Shaw" (114). In any case, Ellmann minimizes the implications of Joyce's epistolary encounters with Shaw. He reports Shaw's response to *Ulysses* in a lengthy footnote (JJ1 588), accepting Claud W. Sykes's word that Joyce thought Shaw was a "mountebank" (JJ1 454)—a description that might have actually confirmed Joyce's feelings of kinship with G. B. S. In his preface to *Three Plays for Puritans* (1898), in a section called "On Diabolonian Ethics," Shaw declared that, "like all dramatists and mimes of genuine vocation, I am a natural-born mountebank" (CP 744).

Ellmann's biography, until recently considered to be definitive, emphasizes Joyce's development as an apolitical, detached, autonomous artist. The thrust of his research was no doubt facilitated by Joyce's deviousness, even though Ellmann himself admits that Joyce tended to hide his real influences. Ellmann may also have been put off the scent by Joyce's equivocal relations to his official biographer, Herbert Gorman, to whom Joyce did not mention Shaw except in relation to the evidences of his own talent. Thus Gorman reported Joyce's review of *The Shewing up of Blanco Posnet* (1909), which is a matter of public record. He also wrote that *The Dark Lady of the Sonnets* (1910) and *Mrs. Warren's Profession* (1894) were produced by Joyce's English Players in Zurich in 1918, but, no doubt because Joyce avoided admitting his culpability, Gorman did not mention Joyce's piracy of the plays—an event that cannot be underestimated in terms of its impact on the prodigal son's changing attitudes toward the paternal playwright. Instead Gorman reported of the performance of *Mrs. Warren's Profession* that "such a production was an adventure at the time for the theme [prostitution] of Shaw's play was so delicate that most managers shied away from publicly presenting it" (260). Thus the daring Joyce gets kudos for his bravery.

Critics influenced by Ellmann have thoroughly examined the cosmopolitanism of Joyce's writings, the relationship of his work to Catholicism and to various modes of criticism—New, structuralist, poststructuralist, deconstructionist, neo-Marxist, psychological, feminist, and new historicist. But most have avoided discussing the political context of Joyce's thought, which inexorably leads to links or parallels to Shaw. In *The Exile of James Joyce* (1972), after laying the groundwork for the chapter "Politics as Temptation" (182–204), Cixous mentions Shaw twice, once as a supporter of the idea of the hero as renegade (224) and once as one of the court jesters of the English of whom Joyce disapproved (451). After researching *The Consciousness of Joyce* (1977), Ellmann became aware of the political content of Joyce's library and began to revise his notions about Joyce's exclusive concern with art for its own sake. Nevertheless, he continued to overlook the

Shavian connection, despite having documented the presence in 1920 of many of Shaw's works in Joyce's Trieste library: Fabian tracts, two early Shaw novels—*Cashel Byron's Profession* (1886) and *Love among the Artists* (1887)—and an extensive collection of the prefaced plays: *Mrs. Warren's Profession* (1894), *Widowers' Houses* (1898), *The Philanderer* (1898), *The Devil's Disciple* (1898), *John Bull's Other Island* (1904), *Major Barbara* (1907), *The Shewing up of Blanco Posnet* (1909), *Getting Married* (1910), *The Dark Lady of the Sonnets* (1911), *Fanny's First Play* (1911), and *Misalliance* (1914) (*Conciousness* 127–28).

To qualify the emphasis of his biography, which stresses Joyce's cultural isolation, Ellmann encouraged Dominic Manganiello to write *The Politics of Joyce* (1980). Apparently influenced by his mentor, Manganiello continued to downplay Joyce's relationship to Shaw. Passing over the ties that virtually bind his findings to Shavian connections, he concluded that Joyce was an anarchist, albeit not a violent or committed terrorist who believed in the *Attentat* to get media attention for the disenfranchised. Joyce's nonviolent, individualistic "anarchist" sympathies were, in fact, a clone of Shaw's, which, like Joyce's, did not extend to belief in planting bombs or dismantling governments. In his preface to *Major Barbara* Shaw wrote that "all men are anarchists with regard to laws which are against their consciences, either in the preamble or in the penalty" (CP 135). The pacifist gradualist continued to believe, however, in "the advantages of living in society with laws" (CP 136). Furthermore, although, unlike Shaw, Joyce was not politically active, his admiration for American anarchist Benjamin Tucker echoed Shaw's. It was for his friend Tucker that Shaw wrote an essay on art that probably influenced the adolescent Joyce deeply. At Tucker's request, Shaw wrote *The Sanity of Art* (1895) to defend artists, thereby continuing to advocate the personal aesthetic freedom that he championed in *The Quintessence of Ibsenism,* a little book that Ellmann admits Joyce read. He disregards, however, its profound influence on Joyce, concluding instead that the young man's interest in Ibsen stemmed from his "spirit of wayward boyish beauty" (JJ1 55). Thus Ellmann hints that Joyce was an artist more like Shaw's Marchbanks in *Candida* than the artist whom current reevaluations give a less waifish portrait. The revised edition of his biography (1982) continues to marginalize Shaw's relationship to Joyce.

Although much Joyce criticism, influenced by Ellmann, reinforces the impression that the jejeune Jesuit was a recluse who rejected the "nightmare of history" and that his self-reflexive writing, even *Dubliners*, might best be studied without regard to historical context (even though most concede that a map of Dublin helps), many Joyce scholars touch upon Shaw in passing, whereas others, like Michael Patrick Gillespie, who promises to "pay close attention to associations with . . . [Joyce's] antecedents" (200), ignore him. William York Tindall remarks on the similarities between *Candida* and *Exiles* (108–9), and Rhoda B. Nathan points out the remarkable parallels in an article that does not, however, argue that Shaw's play influenced *Exiles*. On a more general note, Marvin Magalaner and Richard M. Kain observe that, "like the clownish antics of Shaw, Joyce's artistic perspectives rest on a dazzling display of paradoxes" (175). Zack Bowen notes that Joyce follows Shaw in his penchant for the comic (84). Seamus Deane is certain that Joyce would have found the quick-witted "linguistic self-consciousness" of the Irish in "its more sophisticated variations in the works of Wilde and Shaw" ("Joyce the Irishman" 42–43). Christopher Butler admits that Joyce "had questioned conventional morality with help of Ibsen and Shaw" (264). Richard Brown avers that Joyce's "portrayal of sexuality has its play in the array of possible contemporary positions alongside the discussion of modern morality in Ibsen and Shaw" (4), whereas Patrick Parrinder notes that "both Joyce and Shaw delighted in Ibsen's courageous exposures of corruption, hypocrisy, the suppression of truth, and the oppression of women in his native country" (24). Robert Scholes prods Joyceans in the directions of Joyce's political persuasions but does not develop the Shavian parallels.

Influenced by Bakhtin, R. B. Kershner notes similarities between the thought of Shaw and Joyce (and between that of Joyce and Havelock Ellis, the sexologist and socialist who was a friend of Shaw) (259) but considers Shavian ideas as part of Joyce's general intellectual milieu, as indeed many of them were. In studying the cultural context out of which Joyce derived his work, Cheryl Herr uses evidence of Shaw's admiration for Edward Royce, the pantomime harlequin to whom Joyce refers in *Ulysses* (118). But since her emphasis is elsewhere, Herr does not pursue the noteworthy Shavian parallels. Many interpreters of Joyce have thus touched on the similarities of the two Irishmen. John Benignus Lyons reports that Robert McAlmon met Joyce almost every night in Paris "for apperitifs" while he was writing *Ulysses.* They talked into the night of "Sir Thomas Browne, not to speak of Ezra Pound and Eliot and [George] Moore and Shaw" (126). One of Joyce's frequent visitors in Paris during the 1920s and '30s, Adolf Hoffmeister, even went so far as to describe Joyce as a "quiet, indulgent, somewhat dreamy Bernard Shaw" (127). Virginia Woolf also noted the resemblance (*Diaries* 2:68). While writing the *Wake,* Joyce may have been aware of the similarities, for in the Parable of the Prankquean he wrote, "Mark the Twy" (alluding simultaneously to Mark Twain and to variants of the brothers Shaun and Sham): "Why do I am alook alike?" (22.5).

Shaw's influence on his "somewhat dreamy" double is perhaps most obvious in his first and last prose works, *Stephen Hero* (the first version of *Portrait*) and *Finnegans Wake.* When Joyce found his own voice in *Dubliners, A Portrait of the Artist as a Young Man,* and *Ulysses,* he assimilated Shavian theory into literary practice almost antipathetical to Shaw's. However, in the *Wake* the kinship and the polarity of the two Irishmen become, I believe, almost an obsession to Joyce. After my epiphanic realization that Joyce's "NIGHTLETTER" (308.21), never sent to Shaw, begins to make sense as a parodic portrait of Shaw, I overcame my resistance to the "Allmaziful" text by admitting that G. B. S. is a major presence at the wake. Extrapolating from the definite allusions to Shaw (insomuch as anything is clear in the murky nightworld of Joyce's subconscious), I realized that the complex, multiplayered puns make perverse comic sense when one discovers that Shaw is often cloaked in them and that the character of Shaun and the Shaun side of the father, H. C. E., combined with other figures from myth, history, and Joyce's life, is a portrait of the polemical artist as a young/old man interfused with a portrait of the penman as his conscience-stricken, lascivious rival and kinsman. Considering that Shaw was the subject and model of many other artists such as Rodin, Jacob Epstein, and Augustus John, of caricaturists like Max Beerbohm and obliging biographers like Archibald Henderson, Frank Harris, and St. John Ervine, it seems that Joyce, having covertly turned to Shaw throughout his career, competed in the *Wake* with other artists and writers, making a kaleidoscopic portrait that would outdo them all—especially because he made his decentered subject (like everything else in his "nightynovel" [54.21]) almost unrecognizable. The "incorrigible and continuous actor" G. B. S. had cheerfully discussed his career as a model in his correction to Frank Harris's "Contemporary

Portraits—How Frank Ought to Have Done It" (SSS 123–28); in supervised, so-called authorized biographies by Henderson in 1911 and 1932; and in 1931 in "my autobiography," by Shaw's fellow Irishman Frank Harris—the sex-obsessed biographer who intended to give Shaw not "an inch of credit" more than he deserved—G. B. S. leaves slapstick and caricature "to himself and an army of agile illustrators who have made his sardonic profile world-famous" (xxvi).

Shaw's second sex-obsessed biographer, Joyce, devised a decidedly unauthorized slapstick portrait, "circumveiloped by obscuritads" (FW 244.15). From the Joycean collage emerges a pattern of Oedipal rebellion against Shaw as surrogate father—one who was chosen, unlike John Joyce; sibling rivalry with the fraternal writer who was a better fantasy competitor, a better comic foil, and a better measure of the grandiosity of Joycean ambitions than his real brother Stanislaus; and "anxiety of influence" that parallels the contours outlined by Harold Bloom. Although their connections were, as Stanley Weintruab observes, slight in the real world (see Weintraub, "Respectful Distance"), in the labyrinth of Joyce's psyche their debates were endless and endlessly obscure. As a young man, Joyce admired "the paradoxical and iconoclastic writer of comedy" for his "lively and talkative spirit" and his courage in fighting censorship, but he eschewed the sermonizing that he found in *The Shewing up of Blanco Posnet* (CW 171, 208), blamed Shaw for the failures of *Exiles* (perhaps secretly sensing that Shaw recognized his thefts from *Candida*), and resented his refusal to support the publication of *Ulysses* or to defend it from plagiarism. Such responses may be those of a "stolenteller," for, according to Thomas Mallon, the plagiarist convinces himself "of his own innocence partly by convincing himself of the other's guilt" (31–32). Thus the borrower is a master of psychological projection.

In his last two psychological novels, Joyce became in extremis a paradoxical and iconoclastic writer of comedy, like Shaw. After he pirated two of Shaw's plays in Zurich, he turned on the old playwright and overreacted to Shavian criticism of *Ulysses*. When his stolentelling was clearly a success, however, even if the *Wake* wasn't, Joyce seems to have privately reconciled himself with the Shavian scapegoat imago. When the "biografiend" (FW 55.6) finished writing his "tale told of Shaun or Shem" (215.35), Shaw was eighty-two and Joyce was fifty-six, but the younger man was feeling as old as Methuselah and as forgiving as the octogenarian had always been with his enemies. In the *ricorso* of the *Wake* and in many of its foreshadowings, Shem/Jim begins to accept his loved/hated paternal brother, after several acts on Shaw's part that may have taken the sting out of Joyce's resentment, among them G. B. S.'s 1926 defense of *Exiles* and, in 1932, an invitation to become an honored member of the newly founded Academy of Irish Letters, of which Shaw was president. The old man's testimonial to Joyce's genius no doubt dispelled Joyce's rivalry and facilitated a resolution of the mocking hostilities of the *Wake*.

In the decentered portraiture and deception of his "nightmaze" (411.8), Joyce covered his tracks effectively through his new approach to language, whose "quashed quotatoes" (183.22) obscure his "doblinganger . . . with a sandy whiskers" (490.17–18). Because the evidence in the *Wake* of Joyce's doblinganger is so compelling, my study expands on its dialogic relationship with Shaw, prompted by the discrete findings of other scholars. In his study *The Books of the Wake* (1960), James S. Atherton cites references to *Man and Superman, Back to Methuselah*, and *Saint Joan* (279). Adaline Glasheen finds in *The Second Census of "Finnegans Wake"* (1963) "many perhaps all" of Shaw's dramatic characters in the *Wake* (236). Stanley Weintraub, while emphasizing the "respectful distance" between the two writers, also notes many Shavian allusions in Joyce's nightbook ("Respectful Distance" 73–74). In his *Annotations to "Finnegans Wake,"* Roland McHugh discovers Shaw references and, notably, identifies a footnote referring to Shaw's phonetic spelling of *fish* (299), part of a network of references to "Old Parr" Shaw, who noted that writing popular novels such as he had written was "the fish stage of your Jonathan Swift" (Harris 95) (he thus identifies himself with Swift, another important component of the *Wake*). Matthew Hodgart observes that Shaw had prefigured Joyce in pointing out the Irish penchant for betrayal (52) and that in the eleventh question of part one, chapter 6 of the *Wake,* the polemical Shaun "holds forth in the style of George Bernard Shaw's prefaces to the plays" (146–47), a fact that Glasheen had observed in calling the Burrus/Caseous skit a "burlesque" of Shaw (*Second Census* 68). Hodgart also notes that "Shem's house is Shaw's *Heartbreak House*" (150) and asserts that "Showting up of Bulsklivism" "refers to *The Shewing up of Blanco Posnet* . . . [and] to a Bolshevik interpretation of 'How Buckley Shot the Russian General'" (144). In a random remark on G. B. S., Bernard

Benstock interprets the "Showting up of Bulsklivism" as a "dig" at Shaw (*Joyce Again's* 46). In documenting Joyce's desire to mold Nora Barnacle into a preferred female image, Mark Shechner refers to the *Wake* line "You cannot make a limousine lady out of a hillman minx" (376.3) as an allusion to *Pygmalion* (75). Thus, as Mary Reynolds, author of *Joyce and Dante,* told me a few years ago when this study was in its infancy, Joyceans have been skirting the Shaw precincts of Joyce's mind for years.

Although the *Wake* resists closure and its strobe-light quality is its indeterminacy, its guessing games take on added significance if the double crostic has possible biographical references, not just those inside the networks of the dreamer's consciousness. All of Joyce's work starts in "objective" reality, even the *Wake,* and all of it has autobiographical overtones and undertones that have the Shavian imprimatur. As Shaw said, "The best autobiographies are confessions: but if a man is a deep writer all his works are confessions" (SSS 19). To retrieve and participate in the comedy of Joyce's linguistic caper, readers not given over wholly to intratextual study privilege themselves and their reading by finding glimpses, shadows, signs, allusions that seem historical or biographical. Joyceans who consider the corpus of his works to be semiautobiographical continue playing hide-and-seek with the *Wake* in an effort to identify the mysterious, slippery Shaun and H. C. E. into whom the dreamer finally melds himself. Shem seems almost universally accepted as a self-portrait of Joyce, but critics differ on the identities of Shaun and H. C. E.

Among the many models offered for Shem's male relatives, some are ludicrous and some tantalizing because Joyce provided multiple and ambiguous clues to tempt readers to penetrate his linguistic disguises. Following Tindall's reasonable assumption that Joyce's characters represent his own family, John Gordon wrote *Finnegans Wake: A Plot Summary* (1986), in which he stresses the presence of Joyce's immediate family. According to Grace Eckley, William Stead is Shaun/H. C. E. Following Ellmann's lead, some critics identify Wyndham Lewis with some of Shaun's avatars. But the main candidate for the rival who is both father and brother in Joyce's "meandertale" (18.22) of Dublin is Irish. Hence tenor John McCormick, politician Eamon De Valera (Manganiello's choice), and political martyr Charles Stewart Parnell have been advanced as possible historical models for Shem's masculine

Other. And doubtless at times Joyce associated these figures with Shem's alter egos. Indeed, Yeats, Wilde, Swift and many other Irish writers—including, among others, Goldsmith, Bishop Berkeley, Edmund Burke, Sheridan, Sterne, Thomas Moore, LeFanu, Maturin, Dion Boucicault, and A. E.—are sprinkled throughout the text, but close reading reveals that on nearly every page there is an allusion to Shaw, who is not only Shem's "Grand Precurser" but also his "hoary frother."

In interweaving his night portrait of himself with his pastiche biography of his rival, Joyce may have been taking up a Shavian dare, for as early as 1898 Shaw had declared, "All autobiographies are lies. I do not mean unconscious, unintentional lies: I mean deliberate lies. No man is bad enough to tell the truth about himself during his lifetime.... And no man is good enough to tell the truth to posterity in a document which he suppresses until there is nobody left alive to contradict him" (SSS 41). In retort, Joyce audaciously told his autobiographical lies but suppressed the identity of his secret literary father by inventing a style that would accommodate his intention to absorb and evade him. In order to expose Joyce's auto/biographical method, I give considerable attention in this book to the *Wake* and its intertextuality with Shavian works, especially *Back to Methuselah* (1921). Because *Finnegans Wake* is not linear, because it subverts syntax, and because its metonymic parts are both synchronic and paranomastic, my method has been to dip my sieve into Joyce's stream of consciousness to strain out from the debris the recognizable broken bits stamped with the Shavian logo. Indeed, in order to suggest the organic unity of the corpus of Joyce's co-optations of Shaw, my chapter titles and most subsection titles are taken from the *Wake*. For the pattern and text of *Finnegans Wake* reveal that it is the subterranean climax and resolution of Joyce's ambivalent altercation with his fraternal father, conjoined with *Back to Methuselah* in much the same way as *Ulysses* relates to the *Odyssey*. In examining Joyce's dialogic relationship to his opposite and double, I hope in *"The Last Word in Stolentelling"* to map the course of Joyce's expropriations and of his secret struggle with his literary progenitor, to retrieve the spoils of his pickpocketing and reveal the forms of his rebellion and aesthetic takeover. Intended to give Shaw the credit out of which moderns have often bilked him, this book is for Shavians and Joyceans alike. It examines Joyce by Shawlight to disclose G. B. S.'s relevance and relationship to Joyce and, while emphasizing the Irish connections of both Dubliners, to make Joyce's fictions, especially *Finnegans Wake,* more accessible to the Joyceophilic lay reader.

Like A. S. Byatt's *Possession*—a detective story about scholarly sleuths possessed by the desire to solve literary mysteries—my book is concerned with the quest to uncover the mysterious links between creative genius and its sources. Furthermore, in an age whose literature and criticism are often nihilistic, an age in which the old bourgeois solutions regarding self-realization through the family romance no longer pertain because families are often even more dysfunctional than those of Shaw and Joyce, the relationship of the two Irishmen may be instructive. Because of Shaw, this book is not just an exercise in literary criticism. It concerns the way in which one man's ideas can shape another's. The curve of Joyce's development as secret sharer with Shaw illustrates that reading can lead toward self-definition and the full exercise of one's talents. Furthermore, if Elaine Showalter is correct in her recent study, *Sexual Anarchy,* our fin de siècle replicates many of the problems that plagued the end of the last century, when Joyce was finding out who he was by studying Shaw, who dared to express his ideas on just about everything. Therefore, *"The Last Word in Stolentelling"* may reveal relevant messages (an unpopular word, but one that studying Shaw has given me the courage to use) from Shaw translated into Joyce's fiction. Although Shaw has been passé among the literati, perhaps because we remember him as a white-bearded, twinkly-eyed leprechaun in a television documentary or because his writing seems too logocentric, his wit and wisdom are as germane to us as they were to Joyce, who was, as some of my readers may be, discomfited by the thought of admitting the value of his incorrigible sallies into the realm of ideas. Although sophisticated Joyceans may not want to admit Shaw's presence in Joyce, my book illustrates his ubiquity in the younger Dubliner, in whose fictions the irrepressible, waggish laughter of G. B. S. turns into parodic tributes that reveal the lessons of the *"Immensipater."*

CHAPTER

"Sonny" George and "Sunny" Jim:
"Frother" and His "Doblinganger"

Two

GIVEN THE fact that the pugnacious Protestant admitted that he wrote to preach and teach and that the wily Catholic served his craft so devoutly that we might call it his only serious ideology, George Bernard Shaw and James Joyce nevertheless had much in common. Even as a teenager being educated by Jesuits, Joyce would have had to be a total solipsist to ignore the notorious playwright and polemicist who was already an infamous iconoclast. The biographical parallels of their childhoods, which the adolescent Joyce could have discovered in newspapers and periodicals, are striking. Furthermore, in his teens Joyce paid more attention to the subversive voices of writers who were not in the curricula of Belvedere College and University College, Dublin, than to his official assignments. In the 1890s, news of the famed subversive expatriate Irishman in London was readily available. From Shaw's own "self sketches" "In the Days of My Youth" (1898) and "Who I Am, and What I Think" (1901), young Joyce could have learned of their similarities. Both started life in the same provincial capital of a part of the British Empire, on the southern strands of Dublin Bay, Shaw in Dalkey and Joyce in Bray, seaside villages within walking distance of one another. Shaw recorded the "happiest hour" of his childhood, when at age ten his mother told him they were " 'going to live on Dalkey hill' " (Winsten,

Days 219). There he became "a prince of the world" of his "own imagination" (BSL 2:714). In later life in London he attributed his optimism to Dalkey: "I am a product of Dalkey's outlook" (H1 28). If Joyce knew that his real father, John Joyce, had as a young man "spent a good deal of time sailing around Dalkey, where his mother had taken a house" (JJ1 14), he probably would have been impressed by the Dalkey connection between his real and his chosen sire. Called Sonny by his family, Shaw was shy and sensitive as a boy. He lived life through imagination and despised the dirty slums of Dublin. Born a generation before James Joyce, "Sonny" George was a lot like "Sunny Jim," as Joyce's parents called him.

Both boys did not have a lot to be sunny about, for they were sons of alcoholics, whose fecklessness made each, as Shaw put it regarding himself, a "downstart" on the social scale. The bibulous misadventures of George Carr Shaw were tempered by a sense of humor that his son believed he inherited, but Sonny Shaw repudiated the paternal behavior patterns—his drinking habits, his irresponsible ineptitude in business, and his passivity toward his wife's suspected adultery with her music teacher. The son learned to prefer the part of Oedipal Don Juan. In his early quest for love, he usually took on the role of George Vandeleur Lee as a third party inveigling his way into the home of a married couple. For Lee moved in with the Shaw family and gave Lucinda Shaw, his most industrious and talented pupil, the use of Torca Cottage in Dalkey, thus allowing Shaw to escape from the gloom of Synge Street and environs in Dublin. Always concerned, like Joyce, about the problem of paternity, Shaw declared that he had three fathers as a boy—his ineffectual sire; the dynamic, mesmeric Lee, whose largesse kept the family solvent; and an irreverent, waggish uncle, Walter.

Joyce, on the other hand, had many surrogate fathers in his intimidating Jesuit teachers, but, like young Shaw, he was ashamed of his father's insolvency and humiliated by his alcoholism. Although John Stanislaus Joyce's amiable habit of drinking with compatriots in Dublin pubs and playing the boozy raconteur embarrassed young Joyce, in spite of his shame he identified with his father. As the favorite in a family of at least eleven children (the number of children that May Joyce bore remains uncertain)—unlike Shaw, who was an only son with two sisters—Joyce despised his father's dereliction but admired his ability to tell a witty story. And although he hated his father's abuse of his mother, he seemed to identify with his father when May Joyce's inflexible morality conflicted with her son's need for the kind of freedom that Shaw's writing championed. Joyce's guilt was compounded by his refusal to comply with his mother's wishes while she lay dying. Because he had left the Church, he would not kneel down and pray by her deathbed.

The young Catholic might have been following the example Shaw described in fiction. In his early novel *An Unsocial Socialist* (1886), the hero refuses to grant his dying wife customary sympathy and later denies her the expected obsequies. Shaw's unconventional childhood had, it seems, prepared him to reject conventional grief, but Joyce suffered remorse of conscience, the "agenbite of inwit" that troubles Stephen Dedalus in *Ulysses*. Such guilt helped him, however, to identify with his abusive father and gave him the excuse for similar drinking habits. Contrarily, Shaw responded to his father's neglect in a very different way—by imitating his mother and the enterprising George Vandeleur Lee. He became a teetotaler and a workaholic. But the social pretensions of both proud young Dubliners were dashed by paternal intemperance. In 1898 Shaw revealed that his father was "an Irish Protestant gentleman of the downstart race of younger sons" whose "every rag of excuse for gentility . . . [was] stripped off by poverty!" (SSS 44–45). Shaw wrote, "I sing my own class: the Shabby Genteel, the Poor relations, the Gentlemen who are No Gentlemen" (CP 659)—"Gentlemen" who, despite the religious differences, were very like John Joyce. For Joyce's father also claimed genteel ancestors—"descent from a distinguished clan of Galway." To atone "for squandering his family's fortune," he had a family coat of arms made and ostentatiously carried it "on his frequent enforced *déménagements*" (JJ1 9). Thus both boys experienced the bitterness of believing that they had noble ancestors and the disillusioning reality of ineffectual fathers.

The mothers of the two geniuses no doubt accounted in part for their different preoccupations and relationships with women. Both Lucinda Shaw and May Joyce had musical talent, but Shaw's mother developed hers under the tutelage of Lee, whom, according to B. C. Rossett (and Demetrius O'Bolger, whose research Shaw squelched), Shaw suspected to be his father (with two Georges in the paternal constellation, he often preferred to call himself Bernard Shaw). Nevertheless, music was the great liberating force of his childhood. The musical rehearsals and soirees in the Shaw house educated him to be a cosmopolitan and inspired him to make art his religion. Contact with the Dublin music world and Lee, who was a Catholic, also taught him to respect people on the basis of their talents and merits rather than their class or religion—an important and emancipating lesson in Ireland, where Protestant prejudice against Catholics was the last bastion of a privileged group that needed to vindicate its oppression of the majority. Shaw's 1898 self-sketch made his stance clear. It must have appealed to the young Catholic, "Sunny" Jim: "Imagine being taught that there is one God, a Protestant and a perfect gentleman, keeping Heaven select for the gentry against an idolatrous imposter called the Pope!" (SSS 45–46). Because many (according to Shaw, most) of the accomplished singers in Dublin were Catholic, Shaw learned in the family parlor that Protestant snobbery was absurd. But equally important, music made him a citizen of the world and prepared him to become a music critic in London, a defender of the avant-garde music of Wagner, and a contrapuntal playwright whose dramatis personae operate like musical leitmotifs for expressing political, religious, and even metaphysical themes.

Music in Dublin was almost equally important to young James Joyce, even though the Catholics in his circle were not singing *Don Giovanni,* as Lucinda Shaw was. A promising young tenor, Joyce sang in Catholic parlors. Although the lyrics and piano selections that he sang and heard at home, at the home shared by his aunts (the Misses Morkan of "The Dead"), and during evenings of house music at the Sheehys were often ballads like "The Croppy Boy" or "Blarney Castle" (JJ1 53), Joyce must have found yet another point of kinship with Shaw in his admitted derivation from the Dublin music world. Occasionally in London, the young journalist was a substitute performer with his sister Lucy. That Joyce considered a career as a tenor and performed with John McCormick indicates the similarities of his interests and Shaw's. Like G. B. S., Joyce exploited his knowledge of music throughout his writing.

Although Joyce's mother played the piano, she could not have pursued a career as an amateur musician as Lucinda Shaw did, even if she had wanted to (and doubtless she didn't, because she accepted the conventional roles of wife and mother). May Joyce had so many children that she had little time for music (and, a proper Catholic woman, no inclination like Molly Bloom and probably Lucinda Shaw for adultery). Both Shaw and Joyce were, however, profoundly influenced by their musical mothers, Shaw by his feeling of rejection as well as admiration for the coldly efficient and independent music teacher and Joyce by another sort of ambivalence. Although he was the favorite of both parents, Joyce defined himself by repudiating the conventional Catholic life and religion that his mother stood for.

If music was a liberating force for both young Dubliners, perhaps the most repressive for both was religion. Despite being deeply engaged by the literature of Christianity, both defected from orthodox religion, Shaw from the Anglican Church of Ireland and Joyce from Irish Catholicism. Shaw's rejection was facilitated by his family's laxity: "In my childhood I was sent every Sunday to a Sunday-school where genteel little children repeated texts," but when "we went to live in Dalkey we broke with the observance and never resumed it" (SSS 45). The irreverence of his father and uncle no doubt encouraged his dereliction, even though another uncle was the vicar of St. Bride's Church in Dublin. Joyce's revolt was, on the other hand, in part the result of the dilemma that confronts young Stephen in the Christmas dinner scene in *Portrait*. The quarrel mirrored in the confrontation between Mr. Casey, for whom Parnell is "dead King," and Dante Riordan, who defends the priests who condemned Parnell's adultery, was deeply disturbing to young James Joyce. Called upon to choose between nationalism and religion—his father's politics and his mother's Catholicism—and having read *The Quintessence of Ibsenism,* Joyce pronounced a plague on both houses, emulating Shaw. But like the older Dubliner, he was throughout life preoccupied with Christian theology and symbology that he had supposedly rejected. The "crisscouple . . . crosscomplimentary" (FW 613.10–11) imagined the redeemer as the antagonist of established religion and the artist as a scapegoat martyr, preacher, priest of art, and, finally, prophet. "Sonny" George, the boy who painted the whitewashed walls of his Dalkey bedroom with watercolor frescoes of Mephistopheles (H1 42), set an example for Stephen Dedalus.

In going into voluntary exile, Shaw offered Joyce yet another pattern for emulation. At home "only in the realm" of his imagination (CP 680), at age twenty Shaw left Ireland, which Joyce called "the little green place" and Shaw "the little green patch." By the time his novel of his nonage, *Immaturity* (written in 1879), was published in 1930, Shaw had also read part of *Ulysses* and made it clear that his assessment of Dublin in 1876 had matched that of Joyce in 1904: "James Joyce in his *Ulysses* has described, with a fidelity so ruthless that the book is hardly bearable, the life that Dublin offers to its young men, or, if you prefer to put it the other way, that its young men offer Dublin. . . . I am not enamoured of failure, of poverty, of obscurity, and of the ostracism and contempt which these imply: and these were all that Dublin offered to the enormity of my unconscious ambitions" (CP 673–74).

Harboring feelings about his hometown almost identical with Shaw's, Joyce, like Shaw before him, left Dublin at age twenty. Feeling guilty about leaving his mother, whereas Shaw felt guilty about abandoning his father, Joyce stopped off in London on his way to Paris, distinguishing himself from Irishmen like Shaw, who had chosen London as the mise-en-scène for exile. Joyce was to leave Ireland permanently in 1904, repulsed, as Shaw was, by the narrowly provincial life of Dublin. Both were proud and poor. Neither was certain of his vocation, but both were sure of one thing—that they had to get away from Ireland. Subsequently, both expatriates distinguished themselves for their insistence upon their Irishness and for recording in their writings their responses to their mother country.

The first years in voluntary exile were hard for both young émigrés. Shaw spent eight impoverished years struggling without recognition to become a novelist. Joyce struggled for ten to get *Dubliners* published. Their circumstances differed, however, for Shaw had followed his mother to London and lived on a subsistence level on the top floor of her quarters, while she taught music to earn their rent. He worked briefly for the Edison Telephone Company and, by his own account, "earned a few pounds by counting the votes at an election" but admitted, "I was an Unemployable, an ablebodied pauper in fact if not in law, until the year 1885, when for the first time I earned enough money from my pen to pay my way" (CP 676). Meanwhile, encouraging the myth of himself as a ruthless artist-superman, he averred that he "threw" his mother into the "struggle for life. . . . My mother worked for my living instead of preaching that it was my duty to work for hers" (H1 80). By the time Joyce left Ireland, Shaw had announced behavior that might have given him the heart to do so. In a column in the *World* on July 18, 1900, entitled "Celebrities at Home," Shaw announced that "any place that will hold a bed and a writing table is as characteristic of me as any other. . . . I have no more home instinct than a milk can at a railway station" (I&R 428).

Four years later Joyce eloped with Nora Barnacle, who assumed the role of wife if not the legal title. Joyce's life was even less stable than the one that Shaw found acceptable, for, whereas Shaw wanted a table, Joyce often had to settle for writing on a suitcase. And soon the young man was confronted with paternal obligations. At the age of twenty-three he became a father. At age twenty-five, with Nora and now two children to support, he struggled in poverty as a teacher in Berlitz language schools. At the same age the seedy Shaw had sequestered himself to write five novels and emerge on the London political scene on a washtub, preaching Fabianism on street corners and later writing music, art, and drama criticism. In copying Shaw, Joyce did not develop the older man's political activism and his great ability as a public speaker. In Trieste he wrote essays and gave lectures at a time when Shaw had already become a famous journalist, an infamous socialist debater, and a major playwright. Shaw had given up the idea of becoming a novelist while Joyce was still a boy.

All of Shaw's early novels were portraits of the artist as a young man and a budding socialist. Indeed, as the title of Richard Dietrich's study of the five fictions puts it, they were a *Portrait of the Artist as a Young Superman.* Published serially when Joyce could have read all but the first, *Immaturity,* they presage Joyce's life choices and his fiction. In Shaw's second novel, *The Irrational Knot* (1890), a woman runs away with her lover, defying conventional morality. Shaw condoned the act; Joyce carried it out with Nora Barnacle. The hero of Shaw's *Love Among the Artists* (1887) attacks old-fogy pedants while defending avant-garde art, as Joyce would do in *Stephen Hero* and *Portrait.* This novel, like *Candida,* prefigures the artistic declaration of independence in *Portrait.* Intolerant of reins upon creativity, Shaw's artist could be an adult model for the youthful Stephen Dedalus. Joyce may have thought so, for he purchased *Love Among the Artists* as well as *Cashel Byron's Profession* (1886), neither of which was a best-seller or recognized as innovative fiction. Even in its title, the novel about Cashel Byron suggests two important aspects of the Shavian persona that must have commanded the ephebic Joyce's attention: his distinctively Irish first name and his surname after the exiled romantic poet whose audacious rebellions against conventional morality both Irishmen defended. Naming his hero for the Rock of Cashel in County Tipperary was young Shaw's attempt to give his pugilist archetypal fighting stature, for the rock and its imposing castle remains seem to symbolize the brutal strength of the ancient Irish. As a novel of vocation, *Cashel Byron's Profession* anticipates *Portrait,* for, while celebrating the combative stance that became identifiably Shavian, its theme is, at bottom, the subject of Joyce's first novel—the special claims of vocation even if they alienate the hero from family and society.

Shaw's fifth example of fictional juvenilia, *An Unsocial Socialist* (1887) (first entitled *The Heartless Man*), could be an epithet for Joyce himself and his youthful avatars, for the younger man avowed that he was a socialist, though in actuality he produced little evidence of such political commitment. Moreover, Shaw's hero adamantly repudiates bourgeois loyalties, just as Joyce's fictional alter ego does. Although Shaw's preachy style and lectures on politics disguised as dialogue might have offended Joyce, *An Unsocial Socialist*'s message would have suited him. Even before he began writing dramas, Shaw aimed to preach and teach; but he preached both (sometimes all) sides of an issue, creating mouthpieces, as Joyce would in *Portrait,* to orchestrate different perspectives. The privileged character in Shaw's novel embodies an outlook that Shaw and Joyce found in themselves: a recognition that talent and intelligence are not equally distributed in the world but that persons of conscience should stand up for social equality. Both young Irishmen were aware of their superior gifts, and both resented being held back by poverty.

Shaw's unlovable hero Trefusis is a mask for his own insistence upon telling the truth. A very early example of the bifurcations that appear in Shaw's characters and in his personality—his irreverently brash public persona G. B. S. and his sensitive private self—Trefusis plays two roles, himself and a rusticated version of himself. As a young man from provincial Ireland, Shaw was busy creating himself as a sophisticated socialist. As Michael Holroyd notes, in his "first socialist hero and Don Juan figure" Shaw "attempts to reconcile his sexual and political attitudes" (H1 18), but it is important to observe that, rather than reconcile them, Shaw allowed his central character to be both himself and his double. As the son of a millionaire, Trefusis was for young Shaw a form of prophetic wish fulfillment, the kind that might have amused his impoverished young disciple. In Shaw's own mocking description of the protagonist, the younger Irishman would have found renegade affinities. Shaw called Trefusis "a Red, an enemy of civilisation, a universal thief, atheist, adulterer, anarchist, and apostle of the Satan he disbelieved in" (H1 119).

Because of its socialist hero and the love borne to his creator by its editor, Annie Besant, *To-day,* a magazine of "Scientific Socialism," serialized the novel in 1884, when Joyce was an infant, but he might have found back issues at the Liffey quay bookstalls that specialized in used periodicals, for apparently such literature reached Dublin and influenced young men like Joyce's classmate Francis Skeffington.

Despite the oppressive and narrow life of Dublin, popular literature was available to boys and teenagers. In *Dubliners* Joyce described British boys' magazines and romantic literature in "An Encounter" and exotic escape literature in "Araby." Such reading was not part of the prescribed education for Catholic youngsters any more than *An Unsocial Socialist* would have been. But, whether Joyce read Shaw's subversive novel or not, he came to accept the rebel values that Shaw was preaching. Shaw argued that social institutions and customs had been set up by "idealists" to control complacent "philistines"; he listed as "the Seven Deadly Sins" "respectability, conventional virtue, filial affection, modesty, sentiment, devotion to woman, romance" (GBS 77)—all "sins" that Stephen Dedalus finally eschews. Shaw's antisocial socialist opposes marriage as "a violation of the sanctuary of the soul . . . shameful surrender, ignominious capitulation"—scripture for Joyce, who did not marry Nora Barnacle until he had sired two children by her and lived with her for twenty-seven years. Although other writers offered discrete theories that Joyce incorporated in his worldview, no other Irishman propounded such a complete rationalization and program for revolt. As Seamus Deane writes, "It is well known that Joyce, like Stephen Dedalus, considered himself to be the slave of two masters, one British and one Roman. It is equally well known that he repudiated the Irish Literary Revival" (*Celtic Revivals* 92). It is less well known that his analysis of the two masters, his rejection of Yeats's literary movement, and his escape from Ireland replicated Shaw's.

The works of Ibsen, however, offered patterns for rebellion that were not specifically Irish. In 1891 Shaw distinguished himself for championing Henrik Ibsen, though the critic's analyses were shadows of his own substance. Nine years after the publication of Shaw's study, Joyce became the second dissatisfied Dubliner to champion the Norwegian. In looking for a spiritual father, Joyce pretended to ignore the Irishman who qualified for the role, but he chose the same artistic progenitor that Shaw did. Moreover, despite Joyce's avowed youthful worship of Ibsen, his work is, at bottom, closer in spirit to Shaw's. As George Watson points out, Ibsen's writings are very "different from Joyce's own—not least in the almost total absence of humour and the comic spirit" (161). It seems that, perhaps not yet fully aware of his own gifts for humor and comedy, Joyce, whether expediently or inadvertently, diverted his hero worship from his fellow countryman to another controversial father figure. But it is hard to believe that the keenly perceptive Joyce was not aware of his own motives, even as a youth. Thus the wily writer who was to make Shaw into his brother Shaun later in life already symbolically admitted fraternity, at least to himself, by ostensibly choosing the same paternal artist for adulation. For Ibsen could have been the father to both Shaw and Joyce, as well as Joyce's grandfather. When Joyce began to defend him, Ibsen was seventy-two years old.

In 1899, while he was an undergraduate at University College, Dublin, Joyce delivered a paper entitled "Drama and Life," in which he bravely defended the Norwegian dramatist at a Catholic school that condemned Ibsen as immoral. Perhaps Joyce had just read *The Perfect Wagnerite* (1898), for in his debating society speech he approved the German composer. In paying homage to the "new school" of drama, Joyce posited Wagner as an analogue of the "immeasurably higher calibre" of the newer art. Of course, Joyce's unauthorized teacher was not the only defender of Wagner at the time, but he was the most famous, and he was from the teenager's hometown. Aware that his article would be scrutinized by his priestly instructors, the embryonic writer argued in his essay that art should be amoral, whereas the brazen Shaw had argued that it should be frankly immoral by current hypocritical standards. While writing plays that assaulted nineteenth-century tradition, Shaw argued for rejecting old forms of drama. Echoing him, Joyce asserted that the public's "palates have grown accustomed to the old food" and thus "cry out peevishly against a change of diet." He contended that drama should be a portrayer (but not a purveyor) of "truth" and the embodiment of a "spirit" that sounds like Shaw's Life Force. Disapproving of outright sermonizing, the undergraduate declared, "Drama will be for the future at war with convention," which is precisely the thrust of Shaw's studies of Ibsen and Wagner. Reiterating Shavian argument without crediting Shaw, Joyce contended that plays like Ibsen's "clear our minds of cant and alter the falsehoods to which we have lent our support" (CW 40–42).

As Shaw wrote in *The Sanity of Art* (1895), "Every step in morals is made by challenging the validity of the existing conception of perfect propriety of conduct" (MCE 328). Like Shaw, the youthful essayist asserted that drama was the "head of all artistic institutions," agreeing with the older writer that beauty is less important than truth in drama and rejecting "the fetters of convention" made by "the compact majority" (CW 42–44), which Shaw named in *The Quintessence of Ibsenism* as the chief support of the false ideals of society. Shaw's chapter entitled "Ideals and Idealists" contends that as man "raises himself from mere consciousness to knowing by daring more and more to face facts and tell himself the truth," he pulls off the "masks" of society's "ideals" (MCE 47). The Shavian disciple wrote, "Art is marred by such mistaken insistence on its religious, its moral, its beautiful, its idealizing tendencies," for this doctrine of realism in art frightens audiences who "dive under blankets at the mention of the bogey of realism" (CW 44). The tyro's definition of realism is Shavian, referring not so much to a style that documents objective reality as to facing life's realities without the blinders of convention or socially indoctrinated ideals. Joyce thus preempted the main thesis of Shaw's tract on Ibsen as well as its vocabulary; he called the blind followers of past ideals "the Philistine chorus" (CW 44), echoing Shaw's description of "philistines" who "comfortably" accept ideals without questioning them (MCE 49). Like his mentor, he could have read Matthew Arnold's analysis of philistinism in *Culture and Anarchy* (1869), but Joyce's emphasis is Shavian.

Following Shaw's precept regarding Ibsen's "objective Anti-Idealist Plays," Joyce insisted that we must accept "life ... as we see it before our eyes, men and women as we meet them in the real world, not as we apprehend them in the world of faery" (CW 45) that appealed to Yeats. Prefiguring Joyce, Shaw wrote that theater audiences were conditioned to prefer false heroics and empty romanticism to the "inevitable return to nature" and "the everyday" in the new drama (MCE 165). Joyce aligned himself with Shaw against the enemy, Victorian "idealism." While eschewing the fairy tales of commercial theater, he also supported the Shavian objection to romantic clichés. Even though Joyce soft-pedaled the importance of discussion in dramas such as Shaw's, which, G. B. S. affirmed, aim to play "upon the human conscience" (MCE 172), in quoting Ibsen at the end of his essay—"I will let in fresh air"—Joyce emulated Shaw. In *The Quintessence of Ibsenism* he had written that the great artist aims to clear the world of "lies" (MCE 62). Later in *Portrait* the young man would announce a goal even more exalted than the Shavian aim at "conscience": godlike Stephen Dedalus wants to "create the uncreated conscience" of his race (203).

Although *The Quintessence of Ibsenism* and *The Sanity of Art* provided secret stimulus for his insurgency, it was his allegiance to Ibsen, not Shaw, that Joyce advertised. The idea of defending the cosmopolitan exile no doubt appealed to his adolescent pride, whereas admitting allegiance to the iconoclastic Anglo-Irish Protestant would perhaps have seemed less daring and, in Catholic Dublin, even more susceptible to criticism. And in covering up his indebtedness the young Catholic may have been influenced by vestigial prejudice against Protestants. Joyce sent his hero-worshipping review of *When We Dead Awaken* to the *Fortnightly Review,* to which Shaw was a prominent contributor. The periodical published Joyce's essay on April 1, 1900, under the title "Ibsen's New Drama" and paid the new writer the astounding sum of twelve guineas. After Shaw's friend William Archer, Ibsen's English translator, sent the review to Ibsen in Christiania, the old playwright wrote to Archer, complimenting his benevolent reviewer. Joyce was understandably overjoyed when Archer passed on his thanks. The fledgling critic was, however, certainly aware that his literary career started in the shadow of Shaw, with the blessings of Shaw's dramatic hero and of Archer, his mentor. In an 1896 article Shaw noted that Archer had discovered him in the British Museum Reading Room reading Karl Marx and contemplating a musical score of Wagner (I&R 25). Perhaps Joyce had read Lady Cicely's words in *Captain Brassbound's Conversion* (1898): "Getting patronage is the whole art of life. A man cannot have a career without it" (Plays 330). It is hard not to infer that the astute, well-informed, opportunistic young literary Dubliner was copying the older Irishman, but it is also not hard to understand that the teenager did not want to detract from his success by admitting that he was modeling himself on Shaw.

Joyce's essay on *When We Dead Awaken* reiterates Shavian complaints regarding "the common lot of plays . . . for the most part reheated dishes—unoriginal compositions, cheerfully owlish as to heroic insight, living only in their own candid claptrap—in a word stagey" productions (CW 49). In his drama criticism Shaw had been hammering away at conventional drama in order to expose the "naive machinery of the exposition." He called "well-made plays . . . mechanical rabbits, clockwork mice." He even complained of the "stagey element" in Shakespeare (Meisel 79–81). Joyce, the student critic, noted, after summarizing Ibsen's plot, that the Norwegian's plays "do not depend for their interest on the action, or on the incidents," but rather on "the perception of a great truth, or the opening up of a great question, or a great conflict" (CW 63). Like Shaw, who described the new drama as without conflict "between clear right and wrong," with "a villain . . . as conscientious as the hero" and, in fact, with "no villains and no heroes" (MCE 65), Joyce lauded Ibsen for not writing a "speciously" lofty play with a "legitimate hero" (CW 63).

By the time Joyce wrote these words, Shaw was writing plays that subordinate incident to "a great question" and omit or satirize the conventional "legitimate hero." Nevertheless, his young rival tried to denigrate the sort of critical study that *The Quintessence of Ibsenism* represents. The aspiring writer snidely dismissed Shaw's lengthy study by giving unstinting and unqualified "appreciation" to Ibsen while declaring that "that species of criticism which calls itself dramatic criticism is a needless adjunct to his plays. When the art of the dramatist is perfect the critic is superfluous. Life is not to be criticized, but to be faced and lived" (CW 67). Thus Joyce managed simultaneously to dismiss Shaw's dramatic criticism, to rationalize his own uncritical and relatively uninformed acceptance of Ibsen (an approach often taken by the young), and to copy the commandment of Shavian gospel—to face life and live. However, by congratulating Ibsen for "his reticence and refusal to join battle with his enemies" (JJ1 76), Joyce was choosing sides with a dramatist less pugnacious than Shaw and hence trying to distance himself from him. Later in life Joyce would expend a lot of energy combating real and imagined enemies—one of whom he came to believe was Shaw—while his opposite, always fighting public battles with his pen, was invariably and amazingly above petty revenge.

In his analysis of Ibsen's late play, Joyce admired the "awakening" at its conclusion. Such epiphanic culminations typify Shaw's early plays, although like *Dubliners* they end without the dramatic catastrophes that characterize many of Ibsen's problem plays. In *Mrs. Warren's Profession* (1894), Vivie Warren awakens to her true position in society and rejects it. In *Arms and the Man* (1894), Raina rejects romantic in favor of realistic love. In *Candida,* after a moment of truth, the young artist is freed to pursue his art. In *Captain Brassbound's Conversion* (1898), Brassbound is freed from the "ideal" of revenge. In *The Devil's Disciple* (1898), Reverend Anderson is converted to commitment to the real world. Unlike Ibsen, Shaw usually disdained melodramatic endings (except in *The Devil's Disciple,* itself a satire on melodrama) in favor of moments of truth, even though they are not so subtle as the epiphanies described by Stephen Hero as sudden spiritual manifestations of "the most delicate and evanescent moments" (SH 216). Nevertheless, when Joyce began writing his stories of Dublin in his "scrupulously mean" style (JJL 2:134), he shunned the catastrophes that are the stuff of Ibsen's problem plays, using a Chekhovian realism flatter than Flaubert's and arriving at moments of ironic truth. In his youthful essay Joyce revealed the influence of Shaw as well as his desire to annul his importance. He implicitly admitted having read "needless" dramatic criticism of Ibsen while failing to acknowledge his expropriations from his fellow Dubliner.

In 1904, when Joyce was expounding "a neo-paganism that glorified selfishness . . . denounced . . . 'domestic virtues,'" and gave him the imprimatur "to think of himself as a superman" (JJ1 147), he was imitating Shaw, whose *Man and Superman* had been published in 1903. The Fabian superman had made it clear that the one "realist" in a society of "idealists" and "philistines" was probably a communist who put his superior qualities to work toward creating a better society. While congratulating himself on being such a superior person, Joyce was also attending socialist meetings "where milder prophets of the new day than Marx were discussed" (JJ1 44). The most famous prophet of this mild, nonviolent socialism was the noted Irish Fabian, who befriended Joyce's former classmate Francis Skeffington—a pacifist radical from whom Joyce distanced himself after Skeffington disapproved of Joyce's illicit liaison with Nora Barnacle. Shavian theory supported, however, *all* of Joyce's heterodoxies. The preface to *Man and Superman,* as well as his studies of Ibsen and Wagner's Siegfried, whom Shaw compared to anarchist "Bakoonin," confirm Joyce's program for himself, for "the spirit or will of Man is constantly outgrowing . . . ideals, and . . . thoughtless conformity to them" (MCE 154).

When Joyce turned from poems and epiphanies to begin writing *Stephen Hero,* he was full of Shavian ideas. The first draft of his tentative novel replaced religious zeal with redeeming egoism. The hero rejects idealistic meditations on abstractions and turns to the "beauty of mortal conditions." Shaw favored the anarchist Proudhon's thesis that property is theft—an appealing idea to the alienated young graduate without property. In his earliest draft of *Stephen Hero* he wrote, "Man and woman, out of you comes the nation that is to come, the lightening of your masses in travail. The competitive order is employed against itself, the aristocracies are supplanted, and amid the general paralysis of an insane society, the confederate will issues in action" (quoted in JJ1 152). This opaque peroration cannot disguise the emphasis on the active will advocated by Shaw.

In his 1904 broadside, "The Holy Office," Joyce attacked the Irish literary renaissance, using Shavian criteria. According to Richard Ellmann, he declared that he "would pursue candor while his contemporaries [but not Shaw] pursued beauty" (JJ1 171). Against Yeats's nostalgic movement, he aligned himself with the author of *Candida* (named for her candor) without acknowledging the alliance. Shaw had no sympathy for the "neo-Gaelic movement, which is bent on creating a new Ireland after its own ideal" (CP 441). His 1904 preface to *John Bull's Other Island* apparently offended Yeats enough to prompt him to veto its proposed Abbey Theatre production. Tactfully, Yeats did not attack Shaw directly. Instead he complimented him on having "a geographical conscience." The phrase may have inspired the author of *Dubliners, Portrait,* and *Ulysses,* all of which display Dublin's geography and concern Irish conscience (or lack of it), for Joyce tracked the literary pronouncements of both Shaw and Yeats. The poet and manager of the Abbey did not consider Shaw's Irish drama dangerous, but the Abbey decided not to perform the play, for its spirit was, according to Shaw, "uncongenial to ... the neo-Gaelic movement ... [because it is] a very uncompromising presentment of the real old Ireland." Shaw objected to the "quaint little offshoot of English Pre-Raphaelitism ... [which] has got a footing by using Nationalism as a stalking horse" (CP 441, 457).

G. B. S.'s reasoned repudiation of the revival parallels Joyce's angry assessment in "The Holy Office," composed as a parting shot at the literary establishment before he left Dublin for good. The broadside scorns Yeats and his followers but not Shaw. Admitting himself to be a diabolonian leviathan, Joyce identified with "that high spirit [who] ever wars / On Mammon's countless servitors" and went on to proclaim,

> Where they have crouched and crawled and prayed
> I stand the self-doomed, unafraid,
> Unfellowed, friendless and alone. (CW 152)

The posture, for all of its proud assertion of singularity, is Shavian if one overlooks the self-pity. In his view of Ireland, Joyce was not "unfellowed," though he was too arrogant and perhaps also too timid to approach his mentor in such apostasy. Dick Dudgeon, Shaw's devil's disciple, might have joined Joyce in "The Holy Office" if he could bear the doggerel: "And though they spurn me from their door / My soul shall spurn them evermore." Among Irish writers of the time, Shaw was the devil's advocate, but Joyce was the devil's disciple.

After leaving Dublin in 1904, Joyce continued to find incentives in Shaw. In 1906, while teaching at the Berlitz School in Trieste, he wrote about his country, expatiating upon ideas that Shaw expounded in his preface to *John Bull's Other Island*. In describing two of his principal characters, Irishman Larry Doyle and Englishman Tom Broadbent, Shaw wryly insisted, "No doubt, when the play is performed in Ireland, the Dublin critics will regard it as self-evidence that without Doyle, Broadbent would have been bankrupt in six months" (CP 442). Thus with tongue in cheek Shaw argued that Irish brains make for English success. Joyce wrote, "Ireland remains the brains of the United Kingdom. The English judiciously practical and ponderous furnish the overstuffed stomach with a perfect gadget—the water closet. The Irish, condemned to express themselves in a language not their own, have stamped on it the mark of their own genius and compete for glory with the civilised nations. This is then called English literature" (quoted in JJ1 226).

The character of Broadbent is the English stereotype to which Joyce referred in his musings, an efficient pragmatist promoting hotels, speedboats, and golf links to make life better for tourists. He is, in fact, a "civil engineer." The Irish geniuses to whom Joyce referred as dominating English literature were Yeats and Shaw. And the young writer competing for glory was Joyce himself, at the time fighting to get *Dubliners* published. Throughout his Dublin stories the motifs of English usurpation and Catholic domination of Irish life appear, echoing Shavian diagnosis of the symptoms of Ireland's severest ailments. Joyce's 1907 article in *Il Piccolo della Sera,* "Ireland at the Bar," once more corroborates Shaw's analysis of the Irish problem as stemming from the complicity of British imperialism and Roman Catholicism. Echoing Shaw, Joyce wrote that "the true sovereign of Ireland, the Pope" has no more sympathy with the Irish than the English do; the Holy See favors messengers of the British monarch over those of the Irish people (CW 198).

Earlier in 1907 Joyce gave a lecture in Trieste titled "Ireland, Island of Saints and Sages," which further substantiates his relationship to Shaw, especially to *John Bull's Other Island.* In his preface to that play G. B. S. avers that " 'the island of the saints' is no idle phrase" (CP 454), even though the country is paralyzed by Catholicism and British rule. One of Shaw's main characters, the defrocked priest Keegan, is the prototype of the saint and sage to whom Joyce refers. The expatriate Larry Doyle, Shaw's principal alter ego, could have been Joyce's double. His "special contribution was the freedom from illusion, the power of facing facts, the nervous industry, the sharpened wits, the sensitive pride of the imaginative man who has fought his way up through social persecution and poverty" (CP 442). Joyce no doubt recognized much of his ideal self in Shaw's portrayal of the judgmental expatriate. In his lecture he said that the "pejorative conception of Ireland is given the lie by the fact that when the Irishman is found outside of Ireland in another environment, he very often becomes a respected man" (CW 171). Shaw conceived Doyle as such a character, successful in London but reluctant to return to Ireland, "an Irishman who knew the world and was moved only to dislike, mistrust, impatience and even exasperation by his own countrymen" (CP 441). He believes that any self-respecting Irishman should "learn to do something and then . . . get out of Ireland and have a chance of doing it" (Plays 414). Joyce told his audience that "no one who has any self-respect stays in Ireland" (CW 171). In 1906 Joyce wrote his brother that he was "nauseated by . . . lying drivel about pure men and pure women and spiritual love and love forever: blatant lying in the face of truth" (JJ1 247)—lines that could be mistaken for Larry Doyle's indictment of the Irish for preferring romantic illusions to reality.

Furthermore, Keegan's remark that Ireland "produces two kinds of men in strange perfection: saints and traitors" foreshadows the Joycean attitude toward Ireland. While both writers adumbrate the *insula sanctorum et doctorum* of medieval Ireland, both alienated Celts suspected that wisdom required betrayal of Ireland, paradoxically because the Irish themselves were such turncoats to their kind. Shaw anticipated Joyce's persistent theme of Irish betrayal. In his lecture Joyce alluded to such self-defeating treachery in his summary of two significant events in Irish history—the Anglo-Norman invasion, which brought the English to Ireland "at the repeated requests of a native king," and the Act of Union (1800). Such self-betrayal, he pronounced, was "not legislated at Westminster but at Dublin, by a parliament elected by the vote of the people of Ireland, a parliament corrupted and undermined with great ingenuity by the agents of the English prime minister, but an Irish parliament nevertheless" (CW 162).

The text of Joyce's lecture ranges over Irish history; the ethnic and racial mix of Protestants like Shaw and Catholics like Joyce; and the political backwardness of the people, "Catholic, poor, and ignorant" (CW 167) because the British Empire, in collusion with their religion, made them that way. Thus the devil's disciple covers much the same territory as Shaw's preface to his first Irish play. Listing Ireland's contribution to British culture, Joyce named George Moore, Oscar Wilde, and Shaw but not Yeats or any of the participants in the Celtic revival. At the time of Joyce's speech, which credits Shaw's "contribution to English art and thought" and refers to Shaw as a "paradoxical and iconoclastic writer of comedy" (CW 171), Joyce was trying to publish stories with the same professed aim as *John Bull's Other Island*—to present, as Shaw wrote, an "uncompromising picture" of the "real" Ireland (CP 441).

Meanwhile, in trying to get *Dubliners* published, Joyce had first approached Grant Richards, Shaw's friend and the first publisher of his *Plays Pleasant* and *Plays Unpleasant* (1898). If Joyce had seen a copy of *Plays Unpleasant,* he would have found in it the name of an English publisher interested in subversive Irish talent. Richards, to whom Shaw was a hero, had volunteered to publish his plays. Hoping to be discovered himself, Joyce first sent Shaw's admirer *Chamber Music,* lyric poems that might have been written by young Marchbanks of *Candida.* Then he sent his stories. In seeking out Shaw's publisher and corresponding with William Archer between 1900 and 1903, Joyce warily circled G. B. S. without approaching him directly. Richards's reluctance to publish *Dubliners* because of language and innuendos discovered by his printer may have initiated Joyce's special prejudice regarding Shaw, for, although he did not openly blame him for Richards's rejection of *Dubliners* (or credit him for its ultimate publication by Richards in 1914), Joyce's belief that Shaw was a puritan developed during his difficulties with Shaw's publisher.

Joyce's arguments to persuade Richards to print his endangered stories may have been designed to convince a Shavian, for they promised that his early views of the ends of art matched Shaw's. In defense of his stories, Joyce used the Shavian argument (not Shaw's property, but his distinctive stance at the turn of the century) that literature should have a moral or social purpose. In 1906 Joyce contended that he was writing a "chapter in the moral history" of Ireland, "the first step toward the spiritual liberation of my country"—a laudable aim that Joyce knew corresponded to Shavian artistic goals. He wrote further, "I seriously believe that you will retard the course of civilisation in Ireland by preventing the Irish people from having one good look at themselves in my nicely polished looking-glass" (JJL 1:63–64). But in 1906 his justifications did not prevail with Richards.

When in 1909 the Abbey Theatre performed Shaw's latest challenge to British censorship, *The Shewing up of Blanco Posnet*, both Irish expatriates were in Ireland. After attending the opening, Joyce sent a review to *Il Piccolo della Sera* in Trieste, but he did not meet the infamous dramatist. In his preface to the play, Shaw admitted that it was a dramatized sermon. In his judgmental review, Shaw's former fan disapproved of the "born preacher" in the play. Although his title, "Bernard Shaw's Battle with the Censor," implies admiration of the pugnacious playwright, "His lively and talkative spirit," Joyce wrote, "cannot stand to be subjected to the noble and bare style appropriate to modern playwriting." To Joyce, who clearly esteemed Shaw's "lively" spirit, the play was not convincing as a sermon or as a drama. In it the heroic champion of "all the progressive movements in art and politics" was, Joyce feared, "shewn up" as touched by religion (CW 208)—from whose influence, Joyce no doubt knew, G. B. S. had once abetted his escape. A copy of the review was sent to the publicly feisty and privately mild-mannered Shaw, who was requested to "do what he could to help promote the fortunes of the same author's coming book *Dubliners*" (JJ1 299). Shaw, however, held his forked tongue.

Joyce knew, nevertheless, that Shaw's play had been performed in Dublin because it was under ban of the censor in England. Shaw strenuously opposed censorship because, as he said in his preface to *Mrs. Warren's Profession,* "All progress is initiated by challenging current conceptions, and executed by supplanting existing institutions. Consequently the first condition of progress is the removal of censorship. There is the whole case against censorship in a nutshell" (CP 226). Joyce himself was about to encounter trouble with censorship in Dublin. During the visit to Ireland when he reviewed Shaw's play, he signed a contract with Maunsel and Company for the publication of *Dubliners;* but soon the editor, George Roberts, began to fear its "disrespectful references to Edward VII . . . pornographic elements that might evoke legal penalties . . . ecclesiastical disapproval, and . . . law suits from the dozens of tradesmen, public figures, and even private citizens, either specifically named or barely disguised" (Walzl, "Dubliners" in *Companion* 163).

After three years of haggling, in 1912 Joyce wrote the venomous doggerel of "Gas from a Burner," attacking the Irish characteristic that Shaw had already espied and that Joyce, smarting from wounds inflicted by the reluctant publisher, felt he had experienced first-hand—the Irish penchant for betrayal. He wrote with heavy irony of

> This lovely land that always sent
> Her writers and artists into banishment
> And in the spirit of Irish fun
> Betrayed her leaders, one by one. (CW 243)

In the preface to *John Bull's Other Island,* Shaw had written, "If you put an Irishman on a spit you can always find another Irishman to baste him" (CP 456). Joyce's persistent accusation that in Ireland "Christ and Caesar are hand in glove" replicates Shaw's coupling of the "British government and the Vatican" (CP 449), who collude in supporting censorship. In the younger man's bitter tirade, Shaw is not included as a victim of Irish perfidy because he had not tried to publish in Ireland. Shaw's lengthy attack on censorship, however, which constitutes the preface to *The Shewing up of Blanco Posnet,* is comparable to Joyce's in substance although completely different in form and tone. And, like *Dubliners,* Shaw's play about the Irish, which documents and ridicules Irish submission to Church and the British usurper, was as unacceptable in Ireland as were Joyce's short stories. Shaw's persecution by the censor over *Mrs. Warren's Profession* and *Blanco Posnet* would no doubt remind Joyce of his kinship to the older Irishman years later when *Ulysses* was banned in the United States.

Meanwhile, Joyce continued to study Shaw. Between fall 1913 and spring 1914, while working on *Portrait,* he bought copies of *Major Barbara* and *The Devil's Disciple* as well as Henri Bergson's *Creative Evolution* (JJ1 788), perhaps in an effort to understand the philosophy for which Shaw had made himself spokesperson. Two years later, in the privately printed poem "Dooleyprudence" (later included in *Critical Writings*), Joyce seemed to have formulated his response to G. B. S.'s *Common Sense about the War* (1914)—its title an ironic allusion to Thomas Paine's radical call for the American Revolution. Shaw's explosive analysis of World War I, which appeared in the *New Statesman* and later in the *New York Times,* triggered worldwide controversy and angry rebuttals. Upon publishing Shaw's attack on the war in November 1914, the *New Statesman* announced that Shaw had "probably done more than any other living man to influence and to create opinion on an immense variety of subjects" (quoted in H2 359), but in 1916, taking its cue from the outraged public response to Shaw's unpopular, seemingly unpatriotic assessment of the war, the periodical blackballed his articles. No one who kept abreast of world news could have avoided Shaw's challenge. His carefully researched political pamphlet attacked both the British and the Germans, exposing Machiavellian motives on both sides. G. B. S. scorned politicians who still believed that the war "was a question of Union Jacks and Tricolours and Imperial Eagles," which he described as "merely toys to keep them smiling." "There are only two real flags in the world henceforth," Shaw said, "the red flag of Democratic Socialism and the Black flag of Capitalism" (*What I Really Wrote* 90). The Fabian chastised governments, belabored the public at large, and ridiculed "Junkerism [in both Germans and English] and Militarism" (26), attacking all and sundry Jingoist war-mongers with the battering ram of his informed wit. He despised the leaders for treating war as if it were "an Olympic game conducted with ball cartridges" (53) or a chess match (55), when in reality ordinary citizens were the pawns of greedy, organized murderers. Disdaining hypocrisy and false heroics on both sides, he trivialized the opposed forces as two pirate fleets out for booty (78). He pronounced it monstrous that an enlisting soldier had to "Swear by Almighty God" in order to go out and commit atrocities against his fellow men, women, and children. He despised the Church for acquiescing to the slaughter and thus turning Christ into "Mars" (100).

In summarizing the incendiary political pamphlet, Hesketh Pearson writes that Shaw "simply pointed out that the violation of Belgian neutrality was a trumped-up excuse for British intervention, and a poor one; that if the soldiers of every army engaged were wise they would shoot their officers and return home; that if the citizens of every belligerent country were wise they would refuse to pay for diplomatic wars; that there were Junkers [country squires] and militarists in England as well as Germany . . . that self glorification and abuse of one's enemy were not the best ways of winning a war" (343). Such honesty soon produced printed attacks, personal ostracism, and heated patriotic invective that stigmatized Shaw. Rebecca West wrote that "Shaw's spirit of mockery" caused him to be outspoken in his ridicule of the war (quoted in Terry, 453). His fierce, Swiftian commitment and outrageous (and outraging) sense of humor produced hysterical counterattacks from jingoist patriots. Challenging the English to distrust him, he established at the outset of his scathing analysis his Irish credentials: "Besides, until Home Rule emerges from its present suspended animation, I shall retain my Irish capacity for criticizing England with something of the detachment of a foreigner, and perhaps with a certain slightly malicious taste for taking the conceit out of her" (*What I Really Wrote* 23).

While Shaw's ideas were causing a furor around the world, in late 1915 Joyce took a job as translator for "a bearded messianic professor from Vienna," Sigmund Feilbogen, one of the few people who dared publicize ideas like Shaw's. A neutralist, Feilbogen was publishing his *International Review* in neutral Switzerland. It aimed to prove that stories of both British and German atrocities were greatly exaggerated. The British and Americans effectively squelched the periodical by refusing its entry into the United Kingdom and the United States. Although, according to Ellmann, Joyce at first disappointed Feilbogen (JJ1 410), Feilbogen's political views could not have failed to remind the Irish translator of his rival's. In "Dooleyprudence" Joyce disparaged Dooley's neutrality while at the same time ridiculing the war. The poem's double-edged irony suggests that Joyce thought he should be committed like Shaw to issues beyond his private life and had to make (as he often did) a self-mocking *apologia pro vita sua*.

Later in life Shaw admitted that his cold-blooded analysis of the war was partly motivated by his being Irish, for England's trouble was, to a Hibernian, Ireland's opportunity (see Pearson 345). "Dooleyprudence" seems to take its cue from Joyce's dual stance: it defends neutrality with two prongs of irony—one of them self-irony directed at Dooley, who has retreated from political engagement; and the other a mocking attack, like Shaw's, on self-serving warmongers. The name Dooleyprudence implies "substituting private good sense for the folly of society's legal code" (CW 246). In both defending and ridiculing neutrality the broadside is the passive side of Shaw's courageous analysis of the vested interests of the power brokers and the victimization of ordinary citizens by war. "Dooleyprudence" is a diatribe against war, just as Shaw's *Common Sense* is; but Shaw's is a notoriously public manifesto, whereas Joyce's private poem is not so fearless. It conveys the unpopular heterodoxies of Shaw while setting Joyce off from his mentor by ostensibly doing the right deed for the cautious, noncommittal, selfish reason.

While Shaw the teacher was busily pointing out the faults on both sides, "Dooley" was dismissing both with obloquy. His poem jests about war in much the same way as Shaw had, opposing "all the gallant nations" that "run to war." Like Shaw, he satirizes the institutions that supported the war—Britain, Germany, and the churches for teaching "their flocks the only way to save all human souls / Was piercing human bodies through with dumdum bulletholes" and thus creating a "Jingo Jesus." As a "meek philosopher" Dooley is a lot like the bold one except in protesting that he "doesn't care a damn. . . . And disbelieves that British Tar is water from life's fount / And will not gulp the gospel of the German on the Mount." In crying, "The curse of Moses / On both your houses," he apes Shaw, intending to discomfit nearly everybody. Ironically, because the poem was not widely circulated, it threw down the gauntlet to no one but himself. It anticipates, however, the association between Shaw/Bloom and Moses that Joyce was making in *Ulysses,* a connection that he would develop in the *Wake* after reading Shaw's audaciously titled "Pentateuch," *Back to Methuselah.* In defending himself for paddling his own canoe "down the stream of life," Joyce, in the persona of Dooley, admits in ironic self-deprecation that he is not, like his prophetic Other, *engagé*. But on the war craze, Dooley's private attack matches Shaw's public one: "Poor Europe ambles / Like sheep to shambles." Paradoxically and defiantly apolitical, however, Dooley vows that he will not be a passive resister like "the tranquil gentleman who won't salute the State [Shaw?] / Or save Nabuchodonosor or proletariat" (CW 248). During months of being mercilessly scapegoated in the press and snubbed in arenas such as the Society of Authors, where he had once been a featured attraction, Shaw played the gentleman, tranquil and self-assured.

As the war went on, the fickle public and perfidious intellectual community began to realize that Shaw's uncompromising position was, paradoxically, the manifestation of realistic patriotism. The news media did an about-face, recognizing Shaw as a saintly seer. Although initially his pronouncements convicted him in England of pro-German sentiment (a misreading that at first led the Germans to believe that he was on their side), as condemnation of the war became more general, Shaw began to be praised as a prophet rather than scorned as a traitorous pariah. Though he was not aware of it, the pacifist-activist was setting himself up as a strategic opposite to Joyce—in some respects Leopold Bloom's fantasy self to Joyce's Stephen Dedalus and later Shaun to Joyce's Shem. Joyce's ironic portrayals of Stephen in *Ulysses* and of Shem in *Finnegans Wake,* tinged with "Dooleyprudence," are facilitated by their contrasts to Bloom and Shaun, foolhardy in fantasy. Joyce, apparently ambivalently, approved of Shaw because at bottom they shared, among many common experiences and interests, disdain for the hypocritical political scene, but the equivocal Joyce despised Shaw because his activism, his success, and his ability to get the public spotlight, whether as scapegoat or redeemer, were reproofs and reminders of his own inadequacies.

As has been noted, while Joyce's Dooley rejects the energetic commitment of the Shavian propagandist, he scorns the same international faults that Shaw had outlined. H. G. Wells's verdict that Shaw had proven himself to be "one of those perpetual children who live in a dream of make-believe" (Weintraub, *Journey* 78) may actually have recommended him to his rival as an opposite with whom he shared a basic kinship, a consanguinity that would lead him to dream of Shaw as one of the perpetual brothers of the *Wake.* Furthermore, underlying all of G. B. S.'s argument had been his Fabian goal of eliminating nationalistic warfare and working, like Leopold Bloom in his fantasies, toward an international league of governments. Like the dapper preacher, Jaun, in the *Wake,* Shaw claimed that he was "not the man to lose an opportunity of preaching at the utmost admissible length when I find myself installed as a great prophet" (quoted in H2 367). He began to campaign for a league of nations, while the envious Joyce retreated into "Dooleyprudence"—at once a lampoon, self-vindication, and self-condemnation. While attacking the bad faith of partisan church and state, he mocked himself for being a trimmer. The pugnacious and persistent daring of the "doblinganger," who, like himself, despised "the blatant bulletins of the rulers of the earth," could only have reminded "Mr Dooley-ooley-ooley-oo" (CW 248) of his own meek escapism.

Having made up his mind that Shaw must disapprove of him, the retaliatory Joyce was quick to believe that the famous propagandist would subvert him. In 1916, when the younger Irishman was trying to get his play *Exiles* staged in London, the Stage Society rejected it because of its " 'Filth and Disease,' as one member called it" (JJ1 429). No doubt feeling guilty because of his surreptitious use of *Candida* as a model for *Exiles* (discussed further in chapter 3 of this book), Joyce promptly concluded that Shaw was a purity-snooper. Among those who opposed *Exiles* was, in fact, William Archer, whose aid Joyce had often solicited, whereas Shaw had actually approved of the play. Meanwhile, while Shaw was in limbo in London for his attack on World War I, he was a hero in Dublin because of his vociferous defense of the 1916 Easter Uprising. In 1917 the Abbey Theatre began a major retrospective of his plays, which must have exacerbated the jealousies of his undisclosed rival. In 1918, when *Exiles* was again refused a showing in England, Joyce—"apparently without direct evidence" (JJ1 437)—once more projected the blame onto the literary giant. Still nursing his wounds in 1919, he wrote Carlo Linati that his play had been "removed following the protest of Bernard Shaw who found it obscene" (JJ1 429). Biographers cite no source for such a rejection, but Joyce was quick to rationalize injuries. He was especially sensitive regarding Shaw, but although he felt stung by the literary patriarch's pandybat, Joyce still wanted to assert himself in what was to him no doubt a literary competition.

When Joyce faulted Shaw for the failure of *Exiles* in 1919, it was a year after his most reprehensible behavior with respect to Shaw. In Zurich, perhaps to compete with Yeats's work at the Abbey and Shaw's earlier accomplishments at the Court Theatre in London, Joyce founded a theater group called the English Players. In 1918 he was fighting to stage performances of J. M. Barrie's *The Twelve-Pound Look,* J. M.

Synge's *Riders to the Sea,* and Shaw's *The Dark Lady of the Sonnets* despite his criticism of his two fellow Irishmen (JJ1 454). At the time—ironically, since Shaw's play was designed to create interest in a national theater and hence had a purpose far removed from art for art's sake—Joyce declared himself "TOUT POUR L'ART" (JJ1 454). While ostensibly applying his energies to the project with intentions antithetical to Shaw's, he produced illegally two Shaw plays that were blatantly propagandistic in their aims to bring about social change. Thus Joyce's declaration of purpose might have been a joke, a wily inconsistency, a declaration of his difference from the likes of Shaw, a rallying cry meant to satisfy supporters like Ezra Pound, or a combination of such motives.

The English Players opened their fall season in 1918 with a production of *Mrs. Warren's Profession* without Shaw's consent and without paying royalties. Joyce was in the midst of a legal battle with an actor from the British Consulate, who claimed that Joyce had underpaid him. In this peccadillo he expended a lot of physical and emotional energy—more, it seems, than he did in responding to the charge of piracy. When the secretary of the Society of Authors (from which Shaw had retreated when fellow dramatists treated him like a leper because of his stance on World War I) contacted Joyce, the literary larcenist defended himself by arguing "that no rights could exist for a play whose production in England was an indictable offence." Upon consulting Shaw, however, the secretary confirmed that the play had been licensed by the Lord Chamberlain in a "modified version"; he wrote an angry letter to Joyce, insisting upon his culpability. Joyce's excuses were perhaps especially ungrateful considering that Grant Richards published *Exiles* in England in 1918. Nevertheless, in denying his guilt, the all-too-human Joyce rationalized in order to exonerate himself. Whereas, according to Ellmann, the exiled penman was litigious, Shaw was not, even though he was impishly and pragmatically capable of threatening legal action. In Joyce's case he did not even use his playfully poisoned pen to retaliate. Nevertheless, in a 1920 letter to his American patron, John Quinn, Joyce continued to accuse Shaw for the failure of *Exiles:* he wrote that the play was not produced "owing to the veto of Mr Shaw as I am informed" (JJ1 791). Yet even as the younger writer protested that Shaw had violated his own principles regarding freedom of expression, Joyce continued to read his works. In a 1921 letter to Harriet Weaver he apologized for sounding like a digressive Shaw preface (JJL 2:234).

In spite of his real or feigned reservations about G. B. S., Joyce was defensive if the older artist criticized him. During his attempts to publish *Ulysses,* he prompted Sylvia Beach and Ezra Pound to approach Shaw for a subscription. Pound and Shaw got into a "letter battle" that Joyce followed with relish. Although he was a millionaire at the time, Shaw waggishly insisted that he wouldn't pay three guineas for the book. On the basis of his reading of parts of it in the *Little Review,* he acknowledged Joyce's literary power but criticized him for his use of "blackguardly language," admitting that he himself was "old fashioned and squeamish" and could not "write the words Mr. Joyce uses" (JJ1 588). Having repressed his own sexuality after his unconsummated marriage in 1898 and suppressed temptations to dwell on bodily functions whose descriptions could have no social or philosophical use to him, Shaw pleaded prudishness and lack of interest in "infantile clinical incontinences, or the flatulations which he thinks worth mentioning." But as a Dubliner himself, G. B. S. recognized the veracity of *Ulysses* as a social "document" of remarkable accuracy: "The Dublin Jackeens of my day, the medical students, the young bloods about town, were very like that!" On the basis of his reading (which did not, it seems clear, include Molly Bloom's infamous and supposedly pornographic monologue), Shaw said he would not pay "a penny beyond seven and sixpence" though he was attracted to the novel because it confirmed the life that he had lived in Dublin and had "literary power . . . of classic quality" despite its "indecent exposures" (JJ1 588). Indeed, he defended *Ulysses* against censorship: "Suppress the book and have the ribaldry unexposed and you are protecting dirt instead of protecting morals. If a man holds up a mirror to your nature and shows you that it needs washing—not whitewashing—it is no use breaking the mirror. Go for soap and water" (JJ1 588). Nevertheless, when Joyce organized an international protest against the plagiarizing of *Ulysses* in the United States, Shaw's signature on the petition was conspicuously absent. No doubt he remembered the American piracy of his own early novels, which he was helpless to stop, as well as Joyce's thefts from him in Zurich.

In the 1920s, while he was writing his "Work in Progress," Joyce's guilty hostilities underwent a subtle transformation. On November 26, 1926, he wrote a brief letter congratulating Shaw for winning the Nobel Prize for literature and indicating his "satisfaction that the award . . . has gone once more to a distinguished fellow townsman" (JJL 3:146). The conciliatory letter perhaps resulted from the fact that in February 1926 *Exiles* had been produced at the Regent Theatre in London. In the Stage Society's public debate over the play, Shaw defended it. Whereas reviewers panned it, Shaw admired Joyce's talent "but distrusted his subjects and language" (JJ1 588). While shrinking from Joyce's overtly sexual subjects and finding little in the mature Joyce that seemed socially redeeming, the vestigial Victorian revealed his biases concerning the didactic functions of drama but also his own magnanimity regarding the genius of his fellow Dubliner. In vindicating the dramaturgy of *Exiles,* Shaw may or may not have recognized that the form and even the content of Joyce's play about a marital triangle were remarkably like those of his own play *Candida*.

During the seventeen years he was writing the *Wake,* Joyce seemed to think of Shaw as a figure both punitively patriarchal and potentially protective. In 1931 Joyce planned, according to Weintraub, to use Shaw's name, along with that of H. G. Wells, "in protecting the inadvertent use of the Joyce byline by the *Frankfurter Zeitung* . . . over the German translation of a story by the younger and little-known writer Michael Joyce. Other than sowing brief and minor confusion, the mistake did Joyce no harm but he wanted to seek damages until his lawyers warned him that he would win £25 at best." He changed his mind about using Shaw's name before the old man could refuse him ("Respectful Distance" 71). Clearly feeling some sort of kinship with the aged laureate, Joyce encouraged his daughter Lucia to send the three lettrines G. B. S. to Shaw on his July 26 birthday in 1932, hoping that the old man "might like her talent" (JJL 3:250). To divert his daughter from her symptoms of schizophrenia, the father induced her to create elaborate, ornate alphabetical letters to amuse herself and others. Either Lucia did not send the lettrines or the aging playwright ignored them. In the fall of that year, perhaps smarting from one more apparent rebuke, Joyce declined W. B. Yeats's invitation, underwritten by Shaw, to be at the top of the list of nominees for membership in the Academy of Irish Letters that they were founding. In effect, Joyce snubbed the two famed Irishmen.

Nevertheless, the venerable old dramatist championed the younger writer one more time. In a letter published in the *Picture Pose* on June 3, 1939, he assailed Geoffrey Grigson for reporting that G. B. S. had been "disgusted" with the "unsqueamish realism" of *Ulysses* and consequently had burned it in his fireplace. Actually, Shaw's wife Charlotte had been so repulsed by the sensuality of Frank Harris's *My Life and Loves* (1922) that she had burned *it,* but even in his eighties Shaw was a defender of truth. Charlotte perhaps thought that one sexually obsessed Irishman's book was like another's, but not her husband. Perhaps Grigson had confused Charlotte's book burning with Shaw's criticism of *Ulysses*. The old playwright, in an effort to set the record straight, retorted that Grigson's story was humbug. He insisted that he admired both the realism and the poetry of Joyce's novel and that "if Mr Joyce should ever desire a testimonial as the author of a literary masterpiece from me, it shall be given with all possible emphasis and with sincere enthusiasm" (JJ1 588–89). Even though Joyce continued to let his biographer Herbert Gorman depict him as a persecuted artist, he was especially gratified by Shaw's approval. He urged his friend Paul Leon to enclose in a letter to Gorman the proof of Shaw's "emphatic denial" of gossip concerning the Shavian appraisal of *Ulysses*—a denial that could only please (and amuse) Joyce, who had avidly read Shaw to co-opt and corroborate ideas (and, in *Ulysses* and *Finnegans Wake,* to kidnap his public persona) as well as to seek evidence of his own artistic superiority.

The letter probably confirmed for Joyce the reconciliation that emerges in the dreamwork about warring brothers and the formidable father and envious son upon which Joyce focused in his "Work in Progress"—finally entitled *Finnegans Wake*—as a "funferal" celebration instead of a condemnation of a rival father/brother Irishman. In the end of the *Wake,* which "reamalgemerges" Shaun/Shaw and Shem/Jim in Joyce's psyche, the cunning penman had, it seems, realized that Shaw had always simply told the truth as he saw it, without malice, and that the grand old Irishman who seemed to be his opposite and equal was really more kin than enemy. He had no doubt awakened to the fact that the jocular literary giant's random remarks about his own work were usually description, not prescription—that, indeed, his basic assessment had from the start given Joyce the recognition that his genius craved. Clearly, in the year of the publication of the *Wake,* Joyce was gratified by Shaw's testimonial. It must have seemed like poetic justice that the unwitting model for Shem's great "Adversarian" had reached out to applaud his work.

In any event, in his last years Joyce did not have the stamina for literary battles. He worked out their resolutions in the shamantics of the *Wake,* at times when there was little cause in his private life for laughter. His daughter Lucia was in a sanitarium, having had a mental breakdown, and he was all but blind. Drinking heavily, spending money irresponsibly, and showing signs of the duodenal ulcer that would kill him, Joyce was tormented by personal problems that led to his death in January 1941. Methuselan Shaw, unaware of the crucial role that he had played in Joyce's life and fiction, would complete four more plays and outlive Joyce by nine years, dying at the age of ninety-four.

CHAPTER

Three

The Devil's Disciple and His Great *"Immensipater"*: *Stephen Hero*, *A Portrait of the Artist as a Young Man*, and *Exiles*

 T HE FACTS barely scratch the surface of the bridge between the two Irish geniuses. The gadfly was usually too busy stinging the state to take serious notice of his cunning apostle, but the young artist was profoundly marked by reading Shaw. In the renegade Protestant who shared his Dublin heritage, Joyce found intellectual underpinnings that he could not get from his Jesuit teachers, as well as a program for rebelling against them. Shaw's propaganda was an antidote to the rigors of a strict Catholic education. Reading it was itself an act of insurrection, for, as Shaw maintained, all the books worth reading in Ireland were on the Index. Among the subversive literature that we know young Joyce read, as has been noted, was *The Quintessence of Ibsenism*. The internal evidence in *Stephen Hero* and *A Portrait of the Artist as a Young Man* suggests that Shaw's 1891 tract whetted Joyce's appetite for Shavian propaganda—pamphlets, prefaces, and plays. By the time he was a de facto husband, Joyce had been reading Shaw's plays, among them *Candida;* its interfacings with *Exiles* disclose that Joyce was a stealthy student of Shaw's parlor play about adulterous, triangulated love, a subject that compelled both Irishmen. Indeed, Joyce's drama borrows both structure and theme from *Candida*. Furthermore, both *Stephen Hero*, the incomplete version of Joyce's first novel, begun in

1903, and *Portrait,* begun in 1907 as a radical revision of his earlier effort and completed in 1915, are informed by Shavian ideas and experience that paralleled Shaw's as a young man, just as Joyce's autobiographical play is informed by theory and events corroborated in Shaw's life—a life well known to the public because of his relentless self-promotion and self-exposure. Amid accurately observed scenes of Stephen's life in Dublin, the lengthy, diffuse fragment of Joyce's first *roman à clef* presents and tests Shaw's credo for liberation through heterodoxy, whereas the finely honed and carefully compressed stream-of-consciousness *bildungsroman, Portrait,* alludes to Shaw in its patterns of reference, its archetypal symbols, and its supporting characters, even as it creates aesthetic distance from the emancipating paternal writer while at the same time choosing him. It defines, without crediting, the areas of kinship between the playwright and his wily disciple.

Although the beliefs of the artist hero concerning personal development echo those of G. B. S., the autobiographical and confessional implications of *Stephen Hero* and *Portrait* have many literary antecedents besides Shaw, notably St. Augustine's *Confessions,* which reveals, as an act of contrition, the growth of Augustine's faith. Whereas the *Confessions* concerns the search for a father, its outcome is the inverse of Joyce's, whose spiritual self-studies move through rejection of the Christian Father to triumphant artistic faith in a chosen father. The young man in *Portrait* chooses his own mythic paternity, one that suggests, at the same time that it hides, his kinship with Shaw. Rousseau's *Confessions,* to which Stephen Hero and Stephen Dedalus admit an affinity, is also the self-absorbed revelation of an alienated young man's growth, but its neurotic self-consciousness is perhaps less relevant than the soul-searching of other romantic precedents, from Blake to Shelley (heroes to young Shaw) to *Jane Eyre* and Baudelaire's *My Heart Laid Bare.* Charlotte Brontë (whose father was Irish) anticipated Joyce by depicting Jane as a dependent child, a "rebel slave" who grows up by refusing to be a "servant" to the unjust tyrannies of religion and patriarchal society. Nevertheless, that her tribulations end in a happy marriage makes her tale the antithesis of Shavio-Joycean antiromanticism—the sort that led Shaw to conclude that artistic independence was preferable to the "small beer" of domestic happiness. While Joyce was coming of age, Shaw fulminated against the romantic; Stephen Hero burned his poems because "they were romantic" (226). For, although romantic literature is full of fictionalized or directly confessional poetry and prose, its rebellions and its confessional mode were just about the only aspects of romanticism that both Shaw and Joyce iterated; as Stanley Weintraub writes, Shaw wrote his "autobiography—all his life" (*Unexpected Shaw* 16), not only in his "self-sketches" and supervised biographies but covertly in his dramatic characters. Like the hero/ine of romance, both Shaw and Joyce described themselves as sensitive outsiders, like Thomas Mann's Tonio Kröger (1903), confronted by respectable bourgeois society. A variant of the heroes of romance, Eugene Marchbanks in *Candida* is the Shavian portrait of the artist as a young exile, one who anticipates both of Joyce's portraits of Stephen.

Even though Joyce did not lack for thematic precedents, he found some very near to the bone of his contentions with society in his fellow Irishman, whose first efforts as a writer—portraits of himself as artist, socialist, even pugilist—were serialized in periodicals. *An Unsocial Socialist,* published serially between March and December 1884, caught the eye of William Morris while Joyce was still an infant. *Cashel Byron's Profession* was also published serially in *To-Day* as well as in "a misshapen 'Modern Press' edition of two thousand five hundred copies in March 1886" (H1 120). Annie Besant's socialist magazine *Our Corner* published *The Irrational Knot* and *Love among the Artists* between 1885 and 1888, and the novels were pirated in America. Joyce was, of course, still a child when Shaw's novels found their way into print, and there is no hard evidence that he read them as a youth, but the fact that he owned copies of *Cashel Byron's Profession* and *Love among the Artists* before 1920 attests to his interest, for Shaw's early novels were not exactly best-sellers or required reading for an avant-garde artist. His problem play *Candida*—a model of stage success on the mysterious subjects of woman and masculine vocation—also anticipates themes in Joyce's three most obviously autobiographical works. Like *Stephen Hero* and *Portrait,* it explores the sources of artistic inspiration and the fledgling artist's quest for independence.

"Fruting for Firstlings"—"A True Covenanter against the World": *Stephen Hero*

Like Shaw's novels of his nonage, the younger Dubliner's first effort to write autobiographical fiction concerns the quest for vocation in an alienating environment. Young Joyce seems to have conceived of his alter ego as a member of Shaw's "Order of Heroes" (MCE 14) like Dick Dudgeon, "the Devil's Disciple"—"a true Covenanter against the world" (CP 746). The first fruit of Joyce's selective self-disclosures describes action in a realistic style that foreshadows *Dubliners,* ranges over ideas in discussions that parallel the techniques of Shaw's novels, and uses dialogue as a means to reveal the character of the young hero, auguring the subjectivity of his later works, just as Shaw's first fiction predicted drama to be his forte. Joyce's rambling confessions are, however, less effective than Shaw's early novels—as Joyce no doubt recognized when he junked his first manuscript and began to create *Portrait.* Neither young Irishman had in his first fiction developed an idiosyncratic style, though Shaw's witty, protracted dialogues for the debate of ideas anticipate his discussion dramas, whereas Joyce's discursive third-person-limited narrative only hints at the methods of presenting and organizing experience that he would develop. Despite its effective use of details and its convincing dialogue, his juvenilia seem less orderly and more tentative than any of Shaw's prodigious first inventions, perhaps because *Stephen Hero* is incomplete. Although Stephen vaguely promulgates an aesthetic, Joyce's manuscript does not use it. But the range of *Stephen Hero* is Shavian, its conflicts those that Shaw had already discussed in print: disaffection with his homeland, his family, and his religion; the subversive route to artistic freedom; and the function of art.

As an apostle of art and a rebel against Irish institutions, Joyce's alter ego derives from Shaw and from Ibsen largely as the older Irishman interpreted him. Both Dubliners took the advice of the anarchic Ibsen, who wrote to Georg Brandes, "What I chiefly desire for you is a genuine, full-blooded egoism, which will force you for a time to regard what concerns you yourself as the only thing of any consequence.... [W]hen the whole history of the world appears to me like one great shipwreck ... the only important thing to do is to save yourself" (Ibsen, *Letters* 218). In discussing Stephen's drama essay with the young student, the president of the college tells Stephen that his theory, "if pushed to its logical conclusion—would emancipate the poet from all moral laws" (95). Because Shaw questioned and disdained the morality of the majority, he propounded the emancipation that the priest fears—a morality that confers upon the artist the right to freedom from middle-class constraints and the privilege of exposing the failures of bourgeois beliefs. The president calls Stephen a "paradoxist" (96), which is the title Joyce gave to Shaw (CW 208). The first draft of Joyce's self-portrait struggles between Shavian commitment to social reform (a commitment that he foisted on Ibsen) and Joycean desire for self-expression, even as it exposes social problems, as the means to personal redemption.

A self-styled revolutionary writer and enemy of the existing society, Shaw was enjoying immense popularity among the intelligentsia as Joyce started out on his literary career. After reading *The Quintessence of Ibsenism,* William Archer's translations of Ibsen and, Joyce claimed, a French translation of *When We Dead Awaken,* so great was his enthusiasm for the Norwegian playwright that his alter ego "suffered the most enduring influence of his life," Henrik Ibsen, but he did not mention his Irish champion. Slyly ignoring Shaw's adulatory study, Joyce averred that "Ibsen had no need of apologist or critic" (SH 40). But the interpretation of Ibsen to which Stephen adverts comes from Shaw's tract. In *The Quintessence of Ibsenism* he had argued that the new dramatist surpassing Shakespeare and Goethe was Ibsen. Copying Shaw and adding his own Catholic interpretation of the literary apostolic succession, Stephen Hero argues that Ibsen, not Shakespeare or Goethe, was "successor to the first poet of the Europeans," Dante (SH 41). In a section entitled "Better than Shakespear?" in his preface to *Three Plays for Puritans,* Shaw denigrated "Bardolatry" and argued that "the right to criticise Shakespear involves the power of writing better plays." The modern "Shakespear or Goethe" must give us a "new drama" with "new philosophy" (CP 750). In discussing his own *Caesar and Cleopatra,* G. B. S., with characteristic public immodesty, offered himself as the purveyor of the new philosophy.

Joyce's meandering manuscript mysteriously mentions but does not name the author of a "tract" so important, it seems, to Stephen's "insufficiently scanty knowledge" that, upon reading it, he determines that "Ibsen was the first among the dramatists of the world" (SH 41). The undisclosed inspiration for his Ibsenist enthusiasm was undoubtedly Shaw's tract *The Quintessence of Ibsenism.* Like the exiled autodidact who educated himself in the British Museum Reading Room, Joyce's young hero, seldom attending university lectures or taking exams, was "educating himself" (38). Stephen "examined all the bookstalls," where he found cheap, no doubt used, "old directories and volumes of sermons and unheard-of treatises" (145). Among them may have been treatises by Shaw, unheard of in Ireland. Stephen's arduous "research" was all the more ardent because "he imagined they had been <put under ban>" (34). With a reluctance to name sources that might jeopardize his appearance of originality, Joyce left out the antecedent of "they," thus omitting the identity of his unauthorized reading.

Further suggesting the forbidden nature of Stephen's studies, his father condemned as "inopportune . . . his son's wayward researches into strange literature" (87)—which no doubt included the alien dramas of the Scandinavian as well as the iconoclastic writings of the runaway Irish Protestant, whose subversive morality was just as daring, strange, and cosmopolitan as Ibsen's and even more relevant in provincial, Catholic Dublin. Because Stephen's friend Cranly read newspapers in the library, we can assume that James Joyce also did, at a time when Shaw was a regular contributor to newspapers and periodicals such as the *Fortnightly Review*, whose editor, the Irishman Frank Harris, was Shaw's friend. In 1900, it will be remembered, the *Fortnightly Review* published Joyce's first essay. Significantly, however, the fictional Stephen enjoyed notoriety because his classmates did not understand "what manner of ideas he favored" and therefore "rewarded" him for "originality" (39)—an originality preempted from Shaw but carefully cultivated as Stephen's own. Without jeopardizing his reputation for disconformity by ascribing sources, Stephen disdained "orthodox study."

In *Stephen Hero* the fledgling writer seems so busy responding to Shavian ideology that his "taste for elegance" is lost and his taste for "detail" too often smothered by abstract ruminations. Although Joyce would later distinguish himself by the efficacious arrangement of the concrete and sensuous details of his style, the young man was, despite claims of inventiveness, preoccupied with the theme of rebellion recommended by Shaw, whose writing distilled the advanced thinking of the time. While expropriating the arguments of the established playwright and polemicist by assaulting social institutions in *Stephen Hero*, Joyce also described his persona's sporadic attempts to distinguish himself from artistic purposes that Shaw espoused. Joyce's views are not clearly formulated in the ur-*Portrait*, but he co-opted the Shavian rejection of romanticism: the "romantic temper is an insecure, unsatisfied, impatient temper which sees no fit abode here for its ideals and chooses to behold them under insensible figures" (78). Shaw embraced the dissatisfaction and impatience of romanticism but disdained its inclinations toward abstraction. In rejecting the romantic predilection for "insensible figures," Joyce aligned himself with Shaw, who had a lifelong quarrel with Yeats over the poet's preference for abstract symbols—the "circus animals" that deserted the Nobel laureate poet in his old age. While groping toward the Shavian insistence that a writer must look at "abodes" (like *Widowers' Houses?*) in this world, Stephen nevertheless objected to the "profane" artist who aimed "to instruct, to elevate, and to amuse" (79)—perhaps the Shavian artist. Shaw advocated art that instructed and amused, but he opposed drama that pretended to "elevate," for he believed that the artist's business was to repudiate supposedly ennobling ideals. He had written that "as Man grows . . . he also raises himself from mere consciousness to knowledge by daring more and more to face facts and tell himself the truth" (MCE 47). *The Sanity of Art* argues that "every step in morals is made by challenging the existing standard of perfect propriety of conduct" (MCE 328). Stephen decides to call his subversive essays for the Literary and Historical Society "Art and Life" (81)—the subject of Shaw's tract in defense of the artist. He hopes that his paper will be a "trumpet call" to liberty (49), which was what Shaw, emulating Shelley, wanted his works to be.

Young Stephen wavers, however, between Shavian commitment and the bent of his own nature. Dubbed (perhaps ironically) by his creator "the fiery-hearted revolutionary" (an epithet more suitable for Fabian Shaw), Joyce's "heaven-ascending essayist" at times elected "the *revelation* of the beautiful" (SH 80). The conflict is not surprising, for Joyce's secret mentor urged his devil's disciples to fulfill "the individual will, upon which all duty is a restriction, founded on the conception of the will as naturally malign and devilish" (MCE 61). Young Stephen "cultivated an independence of soul which could brook very few subjections" (111). His "unapologetic egoism, his remorseless lack of sentiment for himself no less others" (151) is Shavianism par excellence, revealed emphatically in *An Unsocial Socialist* and refined and developed in *The Devil's Disciple* and *Man and Superman*. Shaw's secret student decided, like Dick Dudgeon and Don Juan, that "the life of an errant seemed to him far less ignoble than the life of one who had accepted tyranny of the mediocre because the cost of being exceptional was too high" (SH 179). He wanted to escape the "world in thrall" (described in Shaw's "Don Juan in Hell" in *Man and Superman*) to live according to "the voice of a new humanity, active, unafraid and unashamed" (194)—one implicit in

Ibsen and explicitly propounded by the self-proclaimed diabolonian Shaw. In the discussion of Stephen's paper on drama, Father Butt says that he will "be *advocatus diaboli*" (103), implying that Stephen takes the diabolonian position and that he is indeed a devil's disciple.

Stephen's high social purpose sounds like that of the author of *The Devil's Disciple* and "The Revolutionist's Handbook" appended to *Man and Superman,* except that the role of political activist was not congenial to him: "He was not sufficiently doctrinaire to wish to have his theory put to the test by a general revolution of society but he could not believe that his theory was utterly impracticable" (SH 203). Not a violent Marxist revolutionary, Stephen took the Shavian stance, despising "the strength of walls and watch dogs" (183) that entrap the timid multitudes and opaquely accepting the famed Fabian's "advanced" philosophy: "All modern political and religious criticism dispenses with presumptive States, [and] presumptive Redeemers and Churches. It examines the entire community in action and reconstructs the spectacle of redemption" (186). The Fabian Society, of which Shaw (with Beatrice and Sidney Webb) was the most famous member, aimed at "the prompt 'reconstruction of society in accordance with the highest moral possibilities'" (GBS 105). No doubt aware of the Shavian reputation as Devil's Disciple, young Joyce wrote in *Stephen Hero,* "Civilisation may be said indeed to be the creation of its outlaws" (178). Among them the Mephistophelian Shaw was, at the time when Joyce started writing, the most notorious Irish example, leading the attack on "the current morality" (BSL 1:277).

Having considered political activism, however, Stephen separates himself from Shaw's Fabian polemicism while still identifying with his heroic rebellion: "It was not part of his life to undertake an extensive alteration of society, but he felt the need to express himself such an urgent need, such a real need, that he was determined no conventions of society . . . should be allowed to stand in his way, and though a taste for elegance and detail unfitted him for the part of demagogue. . ."; his "general attitude" made him "an ally of collectivist politicians"—socialists, like heretical Shaw—who "are often very seriously upbraided by opponents who believe in Jehovahs, and decalogues" (147). Shaw had targeted Jehovah and the Ten Commandments because they oppose the very purpose they were institutionalized to serve, "human happiness" (BSL 1:277). In *The Sanity of Art* (1895), he wrote,

> Art should refine our sense of character and conduct, of justice and sympathy, greatly heightening our self-knowledge, self-control, precision of action, and considerateness, and making us intolerant of baseness, cruelty, injustice and intellectual superficiality, and vulgarity. The worthy artist or craftsman is he who serves the physical and moral sense by feeding them with pictures, musical compositions . . . poems, fictions, essays and dramas which call the heightened senses and ennobled faculties into pleasurable activity. (MCE 343)

Always drawing back from complete identity with Shavian politics and hence from loss of identity in his secret source, Stephen remonstrates with himself that he must distance himself from the "demagogue" and "phrases of the platform." He disaffiliates himself from anarchosocialists like Shaw, who announced, regarding his Fabian phase, "I was a man with some business in the world. . . . [M]y main business was socialism" (BSL 1:486–87). To prove it, Shaw led socialist demonstrations and through his incendiary street-corner oratory earned the reputation of a demagogue. Veering away from his precursor and arrogantly attempting to plant himself on aesthetic grounds, Stephen "acknowledged . . . in honest egoism that he could not take to heart the distress of a nation, the soul of which was antipathetic to his own, so bitterly as the indignity of a bad line of verse" (146). Contrarily, Shaw had declared in *The World* that "you might as soon divorce mathematics from astronomy . . . as art from morality" (H1 142). Art, he argued, should be useful, not merely beautiful. Whereas Stephen admired "a song by Shakespeare . . . remote from any conscious purpose" (79), thus setting himself off from Shaw, he identified with the thesis of *The Sanity of Art* by arguing in favor of the high calling of the artist: "Every age must look for its sanction to its poets and philosophers." The "realities" of art "alone give and sustain life" and vivify "the force of life" (80), which Shaw called the Life Force. Thus revealing the uncertainties of a young man, torn between the social purpose of the iconoclastic ideologue and his narcissistic desires for self-gratification through art, Stephen declares that "he wished to express his nature freely and fully for the benefit of society which he would enrich and also for his own benefit" (146–47).

Already Joyce had recognized that Shaw was his opposite as propagandist and "kinetic" artist and his equal in his view of what matters in life. Stephen wants "to walk nobly on the surface of the earth, to express oneself, without pretense, to acknowledge one's own humanity!" (142). Shaw's vitalism identified the Life Force with "man's God [which] is his own humanity." Young Joyce had listened to the admonition that a person's "first duty [is] to himself" (MCE 46): "He had first of all to save himself," abrogating "vague inactive pity from those who upheld a system of mutual service association towards those who accepted it" (SH 127). Stephen follows the lesson of the master by refusing to pity his pathetic, conforming Catholic sister and by being "cold-hearted" at her funeral, even though he rebels against the "entire apparatus of the State" (168) which seemed to denigrate the dead girl. Shaw admired above all else the courage to face up to such unjust authority. The boyish need for such self-assertion motivates Stephen in both of Joyce's *bildungsromans*.

Shaw exhorted his disciples to assert themselves by overthrowing religion, the first repressive ideal designed to enslave a person's soul: "First there was man's duty to God, with the priest as assessor" (MCE 45). In *Stephen Hero* one of Stephen's antagonists, Madden, defends Irishmen for being "true to the Church because it is our national Church, the Church our people have suffered for and would suffer again" (64). Stephen replies, "I'll put the priest on Tom an' I'll put the polisman on Mickey," to which Madden answers, "—I suppose you heard that sentence in some 'stage-Irishman's' play. It's a libel on our country" (64). Such a libel is perpetrated by G. B. S. in *John Bull's Other Island*. In *The Devil's Disciple* he compounded his criticism of institutionalized religion by making his hero the devil's advocate. While still at University College, Dublin, Joyce was a passive supporter of such apostasy. He distinguished himself by refusing to sign a petition against the seeming blasphemy of Yeats's *Countess Cathleen,* in which the countess sells her soul to the devil in order to save Ireland—hardly a stage Irishman's theme. Joyce preferred a secret pact with the Irish devil in London, whose stage Irishmen in *John Bull's Other Island* were comic libels on Irish character. Although in *Stephen Hero* Joyce could have been thinking also of the stage Irishman promulgated by Dion Boucicault on the English stage in the late nineteenth century, the stereotype uppermost in Joyce's mind after he began writing his novel probably derived from Shaw's 1904 play, which exposes the stage

Irishman as a hoax. While Shaw's comedy satirized the power of the parish priest in collusion with the visiting Englishman, Joyce's journeyman novel makes the priest-president of the college an idealist defender of religion. He declares that "our people have the faith and they are happy" (97). When the Very Reverend Dr. Dillon fears that Stephen's ideas are a danger to Catholic morality, Stephen recognizes an "importunate devil" inside himself, "whose appetite . . . for the farcical" (94) reminds the reader of Joyce's jesting *doppelgänger,* the diabolonian Shaw.

In disapproving of all didactic purposes as "Puritan," however, Stephen may be refuting the author of *Three Plays for Puritans.* Although admittedly a subversive preacher himself, Shaw disdained the hypocrisy and self-serving of "Crosstianity" (MCE 81), which is, perversely to Shaw, based on the symbolism of the cross, an instrument of torture. He parodied the Lord's Prayer, calling God "our blunderer which art not in heaven" and asking to be led "into all sorts of temptations" (MCE 100). Stephen, like Shaw, objects to the depiction of Christ as "a crooked ugly body for which neither God nor man have pity" (117). The young hero tries to imitate Shaw's blasphemous jibes by asking his mother why the Savior didn't "go by balloon" in his Ascension (132). He tells her that Christ's miracles are "Barnum"— circus stunts to entertain the public (133). His mother fears, no doubt correctly, that "it was those books" that led him "astray" (133–34). *The Quintessence of Ibsenism,* backed up by *The Devil's Disciple* and *Man and Superman,* would have sufficed as incentives. Don Juan's mocking jests seem to suit the temperament of the young Irishman better than the straight-faced seriousness of Ibsen and the strident egoism of libertarian Max Stirner and philosopher Nietzsche, parallels in *Stephen Hero's* background, to which Dominic Manganiello refers ("Politics" 243).

In telling Cranly, his secular confessor, of "his latest conflict with orthodoxy"—Shaw's persistent theme—Stephen announces, "I have left the Church" (138). As early as 1898 Shaw had publicized his defection from religion, as well as the power "in Ireland religious enough to redeem me from this abomination of desolation"—"the power of art" (SSS 46). Like Shaw, Stephen does not repudiate Christ the man but rather the Church under "his lieutenant in Rome" (141). Like Shaw in the preface to *John Bull's Other Island,* Stephen "cursed the farce of Irish Catholicism: an island [whereof] the inhabitants of which entrust their wills and minds to others that they ensure for themselves a life of spiritual paralysis, an island in which all the power and riches are in the keeping of those whose kingdom is not of this world, an island in which Caesar confesses [professes] Christ and Christ confesses Caesar that together they may wax fat upon a starveling rabblement" (146). These are imprecisely the sentiments of Shaw, who had in 1904 with the publication of *John Bull's Other Island* exposed this partnership between Christ and Caesar in Ireland. Stephen's speech seems to be an inversion of ex-priest Keegan's utopian ideal for Ireland in Shaw's Irish play, "where the State is the church and the Church the people . . . work is play and play is life . . . a temple in which the priest is the worshipper and the worshipper the worshipped . . . a godhead in which all life is human and all humanity divine" (Plays 452). In opposing "the watchcry . . . [of] Faith and Fatherland" (53), Stephen emulates Shaw.

Like his secret mentor, young Joyce scorned submission to church and alien state but also rejected physical-force patriotism and romantic nationalism. Stephen spurns students he believes are being trained to be philistines: "They respected spiritual and temporal authorities, the spiritual authorities of Catholicism and of patriotism, and the temporal authorities of the hierarchy of the government" (172–73). The author of *The Quintessence of Ibsenism* would have classed a paper delivered by Moynihan as the words of a deluded idealist: "Moynihan's paper showed that the true consoler of the afflicted was not the self-seeking demagogue with his ignorance and lax morality but the Church and that the true way to better the lot of the working class was not by teaching them to disbelieve in a spiritual and material order, working together in harmony, but by teaching them to follow [Christ] in humility" (SH 172).

Echoing the Irish demagogue in London, Stephen derides "patriotic and religious enthusiasts" as "fit to inhabit the fraudulent circles" of Dante's hell (or Shaw's hell in *Man and Superman*): "The spirit of the tame sodalists, unsullied and undeserving, he would petrify amid a ring of Jesuits in a circle of foolish and grotesque virginities and ascend above them and their baffled icons to where his Emma, with no detail of her earthly form or vesture abated, invoked him from a Mohammedan paradise" (159). Although, like G. B. S., Stephen condemns the tame conformists, he is, like Marchbanks in *Candida,* still tempted by romantic adoration of the female, unlike Shaw's Don Juan, who wants to escape from the worship of women. Like Marchbanks, Stephen momentarily gives in to the idolization of the Other (who remains, however, in her physical form) that he despises in his more realistic moments, because, like Don Juan, he believes that woman will distract him from his quest to become the artist-philosopher.

Defining himself as a critic of social hypocrisy (like Shaw), Stephen insists that Hughes, the nationalist, would become a barrister in the service of Britain, "yet he sneers at the Parliamentary Party because they take an oath of allegiance." Some Irishmen train in English militia camps while hurley players ostentatiously refuse "to wear the redcoat" and many Gaelic Leaguers are in the Civil Services, hence are servants in the pay of the colonial government (63–64). Such disingenuous patriotism was one of Shaw's targets. Stephen particularly dislikes Hughes, the Gaelic teacher whose rabid nationalism is the kind that Shaw rejected as "quaint." When Stephen refuses to sign a testimonial for the tsar's peace initiative, however, he makes a feeble attempt to be apolitical and to cultivate his own garden, while at the same time protesting against the hypocritical proposal of a despot. In his passivity, he reveals himself to be the opposite of the activist Shaw, even though his disapproval of the tsar matches that of the Fabian activist. The inspirational Fabian had indeed led a demonstration against the tsar in 1896. Stephen's essay "Drama and Life" is, however, a concerted effort to veer away from the anxiety of influence by denying that the chief aim of literature is education. Stephen does not want to "prejudice his success by oaths to his patria," in context his country, but perhaps also to his spiritual father, for he argues that the ends of art are "esthetic" (77). His friend McCann, though, views Stephen's essay from a Shavian perspective: "The modern world had to face pressing problems; and he considered that any writer who would call attention to these problems in a striking way was well worthy of every serious person's consideration" (102).

The model for McCann was Francis Skeffington, who probably recommended Shaw's writings to Joyce. After Skeffington was jailed for agitating against conscription into the British army at the start of World War I, Shaw wrote a "strong letter" in his defense that was published— could the Ulyssean date be significant?—in the *Freeman's Journal* on June 16, 1915 (see Weintraub, *Unexpected Shaw* 164–65). The pacifist became Sheehy-Skeffington when he married; as a feminist, he took his wife's name, combining it with his own. A nondrinker, vegetarian, and antivivisectionist like Shaw, he differed from the older Irishman in an area crucial to Joyce. Because Skeffington remained a Catholic and believed in personal chastity for both male and female before marriage, his friendship with Joyce cooled after Joyce's elopement with Nora Barnacle. However, to Sheehy-Skeffington's puritan morality, the dramatist who wrote *The Philanderer* clearly did not subscribe. If Joyce needed a foil for Stephen's aesthetics and a model for his sexual rebellion, he found both in Shavian theory and praxis.

Upset by the hypocritical connections between propriety, property, and prostitution, Stephen argues with the "patriots." He avers that Madden's medical school teacher who lectured on "Sanitary Science or Forensic Medicine . . . is at the same time the landlord of a whole street of brothels" (65). Thus Joyce makes a stab at the hypocrisies that Shaw attacked in *Widowers' Houses* and *Mrs. Warren's Profession*. Longing for sexual experience without wedlock, Stephen opposes marriage as "simony"—trafficking in holy objects. As Shaw, concurring with Engels and John Stuart Mill on the matter, had clarified in *Mrs. Warren's Profession*, Victorian marriage, like prostitution, treated a woman's body as property sold for monetary gain. Young Stephen agrees with Shaw in opposing the commodification of female flesh, which is, under capitalism, "a corporate asset of the State: If she traffic with it she must sell it either as a harlot or as a married woman or as a working celibate or as a mistress" (202). While Joyce was revising *Stephen Hero* (making it into *Portrait*), Shaw wrote in the preface to *Getting Married* (1908) that bold free-thinkers "can no more bring themselves to commit adultery than to commit any common theft, while women who loathe sex slavery more fiercely than Mary Wollstonecraft are unable to face the insecurity and discredit of the vagabondage which is the masterless woman's only alternative to celibacy" (CP 41). Claiming himself to be "like most Socialists, an extreme Individualist," Shaw defended *Mrs. Warren's Profession* as an exposé of sex as trading in women's bodies without a "moral minimum" wage (CP 726–27). In *The Quintessence of Ibsenism* he argued that a woman is a human being, not an object of commerce, but in both marriage and prostitution her favors are for sale.

Stephen Hero emulates his belief: "A woman is (incidentally) a human being and a human being's love and freedom is not a spiritual asset of the State" (202). Moreover, like Shaw, who protested against binding himself by patriarchal oaths such as marriage vows (though he gave in to Charlotte Townshend), Stephen "had what he called a 'modern' reluctance to give pledges" (204). Orthodox in his iconoclasm, Stephen declares bitterly that "there is no such thing as love in the world"; hence, as in sound Shavianism, romance gives way to the reality of Stephen's inept proposition to Emma Clery. Above all he does not want to get trapped by "duty," the villain of *The Quintessence of Ibsenism*. Recognizing the dangers of the path taken, Stephen "was convinced . . . that a dull discharge of duties, neither understood nor congenial, was far more dangerous and far less satisfactory" (179) than the rebel course he follows.

Stephen Hero may be influenced by Shaw's *Candida,* which was the talk of London in 1904 when Joyce was writing his tentative novel. Emma Clery is, like Candida, a strong, independent, but ultimately conventional woman who holds her own in discussion with a young man, even though he patronizes her as a philistine. Unlike Candida, Emma does not have a leading role, but, like Marchbanks, Stephen reads to the woman of choice, who gives little sign of understanding her intense young admirer. Nurturing sympathy, as well as the desire for masculine attention, prompts both women to encourage their wooers, but acceptance of the stereotypical role prescribed for women prompts them to turn their unconventional suitors away. Stephen tries to tempt Emma away from her Catholic obligations, just as Marchbanks tries to lure Candida away from her preacher husband and hence from her allegiance to Protestantism. When Stephen berates Emma for her social conformity, he tells her to "apply to McCann who was the champion of women" (67)—to Sheehy-Skeffington, a feminist like Shaw but one who championed chastity. Whereas Candida turns to her minister husband Morell after rejecting her importunate suitor, Emma turns to the priest Moran, who will perpetuate her image as frigid Madonna, a parallel to Candida, whom Shaw admittedly compared to the Virgin Mary. In *Stephen Hero* Emma's conventionality annoys her proud pursuer, whose proposal of a night of "love" frightens her away and in effect pushes Stephen toward liberation.

In rejecting conventional courtship and marriage, Stephen also denies another Shavian humbug: the family. Stephen grows "against the tendency of his family" (48). He "did not consider his parents very seriously" (111)—a defensive remark that Shaw might have made. Stephen is stung by the very idea of "*paterfamilias*" (52). Like the Irish dreamer whom Shaw's Larry Doyle condemns for living by imagination helped along by alcohol, Stephen's father lives in his illusions: "He knew that his own ruin had been his own handiwork but he had talked himself into believing that it was the handiwork of others. He had his son's distaste for responsibility without his son's courage" (110)—the key virtue in Shaw's ethical code: "Courage," he wrote, is "the virtue of virtues" (CP 164). Stephen's father "had not an acute sense of the rights of private property; he paid rent very rarely" (15). The young man is aware that "union between father and son had been worn away by the usages of daily life" (110). The ephebic intellectual is deeply annoyed by his father's disdain for books (85). He "avoided his father sedulously because he now regarded his father's presumption as the most deadly part of a tyranny, internal and external, which he determined to combat with might and main" (209). He was following advice that Joyce found in the literary father whose presence he sedulously covered up. While Stephen's father presses his oldest son to redeem him (111) and his mother tries to impose her narrow Catholic morality upon him, Stephen expostulates to Cranly on "the tyranny of the home" (126), discussed by Shaw in *The Quintessence of Ibsenism* and the prefaces to *Getting Married* (1908) and *Misalliance* (1910). He wrote of "marriage as a useless sacrifice of human beings to an ideal" and the destructiveness of belief in "the purity of home life" (MCE 89).

Stephen reproaches himself for lack of sympathy with his sister but cannot "honestly" admit that the reproach is just (126). Isabel is the quintessential representative of the docile majority, and Stephen, like an orthodox Shavian, thinks she is spiritually dead, for she "had acquiesced in the religion of her mother" and accepted all of her values without question. "She had exactly the temper for a Catholic wife of limited intelligence and of pious docility" and was promised heaven if she died. Stephen recognizes her hopeless entrapment (which is probably the basis for his story "Eveline") but does not feel kinship or natural affection for her. In this he replicates the seemingly heartless "Unsocial Socialist" of Shaw, with whose insensitivity the Stephen of *Portrait* armors himself at the novel's close. True to his image of "The Heartless Man" who will not pray over his wife's corpse, Shaw made headlines when his mother died in 1913 and again when his sister Lucy died in 1920: he refused to be maudlin or grave and, in fact, took toward their deaths the festive attitude of an Irishman at a wake.

Joyce's hero is estranged from his family. The tyro's first attempt to define himself in prose disdains the father and describes Stephen's mother as a symbol of wifely duty and motherly moral pressure. When she wants Stephen to make his "Easter Duty," he is "much annoyed that his mother should try to wheedle him into conformity by using his sister's ill health as an argument" (131–32). When mother and son quarrel, she accuses him of "pride of intellect" (134) and threatens to burn his books. Probably the main book that would be thrown into the fire would be *The Quintessence of Ibsenism,* which proclaims young Stephen's credo: "The realist declares that when a man abnegates the will to live and be free in a world of the living and free, seeking only to conform to ideals for the sake of being, not himself, but 'a good man,' then he is morally dead and rotten" (MCE 53). Whereas Shavian theory buttresses all of Stephen Hero's resolves, Joyce's protagonist does not contemplate the idea of elective paternity. Indeed, perhaps the most significant factor missing in *Stephen Hero* is the surrogate and symbolic father who informs *A Portrait of the Artist as a Young Man*. If, like Stephen Hero who begins to study Irish, Joyce had learned by the time he began to revise his novel that he shared a Gaelic surname with Shaw, the realization may have influenced the structure and substance of *Portrait:* in it the search for a father of Joyce's heterodoxy ends in Stephen's epiphanic recognition of his spiritual father, upon whom he relies to be with him "now" as he prepares to exile himself from Ireland.

A Portrait of the Artist as a Young Shavian: "O Foenix Culprit!"

In its often desultory and too often murky prose, occasional dramatic dialogue, and encounters with the banal realities of Dublin's streets, *Stephen Hero* foreshadows the themes implicit in *A Portrait of the Artist as a Young Man,* in which Shavian influence is more subtle but equally pervasive. Fortunately for Joyce and his admirers, when he began to rewrite his novel, he had assimilated Shavian ideas sufficiently to graft them onto the patterns of imagery and archetype that evoke and interface with the growth of the youthful artist's consciousness. Shaw stated that "the real slavery of today is slavery to ideals of goodness (MCE 141). His preface to *John Bull's Other Island* asserts that an Irishman's only hope is to get out of Ireland in order to exercise his talents. Shaw contrasted the Protestant spirit with the docile self-abnegation inculcated by the Roman Church and supported by Dublin Castle in the Irish populace: "The Protestant is . . . an individualist, a free-thinker, a self-helper . . . a mistruster . . . of the State, a rebel" (CP 448–49).

Repudiating the Irish Catholic stereotype that Shaw set up, Joyce created a "Protestant" rebel, but he no longer needed stealthily to restate Shavian hypotheses. Instead he illustrated them in the episodes that refract Stephen Dedalus's psychological development. Young Stephen grows as he develops Shavian courage. Whereas Shaw proselytized for the end of "idols, domestic, moral, religious and political" (MCE 140), Joyce had discovered that he could communicate his feelings regarding these idols by grounding them in the experience of his protagonist and by referring to their objective correlatives and to archetypal iconoclasts who broke them.

Among the light-bringing renegades upon whom Joyce patterned his psychological novel were Prometheus, Lucifer, and Siegfried, all of whom Shaw touted as hero-redeemers, heroic scapegoats bringing a boon to people by providing the fire and light of artistic heterodoxy. Shaw's commentary in *The Perfect Wagnerite* that "we must, like Prometheus, set to work to make new men instead of vainly torturing old ones" (MCE 249) puts an ironic light on Dante Riordan's unwitting allusion to Zeus's torment of Prometheus; in threatening Baby Tuckoo she warns that the "eagles will come and pull out his eyes" (P 2). The line alludes to Prometheus, who stole fire for mankind and was punished for his benefaction by Zeus in the form of an eagle who attacked the hero's liver. Eyes, far more vulnerable for the young boy whom we discover in the second episode wearing glasses, relate to the network of images of potential blindness and Stephen's climactic vision of mortal beauty and conversion from the *lex talionis* religion of Ireland. The "eagles will . . . pull out his eyes" alludes simultaneously to the Biblical threat of punishment for failure to honor parents—in Shaw's gospels a failure that is a virtue if the individual is to become a "free-souled" person. Proverbs 30:17 warns that "the eye that mocketh at his father, and despiseth to obey his mother, the ravens of the valley shall pick it out, and the young eagles shall eat it." Although *Portrait* mocks Simon Dedalus, Stephen's father, and describes Stephen's disobedience to his Catholic mother, his rebellions do not finally produce the promised torture.

The sermon at the beginning of chapter 3 thunders that the disobedient sinner, like Satan, will plunge "headlong through space" (124) into perdition. It promises ominously that the Adamic sinner, comparable to the fallen angel, Lucifer, will be "scourged with five thousand lashes" (119) for the sin of disobedience. Shaw's "Diabolonian Ethics" (CP 744–48), relying on William Blake (whose Devil, he wrote, "is a Redeemer"; 746), argues that disobedience in the service of self-realization is a rare virtue and that "duty," not disobedience to God's edicts, is "the primal curse from which we must redeem ourselves" (MCE 46). While writing *Portrait,* Joyce owned a copy of *The Devil's Disciple* (1898), which makes a hero of the self-willed, Luciferian outsider opposed to the orthodoxies of religion, state, and obsequious colonialism. Shaw described the stance of Dick Dudgeon, the Devil's Disciple, as the "Diabolonian position," new to theater but not to literature: "From Prometheus to the Wagnerian Siegfried, some enemy of the gods, unterrified of those oppressed by them, has always towered among the heroes of the loftiest poetry. Our newest idol, the Superman, celebrating the death of godhead, may be younger than the hills but he is as old as the shepherds" (CP 746).

Shaw referred to Nietzsche and to "The Marriage of Heaven and Hell" for corroboration, which Joyce also found in Blake, while rejecting the mysticism and private mythology that attracted Yeats to him. Shavian allusion to Nietzsche is paralleled in Joyce (see Buck Mulligan's mocking reference to himself and Stephen as supermen in *Ulysses* 1.709). But young Joyce was probably more interested in reading his fellow Dubliner's plays and prefaces than in studying the German philosopher, for Shaw's Irish experience and his insurrections validated Joyce's own. In Dick Dudgeon he would have found an instigation for Stephen, for Dick is "impassioned only for saving grace, and not to be led or turned by wife or mother, Church or State, pride of life or lust of flesh" (CP 747). Despite the necessity for Joyce to demur regarding Stephen's "pride of life" and "lust" in charting his protagonist's growth, the writer shows how his persona refuses to be led by women, family, Catholicism, and nationality in his quest to identify with the Dedalian father, whom Joyce associates with the rebellious archetypes that Shaw preferred. Shaw's "Revolutionist's Handbook," appended to *Man and Superman,* gives advice that Joyce's hero takes: "Never resist temptation." "Do not love your neighbor as yourself. If you are on good terms with yourself, it is an impertinence, if on bad, an injury." "Liberty means responsibility. That is why most men dread it" (CP 188–89).

Joyce's portrait of the artist as a fallen, light-bringing pagan iconoclast approximates the views of Shaw, who wrote, "Beware of the man whose god is in the skies" (CP 191). Like Shaw, Stephen is a "foenix culprit"— one reborn in the *felix culpa* of a happy fall.

A third hero who fights the god of the skies is Siegfried. In *The Perfect Wagnerite* (1895) Shaw examines Wagner's characters as parallels to society. In *Siegfried* there are philistine giants and dwarves; an "idealist" god Wotan, comparable to the patriarchal god of Judeo-Christianity; and the "realist" superman Siegfried, who must overthrow Wotan. The hero overthrows the establishment as Stephen Dedalus does, for the sake of self-realization. In chapter 2, "Wagner as Revolutionist," Shaw categorizes giants as smugly narrow conformists, gods as idealists stuck on illusions that support their hegemony, and the hero as the highest form of creative realist. In *Man and Superman,* the Devil remarks that he once entertained both Nietzsche and Wagner, the first of whom "raked up the Superman, who is as old as Prometheus," and the second of whom "invented a Superman called Siegfried" (Plays 293).

In *The Perfect Wagnerite* Shaw admires Siegfried as the "totally unmoral person, a born anarchist, the ideal of Bakoonin, an anticipation of the 'overman' of Nietzsche" (MCE 227). In a chapter entitled "Siegfried as Protestant," Shaw lauds him as "the healthy man raised to perfect confidence in his own impulses by an intense and joyous vitality" characteristic of "the man who is delivered from conscience" (MCE 24). With a strategically placed reference in *Portrait* to Wagner's opera, Joyce evokes Siegfried as well as Shaw's analysis of him as a subversive hero. As Stephen walks across the quadrangle with Cranly, "the birdcall from *Siegfried* whistled softly followed them" (237). The courage and vision of Siegfried are called up, as is the plot of Wagner's opera, in which, after slaying the dragon Fafner, Siegfried is able to communicate with the forest birds—no doubt related in Joyce's network of images to the dove woman, vision of whom elicits in Stephen an ecstatic epiphany. Siegfried is vouchsafed such communication because he has a drop of dragon blood in his mouth. Having undergone a fortunate fall that inverts the role of St. George, he has slain the dragon of religion. The birds tell him of the Rhinegold, which makes its wearer invisible, and of the ring that will make him ruler of the world if he forfeits love.

All of this reflects upon the action and the richly allusive method of

Portrait. Stephen resists the priesthood and Cranly, the representative of religion. He has an intimation of his vocation as the artist-hero who will be invisible in his creations and of the fictional world over which he will, as creator, be ruler. Like Siegfried, Stephen forfeits love in order to fulfill his destiny. Like Shavian heroes Dick Dudgeon and Don Juan, Stephen rejects romantic love in exchange for subversive power. Like Don Juan, Stephen opts to "steer" instead of to "drift" in hell (Plays 388), even though in *Man and Superman* John Tanner, Shaw's Don Juan, is trapped, like Shaw himself, into marriage (his apt pupil would outdo him in the application of his principles). Like a Shavian realist determined to live "by the laws of his own nature" (CP 747), Stephen Dedalus escapes the nets of romantic love and philistine conformity to ideals.

Joyce's protagonist is confronted by idealists, like Dante Riordan, who blindly assert the ideology of the priests. Dante, who shares the name of the author of *The Divine Comedy,* represents punitive Catholic orthodoxy in *Portrait.* A parallel to Mrs. Dudgeon, the arch-Puritan of *The Devil's Disciple,* she represents a sterile, bitterly vindictive Christianity. Both the Puritan and the Catholic pride themselves on demanding the letter of religious law. Both are scandalized by male impropriety, Mrs. Dudgeon by the illegitimate child Essy and Dante by the adultery of Charles Stewart Parnell and Kitty O'Shea. Dante reacts to Baby Tuckoo's innocent attraction to Eileen Vance, a little girl whose parents are Protestant, by threatening punishment. In a Catholic household even baby talk about such a marriage was apocryphal. Shaw wrote that in Ireland, in Protestant households, similar prejudices pertained (SSS 45), and like Shaw's self-sketches, *Portrait* depicts juvenile responses to such bigotry.

In Joyce the embryonic Promethean is threatened with blindness, after Stephen's mother urges him to apologize and Dante intimidates him. Unimaginative "people told me," Shaw declared, that "I should go to hell if I did not make myself agreeable to them" (CP 48). The author of *Portrait* was already aware of Shaw's warning that ideals are "only something to blind us." "The realist at last loses patience with ... [them] altogether" (MCE 53). Furthermore, to represent "cruelty as the beneficent act of God, which is exactly what all floggers do, is to add to the torture of the body ... the maiming and blinding of the child's soul" (CP, 49). Against such maiming, Joyce's young Stephen responds after being pandybatted for breaking his glasses. Joyce put the blindness-vision paradox to work in manifesting Stephen's development from the menace of blindness to his epiphanic vision at the climax of the novel, which occurs after he repudiates the blindness—the eyeless obedience (P 160)—demanded by the priesthood. Paradoxically, his epiphany is elicited by a vision at once pagan and Christian: "A girl . . . in midstream alone and still, gazing out to sea." Like a pagan Venus and profane "crane" trailing "emerald" seaweed (for Ireland), the girl is also a dove-like third person of an earthly trinity, a holy ghost to Stephen, who becomes one with a mythic progenitor. Her flesh, like Mary's, is "softhued as ivory" (171). In his paradoxical moment of revelation, the young man has an ecstatic moment of At-one-ment with the flesh.

But before his conversion to what Shaw called the "religion of art," the young "paradoxist" (as the president of the college calls him in *Stephen Hero;* 96) undergoes trials described by the paradoxical Shaw. The heterodox playwright argued that "duty arises at first, a gloomy tyranny, out of man's helplessness, his self-mistrust, in a word his abstract fear. He personifies all that he abstractly fears as God, and straightway becomes a slave of his duty to God" (MCE 45). Of course, Joyce did not need Shaw to remind him that religion was a pervasive and repressive influence on his life, but Shaw probably helped him to realize that it was the major despotism that confronted him in his youth. Joyce's youthful persona is repeatedly assaulted by the authority of the Church, represented by Dante and his mother, his Jesuit teachers, and his college classmate Cranly. Shaw, indeed, blamed the grownups. In his 1910 preface to *Misalliance* (a book in Joyce's library), entitled "Parents and Children," he denounced corporal punishment as "a sham." "The improvement, the beating, and caning, the breaking of young spirits, the arrest of development, the atrophy of all inhibitive power, except the power of fear, are real" (CP 73). Shaw admitted to not learning his "school lessons, having [like the truants in "An Encounter"] much more important ones in hand" (55). He pointed out that nonconforming boys were deemed "disloyal wasters and idlers" (56), anticipating the Prefect of Studies at Clongowes Wood who calls his young students "lazy idle little schemers" (P 49). Shaw urged that "a child should begin to assert itself early" (CP 78), advice that Joyce took in portraying Stephen's courageous confrontation with the rector after being cruelly and unjustly abused by the Prefect of Studies, who accuses him of lying—

"Broke my glasses! An old schoolboy trick!" (P 50). Shaw advocated "Children's Rights" and "A Child's Magna Charta" (CP 84) such as the reader of Joyce's vivid pandybatting episode might want to sign.

An Unsocial Socialist presents the pattern of youthful, heroic defiance that informs Stephen's development at Clongowes Wood. Shaw's early novel begins with a description of the encounter between a girl about to be expelled from school and her principal. Like Stephen Dedalus, unjustly accused, she triumphs in her interview. A defender against tyrannical teachers, Shaw insisted that in school he learned "lying, dishonorable submission to tyranny, dirty stories, a blasphemous habit of treating love and maternity as obscene jokes" (CP 56). At Clongowes Wood, boys were learning much the same things. Stephen humiliates himself by covering up his love of his mother in order to escape the ridicule of his classmates. Shaw attacked the "violation of children's souls" by those whose "cruelty must be whitewashed by a moral excuse . . . hypocrisy as well as cruelty." Such "pious fraud," he wrote, "is an attempt to pervert that divine mystery called the child's conscience into an instrument of our own convenience . . . a sin . . . impudently practised by popes, parents, and pedagogues" (49).

According to Shaw, if the adolescent is sufficiently frightened by guilt, he will submit briefly to "duty" to what Shaw called the "God of Wrath." Guilt over his sexual "sin" causes Stephen's terrified response to the sermon on hell that he hears while on a religious retreat; this would, to a Devil's Disciple, represent, by its very nature, the withdrawal from real life, with which the budding realist should be grappling. The hellfire sermon condemning Lucifer, a hero to Shaw, frightens Stephen into becoming, for the nonce, the servant of God. *Portrait* vividly depicts the teenager's sense of sin: "His soul sickened at the thought of a torpid snaky life feeding itself out of the tender marrow of his life and fattening upon the slime of lust" (140). While blaming the snake as a parasite feeding on his sin, Stephen does not know that later he would identify with the serpent, aware that the ideals tormenting him with guilt were avatars of the *lex talionis,* comparable, so Shaw averred, to "man-eating idols red with human sacrifice" (MCE 97). Joyce was also no doubt aware that in attacking the rebel angel for the sin of pride, the priest assailed a virtue in the Shavian gospel.

Before accepting his pride as a merit, Stephen becomes a servant of God, following the path outlined by Shaw: the servant of the angry God evolves, as his fears diminish, into a devotee of the God of "love," duty to whom pressures him to become an "altruist" (MCE 45). After the repentant sinner turns to religion, he tries to be a model of Christian virtues, all of which coerce him into suppressing his instincts, no longer "for hours sinning in thought and deed" (P 115). Stephen "would be one with others and with God. He would love his neighbour. He would love God Who made and loved him. He would kneel and pray with others and be happy" (134). He would, in short, become part of the compact majority, subservient to their religion. In humbling himself Stephen turns to self-sacrifice—loving "his neighbour" and the God who "loved him." Submissively, he becomes a slave to religious duties, abstract demons to the Devil's Disciple—Sunday "dedicated . . . to . . . the Holy Trinity, Monday to the Holy Ghost, Tuesday to the Guardian Angels" (147)—all "abstractions invested with collective consciousness or collective authority" (MCE 97), which Shaw taught the realist to disdain.

The guardian angel for Dedalus would turn out, however, to be a fallen one like Shaw—the Icarian son who preempts the father's power by daring to disobey. For Stephen passes "beyond the challenge of the sentries who had stood as guardians of his boyhood and had sought to keep him among them that he might be subject to them and serve their ends" (P 165). But like Dante leaving the Inferno—which is, according to Keegan in *John Bull's Other Island,* Ireland—Stephen had found "an unseen path" of escape, one that Joyce forbade his readers to see. An avatar of Virgil leading Stephen out of the Hibernian hell of ignorant philistines and conforming idealists, Shaw was a shadowy guide.

According to the Shavian model, if a person's courage grows sufficiently, he can repudiate "duty," "the primal curse" (MCE 46) from which he must redeem himself in order to discover the god inside him. Motivated by his own godlike will, the realist will vow, as Joyce put it, summarizing his own and his undisclosed mentor's positions, "not to serve" that in which he no longer believes (P 247). According to Shaw, however, the "Covenanter against the world . . . becomes, like all genuinely religious men, a reprobate and an outcast" (CP 746). Such a rebel will, Shaw wrote, be persecuted by "idealists" like Father Dolan, who hits Stephen with his pandybat, and their philistine followers. Thus Heron, Boland, and Nash pummel Stephen for preferring the immoral "heretic" Byron to Lord Tennyson, the representative Victorian poet of the British Empire. Shaw had praised Byron as a greater poet than Wordsworth because of his "unscrupulous freedom of thought" (CP 52). Also while denigrating Tennyson as the poet of the establishment, Shaw praised Shelley, although idealists attacked him as a depraved "fiend" (MCE 51). An admirer of Shelley, like Shaw, Stephen is punished for defending one of his devilish forerunner's heroes—as Shaw informs us—the artist who tries to "adapt the world to himself" and to unmask the idols of the bourgeoisie (CP 164).

In the climactic epiphany scene of *Portrait,* Stephen redeems himself from the "primal," the original sin, by interpreting his fall as fortunate—what Joyce would call in *Finnegans Wake* "Felicitous Culpability." After going through the dark night of his soul because of his fall into sin with a prostitute, he recognizes his kinship with common humanity and becomes an exultant Shavian "realist"—"alone ... happy and near the wild heart of life," which Shaw identified with female fecundity and, in creations like Candida and Ann Whitefield of *Man and Superman,* female beauty. Shaw called the heart of life the "Life Force." After Stephen's conversion into the free-souled exponent of the religion of art, he vows "to live, to err, to fall, to triumph, to recreate life out of life" (171), like a "foenix culprit" in the *Wake*—in short to be a Devil's Disciple, the iconoclastic artist-hero, fearlessly alone and devoted to the spirit of "mortal beauty."

Shaw argued in the preface to *John Bull's Other Island* that one of the constraining idealisms that can entrap the lone artist-hero is sentimental patriotism. At the time of Parnell's political fall, in personal letters and a letter published in the *Star,* Shaw "defended Parnell against the outcry 'Parnell Must Go!'" and, according to Michael Holroyd, probably published *The Quintessence of Ibsenism* as an attack on the conventional morality that deposed the Home Rule leader (H1 198). Nevertheless, by 1904 Shaw was pointing out the danger of retrograde, hero-worshipping nationalism. He entitled one section of his preface "The Curse of Nationalism" (CP 456) and contended in it that "Nationalism stands between Ireland and the light of the world. Nobody in Ireland of any intelligence likes Nationalism" (457). Shaw analyzed and repudiated such patriotism as ineffectual and self-defeating because, in Ireland, the power of the Church conspires with the colonialist government in vitiating its effect, while its backward-looking nostalgia for the past and for the dead Gaelic language is an opiate instead of an instigation toward assertion of freedom from England. Except in Stephen's anguished cry that his "soul frets in the shadow" of the language of the English Jesuit Dean of Studies (P 189), Joyce's response to the Irish situation concurred with Shaw's. The idealistic Parnellism of Stephen's father and Mr. Casey, revealed in the Christmas dinner conflict with Dante, is another net for Joyce's alter ego. He escapes its tyranny, but not without arguing with friends who represent Ireland's conflicting and afflicting beliefs.

Although in *Stephen Hero* Joyce did not self-consciously present these ideals in single, representative characters, in *Portrait,* as in a Shaw discussion play, the valorized character engages in dialectic with peers, each of whom promotes the claims of a restraining ideal. The peasant nationalism of Stephen's fellow student Davin, who "worshipped the sorrowful legend of Ireland" (181), is a net "flung" at "the soul of a man" born in Ireland "to hold it back from flight" (203). His friend MacCann pressures Stephen to recognize the "dignity of altruism" (298), another ideal that would divert the tyro artist in his quest for freedom. Like the priests who are his teachers, the layman Cranly is a confessor for Stephen; he represents the conventional ties of family and religion, which collude to form yet another snare. A religious idealist, Cranly attacks Stephen for failing in his duty to his mother—"on the score of love for one's mother" (247)—and denigrates his rebellion.

Like a Shavian debater out of "Don Juan in Hell," Lynch, the tempter to aesthetic knowledge, enters into an almost Socratic dialogue with Stephen (Shaw called his dialogues "Shavo-Socratic"), which gives the budding artist the opportunity to test his aesthetic system. Its theory, derived from Aristotle and Aquinas, differentiates Joyce's persona from Shaw, who argued that art is "kinetic" because it aims to communicate truth and move people toward action rather than merely to convey beauty to the beholder. Stephen argues for the aesthetic "stasis" that gives the art object the venue for revealing its own "*integritas, consonantia, claritas*" (its own "wholeness, harmony" and essential "whatness"; P 212–13), qualities that distinguish the method of *Portrait* from the intentions of Joyce's ideological sire. During the dialogue with Lynch, the young artist is at pains to develop an aesthetic theory antipathetical to Shaw's, a theory that informs Joyce's novel.

However, the images of flight in *Portrait,* supported by the Icarian archetype that Joyce contributed to build his story about the search for the father, have their precedent in Shavian prescription. While discussing marriage, Shaw urged the greenhorn "free-souled person" to "fly" from captivity (MCE 61). Indeed, wedlock is the third ideal Shaw urged the novitiate realist to escape, for he believed that the ideal of the family as a "holy and natural" institution was another illusion to be swept away. His chapter "The Womanly Woman," like most of his early writings, rejects the conventional "idealization of marriage," for "love loses its charm when it is not free" (MCE 56). As Kershner notes, Stephen Dedalus "is at pains to present as radical and self-generated" his stance on marriage (9), but it reiterates Shaw's radical view. In *Stephen Hero* Joyce's persona tries to tear off the mask of conventional courtship by proposing to Emma Clery that she spend a night with him. Revealing herself to her unconventional suitor as a benighted philistine, she is shocked by his proposal and subsequently snubs him to flirt with a priest, who supposedly could not make an indecent offer. Joyce attributes to his young hero the sexist motives that Shaw disapproved when a man regarded "Woman, not as an end in herself like Man, but solely as a means to minister to his appetite" (MCE 58). In any case, in *Portrait* Joyce rejected the traditional novelistic courtship that, to Shaw, disguises "the brutalities of the sex instinct" with contrived happy endings.

The dialogic relation of Shaw's *Candida* to Joyce's roman à clef is effaced in *Portrait,* but Stephen's liberation parallels that of Shaw's Marchbanks. The young poet, expelled like Candide from a Westphalian Eden, shares many of Stephen's idealizing tendencies. Like Stephen, Marchbanks goes about "in search of love" and, frustrated, speaks "foolish lies" (Plays 135). Preferring romance to reality in her relationship with her young suitor, Candida urges Marchbanks to "talk moonshine as you always do" (144). In his romantic moods, Joyce associated woman with "the moon's grey golden meshes" in *Chamber Music* and other poems. In verses that circumvent sexuality with clichés of courtly love, Stephen's amorous desire for Emma is distanced by "the maiden lustre of the moon" (P 70). He associates Emma with lunar beauty, thus imitating Marchbanks, inheritor of the aesthetic sublimation in the moony romanticism of Keats's *Endymion*. As Suzette Henke observes, "in Chapter Two, Stephen vainly searches for the romantic figure of a woman who will mediate his artistic transfiguration" (50). Candida mediates, indeed precipitates, such a transformation for Marchbanks.

Marchbanks, however, vows that "nothing that's worth saying is proper"—perhaps providing the imprimatur for Stephen Hero's carnal proposition. Marchbanks's speech to Morell—"Why should she have to choose between a wretched little nervous disease like me, and a pigheaded parson like you? Let us go on a pilgrimage, you to the east and I to the west in search of a worthy lover for her—some beautiful archangel with purple wings" (Plays 147)—is related more to the conclusion of "The Dead," in which (archangel) Gabriel tells himself that he must begin a voyage westward, than to Stephen, but it sets up the choice that E. C. faces between poet and priest. Even Morell's description of Marchbanks could be applied to Stephen. He says that "the foolish boy can speak with the inspiration of a child and the cunning of a serpent" (150), qualities that Joyce exploits in *Portrait*. After the maternal Candida's rejection of young Marchbanks, he departs the Morell household, ecstatically free to meet the impatient "night outside" (Plays 152). Indeed, both *Candida* and *Portrait* end as the young artists prepare to go forth into the world, having surmounted the greatest temptation—the pull of a maternal figure.

A composite of all of the females in *Portrait* except the prostitute, Candida exercises more power than any of Joyce's females, whether they are icons, fantasies, or fictionally purported to be real. Stephen's escape from female snares is reified, so that the female principle compacted in the Great Mother/Madonna/Circe/Candida is represented discretely. In *Portrait* one aspect of the Eternal Feminine is the Virgin Mary, whom the potential priest adores as the "tower of ivory" associated with the idealization of real women like Eileen and E. C. Shaw admitted that the Madonna was his model for Candida. Marchbanks has presented her with a print of Titian's *Assumption of the Virgin* that establishes the connection. Candida is also a nurturing mother who, like Stephen's, upholds marriage. She attracts the young poet sexually but remains, like E. C. in *Portrait,* chaste with him. Like Mercedes, heroine of *The Count of Monte Cristo* and one of Stephen's female fantasies, Candida is Marchbanks's romantic fantasy, besmirched in his imagination when he thinks of her peeling onions. Like the bird woman in *Portrait,* Candida is a catalyst for the young artist.

Like Shaw's beautiful, unattainable female, in *Portrait* E. C. and her fantasy double Mercedes have tantalized the adolescent wooer. Candida fears, however, "abandoning" Marchbanks "to the bad women for the sake of my goodness—my purity" (Plays 141). When Marchbanks approaches her, at the "gate of heaven" he finds, like Tristram as Adam, a "flaming sword" turning him away; and he "saw that the gate was really the gate of Hell" (145)—the hell of captivity to the worship of women, which, Henke notes regarding Stephen, threatens the young artist: "The artist must paradoxically renounce the flesh and blood female in order to free the spur of desirability from the dangers of possible satisfaction." Both Shaw and Joyce suggest that the art of such young aesthetes will, as Henke puts it, develop "through a poetics of erotic absence, [and thus] spur the poet to nostalgic compensatory creation" (63). After Stephen, abandoned by the chaste E. C., turns to a prostitute for sexual initiation, he enters the gate of hell without regard for the consequences. Such "oral-regressive" surrender to sex that approximates return to the maternal womb (Henke 66) is, of course, a pivotal difference between Joyce and his secret literary progenitor. After a revelation that illicit sex is infernal, the Shavian artist is saved from the hell of romantic love by the advanced Victorian "womanly woman" (as Shaw called such females), who is, though Victorian, a tease, representing at once the aggressiveness associated with masculinity, the purity of the Virgin, and the erotic lure of the whore. Marchbanks, apparently an avatar of the young Shaw superimposed upon Yeats, does not enter the sexual gate of a forbidden partner, whereas Joyce's hero willingly succumbs to the hell of sensuality in order to satisfy his lust and, thereafter, to suffer the damnation that Marchbanks foresaw—"a hell of lecherous goatish fiends" (P 138).

Nevertheless, Stephen's conversion into an apostle of art, like that of Marchbanks, comes about through the agency of a woman. The dovelike woman in *Portrait* is, like Candida, the catalyst to artistic liberation. Spellbound by Candida, Marchbanks does not, however, make his own choice. Instead, the goddess of mortal beauty makes it for him, whereas Joyce's bird-like image—a passive manifestation of mortal beauty transformed by the masculine gaze—provides the occasion for Stephen's epiphany. *Portrait* may thus be a sly retort to Shaw's improbable young artist; Joyce's novice is more plausible than Shaw's. Whereas Stephen's artistic conversion and his final appeal to the Old Artificer are carefully foreshadowed in the patterns of Joyce's prose, Marchbanks's transformation is abrupt and peripheral, even though it is vital to Shaw's theme. As Richard Dietrich pointed out to me in a recent letter, "Shaw's dramatic fables customarily opt for the sudden conversion or revelation appropriate to that form," and G. B. S. may have been twitting Yeats for his implausibly sudden revelations. Indeed, while emphasizing the mysterious, enigmatic power of the archetypal female, Shaw does not prepare his audience for Marchbanks's assertion of maturity, whereas Joyce's solipsistic novel centers entirely on psychological growth, revealed through the language of Stephen's consciousness, associated patterns of imagery, and the content of his confrontations with others. Shaw is ironic with both of his males: the socially engagé preacher Morell is emasculated by his wife, who, in choosing to nurture him, frees the young artist who does not need her. Marchbanks is acted upon by Candida, but Stephen escapes the nets of environment after the ecstatic revelation that gives him the courage to depart.

Like E. C. in *Portrait,* Candida is, as Henke describes "the phallic mother," an "eternal temptress, who tantalizes with nurturant pleasure, then obstinately withholds satisfaction" (81). As strong surrogate mother, Candida is the fate to which Marchbanks must respond, whereas Stephen—closer to the Shavian archetypal hero whom Shaw defined at the turn of the century—works out his own destiny. Like Marchbanks, leaving Candida to her preacher mate, Stephen congratulates himself for leaving E. C. "to flirt with her priest, to toy with a church which was the scullerymaid of christendom" (220). Although Marchbanks was appalled because Candida took on the duties of scullerymaid for Morell, Shaw does not make the socialist preacher's religion a total mockery.

In *Candida* the struggle between the religious or reformist vocation and art is revealed in the contrast between the moral, socialist preacher Morell and the youthful poet. The conflict between religion and art is, in *Portrait,* internalized in Stephen, while one side of the dialectic is distributed among several characters whom Stephen encounters. Joyce creates an authentic, even ironically prideful young artist who could renounce what *Candida* rejects—the "infatuated amorism of the nineteenth century" (I&R 17). At the same time, Shaw spoofed love stories of Irish myth in which the female, as Grania or Deirdre, rejects her mature husband-hero for a young, romantic love and thus acts out the *liebes tod* leitmotif, one that both Shaw and Joyce refused to take seriously in Wagner. Joyce discards such retrograde ideals, as does Shaw, while perhaps treating his young poet-hero with indulgent irony.

No one, however, disputes Joyce's psychological plausibility, whereas Shaw himself admitted that he did not always know where his plays were going and at the last moment did "not foresee the way out" (BM 307). Joyce's *Portrait,* however, unfolds from the embryonic artist's point of view what Shaw dramatized in *Candida*—the emergence of the solitary artist, destined for a higher calling than domestic happiness.

In spite of his ambivalence over women, Joyce could have gone to Shaw's feminist drama, *Fanny's First Play* (1911), a copy of which he owned, for additional parallels to his theme, even though Shaw's central character is female. Surrounded by philistines who substitute "mere morality, or . . . custom for conscience" (CP 138), Shaw's heroine aims to shock her patriarchal father "morally" and "artistically" in her play (Plays 656). After a Salvation Festival at the Albert Hall, the anti-ingenue of Fanny's play wanted "more music—more happiness—more life" (666), so she went to a theater and picked up a Frenchman with whom she went dancing and got involved in a drunken riot. After being jailed for defying the law, she had an epiphany. Upon returning home, she declared herself to be "a heroine of reality . . . pretty brutal, pretty filthy, when you come to grips with it. Yet it's glorious all the same. It's so real and satisfactory." She had made a "descent into hell" and emerged from her rite of passage free. Thereafter she rejects her conventional fiancé, her parents, and their religion: "I've been set free from this silly little hole of a house and all its pretenses. For good or evil I am set free and none of the things that used to hold me can hold me now" (667). Thus liberated, she is ready to choose her own future, without regard to the middle-class values of her parents.

Granted that Shaw's tone differs entirely from Joyce's and that the play ends in contrived couplings that typify romantic comedy, the playwright nevertheless insists on the value of dealing with real life. His audacious heroine chooses a mate on the basis of her attraction to him instead of on the basis of class. Shaw argued that young people are better off having "their souls awakened by disgrace . . . than drift[ing] along from their cradles to their graves doing what other people do for no other reason than that other people do it, and knowing nothing of good and evil. . . . I hate to see dead people walking about. It is unnatural. And our respectable middle class people are all as dead as mutton" (CP 138). Thus *Fanny's First Play* and its preface corroborate *Portrait* and summarize the theme of Joyce's stories about the living dead, the petty bourgeoisie of Dublin.

Joyce apparently agreed with Shaw that "Life and not Love is the supreme good" (MCE 249). Disapproving of the "love panacea," Shaw answered the call of the Life Force, which Stephen hears at the climax of *Portrait*—to celebrate life, to recreate life without wallowing in guilt or the romantic yearning that Stephen associates with *The Count of Monte Cristo*. Like a Shavian hero, Stephen outgrows the Count's obsession with romantic love and with revenge. Dick Dudgeon, "The Devil's Disciple," has the Count's derring-do but not his ideals, for Dick has repudiated the motive of wounded love and escapes the snare of the beautiful Mrs. Anderson. The melodramatic conclusion of *The Devil's Disciple* is as implausible and thrilling as the events in Dumas's novel, but both Shaw and Joyce treated romantic heroism with irony. Shaw used it as a theatrical device upon which to hang his play, hoping to amuse his audience with its melodramatic implausibilities. Joyce used the Count as a correlative for Stephen's adolescent yearnings for courtly romance, but as he develops courage to take control of his own life, he comes close to emulating Duck Dudgeon. In rejecting the Count's motive of revenge, he emulates the hero of *Captain Brassbound's Conversion*.

Joyce's portrait of the artist as a light-bringing pagan iconoclast approximates the views of Shaw. His disdain for the sky god of Judeo-Christian tradition must have appealed to the creator of Stephen Dedalus, whose hawk-like hero's spirit soars only as prelude to falling into the waters of mortal existence. Shaw often associated himself with light-bringing solar deities like the Egyptian sun-god. In the prologue to *Caesar and Cleopatra* (1906), Ra proclaims, "Look upon my Hawk's head; and know that I am Ra" (Plays 250). He lauds Caesar over Pompey because Shaw's Caesar, like Joyce's Stephen, will not serve the old laws, whereas Pompey—like the characters with whom Stephen interacts—serves them. Caesar knows that he must "break the laws of old Rome," but Pompey, anticipating the thrust of the Daedalus myth before Joyce deconstructed it, insists, "The [patriarchal] law is above all; and if thou break it thou shalt die." Caesar replies, " 'I will break it; kill me who can.' And he broke it . . . [and] fled across the Adriatic sea" (251), prefiguring the flight of Stephen Dedalus. As Albert Moreiras writes, "Joyce is clearly associating Daedalus with Egyptian solar divinities" ("Pharmaconomy" 69). He is also associating him with Shaw. If Joyce already knew that he shared a Gaelic surname with Shaw,

Stephen's recognition of "the hawklike man whose name he bore" (P 225) may be cunning admission of Joyce's literary paternity. For, in identifying with the profane god in him, Stephen attributes his patrimony to Daedalus, the creative maker who found his materials in the real world and used his skills to escape the labyrinth, not of Minos, but of Dublin. The mythic Daedalus was a maker, an architect, something of a town planner and "civil engineer" like Shaw's two alter egos in *John Bull's Other Island,* but he was also a victim of ingratitude, betrayed by Minos, the power figure for whom he was master builder—an Ibsen/Shaw correlative comparable to the playwrights who wanted to build a better society.

It is significant that the Daedalus myth is a story of patrimony in which the mother is missing. Both *Candida* and *Portrait* end with the flight from the mother, and the author of *Candida,* itself a rejection of maternal nurturing, had, by example, already rejected Mother Ireland and the Church, even though in the Protestant Church of Ireland the Virgin Mother was not so powerful a symbol as she was in Catholicism. In the Daedalus myth the maker and his son are betrayed on Crete, which has legendary associations with goddess worship. Like the heroes of the myth escaping the womb-like labyrinth, the young artists in *Candida* and *Portrait* flee the mother. In their escapes from Ireland, both Shaw and Joyce were freeing themselves from unhealthy bondage to Ireland, their mother country, and to its patristic institutions.

Like Icarus, Stephen is both inheritor of the maker's genius and the disobedient son who does not follow the father's orders. Like his mythic model, he flies too near the sun and falls—though conveniently not to drown but, in Joyce's revision, to die into a life devoted to recreating "life out of life" and thus creating "mortal beauty." This is not what the practical father figure, if he is Shaw, prescribed. Saving his own life and that of his son was the escaped Daedalus's aim. Recreating them in art is the son's. If Shaw's early writings provided wings for Joyce's escape from Dublin, he may be the Old Artificer of *Portrait*. Although Stephen/Icarus has disobeyed the father, he has also chosen him. Significantly, the Daedalus myth is a prototype of the relationship of father and son, one that all of Shaw's early pronouncements revised in favor of the disobedient son who usurps the father's place while using the older man's skills. In *Portrait* Joyce created a surrogate father to lead him out of the labyrinth of Dublin—an exemplum against whom he could rebel to define himself. In Joyce's deconstructed script, Icarus is not punished for his audacious revolt against the father, who is, like Shaw, a famed maker. Instead, for his daring he undergoes a fortunate fall and rebirth, a fall that could not have come about without the help of the father. At the end of the novel Stephen addresses the chosen sire, the source of his strength, who provided the means of his rebellious escape. Having elected him, the young artist pointedly does not address the patriarchs who had tried to claim him—the Father in Heaven or the one in the pub. Having become a foe of the Blakean Nobodaddy, Stephen's emancipated soul luxuriates in freedom. The young man has also rejected the collective authority of Minos that, according to Shaw, betrays talented makers to cannibalistic idols (see MCE 97).

G. B. S. argued that, like Tolstoy and Ibsen, the "realist" rebels against such sacrifice and exposes it for what it is, upsetting the "moral complacency" of his audiences. Stephen's motto—*non serviam*—is the apostate badge of Shavian heterodoxy. Stephen chooses a pagan spiritual father like Shaw, who defied the powers of the minotaur majority. Apparently because the issue of paternity was as important to Joyce as it was to Shaw, Joyce used the Icarus-Daedalus archetype to inform his novel. Like the older Irishman Joyce was unique in his need to reject his mundane father and to create his own paternity. G. K. Chesterton criticized Major Barbara in 1909 for insisting, "I will never have a father unless I have begotten him" (110). Like Joyce, deeply discontented with his own father, Shaw argued that "the child develops in spite of the parents, not because of them," with "a right to find its own way . . . *as if it were its own father*" (CP 45; italics mine).

Joyce created himself with a little unacknowledged help from his rival and elected sire. Daedalus's fatherhood in myth, as reinterpreted by Joyce, adumbrates the connection between the two Irishmen. Probably secretly relating to his literary progenitor the adopted Old Artificer whom his hero has elected as father, Joyce parallels young Icarus to rebels privileged by Shaw: Prometheus, Lucifer, Siegfried, Dick Dudgeon, and Don Juan, all challengers of patriarchal institutions. Thus Shaw, who showed Joyce the way out of the imprisoning Dublin maze, was a covert model for the Old Artificer and social architect whom Stephen chooses as his paternal model. Dismissal of "my home, my father or my church" defines him as a defiant Shavian, but reliance on "silence, exile, and cunning" (P 247) suggests that Joyce, shrewdly keeping his own counsel, would not acknowledge his spiritual father before the world.

When Stephen welcomes life at the end of the novel, his stated aim and even the language he couches it in imply the realist goal and moral purpose that Shaw prescribed for rebel genius: "I go to encounter . . . the reality of experience and to forge in the smithy of my soul the uncreated conscience of my race" (252). Significantly, Stephen's final avowal is not that of an aesthete who creates art for its own sake, for it alludes to Hephaestus and Vulcan, who made armor for gods preparing for combat, and to Blake's Los, the militant smith of the prophetic imagination. Like the Fabian gradualist, Stephen Dedalus aims to use his literary art to expose social illusions and thereby to teach a higher morality to the Irish. The concluding prayer to the "Old Father Old Artificer" whom Stephen chose over his blood sire and over God signifies his apostate redemption and self-realization. The most significant living Irish rebel who preached a pagan gospel for such artistic liberation was Joyce's famous but unacknowledged literary father, the great *"Immensipater"* (FW 342.26), George Bernard Shaw.

Carmen in the Drawing-Room: "Annadominant" "Candidatus" in *Exiles*

In the preface to *The Irrational Knot* (1905), Shaw remembered that Bizet's *Carmen* was new in London while he was writing this novel of his nonage: "I used it as a safety-valve for my romantic impulses. When I was tired of the sordid realism" of the unromantic hero of the novel, "I went to the piano to forget him in the glamorous society of Carmen and her crimson toreador and yellow dragoon." Not "infatuated" with Bizet's music, Shaw thought nevertheless that it was "exquisite" enough in places to "enchant a young man romantic enough to have come to the end of romance" before he began to create quite another sort of art for himself (CP 681). Although in 1905 Shaw was "cool" toward *Carmen*, he admitted that his younger self was taken in by the femme fatale and her two lovers. In Joyce's largely autobiographical *Exiles* (1918), the dominant male character also admits to having been taken in by the romance of passion in his youth. In the first scene of the play he points out a portrait of his father. Joyce, who chose his own paternity in *Portrait,* created a benevolent father for Richard Rowan, one who on his deathbed generously gave his son money to attend *Carmen*. Indeed, a crayon drawing of the father, like General Gabler's portrait in *Hedda Gabler* and Titian's *Virgin of the Assumption* in *Candida*, dominates the set of *Exiles*. The opera to which the revised father (unlike the impecunious John Joyce) sent young Richard is dialogically related to *Exiles*, as Joyce was no doubt fully aware. Joyce's play is the covert recipient of the Shavian view of Bizet's opera as well as Shaw's deconstruction of the *Carmen* theme in his *Candida*.

Like *Candida*, *Exiles* is a drawing-room *Carmen*, whose central female figure is an "annadominant" Circe—representative of the Life Force, like Ann Whitefield in *Man and Superman* and Anna Livia in *Finnegans Wake*. Like Bizet's opera, both plays revolve around a love triangle, but both at once call up the conventional trichotomy to examine its implications and dismiss the crimson toreador without histrionics. Both dramas are realistic problem plays that eschew the exaggerated affectations of melodrama: there are no strained, impassioned duets, no physical violence, no death scenes; no duel, no bullfight, and no stabbing, although the leading men end up with psychic wounds. The heroines of the Shaw and Joyce plays both parallel and gainsay the Gypsy temptress of Seville. Both embody her seductive female allure while lacking her fiery wildness. Richard Rowan in *Exiles* has been insubordinate to the ruling powers of Ireland, just as Don José, Carmen's lover, has been insubordinate to his superiors; both swains go into exile with their Carmens, neither of whom is her man's social equal—a fact that distresses both males. Moreover, like Robert Hand in pursuit of Bertha and Eugene Marchbanks in pursuit of Candida, Don José's rival, the toreador Escamillo, woos Carmen despite her attachment to the yellow dragoon.

Marchbanks and Robert Hand, like Escamillo, challenge the competing male to a duel, but both use words to win. In *Carmen* the rivals actually fight, but Don José (shades of Joyce himself) is called away by news that his mother is dying. (*Exiles* eliminates the factor of the biological mother, for Richard's mother is dead). The fickle Gypsy girl forsakes her love partner to go to a bullfight starring her new suitor, Escamillo, but she waits for Don José outside of the arena. When he gets there, like Candida's husband James Morell and unlike the proud Richard, Don José begs Carmen to be faithful to their love. When she will not promise to be true, her lover, in an excess of jealousy, stabs her as her toreador comes, victorious, out of the bullring. Shaw and Joyce eschewed such carnage and such male violence, reversing the roles of the impassioned lovers. Candida chooses to stay with her importunate husband; Bertha begs Richard to love her again. Nevertheless, the males sustain wounds because of the real or dreamed unfaithfulness of their spouses. In *Candida* it is the husband who returns triumphantly from the "bullring" of a political rally; in *Exiles* Robert, the suitor who fights in the journalistic rings of Dublin, leaves town, like poet Marchbanks in *Candida*. Carmen is a model deconstructed in *Candida* and *Exiles*: although Carmen/Candida/Bertha chooses her Don José/Morell/Richard, the males suffer for what they have done to their women.

Like Joyce's Bertha, Carmen is an unconventional exile from middle-class proprieties. Bertha is also a reckless gambler who staked everything on her lover. Her relationship to Richard, like Carmen's to Don José, has a basis in Gypsy law: their union can be ended only by mutual consent. Like Carmen, Bertha is isolated from ordinary society, but Joyce's heroine is far more passive in her self-admitted "simplicity" (*Exiles* 52) than the passionate Gypsy. Whereas Bizet's wild temptress is the epitome of untamed freedom, Joyce compares Bertha unromantically to a cow. In telling young Archie, his and Bertha's illegitimate son, about how cows give milk because of bulls, Richard adds that a "robber" (like Robert) could steal a cow in the night (46–47). This debasing image of woman makes the bovine female a prize; it suggests obliquely an unheroic, devious prowler contending for the bull's mate.

Richard's reference foreshadows the content of *Exiles*. He fears that Bertha may be stolen by a thief in the night. Later he calls his rival Robert "a liar, a thief, and a fool!" (51). Richard himself has, he notes, matured beyond the passion of a Don José, but he remembers it as the mark of his youth. Robert is, however, a middle-aged Escamillo. Nevertheless, he insists that he still believes in "the blinding instant of passion alone—passion, free, unashamed, irresistible—that is the only gate by which we can escape from the misery of what slaves call life"; Richard recognizes in his declaration "the language of my youth" (71). It is also the language to which Shaw assented in his youth when he loved *Carmen*. By the time he wrote *Candida,* he had become the avowed enemy of the romanticism typified in Bizet's opera. When Joyce wrote *Exiles,* he had learned through experience corroborated by Shavian writings the lesson of the master. He was also trying to learn another sort of lesson—how to construct a discussion play. Joyce's drama appropriates both the Shavian method and the antiromantic revisionism of Shaw's theme. Whereas *Carmen* acts out the grand passion of a spurned lover, in *Candida,* as in *Exiles,* an amorous suitor challenges the "complacent" and "superior" (Plays 194, 196) mate of an alluring woman, without visible catastrophe.

To point up the annadominant qualities of their seductive heroines, both Shaw and Joyce, like Bizet, created foils for the Eternal Female. In *Candida* Prossie, Morell's secretary, is in love with her boss; in *Exiles* Beatrice, little Archie's piano teacher and former object of Richard's affections, carries the wound of love for the exiled writer. In *Carmen,* the foil to the heroine is Micaela, a parallel to Beatrice. Modest, maidenly, proper, but loyal and brave enough to seek out her former lover, Micaela goes to Don José in the smugglers' den where he is living with Carmen, just as, in *Exiles,* Beatrice seeks out Richard in the lodgings of the common-law Irish couple. Once Richard's beloved, Beatrice had been abandoned for Bertha; once Don José's beloved, Micaela had been deserted for Carmen. In act 1 of *Exiles* Beatrice is portrayed as a nun-like Protestant who shares some of Candida's qualities. Although she is unresponsive to Richard's renewed interest in her, the scene between the former friends interfaces with Bizet's musical score: in both opera and play the affection between the amorous friends seems to border on desire. Moreover, the duet of Micaela and Don José, "Parle-moi de ma mère," is the subject of the revisionist dialogue between Beatrice and Richard. But, unlike the Spaniard, the Irishman has no nostalgic love for his hometown or his mother.

Richard is, however, like Don José, irretrievably enamored of his Carmen and afraid that he will lose her. And like the tenor, having chosen exile with his beloved, Richard fears that his Gypsy sweetheart is getting tired of him. Like Candida's husband, Don José and Richard are jealous of and outraged by their rivals. For the opera and the two plays focus on love triangles in which a romantic agonist generates the dramatic conflict. In all three works, the tempting female flirts with a rival but is faithful in her fashion to her mate. In the finale of the opera, Carmen responds to her menacing lover, "Je t'aime encore"; in the denouements of *Candida* and *Exiles,* the heroines still love their mates. The problem plays introduce a critical difference, however. Whereas Carmen dies for her seeming inconstancy, in the drawing-room dramas, Morell and Richard suffer. Like Candida's husband, Bertha's common-law mate is deeply pained by doubt. Bertha, who possesses her man in the flesh, pleads for his return as the wild, passionate lover she first knew. Although Candida stays with her husband, he, like Richard, has sustained an emasculating blow.

In the preface to *The Irrational Knot,* in which he defined *Carmen* as an escape valve for his early romanticism, Shaw also argued that his novel anticipated Ibsen: "The revolt of the Life Force against ready made morality in the nineteenth century was not the work of a Norwegian microbe"; he contended that his novel had expressed female insurgency in English literature before Ibsen did so in Scandinavia. And, unlike Ibsen in *A Doll's House,* he did it "without any melodramatic forgeries, spinal diseases, and suicides" (CP 689). Elsewhere Shaw argued that *Candida* was his answer to *A Doll's House,* revealing that the person infantilized in marriage is not necessarily the female. Implicit in *Candida* also is his realistic reply to chivalric romance. His play anticipates *Exiles* in its ironic, dialogic relationship to *Carmen,* which is itself a popularized variant of the courtly love theme, in a nineteenth-century version that emphasizes its illicit nature. Both Irishmen aimed to shock rather than titillate the bourgeoisie by questioning conventional moral standards. Both also implied in their parlor dramas that the *liebes tod* theme of opera and theater could reveal itself without stagy tragedy, for in reality assaults on love are not always fatal.

As Benstock observes, *Exiles* is "a basically naturalistic play with certain symbolist touches, a domestic situation with extended social ramifications, a bourgeois setting with a box-stage structure" (*Exiles* 363). Ibsen's influence is, however, less pervasive in Joyce's play than is Shaw's. Like *Candida,* Joyce's realistic drama is all talk, has virtually no action, and lacks a catastrophic conclusion. Its overall pattern is closer to Shaw's late Victorian drama than to any Ibsen play. Ibsen's love triangles usually end in more than spiritual disaster: Hedda Gabler commits suicide; in *The Wild Duck,* Hedvig shoots herself; in *When We Dead Awaken,* the artist and his beloved immolate themselves in a tumultuous snowstorm high in the mountains. Nonetheless, *Exiles* is, like *Candida,* related to *Hedda Gabler.*

Joyce's quasi-husband Richard is, like Hedda's husband Tesman, a would-be professor, but Richard has none of Tesman's stodgy bourgeois qualities, qualities that lurk in the character of Candida's husband. Richard is, in fact, more like Tesman's unwitting competitor Lovborg, who does not woo Hedda during Ibsen's play. According to his romantic rival, Robert, Richard deserves (ironically) "the chair of romance literature" (38). Rowan is a writer, like Lovborg, whose spiritual history of the present is comparable to *Dubliners,* the unnamed work that Richard, in *Exiles,* has just published. An adumbration of Lovborg, Richard seems also to be in part an adult Eugene Marchbanks, just as Shaw's Morell is an adumbration of Tesman before his marriage—a man spoiled by women. According to Padraic Colum, in Joyce's deconstruction of Shaw middle-aged Robert Hand vaguely resembles Judge Brack in *Hedda Gabler* (*Exiles* 8); but the romantic rival who seeks to destroy a marriage and win another man's wife is closer to Marchbanks than to the lecherous judge.

Like *Hedda Gabler,* but also like *Candida, Exiles* begins with the return of a woman who has been away. In Ibsen's play Hedda and Tesman return from their honeymoon; in *Exiles* Bertha and Richard have returned from the continent; in *Candida* the heroine and her young admirer return from the country, like Beatrice in *Exiles,* who arrives alone. Beatrice, Bertha, and Candida do not copy Hedda by committing suicide, though Beatrice seems to have undergone symbolic suicide since Richard's departure from Ireland. Joyce's two women share, however, some of the qualities of Thea and Hedda: Beatrice (like Shaw's Prossie) is an intellectual helpmate and inspiration, like Thea, but Beatrice is frigid and emotionally distant like Hedda and Candida. It is Bertha who, like Thea, has had the courage to run away from the old life because of a romantic writer—a fate that the bourgeois Candida rejects. Unlike Hedda, who envies Thea's abundant hair and cruelly despises her as a rival, Bertha admires Beatrice's "long eyelashes" but, after admitting her jealousy, wants "to be friends" (101).

In his notes to *Exiles* Joyce compared Bertha to Isolde, emulating Shaw's comparison of Candida to Tristram's beloved. In Shaw's play, however, Marchbanks—the Tristram figure—recognizes the "flaming sword" preventing him from consummating his love. Its flames also suggest that he is Adam deprived of an Eden in which the female (Candida with a fire poker in her hand) plays God. For Candida is the "annadominant" phallic mother, whereas Bertha, whose name suggests birth and earth, is a less threatening, more malleable Earth Mother. Indeed, Marchbanks fears the poker raised in Candida's hand as if it were the rod of the Almighty: he shrinks from it as if it were "a weapon.

If I were a hero of old, I should have laid my drawn sword between us" (Plays 144). Thus the courtly Tristram proscribes illicit sex with thoughts of the masculine blade threatened by the patriarchal rod in the hands of a phallic female protector. When Candida's moral husband interrupts the wooing, Marchbanks admits that he neared the "gate of Heaven," but the flaming sword blocked him and he saw it was "the gate of Hell" (145). Contrarily, Robert, his counterpart in *Exiles,* tries to enter the "gate" and, because Joyce left the potential lovers together, may or may not have succeeded. After Marchbanks wonders how Morell "got past the flaming sword that stopped" him (146), Morell responds that he earned the right to love Candida "in the scullery, slicing onions and filling lamps," and admits to using the pulpit, where he "scrubbed cheap earthenware souls," to impress her. He asserts that he did not, however, woo her "to steal another man's happiness" (146), like Marchbanks and like Robert in *Exiles.* Robert's confession in act 2—"I love her and I will take her from you, however I can, because I love her" (62)—parallels Marchbanks's declaration to Morell at the end of act 1 of *Candida:* "There is something that must be settled between us." "I love your wife" (132). "I can't fight you for your wife as a navvy would. . . . I'll fight your ideas. I'll rescue her from her slavery to them" (134). He vows to take Candida from Morell because he loves her.

Both *Candida* and Shaw's lesser known farce, *How He Lied to Her Husband* (1904), parallel *Exiles:* a suitor of the wife enters the home of the couple, woos the wife during the husband's absence, is interrupted by the spouse, and departs. After the romantic suitor leaves, there is a bittersweet—comical in *How He Lied to Her Husband*—reunion of wife and husband, who have faced the unromantic truth about their relationship. In the brief preface to his farce, Shaw boasted that he used the "hackneyed stage framework" of "doctrinaire romanticism" to present "an observed touch of actual humanity." Although "nothing in the theatre is staler than the situation of husband, wife and lover," Shaw claimed to have written "an original play" by refusing to plagiarize *Othello* "and the thousand plays that have proceeded on Othello's romantic assumptions and false point of honor" (CP 282). In *Exiles* Joyce copied Shaw: his notes argue that "Shakespeare's *Othello* is incomplete as a study of jealousy" (114). For Joyce's play is, like Shaw's, a problem play airing "advanced" ideas about jealousy and about women. As an aspiring dramatist and unadmitted disciple of Ibsenist

Shaw, Joyce wrote that the new drama aimed to "open ... up a great question" (CW 63). In *Candida* and *Exiles,* the great question concerns the hegemony of women, for both Candida (called Candidatus in *Finnegans Wake* to ridicule her dominance with a masculine ending) are annadominant—variants on the New Woman, *Anno Domini,* adumbrations of female archetypes of the Christian era. Like Anna Livia in the *Wake,* they represent the dominant Life Force. They also stand for honesty, the candor for which Shaw named his heroine: both prefer truth to deception and romantic intrigue.

Both Candida and Bertha are associated with Christian symbolism. Both are Eves, but Candida is compared to the Madonna and Bertha to the penitent Mary Magdalen. Shaw admitted that he purposely compared Candida to the Virgin Mother (see H1 314–15) and stressed the comparison by making a copy of a Titian painting of the Madonna a central prop. Marchbanks and his creator think of Candida as an exalted and mysterious Virgin Mother—with "her shawl, her wings, the wreath of stars on her head, the lilies in her hand, the crescent moon beneath her feet—" (146). Her youthful suitor "throws back his head across her knees," putting himself in the pietà posture of the savior/son of Mary. Like Robert, paradoxically playing Lucifer as possible redeemer, Marchbanks wants Candida's permission to "say some wicked things" (144). The Eternal Mother leads him on by insisting only that he be candid: "I am not afraid, so long as it is your real self that speaks and not a mere attitude—a gallant attitude, or a wicked attitude, or even a poetic attitude. I put you on your honor and truth" (144–45). The enamored young man (anticipating the protagonist of Joyce's "Araby") tells Candida that he has repeated her name "a thousand times" and "every time is a prayer to you" (145). Shaw's stage directions before Candida's entry describe some of the maternal qualities that she shares with Bertha, but they also distinguish her from the more compliant Joycean female. Candida looks on others with "amused maternal indulgence.... [S]he can always manage people by engaging their affection, and ... does so frankly and instinctively without the smallest scruple" (129). Her behavior toward the two men prompted Beatrice Webb, however, to call her a "sentimental prostitute" (Terry 108).

This aspect of Candida suggests Joyce's conception of Bertha. Robert calls her "a strange and beautiful lady.... A young and beautiful queen" (26), but not the Queen of Heaven to whom Shaw compared Candida.

Instead, Joyce associates Bertha with Mary Magdalen—the loose woman who redeems herself through her association with and love of Christ—to whom Joyce did not hesitate to compare Richard. His stage directions as well as his notes make the comparison to the penitent Magdelan clear: in act 3 Bertha is directed to appear in a "loose saffron dressing gown. Her hair is combed loosely over the ears and knotted at the neck. Her hands are folded in her lap" (89). Thus Joyce creates her in the image of late Renaissance painter Georges de la Tour's *The Penitent Magdalen.* Joyce's notes describe her with "tears . . . of worship, Magdalen seeing the rearisen Lord. . . . She is Magdalen who weeps remembering the loves she could not return" (118). Whereas the Madonna Candida (in Marchbanks's romantic view) "wants somebody to protect, to help, to work for. . . . Some grown up man who has become as a little child again" (147), Bertha wants to give herself to her man, to someone in whom she can lose herself, her identity, her will; she tacitly accepts the credo that Richard has been her sacrificial redeemer, and at the end of the play is repentant.

Both writers, however, associate the desirable annadominant woman with the moon and with romantic escape. When Marchbanks reads poetry to Candida in her husband's absence, she asks him to "sit down on the hearth-rug [below her], and talk moonshine as you usually do" (144). Shaw's young poet tells Proserpine, who is languishing for love of Morell, "We all go about longing for love: it is the first need of our natures, the loudest cry of our hearts." He fantasizes "a boat—a tiny shallop to sail away in, far from the world. . . . Or a chariot—to carry us up into the sky, where the lamps are stars" (135, 139). The notes for *Exiles* define Bertha as "the earth, dark, formless, mother, made beautiful by the moonlit night, darkly conscious of her instincts" (118). Like Shaw, ostensibly inspired by Thomas De Quincy (see H1 315), and Joyce, admittedly inspired by Shelley (117), Robert—as worshipful as Marchbanks—compares Bertha to the moon (31): "I think of you always—as something beautiful and distant—the moon and some deep music" (32). Like a poet in the grips of the romantic agony (Keats "half in love with easeful death" and Shelley panting for "music which is divine"), he complains that his life is "over"—that he wants to end it "listening to music, and in the arms of the woman I love—the sea, music and death" (35). At the end of act 2 Robert woos Bertha with images of fertility—"Summer rain in the earth. Night rain. The darkness and warmth and flood of passion. Tonight the earth is loved—loved and possessed" (87). With the room "quite dark," Robert—more experienced than Marchbanks—embraces Bertha and "kisses her hair" (88).

The unresisting Bertha who permits Robert such familiarities differs from the Shavian woman. In *Candida* Morell decides that Candida "must choose between us now" (150)—a choice not given unequivocally to Bertha by Richard. The idea that the males assume the power to grant the females the right to choose is fundamental to both plays. Whereas Bertha is timorous, Candida has long since seized the controls. Even the reader is warned that she may use her power for "trivially selfish ends" (129). When Candida is hardened by her husband's "rhetoric" into realizing that he thinks she must "belong to one or the other," Marchbanks understands that "she means that she belongs to herself" (150). Richard only half-heartedly tries to affirm to Bertha that she belongs to herself. He takes the initiative, but when it becomes apparent that she has no intention of leaving him, she is strong enough to castigate him for using her and Robert and for taking "advantage" of her "simplicity" (52). Richard is, indeed, a controller like Candida, even though he avers that he has allowed Bertha "complete liberty" (52). Whereas in *Exiles* the leading male uses the other characters, in Shaw's drama the female lead is in control.

The manipulative Candida chooses Morell, knowing full well that he was as a male "spoiled from his cradle"; she announces that she has built "a castle of comfort and indulgence and love for him, and stand[s] sentinel always to keep little vulgar cares out. I make him master here" (151). Shaw's play ends as *Pygmalion* in reverse: the phallic mother has made the man, whereas in *Exiles* Richard likes to think that he has formed Bertha, but Bertha asserts that she "made him a man" (100). Her methods, however, differ significantly from Candida's. Bertha seems to have made Richard sexually, as well as by needing him to form and guide her. Thus, despite the fact that she becomes the interrogator with Beatrice, the suspected "other" woman, Bertha produced the egocentric male out of her weakness, dependency, and need. She is unlike the efficient Candida, who is a Nora Helmer (as Shaw quipped) in reverse. Shaw's answer to *A Doll's House* shows that the strong womanly woman with a vocation for caretaking creates the male. Morell accepts her maternal power with the statement "You are my wife, my mother, my sisters: you are the sum of all loving care to me" (151)—even though

Candida's puissance seems castrating. Contrarily, Bertha accepts Richard's masculine power over her, and perhaps having withstood the temptation to infidelity, she continues, like Candida, to love her mate.

Despite the paradoxical power that women get through the weakness of their position in society, both Robert and Bertha accuse Richard of being selfishly manipulative. Marchbanks accuses Morell: "You have selfishly and blindly sacrificed her to minister to your self-sufficiency—" (Plays 132). The audacious young man attacks Morell's "complacent superiority," a sense of superiority shared with Richard. Morell replies by accusing Marchbanks of being Satanic: "To break a man's spirit is devil's work." Like the envious marplot of Eden, Marchbanks admires the archetypal mother as "a woman with a great soul, craving for reality, truth, freedom" (133). Richard has tried to make Bertha into such a soul, but the candid Bertha is a passive plaything to Joyce's men. Candida, on the other hand, patronizes the men as boys. Her behavior is not, however, transparent to her starry-eyed admirer at the start of the play. In act 1 Marchbanks challenges Morell, "You are driving me out of the house because you daren't let her choose between your ideas and mine. You are afraid to let me see her again" (134). After the truth of the romantic seducer's motives is known to him, however, Morell, like Joyce's Richard, deliberately lets his spouse choose. Marchbanks, idealizing honesty, first confesses to Morell and later to Candida; in *Exiles* Robert first confesses to Bertha, then Bertha confesses to Richard, and—only when he is trapped—Robert confesses to Richard. The devious dishonesty of the males in *Exiles* is a cynical corrective to *Candida*.

Despite Shaw's avowal that Candida was the Eternal Mother to whom worshippers confess, he admitted her to be "immoral," "bound by no law and . . . seducing Marchbanks to exactly the extent she wishes. 'Without brains and strength of mind she would be a wretched slattern & voluptuary'" (BSL 2:40). She is indeed a subtly cruel manager of her mate—as Marchbanks begins to learn when he realizes that she is, like Richard in Joyce's play, torturing her mate diabolically. In Joyce's triangle, the husband, not the wife, abuses power. Candida commands Shaw's drama, but Richard Rowan controls the minimalist action of *Exiles*. Like Candida, he torments his mate: he recalls waking Bertha to tell her of his infidelity, "feeding the flame of her innocence with my guilt" (67). The proud exile, no doubt addressing Joyce's own fears regarding Nora Barnacle, is afraid that he has killed "the virginity of her soul" (67), whereas Morell and Marchbanks know that they exercise no such power over the phallic mother Candida, even though Marchbanks has worshipped her virgin soul.

While the maternal goddesses exert seductive influence over the opposite sex, the husbands in the two plays test the loyalty of their wives. Shaw's Morell, like Richard Rowan, insists upon leaving his spouse with his competitor; but Morell is dense, self-satisfied, and open, while Richard is cunning, anxious, and ulterior in his motives. Because Shaw's young poet puts candor on a pedestal, Morell is aware of Marchbanks's designs, but Richard is aware of Robert's because he plays inquisitor to Bertha, who ingenuously gives him a running account of Robert's pursuit. Richard, like Marchbanks and Candida—the souls of candor—insists upon honesty, but only from his mate. Replicating Joyce's attitude toward Nora, Richard likes to think that he created Bertha, but in truth her sexual power arouses his jealousy—an anguish that he brings upon himself by willfully encouraging her assignation with Robert. Similarly Morell sets up the romantic scenario between Marchbanks and Candida. As a consequence of their patriarchal presumptions, both husband figures are punished: Richard suffers because he will never know certainly whether Bertha was unfaithful (neither does the audience); James suffers because of his humiliating admission that Candida is the master/mistress who makes his successes possible.

Shaw's rival males are less complicated and less devious than Joyce's pair. Sadomasochistically, Richard enjoys trapping his disloyal friend. Marchbanks tries to keep his oath to Candida's smug husband, even when Candida offers the ultimate temptation ("Do you want anything more?"; 145), but Robert Hand is treacherous while at the same time acting out the script for seduction in unspoken collusion with Richard. Rowan ensnares Robert through Bertha, but Robert, without copying Marchbanks's bold first-act challenge to Morell, stealthily arranges a rendezvous. He chooses his cottage as the setting for the tryst instead of the parlor of the couple whose union he seeks to undermine. Significantly, Marchbanks reveals his amorous intentions in the female domain of Candida's sitting room, but Bertha's potential ravisher pursues her in territory once shared—as Bertha may be—with Richard. Neither Bertha nor Candida, despite her menacing appearance with the fire poker in her hand, repulses her wooer. The submissive Bertha acts, however, with Richard's imprimatur, whereas Morell assumes that

Candida is a free agent and Marchbanks discovers to his simultaneous dismay and relief that she can be controlled by no man.

The "accepted moralities" beyond which Padraic Colum (8) says the characters in *Exiles* have moved are those that Shaw's early dramas challenged. An admitted immoralist, Shaw denounced marriage as possession and enslavement of woman as well as man. He rejected the jealousy of Julia Craven, the cowardly womanly woman who wants to possess the early Shaw persona, Charteris, in *The Philanderer* (1893)—one of many Shaw plays about amorous triangles. In *The Philanderer*, as in *Candida* and *Arms and the Man*, Shaw squares the triangle by providing a fourth party to make two heterosexual couples, a feat that Joyce tries weakly to imitate by introducing Beatrice into *Exiles*. In *Arms and the Man* two men pursue Raina, who is affianced to Sergius but attracted to Bluntschli, while Sergius is attracted to the maid. In *The Philanderer* the central discussion concerns the pursuit of Charteris by two women—a chase that appears lamely in *Exiles* when Beatrice, like Shaw's Prossie, arrives at the beginning and Bertha woos Richard in the end. Shaw's Charteris schemes to provide a diversionary male for Julia. The fraternal and Oedipal rivalry of *Candida* is anticipated by the presence of a competitor who gets Julia off of Charteris's hands. Richard's complex and inadequately dramatized motives in *Exiles* may also include his half-hearted desire to get free of Bertha, as well as his anti-social, vaguely homosexual desire to share her with his false friend; Robert declares to Richard, "You are so strong that you attract me even through her" (62). In spite of compelling fraternal pairs in some of his plays—Higgins and Pickering (who probably owe something to Sherlock Holmes and Doctor Watson) in *Pygmalion* and Undershaft and Cusins in *Major Barbara*—Shaw avoided such sexual ambiguities, although he was not above hinting at them or parodying them. In *How He Lied to Her Husband*, the farcical version of *Candida*, Shaw humorously suggested motives that foreshadow those of Richard and Robert.

In *How He Lied to Her Husband*, the lover is, unlike Joyce's middle-aged lothario, "a beautiful youth of eighteen" who has, like Robert, brought his beloved, a married woman, a bunch of flowers. The wife, like Candida, is more than twice the young man's age (whereas in *Exiles* Robert is considerably older than Bertha). In Shaw's farce, the woman has lost romantic poems addressed to her by her young swain and fears that her husband or in-laws will find them. In *Exiles* Richard seeks out the written evidence against Bertha. Shaw's young romantic, beyond good and evil, like Richard Rowan and his rival, wants to proclaim his love publicly and "to declare it" to Aurora's spouse, believing that this is "the only honorable" way of behaving (Plays 454). Unlike the Joycean males, Henry wants to be free and open. Although Richard wants freedom for himself and is, at his convenience, open with Bertha, he is not candid with his friend any more than Robert is with him. In *How He Lied to Her Husband,* Shaw's artless young Don Juan, however, anticipates the Joycean *immoralistes*. He agrees that after Aurora's divorce, "we shall go through whatever idle legal ceremony you may desire. *I* attach no importance to the law; my love was not created in me by the law, nor can it be bound or loosed by it" (454). Although Aurora, unmasked as a philistine, fears that her husband Teddy will kill the young man when he finds out about her infidelity, Shaw's comedy ends up wittily and incongruously supporting the unconventionality and the amour propre that underlie Joyce's oppressively serious play. Aurora turns out to be thoroughly bourgeois, expecting her lover to be "a man of honor"—by which she means, "As a gentleman, you wouldn't tell the truth: would you?" (456). Shaw's young gallant, on the other hand, unlike Joyce's inconsistent would-be romantics, is eager to tell the truth. When the husband arrives, his romantic posturing gets its comeuppance.

Teddy has the poems addressed to his wife, just as Richard has seen Robert's note to Bertha. Confronted by Teddy, Shaw's youthful idealist lies to protect "Rory" and himself, but the cuckold is, unpredictably, not jealous but glad that the "little puppy" has taken his wife off of his hands. He attacks Henry because the impertinent young man pretends not to admire Aurora. Thus the young poet, like Marchbanks and Robert in *Exiles,* is liberated from his infatuation and disgusted with himself for stooping to tell lies for his inamorata's sake. Finally, exasperated by the husband, the courtly lover blurts out the truth: before his epiphany he "thought her the most beautiful woman in the world, and I told her so over and over again. I adored her; do you hear?" (459). In response to this confession, the husband is *"gratified"* and wants to print Henry's poems. Thus Shaw's satirical farce reverses the implication regarding jealousy over which Joyce's husband figure is ambivalent. Teddy happily participates in his own cuckolding out of self-regarding motives akin to Richard's masculine egoism, which requires other men to do homage to his choice. Joyce's motives, however, are more complex than those of the comic types whom Shaw ridiculed. In his attempt to write a psychological drama, Joyce hinted at Richard's sadomasochism and repressed homosexuality as well as his demonic need to control his friend and his beloved. Nevertheless, in spite of being as heavy as an Ibsen drama, *Exiles,* like *How He Lied to Her Husband* and *Candida,* ends with the couple shakily reunited and the rival preparing to depart.

Like the comic husband in Shaw's farce, Richard Rowan leaves Bertha with her suitor for his own sake. Bertha accuses him: "If you loved me or if you knew what love was you would not have left me" (103). She calls him a "Woman-Killer" (the male version of Candida and of Carmen, who suffers, however, more permanent retribution than Richard does). Richard has been cruel to his mother, Beatrice, and Bertha. Sadistically he interrogates his beloved and prods her, "freeing" her for her "lover," until she bursts into tears. Like Nora Helmer, she realizes that she is "living with a stranger" (104); but unlike Nora, Bertha does not have the courage or the desire to leave Richard, even though the exiles are alienated from one another at the conclusion of the play. Moreover, Robert, her self-regarding suitor, behaves ignominiously after their assignation. An older version of Marchbanks, Robert admits to doing what Candida fears Marchbanks will do if she rejects him: he describes having sex with a divorcée in a cab; the divorcée is a polite version of the "bad," whorish female from whom Candida believes she is saving Marchbanks. Bertha is herself a sacrifice to, rather than an intercessor for, such self-indulgent, self-flagellating egotism.

In confessing to Bertha (having acted out what Candida in Shaw's play fears), Robert reveals that Joyce's conception of relations between men and women differs from Shaw's. Although Morell takes advantage of Prossie's unspoken adoration in order to keep her as his efficient secretary, Shaw's men do not use women as sexual objects. Whereas in *Candida* Marchbanks sits in a child's chair at Candida's feet, Bertha sits on the floor "on a mat," and Richard sits above her on the lounge. Such postures communicate the power relations of the couples. Although some of Robert's rhetoric regarding Bertha is naively and stereotypically romantic, much of it is sexist. He compares the earth goddess to "a work of nature . . . a stone or a flower or a bird." "It is silent, it suffers our passions; and it is beautiful." Even though to Robert "a kiss is an act of homage" (41), his metaphors demean Bertha, making her a neuter *it*—an indeterminate thing instead of a person. Misogynistically, Robert argues that a woman's chief qualities are her "commonest"—her body's developing heat when "pressed," her "blood," and her alimentation (42)—hardly qualities that Shaw admired in a woman or ascribed to Candida. Moreover, as if to substantiate the masculinist evaluation of her as inferior, Bertha accepts the blame that she does not deserve. She is remorseful, but Candida is remorseless. Submissively Bertha vows to follow Richard wherever he wishes to go, despite his "deep, deep wound of doubt" in her (111–12). Morell's wound at the end of *Candida* is very different, for he discovers that Candida is the power in their marriage. Candida tells Morell, "You're spoiled with love and worship" (141)—as Richard seems to be. When she admits that James taught her "to think" for herself "and never to hold back out of fear of what other people may think of me. It works beautifully as long as I think the same thing he does" (142), her words might be a gloss of the relationship of Richard and Bertha. Both male mates want to be Pygmalion but are frustrated.

Before Joyce's temptation scene, anticipated in *Candida,* the amoral Richard departs after giving Bertha permission to "love him, be his, give yourself to him if you desire—if you can" (75). But Bertha is not as self-assured as Candida; nor is she as proper. She trembles and is "afraid" (79), for she "could not keep things secret from Dick. Besides what was the good? They always come out in the end" (80). Although Dick is "excitable" when "he is not lost in his philosophy" (81), "we all confess to one another here" (82). This is what happens with fewer cunning deviations in *Candida*. Robert offers "the common simple gift" that Morell gave to Candida, whereas nine years before an impetuous Richard had eloped with the simple, unsophisticated woman he had courted. Suggesting an unconventional triangle in which Bertha would mediate between males, Richard implores her to "love us both: him and also me" (88), but Morell and Marchbanks insist that Candida must choose between them. Marchbanks, however, anticipates the amorality of Joyce's males and, by freeing himself from the worship of woman, achieves what Richard seeks—freedom from "every bond"; "Laws are for slaves" (87). This is a sentiment of the early Shaw. "The Perfect Wagnerite" admired Wagnerian heroes who are, like Nietzsche's *Übermensch,* beyond good and evil.

In act 2 of *Exiles,* while Robert waits for Bertha, he plays strains from act 2 of *Tannhäuser*—no doubt "O du mein holder Abendstern," the

"Song of the Evening Star." Robert is playing the role of Wolfram, whose love of Elizabeth is hopeless because she loves Tannhäuser. While Wolfram sings, the hero—like Richard—appears, having been on a pilgrimage in exile because he praised the pagan eroticism of Venus, whose avatar in *Exiles* is Bertha. Unforgiven by the pope for lauding profane love, Wagner's hero is saved by his self-sacrificing lover, Elizabeth. Beatrice, her parallel in *Exiles,* does not live up to the promise of her name: unlike Dante's saving grace, she does not redeem Richard. In *Tannhäuser,* Elizabeth's prayers save the unregenerate knight-minstrel, but she dies and, because of her purity, ascends to heaven. An archetypal Madonna, like Candida, who saves Marchbanks, Elizabeth is more like Beatrice than the innocent but amoral love goddess Bertha. Although the opening of *Exiles* suggests that Joyce was aware of Beatrice as intercessor, he did not sustain the significance. He seems to have placed Beatrice in dialogic relationship to Micaela of *Carmen,* Elizabeth of *Tannhäuser,* and Prossie of *Candida.* But, like Shaw, who introduced Prossie as a rival for Candida, Joyce left the foil for his Circe dangling, apparently because he was absorbed with the annadominant temptress.

The Wagnerian pair Elizabeth and Wolfram are comparable to Beatrice and Robert in *Exiles*. When Elizabeth and Tannhäuser meet upon his return to earth (for Joyce, Ireland) after his affair with Aphrodite, their old mundane love is rekindled. When Wolfram witnesses the scene (like Robert arriving to find Beatrice and Richard together), he realizes that his relationship with Elizabeth is over. Wolfram sings of chaste, innocent love (like Beatrice's for Richard), but Tannhäuser praises earthy, sensual love, like Bertha's, horrifying the pure Elizabeth, whom Beatrice parallels. For his defense of such love the hero had been banished. Similarly, the penalty for Richard's elopement with his "wild flower" was exile. Using parallels to the opera only to subvert them, Joyce in *Exiles,* like Shaw in *Candida,* avoids the melodramatic, orthodoxly Christian finale of Wagner's musical drama. Instead, he allows the knight-quester-minstrel Richard to live and to refuse to be reconciled with the Church. To the Madonna-figure Elizabeth/Beatrice, Joyce contrasts his own earthy female archetype—a placid, wayward Venus.

In *Tannhäuser* as well as *Candida* and *Exiles,* a woman is mediatrix, but the Irish realists do not demand any sacrificial martyrdoms. Nevertheless, the comparisons of the pairs Morell and Marchbanks and Richard and Robert to Christ and the apostles imply masculine death and rebirth through the mediation of the female. The stricken husbands represent one half of the equation—the betrayed martyr—but their doubles and rivals are resurrected and reborn in the denouements of the dramas. Robert admits to being Richard's disciple, but Richard says that a faith "stranger" than that of "a disciple in his master" is "the faith of a master in a disciple who will betray him" (44). In *Candida* Marchbanks is disciple to the Madonna Candida, not her husband; he tells the preacher and man of God that "it is in the poet that the holy spirit of man—the god within him—is most godlike" (136). But, a Judas like Robert, he betrays the husband who imagines himself to be a redeemer: the Christian socialist preacher thinks of himself as a social savior, while Richard Rowan dimly views himself as Bertha's scapegoat messiah.

When Robert urges Richard to dine with the vice-chancellor of the university because "tonight will be the turning point of your life" (42), Joyce was using dramatic irony, for the audience and Richard know that his Judas intends to seduce and win Bertha, replicating Marchbanks's betrayal while Morell is out satisfying his worldly ambitions. But the bumptious preacher has none of the guilt of Richard, who anguishes over denying Bertha freedom "to give to another what was hers and not mine to give, because I accepted from her loyalty and made her life poorer in love" (69). The darker, psychological motives of Joyce are revealed, however, in Richard's admission that he courts martyrdom: he wants "to be betrayed by you, my best friend, and by her. I long for that passionately and ignobly, to be dishonoured forever in love and in lust," so that he can "build up" his soul "out of the ruins of its shame" (70). Such convoluted motives suggest the obscenity that Joyce believed Shaw found repulsive in *Exiles*. Since the immoralistic *Candida* and *How He Lied to Her Husband* parallel Joyce's parlor play, it is hard to believe, as Joyce did, that Shaw could have found any other "obscenity" in *Exiles*. Shaw's attack on Joyce's works in Dublin in 1918, after Joyce pirated his plays in Zurich (see Weintraub, *Journey* 322), probably centered on *Ulysses* but may have been tinged by his awareness of the perverse sexual motives behind *Exiles*.

In his overt admission of desire to be betrayed, Joyce entered forbidden psychic territory from which Shaw (his own father having been betrayed by George Vandeleur Lee) distanced himself, though his works are full of triangular, Oedipal rivalries. Both Irishmen wrote revisionist autobiography in their plays about adultery; however, their positions in the triangles they described differ. A supporter of free love and enemy of marriage, young Shaw had several brushes with Oedipal adultery in which he played Marchbanks to the husbands of his inamoratas. When he had his affair with Annie Besant, she was still legally wed to Reverend Frank Besant. She wanted to enter into a free love contract with Shaw, but he refused. Shaw recognized himself as "creator of an atmosphere subtly disintegrative of households.... [A]ll the women I really cared for were already married" (DuCann 118). William Morris's daughter May, whom Shaw had courted, married Henry Sparling. The Fabian orator stayed with the couple, considering himself mystically married to May, but Sparling was his friend and fellow socialist, so Shaw "vanished" (DuCann 128), like Marchbanks. Shaw was a familiar in the household of Hubert Bland, a famous Fabian essayist, and Edith Nesbit, his wife, who "graciously humored the reckless Bohemianism" of young Shaw (PP 165). Holroyd describes Shaw as "easing out of the Avelings' home," in which he courted Karl Marx's daughter Eleanor, who was living in "sin" with Edward Aveling, himself a notorious philanderer. Having withdrawn from that triangle, Shaw "started to infiltrate . . . the marriage of the Blands" who were perhaps the models for the Morells (H1 155). Among other couples that Shaw infiltrated were the Webbs and the Charles Charringtons. All of these relationships seem to replay George Vandeleur Lee's accession in the household of Shaw's youth; but, Hamlet-like, Shaw took the role of Oedipal son/lover who could not act out his desires.

Joyce's case, if not the configuration of his erotic problem, differed: he imagined himself as a wronged husband, despite his own dalliances. As Shaw compacted in Morell all of the older husbands, socialists like himself, whose wives he pursued, Joyce compacted in Robert the rival pursuers of Nora: Robert Prezioso, a Triestine journalist friend who wooed her; Michael Bodkin, the Galway beau of Nora's youth; and Vincent Cosgrave, who competed for Nora's attentions when Joyce first met her in Dublin. It was Cosgrave who aroused Joyce's jealousy. In 1909, while Joyce was in Dublin, his friend told him that even after Joyce's love affair with Nora began, she "had gone for walks in the darkness along the river bank" with him (JJ1 288). Suspicions of Cosgrave's treachery and Nora's unfaithfulness inspired *Exiles,* but it seems that Candida provided a model for its structure, while *How He*

Lied to Her Husband confirmed Joyce's perverse postulate that a husband might want to be betrayed.

Shaw despised "the plague of the stage . . . the intolerable stereotyping of the lover" (OTN 241). He credited *Hamlet* because it revealed Shakespeare's best "effort to think out the revolt of his feeling against ready-made morality" (CP 688). In his own plays about illicit love, he pointed the way for Joyce, refusing to make his females conforming romantic heroines, his lovers stereotypes, or his wronged husbands conventional revengers. Bertha's unorthodox, aspiring lover acts like Marchbanks in challenging the husband figure. He says to Richard, "Have you the courage to allow me to act freely?" Like Morell and Don José in *Carmen,* Richard replies, "A duel—between us?" (70). Robert retorts, "A battle of your soul against the spectre of fidelity, of mine against the spectre of friendship. All life is a conquest, the victory of human passion over the commandments of cowardice" (71)—a sentiment distinctly Shavian. Even though Shaw disdained making women pawns or booty, he was ever ready to challenge the "commandments of cowardice," just as Marchbanks does in *Candida. Exiles* is a subversive palimpsest of Shaw's challenge of the conventions of love in the Western world.

The striking parallels between *Candida* and *Exiles* have been noted by other scholars, including William York Tindall and Rhoda Nathan. In her study of the connections, Nathan discovers the "uncanny resemblance" between the two plays in "subject matter, sources, and casts of characters" but concludes that the remarkable similarity of the dramas by "two towering Irish geniuses who stood outside and above any 'set' or 'circle' and had little to do with each other is worthy of note" (10). Nathan's analysis is discerning, but her conclusion overlooks, while at the same time suggesting, Joyce's link to Shaw, the Irishman most like Joyce precisely because he was what Joyce considered himself to be—a solitary and towering literary giant from Dublin. The connections between *Candida* and *Exiles* are almost certainly not a coincidence. The notable analogues between the two dramas of triangulated love actually substantiate Joyce's sly arrogations of Shaw. In his play, as in his fiction, he turned in silent cunning to his undisclosed preceptor as guide. Although he criticized Shaw to Padraic Colum for writing prefaces to explain what his plays should have communicated (Colum and Colum

221), Joyce added notes to *Exiles* that are comparable to notes Shaw appended to such plays as *The Devil's Disciple, Caesar and Cleopatra,* and *Captain Brassbound's Conversion.* In his addenda Joyce explained his characters, symbolism, and themes, like a Shavian disciple. He did not, however—as Shaw was wont to do—also write a prefatory essay to challenge accepted morality, to preach his own heterodox theories, or to defend the social and political philosophy implicit in his work. Nor in secretly emulating Shaw's dramatic technique did Joyce succeed nearly so well as he did in appropriating Shavian theories in his fiction.

Nevertheless, Robert's self-exonerating article praising Richard as "A Distinguished Irishman" (which is what Joyce called Shaw in his letter congratulating him for winning the Nobel Prize; JJL 3:146) could refer to Joyce himself as well as to his precursor and Dublin double. To expiate his sin against Richard, while at the same time insinuating Richard's betrayal of Mother Ireland, the journalist describes self-exiled Irishmen such as Shaw and Joyce—spiritual exiles—as Ireland's "most favoured children, who left her to seek in other lands that food of the spirit by which a nation of human beings is sustained in life." According to Robert, Richard is comparable to Swift in his own epitaph, as translated by Yeats: "fierce indignation" has "lacerated" Mr. Rowan's "heart" (99). Richard's indignation is personal, however; Shaw's was, like Swift's, an indictment of the larger political and human scene. A political propagandist like Swift, Shaw always undercut his fierce indignation with wit and self-parody such as Joyce would discover in his own talent when he began to write *Ulysses.* Even in his parlor play, Shaw did not write about his romantic misadventures and epiphanies with such seriousness as Joyce did in *Exiles.* But like his covert disciple, in what G. B. S. called "THE Mother Play" (Pearson 204), he examined the annadominant female and an atypical love triangle that deconstructs, like *Exiles, Carmen* and its kind, to move from romance to reality.

CHAPTER Four

Tripartite *Dubliners:*
"Circumcivisizing" the Quintessential Dublin

IN AN 1896 review Shaw noted that Balzac and Maupassant had done for France what needed to be done for Ireland—"painted for us [pictures] of the spiritual squalor of the routine of poor middle class life, in which the education, the income, the culture of the family are three quarters abject pretense." Shaw volunteered to be part of a wrecking crew to reduce the Ireland of "sham" romance to "unsightly ruins: When this is done my country can consider the relative merits of building something real" (PS 114). In his short stories about Dublin, Joyce joined the Shavian urban renewal campaign. He wrote *Dubliners* (1914) in the spirit of G. B. S.—as Shaw put it in another context, as "an enemy of the existing order" (CP 136), which indoctrinates, constrains, and thereby diminishes ordinary people. He wrote his stories, however, from the stance of the Shavian superman: Shaw wrote that "the real Superman will snap his superfingers at all Man's present trumpery ideals of right, duty, honor, justice, religion, even decency" (CP 173–74). As the artist-god (as Stephen Dedalus would have it, paring his fingernails instead of snapping them), Joyce made Dublin the microcosm of social problems, grounding his stories in the reality that Shaw argued to be the basis of the new art. Most of the stories illustrate a Shavian (and socialist) dictum: "Society, and not any individual is the villain"

(CP 235). Moreover, the avowed aim of *Dubliners* is Shavian: Joyce wanted to disturb the "complacency" of his countrymen.

In his preface to *Plays Unpleasant* (1898), Shaw declared his intention "to force the spectator to face unpleasant facts . . . and . . . social horrors" to which the average citizen "will shut his eyes" (CP 726). He argued that his plays were "simply dramatic illustrations of the terrible mischief made everyday, not by scoundrels, but by moral people and idealists in their inexorable devotion to what they call their 'duty' " (BSL 1:278). The stories in *Dubliners* illustrate similar "terrible mischief" done by and to ordinary people in the name of ideals and duties. When Joyce was trying to get his stories published in 1906, he wrote Shaw's publisher Grant Richards, stressing the social and moral purpose of his fiction. He argued that rejection would "retard the course of civilization in Ireland by preventing the Irish people from having one good look at themselves in my nicely polished looking-glass" (JJL 1:64). His avowed intention is prefigured by Shavian argument. The preface to Shaw's *Plays Pleasant* (published by Richards in 1898) asserts that the artist can't "explain . . . he can only shew . . . you as a vision in the magic glass of his artwork" what is wrong with society (CP 732). Shaw explained that "theatrical art begins as the holding up to Nature of a distorting mirror," but people mature "to demand that the stage shall be a mirror of such accuracy and intensity of illumination that they shall be able to get glimpses of their real selves in it, and also learn a little how they appear to other people" (CP 112). Moreover, Shavian dramatic theory supports the impasse structure that informs Joyce's fictions. Of the new drama he wrote,

> The moment the dramatist gives up accidents and catastrophes and takes "slices of life" as his material, he finds himself committed to plays that have no endings. The curtain no longer comes down on a hero slain or married: it comes down when the audience has seen enough of the life presented to it to draw the moral. (CP 200)

In order to achieve the semblance of realism, Shaw announced that in his first play, *Widowers' Houses,* "I told the story, but discarded the plot" and created neither a "beautiful or lovable work" but rather an honest one (CP 701–2). Such mimetic theories of art had, of course, been discussed from the beginning of Western civilization: Plato objected to mimesis and Aristotle championed it. But the aesthetics of representation that developed with the rise of the novel (and of photography) and, subsequently, of naturalism influenced Shaw and his young disciple. By the late nineteenth century, Stendhal's formula that a novel is a mirror walking along the road had become the property of all realists. Shaw wrote, for example, that Zola, in whose tradition most critics would place *Dubliners,* "wanted, not works of literary art, but stories he could believe in as records of things that really happened . . . to the people he wanted to get at—the anti-artistic people . . . [for whom] he made it readable" (CP 199). Aware of theories of representation that were becoming commonplace in their age, both Irishmen aimed in their early works to hold the mirror up to nature, though not just through naturalistic documentation. Shaw, never afraid to be inconsistent, also argued that "stage realism is a contradiction in terms" (*Today,* April 28, 1984). He insisted that "drama is no mere setting up of the camera to nature: it is the presentation in parable of the conflict between Man's will and his environment: in a word, of problem" (CP 228). Denying that he was ever strictly "what you call a representationalist or realist," he wanted to differentiate himself "from a gramophone and a camera" (Meisel 435). The stories of his fellow crusader for a new Irish conscience were, in the Shavian sense, also not naturalistic, for both Irishmen carefully selected the details through which they would explore a problem without didactic declaration and sentimental dilutions. Shaw chose to do this in dialogue.

Though Shaw focused on content, admitting that his plays were propaganda, he believed that "style" could not be divorced from content; if it was not integral to the work's message, he held, it was "vain." In his preface to *Widowers' Houses* he introduced the duality of purpose with which he struggled—a conflict that Joyce shared but resolved differently: Shaw wanted his drama to be as much "a work of art" as any Molière play, but he also wanted to expose "a burning social issue" (CP 710). Robert Scholes's perception that in 1906 Joyce was judging literature "by a standard in which realism and aestheticism are allied rather than antagonistic" (106) suggests Joyce's covert discipleship and alliance with Shavian intentions. But for the purpose of examining the dialogic relationship of Shaw to Joyce, it is important to note that Joyce had read the fiction of realists like Flaubert, Chekhov, and Maupassant for style and could have found in George Moore's short stories, collected in *The Untilled Field* (1903), attitudes toward Ireland that Joyce shared with both the aristocratic landowner and with Shaw, his fellow declassé Dubliner.

Moore's stories corroborate Joyce's anticlericalism, his views of "the ignorance of the ordinary Irish, [and] the necessity of flight by emigration" (Magalaner and Kain 75). Shaw had anticipated these themes, and he developed and illustrated them in 1904 in *John Bull's Other Island*. Joyce, a Dublin "downstart," no doubt identified more closely with Shaw than with Moore, despite the fact that Moore was a Catholic (one who would, however, convert to Protestantism). For Shaw and Joyce judged people on merit, not on class, whereas in *Hail and Farewell* (1911) Moore was to make his elitist position clear: he wrote, "We looked upon our tenants as animals, and . . . they looked on us as kings" (Cahill and Cahill 144). Shaw's socialism was far more compatible to young Joyce. Indeed, the *Dubliners* stories are exempla of Shavian ideas, even though they are written in an understated, concrete style very different from that of the discursive generalist Shaw. When *Fanny's First Play* (1911) became one of Shaw's most popular dramas, Joyce purchased a copy while he was writing *Portrait*. In it, he might have noted with secret satisfaction one more corroboration of the similarity between his own and Shaw's thought. G. B. S.'s preface expresses distress over "our respectable middle class people . . . all as dead as mutton" (CP 138). As critics of *Dubliners* have noted, Joyce's Dubliners are the living dead, paralyzed by the values with which they have been indoctrinated.

At the start of his career, Joyce (albeit inconsistently) believed in the didactic ends of art and contended that his writing, like Shaw's, held a mirror up to reality—a mirror that had become in *Ulysses* "the cracked looking-glass of Irish art" (1:146). Both Irishmen were highly selective as to the reality that they represented. Shaw's talky dramas debate issues, whereas Joyce's stories record the environments, gestures, and speech of Dubliners while refracting their thoughts. Joyce arranged details to convey messages that Shavian characters state and Shavian polemics argue. Whereas Shaw tells, Joyce shows. But what he illustrates is often backed up by Shavian theory. Although Joyce's self-declared "scrupulous meanness" of style seems on the surface objective, its carefully selective documentation of the deadening realities of Dublin interfaces with Shavian lessons. Joyce demonstrates what makes the middle class into what Shaw called "dead people walking about" in a "counthry" that is an Irish "hell" (Plays 416).

Joyce told his brother Stanislaus that he intended "to give people some kind of intellectual pleasure and spiritual enjoyment by converting the bread of everyday life into something that had permanent artistic life of its own . . . for their mental, moral and spiritual uplift" (JJ1 169)—hardly the aim of a pure aesthete. In comparing himself to a secular priest performing a transubstantiating sacred rite, Joyce emulated Shaw, who irreverently compared his mission to that of a preacher and redeemer (CP 746). The paradoxical diabolonian savior believed that iconoclastic art "is the subtlest, the most seductive, the most effective instrument of moral propaganda in the world" (CP 221). While Joyce was writing *Dubliners,* Shaw's ideas were apparently congenial and surely useful, for in defending his stories, the younger man made his well-known declaration that he was writing "a chapter in the moral history" of his country. In asserting that his stories exposed the "paralysis" of Dublin, Joyce presented from the other side of the coin the Shavian insistence that his writing criticized society in order to be "medicinally salutary" (CP 717). Joyce described the problems, while Shaw diagnosed them and prescribed remedies.

Dubliners illustrates the social paradigm that Shaw charted in *The Quintessence of Ibsenism* (1891). There the Ibsenite gave a skeletal analysis of a tripartite society made up of three kinds of people—out of a sample of 1,000 people there would be 700 "philistines," 299 "idealists," and 1 lone "realist" who sees society and its unhealthy values for what they are. In the preface to *Plays Unpleasant* Shaw opposed "political and religious idealism" and "fictitious morals" that contaminate society. He urged idealists to "learn respect for reality, which would include the beneficent exercise of respecting themselves" (CP 734–35). Both writers wanted to translate real life—men and women "as we meet them in the world" (CW 45)—into literature. Thus in emulating his secret mentor, Joyce used the terms *philistine, idealizing,* and *realism,* filtering Shaw's vocabulary into his 1900 essay "Drama and Life" and his theories into his stories. Both Irishmen defined idealism not as a system of thought providing a priori, Platonically perfect forms or patterns of behavior but as misleading ideology. As Shaw put it, abstract words for ideals shed "fictitious glory on robbery, starvation, disease, crime, drink, war, cruelty, cupidity" in the names of "progress, science, morals, religion, patriotism, imperial supremacy, national greatness" (CP 734).

In the social model of *The Quintessence of Ibsenism,* the sheep-like majority are philistines; devotees of stale, accepted values are often their misguided and misguiding idealist shepherds. But there is the minority of one—a blacksheep precursor of the superman, a freethinker, and a realist pioneer "bold enough to seek the fulfillment of the individual will, hardy enough to prefer the naked facts of life to the comforting illusions of the imagination." Self-deluded idealists disdain or rationalize the brutal facts of life, whereas the singular hero dares to face and expose the truth behind the masks worn by idealists. Philistines, incapable of questioning the illusions inculcated in them by guardians of given beliefs, go through life with blinders imposed by their conditioning. The lone creative realist, having awakened to the truth behind the social facade, has the Promethean and Ibsenist mission of bringing knowledge to humanity and clearing the world of lies. Shaw identified himself with such antiestablishment realism. He declared in his preface to *Plays Unpleasant* that he had "no taste for what is called popular art, no respect for popular morality, no belief in popular religion, no admiration for popular heroics. As an Irishman I could pretend to patriotism neither for the country that I had abandoned nor the country that ruined it" (CP 716). Such declarations anticipate the subjects of Joyce's stories, which examine how "popular art . . . morality . . . religion [and] . . . heroics" entrap Dubliners.

By affirming the artist whose estrangement from social institutions is the mark of his genius, Shaw became an agent provocateur for Joyce. In writing *Dubliners,* Joyce took on the mission of the lone realist questioning popular ideals and depicting the compact majority who routinely serve their ends. Dubliners in Joyce's symposium of stories are aware to varying degrees of the significance of their ideals. Among the idealists are Fathers Flynn, Butler, and Purdon, who serve Catholicism. The old pervert in "An Encounter," Little Chandler of "A Little Cloud," and Duffy of "A Painful Case" live on illusory ideals derived from literature. Mrs. Kearney of "A Mother" supports the cultural revival, Joe Hines of "Ivy Day in the Committee Room" is a sentimental Parnellite, and Miss Ivors of "The Dead" is an Irish Irelander. Most Dubliners are, however, unwitting, trapped philistines, acting out their socially programmed scripts. Among them are women like Eliza and Nannie in "The Sisters," the central character of "Eveline," Maria of "Clay," Polly Mooney and her mother in "The Boarding House," Kathleen Kearney of "A

Mother," Mrs. Kernan of "Grace," and the women (except for Miss Ivors) of "The Dead." Philistine men include Jimmy Doyle of "After the Race," the eponymous "Two Gallants," Farrington of "Counterparts," the political canvassers of "Ivy Day," and the bourgeois Catholics of "Grace." In Joyce's sampling of Dubliners, there are only four incipient realists—the boys whose points of view inform the first three stories and Gabriel Conroy in "The Dead." By Shaw-light, however, Gabriel's ambiguous epiphany is prompted by one of the most destructive ideals of all—the *liebes tod,* love-death motif of romanticism. Nevertheless, in becoming aware of his failures Gabriel is, we shall see, a surrogate for the realist author of *Dubliners.* To Shaw, the disillusion of the embryonic realist was the beginning of wisdom. In each of Joyce's first three stories—"The Sisters," "An Encounter," and "Araby"—the fledgling realist is awakened from devotion to a crippling ideal that Shaw had denounced.

"Yung and Easily Freudened": Dublin Boys

By the time Joyce had written the third revision of his first story, "The Sisters," its characters paralleled the paradigm of Shaw's tripartite society. Like the geometrical gnomen mentioned on the first page of the story, the characters are a representative part of society, the remainder of a parallelogram after the removal of a similar parallelogram containing one of its corners: hence they are a microcosm and indicator of the whole. The mix almost approximates the Shavian divisions of the triune society: two priests (Father Flynn and Father O'Rourke); five philistines (Old Cotter, the boy's uncle and aunt, and Father Flynn's two sisters); and the incipient realist, from whose point of view the story is told. The priest is a failed religious idealist who tries to pass on his duties, rituals, and deadening beliefs to the next generation, represented by the boy. The women personify conforming Christianity, whereas the men stand for bourgeois, masculine values. The portraits of the sisters reveal another Shavian theory with which Joyce concurred: his argument in the preface to *John Bull's Other Island* that devotion to Catholicism had reduced the ordinary Irish believer to "penury and servitude" (CP 449). The sensitive boy is, however, an ephebic realist.

Shaw's emancipation proclamation in *The Quintessence of Ibsenism* insists that to gain freedom, one must "repudiate duty" (MCE 48), for "every step of progress means a duty repudiated, and a scripture torn up" (140). The boy does not tear up scripture, but he rejects the mysteries of priesthood in favor of his instinct for life. Although the priest had been indoctrinating him into the arcane rituals of Catholicism, the child feels "freed" by the priest's death and chooses to walk "slowly along the sunny side of the street" (D 11). Not yet ready for discourses on the Life Force, he intuitively opts for life. Ironically unaware that he is repudiating religion and still trying to conform politely to the rituals of the wake, the boy kneels at the foot of the bed where the coffined priest lies. He pretends to pray and declines to participate in the mock communion offered by Father Flynn's sisters, refusing the cream crackers that, the reader realizes, ironically represent the wafer of Christ's body. Although the boy meekly refuses, because he thinks he "would make too much noise eating them" (14), he has symbolically rejected participation in the spurious mass administered by Father Flynn's unannointed surrogates. Without knowing it, the boy has disputed the spiritual hegemony of the sisters and retreated from identification with the priest, hence from Christian communion. In refusing the proffered wafer, he abjures what Shaw called "sanctified . . . Duty," for "the impulse toward greater freedom . . . [is] sufficient ground for the repudiation of any customary duty, however sacred, that conflicts with it" (MCE 45, 48).

Turning away from "slavery" to religion is, by Shaw-light, the first step toward recognizing one's "duty" to oneself, "assessed" by oneself instead of others (MCE 45). Thus Joyce's boy passes beyond the "infancy of helplessness and terror" that Shaw believed prevents youngsters from looking reality in the face. In revealing the boy's confrontation with stultifying religion, Joyce emulated Shaw, who advised the artist to tear off "the masks created by idealism." Significantly, the unnamed persona of the story gazes on the dead priest, even though a corpse symbolizes the "spectre"—in Shaw's terms—whose worst form is "the king of terrors, Death . . . the Arch-Inexorable." Shaw exhorted his disciples to look "the spectres in the face" (MCE 47). A Joycean alter ego, the boy in the *Dubliners* story looks and then chooses life. When he peers at the dead priest, he sees "that he was not smiling. . . . his large hands loosely retaining a chalice. His face very truculent, grey and massive" (14). When the boy fancies that the priest is smiling in his coffin, he instinctively feels that Father Flynn must believe himself well out of his depressing existence; but when he actually looks at the corpse, he sees that its expression is "truculent." Illusion and reality conflict in the story, producing its painful ironies. The evidence counters the conventional wisdom of the devout mourners who say that Father Flynn's death was "beautiful" and that he "has gone to his eternal reward" (15–16). The potential realist recognizes that the dead priest, like the religion for which he stands, is ugly and ineffectual ("his hands loosely retaining a chalice") but still somehow larger than life—"massive." Whereas the boy does not understand the symbolism of the chalice, Joyce's strategic references urge it upon the reader as the symbol of the priest's failed communion with Christ and of his failure, therefore, as Christ's emissary.

In Shavian terms, Father Flynn comes near to being a villain. In his "Maxims for Revolutionists," appended to *Man and Superman,* Shaw wrote that "the vilest abortionist is he who attempts to mould a child's character" (CP 189). The symbolic simoniac had tried to mold the child, in fact to sell his church office to him—in effect, to reverse roles with him, after teaching him "the duties of the priest towards the Eucharist and towards the secrecy of the confession" (12), two duties that the priest may have profaned. Such priestly duties tempt the boy because they seem to require courage and offer magical power. But, ironically, the priest—a disillusioned idealist—had failed precisely in his duties toward the Eucharist, for in breaking the communion chalice he had severed his covenant with Christ and estranged himself from God. Subsequently, he "sold" his office to the boy, committing the heresy of simony by insinuating into the boy's awareness the notion that he must hear the cleric's confession. He offered his office to the boy in exchange for his company and to expiate his guilt over breaking the chalice years ago during mass and blaming an altar boy.

But projection of adult responsibility onto a child is reprehensible, and the boy senses the imposition. Indeed, the priest instilled in the young novitiate the feeling that he was the old man's confessor. Awareness of such an obligation makes the boy feel uneasy. He dreams that the "grey face . . . desired to confess something" (10). Suggestions of exotic romance in far away Persia—an escape into alien and romantic unreality—attend the dream. Simultaneously tempted and frightened by the priest's transference of his office to him, the youngster (or his adult imago interpreting the unhealthy and iniquitous role reversal) senses that the paralytic wanted him "to absolve the simoniac of his sin" (10). The boy, however, resists such self-sacrifice, instinctively refusing to become Isaac to the priest's Abraham, for he has associated "simony" with the descriptions "maleficent" and "sinful" (9). Thus he intuits his fears and anticipates his resistance to the old man's malignant temptation.

Although the boy cannot articulate the problem, the priest's mental and spiritual paralysis is a mockery of religion, to which the religious idealist had devoted his life. His faith, like that of the disillusioned idealists whom Shaw described, was empty and useless. Like other idealists, the "disappointed man" (18) did not have the realist's courage to repudiate that in which he no longer believed. Father Flynn is one of the idealists whom Shaw recorded—"temperamentally dissatisfied with their lot, yet seeking refuge from the spectacle of their own failure in . . . the self-delusion that to see the world thus is noble and spiritual" (GBS 273). When Father Flynn laughed in the confession box, however, his illusions were gone, for his disappointment and disease had reduced him to senility. The failed priest's "idle chalice" is "empty"; the "duties of the priesthood was too much for him." As Eliza says, "his life was, you might say, crossed" (17–19). His ironic martyrdom resulted from his submission to what Shaw called "Crosstianity" in his 1905 preface to *Major Barbara* (CP 116). Shaw abhorred self-sacrifice to "religious idealism" because it is selfdestructive and dangerous to others: "Self-sacrifice enables us to sacrifice other people without blushing" (CP 195).

Enfeebled by his own martyrdom to an ideal, Father Flynn tried to atone by sacrificing the boy. He had already sacrificed his sisters, Nanny and Eliza. These women represent the majority, who, according to Shaw, do "not yet dare to do without" masks that cover up the bitter reality of failed idealism. Their brother's profession brought only poverty to the nun-like sisters, who are as crippled as Father Flynn was in life. Their acceptance of the sale of the church office is ironic, for women are not allowed to administer the sacraments. The communion that they offer at the wake is secular and unconsecrated. There has been no spiritual rebirth, only the continuation of empty lives of sterile devotion to a dead ideal. According to the boy's philistine aunt, Eliza's comfort has been to serve her brother: "At any rate it must be a great comfort for you to know that you did all you could for him" (15). But in reality service to the priest has crippled them. Although they have spent their lives as caretakers, the pathetically ineffectual sisters are incapable of handling the funeral arrangements. Still dependent upon the church, they require the guidance of Father O'Rourke. Deprived of education and abased by her subjection to religion, Eliza is platitudinous: "I don't know what we will have done at all," she says, telling the truth about her helplessness (15). The sisters have indeed taken the vows of poverty for their brother and become his nearly illiterate nursemaids (as Nannie's name suggests). Their seedy dress and bad grammar convey their impoverishment: "poor Nannie . . . [is] wore out." Nannie's "muttering"—a bad imitation of the priest at mass—"distracted" the boy, who notices "how clumsily her skirt was hooked at the back and how the heels of her cloth boots were trodden down all to one side" (16). Ironically, the sisters take the priest's place, with "Eliza seated in the arm-chair in state" and Nannie stolidly offering wine and crackers.

The language of the adult Dubliners, fragmented and stereotyped, is trite. The philistines cover reality with truisms. Using conventional clichés to hide the ugliness of Father Flynn's life and death, Eliza says, "He had a beautiful death, God be praised." She evades the reality of his "truculent" face by asserting, "No one would think he'd make such a beautiful corpse" (15). To the budding realist willing to look reality in the face, he seems no more beautiful in death than in life. His pupil remembers his "big discoloured teeth and . . . big tongue" lying "upon his lower lip"—evidence of his gross paralysis. The boy's aunt, instead of facing the ugly truth, asserts euphemistically that "he's gone to his eternal reward" (16)—a reward that might, indeed, be in hell, which is the symbolic setting of *Dubliners*. Putting Shavian theory into practice, philistine Dubliners make themselves believe "that all illusions . . . are realities" (MCE 48).

Like all philistines (in Shaw's view), the pathetic sisters, who have neither the privileges nor the status of nuns, are paralyzed, sterile, poverty-ridden cases of blindly obedient sacrifice to an ideal. Setting the pattern for many Dubliners, they sentimentalize the past rather than break with it to make a better future. Thus Eliza speaks of "going out for a drive one fine day just to see the old house" in "one of them new-fangled carriages . . . them with the rheumatic wheels" (17). Even as a young man Joyce made skillful use of irony that borders on the comic, for Eliza's malapropism reveals her ignorance, while at the same time it suggests the painful condition of the old joints and muscles of Dublin, whose decadent religion the dead priest and his sister communicants symbolize.

The two adult, secular males in "The Sisters" represent another form of social indoctrination. The "tiresome old fool" Cotter, who has spent his life working in a brewery, would have the "lad run about and play with young lads of his own age and not be" (10). In front of the boy, he cannot or will not define what is wrong with the boy's unconventional friendship with the priest. Like the uncle, Cotter has little respect for education. The uncle seconds him with an Irish cliché: "Let him learn to box his corner," meaning, "Let him go out and learn to make a living and get ahead in the world" (Gifford 30). He labels the boy a Rosicrucian because of his nonconforming tendencies to be dreamy, withdrawn, and attracted to what seems to Cotter to be esoteric knowledge. The reader realizes, however, that the boy may be a potential Yeats (who was in his early phase a Rosicrucian)—to the conforming, witless uncle an eccentric, but to the reader perhaps a fledgling mystical poet. The men offer the limited and limiting bourgeois cure-all of masculinity—"Take exercise" (11). Both advise that he become a normal, normless clone of every other callow philistine.

In "The Sisters" the juvenile protagonist rejects what Shaw called "Duty to God, with the priest as assessor" (MCE 48). In "An Encounter" another truant rejects duty only to be disillusioned by an alternative ideal. In "Parents and Children," the 1910 preface to *Misalliance,* written after *Dubliners* had been refused by Grant Richards for publication, Shaw attacked school, calling it a prison. This position is implicit in his earlier work *The Quintessence of Ibsenism.* Shaw opposed all forms of authoritarian indoctrination. "An Encounter" demonstrates the proximity of Joycean to Shavian thought on education. Shaw declared that "pious fraud is an attempt to pervert that divine mystery called the child's conscience into an instrument of our own convenience, and to use that wonderful and terrible power called shame to grind our own axe" (CP 49). His definition of "pious fraud" provides a segue between Father Flynn and Father Butler, who represents the parochial educational establishment in "An Encounter." He shames Leo Dillon in class for reading *The Apache Chief* instead of studying his Roman history. Such chronicles of empire form young minds to accept their modern equivalent, the British Empire, which is Ireland's oppressor. Religion and secular history collude to train Irish boys for self-betrayal. Like Shaw, Joyce implicitly condemned classroom texts that coerce students into accepting the official ideals of an alien society. G. B. S.

disapproved of the "dogmatic and coercive schoolmaster" but understood that a teacher was defending his own vested interests (CP 59).

Shaw, however, had faith in the child, whereas most adults, he wrote, assume "that the child does not know its own business" and the adult does. "In this you are sure to be wrong: the child feels the drive of the Life Force" (CP 50). This is perhaps what tempts the boys to play hooky in "An Encounter." To Shaw, school is even worse than prison, because in jail "you are not forced to read books written by the warders and the governor ... and beaten or otherwise tormented if you cannot remember their utterly unmemorable contents" (CP 54). In school,

> you are forced to read a hideous imposture called a school book. ... With millions of acres of woods and valleys and hills and wind and air and birds and streams and fishes and all sorts of instructive and healthy things easily accessible, or with streets and all sorts of city delights at the door, you are forced to sit, not in a room with some human grace and comfort ... but in a stalled pound with a lot of other children, beaten if you talk, beaten if you move, beaten if you cannot prove by answering idiotic questions that even when you escaped from the pound and from the eye of your gaoler you were still agonizing over his detestable sham books instead of daring to live. (CP 55)

This Rousseauistic view of education roughly summarizes the attitude that Joyce depicts in "An Encounter." Joyce's boys want to dare to live. The narrator is, upon escaping from school, delighted with nature, which reflects his joy: "All the branches of the tall trees which lined the mall were gay with little light green leaves and the sunlight slanted through them on to the water" (D 21). The foliage and sunlight on the water are objective correlatives for the truant's delight. The sensitive youngster wants the adventure and freedom that Shaw promised awaited an enterprising, urban truant who could be encouraged by his subversive reading.

"An Encounter" contrasts the conflicting ideals of two written forms of history—the accepted cultural ideal of empire promoted by Father Butler and the ideal depicted in glamorized, popular stories of renegade underdogs who have been, like Indians in America and the Irish in the British Empire, colonized by the usurping invaders of Western civilization, built on the Roman model. Most of the schoolboys who "banded together" to play cowboys and Indians are cowboys, on the winning side. The losers, the "reluctant" Indians, like the narrator, are pressured to conform, so that they won't "seem studious or lacking in robustness" (20). Most of the boys are philistines. Joe Dillon's "fat young brother Leo the idler" and Joe, who enjoys pretending to be the fiercest Indian, are in reality tame, conforming Catholics. Joe supposedly has "a vocation for the priesthood" (19). As Shaw put it, "The red scalp-hunting braves of North America were the sportingest race imaginable; and they were conquered as easily as the bison they hunted" (CP 146). Ironically, the most vocal, wildest "Indian"—ringleader Leo Dillon—backs out of the proposed day of truancy because he fears reprisals. Although he denigrates it, the timid narrator is afraid to repudiate fully the ideal of masculinity that is the concomitant of imperialism. Mahony, who shares the day of "miching" with the narrator, is a schoolboy version of the stereotype.

Mahony imitates the ideal of rugged manhood by bringing along his catapult to shoot birds. This masculine code was repugnant to Shaw, partly because of his "sense of kinship with animals" (CP 140) but mostly because he objected strenuously to killing for sport. After mentioning his aversion in passing in his prefaces, he wrote an essay in 1914 called "Killing for Sport" (CP 138–48). In it he set up adult models comparable to the two boys whom Joyce describes. In reading Shaw's essay, Joyce must have recognized his own predisposition. "Which is the superior man?" Shaw asked—"the man whose pastime is slaughter, or the man whose pastime is creative or contemplative?" (146). Preferring the latter but admitting that the other was "necessary," Shaw despised those who enjoy killing for the sport of it (146): "To kill . . . merely to pass away the time . . . is to behave like an idiot or a silly imitative sheep" (148). Thus scorning the accepted male ideal, Shaw despised the model upon which Mahony's youthful aspirations seem to be based. Mahony apes chauvinist behavior by chasing "a crowd of ragged girls" (D 22) and bragging to the old man whom he and the narrator meet that "he had three totties" (25). He escapes talking to the "old josser" by springing up and chasing a cat "across the field" (26). At the end of the story the narrator, an embryonic "creator and contemplative" like Shaw, calls to his friend for help. Though he admits that he had "always despised" Mahony "a little," the juvenile persona as yet lacks the bravery Shaw named as the greatest virtue. Even as the boy tries to muster courage, he acknowledges that his "voice had an accent of forced bravery in it, and I was ashamed of my paltry stratagem" (28). The stratagem was necessitated by the ominous behavior of the pederast who had engaged the innocent narrator in conversation. Ironically, the narrator, who disdains mesomorphic inclinations, recognizes Mahony as his rescuer.

The young protagonist whose perceptions shape "An Encounter" is tempted by a third literary ideal—an escapist, adult variation of the schoolboy adventure stories that inspire the truants. G. B. S. viewed such "romance as the great heresy to be swept from art and life" (CP 732). He urged theater to turn "from the drama of romance and sensuality to the drama of edification" (CP 737). As Arland Ussher observes, Yeats wrote of his friends in the literary revival, "We were the last romantics," but Shaw "might have said, 'I was the first Unromantic'" (63). Joyce was not far behind him. In "An Encounter" he emulates Shaw in exposing the decadence of romanticism. Escape literature for boys—fantasies of wild, exotic Western adventure in *The Union Jack;* daring deeds of British heroes and romance with violent details in *Pluck;* and cheap, sadomasochistic sensationalism in *The Half-Penny Marvel,* all masquerading as wholesome literature (see Kershner 33)—depicted the romance of phony heroism that Shaw despised. Joyce's young narrator prefers "American detective stories" with "unkempt fierce and beautiful girls" (20). Thus we are prepared for his receptivity to the old man whom he and Mahony encounter in Ringsend.

The literature that the "old josser" reads includes the requisite beautiful damsels, although like the little boy himself, they are not unkempt and fierce. Instead they are (like the boy?) damsels in distress. The old reprobate's decadent literary preferences are as escapist and dangerous as the glorifications of violence in boys' magazines. The shabby stranger asks the boys whether they have read Thomas Moore, Sir Walter Scott, or Bulwer-Lytton, all romantic writers and only one of them, Moore, Irish. Although he was a shallow, sentimental patriot who idealized Tara's halls from the safe distance of London, Moore was a commercially successful Irish romantic. He evoked the past glory of the silenced minstrel's harp and of Ireland's dead heroes as well as self-indulgent sorrow over loveliness faded away. Although, according to Terence Brown, Joyce admired Moore's *Irish Melodies,* which resonate in his writing (16), he did not do so unreservedly. As a young tenor Joyce may have been attracted to Moore's lyrics, but by the time he wrote "An Encounter," he recognized their maudlin and even dangerously retrograde sentimentality as well as the decadence of the exotic, voluptuous Orientalism of *Lalla Rookh*. This is evident in the fact that Joyce makes Moore a favorite of the self-indulgent onanist with whom Mahony and the narrator have a distinctly unromantic encounter. (In *Ulysses* Joyce again treats Moore ironically, by commenting on the fact that the Dublin statue of the author of "The Meeting of the Waters" stands over a public urinal: see U 8.414–17).

That Moore was an Irishman who sold verse by catering to an English preference for harmless, nostalgic, unthreatening Irish lyrics and flattered their worst bourgeois inclinations for romantic escapism suggests that the tastes of the stranger the boys meet, the old man with "yellow teeth" (25) and "bottle-green eyes" (27), are not trustworthy. His preference for the Irish poet who was a sycophant to the English hints to adult readers that he is a betrayer. His choices of novels that are officially British are conclusive. But the boy, if not his creator, is innocent of such sophisticated, Shavian perceptions. To prove that he is grown-up, he lies to the old man, pretending that he has read the works the seedy fellow names—works not esteemed by Joyce or his mentor. Kershner notes that Scott was especially noxious to Joyce, for the priest in "Araby" and the monkey-faced captain in *Portrait,* like the old onanist, like his works (39). Scott's historical novels of crime, terror, and forbidden love as well as slightly off-color morality were standard romance. His novels glamorize chivalric quests. Heartrendingly happy endings, like those in Scott's novels, were repugnant to Shaw, opiates that distracted readers from the real problems they should face. The popularizer Bulwer-Lytton represents an even more decadent romantic tradition that commercialized melodramatic fiction. As Kershner points out, the plot of his novel *The Last Days of Pompeii* (1834), "an interminable melodrama of decadent Roman Empire society," is in many ways ironically analogous to the action of "An Encounter" (39–40), especially in its "sexual confusion," which is replicated in the behavior of the old pervert. Interestingly, Shaw advocated confusing the sexes, creating manly women and womanly men, but he tested his androgynous characters in comic social situations that had only traces of the possibly perverse implications of such disturbance of the old gender stereotypes. The ominous, deranged old sadist in "An Encounter" bears no resemblance to Shaw's extroverts. Having surrendered himself completely to the illusions of his romantic "ideals," he ritualizes the sick, decadent love suggested by stale romantic literature; he makes autoerotic love into a mechanical fetish to accompany his onanism. His irrational repetitions are vaguely reminiscent of the mutterings of the bogus mass in "The Sisters."

Having educed the sickly implications of his romantic reading, the pederast has made sadomasochistic sex into a religion, and he preaches it and demonstrates its rites to the truants. Both are understandably repulsed and afraid. The boys' illusions of escape have turned into the ugly reality of a frightening encounter with perverse sexuality. Although romantic literature had seemed to be an attractive escape to the youthful narrator, his brief meeting with the decadent old "idealist" is almost as dangerous as friendship with Father Flynn and more disturbing because it represents a confrontation with the sinister unknowns of sex. The "old josser," who, like the priest in the first story, alienates the boy he wishes to win, is a skewed parallel to Father Flynn; "josser" is pidgin English for "God." His decadent ideal of mysterious worship of unsavory romance exposes yet another false palliative that the budding realist faces and rejects.

In "Araby" the representative of decayed ideals is not present as a foil. A priest now dead was, however, the former tenant of the house in which the young protagonist lives. Like "An Encounter," the story deflates romanticism and suggests theory propounded by Shaw. In his preface to *Plays Pleasant* (1898), Shaw remarked that romance pretends to make a man "courageous and kind and friendly" while he is "infatuated in love," but actually "the blinding and narrowing power of lovesickness" makes "princely heroes unhappy and unfortunate" (CP 741). Readers of "Araby" recognize that its title refers to the bazaar in the story and that it also suggests the exotic romance of the Middle East. Gifford points out that "Araby was a poetic name for Arabia and was suggestive of the heady and sensuous romanticism of popular tales and poems about the Middle East" (40). He notes the bazaar's theme song with its "rainbow visions" and Thomas Moore's ballad "Araby's Daughter" as analogues that enrich the implications of the title (42).

Shaw's preface to *Three Plays for Puritans* (1898), however, intimates a somewhat different significance for the title and theme of the story. Shaw wrote that there are two kinds of love stories "that seem to me to be not only fundamentally false but sordidly base. One is the pseudo-religious story in which the hero . . . does good on strictly commercial grounds, reluctantly" exercising a little virtue on earth in order to get credit in heaven. "The other is the romance in which the hero, also rigidly commercial, will do nothing except for the sake of the heroine. Surely this is as depressing as it is unreal. Compare with it the treatment of love, frankly indecent according to our notions, in oriental fiction. In The Arabian Nights . . . love is treated . . . as naturally as any other passion. . . . These tales expose . . . the delusion that the interest of this most capricious, most transient, most easily baffled of all instincts is inexhaustible" (CP 742).

Such words might be a commentary on "Araby." Shaw's analysis of *Arabian Nights,* to which "Araby" probably alludes, puts a different cast on the irony of Joyce's title. Although a few of the fairy tales "are based on the traditional plot of the young prince compelled to undergo arduous tasks before he is allowed to marry the princess of his choice" (Zipes 590), in Scheherezade's tales love is expressed in frank sensuality. Love is not comparable to a religious quest, nor is it eternal. Beginning with disillusion regarding women, the aim of the tales is to cure a man of lovesickness. Joyce's tale has a similar aim: it illustrates a cure for adolescent infatuation. The boy at the center of Joyce's free indirect discourse (see Gillespie 215–16), led on by his illusions, thinks of Araby as a symbol of romantic love, but his consciousness is influenced by the Western tradition of courtly love. He lives, like the hero of romance, for the heroine. Finally, however, in a tale in which "Araby" is both title and terminus, West meets East. The boy's illusions regarding the Araby into which he enters—the dark night of the closing bazaar—are dissipated. Having imagined himself as a knight quester, he encounters eroticism "treated," as Shaw put it, "as naturally as any other passion." He discovers, through confronting the Arabian night of the street market, that romantic love is indeed, as Shaw wrote, "capricious . . . transient . . . easily baffled." He also intuits that it is commercial—a commodity exchange in which favors are bought and sold. That he does not buy a gift to purchase the favor of Mangan's sister suggests that he is becoming a Shavian realist. He has an intimation of the reality of what Shaw called the "frankly indecent" treatment of love in *Arabian Nights* when he hears the vulgar shopgirl's flirtatious gambit with her admirers.

Shaw was convinced that because "man's intellectual consciousness of himself is derived from the descriptions of him in books, a persistent misrepresentation of humanity in literature gets finally accepted and acted upon" (CP 743). In *Dubliners* Joyce accepts this premise as axiomatic; he shows the inevitable deleterious effects of being conditioned by reading popular literature. As Kershner points out, in "Araby," as in "An Encounter," Joyce includes books dialogic to the boy's romantic quest but in an ironic context. Two of them are inappropriate for the dead priest, their former owner, and the third is related to the prepubescent protagonist, who is, with regard to love, a "Devout Communicant." The dead priest left behind "a few paper-covered books ...: *The Abbot* by Walter Scott, *The Devout Communicant,* and *The Memoirs of Vidocq*" (29). Although *The Devout Communicant Or Pious Meditations and Aspirations for the Three Days Before and the Three Days After Receiving the Holy Eucharist* (1813) is an appropriate book for a priest to own, its discussion of the priestly preparation for participating in the Eucharist ceremony suggests the quasi-religious aspect of the boy's romance, for he carries the image of Mangan's sister as a "chalice" (31).

Although Jesse Weston's *The Quest for the Holy Grail,* which posits the relationship between the Grail and female fertility, was not published until 1913, Joyce, with or without the help of Freud and Jung (his disclaimers notwithstanding), understood the relationship between the Eucharist cup and woman. He was also aware that the quest for the Holy Grail necessitated spiritual purity in the quester; such virtue would make him worthy of love. Riane Eisler's thesis in *The Chalice and the Blade* is that the chalice, in contradistinction to the destructive, masculine blade, symbolizes the creative, life-generating female. Her observation would not have surprised Joyce (or Joyceans) used to gazing at the omphalos of Molly Bloom. But in "Araby" the boy has substituted the symbol for the actual, earthy tureens of the female. And he vaguely imagines himself as a questing knight tested by a hostile environment.

Joyce's 1902 essay on James Clarence Mangan prepares the way for his conception of his prepubescent protagonist—an "innocent Parcifal"—as well as that of Mangan's sister. In Mangan's conception of the female, "East and West meet" in "an imaginative personality reflecting the light of imaginative beauty." Images of beauty—"Vittoria Colonna and Laura and Beatrice . . . and Monna [sic] Lisa—embody one chivalrous idea, which is no mortal thing, bearing it bravely above the accidents of lust and faithlessness and weariness" (CW 78–79). The inexperienced boy of "Araby" fancies himself bearing his Holy Grail, the purity of his holy love for Mangan's sister. The "white curve of her neck" (D 33) suggests that she is the Irish equivalent of the Pre-Raphaelite "Blessed Damozel," Rossetti's Madonna-like lady to whom lovers address their idolatrous love. Mangan's sister is to Joyce's early adolescent narrator very much as Candida is to the romantic young poet Marchbanks in *Candida;* the poet's gift of a copy of Titian's *Assumption of the Virgin* clarifies his quasi-religious and courtly adoration. Marchbanks's idealistic perception of Candida, until the last scene of Shaw's play, enthrones the woman as an ideal rather than a real person, just as Joyce's story does. In both the play and the story, confrontation with reality frees the young suitors from fealty to the courtly ideal. In "Araby," the Western tradition of courtly love meets the frankly erotic tradition of *Arabian Nights*.

Whereas Joyce's inclusion of *The Devout Communicant* among the books left by the dead priest slyly suggests the Western confusion of love and religion, his other two books are escapist and therefore suggest diversions from religious vocation. They also hint at the simulacrum of the boy's quest: it is a diversion from growth to maturity. Kershner shows that *The Abbot* is an ironic and romantic parallel to the action of the story. *The Memoirs of Vidocq,* about a secretive, egoistic detective who invents adventures for himself, thus engaging in narcissistic self-romance (a variation on that of the old pervert in "An Encounter"?), makes ironic dialogic commentary on the action of "Araby," deflating the boy's romantic adventure. In the bitter end the boy repudiates such vanities. The disillusioning "porcelain vases" and "great jars that stood like eastern guards at either side of the dark entrance to the stall" (35) are debased and enlarged symbols of the female whose image he had carried like a chalice. At the bazaar the religion of romance and its rituals are vulgarized and cheapened. The bazaar is as silent as "a church after a service," and the boy arrives at the Café Chantant, whose name intimates French wickedness. There his elevated quest is reduced to *cherchez la femme*—the real subject of *Arabian Nights.* Englishmen seek the shopgirl, and "two men," like the money changers Christ expelled from the synagogue, are "counting money" (34). The reality of the commercial bazaar, like that in the exotic but sexually explicit *Arabian Nights,* destroys the boy's illusions.

Shaw wrote, "If the conventions of romance are only insisted on long enough and uniformly enough (a condition guaranteed by the uniformity of human folly and vanity) then, for the huge compulsorily schooled masses who read romance or nothing, these conventions will became the laws of personal honor" (CP 743). Significantly, the thoughts and actions of the protagonist of "Araby" indicate that he has been schooled in romance and its connection with Christianity, knighthood, and the quest for the Grail. When he realizes that he has been "driven and derided by vanity" (35), "Araby" reveals Shavian theory in practice. The story is an exemplum of initiation through disillusionment into the select fraternity of Shavian "realists." The false lure of romance, parodied in *Arms and the Man,* is the major theme of Joyce's story. The prepubescent hero's ideal of courtly love is shattered. In confronting the East of the bazaar, Joyce's boy is deeply disillusioned. "Araby," which begins in a "blind" alley foreshadowing its ending with the boy's eyes opened to the darkness surrounding him, suggests a Shavian rite of passage from romance to reality. Ironically, in the end, when the lights of Araby are out, the boy is no longer blind. Shaw had indeed written of Ibsen's developing awareness, that idealism blinds us and that "with his eyes . . . opened, instances of the mischief of idealism crowded up on him" (MCE 82). Similarly, when Joyce's eyes were opened, he created alter egos for whom disillusionment was the beginning of wisdom. His mentor Shaw distrusted romanticism because "it is dangerous; people may mistake it for Reality, and believing it swallow it whole" (Colbourne 40), no doubt to be poisoned. The boys in Joyce's first three stories are learning the Shavian credo—to respect reality over illusion, fact over fantasy, because recognition of the truth is liberating. His protagonists have enacted two parts of the mythic initiation of the hero-redeemer, who, according to Jungian Joseph Campbell, undergoes separation, initiation, and return with a boon for his people. In "Araby" the boy separates himself from the other Dubliners. He undergoes the trials and testing of the hostile terrain of Dublin streets at night. He has his moment of ironic enlightenment at the bazaar, where Western chivalry meets the "frankly indecent" erotic reality of *Arabian Nights.* Although the boy does not return to his people, the story is itself the boon that Joyce brought to the Irish.

Like the knight quester, Joyce's protagonist is tested by a hostile environment. Shaw had been accused of exploiting squalor, of creating characters "unsympathetic, sordid, soulless—ending worse than they began," and of being preoccupied with "the seamy side of life" (CP 706, 733). In *Dubliners* Joyce appears to compete with Shaw for similar critical evaluation. Though the boy in "Araby" is not soulless, his environment is antagonistic and ugly. The garden behind the house is an unkempt adumbration of Eden after the Fall. Despite its central apple tree, its snake-tempter is a "rusty bicycle pump" whose phallic and religious significance is corroded. The air is cold, the lanes are dark and muddy (30), the Dublin streets are "hostile to romance." Vulgar, commercial, noisy, "litanies" of the marketplace and of patriotism are competing discourses and "foe" to the quester seeking the fulfillment of romantic love (31). The journey to the bazaar is equally depressing "in a third-class carriage of a deserted train" (34), which is an ironic contrast to the mighty Arab steed in the poem the boy's drunken uncle begins to recite as the boy departs on his symbolic pilgrimage. Significantly, the sentimental poem alludes simultaneously to East and West, for the steed suggests the knight quester, and the owner lamenting his loss is an Arab. The song, of course, obliquely foreshadows the boy's farewell to chivalric romance and his disillusioning awareness of the triumph of commerce and the usurping English—the noisy threats of tawdry commerce and politics through which he had borne his "chalice." The train arrives at "an improvised wooden platform" that suggests the insubstantiality of the illusory Araby. The bazaar is almost over, but the rituals of the corrupt and corrupting commercialism of the marketplace—which Shaw related to the commodification of women—continue.

The reticent boy senses the vulgarity of the scene. The debased transactions of trade are juxtaposed to the vulgar rites of fraternizing courtship. The boy hears the language of the usurpers, "English accents," flirting with the salesgirl, whom he romantically thinks of as a "young lady." Whereas the philistine shopgirl comes to him out of a sense of "duty" (the Shavian shibboleth), the boy finally rejects venal romance by saying, "No, thank you" to her query as to whether he wishes to "buy anything" (35). In the impasse at the end of the story the boy has an epiphany, the content of which is Shavian: he recognizes the "vanity" of his mercantile, romantic aspirations. In "Araby" a young idealist, innocently ensnared by one of Shaw's *bêtes noires*—as Shaw put it, "the deification of love" as "the holy of holies" (CP 744)—tries vainly to maintain his adolescent fantasy despite the alien, impoverished, and coarse materialism of his surroundings. His disillusioning moment of truth awakens him to "the blinding and narrowing power of lovesickness." When the boy articulates his deluded vanity, his initiation as a Shavian realist is complete.

Joyce's stories of "yung and freudened" boys illustrate the Shavian theory that growth is possible only when one becomes realistic. Indeed, in conversation with his young Irish admirer Arthur Power, Joyce reiterated, without crediting his source, the dictum that was the first commandment of Shaw's credo until late in life: "In realism you get down to the facts in which the world is based; that sudden reality which smashes romanticism to a pulp. What makes most peoples' lives unhappy is some disappointed romanticism, some unrealisable misconceived ideal. In fact you may say that idealism is the ruin of man" (Power 98).

"Lawanorder on Loveinardor": Dublin's Destructive Ideals

Several of the characters in *Dubliners* can be categorized as self-destructive idealists, entrapped by the inflexible and unrealistic beliefs to which they give their allegiance. In accordance with Shaw's analysis, the work of the realist is to expose the maladies of society, the misguided idealists who perpetuate social ills or sustain themselves by defending them, and the determining and misleading ideologies that have enveloped them. To Shaw ideals are, as they are in Joyce's stories of young boys, illusions, "only swaddling clothes which man has outgrown, and which insufferably impede his movements" (MCE 31). Prevalent in the young boys' stories, as in the others in *Dubliners,* is the sort of "greyness" and "gloom . . . unbroken and hopeless" of which Shaw was accused in the *Athenaeum* on December 17, 1892 (reprinted in Evans 4). Like Shaw's *Plays Unpleasant* (1898), Joyce's portraits of the stultifying effects of inflexible ideals aim to raise the consciousness of readers capable of developing a new and radical conscience, for, like Shaw, Joyce paradoxically averred that his writings intended to develop in a supposedly moral people their "undeveloped conscience." Shaw maintained that he intended "to force the spectator to face unpleasant facts" (CP 716). He regarded as "silly and often treacherous delusions about Womanliness and Manliness, Marriage and the Family, Goodness in morals, Propriety in business" (Carpenter 14). Joyce tried to make the Irish confront the abuses of idealism by depicting believers who sometimes have belated intimations of the unpleasant facts, being no longer able to shut their eyes to them. Among the proponents of paralyzing beliefs incapable of such vision are, as we have seen, Father Flynn, the failed priest of "The Sisters"; and the dirty old man of "An Encounter," who, fixated on romantic literature, is palsied in self-perpetuating onanism—itself an ironic comment on the pornographic provocations and self-absorption of such literature.

The dirty old man is not, however, the only alienated Dubliner who idealizes literature. In "A Little Cloud," a timid family man idealizes English-language Celtic Twilight poetry and envies the escape and freedom of his old school chum Ignatius Gallaher. The brash, expatriated journalist is a foil for Little Chandler: the boyishly immature clerk is in reality a beleaguered husband and father, pathetically aware of his entrapment. He lacks the will or talent to make his dream more than "a little cloud." The story dramatizes from the point of view of Chandler's sensibility the insubstantial illusions that are a minor storm warning. Chandler's ineffectuality is motivated by three Shavian taboos: unsatisfied imagination, sentimental nostalgia, and fatalism. First, he is the sort of Irishman whom Larry Doyle of *John Bull's Other Island* believes to be trapped by "the dreaming! the torturing, heartscalding, never satisfying dreaming," for his "imagination never lets him alone, never convinces him, never satisfies him but it makes him that he cant face reality nor deal with it nor handle it nor conquer it" (Plays 411). Second, his "melancholy tempered by recurrences of faith and resignation and simple joy" (D 73) makes him hope for recognition as "one of the Celtic school" (74)—the school of Yeats and A. E. that Shaw disdained, just as he scorned "faith and resignation" and even "simple joy" that was not in the service of a noble, iconoclastic cause.

Shaw and his secret disciple both rejected the sentimental nostalgia of the Irish literary establishment, even though both were tempted in youth by the role of romantic artist. Marchbanks in *Candida* is an immature Shaw. Joyce, attracted by the romantic Irish poets, like Mangan and Yeats, contemplated renouncing the real world to brood on romantic love (see Stephen Dedalus in *Ulysses,* ruminating on Yeats's "Who Goes with Fergus"; 1.64). But ironically, Little Chandler is not even inspired to write a poem. Instead, he worries about the reception of his unwritten poetry and muses on what his pen name will be, for "Thomas Chandler" is not Irish enough unless he includes his mother's name. Before T. S.

Eliot's "J. Alfred Prufrock," this indecisive young man, painfully aware of his ineffectuality, contemplates calling himself "T. Malone Chandler" (74) and likes its dignified sound. He is in every way the antithesis of a Shavian, sustaining himself on hazy fantasies of how he might, as a minor Celtic voice, disturb the universe or at least the English critics.

He is the opposite of the Shavian artist, for he lacks the will to assert himself, even with his infant son. In the impasse ending, instead of stopping the baby's crying, he exacerbates it by shouting, "Stop" (49), vainly trying to impose his will on his child, whereas in the adult world he is powerless (like Farrington in "Counterparts"). With Gallaher he wishes to "assert his manhood" (80) but fails, just as he does with his son. "He felt how useless it was to struggle against fortune, this being the burden of wisdom which the ages had bequeathed him" (71). Apparently Chandler's reading did not include Shaw, whose romantic poet Marchbanks is not a determinist or fatalist. For, despite his temptation to adore women, Marchbanks does not give in to the "gentle melancholy" that plagues Chandler. Although Chandler's "soul," like that of Shaw and Joyce, "revolted against the dull inelegance of Capel Street" and he knew the Shavian prescription for survival, he did not have the strength and resolve to go against the bourgeois conventions in which he had been brought up. In Shaw's terms, he was too weak to reject the compulsions "of custom and law" that constrain philistines (MCE 56). With a glimmering of truth emerging in Chandler's "tears of remorse" at the end of the story, he seems, like a disillusioned Shavian idealist, to glimpse through his cloudy vision the reality of his situation. As Shaw put it regarding such men, "All his life seems a waste and a failure by the light of it" (MCE 48). Though Chandler asks himself, "Could he not escape from his little house" (83), the question is rhetorical, for he gives up, admitting that he is "a prisoner for life" (84). Whereas Chandler is a scapegoat to his spineless propriety, his wife Annie thinks of her son as her redeemer. Her last words, "Mamma's little lamb of the world" (85), suggest that she relies on him to save her from her narrow life.

Shaw proselytized against such entrapment. In 1904 in *John Bull's Other Island*, Larry Doyle says that before leaving Ireland he "had only two ideas . . . : first to learn to do something and then to get out of Ireland and have a chance of doing it" (Plays 414). In 1906 when Joyce wrote his story, Chandler thinks, "There was no doubt about it if you wanted to succeed you had to go away" (D 73). Furthermore, Doyle tells his friend Broadbent why he did not marry Nora Reilly: "She didn't count. I was romantic about her, just as I was romantic about Byron's heroines or the old Round Tower of Rosscullen" (414). Thus he distinguishes himself as an expatriate from Chandler, who is still obsessed with dreamy Celtic romanticism. In reality, he has not learned how to "do something"—even though he imagines himself as a poet. Unlike Larry Doyle, who rejected the route of marriage, Chandler must "count" his prim wife, even though he fantasizes about a more exotic woman with "dark Oriental eyes" (88). Like Doyle before he left Ireland, Chandler romanticizes over Byron's heroines as a form of escape and over the Celtic past associated with the round towers of western Ireland. At the end of the story, Chandler is, indeed, reading Byron's poem "On the Death of a Young Lady, Cousin of the Author and Very Dear to Him"—a poem in which the dead Margaret in her "narrow cell" is a correlative to the effeminate young man's living death. In identifying with the beautiful dead woman, the self-pitying clerk with the "childish white teeth" (85) is musing on his own spiritual death.

Infantilized by his proper wife, who is an urban Nora Reilly, Chandler is imprisoned by his fatalistic sense of duty to bourgeois marriage. A disillusioned idealist, aware of being caged but also aware that his dream is powerless to be born, he envies Gallaher, the escapee to London. Like Shaw a successful journalist, Gallaher left Ireland out of necessity, not, like Shaw and Joyce, by choice: "In the end he got mixed up in some shady affair, some money transaction: at least, that was one version of his flight" (72). The journalist is thus not a Shavian realist, but he is the antitype of Chandler. An insensitive, egocentric hedonist bent only on his own pleasures, the vulgarian patronizes Little Chandler, bragging about the Moulin Rouge and "Bohemian cafés. Hot stuff!" (76). His diffident friend, who wants to imagine a more refined success story, begins to feel "somewhat disillusioned." Gallaher's "vagrant and triumphant life" (80), as Chandler views it, is the opposite of the life committed to art that Shaw and Joyce espoused. The journalist's attitude toward marriage is, however, similar to Shaw's in *The Philanderer* (1893), but his motives differ completely from those of Shaw's free lover. To the sexist Don Juan, marriage is putting his "head in the sack" (D 81), comparable to emasculating death by guillotine, even though he means "to marry money" if he marries at all. (Unlike the fictional journalist and despite his tirades against marriage, by the time Joyce wrote his story, Shaw had married a rich Irish heiress, though not to facilitate an amoral, debased, epicurean lifestyle).

The sterility of Chandler's orderly life is paralleled by that of another one of Joyce's frustrated idealists, Duffy of "A Painful Case." At the conclusions of their stories, both Dubliners have negative moments of insight into their failures, the result of their withering lack of genuine ardor and their acquiescence to the rules of law and order. Whereas Chandler ambivalently envies Gallaher's brash freedom, Duffy's ideals are even more coercive. He avoids "the society of Dublin's gilded youth" (108), stoically eating a plain "bill of fare" and living on the outskirts of Dublin in Chapelizod, the Chapel of Isolde. This is an extremely ironic setting for an abortive tale which deconstructs courtly love, for the lover is not a heroic Tristram, nor is he aware that he has taken a love potion. Surely he is not prepared to die with or for the married woman of choice; even though her death under a suburban train seems to be a parody of Tolstoy's Anna Karenina's nihilistic suicide, Duffy is not, like Vronsky, a sophisticated roué who has, in effect, debauched a romantic heroine.

Shaw had indicated that a person's reading (or lack of it) forms him—a point of importance regarding the development of Duffy's ideals. Wordsworth, whose romanticism turned into the tame conservatism that Shaw eschewed, seems to be a favorite of Duffy's, for he has "A Complete Wordsworth" (107). Duffy's preference for the poet who achieved a sense of transcendence by worshiping nature, the Magna Mater whose avatar in real life was his sister Dorothy—a forbidden love—is ironic, because Duffy is alienated from nature and rejects the illicit love of Mrs. Sinico, which might have helped him recognize and understand his emotions. Although Wordsworth's "Ode to Duty" seems to interface with Duffy's repressive puritanism, the romantic poet's "egotistical sublime" is the narcissistic solipsism to which Duffy gives barren allegiance. Ironically, in Duffy's library, Wordsworth is coupled with the *Maynooth Catechism,* which implies Duffy's essential conservatism, for he keeps this tome of standard Catholic religious instruction on his top shelf.

The translation of Hauptmann's *Michael Kramer* (108), which seems to be Duffy's current reading, should have been a reminder to him to avoid the rigidity that dominates his personality. In Hauptmann's naturalistic drama, Kramer's inflexibility drives his Bohemian son to suicide. In a play in which the action parallels Duffy's rejection of Mrs. Sinico and his culpability in her death, the elitist and snobbish Kramer, who despises philistines and vulgar souls, realizes that he has failed to love and hence to save his son. Although Duffy is, by the end of his story, driven to recognize his failure to love and hence to save Mrs. Sinico, he had affixed an advertisement for Bile Beans to the Hauptmann manuscript, thus putting the ironic seal of his disapproval on the play.

Duffy is an example of Shavian theory in practice. A puritanical evader of the Life Force, he enjoys Mozart, like Shaw, in opera or concert—"the only dissipations of his life" (109). This preference, like others, is ironic, for Duffy finds himself in the role of an awkward and reluctant Don Giovanni, almost as resistant to his female pursuer as John Tanner, Shaw's Don Juan in *Man and Superman,* and almost as self-righteously unwilling to give in to the female Life Force. Duffy's taste for Nietzsche links with Shaw's interest in the superman, but Shaw had translated Nietzsche's belief in the will to power into Schopenhauer's will to live, without seriously accepting the misogyny of the Germanic philosophers. Incapable of rising beyond good and evil, Duffy is a cautious misogynist, diffident and ineffectual beside the view of women expressed by Nietzsche in one of Duffy's books, *Thus Spake Zarathustra.* In that treatise, the philosopher of the superman writes, "Are you visiting women? Do not forget your whip." Eva Figes writes that "Nietzsche divorces sexuality from emotion" because of "a fear of emotion. . . . [T]he superman not only fears woman but all the aspects of humanity which he associates with woman and which he affects to despise—gentleness, love, sympathy, suffering" (126). Although Duffy's self-exiled, alienated, and self-regarding lifestyle emulates the Nietzschean *übermensch,* Duffy is not in the least Dionysian, and reading *The Gay Science,* by the philosopher who proclaimed the death of God, is an incongruous activity for the owner of the *Maynooth Catechism* (even though he relegated it to the top shelf). Thus Duffy's cultural preferences reveal the conflicts in his character—his Nietzschean fantasies, his distrust of women, his Wordsworthian solipsism combined with the ultimate banality of being a proper, if lapsed, Catholic.

The repressed Dubliner performs "two social duties for old dignity's sake but conceded nothing further to the conventions which regulate the civic life" (109). He dutifully visits relatives at Christmas and attends funerals, thinking erroneously that he has escaped from convention. His interest in Nietzsche and in socialism was prefigured by Shaw, but the Fabian advocated a socially committed superman as well as the "hard-featured realism" that Duffy disapproves in socialists. Although he had "assisted at the meetings of an Irish Socialist Party where he had felt himself a unique figure amidst a score of sober workmen" (110), Duffy dismisses their "inordinate" "interest . . . in the question of wages"—to Shaw the chief issue of socialism. Duffy felt that they were hard-featured realists and that they "resented an exactitude which was the product of a leisure not within their reach. No social revolution, he told her [Mrs. Sinico], would be likely to strike Dublin for some centuries" (111).

In spite of the fact that the Church regarded socialism as atheism, the inconsistency does not seem to bother the supposedly orderly owner of the *Maynooth Catechism* any more than his patronizing attitude toward the workers does. As a bank clerk, he has the "leisure" to rise above the wage question. Considering the incongruities between his vocation and his socialist avocation, it is not surprising that he is not "conscious of any incongruity" (110) concerning his assignations with a married woman. As a condescending and repressed perfectionist, he supposedly rises above Mrs. Sinico's need for love, inflexibly compartmentalizing her along with his other interests. Hence he seems unaware that reading the heroically defiant Nietzsche is incompatible with reading the *Dublin Evening Mail,* an ultra-conservative unionist newspaper whose right-wing journalism is apparently congenial to the narrow egoist.

In his newspaper he comes upon Mrs. Sinico's obituary. After reading about her ignominious suicide, he is at first disgusted and self-righteous, but then he realizes that he had "withheld life" from her. After the would-be affair ended, he was still so self-absorbed that he wrote that "love between man and man is impossible because there must not be sexual intercourse and friendship between man and woman is impossible because there must be sexual intercourse" (113). Duffy is incapable of either love for man or friendship for woman, and his "moral nature" begins to fall "to pieces" (117). Recognizing that he has been thwarted by his rigid illusions of propriety, he experiences an epiphany in which he recognizes that he is a beggar at the banquet of life. He discovers that denial of life has been a denial of himself. Ultimately alone and more estranged than ever because of his insight, the idealist devoted to "rectitude" despairs because he is "outcast from life's feast" (117).

The real painful case of Joyce's title is that of the egocentric, detached Duffy, forever rationalizing his rejection of the vitalism that Mrs. Sinico represented and Shaw propounded. Duffy's life-denying idealism is the kind that Shaw condemned as "self-denying conformity" to ideals (MCE 53). As a letter from Richard Dietrich has reminded me, Duffy no doubt "thinks he's a Realist and would-be Superman." But whereas the realist Shaw preached that one must reject the "artificial conscience" of conventional morality, Duffy is incapable of rising to such a challenge. Joyce, the realist and disciple, treats Duffy like one of Shaw's idealists, "terrified beyond measure at the proclamation of their hidden thought—at the presence of the traitor among the conspirators of silence—at the rending of the beautiful veil they and their poets have woven to hide the unbearable face of the truth" (MCE 50). At the end of "A Painful Case," Duffy is compelled by Mrs. Sinico's death to face the unbearable truth about his empty and impotent life, devoted to the sterile ideal of his own superiority.

Another Dubliner whose sense of superiority is assaulted is Mrs. Kearney in "A Mother." She romanticizes the Irish cultural and language movements but in reality is frustrated by the mendacity and sexism of Dublin entrepreneurs. An accomplished woman who has studied French and music, she sublimates her "romantic desire by eating a great deal of Turkish Delight in secret" (136). Although she pragmatically married a philistine bootmaker—"sober, thrifty and pious" (137)—whom she values as a symbol like "the General Post Office, as something large, secure and fixed" with "abstract value as a male" (141), she "never put her own romantic ideas away" (137). She compares her husband to the Post Office, a symbol of British rule (as was well understood by the 1916 Easter Rising rebels who took over the G.P.O. in order to proclaim Irish freedom) as well as masculinist society. This comparison suggests that she has not thought through the implications of her romantic nationalism, nor has she understood the phallocentric significance of such edifices or the actuality of male power in society. At home she is what Shaw called a "womanly woman," who accepts patriarchal values and the conventional female roles: "She never weakened in her religion and was a good wife" (D 137). But her ideals revolve around accomplishments outside the home—the Irish revival and the Dublin music world.

Mrs. Kearney carries her faith in masculinity into her work for the nationalist cultural concerts at the Ancient Concert Rooms. Just as she accepts her husband without question as a fixture of patriarchal society, like the G.P.O., she accepts the pledge of men who represent the masculine oath culture, even though, like most mothers, she gives her ultimate allegiance to blood ties to her daughter. Joyce's story points up the age-old conflict between patriarchal oath culture and matricentric blood ties. Phallocentric civilization was founded on exogamy—movement away from family and clan to a larger context of legal connections. Exogamy, which required marriage outside of the family, reinforced oath ties which legitimated masculine relationships to women, to offspring, and to one another, while at the same time confining women to familial relations and ties to children. Mother-right was traditionally associated with blood ties and father-right with the importance and validity of oaths, pacts, and contracts made by men. Exogamy "ensures the dominance of the social over the biological, and the cultural over the natural" (Lévi-Strauss 479). In civilization's oath-tie arrangement lawful women "were expected to show all the loving, maternal, giving qualities in support of the masculine world yet without becoming part of the world. They were to abjure power in the world while simultaneously feeling and acting to uphold it" (French 94). Up to the climax of her story Mrs. Kearney epitomizes such a woman, but when her daughter's contract is broken she behaves for a moment like an outlaw, a supporter of mother-right and hence a defender of the daughter tied to her by blood.

For her daughter Kathleen's "services as accompanist at the four grand concerts. . . . a contract was drawn up" (138). Unlike the male organizers, Mrs. Kearney—a true helpmate—"entered heart and soul into the details of the enterprise" (138), the reality of which turns out to be shoddy and mismanaged. The singers are not uniformly professional; the audience, with its stamping and clapping and whistling (146), does not seem interested in culture; and attendance is poor. Because the projected revenues do not materialize, the committee reneges on its contract with Mrs. Kearney's daughter, whereas the other artists are apparently paid. Kathleen suffers discrimination because of her youth, her amateur status, and her gender. Mrs. Kearney's daughter does not get equal pay for equal work, and the committee does not honor her contract. Torn between being ladylike, as she had been trained to be, and asserting her daughter's rights, Mrs. Kearney insists that "she would have to be paid" (144), but the committee gives her the runaround. "Mr Holohan said that it wasn't his business" (144), thus passing responsibility to Mr. Fitzpatrick, of whom Mrs. Kearney has never heard. Throughout the proceedings, the double standard prevails.

The men, who have exploited Mrs. Kearney and who have not worked wholeheartedly on making the concerts a success, are nevertheless in control. Everyone, including the other women, takes Mr. Holohan's side in the dispute over wages. Complacently colluding with masculine assumptions, old Miss Beirne passively accepts the injustice. Instead of showing solidarity and support, Kathleen's peer, Miss Healy, allows herself to be used by the male establishment. In taking Kathleen's place, Miss Healy betrays her friend. With the hyperbole for which Irishmen are noted, "Mr O'Madden Burke said it was the most scandalous exhibition he had ever witnessed. Miss Kathleen Kearney's musical career was ended in Dublin after that, he said" (147). Meanwhile a sexist reporter for the *Freeman* is more interested in the erotic titillation provided by Miss Healy's "bosom which he saw rise and fall slowly beneath him" (145) than in the concert. Other men are "uncorking bottles" (145). The baritone who "had been paid his money and wished to be at peace with men" (147) apparently does not care whether he is at peace with women such as Mrs. Kearney and her daughter. "Mrs Kearney said that the Committee had treated her scandalously" (148), which is the truth, but the patronizing sexist males turn it upside down.

Unwittingly the mother makes a feminist issue of her daughter's contract, one upon which Shaw would have supported her wholeheartedly. He scorned the "underpayment and ill-treatment of women" (CP 35), despising the double economic standard accepted and promoted by men. Mrs. Kearney's consciousness is raised by her experience, for she realizes, "They wouldn't have dared to have treated her like that if she had been a man. But she would see that her daughter got her rights" (148). A man (or boy like Stephen Dedalus at Clongowes Wood) who defended himself against a similar injustice would be considered a hero, but when the angry Mrs. Kearney mimics Mr. Holohan, he attacks her for not being ladylike—"I thought you were a lady"—as if a departure from her designated passive, nurturing role and the prescribed proprieties made her something else. After this chauvinistic reprimand, which displays both sexual and class discrimination, Mrs. Kearney "stood still for an instant like an angry stone image" (149)—a monolithic Earth Mother, perhaps the devouring Sheela na Gig, the Terrible Mother of Celtic prehistory, a hostile chthonic goddess like Dana (whose name was given to a journal to which young Joyce contributed) with power to create and destroy. An adumbration of the fertility goddess, the mother is deeply offended by the gender bias of the male establishment, whose notions of "culture" are less refined than her own.

Joyce's Dublin "mother" has often been accused by critics like Hugh Kenner and even feminist critics like Suzette Henke of being obstreperously domineering. Henke writes that she uses "tyrannical tactics to manipulate a hen-pecked husband" (40). Shaw, however, who advocated and admired self-assertion in women (although at times he feared it), might have considered Mrs. Kearney a strong woman deprived of equal rights in a society that maintains a double standard. In middle-class Dublin, her aims are frustrated by masculine solidarity and female compliance. Significantly, the replacement for Kathleen is her "friend," Miss Healy, whose name is the same as Parnell's betrayer, Tim Healy; this young woman is a traitor to her sex and a disloyal friend who succumbs to the blandishments of men. Sexist males take advantage of the musical daughter and blame the uppity mother. The laws and orders of patriarchal propriety come down on Mrs. Kearney's ardor for fair play and parity.

Thus Mrs. Kearney's belief in masculine institutions like the G.P.O. and her respect for male authority have been severely shaken by the end of the story, in which the men bond in congratulating themselves for not honoring their contract with a mother who demands woman's "rights" (148). Insulted by male betrayal, the mother was, until her confrontation with Holohan, the womanly woman who accepts and promulgates by her example the self-sacrificial female role that Shaw described as one of society's "pestiferous" "idealist abominations" (MCE 55). In her final confrontation with Holohan, Joyce's model of the masculine ideal and stereotype of woman as a "selfless angel" whose proper acts are those of a "lady" (see Gilbert and Gubar, *Madwoman* 24) breaks the mold by parodying Holohan's duplicitous speech. By aping Holohan, Mrs. Kearney simultaneously recognizes his logocentric power and ridicules it. She reveals her ambivalence toward male authority by preempting his language while making fun of it. (Significantly, when the drunk Farrington in "Counterparts" mimics his boss behind his back, his fellow male employees are amused.) Unamused by Mrs. Kearney's demand for Kathleen's money, Holohan, who is definitely not a gentleman, sarcastically judges her for not being a lady: "That's a nice lady! he said. O, she's a nice lady!" Lacking any defense but language, Mrs. Kearney parrots Holohan's lame circumlocutions: "—You must speak to the secretary. It's not my business. I'm a great fellow fol-the-diddle-I-do" (149)—and immediately suffers the consequences of her insurrection. Even though she knows that her mimicry is not acceptable behavior for a woman, her frustration and sense of injustice impel her to speak. Like children, late Victorian women were expected to be seen and not heard unless their words pleased men. According to Brandon Kershner, her "linguistic appropriation" is a "blunder . . . betraying her lower-middle-class origins" (138), but class has less to do with it than gender. Torn between conforming to what Shaw called "the ideal of womanliness" (MCE 55) and her desire for justice, Mrs. Kearney is put in her second-class, powerless place, ostensibly for overstepping the feminine proprieties of a lady. In discussing the inequities of marriage, Shaw wrote that, if the woman "complains, he, the self-helper, can do without her. . . . All this is brought home to her by the first burst of displeasure her complaints provoke" (59). In her contretemps with Holohan, Mrs. Kearney experiences the consequences of the idealized subordination implicit in her decorous role. The parvenu strikes Mrs. Kearney in her most vulnerable spot, for her female social pretensions have been the central buttress of her self-esteem. Although he exploited her superior knowledge and taste, when the mother is no longer an accommodating, altruistic guide and helper, the uncouth Holohan expresses his resentment, and her epiphanic awareness of his chicanery breaks down her gentile facade.

Mr. O'Madden Burke supports Holohan by congratulating him for doing "the proper thing" (149). His surname suggests that he may be a modern, debased version of the Irish conservative Edmund Burke, who opposed the French Revolution and roused Mary Wollstonecraft to challenge him, first with her *Vindication of the Rights of Men* (1790) and then with her *Vindication of the Rights of Women* (1792). Although O'Madden Burke is a member of the "swinish multitude" whom Edmund Burke despised, the Dubliner's dismissal of Kathleen Kearney is reminiscent of that of Edmund Burke as Shaw assessed him, one whose "language gave great offense because . . . [it was] a class insult" (CP 158), in "A Mother" an insult to women. The reactionary O'Madden Burke defends what is considered proper in a supposedly male-dominated society: he condemns the daughter because her mother did not repress her anger over the lies that she had been told.

In most respects a thoroughly indoctrinated Irish woman, Mrs. Kearney is not merely indignant because of her aroused awareness of her inferior position. She is also defending the rights of her child. As Henke notes, Mrs. Kearney "confuses her daughter's desire with her own" (40). Like many frustrated, unfulfilled mothers, she identifies with the daughter, through whom she is compelled to live vicariously; her desires coalesce with those of her offspring, for whom she wishes a more rewarding life than her own. Although Florence Walzl argues that Mrs. Kearney's "mercenariness and unwillingness to take chances . . . overcome her ambition for her daughter" ("Dubliners" 49), it seems that Mrs. Kearney does, instinctively, take a courageous chance. Considering that she has done so much unpaid work behind the scenes of the concerts, with daily visits from Holohan for her help, and has herself purchased tickets for friends, it does not seem mercenary that she wants her daughter to get paid for her work, like the others. The mother had worked hard and efficiently to promote the concerts: "She forgot nothing and, thanks to her, everything that was to be done was done" (139). But the newspaper man proclaims that Kathleen's "musical career" in Dublin is over (even though her interest in the cultural revival persists in "The Dead," where we find that she is going to the Aran Islands with Miss Ivors and other Gaelic enthusiasts). Her mother's dedication to the nationalistic cause of the *Eire Abu* suggests that she is an adumbration of Mother Ireland.

Bonnie Kime Scott notes the wordplay in "A Mother" on the names Kathleen and Holohan (22), which subtly derogates the Celtic revival, as much the target of Joycean scorn as it was of Shaw's in his preface to *John Bull's Other Island*. Joyce's choice of names suggests Yeats's patriotic play *Cathleen ni Houlihan* (1902), in which the fine old woman, symbol of Mother Ireland, persuades a young man to go out to join the 1798 rebellion and thus to sacrifice his personal happiness to fight and probably die for his country. Indeed, as Patrick Keane points out, the setting for Yeats's rehearsals of *Cathleen ni Houlihan*—the Antient Concert Rooms—was the same as the setting of the concerts in "A Mother," and Ben Collins has argued in *Eire Ireland* (1970) that the story is an "exquisite" and "trenchant" burlesque of Yeats's "fervently patriotic play" (45).

Furthermore, Kathleen's behavior is ironically contrasted to that of the eponymous heroine of Yeats's *The Countess Cathleen* (1892), who sells her soul to the devil to save the Irish. If Mrs. Kearney is a Mother Ireland, trying to facilitate the Irish cultural renaissance through her daughter Kathleen while she is herself thwarted by a dishonest functionary named Holohan, romantic nationalism is undercut by vulgar reality. Men like Holohan support the revival as long as Mother Ireland is only a female figurehead and patriotic symbol—an old woman needing help from her young men. When such a mother comes alive in the flesh, like the strong, dedicated, efficient Mrs. Kearney, who manipulates the modern Kathleen—a meek and dutiful daughter—she is threatening to Holohan, even though he exploits her. Because he "was a novice in such delicate matters as the wording of bills and the disposing of items for a programme Mrs. Kearney helped him." He came every day and she offered him secular communion, bringing out "the decanter and the silver biscuit-barrel" (138) and presiding like the Virgin Mother, who was often superimposed, in Irish imagination, upon Mother Ireland. The limping and devious Holohan (a hollow Holohan, a morally as well as physically crippled son of Ireland) used Mrs. Kearney, while she acted as wise, supportive, nurturing female, sacramentalizing their relationship in actions that suggest the Madonna intercessor as well as the nurturing pagan goddess Dana, the Irish Diana.

Mrs. Kearney's foil is the fatalistic old spinster Miss Beirne, a powerless member of the committee, who seems resigned to failure. The old woman sighs and says, platitudinously, "Ah well! We did our best the dear knows" (142)—though the dear Lord knows less about doing "our best" than Mrs. Kearney. If Mrs. Kearney is the fine old woman of Ireland, Miss Beirne is, ironically, the sterile reality of the older generation, and Kathleen is the docile younger variation. Holohan's exploitation of all three women suggests the debased state of Ireland. The mother dedicated to supporting the Irish revival is disillusioned by the ineffectual men in charge. Unlike the heroine of Yeats's *Cathleen ni Houlihan*, Mrs. Kearney is not merely a symbol meant to incite nationalist sacrifice. Ironically, a realistically portrayed mother willing to serve the ideals of romantic nationalism is a threat to feckless Irish men. The Irish illusion is that her males are prepared to die for Mother Ireland; the reality is that they betray her when, like Shaw's "unwomanly woman," she displays some of the strength and courage of the New Woman.

Mrs. Kearney's story is, indeed, a scrupulously mean Irish replay of Aeschylus's *Oresteiad,* replete with modern ironies. The archetypal Greek myth established the hegemony of a patriarchal system of legal justice favoring the male. The subtext of Joyce's story reiterates the components of Aeschylus's trilogy, which dramatizes the shift from matriarchal to patriarchal allegiance in the western world, in which sworn evidence can determine the outcome of a criminal investigation. The trilogy concludes with "a confrontation drama between patriarchal or paternal authority and what appear to be the defeated claims of an earlier order" based on maternal claims (Millett 112). In "A Mother" Holohan, whose name suggests that he could be both husband and son of Mother Ireland, sacrifices Mrs. Kearney's daughter, just as Agamemnon sacrificed his daughter Iphigenia to facilitate his quarrel with the Trojans. The nationalistic concert is, of course, a peaceful means of perpetuating the Irish quarrel with England. After Clytemnestra murders Agamemnon for killing their daughter (in an act perhaps contemplated by Mrs. Kearney when she looks like an angry goddess), their son—and surely Holohan is a son of Mother Ireland—murders his mother and, in a trial by jury, is exonerated, just as Holohan is exonerated by his peers for the character assassination of Mrs. Kearney. The irony implicit in Joyce's replay of the primeval plot is biting, for in fantasy the colonized Irish identify with a maternal figure, Mother Ireland, and despise John Bull, but in reality the Irish son commits the symbolic matricide revealed in Holohan's verbal assault on the mother. In Aeschylus and "A Mother" the masculinist oath culture prevails, despite the presence in the wings of the concert hall of the spirit of a different model of female behavior.

One of the most significant, seemingly inconsequential remarks in the story concerns a renowned unwomanly woman. Miss Healy asks the baritone, one of the performers at the concert, "Have you seen Mrs Pat Campbell this week?" (146). Mrs. Patrick Campbell was Shaw's beloved Stella—a dynamic, successful, and highly acclaimed actress who had achieved artistic fame that was denied to Dublin women. While on tour with Sara Bernhardt, she performed in Dublin in July 1905, starring with Bernhardt (then in her sixties) in Maurice Maeterlinck's *Pelléas et Mélisande*—a production that in itself would have kept sophisticated audiences away from the Ancient Concert Rooms. The tour was a great success except in sexist Dublin, where one critic wrote,

"Mrs. Campbell played Melisande, Madame Bernhardt Pelleas; they are both old enough to know better" (quoted in Peters 260). Joyce's baritone tells Miss Healy, however, that Campbell "was very fine" (146), unlike the elderly Madam Glynn, who "sang *Killarney* in a bodiless gasping voice, with all the old-fashioned mannerisms of intonation and pronunciation" (147). Stella Campbell's acting set a standard of cosmopolitan excellence that the artistes at the nationalist concerts, with their old-fashioned soprano and patriotic recitations, could not rival.

At the time of the Dublin performance, Stella Campbell was a forty-year-old widow and mother who had succeeded without her husband. Although she was already corresponding with Shaw, their love affair was to bloom a few years later. Perhaps also significant as a dialogic contrast to Mrs. Kearney was the headline news in New York nine months before the Dublin performances: "MRS. CAMPBELL DETERMINED HER DAUGHTER SHALL NOT FOLLOW IN HER FOOTSTEPS" (quoted in Peters 251). Whereas Mrs. Kearney was trying to groom her daughter to take compensatory steps that she had not taken, the famed actress did not need to live through her daughter and, in fact, wanted to give her alternatives. Unlike Shaw's own mother (who left Dublin with her daughter, Lucy, also a singer, to give music lessons in London), the disillusioned Mrs. Kearney is trapped in Dublin.

Thus "A Mother" can be read, like *Mrs. Warren's Profession* and Shaw's preface to *Getting Married,* as a protest against patriarchal attitudes and smug male chauvinism. The story exemplifies, in Henke's view, the fact that "women who dare to step out of line and transgress sex-stereotyped codes of behavior are inevitably doomed to suffer harsh consequences for challenging an obdurate patriarchy" (41). It furthermore exposes with irony Irishmen who readily give lip service to their love of Mother Ireland as long as she is distanced from them by myth. Faced with a real Irish mother, they are unwilling to share their prerogatives, even though she is not asking that they give their lives for her, only that they honor an agreement. In Kathleen, the docile daughter, and Holohan, the traitorous male, the old archetype has been reified and degraded, while the real Irish mother is humiliated. In a Shaw play, such a strong, enterprising woman—like Lady Cicely in *Captain Brassbound's Conversion,* Vivie in *Mrs. Warren's Profession,* or Eliza in *Pygmalion*—might have the last laugh, asserting her values in spite of the prevailing sexual politics. Thus, contrary to critics like Walzl who believe that Mrs. Kearney is an obnoxious, pushy mother, the story reveals, in the Shavian arc light, sympathy for the betrayed mother, who is far more courageous and purposeful than the muddling male supremacists who are in charge.

The model for the puissant Mrs. Kearney was probably the mother of Hannah Sheehy, who married Joyce's classmate Francis Skeffington. As a youth Joyce was a familiar in the Sheehy home and seemed to have a romantic interest in Hannah's sister (perhaps a model for Emma Clery in *Portrait*). When Hannah and Frank married, both took the surname Sheehy-Skeffington to assert their belief in equal rights for women. The Sheehy-Skeffingtons supported coeducation, and Hannah was jailed for agitating for women's suffrage. "A Mother" reveals that Joyce honored ideas of his feminist friend and of Sheehy-Skeffington's famous friend and champion G. B. S., for Joyce "saw the emancipation of women as 'the greatest revolution in our time'" (Scott 48). "A Mother" is a feminist story in which Mrs. Kearney is up against the masculine solidarity of vulgar philistines who assume their superiority and bond in male cronyism against the insurgent female.

In "Ivy Day in the Committee Room," Joe Hynes is confronted with the cronyism of uninspired political canvassers who are comparable to the ineffectual *Eire Abu* society sponsoring the "cultural" concerts in "A Mother." A great admirer of the dead hero Parnell, Hynes is a political idealist who is, in the Cyclops scene of *Ulysses,* a barroom crony of the infamous Guinness patriot, the citizen. In "Ivy Day" the official line of the political canvassers in the story is the ideal of nationalism, but in reality they are apathetic philistines, working for an opportunistic candidate whose centrist politics suggest that in order to get elected, he is trying to placate everyone. "Tricky Dicky Tierney" (D 154) lacks genuine commitment to Ireland, and so do the workers whose main concern is that he "stump up" with money for their campaigning.

Joyce wrote this story about Dublin politics before the end of 1905 and revised it in 1906, when he could have had plenty of time to digest *John Bull's Other Island* and its "Preface for Politicians" (1904). Although Joyce's heavily ironic tone differs greatly from that of the farcical comedy, his subject and the attitudes toward Ireland expressed in "Ivy Day" replicate Shaw's. The characters in *John Bull's Other Island* prefigure Joyce's Dubliners. Cornelius Doyle, the land agent, is as bored and boring as the Ivy Day canvassers. Shaw describes "the almost total atrophy of any sense of enjoyment in Cornelius, or even any desire for it or toleration of the possibility of life being something better than a round of sordid worries, relieved by tobacco, punch, fine mornings, and petty successes in buying and selling" (Plays 422). Shaw's maiden aunt Judy anticipates Maria in "Clay" in her "placid" acceptance of her "narrow, strainless life." She reveals her passivity with a platitude that summarizes the apathy Joyce portrays in philistine Dubliners: "What cant be cured must be injoored" (Plays 420)—an Irish adage sung by Stephen's smugly fatalistic father in *Portrait:* "What can't be cured, sure, / Must be injured, sure" (88). In Joyce's spelling, stoic endurance becomes the injury that both Irishmen believed it to be. Shaw's ignorant miller, Barney Doran, has "an impetuous intolerance of other temperaments and other opinions" (Plays 428). Negative social conditioning misdirects his energies. Matthew Haffigan, the farmer who finally owns his land, is, after a lifetime of oppression by landlords, now opposed to "foolish talk agen landlords" (428). The priest who declares that "the Church has no politics" (428) is in the thick of wielding political influence in his parish. Shaw's play ridicules Irishmen from the country for selling out to the English and suggests that in Ireland such history repeats itself. In Rosscullen, where the farmers once hated the English rackrenters who gouged them for rent, evicted them, and set them against each other in competition for the land, the agrarian Irish end up supporting Tom Broadbent. Although he is about to foreclose on their property, they decide to support the rich Englishman as their delegate to Parliament. In a farcical reversal of the intentions voiced in the standard patriotic rhetoric of Irish politics, the Englishman walks off with the local "heiress" (whose pride of place far outweighs her meager inheritance), the votes of the locals, and their land.

Doran says that "there's too much blatherumskite in Irish politics a dale too much" (428). Such self-serving *blague* is the main content of "Ivy Day in the Committee Room," which records in desultory conversation the conflicting motives of the ineffectual canvassers, all, like those of the rustics in *John Bull's Other Island,* with a cash nexus. In Joyce's urban story, Joe Hynes is comparable to Larry Doyle, whom the yokel Doran calls "the bould Fenian." Joe chides the minor political functionaries for their potential betrayal of Ireland: "Don't you know they want to present an address of welcome to Edward Rex if he comes here next year? What do we want kowtowing to a foreign king?" (122). The liberal O'Connor insists that their candidate will be on the Nationalist ticket and hence, as a Home Ruler, opposed to paying homage to the British, but Hynes accuses Tierney of opportunism. He will do what is expedient, like the farmers in Rosscullen in Shaw's play. Like Joyce, Shaw is not above being ironic even with the Irish character whom he privileges as his mouthpiece. The expatriate Larry Doyle sees through the petty self-interest of the locals but is Broadbent's partner and hence a collaborator in British exploitation (considered by Broadbent British aid and social engineering); indeed, he is what Henchy believes Hynes to be. But Broadbent translates manipulation of the Irish into practical aid in getting Ireland's economy working, even if it means destroying the countryside in the interests of "reform." Equally adept at irony, Joyce gives Hynes nationalist ideals but ends the story with his recitation of his retrograde doggerel tribute to Parnell—an example of the nostalgic romantic nationalism that Shaw and Joyce repudiated, though the latter did so ambivalently.

Unlike the liberal Broadbent, but like his partner Doyle, Joyce's Hynes sounds like a Shavian socialist: "The working-man, said Mr Hynes, gets all kicks and no halfpence. But it's labor produces everything. The working-man is not looking for fat jobs for his sons and nephews and cousins. The working-man is not going to drag the honour of Dublin in the mud to please a German monarch" (121). In *John Bull's Other Island* Larry Doyle is prolabor. The workingman is Patsy Farrell, whose first name is apt, for he is a patsy to the other Irishmen; and although he is not dragging "the honour" of Ireland through the mud, he is dragging the luggage of the visiting Englishman. "Intolerably overburdened," he clumsily bears the burdens of the others, carrying the priest's hamper, the estate agent's salmon and a goose, as well as Broadbent's baggage. The peasant drudge, like the workingman of whom Hynes speaks, does the labor and gets very little for his pains except complaints. He labors under the weight of the Church (the priest's hamper), the booty of the local representative of the oppressor (the estate agent), and the invader's luggage. Patsy gets no land out of Wyndham's Land Act, the 1903 land distribution law that made former tenant farmers into freeholders and voters. Instead of favoring the workingman, the farmers, like property-owning voters in Joyce's story and canvassers like Henchy, want to protect their vested interests. In Joyce's story, Hynes thinks that the worker has "as good a right to be in the Corporation as anyone else—ay, and a better right than those 'shoneens' that are always hat in hand before any fellow with a handle to his name" (131). The new landowners in Rosscullen are very like the "shoneens"—would-be gentlemen—willing to court "Misther" Broadbent because he has money.

In Dublin things are even worse, for the canvassers are working, like Henchy (the henchman of unionism), to avoid eviction. Ironically, as a renter, Henchy doesn't qualify to vote, but he wants to get paid for finding voters. He expects "to find the bailiffs in the hall" when he goes home (123–24). A suspicious centrist, Henchy is, like the others, driven by the need of money. A philistine, he is nostalgic for the good old days, preferring the past, like many of Joyce's Dubliners; thus Henchy prefers Joe Hynes's "decent respectable father" to Joe, whom he suspects, ludicrously, of "sponging" (124), of being a spy for the opposition candidate, and even of being "in the pay of the Castle" (125), therefore an informer on the side of the British. All of these suspicions are ironic because Hynes is the only true Parnellite in the group. Ridiculously, considering that Henchy is himself a betrayer of Ireland, operating on the profit motive, he believes that the "hillsiders and fenians"—members of the pro-force Irish Republican Brotherhood that had supported Parnell—are also in the "pay of the Castle," the seat of British government in Ireland. Moreover, suspicious of betrayers on all sides, Henchy readily accuses a "patriot" of being "a lineal descendant of Major Sirr," who could "sell his country for fourpence" (125). His hyperbole refers to the lord mayor of Dublin during the 1798 uprising, a notorious traitor to his fellow Irish who arrested and brutalized leaders of the rebellion. Ironically, Henchy has himself sold "his country for fourpence" or perhaps less, though his betrayal, like that of the other petty canvassers, takes the form of slothful inaction and banal accusations.

The political meeting in act 3 of *John Bull's Other Island* satirizes vested interests and political expediency just as "Ivy Day" does. At the meeting Father Dempsey and Tom Broadbent are the two most powerful players. As J. L. Wisenthal observes, in his "Philistine concerns with money" and his smug self-satisfaction, the priest is the character "most like Broadbent" (98). Together they represent the two masters—England and Catholicism—whom both Shaw and Joyce blamed for Ireland's troubles. But Shaw (and Joyce after him) shows how Irish self-interest contributes to Ireland's misfortunes. Ironically, the agrarian

Irishmen want a new member of Parliament who favors landlords, though, until recently, they had little land to favor. Now that they are freeholders, they are prejudiced against others, like Patsy Farrell "and he like o him" who want the same privileges. The farmers are provincial, prejudiced, hungry for power, and incongruously unhappy with their current M.P. because of his democratic aims. They want to keep cheap laborers in their place, whereas Doyle thinks cheap labor is the problem. Having gotten his land out of the hands of the Anglo-Irish landlords, the new landowner is prepared to perpetuate the old class system. He opposes sharing his good fortune with Patsy, even though not long ago he was an industrious peasant himself. Like Joyce's canvassers, Shaw's rustics are hypocritical "patriots." They oppose government interference but proudly hope to recreate a caste system along the lines of the landlordism that had oppressed agrarian Irishmen for centuries. They want a man in Parliament "dhat knows dhat the farmer's the real backbone o the country, n doesnt care a snap of his fingers for the shoutn o the riff-raff in the towns, or for the foolishness of the laborers" (Plays 429). Absurdly, they are swayed by Broadbent's enthusiasm, despite the fact that they have just gotten rid of Protestant and absentee landlords. Larry Doyle, like Hynes, is aware that economic competition with England is the cause of English usurpation. He wants Patsy to have a fair wage and fair working conditions, but he is aware that greed and self-interest dominate the Irish who qualify as voters. They are, like the voters that Joyce's "riff-raff" Dubliners seek, males over twenty-one with houses valued at ten pounds in annual rent.

John Bull's Other Island satirizes the greed of the Irish locals and their parish priest as well as the fact that political office can, in effect, be purchased. The Rosscullen voters are especially impressed by the fact that Broadbent is rich. He virtually buys his way into candidacy. As Joyce's Henchy observes, a variation on the "little game" of cupidity pertains in Dublin: "You must owe the City Fathers money nowadays if you want to be made Lord Mayor" (D 127). In the country the Englishman buys political power; in Dublin politicos hope to get into office because they owe the government money—money that they can pay once they are elected and salaried. The candidate Tierney—uppity, shrewd, expedient, and cheap—has the "little pigs eyes" of greed but perhaps also of the Ireland that Joyce associated with the "old sow who eats her farrow" (P 203).

Like Joyce and Irishmen before them, Shaw associated Ireland with a pig. *John Bull's Other Island*'s most farcical scene concerns the Englishman's attempt to take a pig for a ride. Farmer Haffigan has just bought the pig from the land agent. Believing that concern for the pig (a symbol for agrarian issues) will be a great election ploy, the optimistic Broadbent offers to drive the animal through the village to Haffigan's farm in his motorcar: "The pig's the thing: the pig will win over every Irish heart to me. We'll take the pig home to Haffigan's farm in the motor; it will have a tremendous effect" (436). The journey of the incongruous couple does indeed have a tremendous effect, for the uncivilized pig is, predictably, not a docile passenger. Broadbent's good-natured interference results in a harmful fiasco. The undomesticated animal in the advanced machine of the British pragmatist causes a hilarious but destructive slapstick accident, in which the pig is killed. The locals laugh at the "bould English boyoh," whereas the ex-priest Keegan, aware of the awful implications of the usurper's co-optation and destruction of the pig, says with grim sarcasm, "There is anger, destruction, torment! What more do we need to make us merry?" (437). The naive Englishman interprets the accident of his encounter with the Irish pig, who is the principal victim of their collision, as an opportunity for the Irish to show their sympathy and magnanimity. After having ridiculed Broadbent behind his back, old Doran says, "An may you never regret the day you wint dhrivin wid Haffigan's pig!" (430). Whether Broadbent will have the sense to rue the day (as the English may now rue the day they took the Irish for a ride), the farcical accident does not deter the Irishmen from supporting the effusive intruder in the election. Like Joyce's canvassers, they are easily swayed into betrayal of Ireland.

Shaw's rural Irishmen are, incongruously, willing to vote a persuasive and optimistic stranger into Parliament. Broadbent will be, like the oppressors of the past, an absentee landlord. Like Joyce's political canvassers, his constituency has no genuine political commitment. Like candidate Tierney, ostensibly a nationalist, Doyle's hypocritical father is ironically "a Nationalist and a Separatist" willing to support an Englishman—one of the agents of Empire—to represent Rosscullen. In "Ivy Day," the paudeen (huckster) Henchy, complaining of poverty that is no doubt real, is similarly willing to sell out for English capital: "The King's coming here will mean an influx of money into this country. . . . It's capital we want" (131)—precisely what the farmers in Rosscullen want from Shaw's Broadbent. This well-meaning but oafish windbag opposes union and in the rhetoric of a political candidate appeals to the Irish by declaring that he hopes "an Irish legislature shall arise once more on the emerald pasture of College Green, and the Union Jack—that detestable symbol of a decadent Imperialism—be replaced by a flag as green as the island over which it waves" (432). Although Broadbent is supposedly for Home Rule, his political rhetoric is comically incongruous, for he is the symbol of "decadent Imperialism," the bumptious "carpetbaggers" that he himself disdains. He makes himself ridiculous to Shaw's audience by averring, artlessly and inconsistently, that "Home Rule will work wonders under English guidance." In Ireland, the more things change, the more the cycle of betrayal perpetuates itself.

Like Joyce, Shaw was keenly aware of the power of the Church to prevent Ireland from changing. Shaw showed that the parish priest, Father Dempsey, uses his authority over his parishioners to maintain his political clout. As local priest, he is the biggest power in the village, because he is not restrained by the laws of the state and because the Irishman is "heavily handicapped" by the Church. "It is the aim of his priest to make him and keep him a submissive Conservative" (CP 449). Piously, Father Dempsey urges the farmer Matthew Haffigan to "think a little more o the sufferins o the blessed saints . . . an a little less o your own" (Plays 432). He is as greedy as his parishioners, wanting to know "how much spoil there is before I commit meself" to Broadbent (433). Like his Catholic constituency, Father Dempsey will support the English usurper if there is money in it for him. And he expects his congregation to follow his political lead. Although Father Dempsey says disingenuously that the Church is not political, he organizes the meeting and agrees to support British capitalism if it serves his ends.

In "Ivy Day," Joyce translates the connection between church and state into urban coefficients. Mr. O'Connor reveals socialist leanings by agreeing with Hynes that the workingman has "as good a right to be in the Corporation as anyone else" (121)—exactly Larry Doyle's belief. Such secularist politics are, however, inconsistent with O'Connor's expedient use of religion to secure votes: he thinks he has gotten the vote of someone named Grimes because he "mentioned Father Burke's name" (123), the implication being that Grimes will vote for the priest's candidate. The defrocked clergyman, "Father" Keon, may be related to Shaw's "Father" Keegan. Keon is an ineffectual "priest"—a "black sheep" stray, silenced by the bishop. Like Keegan, he cannot hear confession or say mass. But, whereas Shaw makes his mystical excommunicant a Greek chorus of his hopes for Ireland as well as his cynicism regarding the self-serving cupidity of the pragmatic Broadbent, Joyce's mysterious Father Keon wanders into the rooms let by the political canvassers, seeking Mr. Fanning on "a little business matter" that does not seem spiritual. Thus, like Shaw's Father Dempsey, even the defrocked cleric in *Dubliners* is more interested in finances than in piety.

In his long, contemptuous disquisition on Ireland in Shaw's comedy, Larry Doyle declares that the Irishman "cant be intelligently political" because he prefers imagination to reality, "and imagination's such a torture that you cant bear it without whisky" (411). Joyce's slothful politicos, whose casual factionalism and unscrupulous self-interest parallel the motives of Shaw's agrarians, have plenty of imagination when it comes to casting doubt on others. Apparently unable to get poteen, the illegal whisky favored by the farmers, they are making the day pass less painfully by drinking stout. Shaw's Doyle provides commentary apt for the men in the committee room: "At last you get that you can bear nothing real at all. . . . [Y]ou hate the whole lot round you because theyre only poor slovenly useless devils like yourself." He adds that in Ireland there is "eternal derision, eternal envy, eternal folly, eternal fouling and staining and degrading" (411–12), often amplified by drink.

In *John Bull's Other Island* Larry, the son of land agent Cornelius Doyle, has escaped from Ireland and returned reluctantly, having become, like Shaw and Joyce, its critic. In Joyce's story the son of Old Jack the caretaker—a young man who has not seen fit to leave Dublin—is worthless. His philistine father believes in parochial education and has sent his son to the Christian Brothers, lay priests who were not renowned for offering the rigorous academic training that Joyce received from the Jesuits. While Shaw urged Irish sons to rebel against the authority of fathers in order to seek self-realization, in "Ivy Day" Jack's son has, indeed, revolted against the authoritarian father who would "take the stick to his back and beat him" (120), using the corporal punishment that Shaw detested as detrimental to forming character. But the behavior of Jack's son attests to the failure of the patriarchal method, for the young man's rebellion only perpetuates the system. The "drunken bowsy" son has inherited the sins of the ineffectual stout-drinking father.

Like Shaw's comedy, Joyce's story of political paralysis shows the pettiness, ignominy, and folly of Irishmen, implicitly contrasting them throughout to the dynamic heroism of Parnell. "Ivy Day" ends, however, with Hynes's recitation of his sentimental patriotic poem about the leader whom the Irish can now respect because "he's dead and gone" (132). An unregenerate nationalist idealist, Hynes hopes that Parnell's "spirit may / Rise, like the Phoenix from the flames," but in the story the remnant nationalists are gathered about a smoldering fire, shirking their obligations—hypocritical, uncommitted traitors to the spirit of Parnell even as Hynes himself is, for his patriotism seems limited to his versifying. The bombastic rhetoric of the poem glorifies the martyred Parnell by comparing him to Christ and decrying his Judas betrayers, but the canvassers have already sold him for whatever silver Tierney will pay them. The maudlin lament for the lost leader offers no program for the present or future. As Shaw's Larry Doyle says, the Irishman "dreams of what the Shan Van Vocht said in ninetyeight" (411) but does not want to face present realities. Joyce's Hynes idealizes the "uncrowned King . . . Betrayed . . . to the rabble-rout" (134), representatives of whom are congregated in the Committee Room, itself an ironic reference to Committee Room 15, in which Parnell's followers betrayed him. Larry Doyle's view of debased Irish politics is thus in dialogic relationship to the subtext of "Ivy Day in the Committee Room." Joyce's tale of political paralysis interfaces with *John Bull's Other Island*. Underlying Joyce's story is the wish of Shaw's alter ego Doyle, who has "learned to live in a real world and not in an imaginary one" (412): "I wish I could find a country to live in where the facts were not brutal and the dreams not unreal" (415). Instead, Doyle is preparing to return to "that hell of littleness and monotony" (413), the microcosm of which is Joyce's Dublin.

"Our Liffeyside People": Philistines in Dublin

The third category in Shaw's analysis of society is the compact majority. In Joyce's stories they are often the lower-middle-class Dubliners who, like the commercial traveler Kernan in "Grace" or Mrs. Mooney of "The Boarding House," live north of the River Liffey, which divided petty bourgeois and poor Catholics from the more well-to-do Anglo-Irish who lived in Georgian houses south of the river. Nevertheless, males like the "Two Gallants," or Farrington of "Counterparts," seek out pleasures in the more fashionable part of the city. Fathers like Farrington, who lives near Sandymount, or Joe in "Clay," who lives in Drumcondra, have families on the outskirts of Dublin. This largest category of Dubliners, philistines who follow the rules of society without question, comprise the minor characters of several stories in which they form a backdrop of conformity or, as in "Eveline" and "Clay," are themselves studies of the emotional deprivations of middle-class life. Thus Father Flynn's sisters, who provide the title of the first story, as well as the boy's uncle, aunt, and old Cotter, represent the blind majority who mouth the platitudes and hackneyed phrases that define their acceptance and limitations. Leo Dillon and his family in "An Encounter" and the uncle, aunt, Mrs. Mercer, "the drunken men and bargaining women" in the Dublin streets (31) and the "young lady" salesperson at the bazaar in "Araby" represent the nonreflective action and talk of people confirming old patterns of behavior. *Dubliners* holds up a "nicely polished looking glass" to the unconverted and unconvertible philistines who accept the "humbug" of what Shaw deemed to be "hell." In 1902 he wrote that his dramas illustrated "the terrible mischief and misery made everyday not by scoundrels, but by moral people and idealists in their inexorable devotion to what they call their 'duty'" (BSL 1:278). In his stories depicting the Dublin majority, Joyce continued to reveal the mischief and misery as well as the hypocritically palliative effect of unthinking acceptance of received codes of behavior, such as the sexual double standard of men in "Two Gallants" and the commercialized power of pardon in "Grace."

Whereas Shaw claimed that *The Quintessence of Ibsenism* "rescued an 'ungrateful generation'" and "was a 'feminist document' . . . which . . . broke up homes and made suffragettes in the most unexpected directions" (H1 198), Joyce could not claim a similar success for the portraits of women in *Dubliners*, because his philistine targets did not read his stories. Nevertheless, Joyce espoused Shaw's aim to "get to the truth regardless of shattered ideals" (BSL 3:602). Shaw battled against conventional ideals that "he felt formed the chief obstacle to the advancement of life's purpose" (H1 199). He argued that middle-class "women, who have not even the city to educate them . . . are positively unfit for civilized intercourse: graceless, ignorant, narrowminded to a quite appalling degree" (CP 722). In Joyce's Dublin, most women, to their own detriment, accept and support the conventional ideals with which religion and family have indoctrinated them.

Despite rare exceptions, like Miss Ivors in "The Dead," Dublin women have restricted options, the preferred being marriage. Usually they are confined to domestic caretaking or dead-end jobs. When Shaw first published his early problem plays in 1898, he hoped that the female "victims"—"the unhappy prisoners of the home"—could make their lives bearable. "If the victims of the hearth may not live real lives, they may at least read about imaginary ones" and perhaps learn to doubt the value of submitting to "home life" (CP 722). Shaw wanted a theater for and a reading public of people "who have some sense that women are human beings just like men" (CP 713). In his Preface to *Widowers' Houses,* he included excerpts from his critics, one of whom wrote that Mr. Shaw "aims to show with Zolaesque exactitude that middle-class life is foul and leprous" (CP 705). In a fiction that has the same aim, Joyce's female victims have such limited education that they do not come into contact with literature like Shaw's. They are not aware of the Shavian dictum that "life is an adventure, not the compounding of a prescription," and "there are no golden rules." Human conduct must "justify itself by its effect on happiness" (H1 202)—a goal renounced by the culturally colonized females of Dublin.

Among the female victims of social stereotyping in Dublin, perhaps none is more pathetic than the antiheroine of "Eveline." Her sad fate illustrates a theme that Shaw found in Ibsen—"the danger of forming ideals for other people, and interfering with their lives" (MCE 100)—a danger that Shaw believed harmful to both those who presume to impose values on others and those who are formed by such indoctrination. He emphasized that he did not traffic in heroes or villains and warned his audiences that his "attacks are directed against themselves, not against my stage figures" (CP 727), who were created to illustrate the problems of society. In much the same way, Joyce tried to touch the conscience of the Irish by creating vignettes of Dubliners like Eveline, incapable of challenging the values imposed upon her by social institutions and by her father, a reprobate whose abuse of his daughter is encouraged by his cultural mandates. Because of his assumptions about the power structure, Eveline Hill's father, like other Dublin men mindlessly supporting the status quo, interferes in the life of his daughter.

In "Eveline" the villainous institutions dominating Dublin life are the patriarchal family and the Church. Nineteen-year-old Eveline has been intimidated by her drunken father and entrapped by her duty to her mother, and she is incapable of summoning the will to escape these determining factors. A womanly young woman whose dreams do not extend beyond the customary female roles of wife and mother, she muses, as her brief tale unfolds, on running away to be married and gaining the "respect" that she believes, against the evidence presented by her own parents, will accrue in being a wife. A deluded and essentially compliant young person, she dreams of a marriage in which "she would not be treated as her mother had been" (37). For her life of quiet desperation derives, ominously, from what we would call now a dysfunctional family background, in which she is endangered by "her father's violence" (38) and desires halfheartedly to escape "her mother's life . . . of commonplace sacrifices" (40), which ended with her mother's dying plea that Eveline "promise" to take care of the family. Obedient to the demands of family (to Shaw an insidious trap for the unwary), Eveline has thus spent her teens doing domestic work at home, caring for "the two young children that had been left in her charge" (38), working to earn money for the family, and dealing with her irascible, good-for-nothing father.

Conditioned by the routine of a "hard life," she nevertheless thinks that she will "miss" her father, even though she remembers only two times when he had been entertaining or thoughtful—once years before at a picnic on the Hill of Howth and once recently when he had treated his obtuse and tractable daughter almost like a wife, reading to her and making "toast for her at the fire" while she was sick (39). More threatening is the fact that her father used to menace the children with his blackthorn stick, hunting them "in out of the field" (D 36) as if they were herd animals. More recently, since her mother's death, she has done her duty, even though invariably there is a "squabble for money on Saturday nights [which] had begun to weary her unspeakably. She always gave her entire wages," but her father squandered the money on drink and was "usually fairly bad" afterward (38). A self-sacrificing philistine, unable to evaluate her circumstances realistically, she is, like a domestic animal, almost content with "shelter and food" and "those whom she had known all her life" (37)—her father and the younger siblings to whom she is a surrogate mother. A substitute domestic drudge, she is reliving her mother's routine and miserable life instead of having one of her own. The "daughter's obligation to reproduce the mother, the mother's story" is a greater obstruction "than even the Father's Law" (Gallop 113) to female growth. Like Joyce's own mother, admittedly "slowly killed" by his father's ill-treatment (JJL 2:48), and like the sister he decries in *Stephen Hero* as docile and religious, fitted only to repeat her mother's life, Eveline has been socialized to renounce her own needs in order to serve those of others.

Many others in her family and neighborhood have escaped, and the house where the family lives has been cut off from the fields in which the children played by a housing project built by a man from Belfast (36). In the brief space of the story, which compresses her insignificant and pitiful life into five pages, Eveline contemplates an escape of her own. Although she has agreed to elope with Frank, she worries about what other people think, for she is, in social scientist David Riesman's terms, partly other-directed, but mostly tradition-directed—obedient to the patriarchal values of Irish society rather than to the inner-direction of her own conscience. She believes that her coworkers might say "she was a fool" for running away, in spite of her brutally authoritarian father. Her self-esteem is so low that she understands "her place [at the store] would be filled up by advertisement" (37). As Henke observes, "The motif of 'home' resounds like a metronome throughout the story, suggesting the moral compulsions that hypnotize the consciousness and preclude the possibility of meaningful change" (22). In the second paragraph of the story, Eveline thinks that "everything changes" (37), but ironically the stultifying traditional valences constitute conditioning to which she, like a dumb animal, is mutely obedient.

Eveline "sacrifices free will to those Irish gods of hearth and home" (Henke 22), duty to which, Shaw argued, must be repudiated if a woman is to be free. In servitude to the requirements of the family, Eveline has to work "at business" and at home as caretaker for her father, who assumes the prerogatives of masculine power even though he does nothing to deserve them. As the story opens, Eveline sits, like an impoverished Emma Bovary who will not have the courage to act out her desires, looking out of the window; she is a spectator on life, the "evening" of which (despite her youth) is already invading the "avenue" on which she lives (36). The props of the little impasse drama suggest the deadly strictures of Eveline's drab life, orthodoxies that make up her refractory superego. On the wall are "familiar objects" that she has "dusted once a week" without understanding their significance. Joyce selected the two that dominate Eveline's repressed psyche—a "yellowing photograph" of a priest who had been her father's school friend and a "coloured print of the promises made to Blessed Margaret Mary Alacoque" (37). These icons prefigure Eveline's martyrdom, for the priest's photo personates the double standard of patriarchal religion (he has escaped to Melbourne, but his code rules the household) to which Eveline turns at the end when she prays to God to show her her "duty." The print, like the masculine *lar,* or guardian spirit, prefigures Eveline's life of suffering sacrifice as a faithful Christian woman.

Margaret Mary Alacoque's career "was marked by a baroque counterpoint of physical and spiritual suffering"; she was beatified and, long after the publication of *Dubliners,* canonized as a saint for her faithfulness to the spirit of the Sacred Heart of Jesus. Her promises are particularly ironic in light of Eveline's benighted, narrow life: the blessed woman is supposed to provide grace, to establish peace in the homes of faithful, "tepid souls," to "secure refuge during life, and above all in death." Clearly the promise of "excessive mercy" through her love (Gifford 49–50) will not be vouchsafed Eveline, whose crabbed life evinces no blessings (considering the family's poverty); no peace (considering her irascible, alcoholic father); no refuge; and, above all, no fervency for her tepid, dead soul. As surely as the guns of General Gabler foretell his daughter's fate in *Hedda Gabler* and the print of Titian's *Assumption of the Virgin* foretells Mrs. Morell's in *Candida,* Eveline's life is figured by the "familiar objects" whose significance she fails to comprehend.

Although it seems likely that Eveline, obedient to her promise to her mother, an adumbration of the female saint, will not die in disgrace or "without receiving . . . [the] Sacraments" as promised by Blessed Margaret Mary Alacoque (Gifford 50), the horns of her dilemma both involve possible disgrace: an inverted, incestuous relationship with her father or escape with Frank that might mean abandonment or—as she fears at her moment of feral panic—that Frank would "drown" her like an unwanted puppy. Her authoritarian and ironically "proper" father, taking the conventional, self-serving patriarchal attitude, is determined to block her chance for happiness. When "her father had found out about the affair," he "had forbidden her to have anything to say" to

Frank (39). Significantly, in the moment of crisis, she cannot speak. In *The Irrational Knot,* Shaw wrote that a parent asserting such "proprietary rights" is "the most unreasonable of adversaries" (151).

Eveline is vaguely aware, however, that her sailor lover will save her from her father and that he represents life. "He would give her life, perhaps love, too. But she wanted to live" (40). Nevertheless, when offered such vitalism—the Shavian Life Force—the young woman cannot take it. In contemplating escape, she expects direction from outside. Unprepared to take responsibility for herself, she thinks at first that Frank will "save" her like the redeemer of her religion of love, but at the crucial instant when she must choose, she relinquishes her own will to God. She cannot be the "free-souled" person Shaw urged women to be in escaping the "cage" of domestic life. Dutiful, paralyzed by fear, in the end she cannot act. Instead of asking the voice of her own humanity, which Shaw insisted is the god in us, "she prayed to God to direct her, to show her what was her duty" (40). And in turning herself over to the Christian God and the duties that his religion imposes upon women, she reveals her essential passivity and submissiveness. Like the servant in Flaubert's "A Simple Heart," she is dumbly docile, destined for a life of self-sacrifice—a resigned and bovine victim who "set her white face to him, passive, like a helpless animal" (41) instead of a moral being whose first duty, according to Shaw, is to herself.

In the section of *The Quintessence of Ibsenism* entitled "The Womanly Woman," Shaw wrote, "The sum of the matter is that unless Woman repudiates her womanliness, her duty to her husband, to her children, to society, to the law and to everyone but herself, she cannot emancipate herself" (MCE 61). In Dublin at the beginning of the twentieth century women often did not have even the option of repudiating a husband, because, like Eveline, they were unmarried captives to duties to the womanly role without the possible incentives of a loved or loving husband. The patriarchal system, supported by puritanical Jansenist Catholicism and British colonialism, encouraged the creation of spinsters, for the breadwinner could not marry until he was able to support a family, and Dublin's economy included a high unemployment rate. Eveline forgoes possible marriage, which might, like Nora Barnacle's elopement with Joyce, turn out to be an illicit liaison. This is the possibility that frightens her: Frank's proposal may be a proposition that she take on the duties that Shaw names but without the status of wife. The tractable young Eveline submits to duty to family and indeed to "everyone but herself." After asking God to tell her her duty, she draws back from the elopement. Instead of going with Frank, she "kept moving her lips in silent fervent prayer" (41), thus giving God the responsibility for her decision. She is in an agony of irresolution, feeling "a nausea in her body," a "frenzy," and issuing "a cry of anguish" (41). Inarticulate and obedient to the patriarchal God, she cannot escape with her lover.

Eveline cannot take the existential leap necessary to achieve the contingent freedom that she might achieve with Frank, a freedom limited because she depends on Frank to rescue her and fears instead that he will destroy her. Joyce may, of course, be ironic in iterating her dread of drowning, for death by water could be baptism into what Joseph Conrad called "the destructive element" of experience, and hence a rebirth, such as Stephen Dedalus undergoes in *Portrait,* into a new life. However, Eveline is not a "Bohemian girl," and her story is not a sentimental operetta. As Kershner has shown in detail (63–68), the light opera to which Frank takes Eveline is a romantic parallel and ironic contrast to Eveline's story, for in it the heroine, although kidnapped by Gypsies, is in the end reunited with both her father and her beloved. The melodramatic, happy ending in which good triumphs typifies the romantic literature that Shaw and Joyce believed to be a ridiculous violation of life's realities. In "Eveline" Joyce ruthlessly documents the central character's pathetic subjugation to the realities of patriarchal religion, familial duty, and assigned roles for females. Whereas Shaw urged his disciples to refuse to make promises that would hamper them and Joyce's Stephen Hero rejects pledges, Eveline is trapped by self-destructive and life-denying loyalty—her promise to her dying mother, whose last words ("Derevaun Seraun!"; 40), perhaps a warning to escape, are incomprehensible to Eveline. The pathetic young Dubliner lacks Shavian virtues—the courage and will to save herself.

Maria in "Clay" is another victim of female conditioning in a society whose religious puritanism magnifies the difficulties of women. She is what Shaw called a "domestic woman" with whose plight ("ill paid, ill organized [and] ill recognized") he sympathized (BSL 1:475). Washing other people's dirty linen in the Dublin by Lamplight Laundry, where "she had become accustomed to the life of the laundry" (100), Maria is a pathetic spinster whose twilight life presages a dead end. A womanly woman whose vocation in life should have been motherhood, she has not married, and Mrs. Warren's profession would be unthinkable for such a proper Catholic female, although she works with reformed prostitutes. She dutifully attends mass and in her early days had acted as surrogate mother, in the role of nanny sometimes alotted to unattached females, for Joe and Alphy. Joe thought of Maria as his "proper mother" (100), though, like the Virgin Mary, for whom she is named, she has not enjoyed a conjugal relationship. Instead she has nurtured a Joseph. In losing the plum cake (a traditional fertility offering) purchased for Joe's family, she has not truly lost her innocence, only misplaced it. It has perhaps been stolen from her, as was her fruitful youth. In accidentally leaving the cake behind with the drunken man who rattled her by speaking to her on the tram, she was acting out her subconscious desire. Moreover, the drinking habits of the man with whom she left the cake parallel those of Joe, attention to whom apparently deprived Maria of eligibility for marriage.

A timid servant to servants who talks over "old times" with Joe and his wife, she is the docile, good-natured butt of the children's joke in their blindfold game. When they give her clay from the garden, which she supposedly chooses with their prodding, she receives the emblem of her failed life, the malleable clay to which she will return, perhaps shortly, in death. Two of the ideals that, according to Shaw, "blind us" with "self-denying conformity" (MCE 52) are troped in the choices in the guessing game—the ring, which promises marriage, and the prayer book, which promises the religious life of a nun. The third option, water (offered to the children but not to Maria), suggests baptismal rebirth as well as life and escape from Ireland. Hence it implies the overseas vitalism for which Shaw and Joyce opted. But, Shaw wrote, "the truth is, that in real life a self-sacrificing woman or . . . a womanly woman, is . . . taken advantage of . . . for her pains. No man pretends that his soul finds its supreme satisfaction in self-sacrifice" (MCE 56–57). Apparently the children intuitively recognize that, as Shaw put it, "the self-sacrificer is always a drag, a responsibility, a reproach" (MCE 56). They take advantage of the kindly Maria by substituting dirt for water, hence unwittingly auguring Maria's fate, the living death in which she is mired as well as her actual death. When the adults make the children present her with a more appropriate fortune, she gets a prayer book, a sign that she "would enter a convent before the year was out" (105). Thus the Life Force she seems to represent is never affirmed.

An ironic Virgin Mother, small and witch-like, Maria has nurtured Joe and his brother. A female scapegoat redeemer, she makes peace among the women at the laundry. She intends to bring the plum cake, a symbol of fructifying communion, to the family, but loses it. Ironically, when she cannot find it, the children act as "if they were to be accused of stealing" (101). Even her attempt to be generous turns into a reprimand. In trying, like the Madonna intercessor, to make peace between Joe and Alphy, she has also failed. Her life has failed because she has not fulfilled the role for which she is fitted, perhaps because she lacks the conventional good looks that might have made her attractive to a man. That Joyce associates her simultaneously with the Virgin Mother and a Halloween witch is not, as Marvin Magalaner and Richard Kain observe, evidence of the uncertainty of "a very young writer" (100). Instead, it suggests the central irony of the story: the discrepancy between Maria's inner self and her surface self. The bountiful, self-sacrificing Virgin Mother is in reality the ugly spirit of self-denial in modern Dublin—a ghost of her powerful mythic archetype. On All Saints' Day, the saintly Maria is both haunter of Joe's family, reminding Joe of his alienation from his brother and his exploitation of Maria, and haunted, for her ineffectual, submissive saintliness alienates her from the life that she deserves.

Maria's pathetic and frustrated hopes are revealed in her rendition of a song from Balfe's *Bohemian Girl*. A sentimental dream of romance, power through marriage, and success through love, the song offers an illusory ideal that few modern women, no women in Dublin at the turn of the century, and surely no aging Irish spinster could realize. Her song choice suggests the painful disparity between her illusions and her reality. It is a means for her of fantasizing over romantic hopes long dead. But the marble halls that await Maria are those of a mausoleum, for hers has been a death in life in which no lover will give her "vassals and serfs" or riches or "a high ancestral name" (106). Although the impoverished woman bears the highest ancestral name of all in female Christendom, she is a vassal and serf, impoverished emotionally and physically by her limited, dependent life. Her cultural conditioning has unfitted her for self-actualization. Her pathetic story is ironic in that the reader is aware of her entrapment, but she is so fully acquiescent to repressive life-denial and self-immolation (Shavian *bêtes noires*) that she seems—until she sings "I Dreamt That I Dwelt in Marble Halls"—to have no inkling of the sterility and emptiness of her life.

Perhaps the greatest irony of "Clay" is that Maria is a nurturing, self-sacrificing womanly woman for whom the vocation of wife and mother would have been natural and fulfilling, but she has been offered up to surrogate motherhood, like Eveline. Shaw wrote that "the domestic career is no more natural to all women than the military career is natural to all men" (MCE 60). As intercessor and maternal caretaker, Maria has the qualities and propensities for "the domestic career," but because she is single, she is a poor outsider who must ingratiate herself with Joe's family. As Shaw also wrote, "At present we . . . condemn women as a sex to attach themselves to breadwinners" or to a life of poverty and loneliness (CP 726).

G. B. S. mentions, however, another option—the one that is the subject of *Mrs. Warren's Profession*. His preface to that play points out the parallels between prostitution, marriage, and commerce. Elsewhere he stated, "Respectability founded on poverty is blasphemy: marriage founded on property is prostitution" (CP 664). In Joyce's story "The Boarding House," mother and daughter collude to assure the daughter's respectability. The working-class temptress, Polly Mooney, has the requisite good looks to make a bargain with a man. As Shaw wrote, "It is no doubt necessary under existing circumstances for a woman without property to be sexually attractive, because she must get married to secure a livelihood" (CP 22). "The Boarding House" documents how the Mooneys, mother and daughter, secure a livelihood for Polly. Joyce's story, like *Mrs. Warren's Profession,* reveals the close connection between sex and the profit motive. As Shaw put it, "until the dependence of women on men is done away with . . . the difference between marriage and prostitution [will be] . . . the difference between Trade Unionism and unorganized casual labor" (CP 23).

Sex has cash value, and cash value translates into social acceptability to the daughters of both Mrs. Warren, the efficient madam who runs successful bordellos, and Mrs. Mooney, who runs a successful boardinghouse that her boarders snidely compare to a bawdy house. Mrs. Mooney's patrons refer to her as proprietress of such an establishment: "All the resident young men spoke of her as *The Madam*" (D 62). Although the Mooney women want respectability, they do not get it, for the vulgar narrator of the Cyclops episode of *Ulysses* asperses both the mother "who kept a kip on Hardwicke street" and the daughter; Polly's marriage to Doran (who is drunk in the pub) has not kept "the little sleepwalking bitch" from becoming a loose woman "open to all comers" (U 12.398–402). Both the Shaw and Joyce businesswomen nevertheless use sex as a means to social and financial advancement. The proper Mrs. Mooney is, like Mrs. Warren, whom Shaw describes as "in complete command of the situation" (CP 219), street-smart and tough. Mrs. Mooney is manipulative and hypocritical but with a less grandiose plan than Mrs. Warren, who educated her daughter to be a New Woman and a lady. The lower-middle-class Dubliner gives her daughter Polly carte blanche in the art of seduction for profit—small profit, but the best Polly can manage in philistine Dublin, where ordinary men serve the proprieties of employer and priest. Like Mrs. Warren, Mrs. Mooney has what Shaw calls "the managing capacity" to survive in a society in which, like Shaw's successful businesswoman, she chooses, "according to her lights, the least immoral alternative" (CP 230) to make a life for herself and her daughter in a society that limits the choices of women.

Both mothers are efficient entrepreneurs. Like Mrs. Warren, Mrs. Mooney is bossy—"a big imposing woman" who "dealt with moral problems as a cleaver deals with meat." An expedient pragmatist, "she governed her house cunningly and firmly, knew when to give credit, when to be stern and when to let things pass" (62–63). A materialist who deals with moral problems insensitively, she has, like Mrs. Warren, her justifications. Decisive and determined, she willingly trades her daughter's body and reputation for the dubious rewards of a proper, petty bourgeois life. In Dublin, the venues for uneducated women were limited: dependence upon men in subordinate work (in Polly's case as a typist), support by a man in marriage, or living off of men in occupations such as Mrs. Warren's or Mrs. Mooney's. The second and third options are tainted by suggestions of trafficking in sex. In light of the action of his little domestic drama, the title of Joyce's story is, indeed, perhaps a sexual double entendre.

In Shaw's *Arms and the Man* Catherine Petkoff's basic aims are the same as Mrs. Mooney's—to get her daughter respectably married. Both mothers are philistines, but Catherine perpetuates romantic illusions, whereas the practical, vulgarly realistic proprietress of the boardinghouse leaves the province of illusory romance to her daughter. Polly, however, seems instinctively to have heeded the Shavian warning that "all attractive unpropertied women lose money by being infallibly virtuous or contracting marriages that are not more or less venal" (CP 219). Mrs. Mooney and her "naughty" daughter are nothing if not venal, even though the stakes in the marriage lottery at the boarding-house are not high. Mother and daughter are as expedient in their unspoken plot to get Polly a husband as Mrs. Warren was in making money to get herself out of the gutter. In "The Boarding House," Polly collaborates with her mother's unarticulated plan for seduction. In Shaw's plays daughters are less complacent than Polly. Unlike Mrs. Warren, who becomes angry at Vivie's noncompliance in the last act of Shaw's play, Mrs. Mooney congratulates herself on the success of her plot, knowing full well that she and her daughter "had connived" and that Polly "had divined the intention behind her mother's tolerance" (64). Like *Mrs. Warren's Profession* as well as *Widowers' Houses*, which Shaw claimed was, in part, a critique of "our marriage laws and customs" (CP 704), "The Boarding House" describes courting customs while revealing the crass hypocrisy that can motivate marriage, but it is marriage Irish style.

The story reveals in mother and daughter the mindless sanctimony of the deluded Irish moral majority. A victim of a bad marriage herself, Mrs. Mooney nevertheless thinks that marriage is the most suitable option for her tempting daughter; she does not succeed as a typist because her drunken father, who once "went for his wife with the cleaver" (61), pestered her at work. Even though her own husband was a drunk, often violent and in debt, Mrs. Mooney determines to marry her daughter off. Wedlock is the only respectable alternative for which Polly displays any talent. Like Mrs. Warren, she takes advantage of her ability as the female with the requisite charms to trade her body. Indeed, the story illustrates the Fabian feminist's belief that, for a woman, marriage is tantamount to selling her body. The wily maternal manager is at first only annoyed that none of her young male patrons "meant business" (63), but she aims to outdo other mothers "who could not get their daughters off their hands" (65).

The plot thickens as mother and daughter collude in entrapping an innocuous boarder. The daughter plays Circe, while the mother, anticipating the scenario that she has orchestrated, awaits developments. In this antiromantic tale, the plot is not suspenseful for mother or daughter. Although the unscrupulous older woman and her shameless offspring are not openly complicit in snaring Bob Doran, both deviously play the roles that powerlessness tempts women to play. Polly is the ingenue antitype of the heroine of what Martin Meisel calls the "domestic Magdalen Play . . . a sentimental drama devoted to a weak but sympathetic woman whose fall was . . . tearfully regretted" (142). In a deconstruction of a marriage melodrama, Polly is not a long-suffering heroine. Though she poses as an angelic woman, she is a "little perverse Madonna" (62), the woman who will fall but who is not portrayed to get the reader's sympathy. Reviewing *The New Magdalen* by Wilkie Collins, Shaw declared it to be "no more a modern 'sex play' than Mercy Merrick [the heroine] is a real Magdalen, or, for the matter of that, a real woman. Mercy is the old fashioned man made angel-woman" (OTN 231). Not a damsel in distress but a real woman, Polly has none of the self-condemnatory qualities of the stereotypical nineteenth-century fallen heroine, but she shares the typical motive of the Magdalen figure—the desire for respectability. In Joyce's domestic drama the sexually impure leading lady (who is not a lady) does not die for her dalliance, nor is the unheroic leading male a hero reformed by love. Instead the philistine Doran is seduced by Polly, the alluring sex trap who goes about her business without getting emotionally involved. An antiromantic, ignoble male such as Shaw might have created, Doran is a victim of his conditioning, without courage to valorize him or undying love to reveal.

And nothing like the stereotypical Mother Macree, Mrs. Mooney is not the self-sacrificing, nurturing, noble Irish mother but rather a phallic mother playing the heavy, the self-serving defender of middle-class morality. She feigns being the matriarchal protector of female virtue— the only sort of virtue granted to woman in a patriarchal society in which the root of so-called virtue is masculinity and woman's greatest asset is her chastity—a "virtue" that Polly handily "sacrifices" to get her man. Polly plays the wronged maiden, but in reality she is as much the active pursuer as Ann Whitefield is in *Man and Superman,* though for more material motives than finding a father for the superman. Polly is, like any "woman seeking a husband"—according to Shaw's Don Juan—"the most unscrupulous of all the beasts of prey" (Plays 382). Perhaps her destiny would have been different had she seen Shaw's discussion drama *Getting Married* (1908) (out of the question, in any event, in puritan Dublin even though Joyce was still revising "The Boarding House" in 1912), but there is no discussion in Joyce's domestic drama, no indication that either Polly or her mother would bother to read a book or see a play, and a play like Synge's *Playboy of the Western World,* whose author stubbornly refused to flatter Irish womanhood, caused a riot at the Abbey Theatre in 1907. As Shaw noted, "the pseudo-Irish, who are still exploiting the old stage Ireland for all it is worth" (*The Matter with Ireland* 65), demonstrated against the play when the Abbey Players took it to America in 1911. It is not surprising, therefore, that Joyce's vignette was having as much trouble getting published in Ireland as *Mrs. Warren's Profession* had in getting licensed in England, for both relentlessly reveal plausible instead of idealized female behavior. Like Shaw, whose method was "systematic counter-convention, by the creation of a genre anti-type" (Meisel 141), the aspiring dramatist who had turned to fiction created ironic antitypes as Shaw did in *Mrs. Warren's Profession.*

Whereas Polly flirts with Doran and, it seems, actually seduces him, the expedient mother exploits the ideals of the compact majority. "To begin with she had all the weight of social opinion on her side: she was an outraged mother.... [H]e had simply abused her hospitality" (64). Appealing to Doran's "honor" (an abstract ideal that Shaw thought to be a humbug), Mrs. Mooney also holds the cleaver over his head—the force of public opinion, to which the philistine Doran capitulates. Shaw's Don Juan in "Don Juan in Hell" would, no doubt, label Doran as a typical man, for "all his civilization is founded on his cowardice, on his abject tameness, which he calls his respectability" (Plays 377). Afraid of losing his job, he fears his employer; having already properly confessed to his priest, he quavers before the authority of the Church; and he cringes at the thought of the "thick bulldog face and ... thick short arms" (68) of Polly's muscular brother. The stern morality of the supposedly outraged mother is the authority that compels the other-directed male to submit.

Like many stories in *Dubliners,* "The Boarding House" stresses the constraints of duty, the cardinal sin in Shaw's heretical ethic. Despite his youthful "wild oats" and "free thinking," Doran has settled into the routine life of a dutiful conformist: "He attended to his religious duties and for nine-tenths of the year lived a regular life" (66). Although his instinct for escape is Shavian—that is, opposed to marriage—he gives in to the pressures of society: the outrage of the mother, fear of his boss, guilt before his priest, and the threat of Polly's brother. Doran is thoroughly conventional but momentarily conflicted about losing his freedom, reasoning that "once you are married you are done for" (68). Shaw wrote in his preface to *The Philanderer* that marriage is "to some that worst of blundering abominations, an institution which society has outgrown but not modified, and which 'advanced' individuals are therefore forced to evade" (CP 726). Clearly the helpless Doran is not an advanced individual even though he has a desperate Shavian fantasy that also suggests the motives of the entrapped Dedalus: he longs "to ascend through the roof and fly away" (67). In *The Quintessence of Ibsenism* Shaw urged advanced people to "fly" from marriage. In *Man and Superman* Don Juan also advocates such flight: "If the prisoner is happy, why lock him in?" (Plays 382).

Yet according to Joyce, even the most feckless young men in Dublin, despite a double standard, cherish the thought of marriage. In "Two Gallants," the voyeuristic Lenehan has a moment of philistine truth, which "embittered his heart against the world" because he recognizes the sterility of his streetwalking life. After eating a plate of peas, he feels sanguine and fantasizes that "he might yet be able to settle down in some snug corner and live happily" (58). A conventional bourgeois at heart, Lenehan muses on his hope to "come across some good simple minded girl with a bit of the ready" (58). His hopes indicate the minimal philistine requirements: shelter, food, female virtue and malleability, ready sex, and ready cash. He would be contented with what Shaw disdained as "the small beer of domestic happiness." Lenehan's mundane and limited expectations are very unlike those of the lone Shavian realist who challenges such commonplace goals. Probably the complacent consciences of such "gallants" would not be awakened by Joyce's story, whose aim matched that of Shaw's plays: "No doubt all plays which deal sincerely with humanity must wound the monstrous conceit which it is the business of romance to flatter" (CP 726).

Lenehan flatters his pal Corley, but both are the "Jackeens" that Shaw recognized and despised in *Ulysses,* vulgar hangers-on who walk the Dublin streets looking for women and scripting themselves as Don Juans: "You're what I call a gay Lothario, said Lenehan. And a proper kind of Lothario too!" (52). Whereas Lenehan cajoles Corley in order to keep company with the insatiable egoist whose sexual "conquests" feed the voyeur's imagination, Corley is an insensitive sexist who exploits young working women if he is lucky. Corley brags about vanquishing menials like the "slavey in a house in Baggot Street" who brought him "cigarettes and cigars" (50–51). Cheap of necessity, he congratulates himself for getting sex for free and without buying women's favors by the expedient of taking them "to a band or play at the theatre or buy[ing] them chocolate and sweets" (52), which was what he did before wising up to the fact that, with a little blarney, he could wheedle sexual favors from women.

The philandering described in this story of narcissistic conquest is very different from the sort Shaw described in *The Philanderer,* in which the sexes are, in theory, equal. Shavian men and women belong to an Ibsen Club meant for advanced, emancipated persons, the opposite of the gallants who protest too much their macho inclinations. An answer to the misogynistic Clubland clubs for men only that grew up in the late nineteenth century as a reaction to New Women (see Showalter 11–13), the Ibsen Club is for manly women and womanly men who are not threatened by the implications of androgyny. In Joyce's story, there is a hint of unsavory androgyny, especially in Corley, who ironically thinks of himself as a sexual "conqueror," for his prey is a flashy, "unabashed" slavey whose attire—a "white sailor hat" with a "ragged black boa" and red flowers—suggests a cross-dresser. She reverses roles with Corley by giving him money after their assignation, and he displays this to his male partner Lenehan with smug satisfaction. The crude lothario has none of the gallantries of a courtly lover. Like his pathetic second, ever ready with a bon mot to tease and to ingratiate himself, Corley is revealed ruthlessly for what he is, with irony and exactitude.

Like Shaw, who had been accused of "making his characters unsympathetic, sordid, soulless" (CP 700), Joyce exposed the tawdry reality of the gallants, which is the inverse of their illusions about themselves. Emulating the Shaw who called the serious artist, himself, a "cynic and paradoxer" (MCE 50), Joyce unmasked the vulgar philistines who equate sex, combat, and money: Corley congratulates himself on his ability to exploit the equation and expects admiration from his friend, whose fantasy life he supplies. Joyce emulated Shaw in remorselessly exposing the pettiness of chauvinist males who fancy themselves romantic. His characters convict themselves with ironies out of their own mouths. Hence, when

Corley describes "a bit of all right," he tells Lenehan, without conviction, that she went out with him and subsequently became a whore—"on the turf." When he rejects culpability by noting "philosophically" that "there were others at her before me," his sycophant buddy makes "a tragic gesture" and, in affected jest, pronounces Corley "Base betrayer!" (53). The real betrayers are the promiscuous Corley and the would-be Peeping Tom, whose admiring approval vindicates and cheers on Corley's sexual athleticism. Shaw condemned such behavior by declaring that "to treat a person as a means instead of an end is to deny that person's right to live. And to be treated as a means to such an end as sexual intercourse with those who deny one's right to live is insufferable to any human being. Woman, if she dares face the fact that she is being so treated, must either loathe herself or else rebel" (MCE 58).

In "Two Gallants" women are such sex objects, but they neither loathe themselves nor rebel. Perhaps the young woman who turned to prostitution had such low self-esteem that she hated herself, but surely the brash slavey who pays Corley glamorizes her debasing role and gratefully compensates the macho male for using her, perhaps because she hopes he will marry her. Her situation is insufferable, but, like other Dubliners who participate in their own victimization, she acquiesces cheerfully and satisfies her own need for sex as commerce in which she has the pittance power of paying a small-time gigolo. Whether male or female, the characters in "Two Gallants" equate sex with the satisfaction of basic needs and the power of money. The story deflates "as monstrous conceit" (as Shaw put it) what Lenehan flatters as the romantic success of a Don Juan. In remorselessly exposing the vulgarity of his philistine Dubliners, Joyce took the Shavian side of what G. B. S. termed "the eternal strife between the artist-philosopher and the Philistines" (MCE 315).

Two of the philistine propensities that Shaw most disdained were the worship of Mammon and the excessive, irresponsible use of alcohol. Indeed, Joyce noted prohibitionism as one of the progressive movements of which Shaw was a sponsor (CW 208). In spite of his tub-thumping for equal distribution of wealth, Shaw approved of wealth when it abetted the "incalculable beneficence" of a character like Andrew Undershaft in *Major Barbara* (CP 120). But he insisted that "'poor but honest,' 'respectable poor,' and such phrases are as immoral as 'drunken but amiable'" (CP 118).

Joyce exposes such a rich but amiable drunk in Jimmy Doyle, the central character of "After the Race." Jimmy, whose father is a wealthy butcher, serves the secular idols of consumer culture. Raised by his father to worship money and status, he may be an answer to Larry Doyle, Shaw's skeptical *doppelgänger* in *John Bull's Other Island,* for, like Larry, Jimmy, whose background, like Shaw's, seems to be Anglo-Irish, has gone to England for education. He has spent a term at Cambridge, which apparently only encouraged his desire to live like an irresponsible, sophisticated cosmopolitan. Unlike Larry, Jimmy was sent to England by his father and is obedient to his rags-to-riches sire, who "paid the bills and brought him home" (D 43). Like other Dublin parents, the father seems to be living vicariously through his child. The butcher controls and emasculates his amiably feckless son through money, a vulgar mistake that the Shavian work ethic disdains. Shaw thought everyone should work for his own good and for the good of society and that intellectual and artistic work were more important than any other. Without a vocational goal, Jimmy is a superfluous person educated beyond his intelligence, programmed by his limited and limiting experience to idealize wealth and high society. His education at Dublin University (Trinity College), has failed to produce the lawyer that his father wanted, but he has accepted his father's nouveau riche values while trying to refine them by attaching himself to cosmopolitan outsiders.

Jimmy's money enables him to associate with Sègouin, a Frenchman who owns a racing car. Joyce encapsulates the young Irish racing enthusiast's epicurean provocations: "Rapid motion through space elates one; so does notoriety; so does the possession of money" (44). If he were committed to politics or excellence in a profession, he might be a hero out of Shaw's early novels, but despite being "at heart the inheritor of solid instincts" (44), the young Irishman is carried away by the vicarious thrill of proximity to the winner, by pride in his continental connections, and by the self-indulgent power and pleasure that his full wallet encourages. With Sègouin and the other young foreigners, Jimmy indulges his preference for life in the fast lane. Apparently the richest young man is the American Farley. Jimmy's attention turns to him as Shaw's preface to *Man and Superman* predicted it would: "Our eyes and hearts turn eagerly to the American millionaire. As his hand goes down to his pocket, our fingers go up to the brims of our hats. . . . Obsequious-ness, servility, cupidity roused by the prevailing smell of money" (CP 160).

And life led on by the smell of money encourages celebrative drinking. As if providing an exemplum of Shaw's theory that the Irishman lives by illusions fired by drink, Jimmy's "imagination," kindled by "generous influences" (46), leads him to talk politics. Jimmy's once idealistic father, like many Irish Protestants, "had begun life as an advanced Nationalist" (43). When his father's nationalism stirs in Jimmy, he begins—reproducing the Shavian paradigm regarding Guinness patriotism—to argue politics with the Englishman Routh. In a microcosm of international relations, the Frenchman, taking the internationalist position that Shaw took, acts as mediator between the antagonists. Sègouin lifts "his glass to Humanity, and when the toast had been drunk, he threw open a window significantly" (46), letting in fresh air. Nevertheless, Jimmy is so inebriated by the end of the night of revelry that he cannot see straight: "He frequently mistook his cards and the other men had to calculate his I.O.U.'s for him" (48). He acts out the Irish inclination for convivial escape; its predictable liability is that Jimmy is bested by the congenial usurpers. During a night of drinking and gambling, the Irishman and the American Irishman (who owns the yacht on which the debacle takes place and hence can afford the dissipation) lose heavily. Jimmy is "glad of the dark stupor that would cover up his folly" (48). "Cover up" is the operative phrase, for Jimmy is other-directed. He gets his cues from others in the group into which he is welcomed, it seems, because of his money and (except in the area of politics) his affability. The dull insensibility brought on by alcohol does not prevent him from recognizing his folly, but even in his drunken state he does not have an epiphany (like the boy's recognition of vanity in "Araby") that will free him from his illusions. He does not want to recognize the significance of his self-destructive behavior and prefers to drown the truth in drink.

Drunk and fatalistically convinced that "he would lose" (48), the inebriate lets the Frenchman convince him to invest in "the motor business," but Sègouin is "at the control" (44–45). Whereas Shaw's Larry Doyle is in active partnership with his English friend, the young Irish scion is manipulated by the more worldly-wise outsiders, and, in the competition over booty in Ireland, loses to the Englishman. In "After the Race" the automobiles represent the technological progress of countries more advanced than Ireland. The Europeans defeat the Dublin Irish, just as the technologies brought by Tom Broadbent in *John Bull's Other Island* master the provincial Hibernians. In Joyce's story, the more cosmopolitan French are "virtual victors" (42). Rivière, "not wholly ingenuously, undertook to explain to Jimmy the triumph of the French mechanicians" (46). The young Irishman drunkenly interprets the fiasco of the day's partying—the "merriment" of false camaraderie—as "Bohemian" (47). He is elated over his contacts with the invaders, just as the locals in *John Bull's Other Island* are. In the play, Broadbent's motorcar gets wrecked by the Irish pig he takes for a ride, but Jimmy—also taken for a ride—gets no revenge. And in Shaw's play the superior business skills and machines of the Englishman, like the racing cars and foreigners in "After the Race," overmaster the Irish. They will be, like Jimmy Doyle, losers to the Englishman.

Another Dublin loser—on a much lower rung of the social ladder than the well-heeled Jimmy—is Farrington of "Counterparts," a father who is an alcoholic. In this story Joyce examines an episode in the life of an angry man who cannot drown his feelings of inadequacy and impotence in drink or articulate them except in violence. A captive of his assumptions about masculinity, which are undercut by his position as a worker, Farrington goes through a series of humiliations brought on by his own escapist alcoholism. Among the counterparts of the story are Farrington and his wife, who trade off roles as bully and victim; Mr. Alleyne, Farrington's nasty boss, who bullies his ineffectual copyist; the artistes in the Scotch House and Mulligan's pub, male and female, who deflate Farrington's ego; and the father and son he abuses to assuage his rage. Farrington forces his son to take on the role of victim, in which he has found himself throughout the day. Unsuited, Joyce implies, for the work of an office clerk copyist, the tall, bulky man deviously escapes to the pub for a pint that will make his demeaning work and his awareness of failure more bearable. He is reprimanded by Mr. Alleyne, his "North of Ireland" boss, a bespectacled little man who wears "goldrimmed glasses on a cleanshaven face" and has a head "pink and hairless" (87). To be put down by such a "dwarf" is an indignity that, like all of the others in this mesomorph's day, enrages Farrington (90–91). Whereas the ugly little man with the power of status and money regularly entertains "Miss Delacour . . . a middleaged woman of Jewish appearance" who comes to the office and stays "a long time" (89), Farrington is rejected by her potential counterpart, an artiste whose eyes meet his later in the day while he is submerging his sorrows in drink. Despite being a married man, Farrington, like Mr. Alleyne, assumes the double standard and, like the "gallant" Corley, lusts after a flashy woman.

Oppugned throughout the day, Farrington is defeated by usurping West British types—Mr. Alleyne, the flirtatious woman with a London accent, and a "young fellow named Weathers who was performing at the Tivoli as an acrobat and knockabout *artiste*" (94). The big Irishman, who has little to pride himself on except his strength, loses in an arm-wrestling contest with the Englishman. When he goes home after a night of drink in which he failed to get drunk, as he wished to do, he is aware that "he had lost his reputation as a strong man, having been defeated by a mere boy" (96–97). He therefore takes out all of his "savage and thirsty and revengeful" (96) sense of humiliation and rage on another mere boy, his small son, beating him sadistically with a phallic substitute, his walking stick (98). To compensate for his losses, he "defeats" a boy who is too small to fight back. Joyce graphically describes the child abuse that he himself had witnessed and that Shaw decried, whether from parent, pedagogue, or priest.

Unlike Joyce, Shaw was a teetotaler who also despised drink as a curse that promotes violence. In *Major Barbara,* first performed in London in November 1905, although Shaw had circulated rumors that might have reached Joyce earlier (H2 115), the playwright created a character who parallels the protagonist of "Counterparts," which Joyce completed by mid-July 1905 but revised in 1906. Bill Walker is a bully like Farrington but less repressed in his hostilities because, being unemployed, he has no job to lose. He strikes one of Major Barbara's lieutenants, Jenny, who promptly begins to pray for him. Her action is not, however, a rejoinder to violence that is made, like Farrington's son's similar defense, out of desperation. The stock response of the young Catholic boy is to promise the drunken man the intercession of the Virgin Mary. Upon hearing the frightened boy's prayer, she would, the boy no doubt supposes, forgive even an angry sinner like Farrington. Shaw's Bill Walker is as furious as Farrington, and Jenny is as forgiving as a Protestant Salvation Army worker as Mary was reputed to be for Roman Catholics. After Bill's unwarranted attack on two innocent women, Shirley, one of the old denizens of the Salvation Army shelter, taunts him for hitting women and challenges him to a match with a man his own size—Todger

Fairmile, "that won £20 from a Japanese wrastler at the music hall by standin out 27 minutes 4 seconds agen him" (Plays 473).

Before his attack on his son, as has been noted, Farrington had lost an arm-wrestling contest. His notions of justice, like Bill's and Shirley's, are physical. He wants an eye for an eye; and, although he does not articulate it, like Bill Walker he despises the doctrine of forgiveness. No doubt if he were as intelligent as Shaw's Professor Cusins, he would argue as Cusins does that "forgiveness is a beggar's refuge" (Plays 500). The little boy in "Counterparts" is such a beggar when he offers to say Hail Marys for his father. Like Bill, who actually menaces Shirley with the threat "Aw'll do you a mischief. Aw'm not dirt under your feet ennywy" (476), Farrington tries to compensate for his low self-esteem by turning his disgraces into violence. The inarticulate male suffers from a sense of injustice because of social inequities just as Bill Walker does. And like Farrington, Shaw's Bill Sykes character (modeled on Dickens's cutpurse cutthroat in *Oliver Twist*) is a bully whom drink turns into a self-righteous avenger defending his amor propre. Walker and Farrington take out their frustrations on innocent bystanders who cannot fight back. The boy bribes his father to stop beating him, with the promise of salvation that the Salvation Army worker makes with her prayers for Bill Walker. Like the boy, who promises prayers if his father will desist, the Salvation Army promises Bill that he will be saved if he repents.

Both Shaw and Joyce were aware, however, that their drunken bullies were blindly acting out the mode of masculine behavior in which justice is strength, a code dominating patriarchal culture since Thrasymachus declared it in Plato's *Republic*. Although he wrote about brutality, Shaw declared that "as a human person I detested violence and slaughter, whether in war, sport, or the butcher's yard" (CP 716). Joyce also had severe reservations about physical force. In 1903 he concurred with Shaw in disapproving of the flogging of sailors (see CW 113). Nevertheless, both created displaced, powerless strong men who turn to abusive, antisocial behavior to bolster their self-respect, which is flagging because of their lack of success in society. Both are impoverished, Walker no doubt because of drink and Farrington clearly for that reason: he pawns his gold watch in order to enjoy a night of carousing in the pubs.

In his preface to *Major Barbara,* Shaw clarified that one of his aims was to expose "the greatest of our evils, and the worst of our crimes . . . poverty" (CP 118). Poverty debases Walker and Farrington, whereas money, which is power, elevates Andrew Undershaft (Major Barbara's father) and Mr. Alleyne, the Anglo-Irishman who employs Farrington. Because Farrington shirks work, lies, and sneaks slyly out of the office to drink in a snug, Mr. Alleyne threatens Farrington, who does not merit his job. As boss, Alleyne expects to be obeyed. Insurrection may cause Alleyne to fire Farrington, consigning him and his family to even worse poverty than they now endure because of his alcoholism. Despite his scorn for irresponsibility and for drink, Shaw would have empathized with Farrington's poverty and condemned the employer's lack of concern for the worker, whose alcoholism the socialist believed to be both the cause and the effect of his poverty. Shaw wrote, "Now what does this Let Him Be Poor mean? It means let him be weak. Let him be ignorant.... Let the undeserving become still less deserving: and let the deserving lay up for himself, not treasures in heaven, but horrors in hell upon earth" (CP 119–20). In *John Bull's Other Island,* it must be remembered, Shaw called Ireland hell. In "Counterparts," Farrington is in the Shavian hell of *Man and Superman* and the Dantean hell of the angry, the intemperate, the slothful, the lustful, the violent, and the fraudulent. Shaw would have been likely to analyze his predicament as he did Walker's, finding that Farrington needs redemption—not the kind that his son naively thinks will come from religion, but redemption from poverty, which creates and feeds his inferiority feelings.

Farrington's guilt at not being a successful "manly man," as Shaw called the masculinist, seems to have driven him to an effort to escape in alcohol, an outlet that Irishmen were taught was a mark of masculinity. Incapable of the imagination that torments the idealist, Farrington fantasizes about getting even with his boss and getting the brassy, sexually alluring artiste he sees in Mulligan's pub. In an effort to aggrandize his masculinity, he stands drinks for his cronies, brashly spending all but two pence (96), and he bases his reputation on proving his strength. Because his stereotyped, macho illusions are undercut by reality, he projects his own failures onto his son. He blames the boy for letting the fire go out, when in reality his alcoholic improvidence is at fault. Like the poor about whom Shaw extrapolates in *Major Barbara*'s preface, he is delinquent because he is "ashamed of ... poverty" and the humiliating powerlessness that it causes. The utopian Fabian, who favored equality of income for all who work, wrote that "money is the most important thing in the world. It represents health, strength, honor, generosity, and beauty conspicuously and undeniably as the want of it represents illness, weakness, disgrace, meanness and ugliness. . . . The first duty of every citizen is to insist on having money on reasonable terms" (CP 121–22).

The hopelessly inebriated and self-absorbed Farrington, like his Shavian counterpart Walker, is incapable of such insistence but vaguely aware that with money he could be generous, prove his strength, and attract a beautiful woman. Frustrated and shamed in all of his self-aggrandizing fantasies, he resorts to the brutality for which his physical nature has equipped him. Although Joyce's Irishman is devious because of his addiction, both Shaw's comic drunk and Joyce's disgusting one believe in physical force. In the microcosmic Ireland, the strong traditionally bully the weak; the upper the lower class; the English the Irish; and, in Joyce's story, the father the son.

Convinced that environment determines much philistine behavior, Shaw argued that what a man "does, and what we think of what he does, depends on his circumstances" (CP 129). Thus the morality of Bill Walker and Farrington differs from that of an employer only in the situations of their backgrounds. Undershaft and Walker have essentially the same worldview, just as Alleyne and all of the men in "Counterparts" do. The difference lies in their material welfare. All believe in patriarchal power and authority, but Undershaft (who is beneficent to his workers) and Alleyne (who is not) "hold the purse strings" (CP 131), as Shaw put it, and hence call the shots, literally and figuratively in the case of Joyce's drunk and Shaw's munitions maker Undershaft. The source of the anger and frustration that exacerbate the alcoholic behavior of Walker and Farrington is their lack of power in spite of their physical bulk, which might serve them in a more primitive society.

For the more tractable citizens, however—often the women and children—religion is, as Marx taught Shaw, an opiate. Farrington's son seems to intuit something Shaw wrote in his preface to *Major Barbara*: "Religious bodies . . . become a sort of auxiliary police, taking off the insurrectionary edge of poverty . . . soothing and cheering the victims with hopes of immense and inexpensive happiness in another world when the process of working them to premature death in the service of the rich is complete in this" (CP 132). Significantly, in Joyce's story, Farrington's wife, who probably expected his drunken rage, is "at the chapel" when he gets home (97). Whereas Farrington's son offers the counterpart of religious distraction for violence, Farrington counterpunches with the chauvinistic law of force, which uses violence and cruelty to assert power. The boy's placating offer suggests that Mother Church will intercede to absolve the abusive father. According to Shaw, this is an old wives' tale related to the mixed messages of Christianity, one part of which supports the idea of "insane vengeance bought off by a trumpery expiation," whereas the other side "forbids the glaring futility and folly of vengeance" (CP 134). Farrington's son vainly relies on his father's hope of the feminine mercy offered by petitions to Mary.

Major Barbara interfaces with yet another of Joyce's stories about adult Dubliners. In "Grace," middle-class Dubliners, almost in the spirit of Shaw's two complacent bums Rummy and Snobby in *Major Barbara,* play a kind of religious confidence game of contrition for blessings. They let themselves be rescued by religion—by a priest who is a sort of Catholic Salvation Army man. In Shaw's play and Joyce's story, confession is good for the soul but far better for the belly and pocketbook. Shaw despised the "nasty lying habit called confession, which the [Salvation] Army encourages." He wrote, "For my part, when I hear a convert relating the violences and oaths and blasphemies he was guilty of before he was saved, making out that he was a very terrible fellow then and is the most contrite and chastened of Christians now, I believe him no more than I believe the millionaire who says he came up to London or Chicago as a boy with only three halfpence in his pocket" (CP 127).

G. B. S. distrusted the hypocrisies, moral constraints, and cupidity of organized religion. He disapproved of the Salvation Army's "advertising" sinners like the "reclaimed drunkard" because of the sordid connection between business and religion—a central theme of *Major Barbara* and the major theme of "Grace." Moreover, Shaw did not think it wise to relieve the alcoholic of responsibility for his own cure. To him "the inexorability of the deed once done should [not] be disguised by any ritual whether in the confession or on the scaffold" (which is what Shaw deemed the Cross to be) (CP 128). He wrote that the

> propaganda of the Cross (which I loathe as I loathe all gibbets) becomes deep indeed. Forgiveness, absolution, atonement, are figments: punishment is only a pretense of cancelling one crime by another: and you can no more have forgiveness without vindictive-

ness than you can have a cure without a disease. You will never get a high morality from people who conceive that their misdeeds are revocable and pardonable, or in a society where absolution and expiation are officially provided for us all. The demand may be very real: but the supply is spurious. (CP 128)

In questioning the motives of the Salvation Army, he was also dubious about confession as a major ritual of the Catholicism of his native land. Shaw used the commercial language that becomes the metaphor for the pardon Father Purdon supplies the "reformed" drunk Kernan in "Grace." When Barbara forgives Bill Walker in *Major Barbara,* "he is placed in a position of unbearable moral inferiority" that he tries to escape. The smug middle-class reprobates in "Grace," however, accept absolution from their "spiritual accountant," confident that their misdeeds are revocable. Mr. Cunningham cheerfully compares the ritual to domestic dishwashing: "We're all going to wash the pot" (163). Indeed, the priest provides a businessman's sermon that whitewashes the guilt of the "children of this world." They are, according to the scriptural text Father Purdon has chosen to launder their guilt, "wiser in their generation than the children of light" (172)—perhaps Luciferian light-bringers like Shaw and Joyce. Such spurious pardon allows the drinkers to repeat the sin. Without a firm purpose of amendment, the philistine Dublin businessmen routinely serve the ends of their religion.

Among these proper bourgeois businessmen, drink and religion are coupled. Robert Adams observes the "spiritual Franklinism" of Father Purdon and points out parallels between "Grace" and Dante's *Divine Comedy* (though Joyce's comedy is anything but divine): Kernan is fallen in the Inferno of the pub toilet, purged in the Purgatorio of the bedroom, and redeemed in the Paradiso of the Jesuit church on Gardiner Street (80). Adams notes too the story's comic parallels to the *Book of Job* (though Kernan's illness is not God's or Satan's test of a perfect and upright man) (81). When the friends come to comfort the ironic Job, they drink stout. Mr. Fogarty brings the sick man a nip of the snake that bit him, a bottle of rum. Such comfort marks the intransigent intemperance that Shaw, the prohibitionist, understood and condemned as self-destructive and humiliating.

More destructive to Shaw, however, was unmerited pardon. Adams points out that Father Purdon is named for "Dublin's notorious red-light district" (81), Purdon Street in Monto; but his name is also, as in medieval allegory, the equivalent of his role. He grants pardon in the spirit of Chaucer's Pardonner: his biblical text is, instead of "*Radax malorum est cupiditas*" (the root of evil is greed), the parable of the unjust steward (Luke 16:8–9). The priest deconstructs the parable to fit his clientele. In calling his congregation into account, as the rich man called his prodigal steward, the priest acts as the steward instead of the rich man, who, in Luke, figures God. The dishonest steward asks "his lord's debtors" to forge their bills, stating only half of their true debt. For asking less—getting something rather than nothing in payment—"the lord commended the unjust steward," apparently rendering unto Caesar what is Caesar's, bribing the children of this world, Dublin businessmen who are also "the mammon of unrighteousness." In his preface to *Getting Married,* Shaw wrote, "In short, Mammon, always mighty, put the Church in his pocket, where he keeps it to this day, in spite of the occasional saints and martyrs who contrive from time to time to get their heads and souls free to testify against him" (CP 39). As "Grace" attests, both Shaw and Joyce are among those who testified against Mammon's hold on religion. Whereas Shaw's Major Barbara is thoroughly disillusioned when she discovers the message implicit in "Grace"—the infernal connections between Salvationism and Mammon—Father Purdon in "Grace" preaches, "Make unto yourselves friends out of the mammon of iniquity so that when you die, they may receive you into everlasting dwellings" (173). Shaw exposed such Salvationism, which offers in exchange for confession "an investment which will bring them in dividends later on in the form, not of a better life to come for the whole world, but of an eternity spent by themselves personally in a sort of bliss which would bore any active person to a second death" (CP 127).

In preaching setting "right my accounts," Father Purdon, as Gifford points out, almost parodies the *Maynooth Catechism*'s "The Examination of Conscience and Firm Purpose of Amendment" (110), which is the prelude to confession and contrition. Like Rummy and Snobby in *Major Barbara,* the Dublin drinkers have no intention of amending their lives. Jesuitical doublethink vindicates them, as well as Father Purdon, for pardoning his intemperate congregation, hence conciliating it and keeping it in his fold while providing for himself and his church. The "grace" given is truly unmerited love, but the exposure of its connections to capitalism is Shavian. Shaw declared that "the world-grasping commercial synthesis we call Capitalism . . . is . . . the bulwark of the Christian Churches" (CP 833). *Major Barbara* favors the Mephistophelian Undershaft because he is not a hypocrite: he frankly improves the lives of workers while making munitions, but he does not offer them religious palliatives. When Shaw's play exposed "the economic deadlock" of the Salvation Army, its officers replied that "they would take money from the devil himself and be only too glad to get it out of his hand and into God's. They gratefully acknowledged that publicans not only give them money but allow them to collect it in the bar" (CP 124). When Major Barbara discovers that "the Salvation Army is the accomplice of the distiller and the dynamite maker" (CP 125), she leaves it, but Father Purdon, still on the side of the Pharisees, prefers to offer his congregation the opiate of salvation with a cash nexus.

Thus Joyce's smug, self-satisfied Catholics defend orthodoxy, the priesthood, Father Purdon as "a man of the world like ourselves" (164), and the doctrine of papal infallibility (167–68). As Mr. Power says, unaware of the devastating irony of his position, "Well Mrs Kernan, we're going to make your man here a good holy pious and God-fearing Roman Catholic" (170). Like Shaw, Joyce ridicules the conventional sanctimony of "God-fearing" religion; Joyce's businessmen would be at home in the "Palace of Lies" that is hell to Shaw. In "Don Juan in Hell" in *Man and Superman,* Don Juan proclaims that the devil's "friends" are

> not religious: they are only pewrenters—they are not moral: they are only conventional. They are not virtuous: they are only cowardly. They are not even vicious: they are only "frail" . . . they are not loyal, they are only servile; not dutiful, only sheepish . . . not kind, only sentimental; not social only gregarious . . . liars everyone of them, to the very backbone of their souls. (Plays 386)

Whereas self-serving, "respectable" philistine males pay lip service to religion, proper women are the victims of the received lies of middle-class society. The wife of the Dublin drunk, Mr. Kernan, who is "saved" by his orthodox cronies, is a womanly woman—the most fully realized minor female character in *Dubliners.* Her sketch matches the stereotype Shaw outlined in *The Quintessence of Ibsenism.* As a young woman, Mrs. Kernan had accepted what Shaw described as the "idealization of marriage" and the "idealistic illusions which the youthful imagination weaves so wonderfully under the stimulus of desire" (MCE 56, 58). Although she is an "active, practical woman" who recently celebrated her silver wedding anniversary (163), "in her days of courtship Mr Kernan had seemed to her a not ungallant figure" (156), for she was, as Shaw described her kind of woman, "an ordinary female conformer to the ideal of womanliness" (MCE 56). Shortly after her wedding, however, she "found a wife's life irksome" (156). Her marriage, like the model Shaw drew in "The Womanly Woman," seemed based on "the romantic ideal," but very soon comes "the breakdown of the plan. The young wife finds that her husband is neglecting her for business: that his interests, his activities, his whole life except that one part of it to which only a cynic ever referred before her marriage, lies away from home: and that her business is to sit there and mope until she is wanted" (MCE 59).

Mrs. Kernan's marriage follows the Shavian curve of development: "The self-respect she has lost as a wife she regains as a mother" (MCE 59). When Mrs. Kernan "began to find it [marriage] unbearable, she had become a mother" (D 156) and hence applied herself to the female duties of *Kinder, Küche, Kirche*. She devoted herself to her children and to keeping house "shrewdly for her husband" (156). Although "she had very few illusions left" (157), she accepted life with a drunkard who was at least, she thought, faithful to his job and "had never been violent since the boys had grown up" (156). She mothers her immature husband, acceding to "his frequent intemperance as part of the climate," healing him "dutifully whenever he was sick," and "always" trying "to make him eat breakfast" (156). Another woman trapped by duty, she has accepted woman's place and has not the strength or desire to repudiate the routine obligations that Shaw insisted held women in bondage.

Significantly, "religion for her was a habit.... She believed steadily in the Sacred Heart as the most generally useful of all Catholic devotions" (158). Her belief in the grace and mercy of the martyred Christ no doubt helps her to bear her own martyrdom in marriage to an alcoholic. But, a mercifully benighted philistine, she is not deeply committed to religion: "Her faith was bounded by her kitchen but, if she was put to it, she could believe also in the banshee and in the Holy Ghost" (158). An Irish stereotype, she blithely accepts pagan superstition along with Christian dogma that requires genuine faith. With her addicted husband she is, in today's terms, an enabler and co-dependent. Her tolerance of her preordained position in life collaborates with religion in valorizing Mr.

Kernan's weakness for drink. Together they guarantee that he will not face the truth of his self-destructive habit or seek a remedy for the sickness, which is a pernicious variation of the bourgeois infirmities that plague the living dead of Dublin.

The final story of *Dubliners,* "The Dead," is a coda and *ricorso,* bringing together characters and reiterating themes that illustrate Shavian theory (which begs a new reading of the story). Aiming like Shaw's early plays *épater le bourgeois*—"the Philistines and sentimental idealists" (CP 711)—the lengthy slice of life of the Dublin music world has its idealists, philistines, and—although by Shawlight not clearly so—one lone realist. For Gabriel Conroy of "The Dead" finally recognizes himself for what he has been, "a ludicrous figure, acting as a penny boy for his aunts, a nervous, well-meaning sentimentalist, orating to vulgarians and idealising his own clownish lusts" (D 220). At this moment of truth, he seems converted from deluded idealism to Shavian realism. But he is surrounded by idealists and philistines. Although his story of the betrayer betrayed is central, the novella explores many Shavian themes: the wasted potential of women, the Church as a negative and controlling influence that puts women in an inferior role and emphasizes death instead of the Life Force, the demon drink, retrograde nationalism, the deleterious effects of romanticism, and finally the role of the would-be artist-philosopher.

"The Dead" celebrates, albeit with some irony, the hospitality of women like Shaw's mother, who developed her musical talent in the "unsectarian" Dublin music world. Shaw found "the religion of ... [his] country in its musical genius, and its irreligion in its churches and drawing rooms" (SSS 47). Hence, although approving Dublin's musicians, he would have disdained, as Joyce's complex ironies do, the gauche worship of the dead in Joyce's story. Mr. Browne's presence as token Protestant at the Morkan party suggests the mildly ecumenical spirit of the Catholic music world in Dublin, a society that Shaw's Protestant mother readily entered because she preferred art to religious prejudice. The conventional Morkans, however, modeled on Joyce's great-aunts, did not have the daring and determination of Lucinda Shaw, whose house on Hatch Street was a center for Dubliners dedicated to music a generation before Joyce.

Joyce's reconstruction of his ambivalent relations with the music world of his hometown recapitulates the leitmotifs of the earlier vignettes of Dubliners, at once deprecating their failures and appreciating the hospitality of the only part of Dublin life that both Shaw and Joyce approved—its love of music. The characters forgathered for the Morkans' festive dinner dance are Dublin's Liffeyside people. The setting of "The Dead" is the home of the Misses Morkan on Usher's Island, on the southern bank of the Liffey quays, where the actual sisters lived who were, though not maiden ladies, models for Kate and Julia Morkan. The cast of characters reflects the themes already suggested in Joyce's life studies.

Lily, the caretaker's daughter, who does domestic work for the sisters and their niece, articulates the fear that Eveline could not put into words: "The men that is now is only all palaver and what they can get out of you" (178). Her cynical word *palaver* at once defines and dismisses men like Corley and Lenehan of "Two Gallants" while at the same time pigeonholing the blarney that young women like the "slavey" and Polly Mooney of "The Boarding House" want from men like Corley and Bob Doran (although, of course, Polly is willing to settle for something else). That Gabriel placates Lily with money suggests the situation at the end of "Two Gallants," even though Gabriel's hush money implies his angst, foreshadowing without revealing any real sin against women. He seems, instead, to patronize them out of both pity and guilt. His Aunt Julia's rendition of the sentimental song from Bellini's *I Puritani* that translates as "Arrayed for the Bridal" (193) is as ironic as Maria's rendition of "I Dreamt That I Dwelt in Marble Halls" in "Clay," since neither emotionally impoverished spinster can hope for a happy rescue by a heroic male. Aunt Kate's protest against the 1903 papal decree that women could no longer sing in church choirs because they could not become ecclesiastics and her self-abnegating withdrawal of the criticism ("O, I don't question the pope's being right. I'm only a stupid old woman and I wouldn't presume to do such a thing"; 195) take us back to the subtext of "The Sisters," in which religion has made women second-class communicants, devout but victimized by the patriarchal authority vested in the priesthood. Aunt Kate's reference to papal decree also reminds us of the smug sinners of "Grace," who complacently vouch for papal infallibility.

Other guests recall characters in other stories. The presence of Freddy Malins and Mr. Browne reminds us of all of the drinkers in Dublin, who escape, like Freddy, into the primarily male preserve of the pub and whose lives, like Farrington's and Kernan's, are being devastated by their escapist addictions. The talk of continental musicians and operas and the Conroys' summers in France, Belgium, or Germany (289) suggests the cosmopolitanism that bests the inebriated Irishman in "After the Race." The musical crowd, one of whom refers to Kathleen Kearney, recalls in a better light than the concert in "A Mother" the Dublin music community that led Shaw into the vocation of music critic and tempted Joyce to become a singer.

Moreover, Miss Ivors provides a link to both "A Mother," with its emphasis on the cultural revival, and "Ivy Day in the Committee Room," but Joyce's last story shows nationalism more favorably than the stories about cultural and political recidivism, perhaps because Miss Ivors is a spirited New Woman with the sturdy independence and directness of a Shavian heroine—the qualities of which Mrs. Kernan was deprived by her ladylike upbringing and conventional marriage. But the fact that Miss Ivors, the self-reliant nationalist, devotes her energy to the Gaelicism whose poetry is honored by Little Chandler in "A Little Cloud" hints that her ideals are misguided. It will be remembered that Shaw, and Joyce after him, dismissed Gaelicism for its retrograde dependence upon a dead language. Miss Ivors's independence may be undermined by her political parochialism, but she provides a conscience for the apolitical Gabriel. Her accusation that he is a "West Briton"—a collaborator and sympathizer with the British oppressor—brings up a leitmotif that occurs in several stories: the theme of betrayal of Ireland by the usurping English. It is revealed in Henchy in "Ivy Day," who is willing to show obeisance to the new English King, Edward VII, if he brings English money to Ireland; in Farrington of "Counterparts," loser to an Englishman in a test of strength; in Jimmy Doyle of "After the Race," the financial loser; and in Duffy of "A Painful Case," who reads a unionist newspaper and fails in love.

Gabriel is perhaps the worst betrayer of Ireland, however, because he is, like the more repressed Duffy, an intellectual, aware that his apolitical writings for the unionist paper display a lack of commitment to his mother country. As an alienated writer he is related to would-be writers Duffy and Chandler, the former preferring continental literature, although he is incapable of acting upon its assumptions, and the latter aspiring to fulfillment by identifying with the romance of the Celtic revival. Like Gabriel, Duffy reads a pro-British paper and, despite his appearance at socialist meetings, has no genuine commitment to his homeland. Moreover, the three boys of the trilogy about childhood ("The Sisters," "An Encounter," and "Araby") seem to have grown up to be Gabriel. As the boy who rejects the priesthood and communion with its devotees might be expected to become, Gabriel is a secularist, but he is thoroughly involved in a spurious communion at the banquet table. Unlike the boy who refused to eat with the philistines, Gabriel is carving the goose for them. Despite his hypocrisy, his values seem to derive from the sweetness and light of the Greek tradition of the "three graces" (204) related to Shaw's Life Force, but he gallantly and ironically relates the graces to his aging hostesses. From a Shavian point of view, his postprandial speech patronizes the philistines by reminding them of their "living duties" (204), abhorrent to the Shavian iconoclast. Gabriel's interest in the cosmopolitan English poet Browning, then in the avant-garde, marks him as a partially enlightened Shavian as well as a betrayer of Irish art: Browning's criticism of decadent Catholicism in "The Bishop Orders His Tomb" and his interest in Renaissance humanism, even its deviant worldliness, interface with Gabriel's view of himself. He thinks of himself as more sophisticated than his aunts and their guests and, like Shaw and Joyce, dislikes Irish provinciality. Like the narrator of "An Encounter," Gabriel wants to escape, knowing what the boy only intuited—that adventure lay outside of Ireland. When Miss Ivors chastises him for ignoring his own country, he retorts, "I'm sick of my own country, sick of it!" (189).

Gabriel is an adult version of the adolescent in "Araby" in that he has supposedly repudiated the romance that lured the boy to disillusioning reality. The *ricorso,* however, comes full circle, for the epiphany of the practical, somewhat stuffy and self-important husband is his discovery that rejection of romantic love has left him self-absorbed, cold, and incapable of deep feeling (which Shaw admittedly sublimated in his writing and his social activism; see Harris 306). In admitting that he has been incapable of love like Michael Furey's, Gabriel falls victim to the heinous ideal from which the boy of "Araby" escaped. Thus he reveals himself to be another worshipper of the dead—the comatose romantic in himself. Gabriel capitulates to a sin in Shaw's ethic, the "deification of love. . . . [T]he substitution of sensuous ecstasy for intellectual activity and honesty is the very devil." Shaw argued that such romanticism is an "infection . . . unbearable" to the realist because it subsists on the illusions of "childish pretendings" (CP 744). Significantly, Michael Furey, an intransigent romantic unenlightened like the boy of "Araby," dies of consumption, the disease of romantic poets. His death symbolizes unregenerate romanticism—the *liebes tod* that underlies the tradition of courtly romance. It is implicit in the picture of the balcony scene of *Romeo and Juliet* that Gabriel notices while Mary Jane is playing her kitsch "Academy piece" (186). Later his lust for his wife Gretta rises as he watches her standing at the top of the stairs like Mangan's sister in "Araby" and Juliet on her balcony. Gretta, who figures the Life Force in *Dubliners* as no other woman does, is nevertheless an incurable but compassionate romantic. She weeps for an irretrievable past, compelled by what Shaw called the "heartscalding" Irish romantic imagination of what might have been.

The sentimental ballad that elicits Gretta's tears is a variation on the *eros-thanatos* dialectic. In this obsession of blighted romantic lovers, the male is a sadomasochistic narcissist and the female is "La Belle Dame Sans Merci"—no doubt what Gretta imagines herself to have been with Michael Furey. It is important, however, to note that, like any philistine girl obedient to family, she went to the convent rather than running away with her lover (her real-life model Nora Barnacle, like Shaw's mother, had more spunk). The ballad that Bartell D'Arcy sings, "The Lass of Aughrim," is in dialogic relationship to the story: Gretta identifies with Lord Gregory, who shuts out his needy lover—in this scenario, Michael Furey. But Gabriel is also comparable to Lord Gregory. In the ballad that moves Gretta to tears, the lord will not let his beloved in out of the rain. Even though Gabriel insists that Gretta wear galoshes to protect herself from the elements, he realizes that he has not let her into his life. His failure to achieve the I-Thou intimacy that invites the beloved into the haven of the self parallels the abandonment of the lowborn lass of Aughrim by her highborn lover. Like Joyce with respect to Nora, Gabriel no doubt feels superior to his beloved from the west of Ireland until he awakens to his failure to love her in the old, romantic way. But the melancholy Celtic note that appeals to Little Chandler, who broods on a poem about a dead woman, compels Gretta's sorrow, which she transmits to her husband.

Thus the dead hold sway in Dublin, even over the natural woman who prefers direct contact with the weather and instinctively reveals the climate of her heart. Gretta can articulate her sense of loss by telling

Gabriel about Michael and crying herself to sleep, but the sense of loss is recapitulated in Aunt Julia (no Juliet she), who has, like Maria of "Clay," lived without love. Both old women can hope only to be the bride of Christ, arrayed for the death that awaits them, whereas Gretta may fare better, for Gabriel may be able to offer her a more fulfilling love. He proposes to himself a "journey westward" (223) which is dialogically related to Shaw's *Candida*, which also concerns a love triangle. The journey to the west alludes to the impetuous young Marchbanks's competition for the love of a married woman against her self-satisfied, middle-aged, moral mate. Marchbanks assesses both himself and Morell as unfit lovers for Candida. Not about to die for love, as Gretta fancifully believes Michael Furey did, the young poet urges Candida's stuffy, self-important husband, "Let us go on a pilgrimage, you to the east and I to the west in search of a worthy lover for her—some beautiful archangel with purple wings" (CP 147). Comparable to Michael Furey, who is, like Gabriel, named for an archangel, Shaw's young artist may have sent a message to Joyce's protagonist, who realizes that "the time had come for him to set out on his journey westward" (223). If the allusion to *Candida* is intentional (and even as a young man Joyce rarely made allusions that were not), Gabriel's quest concerns his need to find a fitter love for Gretta or to become that love himself. His journey will confront him, like the bourgeois Morell's, with thoughts of a young lover who idealized his wife.

Although the pilgrimage to the west is extremely ambiguous in the context of "The Dead," its implications take on new meaning in their relationship to the young lover in *Candida*, who at the play's conclusion goes off on a pilgrimage without his beloved, albeit impelled by her. In "The Dead," the west means to Miss Ivors the Gaeltacht of western Ireland. She urges Gabriel to take "an excursion to the Aran Isles" (188), the remote westernmost part of Ireland where Gaelic is the spoken language. The islands off Galway are in Connacht, the area from which Gabriel's wife came (as did Nora Barnacle). Gabriel's voyage west may thus be a trip in his mind to rediscover his Irish wife and thus to confirm his own Irish identity. Although critics are tempted to think of the west as America because Gabriel shares the name of the hero of Bret Harte's *Gabriel Conroy* (1895) (Gifford 113), the archetypal associations of the west with sunset and dying into life relate closely to the implications of Joyce's coda. In any case, Gabriel's decision to go west suggests reversion to the sentimental romanticism to which Gretta succumbed. Fearing that his own feelings have been inadequate, Gabriel tells himself, "Better pass boldly into that other world, in the full glory of some passion, than fade and wither dismally with age" (223).

The passion that he envies is, however, Michael Furey's (even if the boldness is Shavian). In reality young Michael stood in the rain, in a sexual role-reversal of the ballad that reminds Gretta of him. He makes the foolhardy, romantic gesture of a boy playing the part that Shaw's Don Juan rejects, that of "the romantic man, the Artist, with his love songs and his paintings and his poems"—reflecting the infatuated romanticism that had led Don Juan "at last into the worship of Woman" (CP 380). Whereas Marchbanks personifies such worship, thanks to the heroine he escapes its destructiveness. But the passion that seems to haunt Gabriel is the self-destructive romantic ideal of Gretta's fantasy. If, indeed, Gretta's assertion "I think he died for me" (226) alludes to Yeats's *Cathleen ni Houlihan,* in which Cathleen says that a martyred patriot "died for love of me" (see Gifford 125), Michael's death hints at another Irish folly that Shaw and his disciple disdained—the romantic nationalism that led young men to useless deaths for Ireland. Michael's name—the same as that of the hero of Yeats's patriotic play—suggests the militant and angry angel. His death implies abortive martyrdom for Mother Ireland, sacrifice that is paralleled by the demands of romantic love, which may require the masochistic adoration of the femme fatale.

Shaw's Marchbanks apparently alludes to the Archangel Gabriel as the appropriate lover of Candida, considering that he has compared her to the Madonna by presenting her with a print of a Titian painting of the Virgin. In the miraculous Annunciation, the Archangel Gabriel appears to the Madonna to announce her mysterious condition as the Virgin Mother who will bring forth a savior. Both Shaw and young Joyce believed the artist to be a secular redeemer. "Leaning on the banisters" of the staircase, Gretta seems to symbolize the mediatrix Madonna. She has "grace and mystery in attitude as if she were a symbol of something" (209–10). Apparently she is the Magna Mater, who, according to Don Juan, provides "the keystone" of all of man's ideals in "the worship of woman, of mother-hood, of the family, of the heart" (Plays 378) in the idealization of the Madonna. The Archangel Gabriel is the messenger who brings the good tidings to Mary that she is to be the conduit to renewed spiritual life, one that Joyce's Gabriel glimpses after he sees himself realistically in the hotel mirror—an image that, after Gretta's confession, he determines to change. In his journey westward, seemingly he will heed the admonition voiced by Marchbanks so that he will be worthy of the augury of his name.

Gabriel apparently wants to change into "romantic man," who is, according to Shaw, misguided but a model for behavior which is a step above the "tedious failures" of mankind in the development of Don Juan into the philosopher-artist (see Plays 380–81). To renew himself, Gabriel will have to get out of Ireland, the "abysmal void" of hell described in *Man and Superman,* for "to be in Hell is to drift: to be in Heaven is to steer" (Plays 388). Shaw's committed artist-philosopher, Don Juan, leaves hell to become an archangel like Gabriel, but paradoxically he is thus the subversive Son of Light, Lucifer, to be distinguished from the hedonistic Satan of "Don Juan in Hell." Like Don Juan, Gabriel goes through the dark night of his soul to die into life. If he is to emulate the Shavian archetype, he must first examine hell before choosing the heaven of the heterodox from which he can, like Shelley/Shaw, trumpet his prophecies. Significantly, Joyce/Gabriel, like a Shavian, had in *Dubliners* examined the Irish hell and would in *Portrait* identify with the artist, who is, like Shaw's Don Juan, a social iconoclast and superman.

Throughout the evening at the Liffeyside party, Gabriel is like Shaw's Don Juan, who was "suffering amid the pleasure of hell an agony of tedium" (Plays 224, program note). For Joyce's alter ego, the evening ends in capitulation to the dead, apparently the prelude to his Shavian salvation but also an aesthetic necessity in Joyce's coda. In giving himself over to "the vast hosts" of trimmers in the anteroom of Dante's Inferno, where the living dead languish, the chastened Gabriel identifies with the rest of the Dubliners (as well as the denizens of hell in *Man and Superman*). Like them, he has made no commitment to good or evil, God or Satan. Instead of becoming a Shavian realist (as Stephen Dedalus does in *Portrait*), in his final stream-of-consciousness vision, Gabriel coalesces with the inhabitants of the Irish hell in which nothing changes: religion with "its crooked crosses . . . and . . . barren thorns" has failed; the ideal of romantic love is blighted (for Michael Furey was, after all, another sick Irishman, and he is now dead and buried); and Ireland is a wasteland, whose "dark central plain . . . [and] treeless hills" are blanketed with the death-cold snow—the sin that freezes in Dante's hell—which is "general all over Ireland" (223). Thus Joyce's coda recapitulates the spiritual torpor that appears in theme and variations in each of Joyce's stories of the paralysis of Dublin. As Gabriel drifts off to sleep, he likens his soul's swoon amid the "faintly falling snow" to the last judgment—perhaps Joyce's judgment, corroborating Shaw's, of the drift of Dublin's "living and the dead" (D 223).

The Great *"Immensipater"* "Retaled"
in Bloom & Co.: *Ulysses*

Five

J OYCEANS may be reluctant to consider *Ulysses* in the context of Bernard Shaw because of the dominant aesthetic, psychological, and sexual concerns upon which the lapsed Catholic focused in his avant-garde novel. To the casual reader (if there could be one), *Ulysses* may seem antipathetical to Shaw's socialist propaganda and his prophylactic plays. In Joyce's complex, seemingly obscure, but profoundly original artistic experiment, most early readers detected none of the social messages that we think of as Shaw's métier. However, Shane Leslie, who attacked *Ulysses* as "an odyssey of the sewer" exemplifying "literary Bolshevism" by yoking together "Comedy and Blasphemy," unwittingly suggested the Shavian connection as well as the Shavian objection to *Ulysses*. Such "morbidly pornographic" "literature of the latrine" (quoted in Magalaner and Kain 179) would have deterred readers who fellow-traveled with Shaw's leftist peregrinations. It deterred Shaw himself, who commented on the "dirt" in *Ulysses* while at the same time commending its accurate documentation of his hometown. In recommending "soap and water" to clean up the mess (JJ1 588), Shaw implied, as usual, that the test of literature is its effectiveness as social propaganda.

Nevertheless, the description "literary Bolshevism" suggests the subversive social program of Shaw. Although he did not believe a writer needed to sabotage logocentric structure while exposing social problems and thus arguing for radical change, he did argue that a writer is obligated to trash old literary forms to create a medium appropriate to his message. He therefore broke with the structure of nineteenth-century melodrama and well-made plays in order to accommodate discussions that became symposia on public problems. In challenging the phallocentric language of male-dominated society and literature, Joyce did with language what Shaw repeatedly did in his plays—undercut received values and the machismo of patriarchal culture. Because Shaw deliberately used the language of the dominant culture, he may be considered one of the father figures whom Joyce subverts, but in storming the barricades with comedy and ridiculing male arrogance and assumed domination, Shaw was a great, paternal emancipator for Joyce. From different perspectives, each deconstructed old social and literary edifices, Shaw through his revisionist dramas and Joyce through dissident novelistic strategies. But readers of *Ulysses* with Shaw's agenda for reforming the world would have been (and still are) alienated by Joyce's style, which discards obvious linear, social realism and seems inaccessibly and increasingly self-referential as the novel develops. Until Dominic Manganiello's study *Joyce's Politics* appeared in 1980, few critics took seriously Joyce's own avowal that he was a socialist and consequently, like Manganiello himself, did not look for or notice the significant Shavian parallels and parodies in *Ulysses*. In his biography of Joyce, Manganiello's mentor, Richard Ellmann, records without emphasis Joyce's continued assertions of his allegiance to socialism even while documenting his alienation from politics.

Joyce's own designation of his political inclinations suggests his link to Shaw. While he was living in Trieste in 1905, Joyce defended individualistic socialism in his letters to his brother Stanislaus, making it the servant of his own needs. He believed that "a political conscience would give his work distinction" and that "the triumph of socialism might make for some sort of state subsidy of artists" (quoted in JJ1 204). When Shaw was a young, impoverished, aspiring writer, he propounded such beliefs. Without naming his mentor, Joyce insisted that his opinions were those "of a socialist artist" (JJ1 205). In 1906 his sympathy with socialism prompted him to attend the International Socialist Workers' Congress in Rome. (Shaw had attended the organization's conference in Zurich in 1893). Joyce had read Oscar Wilde's *The Soul of Man under Socialism* and wanted to translate it. As Ellmann writes, the subversive "artist pretends to be Lucifer but is really Jesus" (JJ1 283)—precisely the paradoxical stance of the author of *The Devil's Disciple*. As late as 1915 Joyce was still proclaiming political faith opposed to monarchies (JJ1 394).

Despite the many provocations provided by the bold stylistic virtuosity of *Ulysses* and the strategic analogues that Joyce cleverly grafted onto a text that continues to generate interest in the indeterminacies of its form and content, my analysis of *Ulysses* (and all of Joyce) proceeds in the Joycean mode. As Derek Attridge puts it, in the spirit "of Joyce's writing . . . we can, and must, continue to find ways of re-writing ourselves, our history, our future, one another, in a constantly reworded engagement with the nontextual Real" (191). In engaging the nontextual Real, Joyce continued to rewrite himself and his literary father in *Ulysses*. In some important ways the work derives from the Fabian feminist, who had been a literary progenitor to the youthful, secretive Joyce. Its comedy reveals Joyce's conversion to the Shavian worldview. For Shaw was the master of mockery, a comedian for whom the truth "is the funniest joke in the world" (Krause 204). Joyce, always his covert disciple, became converted to comedy in *Ulysses*. Echoing the master, he said, "Not 'in vino veritas,' but 'in risu veritas'—in laughter, truth" (Rodgers 132). As Zack Bowen notes, "Like Shaw, Joyce was most serious and most profound when at his gayest" (xii). In *Ulysses* Joyce's ironic stance vis à vis his characters suggests Shaw. In his preface to *The Dark Lady of the Sonnets* (1910), the dramatist, who considered himself to be a rival of Shakespeare, could not resist making the Elizabethan into his own image. He stressed Shakespeare's irony: "This impish rejoicing in pessimism, this exultation in what breaks the hearts of common men . . . [is] diagnostic of the immense energy of life which we call genius" (CP 764). In his epic of Dublin life, the younger genius, covert competitor and ambivalent admirer of the comic playwright, continued to satirize favored targets of Shaw's impish pessimism—the idealistic illusions promulgated by church and state and social propaganda for romantic love. Furthermore, in scrutinizing the superior common man, Bloom, and the alienated intellectual, Stephen, *Ulysses* brings together, often for purposes of parody, representative Shavian prototypes: the socialist sympathizer and the superman. In the contrast between Bloom, the egalitarian do-gooder, and Stephen, the artistic elitist—good samaritan and prodigal son—Joyce reveals the differences between the father of many of his ideas and himself.

Though his primary model is Oliver Gogarty, Joyce's character Buck Mulligan is somewhat Shavian. He is an irreverent, blasphemous, comic jester without Shaw's Victorian squeamishness. Stephen fears "the lancet" of Buck's "art" (U 1.152), indicating the literary rivalry that motivated Stephen's creator in his dealings with Gogarty as well as with Shaw and other Irish writers. Perhaps because he had read Buck's "ballad of Joking Jesus" and his description of Stephen's "gloomy jesuit jibes" (1.608, 500), in March 1922 Shaw wrote a postcard to Ezra Pound that mocked Joyce for comparing himself to Christ. Shaw captioned the postcard reproduction of Ribera's *The Dead Christ*, which depicts Mary standing over her dead son, "Miss Shakespear consoling James Joyce, who has fainted on hearing of the refusal of his countryman to subscribe for Ulysses. Isn't it like him?" (BSL 2:766). Such a waggish gesture no doubt established Shaw in Joyce's gallery of betrayers, of whom the witty Mulligan is the prototype. In Joyce's mind Shaw was already in a rogue's gallery (even though Joyce was the rogue who had stolen Shaw's plays), for Joyce believed Shaw had sabotaged *Exiles*. One of "the brood of mockers" (U 1.656–57) like Shaw, the obscene Buck Mulligan calls himself "*übermensch* . . . the superman" (1.708), and the self-denigrating Stephen calls himself "toothless Kinch the superman" (1.496), alluding simultaneously to Nietzsche and to Shaw's *Man and Superman*, dated 1904, the year whose June 16 is celebrated in *Ulysses*.

Furthermore, Stephen's cynicism regarding Ireland is reminiscent of that of the disillusioned Larry Doyle. In *John Bull's Other Island*, Larry has, like Stephen, reluctantly returned to Ireland. Shaw's preface to his Irish play names the "two masters" that Stephen bitterly serves, "an English and an Italian" (U 1.638), the British king and the pope. Moreover, Joyce's amiable Englishman Haines, like Shaw's Tom Broadbent, naively and optimistically idealizes the Irish. Like Broadbent, Haines is "bursting with money" (1.52). He proposes making a "collection" of Stephen's sayings (1.480), almost as if they were to rival the revolutionary maxims of John Tanner, the apostate hero of *Man and Superman*.

Bloom's daylight and late-night ideas are often comparable to Shaw's, even in their paradoxes and inconsistencies. Max Beerbohm's assessment of G. B. S. might apply to both the real and the fictional character: "Shaw's judgments were often scatterbrained, but at least he had brains to scatter" (345). In his hallucinatory fantasy in the Circe episode, Bloom wants to be a powerful figure—politician, orator, and reformer—offering panaceas that parallel Shaw's idiosyncratic Fabian socialism. Bloom's nightmare that he will be martyred like Parnell and Christ corresponds to the fate Shaw averted by being good-natured and insensible to attack. During World War I he was repeatedly stigmatized for his unpopular views, Christlike in their judgment, sermonizing to both the Germans and the English. As Henry Arthur Jones told Shaw, "Every Englishman is against you." Christabel Pankhurst (whose suffrage movement Shaw defended) declared that Shaw, "jester of the British public," had gone too far. "Hostility flared up all over the place" (H1 354, 357). Even Shaw's disciples thought his behavior, like Bloom's in his bad dream, to be quixotic. Aware of G. B. S.'s extravagantly incongruous ideals and his tilts with windmills, Joyce wrote to Harriet Weaver that "Shaw has lived too long on the boreal side of La Mancha" (JJL 3:250). In *Ulysses* Joyce created a comedy of dualities like that of Cervantes (Bowen 86), in which Don Quixote and Sancho Panza are both present in Bloom, one of whose shadow selves is Shaw. In body and earthy tastes, Bloom resembles Sancho, but in his conversation and often in his subconscious Bloom identifies with the tall, thin righter of wrongs whose familiar lean body, like Shaw's, was so unlike that of Joyce's androgynous Ulysses.

Both the characters and the setting of Joyce's novel adumbrate Shavian themes. Poldy's social persona and sexual proclivities are tested in the company of various foils—the citizen in Barney Kiernan's pub as a romantic nationalist, a Shavian *bête noire;* Gerty MacDowell as the feminine woman, about whom Shaw wrote a cautionary chapter in *The Quintessence of Ibsenism;* Bella Cohen as the "manly woman" whom Shaw parodied in *Press Cuttings* (1909) and *The Music Cure* (1913); Molly Bloom as a retort to and test of the New Woman whom Shaw advocated; and Stephen Dedalus, the young artist in search of a father. Shavian theory underlies Joycean praxis in his study of the country that absorbed both writers.

In *Back to Methuselah*'s fourth play, "The Tragedy of an Elderly Gentleman" (1921), the old father figure turns to Ireland "with a hungry heart, to the mystery and beauty of these haunted islands, thronged with spectres from a magic past, made holy by the footsteps of the wise men of the West." He calls Ireland "an emerald gem set in a silver sea!" (BM 205)—an epithet that Joyce pocketed for use in the Aeolus section of *Ulysses*. As Karen Lawrence tells us, Joyce added his headlines after the original publication of *Ulysses* (56–58) and, it seems, after he read and lifted the Shavian description. In Aeolus, Ireland became "ERIN, GREEN GEM OF THE SILVER SEA" (U 7.236). Although Gifford and Seidman cite the source of this headline as Thomas Moore's "Let Erin Remember the Days of Old," in which Ireland is "the emerald gem of the western world" (59), or J. P. Curran's "Cuisle Mo Chroidhe," in which "Dear Erin" is "an emerald set in the ring of the sea" (133), Shaw's revision of the two directly prefigures Joyce's borrowing, probably because the speech of the Elderly Gentleman touches on other Ulyssean themes. The old man refers to the Irish claim to Jewish descent and laments (for the year is A.D. 3000) a "world bereft of its Jews and its Irish" (BM 206). Joyce documents a Dublin in which the Jew *is* the quintessential Irishman—good-natured, intelligent, but beleaguered, like the sort that the old man admires: "Think of the position of the Irish who had lost all their political faculties by disuse except that of nationalist agitation, and who owe their positions as the most interesting race on earth solely to their sufferings" (BM 206).

Ulysses amply documents the "interesting" Irish race and the sufferings of its credible Jewish hero, using Shavian theories regarding nationalism. As if slyly to remind us of Shaw's presence, Joyce places strategic allusions to Shaw in his text, each of which suggests a Shavian theory expatiated upon or parodied in *Ulysses*. Two of his allusions are political. In the Cyclops episode, the citizen ends his tirade against the British with a reference to the "Hell upon earth" of ordinary British sailors flogged "on the training ships at Portsmouth. A fellow writes that calls himself *Disgusted One*" (12.1331–32). As Gifford and Seidman point out, the disgusted one is G. B. S., who wrote in the London *Times* on June 14, 1904, "In short, there are certain practices which however expedient they may be, are instinctively barred by the humanity of the highest races: and corporal punishment is one of them. I should blush to offer a lady or a gentleman more reasons for my disgust at it." Although the jingoistic citizen, like Joyce himself in 1903 (CW 113), objects to "corporal punishment" perpetrated by "your glorious

British navy, that bosses the earth" (U 12.1333, 1346), Bloom takes the internationalist, Shavian position, which argues that such disgusting discipline is the "same everywhere" (12.1360), and, like the socialist Shaw, despises "Persecution" for perpetuating "national hatred among nations" (12.1417–18). Yet another political allusion to Shaw in *Ulysses* is Skin-the-Goat's reference to Ireland as the "Achilles heel" of England (16.1360). It refers to *John Bull's Other Island,* which analyzed the Irish political situation in 1904, the year of Bloom's day. In his preface to the play Shaw wrote, "The Irish coast is for the English invasion-scaremonger the heel of Achilles" (CP 451).

In *Ulysses,* Joyce also describes sociosexual roles in terms that Shaw introduced. In the Nausicaa section, Gerty's stream of consciousness employs the categories that Shaw defined in his tract on Ibsen and in *The Philanderer* (1893) to delineate and subvert sexual stereotypes. Gerty is a "womanly woman" (U 13.435) who projects onto Bloom the part of "manly man" (13.210). She emulates Shaw's caricatured feminine woman in the little-known farce *Press Cuttings* (1909). Lady Corinthia Fanshawe is a stereotyped romantic icon who carries a little gun that, according to the lady, is not loaded. She relies on her seductive charms to get her man, trapping Balsquith (a portmanteau for prime ministers Balfour and Asquith), who prides himself on his masculinity. Corinthia lures and enslaves him in a relationship based on hierarchy. The woman pretends to be on the bottom, but through devious manipulation, something like Molly Bloom's, she rules the man. As she says with a smile, "I am one of those women who are accustomed to rule the world through men. Man is ruled by beauty, by charm" (Plays 1101)— patriarchal propaganda of which Gerty MacDowell is a ready consumer.

Corinthia's opposite in Shaw's woman's liberation satire of role reversal is Mrs. Rosa Carmina Banger, a violently aggressive female who bullies men. In the Circe episode Bella/Bello Cohen is the manly woman whom Shaw parodies in Mrs. Banger. H. W. Massingham commented in the *Nation* (April 18, 1914) on "Shaw's fashion of holding romance upside down" (quoted in Morgan 71)—a technique that Joyce develops fully in *Ulysses,* in which Bloom/Flower combines the male and female scripts. Macho Buck Mulligan, "the sex specialist" (15.1772), says that "Dr Bloom is bisexually abnormal" (15.1775–76), and Dr. Punch Costello labels Bloom as "a finished example of the new womanly man"

(15.1798–99)—nomenclature that Shaw used to describe the androgynous male who had rejected the patriarchal model for masculinity. Ten years before Otto Weininger's study *Geschlect und Charakter* (Sex and Character; 1903)—a bigoted attack on both women and Jews from which Ellmann believes the pejorative term "womanly man" derives (JJ1 477)—Shaw had propounded the "new womanly man" as a positive role model, but he did not test it in bedroom or bordello. In *The Philanderer* (1893), in order to join the Ibsen Club, a man has to be a "womanly man" (Plays 53).

Shaw's ideas about politics, sex, and paternity find their way into *Ulysses*. The Scylla and Charybdis episode contains, however, the only direct reference to Shaw, perhaps appropriately, for the section includes Stephen's discussion of paternity. The Quaker librarian refers to the Shakespearean theories of Shaw and his Irish friend (and, later, biographer) Frank Harris: "I hope Mr Dedalus will work out his theory for the enlightenment of the public. And we ought to mention another Irish commentator, Mr George Bernard Shaw. Nor should we forget Mr Frank Harris. His articles on Shakespeare in the *Saturday Review* were surely brilliant. Oddly enough he too draws for us an unhappy relation with the dark lady of the sonnets" (9.438–42). *The Dark Lady of the Sonnets* is the title of Shaw's play about Shakespeare (pirated by Joyce in Zurich) and Mary Fitton—a love triangle paralleling both the triangle in *Hamlet* and the Bloom-Blazes-Molly triangle of *Ulysses* except that it includes, as in Stephen's post-Shavian theorizing, two women and a man, the subject of Shaw's *Philanderer*. In drawing an unhappy triangle, Stephen emulates Shaw and Harris. But more important, the library episode suggests a link between Shaw's and Joyce's ideas about paternity. Both questioned the validity of legal fathers, and both advanced the idea that the creative artist is self-generated. In *Ulysses* Stephen's spiritual father turns out to be the hermaphroditic Leopold Bloom, who is often a surrogate Shaw.

The Credible Androgyne: "Such is Manowife's Lot To Lose and Win Again"

Joyce's womanly man, Leopold Bloom is a test case and sometime parody of Shaw's prescription for androgyny. With statements such as "I always assumed that a woman was a person exactly like myself"; "Why not personify God as a woman?"; and woman is a "man in petticoats," whereas man is "a woman without petticoats" (PP 174), Shaw established himself as an advocate of breaking down gender codes. While late Victorian rebels pressured for acceptance of the New Woman, Shaw perceived what Carolyn Heilbrun has recently confirmed, "that our definitions of the terms 'masculine' and 'feminine' are themselves little more than unexamined, received ideas" (xiv). Records of lectures and interviews with titles like "Bernard Shaw Bossed by Wife" enlarged the picture. G. B. S. pointed out that "we have no word which includes men and women. It just shows how little we realize men and women belong to the same species. No one denies that a stallion and a mare belong to the same species" (I&R 405). He wrote Ellen Terry (September 21, 1896) that "the ideal woman is a man" (BSL 1:659). He averred that "women are an altogether superior species" (Winsten, *Days* 209). Shaw's wife Charlotte went to America without G. B. S. in April 1914 while *Pygmalion* (starring Stella Campbell) premiered. In the *Boston Post* (April 29, 1914), the newspaper of the city from which the mysterious letter in *Finnegans Wake* comes, she revealed her husband's sexual politics: "Mr. Shaw goes so far as to believe [like Molly Bloom] that all government should be by women. He believes women are more capable of management than men and he is a thorough feminist. Women, he says, should be placed on all governing boards" (I&R 180). In proselytizing for woman's emancipation and even gynecocracy, the Fabian believed that he was also fighting for man's freedom from the onus of depriving a fellow creature of liberty and equal opportunity. As Irving Wardle avers, "Feminism was one of his first causes and, fashion aside, you can see why. It applied to his own case. Like Annie Besant and Beatrice Webb, he knew that his only hope of getting into the exclusive gentleman's club was to smash in the door and beat the resident drones at their own game" (165). Although his impish humor sometimes infuriated self-righteous feminists who thought their plight was no laughing matter, Shaw argued vociferously for women's rights and equality of income (albeit not always consistently) and "used Woman the Huntress as a stereotype to combat the Victorian stereotype of the Sexless Angel" (Holroyd, *The Genius* 183). He advised that in the interest of parity and human progress, man should be more "womanly"—sensitive, nonaggressive, cooperative—and woman should be more "manly"—self-assertive, self-reliant, and self-realizing.

Elaine Showalter's study *Sexual Anarchy: Gender and Culture at the*

Fin de Siècle sets the scene for rebellions such as Shaw's. "The 1880s and 1890s," Showalter notes, were decades "when all the laws that governed sexual identity and behavior seemed to be breaking down" (3). In the midst of the "battle against the New Woman" (41), Shaw came to her defense. *The Quintessence of Ibsenism* decries the sexism of purity-snooper William Stead, editor of the *Review of Reviews,* who condemned the emancipated Marie Bashkirtseff for not being "a natural woman with a heart to love, and a soul to find its supreme satisfaction in sacrifice for lover or for child." Such stereotyping was to G. B. S. one of the worst of "idealist abominations" (MCE 55). He championed the woman who naturally exercised "for her own sake all the powers that were given to her" (MCE 53).

Citing many contemporary sources that may have influenced Joyce's view that women are the dominant sex, Richard Brown argues that Joyce was a feminist who drew on "Ferrero, Carpenter, Matthia and Mathilde Vaertine," among others (107). He does not mention Shaw, in whom Joyce found all of the necessary feminist and socialist ideas, as well as the emphasis on androgyny that Joyce deconstructs in *Ulysses.* In the Ithaca episode, Bloom is aware of "the fallaciously inferred debility of the female, the muscularity of the male," and "this feministic recognition of female strength allows him to think his way out of a jealous reaction to Molly's infidelity" (Richard Brown 112). Shaw's *Philanderer* (a copy of which Joyce owned before 1920) no doubt also helped. His plays, late and soon, ridicule jealousy. *The Philanderer* propounds the womanly man, whereas in *The Man of Destiny* (1895), the youth who cleverly connives to get Napoleon's dispatches turns out to be a young female (who is also Irish) whose verbal joust with the male chauvinist general constitutes the play. In *Mrs. Warren's Profession* (1894), the tough-minded madam is as efficient at her business as her male, capitalist friends are at theirs. In *Misalliance* (1910), Lina, the Polish acrobat—designated by the atypical ingenue Hypatia as "the man-woman or woman-man or whatever you call her"—combines forthright daring with female attractiveness, whereas according to Hypatia, Percival, despite having a name designating him as a hero of medieval romance, is a "mean, stupid, cowardly, selfish masculine male man" (Plays 626–27)—which may actually be a realistic summary of the qualities of the medieval hero. Lina's objections to the goings-on in the house of underwear tsar John Tarleton are, however, those that

Shaw could have made to *Ulysses:* "You seem to think of nothing but making love. . . . It is disgusting. It is unhealthy. Your women are kept idle and dressed up for no other purpose than to be made love to" (642). An androgynous outsider like Bloom, she believes (as he does in fantasy) in the importance of taking risks, but she disdains the emphasis on eroticism that preoccupies Mr. and Mrs. Bloom. She is like another Shavian manly woman, the cross-dresser Annajanska, the Bolshevik empress—the title figure of Shaw's 1917 play about a revolutionary amazon princess. In 1920 Shaw argued that "the sexes wear different boots and bonnets, not different souls: that is why I have left the soul out, and concentrated on the boots and bonnets" (quoted in Watson 27). In admiring androgyny, Shaw posited (and sometimes parodied) its social merits. As if in reply to Shaw's phallic women, Joyce documents androgyny in a social as well as sexual and psychological context, making fun of the Shavian model while at the same time paying homage to it.

Shaw's dramas, like *Ulysses,* often center on a social outsider who aims, like the Devil's Disciple or John Tanner, to reform the philistines and remind them of their bigotry and misguided, sometimes fanatical ideals, for Shaw enjoyed taunting the smug, compact majority as much as his covert disciple did. Indeed, one of Joyce's cues for using a Jewish hero in a novel about the Irish might have come from *John Bull's Other Island* (an important book in Joyce's library), for Larry Doyle compares the Irish to Jews to whom "the Almighty gave . . . brains and bid us farm them" (Plays 430–31). G. B. S. admiringly credited "the Jews . . . from Moses to Marx and Lassalle" with inspiring "all the revolutions" (CP 179). His subversive outsiders are, admittedly, rarely as beleaguered as Bloom is, for while representing the social conscience of the indispensable opposition, they add to the pride and haughtiness of Stephen Dedalus a dedication to social activism, a Fata Morgana over which Bloom can only fantasize. In his Jewish antihero Joyce examines the ludicrous, sometimes painful, sometimes heroic consequences of not being accepted by the dominant group. Being a womanly man and a member of a minority group immediately separates such an Irishman from the rest of the male tribe, for, in a conquered country dominated by Jansenist Catholicism, unenlightened males have little to fall back upon except their ideals of manhood, national (and racial) identity, and their supposedly superior position in a patriarchy supported by xenophobic religion. While juxtaposing Bloom and other Dubliners, *Ulysses* unfolds as an interior study of the womanly man and his foils in an entrenched patriarchal society, in which male power is a sustaining illusion for men, despite the fact that their upbringing has often been matriarchal.

Many of Bloom's characteristics are stereotypically female: his personalism; his concern for familial relationships; his nurturing benevolence; his nonviolence; his sensitivity to the loss of his spouse's love, the death of a friend, the painful memory of his dead son. A concerned father of a daughter instead of a son, a lover of cats instead of dogs, he is a caretaker for his wife. He cooks and serves breakfast, runs errands, and looks away—as women were supposed to—from his mate's adultery. Despite his gender, Bloom often functions as mediatrix and intercessor—in Catholic Ireland, the nearest a woman can come to Godhead. Compassionate regarding the misfortunes of others, he leads a blind man across the street. Like the famed Fabian feminist, he is especially sensitive to the suffering of women, like Dignam's widow, for whom he tries to get insurance money. On a mundane level, Bloom's efforts emulate those of G. B. S., for upon the execution of James Connolly, socialist leader of the Irish Citizen Army, in the failed 1916 Easter uprising, Shaw "subscribed heavily to a fund for Connolly's widow and the children, contributing more than a third of the amount collected" (Weintraub, *Unexpected Shaw* 167). Also a do-gooder, Bloom feels sorry for Mrs. Breen, who has to put up with a "Meshuggah" husband (8.314), and Mina Purefoy "in the lying-in hospital in Holles street" (8.281–82).

A sentimental humanitarian, Bloom has "the warmth of heart, true sincerity, the bond of sympathy with love" recommended ironically by Shaw's Devil in *Man and Superman* (CP 388). Mina Purefoy's difficult childbirth prompts him, like Shaw an incorrigible projector, to think that it is "time someone thought about" doing something to ease the pain of childbirth instead of "gassing" about it in evasive, high-toned language—"Flapdoodle to feed fools on" (8.382). Even the word *Flapdoodle* and the fact that on any subject he would talk "for an hour so he would and talk steady" (12.895–96) smack of Shaw (and the "manly," critical side of Bloom's personality). Joyce's fastidious, prudent hero, concerned with social issues, nevertheless hates "dirty eaters" (8.696) and eats "tenderly," turning "a fringe of a doyley down under the vase" to create "Order" (11.614, 637–38). Like Shaw, who denounced "Killing for Sport" (1914) only to be criticized by masculinists, Bloom is ridiculed by the barflies at Barney Kiernan's pub for advocating "humane methods" with animals: "God, he'd have a soft hand under a hen" (12.844–45). Revolted by animal slaughter, Shaw, like Bloom, preferred the "creative" and "contemplative" man to hunters who kill as a pastime (CP 140).

For Bloom's kindnesses, the citizen, a nameless character representing the average drunken Irish nationalist, snidely alludes to him as "a half and half" (12.1052–53), hence a hermaphrodite; and the nasty narrator thinks to himself, after Bloom praises Blazes Boylan as an excellent organizer, "That explains the milk in the coconut and absence of hair on the animal's chest. Blazes doing the tootle on the flute" (12.996–98). Disapproving of cruelty to animals or women, the pacifistic cuckold protects and nurtures Stephen Dedalus, defending him with words, lecturing him—as he does the barflies—on the evils of drink (as the teetotaler Shaw might) and plying the drunken young man with cocoa, perhaps in a scene of fantasy fulfillment for Joyce, who wanted but was denied the wholehearted support of Shaw, who refused to give the novelist financial aid solicited for *Ulysses*. Privately very generous with his time and advice, Shaw may have had reasons—the suspicion that the younger man had looted *Candida* in writing *Exiles* and certainty that Joyce had stolen two of his plays—for not taking his fellow Dubliner under his androgynous wing.

Joyce associated Poldy with potatoes (the *pomme de terre* and an Irish talisman) and melons and named him Bloom, alias Flower—all of which intimates his association with Gea Tellus, the earth goddess. In his Homeric schema, Joyce relates Bloom's genitals to the lotus in the *Odyssey*. The lotus that lures Odysseus' men from their seafaring duties is probably hashish, a plant that induces the nonviolent languor despised by phallocentric societies. Such details mark Bloom as different from his chauvinistic fellow Irishmen, just as his race does. Although critics like Ira Nadel muster evidence of Bloom's "Jewishness" and Erwin Steinberg denies it, others like Bryan Cheyette qualify such assertions with evidence of Bloom's "indeterminate" racial identity (41), which is, like his sex, inconclusive. Bloom's maternity, which throws his Semitic racial identity into question, perhaps relates him to Shaw, for Bloom's mother's name is Ellen Higgins. This may be significant, considering Joyce's hypersensitivity to names; the maternal name may be a sly allusion to the mother of Professor Higgins, the phonetician in

Pygmalion (1914). In a matriarchate, Bloom's alias, Henry, would make him Henry Higgins. Furthermore, Peter Costello writes that Ellen is the daughter of Julius Higgins (10), who may be a portmanteau carrying two Shaw self-portraits, Julius Caesar of *Caesar and Cleopatra* and Higgins of *Pygmalion*. If Mark Shechner is right in asserting that Joyce wanted to play the part of Pygmalion (hence of a male reversing roles with a woman, who gives birth) to Nora Barnacle's Galatea and hence to create her (64–65), the maternal lineage of Bloom is all the more provocative. In the Circe scene he will, indeed, give birth. But in Shaw's drama and Joyce's life women were not so easily sculpted by fellow members of the dramatis personae. Like Eliza Doolittle, Nora turned out to be less malleable than her would-be creator wanted her to be, but in Molly Bloom Joyce had free rein to mold her female consciousness (unlike Bloom, even though he instructs her on the meaning of "metempsychosis"; 4:339). Joyce did so with the imprimatur of his precursor, who argued that the artist uses women, studies them, re-forms them in the service of his art (CP 157).

Combined with Bloom's supposedly female virtues are masculine characteristics that are not epic and masculinist like those of his counterpart, Odysseus (he does not, for example, massacre Molly's suitor). More like Shaw's Androcles in *Androcles and the Lion* (1914), Bloom resembles the "plausible hero" whom Shaw preferred. A bit of the Shavian "pure fool enlightened by compassion" (Carpenter 170–71), a person whose wisdom comes from the heart, one who respects reality and displays consideration and sympathy, a Shaw hero broadly represents "the primal republican stuff of which all true society is made"—"a real man, shorn of the romantic, the histrionic, the chivalric" (GBS 338). Bloom is what Shaw called a "credible hero"—paradoxically an unheroic hero such as the playwright advocated in explaining his conception of Caesar in *Caesar and Cleopatra*. Caesar's "freedom from ideals, natural benevolence, . . . active intellect, and . . . passion for humanity" are the merits of the pragmatic, opportunistic Bloom. Like Shaw's Caesar, he is a "serviceable" modern man scripted in dialogic relationship to past heroism. Joyce treated the archetypal Greek hero in a modern setting; Shaw placed the plausible modern hero in a historical setting familiar to all students of Roman history.

Bloom is a credible protagonist, like Caesar, "in whom we can recognize our own humanity, and who, instead of walking, talking, eating, drinking, sleeping, making love and fighting single combats in a monotonous ecstasy of continuous heroism . . . is heroic in the true human fashion . . . touching the summits only at rare moments, and finding the proper level of occasions, condescending with humor and good sense to all of the prosaic ones, as well as rising to the noble ones" (quoted in GBS 338). Joyce, who was reading *The Devil's Disciple* while writing *Ulysses* (see JJ1 788), also found pertinent advice in Shaw's conception of General Burgoyne, another credible anticipation of the modern Ulysses, whom Joyce places in the banal surroundings of workaday Dublin. In more exotic settings like Africa or Egypt, Shaw situated androgynous virtue in both male and female: his maternal Lady Cicely in *Captain Brassbound's Conversion* parallels the paternal Caesar. In describing Shaw's hero, Richard Dietrich could just as well be outlining Joyce's conception of Bloom—and of Cleopatra as Molly. Dietrich writes that Shaw develops Caesar's identification with Christ through "demonstrations of Caesar's childlike nature (in contrast to Cleopatra's childish nature), of Caesar's loving-kindness, presaging the *filios* and *agape* of the New Testament (in contrast to Cleopatra's possessive erotic love), and of Caesar's selflessness (in contrast to Cleopatra's selfishness)" ("Shavian Psychology" 166). Caesar judges himself, like the Sphinx, to be "part brute, part woman, and part god—nothing of man in me at all" (Plays 25).

The credible hero of *Ulysses* is similarly gender-indeterminate. A survivor who shuns the guileful violence of Odysseus, he supports his family as an advertising canvasser in a profession of which Shaw disapproved: "Exempt from all moral obligations the most respectable newspapers give up the greater part of their space every day to statements which every well-instructed person knows to be false, and dangerously false" (*Essays in Fabian Socialism* 215). Despite his warning, according to Archibald Henderson's 1911 biography *George Bernard Shaw*, during his first nine years in London Shaw earned his "greatest fee—five pounds—for a patent medicine advertisement" (43). As a venal salesman of ideas (unlike Stephen/Joyce, the proponent of art), unruffled by inconsistencies, Bloom writes advertising copy as Shaw did before he became famous. Even as a journalist in London, Shaw sold his ideas while publicizing or playing consumer advocate regarding two of Bloom's consuming interests—music and music drama.

Bloom's work as a profane propagandist is acceptably male, even though, as a service job, it hints of androgyny. Unlike the proud ivory-tower intellectual Stephen, he is willing to violate aesthetic principles to sell his ideas. In "the old advertising impresario" whose "art has a decidedly commercial cast" (Bowen 84), Joyce perhaps satirized publicists like Shaw. Furthermore, in documenting Bloom's postal affair with a typist, Joyce may covertly indulge in self-irony, deflating his own passionate letters to Nora Barnacle in late 1909 (see JJL 2:232–82) as well as celebrated epistolary amours such as Shaw's with actresses Ellen Terry and Stella Campbell. Shaw's notorious and supposedly glamorous letter-writing liaisons were well known among literary gossips while Joyce was finishing *Ulysses. My Life and Some Letters* by Stella Campbell was published in 1922, and while Joyce was writing *Finnegans Wake,* Campbell quarreled quite publicly with Shaw because he refused to let her print all of his correspondence with her, for his wife would have been hurt by the contents of the love letters. Bloom's epistolary amour interfaces inferentially with Shavian and Joycean behavior, but his onanistic stratagem in Nausicaa for satisfying his heterosexual lust veers away from Shavian connection while still distinguishing the plausible hero from the macho missionary of sex, Blazes Boylan.

An all-round man with intellectual curiosity and a scientific bent, reminiscent of the omnivorous Shaw, Bloom is interested in the arts, literature, religion, and especially politics. He takes a Shavian (and Joycean) anticlerical view of religion. The preface to *Major Barbara* satirizes the Salvation Army and delivers a diatribe against confession, whether Catholic or Evangelical. Bloom agrees with the Shavian assessment: "Confession. Everybody wants to. . . . Penance. Punish me please. Great weapon in their [the priests'] hands . . . repentance, skindeep. . . . Salvation army blatant imitation" (5.425–33). Like Shaw, Bloom recognizes that there is little or no difference between the major brands of organized Christianity, except that the Protestants copy the Catholics. Father Conmee sermonizes on missionary zeal ("Save China's millions"), but "the Protestants are the same" (5.325–26). On ethical and political issues Bloom echoes Shaw. Indeed, Bloom fancies himself to be the "born preacher" and "champion" of "all progressive movements" that Joyce found in G. B. S. (CW 208).

Irish Nationalism: "The Vilest Bogeyer but Most Attractionable Avatar"

In the *New Statesman* (July 12, 1913), Shaw declared that patriotism in Ireland is "a morbid condition which a healthy man must shake off to keep sane" (*The Matter with Ireland* 81). In Barney Kiernan's pub, the citizen is a bogey nationalist who has succumbed to the morbid condition, whereas Bloom is an attractive (and, to the citizen, objectionable) avatar of healthy humanistic ethics like Shaw's. The citizen "gladiator" is juxtaposed to the ancient, archetypal Irish warrior—"a broadshouldered deepchested stronglimbed frankeyed redhaired freelyfreckled shaggybearded widemouthed largenosed longheaded deepvoiced barekneed brawnyhanded hairylegged ruddyfaced sinewyarmed hero" who is "seated on a large boulder at the foot of a round tower" (12.151–55). The round tower of Irish monastic antiquity dates back to the eighth century A.D. when monks were trying to save precious sacred objects from the invading Vikings; incongruously, it does not coincide historically with the prehistory and protohistory of heroic myth, but Shaw used this symbol for romantic Ireland as a prop in *John Bull's Other Island*. Ironically, the modern, unheroic citizen fancies himself a patriotic hero like those whom Joyce catalogues (including, inconsistently, several Shaw favorites—Napoleon, Caesar, and Cleopatra—as well as "The Man that Broke the Bank at Monte Carlo" and "The Woman Who Didn't"; U 12.185–87). To the citizen, "having a great confab with himself and that bloody mangy mongrel, Garryowen" (12.119–20), and to his cronies, the unromantic Bloom—a Shavian realist—denounces "force, hatred, history, all that. That's not life for men and women, insult and hatred. And everybody knows that it's the very opposite of that that is really life. . . . Love" (12.1481–85). The citizen puts down such Shavian zeal with heavy irony, calling Bloom "a new apostle to the gentiles" (12.1489).

After *The Shewing up of Blanco Posnet* (1909), which Joyce criticized in his review for its religious good-Samaritanism, and Shaw's pantomime *Androcles and the Lion* (1913), both Shaw's critics and his fans began to associate him with apostolic mission. His Androcles has, indeed, Bloomian qualities. Although his "big strong" wife nags him, Androcles does not complain (Plays 685). A miracle that Androcles can perform is to live with his wife "without beating her." Unlike the fierce, warlike Ferrovius, Androcles worries about the gladiators, even though they are assigned to kill him: "Let them rage and kill; let us be brave and suffer" (698). Like Bloom, he is a friend to animals, even though Garryowen, Mr. Giltrap's surly dog, doesn't treat Bloom with the Christian charity that the lion accords Androcles—as H. G. Wells called him, the "holy silly man" (quoted in H2 287). The holy silly man triumphs over the compact majority, led by the emperor, just as Bloom triumphs over the citizenry, led by their ineffectual champion, whose greatest prowess is displayed in his ability to consume alcohol. Nevertheless, Bloom's faith in love is comparable to that of the little tailor. In a 1913 review of *Androcles,* Desmond McCarthy described him as "the 'pure fool,' the sort of little man who nowadays might go about in fibre shoes and an indiarubber coat to avoid using the skins of animals and drink almond milk with his tea. Yet in him burns a little flame of courage that no wind of misery or torment can make flicker" (Evans 213). In the same year, Dixon Scott declared of Shaw that "a passion for purity, gentleness, truth, justice, and beauty is the force at the base of all his teaching. . . . [H]is message [is] one of the most tonic of our time" (Evans 222). In his mental life, if not in the latrine, Bloom is a lot like Shaw.

In 1904, in his preface to *John Bull's Other Island,* Shaw's passion for truth spurred him to write about how retrograde patriotism and religion kept the Irish in bondage to the British. In this play Larry Doyle analyzes the preference of the average Irishman for "imagination" as an escape from sordid realities. The Cyclops episode in Barney Kiernan's pub presents this type in the citizen who is accompanied by the mutt Garryowen, later revealed, ironically, to belong to Gerty MacDowell's grandpa. The philistine drunk has many of the qualities named by Shaw to mock the Irish stereotype (while putting down the patronizing English): "Ireland is the only spot on earth which still produces the ideal Englishman of history. Blackguard, bully, drunkard, foulmouth, flatterer, beggar, backbiter, venal functionary, corrupt judge, envious friend, vindictive opponent, unparalleled political traitor" (CP 443).

Imitating the "gay, skeptical, amusing, blaspheming, witty fashion which suits the flexibility of the Irish mind very well" (CP 445), Joyce portrays a bigoted Irish Irelander with many of the characteristics of "the ideal Englishman" produced in Erin. Ironically, in a pub on Little Britain Street near the Green Street court where Irish patriots were arraigned and tried, Joyce's loudmouthed Guinness patriot spouts nationalistic rhetoric and clichés that are in dialogic relationship to Shaw's preface to *John Bull's Other Island*. In the section called "The Curse of Nationalism," which defines the citizen's ostentatious, overly ardent, maudlin love of country, Shaw wrote that "Nationalism stands between Ireland and the light of the world. Nobody in Ireland of any intelligence likes Nationalism any more than a man with a broken arm likes having it set. A healthy nation is as unconscious of its nationality as a healthy man of his bones. But if you break a nation's nationality, it will think of nothing else but getting it set again" (CP 457). Moreover, "a conquered nation is like a man with cancer; he can think of nothing else. . . . The windbags of the two rival platforms are the most insufferable of all windbags" (456). Joyce's totemic Irishman fulfills Shaw's definition of the cursed jingoist: "It requires neither knowledge, character, conscience, diligence in public affairs, nor any virtue, private or communal, to thump the Nationalist . . . tub; nay, it puts a premium on the rancor or callousness that has given rise to the proverb that if you put an Irishman on the spit you can always find another Irishman to baste him. . . . [I]n Ireland all political oratory is Jingo oratory" (456).

In the Cyclops section of *Ulysses*, dominated by the uncouth patriot, Bloom is the Irishman who is basted. The episode juxtaposes romantic Ireland (as Yeats wrote, "dead and gone") and its modern, debased counterparts to the reasonable, moderate, prudent outsider, Bloom—like Shaw and Joyce, an Irishman despite the efforts of his countrymen to alienate him. The episode gives a habitat and voice to the Irish political character that Shaw exposed in his 1904 play. In it, it will be remembered, Larry Doyle says that the Irishman "can't be intelligently political; he dreams of what the Shan Van Vocht said in ninety eight. If you want to interest him in Ireland you've got to call the unfortunate island Kathleen ni Houlihan and pretend that she's a little old woman. It saves thinking. It saves working. It saves everything except imagination . . . and imagination's such a torture that you can't bear it without whiskey" (CP 411).

In the first section of *Ulysses*, Stephen associates the old milkwoman at the Martello tower with Mother Ireland, but she does not even speak Gaelic, so deracinated is she. In the pub Joyce's "veteran patriot champion" thinks of Ireland as "the poor old woman" (12.1377–78), Kathleen ni Houlihan, whom Larry Doyle dismissed as the sentimental icon of myth that the Irish substitute for reality. The citizen outdoes himself in singing "A Nation Once Again" (12:917), insisting that "they will come again and with a vengeance . . . the champions of Kathleen ni Houlihan" (12:1374–75). If he, his drunken cronies, and the mangy dog are any indicator, however, the citizen's talk is illusion, underscored by the fact that Joyce's readers would be reminded of the 1916 fiasco of the Easter Rising and by the incongruous contingency of the drunken barroom blather and parodies of the language of epic, romance, and myth—the exaggerated products of the heartscalding imagination. The barflies are ridiculous moderns compared to their inspirations in a once fertile land with epic warriors like Finn MacCool and Cuchulain, whose heroism Joyce deflates through grandiloquence. Apparently for the Irishman, past or present, words take precedence over reality. If the citizen is a metempsychosed Finn and the mutt Garryowen an avatar of Cuchulain (whose totemic animal was the dog: he is the hound of Culann), the cycles of history are winding down. Although, as in *John Bull's Other Island,* history repeats itself, Ireland seems also to be in vulgar decline.

Bigoted, drunken talk passes for patriotism. In the *New Statesman* in July 1913, Shaw wrote that "senseless Fenian maunderings," conceit, ignorance, "insular contempt for foreigners," bad manners, "and the other common weaknesses . . . sometimes masquerade as patriotism. . . . [A] bad Irishman is the vilest thing on earth, and a good one is a saint" (*The Matter with Ireland* 81–82). This could be a gloss of Joyce's conception of the citizen and his parody of saintly Bloom. The designated patriot displays all of the narrowness and prejudice of fanatical nationalism, religious intransigence, and their concomitant, racism. The anti-Semite's pursuit of Bloom for having told him and his pals the truth regarding the ethnic background of their Savior reveals the essential impotence of such irrational jingoism. The citizen—hardly Cyclops throwing a boulder at the retreating Odysseus—throws a biscuit tin—hardly Cuchulain's cudgel either—after the retreating Ulysses figure and sics the dog, a poor excuse for the hero, on Bloom. The barbaric Cyclops thus confirms Larry Doyle's skeptical view of Ireland: imagination and talk, both a cause and effect of drink, characterize the life of the citizenry. Among Irish writers known to Joyce, Shaw was the only one consistently to debunk romantic imposture such as Joyce documents with comic verve in the barroom scene. Yeats had, of course, written a serious poetic drama lauding the fine old woman, *Cathleen ni Houlihan* (1902). George Moore had supported the aims of the nationalist theater until, disillusioned, he wrote *Hail and Farewell* (1911–14) to express his adieu to the literary revival and his disapproval of Catholicism as antipathetic to art. But Moore's ostentatious conversion to Protestantism and his continued association with the elitist landowning aristocracy separate him from the lapsed Christians and downstart, expatriated Dubliners Shaw and Joyce. Both were suspicious of crapulous Irish patriotism—as Shaw put it, "the perversion of fruitful brainpower into flatulent protest" (CP 456).

Shaw had debunked the Gaelic movement for "popularizing itself as an attack on the native language of the Irish people [English], which is most fortunately also the native language of half the world, including England" (CP 457). Through his Shavian hero, Joyce extended the indictment of the cultural renaissance to Gaelic sport, also part of the nationalist revival that occurred after the death of Parnell. Bloom opposes "the resuscitation of the ancient Gaelic sports and pastimes, practised morning and evening by Finn MacCool as calculated to revive the best traditions of manly strength and prowess" (12.909–11). When the drunks discuss Irish athletics, Bloom worries about the athletes instead of admiring the rebirth of indigenous sports. The alienated Irishman prefers tennis to team contact sports that simulate war. Because Bloom shows little enthusiasm for the patriot's game, the narrator berates him, but, undaunted by the barroom cronies, the womanly man pities the "poor" wife of Breen, "the old stuttering fool" whom the barflies are gossiping about (12:1051–62). Bloom also avoids a fight. Arguing that life and love are the "opposite of hatred" (12:145), he finally asserts himself when the tribalistic drinkers reveal their anti-Semitism.

In 1896 Shaw described himself in a letter to Ellen Terry as "the wandering Jew [who] must go in search of someone who can use him to the utmost of his capacity" (BSL 1:676)—a comparison that was published in the year *Ulysses* was published. But Shaw had clarified in his Irish play and elsewhere his stance on the superiority of Jewish and Irish brains. In the *New York Times,* May 14, 1911, Shaw declared, "We have the Christian religion, which is the Jewish religion" (I&R 407). As a Jew, Bloom is, as he tells the citizen, related to the Jew whom Christians worship, one whose qualities were, in late-nineteenth-century iconography, very like those of a charitable androgyne. Joyce's unacknowledged mentor identified himself with the pacifistic, iconoclastic, feminine image of Christ nearly as often as he took on the role of an anti-institutional Satan. He asserted that "Christ stands in the world for that intuition of the highest humanity that we, being members of one another, must not complain, must not scold, must not strike, nor revile nor persecute nor revenge nor punish" (quoted in Winsten, *Days* 316). The sarcastic citizen derides Bloom as "the new Messiah for Ireland! . . . Island of saints and sages" (12.1642). Thus he alludes to Joyce's 1907 essay whose title refers to the legendary name of Ireland and perhaps to Shaw's anticipation of Joyce in the preface to *John Bull's Other Island,* where he declared that " 'The island of the saints' is no idle phrase" (CP 454). After the Easter uprising, Shaw wanted to be a new messiah, doing with the pen what Parnell failed to do in Parliament. While Joyce was writing *Ulysses,* Shaw was especially vocal on Irish matters.

After the Easter rebellion, Shaw defended the insurrectionists, insisting, "I remain an Irishman, and am bound to contradict any implication that I can regard as a traitor any Irishman taken in a fight for Irish independence." James Stephens (whom Joyce would later openly claim as a soul brother) had attacked Shaw for his flippant remark that the damage done in Dublin by British artillery had accomplished slum removal long overdue, but Stephens hastily retracted his attack, praising Shaw for speaking out in favor of the Irish martyrs and hence valorizing the insurrection. G. B. S. went further: he vindicated the morality of accepting German aid against the British oppressor and defended Roger Casement, trying valiantly and abortively to save him from being executed for treason (Weintraub, *Unexpected Shaw* 166–70). Casement was arrested and subsequently hanged for trying to bring German weapons to the Irish rebels. In May 1916 Shaw perhaps inspired Yeats's famous poem "Easter 1916" by arguing that the British were "canonizing their prisoners" by making martyrs of them. He declared that "it is absolutely impossible to slaughter a man in this position without making a martyr and a hero, even though the day before he may have been only a minor poet. The shot Irishmen will now take their places" beside the political martyrs of the world (*The Matter with Ireland* 112). The consequence of Shaw's spirited defense of his countrymen was an apotheosis in Ireland. It took the form of standing-room-only performances of many of his plays at the Abbey Theatre. In his native country admirers began to regard him as a savior. If Herbert Howarth's analysis of Irish literature is correct, both Irish Catholic audiences and Irish writers were, after Parnell's martyr's death, engaged with the theme of messianism. The response of the Irish public to Shaw, who was, like Joyce, drawn to the theme, suggests that the hope of a messiah, political or literary, persisted after the horrors of 1916.

Hope persisted also in Joyce's imagination of Bloom as an adumbration of Shaw and other Irish prophets, parodied in Bloom as saint. By the end of the Cyclops episode, Bloom has been elevated to saintly status, something like that of the Shaw whom Archibald Henderson quotes as declaring, "The final conflict is . . . between the cruel will and the humane will" (GBS 479). In *The Quintessence of Ibsenism* Shaw asserted that "as Man grows through the ages, he finds himself bolder by the growth of his courage: that is, of his spirit . . . and dares more and more to love and trust instead of to fear and fight" (MCE 47). In *Ulysses,* among those catalogued in the "blessed company" juxtaposed to the unholy pub denizens are "S. Leopold and S. Bernard" (12.1678, 1695)—perhaps saints like Leopold the Good and Bernard of Clairvaux, but probably also snide allusions to Poldy and "Saint" Bernard Shaw. For, in proclaiming that love is the answer to violence and charity the appropriate response to greed, the womanly man is identified with a comic scapegoat redeemer, condemned, like Shaw's Androcles, to suffer for his beliefs but also headed for a transforming though incongruously humorous glorification (in the exemplum of Androcles, instead of eating the willing martyr, the lion dances with him). In scapegoating Bloom, the cynical narrator calls Leopold's father "old Methusalem Bloom" (12.1581). The reference must have taken on special meaning for Joyce with the appearance in 1921 of the paternal Shaw's "Pentateuch," *Back to Methuselah.* In it the old messianic seer consciously compared himself to Methuselah as well as to Moses and other Judeo-Christian patriarchs and prophets and "the prophet . . . without honor in his own family" (BM 102). In his apotheosis the pariah Bloom is transformed into Elijah as he escapes with the "jarvey," whose hackney becomes a chariot ascending "to heaven" (12.1900, 1911).

Fireworks on the Beach: "Sunny, My Gander, He's Coming to Land Her"

Before Bloom can begin to think of himself as father consubstantial with an only son of man, he ascends in another way—through his "Fireworks. Up like a rocket, down like a stick" (13.894–95). He has an orgasm on the strand, aroused by gazing at the seductive Gerty MacDowell, who is a Shavian womanly woman. Her acculturation urges her to play the part, like Shaw's Lady Corinthia in *Press Cuttings*, of the beautiful, romantic temptress. Like the fully indoctrinated Lady Corinthia, but younger and less experienced, Gerty imagines herself a romantic heroine who relies on her charms to get her man. To Corinthia, "Love—real love—makes all intentions honorable." She expects General Mitchener to make "advances" to her as "a tribute to romance" and thinks him extremely "vulgar" for blushing (no Bloom he) "at the mention of underclothing" (Plays 1101). More passive than Corinthia, Joyce's heroine of romance wants a hero to ride into her life (on a bicycle, which suggests the reality underlying her fantasies). Gerty admits in Shaw's own terms that she fancies herself to be a "womanly woman" (13.34) waiting for a "manly man . . . who had not found his ideal" (13.210–11). As Suzette Henke indicates, Gerty is Joyce's sentimental heroine (Henke and Unkeless 132–49). She is also a complex, satiric portrait of the amorous young heroine of romance, which is, according to Shaw, "the great heresy to be rooted out from art and life" (CP 737). The "dishonest folly" of "gallantry and chivalry . . . [is] treasonable to women and stultifying to men" (733). Shaw defined Gerty's predecessors in *The Quintessence of Ibsenism* and spoofed their romantic ideals in *Arms and the Man* (1894).

Like Sergius in the romantic imagination of Raina in Shaw's satiric comedy, Gerty's "beau ideal" will be an "unconquered hero" with a "sweeping moustache" (13.209, 237). Utterly unlike Bloom, Gerty's lover will supposedly be, like Sergius, a standard heroic figure—"tall with broad shoulders . . . and they would go to the continent on their honeymoon" (13.225, 237–38). A "votary of Dame Fashion" (13.148–49), Gerty is a narcissist "smiling at the lovely reflection which the mirror gave to her" (13.162), "wearing the blue for luck . . . for a bride" (13.179–80). To her, love is "a woman's birthright" (13.200). She wants "a man among men" (13.207) whom she dreams of marrying according to the ideal that Shaw debunked as unrealistic—the ideal of "till death us two part" (13.216). Modeled on the female stereotype that Shaw defined as the product of romantic illusions endorsed and encouraged by patriarchal society, Gerty fancies herself a nurturing caretaker, providing "creature comforts" (13.222). She idealizes matrimony as a kind of gumdrop heaven with "wifey" at home as a "ministering angel" (13.326). In "The Womanly Woman" section of *The Quintessence of Ibsenism,* Shaw wrote that there are "idealistic parrots [women] who persuade themselves that the mission of a parrot is to minister to the happiness of a private family by whistling and saying 'Pretty Polly,' and that it is in the sacrifice of its liberty to this altruistic pursuit that the true parrot finds the supreme satisfaction of its soul" (MCE 61). Gerty is such a bird.

Both Shaw in *Arms and the Man* and Joyce in the Nausicaa episode achieve ironic effects by juxtaposing romance and reality. Both simultaneously expose and ridicule foolish ideals, but not without sympathy. In G. B. S.'s satiric play, a mysterious stranger shows up in the heroine's bedroom after having escaped the trials of battle. In Nausicaa he shows up on the beach after having escaped his tormentors in Barney Kiernan's pub. One of the most telling comic ironies of the scene is that the man whom the would-be princess's imagination endows with the qualities of the romantic hero is in actuality the object of hateful anti-Semitism, for Gerty's thoughts of her "grandpapa" Giltrap's "lovely dog Garryowen" (13.232–33)—the cur who pursued Bloom from the pub—establish that her grandfather is none other than the owner of the "bloody mongrel" (12.1907). Significantly, in describing his princess, Joyce alludes to the Homeric rather than the Virgilian subtext—to Nausicaa and Odysseus on the beach instead of Dido and Aeneas. In staking out his own epic territory, Joyce chose to expose (pun intended) the private man, whereas Shaw poked fun at the public warrior by borrowing from the first line of the *Aeneid* for the title of his comedy.

While Shaw's punful title targets illusions concerning war and romantic embraces, Joyce combines religious and romantic idolatry by providing for his perverse seduction a backdrop of voices from a church in which the priest is saying Hail Marys. The merciful virgin on the beach responds to Bloom, who seems to beseech her to intercede for him. Pitying the sad "gentleman in black" (as Raina pities Bluntschli), Gerty provides for him a blasphemous solace (13.349). Gerty instinctively associates herself with the Madonna, an ironic litany to whom provides background music for autoerotic fantasy. Gerty's contretemps with Bloom is punctuated by the voices singing "in supplication to the Virgin more powerful, Virgin most merciful" (13.303–4), for Gerty has the "pious Virgin's intercessory power" (13.378–79); without speech, as "Refuge of sinners" (13.442) she can give Bloom a succor that she promises with body language: she "smiled assent and bit her lip," blushed and "just lifted her skirt a little" (13.360–62). The passive, secular Madonna blasphemously patterns herself on "Our Blessed Lady herself [who] said to the archangel Gabriel be it done unto me according to thy word" (13.458–59). Like the Madonna of patriarchal religion who is "queen of patriarchs" (13.489), Gerty is also Eve, for Bloom eyes her "as a snake eyes her prey. Her woman's instinct told her that she had raised the devil in him" and she turned scarlet like the color of sexual sin and then "her face became a glorious rose" (13.517–20) like the color of Christian beatitude. Identifying ironically with the Virgin Mother, Gerty fancies that Bloom is "literally worshipping at her shrine" (13.546). In the "drawer of her toilettable" she kept "her child of Mary badge" (13.639), which makes her a member of the cult of Mariolatry, itself reflected in the ideals of chivalric romance that inform her illusions about love. After their mutually autoerotic orgasms, Gerty continues to identify with Mary: "there was an infinite store of mercy" in her eyes and "a word of pardon even though he had erred and sinned and wandered" (13.748–49). By counterpointing Mary and the lame Gerty, Joyce implies that the ideal of womanhood taught by Gerty's religion is crippling.

Moreover, the deluded sentimentalist had tacked up an almanac with a picture of "a young gentleman in costume . . . offering a bunch of flowers to his ladylove with oldtime chivalry through her lattice window" (13.334–37)—a romantic icon that parallels Raina's view of romance at the start of *Arms and the Man*. It is entirely possible that Joyce's image of "the gentleman . . . in chocolate," looking a "thorough aristocrat" (13.339), alludes to the operetta pirated from *Arms and the Man,* which Shaw first subtitled "A Romantic Comedy" but to avoid misapprehension of his theme changed to "An Anti-Romantic Comedy." Shaw protested that Oscar Strauss's "loathsome plagiarism" *The Chocolate Soldier* degraded "decent comedy into a dirty farce." The "unauthorized parody'" (H1 306) of Shaw's mockery of romance sentimentalizes saccharine romantic ideals. Shaw's chocolate soldier, Bluntschli, carries bonbons to sweeten his hard war experiences and survive them (he prefers them to cartridges, which are "useless" in a real battle); Bloom carries a bar of soap, apparently as a promise to himself that he can wash away his guilt in the sexual war that he is losing. There is an unromantic similarity between the two "credible heroes."

Furthermore, the children in the background on the beach serve the same purpose as the servants in Shaw's play: they remind the audience of unvarnished reality—in Joyce the real issue of marriage, which is the antithesis of Gerty's unrealistic illusions; in Shaw the reality of male-female relations, which Raina at first refuses to recognize. Joyce's whole scene, like Shaw's comedy, is farcical: Gerty's foolish, inflated ideals, imbued in her by romance, advertising, and religion, are comparable to Raina's. Inspired by operas such as *Ernani,* Raina instantly compares Bluntschli to the operatic hero, who, "flying from his foes just as you are tonight, takes refuge in the castle of his bitterest enemy" (Plays 100), like Bloom flying from Garryowen and taking refuge in his owner's granddaughter. Also influenced by pompous notions of heroism derived from the quintessential imperialist and romantic epic, the *Aeneid,* Raina's romanticism is encouraged by her "mamma," who is wildly enthusiastic about the self-glorifying Sergius's supposedly "magnificent cavalry charge" (103–4).

To Sergius, the speciously gallant hero, Bluntschli is "a commercial traveler in uniform. Bourgeois to his boots" (104). Like Shaw's blunt soldier, Joyce's advertising man is a pragmatic, plain professional doing his job and getting "saved" by a young woman enamored of romance. Gerty makes Bloom into a gallant Sergius or Odysseus, transforming him into the hero of her imagination, which is surely not inspired by the goddess of wisdom, Athena, who made Odysseus handsome and alluring to Nausicaa in the *Odyssey.* Starry-eyed over "a glorious world for women who can see its glory and men who can act its romance," Shaw's Raina at first believes in a "higher love" (93). Her double, Gerty, convinces herself that she has found it in the unlikely Bloom, her "dreamhusband" (13.431). Gerty's imagination makes him into an ideal love, and, unlike Raina, she refuses to relinquish her dream. Whereas Raina discovers the difference between the blunt but genuine Bluntschli and her "humbug" heroic fiancé, Gerty clings, as Shaw said Sergius does, to "the old pose, the old cheap heroism" (50).

The realist Bluntschli, like Bloom, is sympathetic to others when their weaknesses are exposed. When he realizes that Sergius, Raina's intended, is none other than the quixotic hero of a foolish cavalry charge as if he were "an operatic tenor" (98), Bluntschli does not ridicule Raina for being taken in by illusions. Similarly, when he realizes that Gerty is "lame," Bloom is sympathetic to the misguided young woman, but her vision of herself as a romantic temptress had worked to his advantage.

Whereas Gerty does not give up her romantic rationalizations, Shaw's drama is about educating Raina. Despite a disillusioning reality far cruder than Sergius's seduction of the maid, Gerty continues to embroider her fantasy, while Bloom, a Shavian realist, has not pretended to be anything other than himself. Shaw debunks false romanticism while exposing its roots in reality. Joyce creates a similar discrepancy between the false and the real, one that unmasks Gerty as a sex-starved cripple (who displays with her admirer the pluck of what we would now call the physically challenged) and Bloom as a needy, voyeuristic masturbator. After the autoerotic climax on the beach, Gerty remains an unrepentant sentimentalist, ironically ecstatic, as Henke writes, over proving that she can "arouse, titillate, and satisfy masculine desire" (Henke and Unkeless 147).

In *Ulysses,* the double-edged song of "a little canarybird that came out of its little house" (13.1299) in a cuckoo clock to tell the time to a cuckold and a young woman caged by her conditioning reinforces Gerty's association with Shaw's womanly woman, whom he compared at length to a bird singing in a cage. The bird underscores Gerty's association with the Shavian woman trying to escape her entrapment—the "selfish bird" who in seeking "its own gratification" comes out of its cage (for reasons, however, unlike Gerty's) (MCE 61). The irony implicit in the contingent symbol for Gerty is that the mechanical bird, like Bloom's phallus inside his clothes, comes out on cue but will retreat into its "little house." In *Arms and the Man,* in which "Shaw defined romanticism as immaturity" (H1 304), the playwright established that Raina will mature to enjoy a loving partnership with Bluntschli, one that is based on a reality that will not be overwhelmed by phony romanticism. Joyce's childishly immature Gerty is, however, left with her illusions. She has relished her conditioned response because she is programmed to give man pleasure, in a role that Shaw thought pathetic and ridiculous when it became a candy-coated trap for women. Although Bloom's perspective of his encounter is antipathetical to Gerty's—he thinks of it briefly as "Beauty and the beast" (13.837)—he rationalizes, like a perceptive Shavian, that brainwashed females need illusion, "the stage setting, the rouge, costume, position, music.... curtain up. Moonlight silver effulgence. Maiden discovered with pensive bosom" (13.855–58). His thoughts dialogue with the opening of *Arms and the Man,* with Raina "in her nightgown" on her balcony, against a backdrop of "starlit snow," "intensely conscious of the romantic beauty of the night" (93). But for the pragmatic Bloom the episode on the beach is a realistic release. Whereas in the Cyclops episode he survives, like Elijah, to ascend to heaven, at the end of Nausicaa he has experienced "a monkey puzzle rocket burst" which "did me good all the same" (13.933, 939).

Bloomo-Shavian Politics: "A London's Alderman . . . Ladled Out by the Waggerful to the Regionals of Pigmyland"

Having eluded his attackers by fleeing Barney Kiernan's pub, and having satisfied his lust on the beach, Bloom displays his talents for survival. In Bella Cohen's brothel they are tested sorely. In the chimerical acting out of desires and fears in the bawdy house, after the whore Zoe urges him to "make a stump speech" (15.1353), Bloom appears in workman's clothes accusing mankind of being "incorrigible" (15:1356) and, like a propagandist on a public podium—a favorite Shaw pose—deplores "our public life!" (15.1361). In his fictional "real" life not an activist like G. B. S., Bloom (in many respects the mature Joyce) imagines himself dedicated to political and social reform. Joyce's portrait of Bloom is prefigured by Shaw's self-portrait in his preface to *Major Barbara* (1905): "Here I am . . . by class a respectable man, by common sense a hater of waste and disorder, by intellectual constitution legally minded to the verge of pedantry, and by temperament apprehensive and economically disposed to the limit of old-maidishness; yet I am . . . an enemy of the existing order for good reasons" (CP 135).

As a spokesperson for politics, Bloom is not an anarchist, as Dominic Manganiello asserts in *Joyce's Politics* that Joyce was, except in the Shavian sense. G. B. S. believed that "both Americans and Englishmen [and some Irishmen] are born Anarchists and, as complete Anarchism is practically impossible, they seek the minimum of public interference in their personal initiative" (CP 307). Although he considered anarchism "a political theory that embraces all that is valuable in the doctrine of Laisser-Faire [sic] and the method of Free Trade as well as all that is shocking in the view of Bakounine," Shaw emphasized that "we clearly cannot, or at all events will not tolerate assassination of rulers" (CP 414). Shaw admired Proudhon, Bakunin, and Benjamin Tucker, whom Manganiello discloses as an anarchist favored by Joyce. But Shaw's covert disciple was anarchistic insofar as Shaw was and, like him, did not applaud anarchist terrorism.

Manganiello notes that in 1845 Max Stirner "had defined egoism as enlightened self-interest, and Tucker, like Joyce, interpreted it to be the only motivating force in human conduct" (*Joyce's Politics* 78). Stirner influenced Shaw, whereas Tucker, Shaw's friend, reiterated ideas that Shaw proposed in *The Quintessence of Ibsenism*. So impressed was Tucker with Shavian argument that he asked Shaw to write a reply to Max Nordau's attack on the degeneracy of artists. Shaw's response became *The Sanity of Art,* in which he duly attributed Tucker's contribution to the debate. According to Manganiello, "Joyce is in league not only with the collectivist . . . but also with the individualists who understand freedom to be essentially self-liberation" (*Joyce's Politics* 77). The most famous "collectivist" among the individualists who prefigure Joyce was his fellow Irishman. Manganiello gives a salient clue to Joyce's behavior by suggesting that the lapsed Catholic reacted to one of Shaw's arguments in the preface to *John Bull's Other Island*. Shaw asserted that the Protestant spirit in Ireland (which was his own) is "theoretically" anarchistic, because the Protestant, in the original meaning of the word, is "an individualist, a free-thinker, a self-helper, a Whig, a Liberal, a mistruster and vilifier of the State, a rebel." The Catholic, on the other hand, is a "self-abnegator, a Tory, a Conservative, a supporter of Church and State one and undivisible, an obeyer" (CP 448). As Manganiello avers, Joyce set out to prove that a member of the Catholic majority could be an anarchistic Protestant (*Joyce's Politics* 211). Nevertheless, despite reminding us that Joyce kept Shaw's Fabian tracts in his library, Manganiello does not develop his observation, which suggests, at bottom, that Joyce behaved like a rival of Shaw. A letter to Stanislaus clarifies that James had been studying Italian socialism and that he knew the "English [that is, Shavian] variety," which seemed to him similar (JJL 2:174). This, of course, establishes that Joyce studied English socialism, which was synonymous with Shaw's Fabianism. As Manganiello writes, "Joyce's conclusions about socialism determined how he viewed the political situation in Ireland to a greater extent than has been generally acknowledged" (*Joyce's Politics* 65–66).

As all of Joyce's fiction illustrates, he agreed with Shaw's assessment of the Irish and, like the older Dubliner, was in a love-hate relationship with his country throughout his life. Bloom embodies the "Protestant" characteristics listed by Shaw. Bloom's advocacy of "reform of municipal morals (CP 489–90, 610) is a mixture of freemasonry and of some of the Utopian Socialist visionary programs at the turn of the century with peculiar Bloomite twists. Political independence is not at all Bloom's primary concern, but radical social reform" (Manganiello, *Joyce's Politics* 111). At the turn of the century, Shaw was the most vocal Irishman promoting radical social reform without making Home Rule the center of his agenda. His Fabian tract *London Programme* advocated "municipalization of milk, gas, pawnbroking, and slaughterhouses, the creation of municipal hospitals, a municipal steamboat service, and the right of women to become members of the Council" (Winsten, *G. B. S.* 90, 153).

According to G. K. Chesterton's 1911 book on Shaw, his views were "essentially anarchy. . . . a worried and conscientious anarchy" (83). Although Bloom is accused in the Expressionistic drama of the Circe episode of being an "anarchist" and "dynamitard" (15.470, 595), he argues for the gradualist revolution through persuasion, for which Shaw was the chief Irish spokesperson. Bloom's mixed bag of social programs may be, as Manganiello argues, a medley of "collectivist, Marxist, and individual anarchist theory" (*Joyce's Politics* 112), but it is just the sort of mélange that the supremely paradoxical individualist-socialist Shaw offered. Indeed, Chesterton described Bernard Shaw as "a great cheapjack with plenty of patter and I dare say plenty of nonsense, but also (which is not wholly unimportant) with goods to sell" in the "plain, pugnacious style. . . . He does not talk about collectivism, but about cash . . . cheese, boots, perambulators" (181–83), the specifics of social need. Bloom emulates the Shavian patter and political sales pitch. Although Manganiello musters considerable evidence and appropriate analogues to reveal Joyce's "anarchism," none of it obviates the evidence that (as Bloom) he is inspired by Shaw. The Fabian's simultaneous advocacy of the lone nontotalitarian superman and of the pacifist socialist prefigures Bloom's beliefs and seems to set the perimeters of Poldy's political enthusiasms. His animadversions on the state of the world and how to reform it imply a Shavian model and source of information, ideological substance, and harebrained utopian schemes.

In his fantasy, suddenly Bloom is running for mayor, advocating a tramline "from the cattlemarket to the river" (15.1367–68). Shaw himself won only one election in his political career. He served as vestryman of St. Pancras from 1897 to 1899. After St. Pancras became a borough, he was elected its alderman in 1899, but when he ran again in 1904, mapping out his own idiosyncratic platform, he lost the election. It is perhaps significant that in June of that year, Bloom, transformed into an alderman (15.1382), makes an impassioned political speech attacking manufacture "produced by a horde of capitalistic lusts upon our prostituted labour. The poor man starves" (15.1394–95), while the rich are amusing themselves. Such sentiments echo Shaw's platform attacks on capitalism. He proposed "the abolition of our capitalistic system to redeem mankind from the double curse of poverty and riches" (CP 345). "Capitalism," he wrote, is "setting up huge vested interests in destruction, waste, and disease" (CP 336). It should, paradoxically, be "called proletarianism which again is but a polite word for prostitution." "The man who cannot see that starvation, overwork, dirt, and disease are as anti social as prostitution—that they are the vices and crimes of a nation and not merely its misfortunes—is (to put it as politely as possible) a hopelessly Private Person" (CP 230).

Although Joyce cultivated an image of himself as such a private person, Bloom is Shavian. An indefatigable talker and debater, Bloom, a *doppelgänger* of Shaw, is "the famous Bloom now, the world's greatest reformer" (15.1459). Shaw fancied himself the world's greatest reformer, encouraged by his followers but also announcing that he feared his fame would defraud him of his "just martyrdom" (CP 165). Although attentive, the world was often more amused by Shaw's gibes than moved by his speechifying and letter-writing campaigns. Like him, Bloom imagines himself to be a political savior, promising to rule by "law and mercy" (15.1480–81) as the successor of Parnell (15.1514), to whom Chesterton compared Shaw (29). No lawless anarchist, Bloom promises a "new era. . . . the golden city . . . in the Nova Hibernia" (15.1542–45), something like the "new epoch" that Undershaft was trying to inaugurate in *Major Barbara* by creating a utopian community for his workers. Bloom copies Shaw, who proclaimed himself "the messenger boy of the new age" (Shaw, *Bernard Shaw: Selection of His Wit and Wisdom* 252). The Nova Hibernia resembles the ideal commonwealth of which ex-priest Keegan dreams in *John Bull's Other Island:* "a country where the State is the Church and the Church the people. . . . in which work is play and play is life. . . . in which the priest is the worshipped and the worshipper the worshipped. . . . in which all life is human and all humanity divine" (Plays 451).

As Shaw's Irish patriotism evolved during World War I, many people, including his sister Lucy, thought his ambitions extended to political office in Ireland. Lucy wrote, "Why does he not offer himself as Lord

Lieutenant for Ireland, he should soon make it anything but the figurehead it has always been" (Weintraub, *Unexpected Shaw* 163). Shaw's reputation was mixed, however. Some, like Bloom's fantasy supporters, idealized him and, like Chesterton, found in him the "strange note of the saint" (15), whereas others despised his heterodoxy. Unionists who believed that Shaw was pro-German because of his ecumenical views in *Common Sense About the War* (1914) were apparently responsible for a raid on the Gaelic Press offices in Dublin in which a copy of *Three Plays for Puritans* was seized (Weintraub, *Unexpected Shaw* 163). In 1917 Shaw tried unsuccessfully to get an appointment to the Irish Convention set up by Lloyd George's government to consider the Irish question. Like the incorrigible Shaw in a Bloom disguise, Joyce's hero is accused of being a fake, even though he insists that he is a charitable ruler and politician.

When Bloom's "court of Conscience" is declared open, he promises to "administer open air justice. Free medical and legal advice . . . in the year 1 of the Paradisiacal Era" (15.1629–32). In this guise, promoting panaceas like socialized medicine and a socialized legal system, Bloom has the answers to everybody's problems, with a self-assurance that is positively Shavian. Like Shaw, whom Chesterton called "a prophet as well as a sanitary inspector" (169) and who during "his apostolate . . . harangued a thousand public assemblies" (Pearson 186) to press for social reform, Bloom stands "for the reform of municipal morals and the plain ten commandments. . . . Union of all, jew, moslem and gentile. Three acres and a cow for all children of nature. . . . Compulsory manual labour for all. All parks open to the public day and night. Electric dish scrubbers. Tuberculosis, lunacy, war and mendicancy must now cease. . . . esperanto the universal language with universal brotherhood. No more patriotism of barspongers and dropsical impostors. Free money, free rent, freelove and a free lay church in a free lay state" (15.1685–93).

Such a state is very like that propounded by Keegan in *John Bull's Other Island*. Despite the inclusion of the incongruous ten commandments in its miscellany of offerings, Bloom's comic plea for social justice roughly summarizes Shaw's political agenda. As we find later, Bloom—like Shaw—honors the "cosmic force" in himself rather than the God of the first commandment of the Decalogue. Even though he is, like Shaw, for some "plain," basic morality, his advocacy of Judeo-Christian ethics seems to be an opportunistic electioneering promise aimed disingenuously at a constituency that, in Ireland, readily mixed church and state. Shaw had reinterpreted "Thou shalt not steal" to agree with the anarchist Proudhon that "property is theft"—an idea that underlies Bloomo-Shavian politics if not Bloomo-Shavian aspirations. Moreover, like Bloom, Shaw perhaps honored the commandment against adultery more in the breach than in belief.

Like Bloom, however, Shaw believed in "union of all." He argued, for example, that "it should be taught that Allah is simply the name by which God is known to Turks and Arabs, who are just as eligible for salvation as any Christian" (CP 97). He advocated intermarriage among classes and races, breaking down "class segregation," alleviating racial discrimination through minority assertion of "equality" or indeed "superiority." Such assertion would, Shaw believed, make racism "patently ridiculous," and "intermarriageable equality" would "establish itself" (SSS 45, 49). In Bloom's perfect society, there would be "mixed races and mixed marriages" (15.1699), such as Shaw advised and later in life blatantly promoted in works like *Back to Methuselah* (1921) and *The Adventures of the Black Girl in Her Search for God* (1932). After 1921 Joyce added a passage to *Ulysses* in which Bloom, turned mother, gives birth to eight yellow-and-white sons (Groden 111) who will be appointed to "positions of high public trust" (15.1829). He may have been inspired by part 3 of *Back to Methuselah,* "The Thing Happens" (published in 1921), set in a future in which blacks and Asians are the brains directing ineffectual Caucasians.

The "three acres and a cow [borrowed from Joseph Chamberlain's 1895 campaign for Liberal Party reform] for all children of nature" parodies offers to Irish peasants, "children of nature," in land agitation that was the focus of political action in agrarian Ireland. For a peasant, the promise of a cow would be a tempting campaign gimmick. The Englishman Chamberlain whose slogan Bloom lifts favored reform in Ireland but not Home Rule. Bloom's solution to the land problem is comic because it is impracticable and unrealistic. It would not appeal to tenant farmers who were finally coming into possession of lands that they did not want to share with the peasantry—a peasantry that, in a catch-22, did not have the vote because it lacked property. The land question is central in *John Bull's Other Island,* which sympathizes with the young peasant deprived of land while recognizing that the farmers who have newly acquired it do not want equal land distribution. The

Wyndham Act forms the background of this play, which exposes the fact that the accession of rural tenants to the roles of petty freeholders did nothing for the ordinary worker, perhaps the disenfranchised child of nature to whom Bloom, ironically, appeals.

Bloom not only offers land distribution but also demands labor. Shaw persistently advocated "compulsory labor for all" (Bentley 19), but not only the "compulsory manual labor" in Bloom's platform, for he also believed in intellectual and artistic endeavors. As local politician in St. Pancras, G. B. S. devoted himself to the general social welfare and to specific projects such as "manure receptacles (maintenance of), horns (blowing of), graves (purchase of) . . . management of ice cream notices, street cries, the sampling of milk-in-transit and all business involving public baths, lighting, tramways" (H1 413). Prefiguring Bloom's fantasies, Shaw served on the Health Committee, hence opposing tuberculosis and lunacy, as well as on the Committee for Electricity and Public Lighting (H1 414) (a fact that does not seem to have escaped Joyce, who dreams of "Lamppost" Shaw in the *Wake*). Joyce's Dubliner might have been especially supportive of Shaw's fight for free lavatories (H1 417). And taking the Shavian view of inebriated patriotism, Bloom in his fantasy stumps to get even with the hypocritical barflies in Barney Kiernan's pub.

In the preface to *Androcles and the Lion*, Shaw contended that "the need for a drastic redistribution of income in all civilised countries is now as obvious and as generally admitted as the need for sanitation" (CP 576). Joyce owned a copy of Shaw's Fabian tract entitled "Free Rents." Shaw often argued for the free rent Bloom advocates: in "The Transition to Social Democracy" he averred that under socialism, rent would be transferred "from the class which now appropriates it to the whole people" (*Essays in Fabian Socialism* 39). Moreover, like Shaw, who argued in favor of a simplified, universal alphabet, Bloom prefers a universal and international language such as Esperanto to the study of a dead one like Gaelic, which isolates national groups instead of promoting "universal brotherhood." In *The Philanderer* Shaw defended the "free love" that Bloom speaks for. His preface to *Getting Married* mocks the "magic spell," the "pathology," and the "criminology" of marriage (CP 21, 36–37), while the preface to *Man and Superman* defends free love as practiced in the Oneida community in America (172–73) and mocks the "matrimonomaniacs" (171). The "free lay church" of Bloom's dream has the paradoxical import of the religio-secular humanism envisioned by Keegan for Ireland in *John Bull's Other Island.*

After Bloom explains his schemes for social regeneration, a priest accuses him of being "an episcopalian, an agnostic, an anythingarian seeking to overthrow our holy faith" (15:1712–13). The heterodox Shaw, born an Episcopalian in the Church of Ireland and become an enemy of Christian orthodoxy, astonished his constituency by working with a Methodist minister who considered their joint effort "an alliance between God and the Devil" (Pearson 189). When Shaw proclaimed to the Shelley Society that he was, like Shelley, a "Socialist, an atheist, and a vegetarian," Holroyd notes, "two pious ladies resigned" (H1 127). Shaw had been severely criticized for his opposition to "Crosstianity" (CP 117), his term for institutionalized Christianity. That one of Bloom's accusers calls him "Stage Irishman!" and "Plagiarist!" (15.1729) hints that Joyce was well aware of one of the chief sources of Bloom's ideas and fantasy self. Shaw had exposed the stereotypical stage Irishman as braggart, parasite, blarney expert, and professional Irishman in *John Bull's Other Island* but had also created a mask in G. B. S. of the shrewd, sly, and clever clown, a new sort of stage Irishman. In Bloom's fantasy, the Veiled Sibyl (a major oracle in "The Tragedy of an Elderly Gentleman," part 4 of *Methuselah*), declares that she is a "Bloomite [Shavian?] and I glory in it. I believe in him in spite of all . . . the funniest man on earth" (15.1736–37). While Joyce was writing *Ulysses,* Shaw was reputed to be a droll stage Irishman and the funniest man around.

However, in the fickle audience of the Shavio-Bloom, the inevitable anti-Bloomite surfaces, like Shaw's detractors who labeled him an agent of the devil (or of the Germans). The calumniator accuses Bloom of being "from the roots of hell a disgrace to Christian men. A fiendish libertine from his earliest years, this stinking goat of Mendes gave precocious signs of infantile debauchery" (15:1754–56). Coming from hell, Bloom seems related both to Shaw's philosophical social reformer John Tanner and to the brigand Mendoza, who are, in "Don Juan in Hell," transformed into Don Juan and the Devil. The "stinking goat of Mendes" is, Gifford and Seidman tell us, a sacred animal of Egyptian mythology, but the passage hints at the polar pagan Shavians in Hell— Don Juan, once a fiendish libertine, and Mendoza, prince of Hades. Like Bloom in his Fata Morgana, Don Juan has forsaken debauchery in his hopes of establishing a better society in "heaven."

When the crowd in Bloom's nightmare turns on the devilish "libertine," Dr. Punch Costello defends him, declaring that Bloom is "a finished example of the new womanly man. His moral nature is simple and lovable. Many have found him to be a dear man, a dear person. . . . practically a total abstainer . . . sleeps on a straw litter and eats the most Spartan food, cold dried grocer's peas" (15:1798–1805). Shaw had argued in *The Quintessence of Ibsenism* that "all good men are womanly men" (MCE 164). Joyce's nightmare womanly man resembles Shaw and his Androcles, for G. B. S. was in private life not the glib, pugnacious stage Irishman that he often presented to his public. His generosity and spartan lifestyle (despite his flaunted wealth) were the obverse of what he portrayed in his media image. As noted earlier, in *The Philanderer,* one of the many Shaw plays in Joyce's library before he moved to Paris in 1920, Shaw advocated the "womanly man."

Shaw's *The Philanderer* concerns a love triangle that reverses the roles depicted in *Ulysses:* two women vie for the amorous attentions of Charteris, the womanly man. He rejects Julia Craven because she displays all of the craven emotionalism, jealousy, and possessiveness of the womanly woman. Bloom seems to have endorsed, reluctantly and painfully, Charteris's "advanced" views regarding relationships, accepting Molly's adultery on the Shavian basis. According to Charteris, lovers reserve "the right to leave" if their "companionship is . . . incompatible with—what was the expression you used?—with your full development as a human being" (Plays 32). Bloom cannot be accused, as Shaw's Julia is, "of habitual and intolerable jealousy and ill temper" (52), and he is more forebearing than Charteris. Julia's father, daunted by derision such as Bloom suffers in Barney Kiernan's pub, calls the Ibsen Club a "cock and hen club" and will not join it for fear of being "laughed out of London." He tells his daughter that he disapproves of "the whole modern movement" and prefers "scenes of suffering nobly endured and sacrifice willingly rendered by womanly women and manly men" (36). The philanderer, however, rejects ideals of noble suffering and self-sacrifice. Like the males Bloom encounters in the pub, Shavian men who deem themselves manly are extremely uncomfortable with Charteris and suspicious of him, not because he displays bisexual tendencies but because he proselytizes for social androgyny, which amounts to equal rights and reciprocity in love relations.

Threatened by the unmanly hero (and perhaps scornful of his election promise of three acres and a cow), evicted tenants in Bloom's nightmare want to punish the womanly man. Meanwhile, he whistles a tune from *Don Giovanni* (15.1886), perhaps giving a clue to Poldy's connection to Shaw's alter ego, Don Juan, the reformist superman. Bloom's hallucinatory fantasy includes the lead roles that tempted Shaw—Chief Pontiff, Lord Mayor, Moses, the Jewish savior whose sermons are for this world, not the next. When Bloom is transformed into an androgynous god figure, he is a female messiah, the god whom Shaw challenged his readers to consider to be a woman. While satirizing the would-be messiah, Joyce also sympathizes with the superior womanly man who wants to be a political redeemer. In the manner of Shaw (and some of his contemporaries, like anarchist Emma Goldman), using Judeo-Christian allusions and archetypes to express secular and heterodox views, Joyce interjects the prophet Elijah, calling, "Are you a god or a doggone clod? . . . [I]t's up to you to sense that cosmic force. . . . You have something within, the higher self" (15.2194, 2196–98). The prophet speaks of god, as Shaw often did, in lower case. The cosmic force or higher self is the vital genius, the élan vital in which, like Henri Bergson, Shaw believed.

Indeed, Bloom preaches his secular religion as if he were a relative of Shaw's reprobate Christ figure Blanco Posnet, redeemed in this life for being a good samaritan who tried to save the life of a boy. Having reviewed the play in 1909 and noted that Shaw was turning toward altruism, Joyce seems, in part, to pattern Poldy's odyssey on Blanco's. That Joyce's black mass takes place in a whorehouse upstages Shaw's trial of Blanco, after which the principals retire to a saloon. But Blanco's chief tormentors are harridan women, and his chief accuser, like Joyce's Bella Cohen, is a woman of ill repute. Despite his faults, Bloom, like Blanco, is a good samaritan. The boy he wants to save is Stephen Dedalus. When his sexual and political ordeal by nightmare in the brothel is over, Bloom rushes to Stephen's aid. After Bella threatens to disgrace the young man, Bloom appeals to her maternal instinct, comparable to that of Shaw's madam, Mrs. Warren. He asks, what if Stephen "were your own son in Oxford?" (15.4306). Joyce knew that Vivie Warren, fictional daughter of Shaw's madam, attended Oxford's chief competitor, Cambridge. When Bloom finds Stephen, who is a student at University College, Dublin, he is babbling Shavian ideas, filtered through Darwin—"Struggle for life is the law of existence. . . . But in here [in his head] it is I must kill the priest and the king" (15.4434–

37)—to Shaw the two great enemies of an Irishman. Like the gradualist Fabian, Stephen would undermine old authorities inimical to the Irish, through intellectual and psychological persuasion. In his drunkenness, Stephen seems to be a convert, for the moment, to Bloomo-Shavian politics. Bloom had addressed Cissy Caffrey, whom he hallucinates that he has found (after having encountered her with Gerty on the strand) in the bordello, as "woman, sacred lifegiver!" (15.4649), as if she were Shaw's Life Force. After Stephen proclaims, "Long live life!" (the Life Force, not the king) (15.4474), Patrice Egan, condemning him as anti-British, calls him a "*Socialiste*" (15.4505), categorizing Stephen with the political group with which Shaw identified. Bloom is, however, the sometimes caricatured bearer of the Shavian message.

In the cabman's shelter, Bloom, still talking about political reform, muses on how "the system really needed toning up." He wants to improve transportation out of the city for "vacationists" (16.541). Equally concerned with transportation, in his Fabian tracts Shaw promoted linking up "entire manufacturing districts with a network of electric trams which will enable English to work in towns whilst their children grow up in the country instead of the slums" (*Essays in Fabian Socialism* 220). Inveterately (although, we shall see, inconsistently) urban like Joyce himself and always interested in pleasure, Bloom is more hedonistic, and his vision is less sweeping than Shaw's, but both look to transportation to improve society. Bloom also pities a "haggard" streetwalker (16.704) and wonders how she could sell herself to any man valuing his health. The pragmatic Bloom, who, the narrator assures us, has no "oldmaidish squeamishness" (16.742) like the "old-fashioned and squeamish" Shaw (as he described himself in responding to *Ulysses;* JJ1 588), accepts prostitution as a necessary evil but thinks there should be licensed medical inspections of whores. Joyce's description at the beginning of the Circe episode clarifies that, like Shaw, he understood the connections between poverty and prostitution. But unlike the author of *Mrs. Warren's Profession,* Joyce presented the sordid nightworld without overtly teaching a lesson. His hero nevertheless adheres, more or less consistently, to Shavian gospel.

Like Shaw, Bloom believes in man's genius but not in "a supernatural God" (16.771). He copies the Fabian in avowing that he is nonviolent but inwardly admires the man "with the courage of his political convictions (though personally, he would never be a party to any such thing)"

(16.1059–60)—the "thing" being physical-force politics. Like Bloom, Shaw opposed war and political violence but supported the English in their wars (though not in their oppression of Ireland) once there was no turning back. Thus, despite his condemnation of the self-interested Machiavellianism of both sides, Shaw favored the English in World War I while issuing polemics opposing international warfare and defending conscientious objectors like Bertrand Russell and Francis Sheehy-Skeffington. Bloom shares such politics. In the cabman's shelter, he delivers a Shavian sermon: "[E]very country . . . has the government it deserves! . . . It's all very fine to boast of mutual superiority but what about mutual equality. I resent violence and intolerance in any shape or form. It never teaches anything or stops anything. A revolution must come on the due instalments plan. It's a patent absurdity . . . to hate people because they live around the corner" (16:1096–1102).

In his preface to *Heartbreak House* (1917), Shaw wrote that "every people has the Government it deserves" and "every government has the electorate that it deserves" (CP 380). In his Fabian tracts he used the metaphor of buying on the installment plan to explain his gradualist socialism. He proposed that "a gradual transfer to Social Democracy means . . . the transfer of rent and interest to the state . . . by instalments" (*Essays in Fabian Socialism* 44). Henderson explained, "Socialism will come by prosaic instalments of public regulation and public administration, enacted by ordinary parliaments, vestries, municipalities, parish councils, school boards and the like, and not one of these instalments will amount to a revolution" (MC 270). Thus, declaring himself a good Irishman and aping the most famous one, Bloom wants to "see everyone . . . all creeds and classes *pro rata* having a comfortable tidysized income" (16.1133–34). Shaw's main socialist platform was a vociferous argument for guaranteed equality of income: "Socialism means equality of income and nothing else" (Shaw, *Intelligent Woman's Guide* 123). In *Socialism and Superior Brains*, a tract that Joyce had in his library, Shaw advocated equal pay for all work (*Essays in Fabian Socialism* 288). Like Shaw, Bloom wants everyone to work but wants all work, even the literary kind, to be gainful.

In the Eumaeus episode, a tired Bloom still holds for being a benevolent leader and a meliorist, but his socialist ideals have become hazier and his socialism, like Shaw's after 1904, less consistent. He imagines himself a leader, not unduly clement or excessively rigorous, just but with "the widest possible latitude," motivated by "an innate love of rectitude" to maintain "public order," repress "public abuses," and control "all perpetuators of international animosities" (17.1617–32). Bloom indicates that (like Shaw) he rejected Irish Protestantism as a boy (17.1636) and advocated the "collective and national economic programme" of Lalor "and others." "And others" includes socialists like Shaw. In inconsistently approving the "constitutional agitation" of Parnell" (17.1646–49), Bloom endorses the Fabian socialist's method of "permeation" through legislation. Nevertheless, his entrepreneurial schemes reveal that, like Shaw, who had become a millionaire while Joyce was writing *Ulysses,* he is not a thoroughgoing socialist. Indeed, he considers the merits of private enterprise. He muses on making money through a private telegraph, by waste reclamation, by exploiting hydraulic power (a Shavian theme), and through tourism (Broadbent's scheme) and the discovery of gold.

Bloom realizes, however, that if he were to lose his middle-class dreams and supports, the reversal of fortune would reduce him to "Poverty. . . . Mendicancy. . . . Destitution. . . . Nadir of misery the aged impotent disfranchised ratesupported moribund lunatic pauper" (17.1936–47). In the preface to *Major Barbara* Shaw announces that "the worst of our crimes is poverty. . . . the evil to be attacked is not sin, suffering, greed, priestcraft, kingcraft, demagogy, monopoly, ignorance, drink, war, pestilence nor any other of the scapegoats which reformers sacrifice, but simply poverty" (CP 118). Even though Shaw, the reformer, attacked all of the sins he mentioned, he most feared poverty as the root of all social and personal problems. Almost as persistent as Shaw, and with Stephen as captive audience, Bloom argues for amending "many social conditions, the product of inequality and avarice and international hostility" (17.991–92).

As a "superior intelligence" whose creator had been reading Shaw's *Socialism and Superior Brains* (1894), the repetitious Bloom tells Stephen that he will work for reforms that sound something like Broadbent's schemes for making Ireland into a tourist attraction. Bloom's enterprises would include "golf links . . . hotels. . . . A scheme for the development of Irish tourist traffic" (17.1716–20)—not in heaven but in a secular utopia. His personal paradise is, however, revealed in his late-night waking dream in the Ithaca episode: he dreams of moving to "Bloom Cottage," something like Wordsworth's Dove Cottage but a lot more like the rectory of Ayot St. Lawrence, near Wheathampton in Herefordshire, where Shaw had moved in the spring of 1904, a few months before Bloom's day. In Holroyd's words, "the red-bearded revolutionary who promoted G. B. S. as a world-wide publicity phenomenon showed himself as a quietly-mannered gentleman in this remote twelfth-century village" (H2 188). He dubbed his country home Shaw's Corner. After 1907 he had private secretaries, a cook, a housekeeper, a maid, two gardeners, and a chauffeur—accoutrements of a lifestyle that belied his socialist politics and one to which Bloom aspires. In *Everybody's Political What's What,* Shaw announced, "Give me a convenient flat in town and a comfortable villa in the country with a few acres of lawn and garden, a couple of cars for long and short distance travel, and a supply of pocket-money not necessarily exceeding a couple of thousand pounds, and there is not a more contented man on earth than I" (*Bernard Shaw: Selection of His Wit and Wisdom* 210).

With regard to Bloom's wish fulfillment fantasy, Karen Lawrence notes "the quaint archaic vocabulary associated with the English country house" (193), the sort of country house the archaic Shaw had made famous. Bloom dreams that, settled in the ivy-covered two-story house with spacious grounds like Shaw's, he will be free to study, garden, cycle, and lecture. Incongruously and humorously, after all of his political rhetoric, he hopes to lecture on the subject of the novel of which he is the credible hero—"exotic, erotic masterpieces" (17.1594–1601) like *Ulysses.* The activities that Bloom wants to take up were, however, well known to be Shaw's occupations at Ayot St. Lawrence. Even the "Harris tweed cap . . . and useful garden boots" (17.1582–83) Bloom foresees himself wearing suggest G. B. S., and the servants Bloom imagines were no doubt amenities that Joyce envied his rich and famous countryman. Bloom concludes that at his country home he will, like the unacknowledged source of many of his ideas, become a local politician (17.1610)—a far cry from the beleaguered womanly man of his Circean fantasy.

Bella Bangs Bloom: "The Morbidization of the Modern Mandaboutwoman Type"

At the same time that the Circe scene reveals Bloom's fantasy of being a hero redeemer, it ridicules Shaw's prescription for androgyny by exposing its sexual implications. Bloom's hallucinatory nightmare in the bordello caricatures Shaw's insistence that in sex woman is the pursuer. Its dramatic form links it to Shavian drama and hints at parallels to "Don Juan in Hell" even though the Expressionistic drama is in dialogic relation to Goethe's *Walpurgisnacht* in *Faust*. Shaw's Hell is a hedonist's paradise in which illusion reigns supreme. Joyce's bawdy house, supposedly a paradise of fleshly delights, is really a kind of inferno for Bloom, who might, if he could, choose (like Don Juan) a more heavenly venue. In Shaw's "Palace of Lies" the only activity is to amuse yourself—supposedly the purpose of Nighttown in *Ulysses*. In Joyce's palace of lies, Bloom is as much an outsider as Don Juan is in Shaw's Hell.

In the bawdy house Bloom is confronted by the manly woman. Joyce's madam, Bella Cohen, is an unmasked Mrs. Warren acting out male fantasies and fetishes in her bordello. In Bloom's phantasmagorical confrontation with her, sex roles are reversed. Such a reversal is prefigured in Shaw's *Press Cuttings,* with "woman developing all the 'manly' qualities of pugnacity and overbearing insolence, man developing womanly qualities of timidity and indecision" to create a "devastatingly comic" play (MC 404). Shaw's *The Music-Cure* (1913) also anticipates Bloom's nightmare of Bella, for the little-known farce, as Gainor describes it, "features a man and a woman exploring their attraction to each other through the realization that . . . the woman wants to behave as a man, and the man prefers the occupation of a woman" (128). Shaw's Reginald is enthralled by the idea that the "muscular" Strega might beat him. He has secretly longed "to be mercilessly beaten by a splendid, strong, beautiful woman" (Plays 1130–31). A satire on the manly woman whom Shaw advocated in the best of all possible worlds, Bella/Bello, whose figure belies the feminine variation of her name, is phantasmagorically bellicose like Shaw's Mrs. Banger and Strega. She is a *"massive whoremistress"* (15.2742) with a *"sprouting moustache"* (15.2746–47).

As "The Fan," she may be related to Lady Corinthia Fanshawe, Shaw's femme fatale in his "Topical Sketch . . . during the Woman's War of 1909"—the war for woman's suffrage that the Fabian feminist supported outrageously with *Press Cuttings* (it was banned, but suffragists gave a private performance). Corinthia Fanshawe dominates in the Molly Bloom fashion. A stereotyped romantic icon, she carries a little gun that, according to the lady, is not loaded. She relies on her seductive charms to enslave her man: she pretends to be on the bottom but through devious manipulation rules him. Joyce's Fan accuses Bloom of being in a marriage in which "the missus is master. Petticoat government" (15.2759–60), a situation to which in real life Shaw lightheartedly admitted. His Mrs. Banger is "a man in petticoats" (1101). Wielding a big gun instead of a whip, Mrs. Banger becomes irresistibly attractive to a general upon whose face she sits (offstage) to prove that she is the dominant, phallic female. He loves it and consequently proposes marriage. In response to Bloom's desire (like General Sandstone's in *Press Cuttings*) for "domination" (15.2777), Bella demands that he tie the laces of her satanic hoof. She threatens him and calls him vile names. As a "grunting, snuffling" pig (15.2852–53), Bloom is treated by this Circe like a "bondslave" (15.2861), in a complete upending of traditional sex roles.

As castrating, phallic woman, Bello administers "correction," calling Bloom "a good girly" (15.2883–84) and forcing him into the stereotypical subservient woman's part: "You are unmanned . . . a thing under the yoke" (15.2965–66). Contrary to the conclusion of Sandra Gilbert and Susan Gubar that Bloom is a "covertly phallic version of the recumbent 'Ewig-Weibliche'" [eternal female] who may turn the tables on the "New Woman" (*Sexchanges* 336), Joyce's scenario implies that Joyce understood as well as Shaw that in a sexist society woman is an enslaved dependent. "By dramatizing the exaggerations of the masculinized woman and the feminized man, Shaw effectively demonstrates the real problems with marriage roles" (Gainor 130). Shaw's preface to *Getting Married* expatiates on "The Economic Slavery of Women" (CP 23–24) and their objectification in their quest to make themselves attractive to the men who will rule them. Bello informs Bloom that he will have to endure what women endure in order to be feminine: he will be "laced with cruel . . . vice like corsets . . . restrained in nettight frocks . . . and things stamped, of course, with my houseflag" (15.2975), having lost his freedom because he will be treated as a female. At night he must cover his "wellcreamed braceletted hands with forty threebutton gloves" (15.3079), nothing like Lina in *Misalliance*, who is revolted by the idea of the helplessness she associates with wearing women's clothes: she despises "gowns" because they "hamper" her (Plays 623). G. B. S. complained that women of Molly's time were not dressed, but "upholstered" (*Platform and Pulpit* 204).

Sex in Joyce's *Walpurgisnacht* is, like that in *Press Cuttings*, sadomasochistic. When Bloom—unlike Tiresias condemned to be female for concluding that women get more pleasure than men from sex—protests meekly that both sexes have "various joys" (15.3019), Bello, the sexual "martinet" (15.3025), accuses him of "insubordination." He addresses her as "Master! Mistress! Mantamer!" (15.3062), thus identifying with the wishful thinking of males like Shaw's General Sandstone, who gets blissfully tamed in *Press Cuttings,* and Reginald in *The Music-Cure,* who is transported by thoughts of Strega (the witch) as "terrible, splendid, ruthless, violent" (Plays 1131). In exchange for his masochistic submission, as Bloom places a ring on Bella's finger, Bella promises, "With this ring I thee own" (15.3068). As she becomes more menacing, she puts her property on the slave market, describing him as "trained by owner to fetch and carry" (15.3088). She compares Bloom to a milk cow and a manx cat and says, "Sing, birdy, sing" (15.3130), almost as if she has been reading *The Quintessence of Ibsenism,* in which Shaw makes his lengthy analogy between a caged pet bird and the womanly woman. This concept of matrimony as ownership and woman as breeder and house pet matches that of the Fabian socialist whose preface to *Getting Married* deems marriage law to be "inhuman and unreasonable" enslavement of woman (CP 1). Mrs. Farrell in *Press Cuttings* knows that marriage is simply unpaid domestic labor for a woman: "every woman's a charwoman from the day she's married" (Plays 1104).

In the mock marriage of Bello and Bloom, the former gives the domestic slave the female agenda: "You will make the beds, get my tub ready, empty the pisspots" (15.3073). She condemns him to do laundry and "swab the latrines." "You will dance attendance or I'll lecture you for your misdeeds" (15.3076). In magnifying the concept of the sadistic manly woman to an absurdity and examining it in a sexual context, Joyce shows how abasing a reversal of sex roles would be for the womanly man, as well as how debasing is the position of woman in marriage. Shaw was, of course, not the only feminist who found such roles debasing. Friedrich Engels and John Stuart Mill advanced similar views, but the Irishman exposed the issue in the popular, public arena of the stage, often suggesting that patriarchy encourages sado-masochistic gender relationships. Joyce may have read into Shaw's spoofs on such relations yet another confirmation of his similarity to his "frother." While suggesting his own attraction to sado-masochism, Joyce projected into the Circe scene anxieties that may also have been exacerbated by his knowledge of the kinky sex examined by Leopold von Sacher-Masoch in *Venus in Furs* (see Restuccia 125ff.). But at the same time Joyce's parody of sex roles bares with Shavian equivocation the underside of the role of the womanly woman. For in fantasy Bloom takes on the role about which Shaw theorized in *The Quintessence of Ibsenism* and which he caricatured in *The Music-Cure* and *Press Cuttings,* where "Rosa Carmina Banger, organizing secretary of the Anti-Suffraget League" (Plays 1098), prefigures Bella by promising to mount her "charger" (1100) and her man.

Molly as Privatized Life Force: "The Bringer of Plurabilities Haloed be Her Eve"

The manly woman, Bella, is in a binary relationship to Lady Corinthia Fanshawe in the same way that the femme fatale is related to Mrs. Banger, the "Bello" of *Press Cuttings:* they are two sides of the same phallic female. Like Molly, both enemies of women's rights are musical: Banger, "A soprano," is "said to be almost a baritone" (Plays 1098), whereas Corinthia boasts that she "can reach F in alt with the greatest facility"—a fact that marks her "as the prey of every libertine" (1100). As the woman who gets power through seeming submissive, Corinthia is less interested in women's suffrage than in her seductive power over men. She is related to Molly Bloom, who relishes her part as feminine woman programmed to give men pleasure. Socialized to please herself by pleasing men, Molly is the antithesis of Shavian females who rise above the level of caricature and people his plays—for example, Mrs. Warren, Major Barbara, and Eliza Doolittle. Moreover, in his preface to *Overruled* (1912), Shaw defined the decadence underlying relationships such as that of Molly and Blazes Boylan. Women, he said, are "the occupation of idle men just as men are the preoccupation of the idle women" (CP 106). Shaw's maxim suggests Molly's mode of life, if June 16, 1904, is a slice of it.

Interestingly, Molly, like Shaw's straitlaced mother, is a singer with a lover whom her husband tacitly accepts. The Eccles Street couple have not, however, gone so far in defying convention as Shaw's real-life parents did, for George Vandeleur Lee moved in with the Shaws in Dublin, and Lucinda Shaw—no doubt shocking her husband and son deeply—followed her lover to London, displaying courage that Molly lacks or that is outside of the omphalic scope of her desires. If Joyce happened upon an article in *Candid Friend* on July 6, 1901, he would have known of the Dublin fame of Lucinda, for Edward McNulty, the childhood friend of the playwright, wrote there in a sketch of G. B. S.'s boyhood that "Shaw's mother was the foremost amateur singer in Dublin" (I&R 19). The resemblances between the real and fictional women stop, however, at their unconventional marriages and their statuses as singers, for the high-toned Protestant soprano was energetic and pragmatic, whereas her warm-blooded Dublin counterpart is passive and slovenly, even if practical in satisfying her private needs.

The pleasure-loving, exhibitionistic Molly hates prudes "down on bathing suits and lownecks" (18.9–10). Almost as solipsistic as Stephen, she judges others in order to vindicate herself. Revealing her proud bad temper with a woman who acted as if "we wernt grand enough," she "gave her 2 damn fine cracks across the ear" (18.1070–71). Accepting the patriarchal lesson that women must rival other women because man is woman's reward in life, she is sexually competitive with them. Foul-mouthed in the stream of her consciousness, even though she prides herself on being a lady, she calls Mrs. Riordan an "old faggot" (18.4), probably "pious because no man would look at her twice" (18.11). The pious old woman (already familiar to readers of *Portrait*) was, however, relatively well educated, whereas Molly is not. Defensively, she calls other female singers "sparrowfarts . . . talking about politics" that they know nothing about, in order to make themselves "interesting" to men (18.879–81)—something that Molly cannot do, though she briefly contemplates studying Italian in order to get the attention of Stephen Dedalus. Unlike her, Shaw females talk about politics and social and ethical issues because they are interested in them or want to change things for themselves or for society, but the skeptical Molly reduces female motivation to her own siren's song. She is polar to a Shavian heroine like Vivie Warren—"the highly educated, capable individual young woman . . . working, smoking, preferring the society of men to that of women simply because men talk about the questions that interest her and not about servants and babies" (BSL 1:566).

An anti-intellectual, Molly "wouldnt give a snap of my two fingers for all their learning" (18.1564–65). Persistently, she refers to men as "them," stereotyping them as the Other, the intelligent species. Nevertheless, like the caged birds in *The Quintessence of Ibsenism,* she lives through, for, and on men—like the pet bird, a parasite in need of treats and coddling in exchange for her singing. Her attitudes are both a retort and a reductio ad absurdum of Shaw's analysis of the womanly woman and his valorizing of the New one; Molly is new only in her domesticated, adulterous, self-congratulatory sensuality. She recalls that an old bishop in Gibraltar preached about "womans higher functions," their riding bicycles and wearing bloomers (18.837–39), but Molly apparently found such insurgencies dull. Shaw, who found little in life dull, had an opinion on the issue of bloomers: whereas they only float through Molly's nocturnal reverie, G. B. S. disapproved of such feminist clothing as "a most irrational, ridiculous and unnatural compromise between male and female attire" (I&R 404)—a pestiferous form of rebellion unworthy of the New Woman. Nothing like the emancipated woman whom Shaw championed, Molly also has few of the scruples that he admired. Impiously, she acts to win male approval. She gave a Claddagh ring, a gift from her Gibraltar lover, to a soldier going to South Africa, where "those Boers killed him" (18.866–68).

A frank sensualist, Molly is less deluded than Gerty MacDowell and less openly cynical than her demonic counterpart Bella Cohen. Molly reads soft-porn popular romances (in Shaw's view, nefariously bad influences that infantilize women) like *Sweets of Sin* but thinks drinking champagne from a woman's slipper is fairy-tale foolishness and is suspicious of an unrealistic Madonna with an infant Jesus too big to be "taken out of her" (18.496–98). The crude sexuality of her character dialogues with the views of Shaw's pragmatic Ann Whitefield in *Man and Superman,* who argues against idealizing women: "If flesh and blood is not good enough for you you must go without, that's all. Women have to put up with flesh and blood husbands— . . . you will have to put up with flesh and blood wives" (Plays 380–81). Molly's coarse sexual vitality, however, has nothing to do with the selective breeding that motivates Ann. Even though Shaw thought of the Life Force as instinctual, even stupid, he gave Ann a sense of purpose that supersedes the amoral quest for narcissistic gratification. Shaw's Tanner, half-humorously trying to deter his pursuer, compares Ann to a boa constrictor and a feline predator. Thus the pert young woman anticipates Molly, who is, like the spider to whom Shaw compared woman, another devouring female and phallic mother. As such, she is a plausible lure, even if there is an element of male fantasy in the joy in sex she expresses in her monologue—which may be perhaps a playful retort to the sexual puritanism to which Shaw confessed. Subverting Victorian sexual morality and suggesting the sort of woman preferred by the people whose deviant sexual practices Steven Marcus studied in his book *The Other Victorians,* Molly enjoys her role as tempting sex object, measuring her value in terms of her ability to lure and satisfy men. Proudly recalling her lactating breasts, Molly admires them as a source of enjoyment for Bloom, who sucked her mother's milk (18.577). Such thoughts arouse her, and she eagerly anticipates her next orgasm with Boylan. Her self-congratulatory dreams of sexual bliss are a masculine projection of feminine desire, beyond, it seems (despite *Press Cuttings* and *The Music-Cure*), Shaw's wildest dreams. When he commented on the "dirt" and "flatulence" in *Ulysses* he had undoubtedly not read Molly Bloom's confession in the coda.

In Molly, Joyce valorizes the id, baring the amoral psyche of the flesh-and-blood female who delights in her orality (like her androgynous husband) and in her conquests. Less sexually liberated than women in literature and life who would succeed her (in, for example, the work of Erica Jong), Molly fantasizes fellatio with a young man to give him pleasure but shows no interest in cunnilingus and wouldn't let Bloom "lick" her "in Holles Street one night" (18.1245), despite the "polymorphous fantasies" of Joyce's letters to Nora Barnacle that dwell on "porcine love" that involves oral sex for both partners (Shechner 91). A "lovely little statue" of a nude male inspires her to muse, "i often felt i wanted to kiss him all over also his lovely young cock there so simple i wouldnt mind taking him in my mouth if nobody was looking as if it was asking you to suck it" (18.1349–53). She likes to sip "richlooking green and yellow expensive drinks" (18.127–28); she remembers cracking nuts with her teeth and "i wished i could have picked every morsel of that chicken out of my fingers it was so tasty and browned" (18.430–31). The singer learned that kissing was sexually arousing when her suitor Mulvey "put his tongue" in her mouth (18.771). Bloom, on the other hand, "does it all wrong thinking only of his own pleasure his tongue is too flat" (18.1249–50). When she got Poldy to propose, the fertility ritual was oral: "yes first i gave him the bit of seedcake out of my mouth" (18.1574).

Molly exemplifies the power and narcissism of women that the artist exploits and fears. In *Man and Superman,* John Tanner says that the artist is to women "half vivisector, half vampire." He becomes intimate with women "to study them, to strip the mask of convention from them, to surprise their inmost secrets, knowing that they have the power to rouse his deepest creative energies" (though he adds that "the great artist" is a "bad husband" who sacrifices his family to his art—an observation that Joyce no doubt recognized as truth) (Plays 341). But Shaw argued that the power of such exploited women is the correlative of their bondage: "The slavery of women means the tyranny of women. No fascinating woman ever wants to emancipate her sex: her object is to gather power into the hands of Man because she knows that she can govern him. . . . The cunning & attractive slave women disguise their strength as womanly weakness, their audacity as womanly timidity, their unscrupulousness as womanly innocence" (BSL 2:260–61). Joyce's portrait of Molly reveals how closely he had studied woman (Nora Barnacle and others; see Maddox, chapter 12) to discover her "inmost secrets."

Molly's monologue spills the intimate particulars of the sort of female about whom Shaw generalizes: because her upbringing is "worse" than a man's she is "an unscrupulous user of her personal fascination to make men give her what she wants" (GBS 367). Like Mrs. Lunn, one of the femme fatales of Shaw's little-known farce *Overruled* (1912), Molly is an "Andalusian beauty" from Gibraltar; Mrs. Lunn's father was a captain in the artillery—not so grand as a major or so lowly as a sergeant, one of which Molly's father may have been. Shaw's seductress is having an affair; however, unlike Molly's, it lacks "volcanic passion." Although Mrs. Lunn, like Molly, is sexually alluring, she is bored by male pursuit and "hopelessly respectable" (Plays 710), despite coming from the exotic background that Joyce attributes to Molly. Lacking personal hegemony, however, Mrs. Lunn, like Mrs. Bloom, uses her seductive power to dominate her husband and attract another man. As Henke observes, Molly "tries to reenact both the pre-oedipal script of infant-mother attachment and the oedipal drama of paternal seduction" (133), for she wants the unqualified love of the mother from the womanly man, while with the manly man, Blazes, she plays the part of temptress, an adulteress like Shaw's Mrs. Lunn, who encourages her illicit lover while assuring him that commitment is unnecessary because of her marriage. Like her, Molly achieves identity and self-esteem through ensnaring males. She needs men to validate her existence and, indeed, seems almost to articulate the penis envy that Freud attributed to women: "God i wouldn't mind being a man and get up on a lovely woman" (18.1146–47). Not interested in ideas, Molly is "new" in a very different way from females who rejected the self-sacrificing, nurturing, Victorian ideal. Selfish, hedonistic, and preoccupied with sex—if her nighttime thoughts are her signature—she has none of the redeeming features of the new person posited by Shaw, the resourceful woman committed to a useful, productive life.

Convinced that even women disdain a woman without a man (18.473–74), Molly defines herself in relation to men, accepting the preconceived patterns provided her by patriarchal values and masculine fantasy. Her portrayal illustrates a Shavian maxim: "The greatest obstacle to the emancipation of women? Lust" (quoted in Harris 227). Exploiting her dependency, she enjoys her consuming role as sex trap. Like Gerty she spends lots of time making herself alluring. Shaw's preface to *The Doctor's Dilemma* scripts the role of such attractive women, who are, in their expedient will to achieve their ends, like the "utterly selfish" artist. With a "genius for personal attractiveness," Shaw wrote, they "expend more thought, labor, skill, inventiveness, taste, and endurance on making themselves lovely than would suffice to keep a dozen ugly women honest; and this enables them to maintain a high opinion of themselves and an angry contempt for unattractive and careless women, whilst they lie and cheat and slander and sell themselves without a blush" (CP 245n46).

Molly is such a self-centered beauty, the female counterpart of the selfish budding artist, Stephen, and, in her anti-intellectualism, his opposite. Her thoughts run to face lotion that she needs to keep her skin from looking old, for if you are old, men will not want you, and you are ready for the "ashpit" (18.747). Unlike her, Shaw believed that "the true joy in life" is "being used for a purpose recognized by yourself as a mighty one; the being thoroughly worn out before you are thrown on the scrap heap" (CP 163). Lacking Shavian motives, the complacent Molly is a convert to the commercialism that encourages the commodification of women. Like Gerty, she ornaments herself to privilege her femininity. Shaw opposed such valorization, for feminine clothes constrict a woman, making her a passive object. In an interview in the *World of Dress,* he wondered how women could put up with the fetters of a petticoat. He advised women to wear "anything that will show how they are constructed and allow them the free use of their limbs. . . . A woman is a biped, built like a man, let her dress like a man" (I&R 404). Of course, Molly is not built like a man and assiduously avoids advice like Shaw's. She covets garters, low-cut blouses, chemises, and lingerie to enhance her sex appeal. She spends "hours dressing and perfuming and combing" (18.149), only to undress to have intercourse with Blazes Boylan. She intends to wheedle an aquamarine and "a gold bracelet" out of Blazes so that she can adorn herself (18.262) like the slave woman to whom Shaw objects. She wears a corset to keep her figure looking like a sensually plump mannikin, even though it must have gores for better sexual access. Molly is like the woman in petticoats whose "system of dressing" Shaw disdained: "If she was not studded with buttons all over her tempting contours like a sort of super-sofa, she was pinched in and padded out so as to produce" the upholstery effect (*Platform and Pulpit* 173–74). Molly worries about her weight and even contemplates giving up stout to maintain the right standard of voluptuousness. She rearranges the furniture, not to please herself or her husband but in hopes of impressing her lover. Like Shaw's womanly woman, she does everything to please men, but unlike her, not everything to please her husband. Her relationship with Poldy is, indeed, like that of Shaw and his wife: Molly and Bloom do not cohabit sexually even though they are married. Nevertheless a songbird with a sexual orientation, Molly is singing for the opposite sex. She cultivates her voice to get applause and male attention, egotistic satisfaction, and the opportunity to carry on her affair with her manager—not because she gets any aesthetic gratification from her "art."

Manifesting a sex drive that the Victorian Shaw recognized as the female's instinct to perpetuate the race but not as hedonistic desire, Molly distinguishes herself from the mother woman because she does not think of herself primarily as a nurturing, self-sacrificing caretaker. In her internal monologue she has few thoughts about her roles as wife and mother. She muses on how to manipulate Poldy to get what she wants from him and disapproves of others for ridiculing him. She seems to enjoy her passive power over her husband, thoughts of whom preoccupy her, whereas she thinks of her daughter Milly only in passing (and then as a rival)—slightly miffed at her because she sent a letter to her father and only a card to her. Displaying no special maternal feeling for her daughter—not so much as Shaw's madam, Mrs. Warren, shows for

Vivie—she notes that Milly is too critical of her: "Her tongue is a bit too long" because she criticized her mother for opening her blouse "too low" (18.1033–34). Blithely unaware of her double standard, Molly in turn remembers lecturing Milly for overexposing herself. Milly is a slip off of the older bloom. As her father tells himself, "Molly. Milly. Same thing watered down" (6.87). To the self-absorbed Molly, Milly's absence is a convenience, for her daughter cannot interfere with her current obsession, her affair with Boylan. When Molly briefly mourns her dead son Rudy, she acknowledges that she will not have another child and is glad that Blazes did not impregnate her. She complains of "clothes and cooking and children" and marital sex as woman's lot (18.1130), but this passing thought seems to apply to the generality of women whose husbands drink, gamble, beat them, or fail to support them—sins that Shaw associated with the poverty caused by patriarchal power.

In what amounts to a female wet dream that distinguishes her from conventional Dublin women, Molly differs significantly from the domesticated mother woman whom Shaw described as trapped in marriage and maternity. Thus she gets greater satisfaction from her amoral adultery than the other women in *Ulysses* get from their inglorious lives. Although Joyce makes Molly a bourgeois sex goddess, the real Magna Mater of *Ulysses* is Mina Purefoy, whose faith in the patriarchal establishment is pure. She is the pelvis bone of the whole social system, an archetypal breeder—different from Molly, who is not a symbol of such rampant, self-abnegating fecundity. By distinguishing the bovine breeder (bovine because the Homeric parallel to her labor is "The Oxen in the Sun") from the sexual siren, Joyce may be documenting his response to Shaw's belief in selective breeding. One implication of Shaw's credo must have alarmed the renegade Catholic, considering that it assumes, like Catholic dogma, that procreation is the purpose of marriage. In Mina Purefoy Joyce reveals the results of accepting Church teaching, teaching that Bloom disapproves in his internal monologue: "Birth every year almost. That's in their theology or the priest wouldn't give the woman the confession, the absolution. Increase and multiply. Did you ever hear of such an idea?" (8.31–33). Shaw agreed, for he approved of birth control while urging careful selection of one's mate, with an eye to the sort of progeny a marriage would produce. Unlike Shaw's Life Force, Mina Purefoy, like Joyce's mother, is the indiscriminately fertile mother, whereas Joyce's Life Force is a venal middle-class temptress whose children, one dead, the other a clone of herself, are not evidence of selective breeding.

A simplistic narcissist whose consciousness valorizes her private responses and whose personalism characterizes the male-made female stereotype, Molly lacks the charity that her husband displays throughout the day, even though she does better than Father Conmee (who offers only a blessing) by throwing a coin out of the window to a one-legged sailor (10.253). She is religious out of fear, saying a Hail Mary after thunder in case the heavens were falling "to punish us" (18.135). She loves kissing, but not confessing. She likes to think that other women would envy her successes with men, for, in acceding to her conditioned belief that women are defined through men, she accepts the idea that women are marketable and quantifiable. She boasts to herself that she knew more at fifteen than others know at fifty about men (18.886–87), the only subject she really enjoys studying. She is proud of having a husband, a daughter, a "swell with money" as a lover, and a voice that attracts male attention. Self-satisfied, she thinks she could have "been a prima donna only i married him" (18.893–96)—a secondhand choice unworthy of a Shaw heroine.

An archetypal Calypso/Circe, Molly is a grown-up Cleopatra who would probably have bored Shaw, who made his temptress a mere girl or, in Candida, a beautiful but ultimately faithful matron who in some respects resembles Molly. Perhaps a recapitulation and an answer to Shaw's Candida, another dominant wife with an admirer, Molly enjoys Bloom's worshipful approach to her, his kneeling down in rain (18.310). She thinks men are "savage" for sex (18.312)—an idea that only once enters Candida's conversation. Like Candida, however, and Ann Whitefield, who tells Tanner that although "you seem to understand all the things I dont understand, you are a perfect baby in the things I do understand" (Plays 348), Molly believes that men are babies. She knows that they need women and "cant get on without us" (18.239–40). Like Candida, she is ironically comparable to the Virgin Mother; "Ave Maria" (18.274–75)—hardly her song—is part of her repertoire. Also, already in a kind of ménage à trois, Molly contemplates taking on the young bard Dedalus as yet another sex partner, thus fantasizing a liaison that the proper Candida courts and then renounces. For Candida, the choice between men is *either/or;* in Molly's greedy, amoral night thoughts, it is *and*. Both women, though, are manipulative, phallic females: the Shavian heroine gets her power through her intelligence, charm, and indispensable maternalism, whereas Joyce's gets hers through her sexual allure. Both control their husbands, but Candida's Morell is an idealist regarding matrimony, whereas Bloom is a realist. Candida supports Morell's ideal of marriage but destroys his illusion that he has the power in it. Perhaps Bloom, as womanly man, never had such illusions. Whereas Molly expects Poldy to spoil her, Candida wants "somebody to protect, to help, to work for," says Marchbanks to her husband: "You don't understand what a woman is" (Plays 147).

Defining woman differently from the way Shaw does, Molly muses that Bloom "understood or felt what a woman is and i knew i could always get around him" (18.1579–80). Nevertheless, like a Shavian disciple, she thinks—although her monologue gives no evidence of the truth of her claim—"itd be much better for the world to be governed by the women in it you wouldnt see women going and killing one another and slaughtering when do you ever see women rolling round drunk or gambling every penny they have . . . because a woman . . . knows where to stop" (18.1434–39). In Molly's night thoughts, her contradictory affirmation of the worthiness of women in the world is incongruous and ludicrous. Because of her habitual dependence upon men, Molly has revealed herself to be singularly unprepared by education or attitude to be an emancipated woman ready to assume a role in society. Instead, she and Leopold agree on woman's association with nature. She is a "flower of the mountain" (18.1576) and, as such, a yea-sayer of the Life Force and a cognate of nature and matter, but her husband, a Bloom whose pseudonym is Flower, combines matter and mind, body and vital spirit, passive nature and active intelligence. Despite Gilbert and Gubar's rejection of the idea that Joyce hints "at the possibility of a nobler and more vital androgyny" (*Sexchanges* 333), in his androgyny Bloom is more complete than Molly. He resembles Shaw himself, who projected, according to J. Ellen Gainor, "a masculine sense of female identification" (126). Although Gainor assumes that Shaw privileges masculinity, whereas like Joyce he may merely be reflecting the social reality of masculine valorization, she concludes that Shaw's work presents "his personal unisexual sensibility" (125)—one like Bloom's. Poldy exemplifies the repeated message of Shaw's plays and polemics: in the mixture of the supposedly feminine and masculine qualities we discover a credible modern form of heroism. At the root of his depiction of Molly as well as of Bloom, Joyce is, like Shaw, gynocentric. In his 1911 biography *George Bernard Shaw*, Archibald Henderson summarized the Shavian view of woman, which prefigures Joyce's: "Recognizing woman as the primal vital agency in the fulfillment of Nature's laws, he has not unnaturally come to regard her as much more formidable than man because she is, as it were, archetypal, belonging to the original structure of things" (81).

Joyce's primal woman is a wish fulfillment fantasy of an ambivalent (feminist?) male chauvinist, perhaps even a detailed comic retort to Shavian feminism, which fails to come to grips with sexuality. Shaw supported forthright eroticism in theory but apparently not in fact. Molly's sexuality might be construed as a form of Shavian realism—the vitalist ability to experience life as it is without being, like Gerty MacDowell, deceived by illusions; but her self-gratifying hedonism seems to be a refutation of Shavianism. The lascivious Molly, unlike her husband, has no real commitment to others, no commitment to ideas or to making a contribution to society. Nevertheless, Henderson's analysis of Shaw's mission and of his limitations corroborates Joyce's theme: Shaw's lifework, he wrote, "may be said to consist in an attack on the conception that passions are necessarily base and unclean; his art works are glorifications of the man of conviction who can find a motive, and not an excuse for his passions" (PP 464). Shaw's "inability to portray sexual passion convincingly," however, may have piqued his cunning competitor, adding to his many motives for depicting in his Penelope coda sexual passion supposedly from a woman's point of view.

Mother, Son, and Hamlet's Father's Ghost: "Anglers or Angelers Coexistent and Compresent with or without Their Tertium Quid"

When Molly muses that the world would be better off ruled by women, she refers to the qualities of her womanly—and ironically Christlike—husband. Bloom's secret dream is of power *for,* not *over,* people, whereas the manly woman, Bella, and Molly, a more benign adumbration of the phallic woman, want power over men, like Shaw's Mrs. Banger and Corinthia, having been taught by them that domination represents strength. The antiauthoritarian Shaw knew better, and in creating the lovable if weak but heroic survivor with a social conscience, Joyce admired his great emancipating precursor's credo while subscripting its ineffectuality in a society prejudiced against womanly men.

Indeed, Joyce's parody of Bloom suggests that the novelist's exaggerations of a Shaw-like persona are not only "stolentelling" but also an expression of Joyce's ambivalence toward Shaw, whom he simultaneously admires and ridicules. Joyce's use of Shaw exemplifies the thesis of Linda Hutcheon's *A Theory of Parody:* parody is an expression of admiration for its model and source. In parodying Shaw, Joyce was imitating Shaw, who even made fun of himself as the acerbic but saintly buffoon G. B. S. Like Bloom, who stammers in Nighttown, "I am doing good to others" (15.682), Shaw was a do-gooder. Despite Joyce's playful attempts to detour the reader from routes to Shaw (by making him more endomorphic than ectomorphic and interested in visceral pleasures, like kidneys for breakfast), Bloom's ruminations indicate that he is, sometimes ambivalently, a parallel to G. B. S., the ethical humanist who was a vegetarian.

Although Bloom enjoys natural functions that Shaw thought "pestiferous," he gets upset over the Lestrygonian lunchers at the Burton. He disapproves of vegetarians like A. E. and Shaw who believe that if they eat a steak, "the eyes of the cow will pursue you through all eternity" (8.535–36). Yet when he sees men eating, he thinks, "Eat or be eaten. Kill! Kill!" (8.703) and reconsiders vegetarianism. "Pain to animal.... Wretched brutes there at the cattle market, waiting for the poleaxe to split their skulls open" (8.722–24). An outspoken vegetarian and antivivisectionist, in his preface to *The Doctor's Dilemma,* Shaw condemned the "humane butcher" who "will cut a calf's throat and hang it up by its heels to bleed slowly to death because it is the custom to eat veal and insist on its being white" (CP 259). He insisted, "I would rather swear fifty lies than take an animal which had licked my hand in good fellowship and torture it" (255). Like Shaw, Bloom is disgusted over thoughts of the slaughter of animals. Despite his love of succulent meats, he gets so upset over the cannibalistic lunchers that he orders a cheese sandwich. In the pub scene, he orders cider, thus nearly emulating Shaw, who wrote, "In refusing to drink maraschino and drinking apple juice instead, I may seem to thoughtless topers as heroically self-sacrificing as St. Bernard and St. Thomas Aquinas when they refused archbishoprics; but the truth is I like apple juice" (*Bernard Shaw: Selection of His Wit and Wisdom* 20).

Bloom thus has many Shavian characteristics and ideas, which Joyce ridicules while paying tribute to them. His novel concerns the search for a father as well as the search for a son. Regarding the composition of *Ulysses,* Joyce's biographer Herbert Gorman wrote, "Joyce himself was a lost son ... in search of the real father" (224). If *Ulysses* can be said to have a plot rather than development through accretions discernible in its thematic patterns, the action concerns the encounter of Bloom and Stephen. Indeed, in their final scene together, in a sacrilegious bonding, the father and surrogate son cross-urinate, their micturation mingling in a comic image of unity that places the two men on the same level, deflating and satirizing the vanities of both while affirming their basic humanity (17.1186–1209). Molly, the tertium quid—temptress Earth Mother and Life Force, more Calypso/Circe than faithful Penelope—is in bed behind the window above them. At the apex of the triangle she completes the trinity, appropriately, for both Shaw and Joyce placed *amor matris,* the anima, the tantalizing fecundity of the eternal female, at the center of creation. In the woman both symbolically reverenced the creative principle. According to Julia Kristeva, Renaissance artist Bellini symbolically gives the Virgin Mary the status of the Father in his painting *The Sacred Allegory* (269). Such valorization of the Virgin is, writes Frances Restuccia, the same in Joyce: "As if suppressing the Masochian supplanting of the Father by the Mother/Virgin, Bellini's *The Sacred Allegory* situates Mary on the throne: she assumes the place of the Father" (176). At the end of *Ulysses,* Molly is enthroned above father and son, where both Shaw and Joyce (and many Irishmen)—whether masochists, as Restuccia argues that Joyce is, or not—placed the maternal Life Force. Both writers recognized, nevertheless, the relationship between female creation and the activity of the creating artist, who, according to Shaw, Havelock Ellis, and Edward Carpenter, considered genius to be "the ability of artists" to interpret the sexes to one another (Gainor, 127). At the National Library, Stephen asserts that the artist is like the fertility goddess, "mother Dana"—a parallel to Molly (9.376).

In celebrating androgyny, both Irishmen also encompassed the trinity in themselves. The family romances of both "Sonny" Shaw and "Sunny" Joyce revolved around fathers who were unsatisfactory role models and weak rivals for an Oedipal triangle; their mothers had good reason to isolate themselves emotionally from their feckless husbands. Although their situations differed, the outlines of the psychological socialization of Shaw and Joyce were similar. Shaw's mother was a strong, phallic woman who seems to have neglected her son emotionally (even though she helped him during his lean years in London). Joyce's mother was a self-sacrificing womanly woman who favored her oldest son and tried, unsuccessfully, to compensate for her miseries through him. Pregnant, like Mina Purefoy, as often as her abusive husband could impregnate her, she tried to mold her son into a bourgeois Catholic like herself. Ineffectual fathers and ambivalence regarding their mothers seem to have prompted in both dissatisfied geniuses the need to create themselves. Among Shaw plays that seemed to stir a deep interest in Joyce was *Candida,* in which, as Arthur Ganz points out, "the father figure is shown to be weak (in effect, he is emasculate), and the mother's sexual fantasy is directed toward the son" (111)—a situation that pertains at the end of *Ulysses,* where the mother's allure reasserts itself after the father and son figures become comically consubstantial, acting out Stephen's Shakespeare theory, which makes the son the father as well as the father's ghost, and the father the son. The artist creates both as he creates himself through his characters.

Both Shaw and Joyce were troubled, as Stephen Dedalus is, by the question of paternity and, it seems, recognized that they were inclined toward the dual sexuality that Bloom barely eludes. Indeed, androgynous sympathies permitted both to create phallic females in their own images, so to speak. The imaginations of both Irishmen were engaged deeply by love triangles—almost a constant feature of Shaw's early and middle plays and in some of his late ones. In *Arms and the Man* Sergius and Bluntschli are Raina's suitors; in *Candida* husband and young lover vie for the heroine; in *Caesar and Cleopatra* the absent Mark Anthony competes with Caesar in Cleopatra's mind; in *The Devil's Disciple* the Reverend Anderson's wife thinks Dick Dudgeon loves her; in *Man and Superman* the romantic Octavius is Ann's suitor, but she pursues the realist Tanner; in *John Bull's Other Island* Broadbent pursues Nora Reilly, but she wishes her suitor were Larry Doyle; in *Pygmalion* Eliza Doolittle and Henry Higgins seem to be a romantic duo, but Eliza chooses Freddy; in *The Doctor's Dilemma* a doctor covets the wife of his artist patient. Irresistibly emulating the Shavian pattern, Joyce's *Exiles* concerns a love triangle, just as *Ulysses* does with more subtle ramifications that are developed obscurely and incestuously in *Finnegans Wake.*

Like the Shaw who wrote *Self Sketches,* Stephen is interested in biographical interpretation. He reads Shakespeare, not just for art's sake or for the spiritual values represented by A. E. in the National Library scene. Stephen relates the principals of *Hamlet*—"dispossessed son . . . . murdered father . . . guilty queen"—to Shakespeare's family (9.179-80). These principals parallel Stephen, Bloom (attacked but not murdered), and Molly—a trinity in which the female "mother Dana, weave[s] and unweave[s] our bodies" just as "does the artist weave and unweave his image" (9.376-78). These are the polar anima and animus, female and male, Molly and Stephen, who are brought together in the womanly man Bloom, the murdered father who is also Joyce. Hamlet's father's ghost is "a voice heard only in the heart of him who is the substance of his shadow, the son consubstantial with the father" (9.480-81). The son is the substance of the father's shadow as Joyce is the substance of ghostly fathers like Shakespeare and Shaw. In his thoughts Stephen parodies the Nicene Creed to indicate that the true creator is the self: "He who Himself begot middler the Holy Ghost and Himself sent Himself . . . and . . . sitteth on the right hand of His Own Self" (9.493-98).

In *Ulysses* Stephen is, like Bloom, fascinated and fearful over woman's sexuality. In the National Library, the young man contemplates female infidelity by referring to Shaw's *The Dark Lady of the Sonnets,* a play that Joyce had illegally appropriated and produced in Zurich—an act that might, in a Freudian context, be compared to stealing the father's substance. Shaw postulated that the lady betrayed Shakespeare with a friend like Robert in *Exiles,* and his comment that the woman waiting to be wooed does so as "the spider does the fly" anticipates Stephen's view of woman. While presenting his symposium on Shakespeare, Stephen argues that Ann Hathaway (like Ann Whitefield with respect to John Tanner in *Man and Superman*) pursued the genius Shakespeare. "If others have their will [that is, William] Ann hath a way" (9.256-57). Woman is the pursuer of the great writer who makes "no mistakes. His errors are volitional and are portals of discovery" (9.228-29)—a Shavian sentiment, despite Shaw's awareness that the willful artist is an egoist. In the preface to his Shakespearean play, Shaw wrote that "the Dark Lady most likely thought . . . [Shakespear] insufferably conceited; for there is no reason to suppose she liked his plays any better than Minna Wagner liked Richard's music drama" (CP 763). Such words would have hit home for Joyce, for they describe his own dark lady, Nora Barnacle, whom Joyce, as godlike artist, re-formed and created in *Ulysses* as Molly Bloom. She is the phallic and omphalic mother who, like Stephen, the aesthetic intellect, is subsumed in Bloom. Three thus become one and creator created.

One of the themes of *Major Barbara,* the title figure of which is a dominant woman, is that character's search to become her own father—a theme that Chesterton noted in his 1911 study of Shaw (146). Barbara, as Ganz observes, is "determined to reverse the traditional roles of child and parent" (169–70). In *Ulysses* Stephen reveals a similar purpose in his discourse on Shakespeare. Like Barbara, Stephen believes that "a father . . . is a necessary evil" (9.828). The issue of paternity that preoccupied the younger writer is often anticipated in Shaw's dramas. *You Never Can Tell* (1898) questions the validity of the biological father. Philip announces to his twin sister, "No man alive shall father me" (Plays 176). The irrepressible twins, indeed, choose the paternal figure of preference, the waiter. In *Caesar and Cleopatra* Caesar chooses two surrogate sons—Apollodorus, the aesthete, and Ruffio, the militarist. In *Misalliance,* young Bentley has adopted the "old josser" John Tarleton as his father, whereas Johnny Tarleton feels an affinity for Bentley's dad. Clever Joey Percival is better off than the other chaps because he has three fathers—one "natural," one a free-thinking philosopher, and one a priest who "didn't believe in anything" (Plays 627, 640). The intruder who appears accuses Tarleton of being his father (628), perhaps acting out Shaw's gravest doubts about his own paternity. With his biographers, however, Shaw tried to suppress the suspected significance of George Vandeleur Lee, his mother's music teacher—an issue that observers of Shaw's life have had trouble ignoring. No doubt the uncertainty that he repressed regarding his sire led Shaw to question the whole idea of fatherhood.

In his preface to *Misalliance* Shaw wrote, it should be remembered, a section entitled "The Child Is Father to the Man." It anticipates Stephen's argument about Hamlet and the identity of father and son. Shaw stated, no doubt to a receptive ear in Joyce, "We are not content with fathers: we must have godfathers, forgetting that the child is godfather to the man. . . . [T]he true representative of God at the Christening is the child itself" (CP 46). Thus the writer gives himself the imprimatur, as Stephen Dedalus does, to create himself. The thrust of the *Misalliance* preface section entitled "Parents and Children" is that the child should father himself, for parents warp and waste children

(50). A child "has a right to privacy as to its own doings and its own affairs as much as if it were its own father" (50), for the family is a "humbug" (52), blocking the child's self-actualization. Shaw would no doubt have supported Stephen's query, "Who is the father of any son that any son should love him or he any son?" (9.844–45).

Shaw, the literary godfather chosen by Joyce, did not go so far as Stephen Dedalus, who announces that "paternity is a legal fiction" (9.844), but such a conclusion must be inferred from his theories. Stephen uses as his authorities the heresiarchs Arius and Sabellius. The Arian heretics argued that the Son is like the Father, but not identical to him. Sabellius, the third-century tritheist, argued that God is at once One and One in Three—Creator, Redeemer, and Sanctifier—all different expressions of the same person—in *Ulysses,* Stephen, Bloom, and Molly. Stephen argues that Sabellius "held that the Father was Himself His Own Son" (9.862–63), thus suggesting that the Creator is also the Savior—an idea corroborating Shaw's notions of the functions of the artist. In orthodox Christianity, the Word consubstantial with the Father is generated by God the Father, though one with him, but Shaw and Joyce reverse the relationship while consubstantiating it: *filiatus* creates *paternitas,* but father *is* son, the incarnate word of the heretical artist. Stephen rejects A. E.'s preference for formless "spiritual essences" in art (9.49), laughing at a formless trinity—"Father, Word and Holy Breath" (9.61)—for the incarnation of the artistic word, the triune sonly/womanly man, creates out of himself and his interaction with the real world, in which surrogate fathers are available even if they do not, like Bloom, offer themselves.

Without the imprimatur of the created father, the godlike artist subsumes his precursor, as it seems Joyce subsumed Shaw in *Ulysses.* Stephen's "unsubstantial father" (9.553) Simon Dedalus is, like Shaw's, an inadequate sire for genius. Furthermore, Stephen argues that Shakespeare sired his characters, drawing even "Shylock out of his long pocket" (9.741–42). Shavian characters were, of course, whether in petticoats or pants, noted to be Shaws. In using the heresiarch Sabellius to fortify his paradoxical argument that "the Father was Himself His Own Son," Stephen asks whether "the father [like Shaw?] who has not a son be not a father can the son who has not a father be a son?" (9.864–65). Apparently Shaw, who had no son, could be sire to the son without a father and be subsumed in him. Stephen asks, like Romeo and Shaw, "What's in a name? That is what we ask ourselves in childhood when we write the name that we are told is ours" (9.927–29). Joyce believed that there is a lot in a name. Although he inscribed himself as Joyce in childhood, he knew by the time he wrote *Ulysses* that he shared a surname with Shaw. The Scylla and Charybdis episode suggests that Joyce's chosen alter ego is Dedalus, "Fabulous artificer. The hawklike man" (9.952) of *Portrait*, who is an avatar of the Shavian spokesperson Ra, whose symbol is the hawk.

Joyce's unacknowledged mentor also invented pseudonyms for himself. In the triangle involving two Georges—George Carr Shaw and George Vandeleur Lee, one of whom he was named after—Shaw avoided questions of paternity: he became Bernard Shaw; then, as music critic, he was Cornetto di Bassetto; and finally he made famous G. B. S., his monogram. Joyce's awareness of the mysterious coincidence that his name in Gaelic was the same as Shaw's provided him with linguistic kinship and thus a potential literary father. Stephen announces, indeed, that fatherhood "is a mystical estate, an apostolic succession, from only begetter to only begotten" (9.837–39). In *Our Theatre in the Nineties* Shaw boldly claimed to be the literary inheritor of the "apostolic succession" that began with the Greek masters (7).

In his murky argument Stephen arrives at the position that "we walk through ourselves . . . always meeting ourselves" (9.1044–46), for the artist is "an androgynous angel, being a wife unto himself" (9.1052)—a womanly man who can create in and through himself both genders ("old men, young men, wives, widows"; 9.1045–46). In his dramatis personae, Shaw prided himself on creating such an array of men and women while ostentatiously pointing out his androgynous disposition. According to Mark Shechner, Stephen's theories about the Bard establish two Shakespeares, one "a middle class actor and playwright whose plays bear the imprint of family intrigue, and the other a metaphysical deity who is transcendent, autonomous father, and yet bisexual" (22). The Shakespeare whom Stephen defines, therefore, has much in common with Shaw, another actor-playwright, bearing the imprint of "family intrigue" and propounding androgyny, the intrapersonal form of bisexuality. Stephen's view of Shakespeare the man relates him to the author of *The Philanderer,* who, in *Man and Superman,* reinterprets Don Giovanni. Don Juan rejects his old role as a waste of creative talent in romantic pursuits. Stephen avers that Shakespeare found that "assumed dongiovannism will not save him" (9.458–59).

In becoming the creative artist comparable to Shaw's Don Juan, no longer merely a womanizer, Shakespeare became free to create *Hamlet*, in which he played both Hamlet's father's ghost and was himself the son. Shaw's inference in the preface to *Misalliance* that the son creates the father and *is* the father is the thesis that animates Stephen's theory. Karen Lawrence notes that Stephen's "elaborate reading of Shakespeare is, of course, an expression of his own feelings about paternity, betrayal and the relationship between the artist and his work. The basic image of the artist fathering himself is a comfort to a young writer who scorns his natural parents and thinks of himself as 'made not begotten' " (81). Her description of Joyce suggests Sunny Jim's link to his secretly elected literary progenitor. He made himself out of the ideas of others, especially Shaw, transformed and transubstantiated by Joyce's gifts for language. As Lawrence points out, Joyce's Shakespearean theory is relevant to his "deliberate use of rhetoric and style to reveal and disguise the sources of his ideas" (82).

Just as Joyce created the father figure Bloom as an adumbration of himself and a chosen father, Shaw created numerous father figures in his plays, all, like his privileged female characters, admittedly Shaws: notable examples are Caesar, John Tanner, Andrew Undershaft, and Captain Shotover. Caesar is more or less a straight presentation of Shaw's scripting of himself. Kind, good-natured, humorous, courageous, unmalicious, he is similar to Leopold Bloom, even though Poldy as father is sometimes ludicrous, like Shavian males whom Shaw admires and parodies as self-portraits. But Shaw also created artist-son figures like Marchbanks in *Candida* and the selfish, egocentric artistic genius Dudebat, scapegoated by the medical establishment in *The Doctor's Dilemma* (1906). Like Stephen Dedalus, Dudebat has chosen his artistic parent; he declares himself to be a "disciple of Bernard Shaw" (Plays 530), an admission that Joyce studiously avoided making. Dudebat aims to be the superman but is, as Ganz notes, "the rebellious child who disputes not only the paternal claim to moral and intellectual authority but the possession of the maternal figure as well" (172). In his rejection of patriarchy by claiming the importance of *amor matris,* Dudebat prefigures Stephen Dedalus.

Preoccupied, like Shaw, with his sense of competition with Shakespeare as a precursor, Stephen tries to appropriate Shakespeare by inventing a theory regarding literary paternity that allows him to identify with the master playwright. Shaw had willfully refused to place *Hamlet* in a historical context, thus reading the drama as an example of his own desire to be sui generis. He wrote that (like himself) Hamlet "felt no impulse to his duty. That was the beginning of modern drama, which challenged moral judgment" (GBS 336). Nevertheless, like Joyce, who pretended to deem Shaw a "blackguard" (JJ1 447), Shaw purported to despise Shakespeare in essays like "Blaming the Bard" (1896), despite the fact that he told biographer Henderson that "Shakespeare was like mother's milk to me" (MC 30). Thus Shaw unwittingly revealed the *amor matris* that can be provided by an androgynous male. Shaw was such a source for the cunning Joyce, who preferred to disguise his literary parentage because he wanted, like Shaw, to be self-generated and was, like his mentor, irresistibly self-generating. In defending the theory of self-creating, willful genius, Joyce emulated Shaw, who admittedly made himself out of literary progenitors—among them Shakespeare, Goethe, and Ibsen. Discovering that a person is his own creator is the business of Shaw's superman, the singular man gifted with subversive intelligence, the drive to use his life for a meaningful purpose, and the vitalism to create himself in words. Thus, even though Stephen/Joyce "gratefully" declines Bloom's "proposal of asylum" in the Ithaca episode of *Ulysses* (17.954–55), quietly asserting his independence, the covetous Joyce had already secretly shared with Shaw by inscribing in Bloom so many of the literary parent's ideas and characteristics.

Buck Mulligan's mockery of Stephen's theory—"*Everyman His Own Wife / or / A Honeymoon in the Hand*" (9.1171–73)—anticipates Bloom on the beach but also alludes to the androgynous artist, male and female, who creates or at least satisfies himself. But in arguing that the male and female are consubstantial, Stephen sets the stage for the trinitarianism of *Ulysses*. Like the tritheist Sabellius, Joyce presents One in Three, who are successive yet coeternal, "coexistent and compresent" expressions of the same person. Whereas Joyce suggests that Father and Son are one at least in their waste body fluids, *Ulysses* presents the sanctifying aspect of the trinity as the tertium quid—the female principle, embodied in the yea-saying Molly Bloom. Thus, as the comically credible hero and androgynous father figure—the mature Joyce—becomes one with himself as Stephen, he also becomes consubstantial with the great "immensipater" Shaw, under the aegis of the sanctifying Life Force.

Thus, in Bloom and company Joyce expropriates Shaw's belief in self-created fatherhood and simultaneously scrutinizes his great emancipating precursor's gender credo and politics while documenting with uncompromising psychological realism their comic ineffectuality in the Dublin of 1904. While ridiculing political and sexual stereotypes and at the same time compelling the reader to admire his womanly man, Joyce reveals that androgynous character can be an affirmation of matrifocal values in a patriarchal society. Contrary to the implication of Gilbert and Gubar in *Sexchanges* that Joyce was a sexist, *Ulysses* illustrates a Shavian feminism that honors (even as it reveals his human foibles) the woman in man as well as Shaw himself. Indeed, in appropriating much of Shaw's valuable substance, Joyce acted out one of Molly's fantasies: she wanted to "borrow" the silverware at a banquet and take it home in her muff.

CHAPTER

Methuselah at the Wake:
"Pelagiarist Penman" and "Grand Precurser"

Six

IN Zurich in 1918, while involved in a libel suit with actor Henry Carr, James Joyce invited further legal trouble, this time with Shaw. His English Players, it will be remembered, performed *The Dark Lady of the Sonnets* and *Mrs. Warren's Profession* in violation of Shaw's copyrights. Considering his superstitions about names, it is possible that Joyce resented Carr for sharing the name and English ancestry of Shaw's father, George Carr Shaw. For Joyce, the student of Shaw who discerned a sinister significance in the shared initials of the two publishers who rejected *Dubliners*, Grant Richards and George Roberts (Gorman 204), would not have missed the confluence of the names of Carr and the older Shaw. If Joyce's vexation over the litigation was consciously exacerbated by his resentment of G. B. S., stealing his dramas may have seemed to the devious penman appropriate revenge. Perhaps because he blamed Shaw for the Stage Society's refusal to produce *Exiles*, thus projecting onto G. B. S. his own guilt over copying *Candida*, Joyce blatantly challenged the old playwright by poaching his plays. Although he was wrong in his accusation—Shaw had, in fact, written that *Exiles* was "just the thing for the S S" (Stage Society) (BSL 2:766), Joyce persisted in transferring guilt onto Shaw. In a letter dated September 19, 1919, he wrote that *Exiles* was not performed because Shaw protested that it was "obscene" (JJ1 429).

Two days later Joyce wrote G. Herbert Thring, secretary of the Society of Authors, to defend himself against Thring's accusation that he had produced *Mrs. Warren's Profession* without Shaw's consent and without paying him royalties. The secretary of the organization that Shaw dubbed the society "for the Prevention of Cruelty to Authors" (*Bookseller,* June 5, 1884), the most prominent of whom was Shaw himself, had accused Joyce of fraudulently appropriating Shaw's drama. The letter protested the illegal production, for although it was still banned in England because of its subject matter, Shaw's play about prostitution was protected by copyright law. The secretary was, it seems, unaware of the spring 1918 piracy of *The Dark Lady of the Sonnets.* When Joyce replied to Thring, he argued, somewhat disingenuously, that the consent of dramatists was virtually impossible to get in Switzerland during the war because of "delays, censorship," and frequently closed borders (JJ1 479). Considering that the war had not interfered with his correspondence with supporters like Harriet Weaver, Joyce's argument seems to have been a plausible rationalization. The secretary's irate response appeared to have no outward effect upon Joyce, who characteristically transferred his own guilt onto Shaw, at least for the benefit of his partisans. In violating Shaw's legal rights, Joyce displayed a typical ambivalence toward G. B. S.: by co-opting the plays, he recognized their merits, but he criticized them publicly and at the same time avenged himself, probably because he was convinced that Shaw had berated his own skills as a dramatist but perhaps because he was suffering from guilt that he transferred to the older Irishman.

When *Mrs. Warren's Profession* opened the English Players' fall 1918 season, Shaw had retaliated without taking legal action. In Dublin's Little Theatre he probably provoked Joyce's belief in his enmity by pointing out the "indecencies" in his work (Weintraub, *Unexpected Shaw* 133). Later, having accused *Ulysses* of "flatulations" and "incontinence," even while recognizing Joyce's genius and praising his documentation of the sordid side of Dublin life (JJ1 588), Shaw unwittingly set himself up to play the role of punitive superego and surrogate parent in *Finnegans Wake.* In its "parricombating" (FW 597.17) with the "*Immensipater*" (342.26), the father figure H. C. E. is often G. B. S., the "renownsable patriarch" (581.5) whom Shaw had promoted into worldwide fame. The *Wake*'s portmanteau words often include Shaw. For example, in one of Joyce's multiple, random, multiplayered allusions, the envious Shem, who is supposedly teaching his brother Shaun geometry, hopes that the "parent" figure will "gift uns his Noblett's surprize" (306.4). Obfuscating the plea by lapsing into German while at the same time suggesting the form of the Lord's Prayer, the narrator wants the father to "give us his Nobel Prize." Although Yeats was also a Nobel Prize winner, Shaw was the recipient who rated a packed portmanteau suggesting Nobel's "blitz"—his role as munitions maker and model for Andrew Undershaft in *Major Barbara*. When Shaw was awarded the Nobel Prize in 1926, the front-page news around the world reported his first response: "I am surprised" (BSL 3:41). Joyce's neologistic layering method, however, is even more complex, for Noblett's Candy Store on O'Connell Street in Dublin was a victim of the British bombardment during the 1916 Easter uprising—a reference that might sidetrack a Dubliner from the typically sly allusion to Shaw. His antiwar stand made him a proponent of "no-blitz" and to his devotees would have qualified him for the Nobel Peace Prize instead of the prize in literature.

The old Nobel Prize winner would have been surprised to discover that in Paris the avid newspaper reader and press clipper was making an epic montage of him in *Finnegans Wake*. He might have been astounded to discover that Joyce's duplicitous book is based in large measure on the five plays which make up *Back to Methuselah*. Because in the 1920s "every word he [Shaw] uttered was cabled across several continents" (Pearson 399), Joyce would have had no trouble in amassing the details for a fractured life study and pastiche of allusions to Shaw's life and works in his parodic deconstruction. Joyce probably read Shaw's magnum opus on Creative Evolution—like the *Wake,* an extravaganza of "far fetched fables" and "true histories that never happened" (Meisel 443)—soon after it appeared in print in the summer of 1921. At the time Joyce was well aware that by the end of World War I, G. B. S. had cast himself in the role of prophet. His public liked him in the part. After Shaw predicted that Georges Carpentiér would beat Jack Dempsey in a July 2 prizefight—a choice that became a media event in American newspapers—as Dan Laurence notes, "there was much chauvinist gloating in the American press" when Dempsey won the fight. Among the gloaters in Europe was Joyce, who mocked Shaw's "spirit of prophecy." He wrote John Quinn that "he is not even a prophet out of his own country" (BSL 3:626–27). A year later, two months after the notable

New York opening of Shaw's prophetic, mythopoeic history of the world, Joyce wrote Harriet Weaver that he intended to write a "history of the world" (JJ1 661). While England prepared for the 1923 production of Shaw's self-proclaimed masterpiece, in London where he could not have avoided the media hype for the Wagnerian cycle of plays, Joyce began in earnest to construct his "Work in Progress."

Circumstantial and internal evidence suggests that, while making sure that its densely layered circuities would make meaning indeterminate, Joyce created in *Finnegans Wake* a "nightmaze" (411.8) and "nightynovel" (54.21) to satirize, surpass, and subsume what G. B. S. subtitled his "Metabiological Pentateuch," without acknowledging his source. Shaw himself had provided the imprimatur for literary pilfering by admitting that his plays were "full of pillage.... In short, my literary morals are those of Molière and Handel." He advised, "Do not scorn to be derivative ... the great thing is to be able to derive—to see your chance and be able to take it" (quoted in H2 334–35). Whereas G. B. S. cheerfully admitted "standing on the shoulders of other writers," his proud, crafty rival wanted—on advice that he probably got from Shaw—to be sui generis and hence remained silent and cunning. But in reading the preface to *Back to Methuselah,* he had seen his chance.

Shaw had persistently argued, "My business is to incarnate the Zeitgeist" (BSL 1:222). In his preface he argued that artists must "recapitulate the history of mankind in their own persons, however briefly they condense it" (CP 511). The sixty-five-year-old admitted gloomily that his own "sands" were "running out," his "powers ... waning." He wished that "a hundred apter and more elegant parables by younger hands [would] soon leave mine as far behind as the religious pictures of the fifteenth century left behind the first attempts of the Christians at iconography" (546). Upon reading the evangel's exhortation, his closet disciple and clever avant-garde literary offspring set out, it seems, to fulfill the old man's wish. The penman took on the role of younger artist who would devise a modern Renaissance art, admittedly "featuring the *chiaroscuro*" (107.29) of light and shade (Shaw and Joyce/Shaun and Shem?). It would make Shaw's religious art a primitive precursor of his own advanced tour de force emulation and evasion of the "medieval" master. To surpass Shaw's flat, recurring allegory, to outdo Renaissance attempts to reproduce three-dimensional perspective, and to leave both behind by recreating the inner reality of chaotic modern consciousness, the younger hand reshaped Shaw's masterwork, forging a new artistic language and a "monologuy of the interiors" (19.32–33) for Hebro-Hellenic culture, a collage grounded in the inner landscape of a complex, conflicted, microcosmic Irish psyche.

Joyce took up Shaw's challenge, furtively internalizing and decentering Shaw's work about progress, probably delighted with the joke that even his working title—"Work in Progress"—alluded to G. B. S.'s gospels. In the linguistic virtuosity of Joyce's elliptical Oedipal "crossroads puzzler" (475.3–4), the trajectories of Shaw and Joyce meet, like Sophocles' Laius and Oedipus, at the crossroads. Indeed, Joyce's counterpoising of many meanings and languages in single words may have been a retort to Shaw, who advocated simplified spelling as an antidote to ambiguity, thus aiming to obviate the condensed equivocations in which Joyce revels. His paronomastic, compacted etymologies illustrate how patently ridiculous it would be to rewrite the world's books in Shaw's shorthand phonetic alphabet, for it would deprive words of their rich linguistic resonances and historical connections. Joyce defied Shaw's pet project by making the *Wake* untranslatable into Shavian phonetics (or into any other logocentric form, current Japanese efforts notwithstanding). Moreover, the younger Irishman's maddening array of debating voices may be a parodic disintegration of Shaw's talky discussion plays.

Because *Back to Methuselah* urges pooling "the legends, the parables, the dramas . . . of . . . the common heritage of the race" in the "MIRACLE OF CONDENSED RECAPITULATION" (CP 540, 515), the notorious Fabian socialist and prophet of progress, one of whose preferred modes of transportation was the bicycle, may be the bustling bicycler of the *Wake*: "A human pest cycling (pist!) and recycling (past!). . . . [H]ere he was again (pust!)" (99.4–6). In G. B. S.'s cycle of dramas "the same types recur generation after generation" (Valency 354), as they do, superimposed upon one another, in Joyce's "piously forged palimpsests" (182.2), which erase Shaw to write over his text. In a letter to Harriet Weaver concerning his "Work in Progress," Joyce referred to "Shem-Ham-Cain-Egan" (JJL 1:214) in the linked form that Shaw used in *Back to Methuselah* for recurring and interpenetrating figures like "Cain Adamson Charles Napoleon! Emperor of Turania!" (207) and "Shakespeare, Shelley, Sheridan, and Shoddy" (211). Joyce repeats and surpasses the performance in "Daunty, Gouty and Shopkeeper" (Dante, Goethe, and Shakespeare) (539.6). When Herbert Gorman wrote that in *Finnegans Wake* "Caesar, Charlemagne, Napoleon and Wellington become one in the mystic interpretation that dismisses chronology and accepts and views history as a whole" (332), he was unaware that he was explaining the method of *Back to Methuselah*. Like the characters of *Methuselah,* the archetypal adumbrations of the *Wake* "are recurrently . . . [met] in cycloannalism, from space to space, time after time, in various phases of scripture as in various poses of sepulture" (254.25–28). Shaw's scriptural Pentateuch and sepulchral sculpture are recycled in Joyce's psychoanalytical self-study in new shapes unlike those of Shaw, who had posed for renowned sculptors such as Auguste Rodin, Prince Troubetzkoy, and Jacob Epstein. In choosing to create interfacing portraits of himself and Shaw as young/old men, Joyce corroborated Shaw's assertion in *The Sanity of Art* that "the man who writes about himself and his own time is the only man who writes about all people and about all time." Providing a provocation for Joyce's method, he continued, "I deal with all periods; but I never study any period but the present . . . ; and as a dramatist I have no clue to any historical or other personage save that part of him which is also myself" (MCE 312).

In the *Wake* the mysterious "M," whose siglum is a capital *E* with crossbars facing downward (see McHugh, *Sigla*), is probably the old father figure behind G. B. S.'s Pentateuch—Methuselah as well as Finn MacCool and Everybody. Like *Finnegans Wake,* Shaw's mosaic Torah is a revisionist Genesis. The *Wake* acts out the idea of Shaw's Belle Sauvage of *Methuselah,* who speaks of "rewriting the Bible in words of four syllables and pretending it's something new . . . [so that] Nobody will understand you" (135). Her description augurs the method and madness of the *Wake*. Savvy has a theory that "all dead people are the new people reincarnated, Nunk. I suspect I am Eve" (BM 132). In both *Methuselah* and the *Wake,* prototypes are reincarnated in what Joyce called "evolutionary clothing" (109.23) or "rise afterfall" (78.7), "(lost leaders live! heroes return)" (74.3). Before Finnegan, Shaw's female Snake says, "Why not be born again and again as I am, new and beautiful every time?" (BM 67). Both the diurnal discussion plays and the nocturnal psychobabble begin and end with the primeval parents. Shaw calls Adam "Old Everybody's Father" (BM 89), to Joyce a "puppetry producer" (FW 219.78) who is "respunchable for the hubbub caused in Edenborough" (29.35–36). In the *Wake* Adam becomes "Here Comes Everybody." The repunchable amateur boxer is probably the author of *Cashel Byron's Profession*, Shaw's novel about a pugilist. The student of fisticuffs responsible for the Eden of *Methuselah* dramatized a pugnacious, Oedipal Cain. In both the discussion dramas and the frenetic dream-narrative, insurgent sons challenge the Adamic father. In *Back to Methuselah*, Eve learns from the Serpent that the voice in the Garden is inside her: "The voice in the Garden is your own voice" (76). Joyce's voice in the *Wake* says, "I have something inside of me talking to myself" (522.26). Both long, wordy works juxtapose and superimpose myth and history on fiction in a dialectic between bifurcated males representing oppositional beliefs and lifestyles. Both examine in many permutations the conflict between extroversion and introversion and altercations between public and private man.

Thus one corridor among the multiples of Joyce's "Allmaziful" tale "of Shaun or Shem" (215.35) is a deconstructed *Back to Methuselah*, as well as a projection of sibling rivalry with the fellow writer and exiled Dubliner, Oedipal assault upon the venerable Nobel laureate, and sublimation of the anxiety of influence that, according to Harold Bloom, preoccupies writers in their confrontations with their dead antecedents. However, the unrepressed obfuscations of Joyce's "NIGHTLETTER" (308.16) may derive as much from the fact that his pugnacious precursor was very much alive as from Joyce's delight in shamantic high jinks, bravura display of punmanship and encyclopedic allusions, or the aim to carry the stream-of-consciousness dream to the ultimate breakdown of the language of rational discourse—an aim that itself attacks the logocentric style of writers like Shaw. Whereas Joyce's aggressive, disorienting style is a denial of influence, on nearly every page allusions, encoded references, and "quashed quotatoes" (183.22) attest to "stolentelling" from Shaw. But at the same time, Joyce's dissident novel is a tacit tribute to the world-famous schismatic, the Grand Old Man of world literature—"the gronde old man . . . [who was] haard of heaering" (332.20)—as well as an epical private prank played on the paternal Irishman who believed that "all great things in literature begin as a joke" (quoted in Harris 14). A "pentshanjeuchy chap" (4.25)—a writer of a pentateuch, a jokey Shaun with a penchant for jokes—Shaw is paraphrased in the *Wake* with "In the beginning [the title of the first play of *Methuselah*] was the gest [which as "deed" simultaneously refers to Goethe's *Faust*] he jousstly says" (468.5). As a joke on Joyce's admirers, the *Wake*'s "decentered text, which seeks to undermine official and authorized language modes" (Parrinder 212), subverts phallocentric prose, of which Shaw was a reigning master.

In another context, Hugh Kenner writes that " 'disguise' is the operative word" for the nineteenth-century writer who conceals "from his audience and from himself what he is writing about." Kenner contends that the romantics exorcised Dr. Johnson "by turning him from an admonitory parent into a ridiculous character in a book by Boswell: a neat piece of ritual father-slaughter" (279–80). Knowing full well what he was doing, the modernist Joyce reiterated such ritual father-slaughter in the *Wake,* but he worked through his repudiation to reconciliation with "Old Parr" Shaw, whose epithet is a synonym for Methuselah as well as a reference to a young salmon, the fish in which Shaw is often encoded in the *Wake.* In topp(l)ing G. B. S., Joyce created a language that replaces the father's while conveniently using the myth of the Adamic family on which Shaw based *Methuselah.* Margot Norris reminds us that the "primary sin in both the Edenic and Oedipal myths is the sin of usurping the prerogative of the father." In the *Wake,* "the son's ability to conceive of himself as a center in the universe of his thought is impaired by his preordained position in the social order, and a struggle for selfhood ensues in the form of a struggle with the father, the end of which is symbolic parricide" (42). As a lapsed Irish Catholic instead of a member of the privileged Anglo-Irish ascendancy to which Shaw belonged (according to his biographer St. John Ervine, "a member of the ascendancy"; I&R 4–5); as native Irishman whose rights and nationality had been preempted by the invasive usurpers—the "Danish, Norman, Cromwellian, and (of course) Scotch" invaders whom Shaw claimed as ancestors (CP 442); as younger experimental writer clamoring for recognition, Joyce resented and envied, while perversely admiring, the world-famous playwright and propagandist who had unwittingly become his mentor. In the *Wake* Joyce exposes his complicated feelings about the paternal writer, whom he also thinks of as a brother.

Like Joyce's Shaun, Shaw touted himself as a reverend, prophet, secular saint, and oracle, whereas his detractors, like Shem, disparaged him as a self-promoting braggart and obstreperous meddler. Shem promises "a most moraculous jeeremyhead sindbook"—both jeering at his inner life (his head) and a jeremiad like that of prophet Shaw, denouncing sins for "all the peoples" (229.31). Shaun tells Shem, "I am a worker, a tombstone mason anxious to please averburies and jully glad when Christmas comes his once ayear. You are a poorjoist" (113.34–36). Shaw was, indeed, a worker; his artists in "As Far as Thought Can Reach" (the coda play of *Back to Methuselah*) are sculptors who recreate dead ancients in stone; the popular "tombstone mason" might be accused of wanting to please everybody and, because he so often compared himself to the Prince of Peace, he would be glad for Christmas. While Joyce was creating his deconstructed portrait, Archibald Henderson's second biography of Shaw, *Bernard Shaw: Playboy and Prophet* (1932), was published. It offered considerable corroboration (and perhaps provocation) for the Joycean montage of G. B. S. as an angelic but also diabolonian do-gooder, stage Irishman, irreverent reverend, and vegetarian mystic. Henderson stressed G. B. S.'s reputation as both dapper harlequin and otherworldly monk and produced illustrations to substantiate his story of the paradoxical Shavian life. On one page he placed a photo of the red-bearded socialist dressed in the Bolshevist manner next to a photo of the white-bearded "Prophet" in a monk's cowl (facing 181). Yet another page displays the socialist savior in a stained-glass window (facing 292), and on another there is Max Beerbohm's caricature showing the Luciferian Shaw holding his forked tail and standing amid flames (facing 213).

In his kaleidoscopic portrayals of H. C. E. and Shaun, Joyce makes mincemeat and bricolage of the older Irishman. Freely associating both Shaw's intimidating power and his seemingly senile foolishness, Joyce's nightbook vents—in fact, almost hyperventilates—his unavowed contest for mastery. The libelous double writing triumphs by confessing and, to escape discovery, concealing his model as well as a guilty conscience—simultaneously challenging detection for his purloined "letters" and carefully camouflaging his thefts. In the *Wake*'s nighttime meanderings, Shaw "Schoen! Shoan! Shoon the Puzt!" (603.4–5) is perhaps the most significant letterman who is, to the scornful Shem, "latterman" (603.3). Although the *Wake* ambivalently asperses Shaw's artistic methods and political practices, it is, in effect, a letter "carried of Shaun"/Shaw but written "of" Shem/Joyce and "uttered for ALP"—the Life Force in whose praise both Irishmen wrote. One version of the letter is "Initialled. Gee" (420.17–19) as in George. The final version is addressed to "Dear . . . Dirtdump Reverend" (615.12). And, if Clive Hart is correct, Joyce's first word, *riverrun,* suggests not only the Life Force Liffey but *reverend* (200)—a title conferred on Shaw by himself and his followers. By the Shavian arc light, the nightbook is thus addressed to the reverend whose montage portrait turns out to resemble the "vegetable souperman" (PP 726) who lived in the rectory of Ayot St. Lawrence and assigned himself vicar of the "New Protestantism" (PP 687) that he preached in *Man and Superman* and *Back to Methuselah.*

The cunning punman Joyce, who was for seventeen years writing and revising the *Wake,* probably deepened the shadowgrams of his manuscript when he read the 1931 biography of Shaw by another Celtic expatriate, Frank Harris. Edited and emended by its subject after Harris's death, the biography is prefaced by Shaw's cautionary remarks about libel: "A man cannot take a libel action against himself and if he is prepared to face obloquy . . . he may even get the sort of Riviera circulation in highly priced top shelf volumes with George Moore and James Joyce. But you cannot write that way about other people. You have a right to make your own confessions, but not to make mine" (xiv). Undaunted and, indeed, probably construing Shaw's words as a challenge, Joyce brashly proceeded to make his own confession and to fantasize fractured dialogues and debates with Shaw, but G. B. S.'s threat that "if you publish a word of mine I'll have the law on you" (vii) probably prompted the guilty Joyce to augment his subterfuges and circumlocutions while making his ruptured disclosures about Shaw/Shaun and himself. Having read G. B. S.'s menacing words, his wily competitor became, it seems, more determined than ever to absorb Shaw's portrait into his own cryptic collages. Also, Shaw's conciliatory postscript to the Harris biography sets the pattern of atonement and forgiveness that surfaces in the brother battles of the *Wake.*

Shaw wrote that he did not alter Harris's text to make himself look saintly and that he bore Harris "no malice" (Harris 421). Nevertheless, Joyce knew that Shaw and the other Irishman who exposed his life and loves had been friends but that he himself had given Shaw little reason for fraternity. Quite the contrary, his negative review of Shaw's "conversion" play, his badmouthing of Shaw as the villain responsible for the misfortunes of *Exiles,* and his theft of Shaw's plays gave Joyce reasons for contriving to make Shaw an adversary, even if he covertly wanted the support of the living Irish writer for whom he felt the deepest kinship and to whom he no doubt secretly believed he was related. Apparently determined to cover up the identity of his "Precurser" and amused by the hoax he was perpetrating, Joyce probably furtively filled up the interstices of his book with diverting and deepening analogues and debris. In his portrait of two artists as old/young men, the proud penman surely wanted to elude discovery but also to avoid the accusation of creating a "ghastly . . . literary shepherd's pie" such as G. B. S. feared would result with "Shaw and Harris horribly messed together" (Harris xviii).

In what he called the "new Irish stew" (190.9), Shaw's bold and devious copyist cooked up a far more complicated dish than Harris did, with many other ingredients, even though the staples are Ireland, himself, and Shaw, who is assigned KP duty for criticizing the "dirt" of *Ulysses*. The creator of *Methuselah*'s Snake—a major figure in "In the Beginning," the overture of Shaw's drama cycle—thus becomes the God-like father, "the Grand Precurser who coiled him a crawler of the dupest dye and thundered at him to flatch down off that erection and be aslimed of himself for the bellance of hissh leif" (506.5–8). Although the God of Genesis and puritans like Stanislaus Joyce, who was until 1915 "savior and chastizer" of James (Cixous 128), broaden and deepen the archetype for the superego, Shaw becomes not only the punitive father but also the "puritysnooper" (254.21), Shaun the Post, whose name in early letters to Harriet Weaver about the new work was spelled *Shawn* (JJL 1:28; italics mine).

The allusion to Dion Boucicault's stage Irishman, Sean the Post of *Arrah-na-Pogue,* adds to the implication of the name as applied to Shaw, for Boucicault was, like G. B. S., an Irish dramatist who won his fame in England. Boucicault developed the character of the clever, resourceful clown so like the public persona Shaw created for himself. Arra-na-Pogue, Nora of the Kiss, is an additional link to Shaw, who named the heroine of *John Bull's Other Island* Nora, alluding simultaneously to Boucicault's play and, ironically, to the heroine of Ibsen's *A Doll's House*. That Shaw scorned Boucicault's melodramas while pilfering from them probably amused Joyce, whose chief self-created *doppelgänger* was a Shaun, John Tanner, Don Juan in *Man and Superman*. Shem's twin melts into H. C. E., the first two letters of whose monogram are one alphabetical step ahead of G. B., as they should be in a work meant to supersede that of G. B. S., whose initials were famed all over the world. Humphrey Chimpden Earwicker's third initial stands for Everybody, like Shaw's Adam, but perhaps also for Methuselah, with his siglum " ⊓ " upended by ninety degrees.

The *Wake* is thus a gargantuan analytical cubist portrait of the teetotaling "teetotum abstainer" (489.17), Protestant, theatrical moralist, preacher, and postman—an inveterate and tireless deliverer of letters. After noting that "the press, the radio, the talking pictures . . . [Shaw's] interviews, his plays, his novels, and his prefaces" kept G. B. S. in the limelight, Harris added that "another medium he ceaselessly pounded was letters. He was forever writing letters to individuals and publications" (387). Defender of Oscar Wilde (himself an important ingredient in the *Wake*ian stew), Roger Casement, Francis Sheehy-Skeffington, Bertrand Russell, and the martyrs of the Easter uprising, the polemical playwright was perhaps the most famous letter writer of the twentieth century, noted also for wooing famed actresses Ellen Terry and Stella Campbell by mail. Like Shaun, "all too unwordy . . . a mere mailman of peace" (408.10), Shaw delivered a barrage of letters and pamphlets opposing World War I, supporting Irish Home Rule, fighting for the League of Nations, and airing his idiosyncratic attitudes on subjects both trivial and sublime. Aware of his role as letter carrier, Shaw made his female emanation, Z, in *Village Wooing* (1934) the daughter of a village postman (*Selected One Act Plays* 152). As G. B. S.'s secretary throughout the years while Joyce was writing the *Wake,* Blanche Patch, explained, "From what some of the newspapers said, one might have thought that Shaw was never out of the Post Office" (33).

In Joyce's "Acomedy of letters" (425.24), informed by the "jollity" of "S. H. Devitt" (489.30)—Shaw the wit—the "Red theatrocrat" hailed by "pink prophets" (29.15–16) of Bolshevism is Shem's chief Dublin opposite and "altar's ego." As Bernard Benstock avers, Joyce's "preoccupation with Russia in the *Wake* is historical rather than ideological" (*Joyce Again's* 51), but the history that preoccupies Joyce concerns the life of Shaw as a touchstone for current events. After the Russian Revolution, the "Showting up of Bulsklivism" (116.6) was the business of the author of *The Shewing up of Blanco Posnet.* Shaun calls Shem/Glugg/Jim, his "someheis brother" who seems to be emulating his politics, a "sposhailiste" (specialist/socialist) (240.3) and a "bogus bolshy of a shame" (425.22), like the Dooley-prudent Joyce a spurious socialist. Shaun is suspected to be, like Shaw, a Russian sympathizer— "Rosskayman kamerad" (89.7). When Shaw visited Russia in 1932, the newspapers reported that the only Russian word he knew was *com-*

rade. In Joyce's paranoid dream, Shaun threatens to send his brother to "Tiberia" (424.9) and, as the Ondt, refuses to give the pickpocket "one pickopeck of muscowmoney" (416.17–18). Joyce misreads Shaw as stingy, in a misprision that Shaw encouraged by writing the importunate Sylvia Beach, "I am an elderly Irish gentleman, and . . . if you imagine that any Irishman, much less an elderly one would pay 150 francs for a book [*Ulysses*], you little know my countrymen" (BSL 2:719). Shaw's refusal to subscribe for *Ulysses* seems to have rankled his impecunious disciple throughout the *Wake*. The wealthy Shaw had, like Shaun, made "friends with everybody red in Rossya" (463.23–24). Moreover, in confusing "Communism with Holy Communion. . . . 'communionistically'" (Benstock, *Joyce Again's* 51), Shaun displays the infamous and paradoxical, but perhaps quintessentially Irish, Shavian penchant for linking politics and religion.

Thus Joyce alludes to Shaw, obscuring and fragmenting his identity and subsuming him in a kaleidoscopic archetype, a "collideorscape" (143.28) that permits Joyce to escape public castigation and legal action by Shaw for his "epical forged cheque" (181.16) while colliding with and checking the fatherly brother who is a victim of Shem's "pelagiarist pen" (182.3). In Joyce's culpable, heretical "traumscrapt" (623.36), a traumatic and at times rapt dreamscript made from plagiarized scraps (Pelagian liked Shaw's plays because both Irishmen denied the doctrine of original sin even while repeatedly describing the events in Eden), Shaun accuses the isolated sexual penman, "penisolate" Shem: "Every dimmed letter of it is a copy and not a few of the silbils and wholly words I can show you in my Kingdom of heaven" (424.32–35). To Shaw's Irish kingdom of heaven, the setting of the fourth play of *Methuselah,* supplicants come to hear the holy ("wholly") words of a sybil. Such "silbils" turn up in the final play as wise Ancients, just as Shaw's syllables and whole words show up in the *Wake*. Although Shem had his "best master's lessons" (539.8–9), he abhors himself "vastly" (539.15) for "mendicity" (541.27); strictly "forbidden by the honorary tenth commandment" to covet his "nighboors wiles" (615.32–33), the shameful Shem, disobeying the Mosaic law, borrows and hence commends the ideas of his wily, occasionally boring Dublin neighbor. His "bardic memory low . . . [he is] covetous of his neighbour's word" (172.30)—the scriptural Word of Shaw's Pentateuch. Shaun blames "Shem Skrivenitch, always cutting my prhose to please his phrase" (423.15–16).

Shem admits the failure of his imagination (as regards his subject but certainly not his language): he feels both guilty and resentful because of his thefts, even though he identifies closely with the twin whose content he has stolen: "The gist is the gist of Shaum but the hand is the hand of Sameas" (483.3-4). Shem, who "was a sham and a low sham" (170.25), no doubt knew that Frank Harris had written that Shaw was "the last word in sham and sham was, I believe, what he cried out most against in the middle years of his life as a dramatist" (390). The "skillfilledfelon" (355.27) and "insufficiently malestimated notesnatcher" (125.21-22) who created "the last word in stolentelling" (424.35) must have taken heart from Harris's assessment of inconsistency in the Irishman whom he had discovered to be his spiritual kinsman as well as his equal in waggish shamming. Shaw, who admitted publicly that his characters were always "composites of several individuals" (I&R 315), was himself, according to Harris, "the most adroit plagiarist, the deftest literary pickpocket in the world" (5). For Joyce, such dubious praise must have sounded the gong for another round with his clever rival, one that he won in the *Wake,* where he outdid Shaw as literary pilferer. His massive borrowings from others are discrete (and discreet), but in counterpunching with his contemporary competitor, he copied method and theme while displaying his mastery of the art of feinting, pulling punches, and administering low blows. In short, he goes the whole ten rounds with Cashel Byron, alias G. B. S. Thus *Methuselah*—a version of "eldorado or ultimate thole" (134.1) filtered through Voltaire's *Candide* to the utopian limits of its journey in the last play of Shaw's cycle, "As Far as Thought Can Reach"—is co-opted into Joyce's dreamwork. Its limits go as far as language can reach, even while revising, disintegrating, and reconstructing Shaw's optimistic creed.

In his preface to *Back to Methuselah* Shaw announced his intention to write the scripture of a new religion. Echoing Shaw, Joyce relied heavily on a reinterpretation of the Old Testament in his "new book of Morses" (123.35)—a coded book of Moses to surpass Shaw's visionary Pentateuch. As James Atherton notes, Joyce "saw himself as the *vates,* the poet and prophet, and his work as the sacred book of a new religion of which he was the poet and prophet" (14)—perhaps as the joking Jesus to Shaw's John Tanner the Baptist. Like Harry Levin, who points out the optimistic faith underlying the *Wake,* Benstock asserts that Joyce's controversial novel celebrates "the possibility of art as the impetus in perfecting man," though Joyce made "no definite insistence upon an achieved perfection as such, as much as . . . an indication of a higher attainment in man's spiral toward perfection in the foreseeable future" (*Joyce Again's* 251). These critics observe in the *Wake* the role and the subject that the prophet of Creative Evolution claimed for himself in *Back to Methuselah*. Supplanting G. B. S.'s Metabiological Pentateuch with his own "Epistlemadethemology" (374.17)—epistolary, epistemological theology—Joyce borrowed Shaw's theme, method, character, and dramatis personae in the *Wake*.

Shaw's five plays, the books of his Pentateuch, discuss and rediscuss the theme that Joyce purloined and recreated based on "the truth" that Shaw's He-Ancient imparts to a young artist: "You can create nothing but yourself" (BM 293). Shaw's introductory play, "In the Beginning," reconstructs Genesis. It becomes in *Finnegans Wake* "guennesses" (4.24) of the "archetypt" of "*paradox lust*" (263.L6) pilfered from the "puraduxed seer" (611.19–20) whose paradoxes Joyce had noted in "Ireland, Island of Saints and Sages" (CW 171). In Shaw's prelude play, Eve takes precedence over Adam, just as the river Liffey runs past "Eve and Adam's" in the *Wake,* thus reversing the biblical, Yahwist order of creation. The Fabian feminist had prefigured Molly Bloom in hoping that, as the *Wake* puts it, "Femelles will be preadaminant" (617.23–24). Like Earwicker, who seems to have been seduced by "Lili Coninghams" (58.30), Shaw had been tempted into making Lilith the creator in *Methuselah*: Eve's teacher is the luminous Snake, an avatar of Lilith, the mother creator who willed herself to "divide into two" because "the labor is too much for one. Two must share it" (69). In making Lilith the creator, Shaw rejected the patriarchal Godhead as well as the demonization of the mythic Lilith in Jewish lore. In his reconstruction, Joyce transforms Shaw's Lilith into Anna Livia, for both Irishmen put their faith in the female Life Force. Although both Shaw and Joyce reached into the past and present and predicted the future to probe the implications of Eden and the Fall, neither accepted the Augustinian doctrine of original sin. In "In the Beginning," Shaw's Adam fears that Eve will die if, like the dead deer that they see, she falls down; but there is no question of a Fall for sin or disobedience. The couple discover death after making up a word for it. In *Back to Methusalah* the main preoccupation of the first parents, before their sons are born, is making up language, as Joyce does in the *Wake*.

When Cain appears in act 2, he is, like Joyce's Shem, "a revolted son who knows that he is not forgiven nor approved of" (79). In front of Eve, the Oedipal son tells Adam that "but for her, I could not resist the sport of trying to kill you, in spite of my fear that you would kill me" (81). Thus Shaw's Cain announces what Margot Norris and other critics conclude to be the main theme of the *Wake*—the struggle of the son against the father. Adam threatens to "shew you that my spade can split your undutiful head open, in spite of your spear" (89). The head of Joyce's Adamic Tim Finnegan has indeed been split open by a loy. Tim fell down a ladder, whereas Adam fell down a whole "flight" of stairs (134). Eve tells Adam and Cain that she prefers sons who "will neither dig nor fight: they are more useless than either of you: they are [like Joyce's Shem] weaklings and cowards; they are vain. . . . They borrow and never pay; but one gives them what they want, because they tell beautiful lies in beautiful words. They can remember their dreams. They can dream without sleeping" (91), as Joyce does in the *Wake*.

The *Wake*'s sly "note-snatcher" must have noted kinship with a son of Eve who borrowed without paying in order to tell beautiful lies. The theological brother and ex-reverend Franklyn in Shaw's second play, "The Gospel of the Brothers Barnabas," explains the *felix culpa* as vindication of the work ethic for the creative sons of Eve in the quest for long life. "Consequently when Adam had the Garden of Eden on lease for ever, he took care to make it . . . a highly desirable country residence." After "he invented death . . . he let the thistles grow," for short life does not demand total commitment to progress. Inventing death was "only the first step of the Fall. Adam did not fall down that step only": by making up "birth," man found that other people were expendable, so Cain became egocentric and ferocious, slaying his "beefsteak eating brother and thus inventing murder," only later to fall down "the steepest step of all" by inventing war (134). Franklyn explains that violence and killing are human inventions and failings that imply, however, that with time and enlightenment human beings can invent a more creative, peaceful existence. The two brothers, like Shaun and Shem, deliver the message of Creative Evolution. Franklyn believes in "the tremendous miracle-working force of Will nerved to creation by the conviction of Necessity . . . under compulsion, as all great efforts are made" (141). Joyce seems to have been inspired to write the *Wake* under similar compulsion.

Whereas Shaw's Conrad translates his brother's "fairy tale" explanation into scientific terms, Joyce transforms Finn's Adamic fall into many variants—H. C. E.'s mysterious sexual dalliance in Phoenix Park, Humpty Dumpty's fall from his wall, the stock-market crash, and various chaotic wars and domestic crises. After his fall from the ladder, Finn, a "foenix culprit" (23.16), "wandered out of his farmer's health and so lost his early parishlife" to experience, like Candide, "foulplay .... hurrigan gales. ... hussites. ... [and] explosium" (589.21–36). No punitive Yahweh drove either Shaw's or Joyce's primeval parents from the Garden. Like his predecessor, writing in the wake of World War I, Joyce recognized that man's own greed and violence brought evil into the world. Both writers superimpose cycle upon cycle of human folly, without interpreting the Fall as implying the human need to throw oneself on the mercy of the unmerited love of a supernatural savior who can grant eternal life. Joyce, however, more fully indoctrinated with Christian dogma than his mentor (who was also deeply immersed in it), riddles his piratical dream monologue with the guilt of biblical brother betrayers, like Cain and Jacob. His "Gracehoper" does not, nevertheless, wish for favor from the Christian deity. Instead he seeks support from a person, an avatar of his father/brother and hence (considering the theories of paternity in *Ulysses*) of himself. Whatever is holy in Shaw and Joyce has a human origin and, the two apostates imply, is created by the vitalism of human fecundity and human genius.

Although seeming to refer to the opening of Genesis with "Inn the Byggning" (17.22) and "Inn the days of the Bygning" (56.20), Joyce alludes to the Shaw play "In the Beginning," (which clarifies that he is a Pelagian heresiarch). Joyce understood Shaw's concept of Eden as part of the cycle of human history—a place where Adam, "our Traveller remote" (156.20–21), like the world traveler Shaw in the 1930s, could stop for refreshment. Joyce's "Mr A" and "these wasch woman ... who had insue keen and able and a spindlesong aside" (336.12–14) are Adam and the Shaw woman: in Shaw's version of Genesis Eve works a spindle and her issue are Cain and Abel. As Adaline Glasheen points out, because of his admonition that the part of *Ulysses* he read in the *Little Review* needed washing up or was, because of its "dirt," a reminder of the need to wash up Dublin, Joyce made an anagram of Shaw that can be suspected in every reference to "wash" in the *Wake* (*Third Census*.261). In Shaw's cycle of plays the Cain figures commit the dirty deeds. The "keen and able" bipolar squabbles that develop between father and son in Shaw's first *Methuselah* play because Cain has murdered Abel continue in "The Gospel of the Brothers Barnabas." The play pits two brothers, an ex-clergyman and a biologist, who propound (like Shaw and Joyce) the same cause from different perspectives, against two hypocritical postwar politicians, one bullish and self-serving and the other doddering and inflexibly complacent. "The Gospel" is adumbrated in the conflicts in the distorted dialogues between brothers in the *Wake*.

After "The Thing Happens" (part 3 of *Methuselah*) in A.D. 2170, Shaw's masculine pairs meld, "as if Nature had made a composite photograph of the two men." Barnabas is "rather like Conrad, but younger, and much more commonplace" (146). Doubles melt into one, as Joyce's paired characters often do in the *Wake*. An Anglican rector who has reappeared as "Archbishop Haslam, Archbishop Sticket, President Dickenson, General Bullyboy and himself into the bargain: all five of them" (162) anticipates the casting method of the *Wake*. Haslam says, "They began to call me the Wandering Jew" because "I had several careers since I began this routine of life and death" (165). He is a *doppelgänger* of the many-faced Shaw, just as Shaun/Jaun/Haun/Yawn/Chuff, the Mookse, the Ondt, and others are in the *Wake*—paired off against adumbrations of Shem/Joyce. Also in "The Thing Happens" two transfigured Long Livers, the rector and a chambermaid from the past, reappear in the future to be contrasted to two childishly immature officials, themselves descendants and composites of figures from parts 1 and 2 of *Methuselah*. The Long Livers have staged drownings in order to be resurrected without arousing the suspicions of ordinary people. Apparently Joyce planned similar resurrections in the *Wake*. The Buffalo Notebooks comment on Shaun, whose siglum is Λ. In book 4, like the hero of Shaw's "The Tragedy of an Elderly Gentleman," Λ pretends to die" (McHugh, *Sigla* 39). Moreover, Joyce suggests the political discussion of "The Thing Happens" in his "Work in Progress": he includes a résumé of Shaw's subject in book 2, chapter 2, marginalia. The book is a "PANOPTICAL PURVIEW OF POLITICAL PROGRESS AND THE FUTURE PRESENTATION OF THE PAST" (272.R1). Shaun's marginal notes seem to gloss subjects in *Back to Methuselah*—"IMAGINABLE ITINERARY THROUGH THE PARTICULAR UNIVERSE" (260.R3)—and its political themes—"EARLY NOTIONS OF ACQUIRED RIGHTS AND THE INFLUENCE OF COLLECTIVE TRADITIONS UPON THE INDIVIDUAL" (268.R1).

The title of Shaw's penultimate futurist play, "The Tragedy of an Elderly Gentleman," could be a subtitle for *Finnegans Wake,* and its subject is the same as Joyce's. It is about the death of an old man, who differs from H. C. E., Joyce's "old man on his ars" (514.34) (it will be remembered that Jim advised Stannie to kick Shaw's "arse" for him) only in being a proper, old-fashioned liberal. The play takes place on the southern shore of Galway Bay (from where Joyce's father believed his ancestors came), where the former chairman of "the All-British Synthetic Egg and Vegetable Cheese Trust," current "President of the British Historical and Archeological Society, and Vice-President of the Travellers' Club" (194), has come on a "pious pilgrimage" (191), which Joyce calls a "salve a tour" (409.31). The Long Liver guardian (shades of Plato's *Republic*) with whom he discusses his predicament can barely communicate with him because she takes his idioms and clichés literally. "Joseph Popham Bolge Blubin Barlow, O. M." (for O'Mulligan, probably no relation to Malachi, but a variant of Methuselah), "Daddy" of the Envoy's Wife and "Grandpa" of his daughter, holds the record in the travel club "for civilized countries" (197). Like Joyce's Shaun the Postman, he has been "round the world in forty mails" (237.14). Like H. C. E., a primal daddy, the world-weary traveler has turned to the "emerald gem" (205) of Erin.

When Zoo, assigned to be the Elderly Gentleman's keeper, tells him that his group are children governed by violence, the old man defends himself by referring to "the galaxy of Christs who arose in the twentieth century, not to mention such comparatively modern spiritual leaders as Blitherinjam, Tosh and Spiffkins," who opposed militarism and taught the golden rule (214). Adumbrations of such leaders, usually associated with Shaun, pop in and out of the *Wake.* Shaw's old man even finds himself defending the Pope: "Even a Pope is not expected to be continually pontificating. Our flashes of inspiration shew that our hearts are in the right place" (219). In the parable of the Mookse and the Gripes (book 3, chapter 1, 414–19; see pp. 329–37), Joyce lets Shaun/Shaw pontificate as Pope Adrian, parodying Shaw's inconsistencies. But throughout the *Wake* he associates Shaun/Shaw with "flashes" of light. Enlivening his "problem passion play" deconstruction of Shaw's, in Joyce's system of polarities, the Mookse is like "Lipoleum" (8.16)

(Napoleon) and "Dalaveras" (De Valera) (9.36), "heroes of Warhorror" set off against the "salvation army" (91.29–32) to resonate and parody the complex conflicts of *Major Barbara*. In "The Tragedy of an Elderly Gentleman," the "man of destiny," Napoleon, seeks the Oracle in Ireland, convinced, however, that the Sybil gets her messages from a three-hundred-year-old man. An avatar of Cain and all seekers of power through violence, he is what Joyce calls him—"a veritable Napoleon the Nth, our worldstage's practical jokepiece" (33.2–3). As one of the mouthpieces of the practical joker who wrote *Man of Destiny* (1895) about Napoleon, in part 4 of *Methuselah*, Napoleon (who has "the power of imagining things as they are, even when I cannot see them"; BM 227) has come to ask the Oracle how he can satisfy his "genius for fighting" until he dies (BM 230). In response the Oracle shoots him, but she misses. The macho sexist falls, but he rises, screaming, "Murdress! Monster! She devil. . . . Bitch! Sow! . . . And missed me at five yards. Thats a woman all over" (231).

Thoroughly disgusted with the self-serving envoys from the continent, Shaw's female Oracle (an avatar of Lilith and Eve), who is served by the druid Zosim, seems to cause *"terrific lightning and thunder"* as if to announce, as in *Heartbreak House* and the *Wake,* a new Viconian cycle. But among "heroes of warhorror," Shaw, like Joyce, preferred the Irishman Wellington, who (G. B. S. wrote) fought Napoleon "without one moment of illusion" (CP 444). In the *Wake*'s "Willingdone Museyroom" (8.10), the "grand and magentic" Willingdone, as "Wounderworker" (8.35), is compared favorably to "the petty lipoleum boy" (8.26). Joyce seems to have shared Shaw's preference for the Irishman who became an English war hero. In *Methuselah* Shaw metamorphoses Cain into Napoleon, who is to Shaw another manifestation of the cycles of violence from which—in the Shavian vision—human beings will evolve into a more peaceful future. The museum guide in the *Wake,* who seems to be pointing out the relative merits of the two generals, is a hazily portrayed cleaning woman named "Kathe" (8.8), perhaps a spoof on Shaw's eponymous *Great Catherine,* considering that everyone cleaning up dirt in Joyce's dream seems to be Shavian. Catherine envies "the scullerymaids" when she has "headaches and colics." The business of her day is to go to the museum (Plays 809). The fact that the dreamer is taking a tour of the "Museyroom" may even relate to the British Museum Reading Room, where the autodidact Shaw provided himself with a thorough education in most of the subjects that his sly disciple borrowed from him. In "The Tragedy of an Elderly Gentleman," the old man parallel to the old man whom Joyce wakes is thoroughly disillusioned with the hypocrisies of warriors and politicians who have come to the Oracle on a quest reiterated in the *Wake*—"a wildgroup's chase across the kathartic ocean" (185.6). He cannot in conscience return to Baghdad with "a blasphemous lie." Thus he implores the Oracle to let him remain in Ireland. Pitying the "poor old shortlived thing," the Oracle touches him and gazes into his face, and he dies. "The Tragedy" ends, like the *Wake,* in death that promises eternal return.

By A.D. 31,920 the Elderly Gentleman seems to have revived as the "ancient sleepwalker." Like H. C. E. in book 3, chapter 4, of the *Wake,* the sleeper's slumber is disturbed: "What was thaas? . . . Let sleepth" (555.1–2). Shaw's Ancient is awakened by youths in a nursery where dancing, singing, and mating are the pleasant "childish games" of adolescence (252)—games with which Joyce peppers the *Wake* (see Eckley)—as, for example, in the competition between "Angels and Devils" in the Chuff-Glugg encounter (see pp. 294–301). Part 5 of *Methuselah* pits the angelic Ancients against the devilish youths whom the sleepwalker meets, just as the *Wake* does. On G. B. S.'s final sci-fi vision, "As Far as Thought can Reach," Joyce's gloss may be, "We are once amore as babes awondering in a wold made fresh where with the hen in the storyaboot we start from scratch" (336.16–18). The play begins when the asexual dreamer is confronted by hedonistic youths in a "nursery" where they are witnessing a human egg birth. The "curious promise of eggs" in book 4 of the *Wake* that marks "the end of night" (Parrinder 233) marks in *Back to Methuselah* the emergence of a nearly ideal future in which oviparous birth has replaced childbirth, freeing women for development into wise, androgynous Ancients. Joyce's Biddy the Hen (perhaps related to Mrs. "Chickabiddy" Tarleton of *Misalliance*), "born to lay and love eggs," is "ladylike in everything she does . . . plays the gentleman's part every time. Yes, before all this has time to end the golden age must return with its vengeance. Man will become dirigible . . . woman with her ridiculous white burden will reach by one stop sublime incubation" (112.13–21).

In Shaw's reprise androgyny prevails. Woman has evolved beyond sexual imperialism. Children are hatched from eggs, already healthy libidinous adolescents. In adulthood ladylike Ancients play reversible roles (like Major Barbara, daughter of Biddy Undershaft). The yin-yang polarity of colonizing heterosexuality is resolved. Sublime incubation results in peaceful androgyny. As Shaw's parodist put it, "the manewanting human lioness with her dishorned disipular manram will lie down together publicly flank upon fleece. No, assuredly, they are not justified, those gloompourers" (112.21–24). The gender confusion in Joyce is both parody and poaching from Shaw, while the ideal of peaceful coexistence, lion lying down with lamb, lioness with ram, hints of the happy conclusion of Shaw's Christian pantomime, *Androcles and the Lion*. In Joyce's paradisiacal future, H. C. E./Adam is reconciled with ALP/Eve: Cain is subsumed in Abel. The sons are reconciled with one another and the father in the upward cycle of Creative Evolution. In this scenario of paradise regained, inventive humankind will be "dirigible," ready, as Shaw's mutant Ancients are, for flight from the biological ties to earth.

Whereas Shaw's Ancients think the body is a "bore," the purpose of life for the youths that the old man encounters in the finale of *Methuselah* are decidedly quotidian. The Long Liver dismisses the infantile preoccupations of young Strephon (who probably got his name from Stephen Dedalus, Gilbert and Sullivan notwithstanding). The Old Man criticizes the youngster's preoccupation with sex and art for their own sake in much the same way that Shaw had criticized Joyce in his correspondence with Ezra Pound over *Ulysses*. The brash adolescent says, "We are always to cheek the ancients on principle" (BM 151). The cheeky Joyce took up this principle in badgering old Shaw in the *Wake*. Strephon tells the Ancient, "You old fish! I believe you don't know the difference between a man and woman" (152)—a statement that may have inspired one of Joyce's twins, at the moment called Dolph, to show Kev, a Shaw clone, what is under ALP's skirts. Noting the epithet "fish" for the old hero redeemer and comic Christ, Joyce wrote a footnote, "Gee each owe tea eye smells fish. That's U" (299n3). The footnote spells "fish" in Shaw's phonetic alphabet and addresses Shaw as "U"— the paternal brother with whom Shem often debates. In Shaw's "abcdeminded" (18.17) phonetical spelling system, GHOTI spells fish (McHugh, *Annotations*).

Shaw's play about the old fish contrasts "childish" art and play with the mature wisdom of committed She- and He-Ancients, philosopher kings who, except in looks, resemble Swift's Houyhnhnms. One of the younger males, Acis, attacks artists like Joyce: "That is the worst of you artists. You are always in little squabbling cliques; the worst cliques are those which consist of one man" (270). This passage suggests that Shaw was as aware of Joyce as Joyce was aware of him. Through Ezra Pound, Shaw had warned Joyce not to become a coterie artist (BSL 2:767). Thus to what he must have perceived as criticism of himself as a "clique" of one, as well as a Yahoo, Joyce retaliated by insisting upon the biological and sexual as opposed to the "metabiological" facts of life. He referred to them, however, in a new duplicitous and multiplistic language calculated to thwart the older Irishman (and all of us). Shaw's He-Ancient finds it "more and more difficult to keep up with your language. Another century or two and it will be impossible. I shall have to be relieved by a younger shepherd" (300). Taking on the role of the relief shepherd of the future, the old man's cheeky rival created a language "difficult to keep up with" while the Ancient was still alive.

The younger leader of the herd often exploited the new language deviously to expose bodily functions—the tyranny of the body, "flesh, blood and bone," from which Shaw's She-Ancient insists we must "free ourselves" (299). Meanwhile, a Shavian maiden who is maturing and thus beginning to reject physical pleasure wandered at night "about the woods, thinking, thinking, thinking; grasping the world; taking it to pieces; building it up again; devising methods; and having a wonderful time" (255). Having a wonderful time, Joyce's dreamer—swerving away from his source—ruminates on the impossibility of transcending the flesh, for it asserts itself willy-nilly in our subconscious and conscious mental life. What Joyce called the "Calumnious . . . Cloaxity" (179.13–14) on forbidden subjects that the squeamish playwright eschewed is, however, balanced in the *Wake* by reference to "Platonic garlens" (622.36), like the setting of Shaw's final Methuselan play, and "a newera's day" (623.7), replicating Shaw's final utopian vision. Whereas Shaw's daydream ends as "night is falling" (BM 302), Joyce's companion night phantasmagoria ends as day breaks.

It is important to reiterate that in her *Second Census of "Finnegans Wake,"* Glasheen finds "many, perhaps all of Shaw's characters" (236), and that Stanley Weintraub has found his own evidence of Shaw's presence ("Respectful Distance" 72–73). Even though all of his condensed and ambiguous allusions are elusive, most, like "Serge Paddishaw" (131.8)—a portmanteau for Sergius of *Arms and the Man* and his Irish creator—imply that Shaw's writing, like Joyce's, was semiautobiographical and that his important characters, whether in pants or shifts, are masks for himself. In 1897 Shaw asserted that "Vital art work comes always from a cross between art and life: art being of one sex only, and quite sterile by itself" (*Bernard Shaw: Selection of His Wit and Wisdom* 15). In his "crosscomplimentary" (613.11) portraits of Shem and Shaun, Joyce acted on the Shavian precept. In 1925 Shaw admitted to Archibald Henderson that he used "living models" in portraits varying "from close and recognisable portraiture to suggestions so overloaded with fiction that the most ingenious detective could not penetrate the disguise" (I&R 315). In Joyce's jigsaw portrait, Shaun gets his "gumpower," like Undershaft's gunpowder, "by the benison of Barbe" (410.25–26) in *Major Barbara*. A defender of androgyny, Shaun swears, ironically, by "Sainte Andrée's Undershift" (147.26)—by Shaw, the saint who created a utopia in Undershaft's Percival St. Andrews, and Andrew Undershaft himself, his unconventionally heroic munitions maker. Joyce's passage about "Major [as in Major Barbara] A. [as in Adam] Shaw," who "got the miner smellpex" (263.7–8), indicates just how much Joyce knew about Shaw. In 1881 he had smallpox and grew his red beard to cover the scars. For accusing Joyce of using "blackguardly" language (JJ1 588), Shaw turns up at the wake with "blackguarded eye and ... goatsbeard" (464.12). "Magnus Spadebeard" (480.12), "Magnus Maggerstick" (535.7), and "Briganteen-General Sir A. I. Magnus" (329.5) are King Magnus, skewed Shavian self-portrait in *The Apple Cart* (1930). The "kerl" Shaun "left behind him" is "Candidatus" (234.8)—Shaw's girl/churl Candida, given a masculine ending to twit Shaw for creating such a phallic woman. Probably to bring up what Joyce perceived as Shaw's silly emphasis on social bisexuality, when Butt and Taff are being called upon to do their act, Taff, the Shaw figure, is called "Barnabas Ulick Dunne" (337.36), thus combining one of the Brothers Barnabas with Ellie Dunn, heroine of *Heartbreak House*. "Imperial Catchering" (498.12–13) is probably Shaw's *Great Catherine* (1913), elsewhere in the *Wake* demoted to the status of "janitrix" (8.8). Joyce reduces to an absurdity what he perceives as Shaw's contradictory preference for womanpower and his prediction of the superman with "Mammy was, Mimmy is, Minuscoline's to be" (226.14–15). In *The Perfect Wagnerite,* Shaw had described the dwarf Mimmy of *Siegfried* as "a blinking, shambly, ancient creature" who needs a hero to help him. He nurses Siegfried (perhaps as Shaw had unwittingly succored Joyce), "an anticipation of the 'overman' of Nietzsche" (MCE 227). The female Life Force, Lilith in *Methuselah* and Ann Whitefield in *Man and Superman,* is to Shaw the creating Mammy. In deflating and denigrating the Shavian optimism, Joyce's dreamer makes contemporary man Mummy—like the Ancients of *Methuselah*—and predicts further diminution with "Miniscoline"—the future miniscule man (who is Shem-Joycean?), whose correlative seems to be the colin, a mere bobwhite instead of the soaring spirit into which Shaw proposed man would evolve. In a more sanguine moment, however, Joyce agreed with his mentor on the evolving female Life Force, subsuming Ann Whitefield and Lilith in the many beauties of ALP: "Anna was, Livia is, Plurabelle's to be" (215.24).

Fragmentary references to the biographical data of Shaw's life are scattered throughout the *Wake*. Significantly, "Allkey dallkey" (317.5) refers to the village of Shaw's childhood where he lived above the Vico Road (and to Vico Road onto whose philosophical path Joyce detoured his readers) and suggests the "Allkey" to the Joycean labyrinth. "How voice you that, nice Sandy man? . . . he dropped his Bass's to P flat" (492.1–3) probably refers to the sandy-bearded music critic whose pseudonym was Cornetto di Bassetto. "Papa Vestray" (26.7) may refer to Shaw, the vestryman from St. Pancras. The catalogue at the end of the supposed geometry lesson—three pages after a marginal notation that contains a Shavian prescription, "service super-seding self" (304.L1)—is interspersed with allusions to causes and subjects upon which the Fabian held forth: "The Shame of Slumdom [the subject of *Widowers' Houses,* elsewhere called "windower's house"; 24.9] . . . The Thirty Hour Week [advocated in Shaw's Fabian tracts] . . . Fistic styles [a subject of *Cashel Byron's Profession* as well as of Shavian letters defending Carpentiér's boxing style]. . . . Should Ladies Learn Music or Mathematics? [in *Methuselah* the answer is yes, both]. . . . Should Spelling? [a fragmentary suggestion of Shaw's argument for simplified spelling]" (307.17–25). G. B. S. is an important adumbration of the "Iro-European ascendances with welldressed ideas who knew the correct thing such as Mr Shallwesigh or Mr Shallwelaugh" (37.26–28), for Shaw represented himself in Europe as a member of the Irish ascendancy. Moreover, Harris mocked G. B. S. for studying etiquette books in the British Museum in order to make himself acceptable to polite

British society (54): thus Shaw must have been learning when to sigh and when to laugh.

Having announced his Scandinavian background, Shaw becomes "Norgeyborgey" (327.30) instead of Georgy-Porgy. As "Diaeblen-Balkley" (326.25)—self-styled "diabolonian" (see CP 744) from Dublin/Dalkey, he is comparable to Bishop Berkeley; the subjective idealism of Shaw's Ancients and the "Irish eighteenth-centuryism" (CP 545) to which G. B. S. admitted relate him to the Irish philosopher. Shaw is the man who "whisk swimmies in Dybblin water" (326.34); his biographies made much of the fact that he risked swimming in Dublin Bay. Moreover, he was charged, "as Harris himself says . . . [with the] undishcovery of americle" (326.31–32). This reference seems to be hard evidence that Joyce read the Harris biography, for it contains a chapter titled "Attitude toward America" in which Harris reveals that, although America discovered Shaw, he did not want to discover it. The pertinent chapter in the Harris biography begins, "Shaw has never gone to America and never will go now" (380). Harris's prediction earned his way into the *Wake,* but as a prophet he failed, for Shaw went to America in 1933—a fact that may be compacted into the Joyce reference to "Sir Tristram," who has "rearrived from North Amorica" at the beginning of the *Wake* (3.4–5). Furthermore, because of his favorable (but perhaps tongue-in-check) remarks about Mussolini and Hitler before World War II, his biographer Archibald Henderson felt compelled to discuss charges against the old playwright as a totalitarian (PP 229, 231). In twitting his rival, who may or may not be all there, Shem begins coaching Shaun in the obscure "Studies" section with "As we there are where are we are we there from tomtittot to teetootomtotalitarian" (260.1–2), collapsing G. B. S.'s notorious teetotalism into totalitarianism and denigrating Shaw as a foolish bird. Joyce was probably referring to the famed orator and self-styled disciple of the devil as "The spiking Duyvil! First liar in Londsend" (535.15)—to Henderson, "The Grand Old Man of Modern Letters" (PP, xix), who in London enjoyed the reputation of being an irrepressible and outright liar who regaled his friends with "incredible anecdotes" (PP 258). In the "pseudostylistic shamiana" into which the "pelagiarist pen" slips "many piously forged palimpsests" (181.36–182.1–3), Joyce is writing over Shaviana to create his forgeries. The "shamshemshowman" (530.3–4), although Showman Shaw is part sham/Shem/Jim, was also known, like Shaw, to be "a disgrace to the homely protestant religion! Bloody old pre-adamite with his twohandled umbrella!" (530.28–29). Among the anecdotes in Henderson's 1911 biography of Shaw is an "umbrella story almost too good to be omitted" (GBS 695). Perhaps "bloody" is germane too, for audiences were scandalized when Eliza Doolittle used the word in *Pygmalion*.

Shaw is, of course, "the shavers in the shaw," just as Yeats is "the yokels in the yoats" and Wilde is "the wasters in the wilde" (41.8–9). Shaw is "Pshaw"—a pseudonym that he appended to some of his early journalism—catalogued with "Steal [Steele] . . . Barke [Burke] . . . Starn [Sterne] . . . Swhipt [Swift] . . . Wiles [Wilde]" and "Doubbllinnbbyyates [Yeats]" (303.5–8). Shaw may be "the lion in our teargarten" remembering "his Nile" and "those liliths undeveiled" (75.1–2)—the literary lion (and perhaps Androcles) in the tea/tear garden and German zoo (Tiergarten) of Eden, who, as author of *Caesar and Cleopatra*, remembers the Nile and as author of *Methuselah* unveiled Lilith. "J. J. and S." (83.3), whose books boys need money to buy, are undoubtedly James Joyce and Shakespeare/Swift/Shaw—all mighty rivals to J. J. The telegram that arrives at the end of chapter 2, book 2, from "jake, jack and little sousoucie" (308.24) refers, according to Glasheen, to J J & S, John Jameson and Sons (whiskey) (*Third Census*.liv), but J. J. and S. also suggest Joyce and his rivals. It is tempting to think that even "Festy King" (85.23) is Shaw—the king of the Malvern Festival established in 1929 in his honor, though for opposing World War I Shaw had been judged by many old men, such as the four gospellers (about whom Shaw wrote at length in his preface to *Androcles and the Lion*) who prosecute Festy, associating him with fish and hence the scapegoat Christ replicated in Shaw. Like Joyce, who was devouring Shaw, Matt, Marcus, Luke, and Johnny seem to be making a meal of the sacred fish: "Pass the fish for Christ sake" (384.15). "Show'm the Posed" (92.13) is Shaun/H. C. E., whose siglum ⊓ is compacted with "M"ethuslan Shaw's stage-Irish pose as well as Blanco Posnet.

Because Shaw was "Turk of the theater," Shem "bepestered the bumbashaws for the alms of a para's pence" (98.10–14): Joyce pestered Shaw for a handout to support his paragraphs while he was writing *Ulysses*. But "Grimshav Bragshaw and Renshaw made off with his storen clothes" (132.10–11): Shaw, the relentless and unmerciful, the boastful, and the sly (who in Joyce's "grim" fairy-tale fable of the

Mookse and the Gripes turns up as the fox), made off with Shem's store clothes, apparently denuding him by exposing the dirt in *Ulysses*. Although the parodied hero Finn MacCool is supposedly portrayed, his description sounds like the exaggerated adulation of a Shaw fan: the hero with the "grand old voice" is "a Colossus among cabbages . . . larger than light [code for Shaw?], doughtier than death Gran Turco . . . the sparkle of his genial fancy, the depth of his calm sagacity, the clearness of his spotless honour, the flow of his boundless benevolence" (132.27–32). As an idealization of Shaw, he is the family forbear and father figure. Of course, Issy, who says, "I'm so keen on that new Free Woman" (145.29), is Shavian, perhaps related to Essie of *The Devil's Disciple* even while she is an adumbration of Isolde. At one point, "Shaw and Shea are lorning obsen" (378.24–25)—Shaw apparently learning obscenity from *Ulysses* while Shem learns Ibsen from the feminist Shaw, as Joyce did by reading *The Quintessence of Ibsenism*.

The "Laurens County's giorgios" (1.8) of page one is probably not merely a reference to a county in Georgia to which the crafty Joyce would send us, or to his son Giorgio, but to the George who lived at Ayot St. Lawrence, to which the text seems to refer while enriching the allusion to Lawrence O'Toole, patron saint (perhaps like Shaw) of Dublin. If John Gordon is correct, a mantel picture presiding over the Earwicker bedroom depicts St. George slaying the dragon—"in a fitting triumph of . . . light over our reptilian heritage" (24). George Bernard Shaw had been caricatured as St. George, and Frank Harris called him St. George because he so conspicuously tried to slay social dragons. The juxtaposition of "Amoricus Tristram Amoor Saint Lawrence" to "Shemus O'Shaun the Post" and "Donn Joe Vance" (211.26, 31–32)— Don Giovanni and Don Juan—suggests the Shaw alter ego Marchbanks in *Candida* whom he compared to Tristram, as well as the hero of *Man and Superman*. Joyce's "Sir Tristram, violer d'amores, fr'over the short sea, had passencore rearrived from North Armorica on this side the scraggy isthmus of Europe Minor to wielderfight his penisolate war" (1.4–6). It is tempting to identify Sir Tristram with Shaw, but when the "Opening Pages of a Work in Progress" appeared in *transition* in 1927, G. B. S. had not yet visited the United States. Tristram's early identity may be that of Irish adulterer and courtly lover Charles Stewart Parnell, who was in North America in 1880 promoting Home Rule and raising funds to support his political program. After his return to Europe, his "amore" with Mrs. Kitty O'Shea blossomed, and he was to fight England for Irish independence. He was not musical, however, and his was not, like Shaw's, a "penisolate" war, a fight by an isolated Irish penman, nor was it the war of an isolated Irishman at times fixated on the penis. Therefore, Joyce must have been gratified by the success of his spindle technique of superimposing one identity upon another when the "oldparr" ("Opening" 9), "Grampupus" (12), "grandfallar, with a pocked wife" who had been "repreaching himself like a fishmummer for sixtyten years" (30) went to North America. In 1926, when he was preparing his "Work in Progress" for *transition,* Shaw was sixtyten, that is seventy years old. His wife Charlotte may have been pocked by empathy for her husband, who hid the marks of smallpox under his beard. When Joyce finished the *Wake,* the opening included many references to Shaw's *Back to Methuselah* disguised as references to the Bible—among them "Eve and Adam's" (3.1), the books of the Pentateuch (4.20–24), and "moses" (4.23).

In 1933 the musical lover from over the short sea (that is, from England) returned from North America while Joyce was writing his book. Shaw returned to continue the isolated war that he (like Joyce, whose combat differed only in linguistic tactics) wielded with his pen. Gordon writes that this return voyage "lacks romance and beauty. We hear of loss of former health ... and an 'icy' woman ... of violated love" (98). When the elderly Shaws ended their world tour after thirty-five years of unconsummated marriage, Charlotte-Isolde might well have been called icy. She was surely a woman whose love had been violated: in 1931 *Ellen Terry and Bernard Shaw: A Correspondence* was published, instantly becoming an international sensation. In the fall of 1931 Stella Campbell told American journalists that "there is absolutely no comparison between Shaw's letters to Ellen Terry and his letters to me" (H3 186–87). She mounted a campaign to get Shaw to permit her to publish his love letters. It lasted until Mr. and Mrs. Shaw began a trip around the world, which ended when they "returned from North Armorica" (1.5).

Joyce's text returns near its close "hoping to Saint Laurans all in the best" (616.34) to send good wishes to "Shaughnessy's mare ... with her strullberghers" (623.22–24). The valedictory may be to Charlotte Shaw and her seemingly saintly, immortal husband, living at Ayot St. Lawrence. Like Shaw's Long Livers in *Methuselah,* when Joyce finished the *Wake* the octogenarian challenged comparison to Swift's immortals, the Struldbrugs, and to his puritanically utopian horses. Joyce's narrator wishes the deistic literary giant whose optimism no doubt reminded him of Voltaire's foolish Dr. Pangloss "all in the best." As the list of ambiguous allusions grows, the reader becomes aware that the tenor of Joyce's tale told in a "plaintiff's tanner vuice" (182.22–23) is stolen from John Tanner, Shavian *doppelgänger* of *Man and Superman*. Were there a libel suit over the plaintive vice/voice of Jim's tenor, Shaw would be the plaintiff. Indeed, in his notes, "Scribbledehobble," apparently in reference to Shaun's Christlikeness, Joyce listed "stage Irishman and pulpit Irishman" (Connolly 103). Shaw was, of course, *the* stage Irishman who was equally famous for his place on platform and pulpit.

As noted earlier, Glasheen observes that, because of his admonition regarding the dirt in *Ulysses*, the anagram for Shaw in the *Wake* is "wash" (3.61). According to Harris, in Shaw's early years, he "dissembled his self-love under many names, even under such absurd ones as 'Redburn Wash'" (388). Henderson notes "Redbarn Wash" as one of his many pseudonyms (PP 261). Such disclosures make Glasheen's theory even more plausible. Thus when one of the twins "disliked anything anyway approaching a plain straightforward standup or knockdown row," the other "the accomplished washout always used to rub shoulders with the last speaker" (174.5–9). Joyce avoided direct confrontation, but Shaw had learned to be an accomplished speaker who bore his opponents no malice and, indeed, was invariably friendly even after the most heated debates. Shem views his rival (some say himself) as a washout, whereas Shaw urged that *Ulysses* was validated because it documented the need for a washup of Dublin. In a significant bogus roll, which is "the radification of interpretation by the byeboys," before Bruno, at the top of the list of "byeboys" of the past who ratify the dreamer's interpretation of things, is "Mr G. B. W. Ashburner" (369.6–8). The name packs together Shaw's first two initials and the Shaw anagram "W. Ash" as well as the "burner" of Redburn Wash and the light and heat with which Shem associates Shaun throughout the *Wake*. It is also a snide allusion connecting Shaw to Joyce's 1912 broadside, "Gas from a Burner," which attacks Joyce's Irish publisher, George Roberts, comparing him to the betrayer of Parnell. In spitefully implying that Shaw too was a "G . . . as [h] burner," Joyce condemned him for finding flatulence in *Ulysses*, such as the puritanical Roberts found in *Dubliners*.

Moreover, the two washerwomen gossiping while they clean up dirty linen are Shavio-Joycean, even though the dirt Shaw wanted to clean up differed from the smelly laundry that attracts Shem/Jim. Shaw had urged readers of *Ulysses* to heed its message that Dublin "needs washing—not whitewashing" (quoted in JJ1 588). A *Wake* translator will find that its references to the washerwomen both wash and whitewash Shaw, sometimes entirely covering him up. That the washerwomen turn into a tree and a stone suggests the two writers, the younger dedicated to organic life and the older, by the end of *Back to Methuselah,* rejecting it while preferring sculpted stone glorifying ancients. Among the titles of ALP's "untitled mamafesta" (104.4) is "*As Tree is Quick and Stone is White So is My Washing Done by Night*" (106.36; 107.1). This includes three of Joyce's shorthand codes for Shaw: stone, white, and wash. Throughout his night thoughts Joyce seems to be "breaking the mirror" that Shaw urged readers of *Ulysses* not to break because it showed that Dublin needs cleaning up. Tree and Stone may further play upon the antithesis between the two Irishmen, for Joyce's ostensible mentor Pound asserted that art "exists as trees exist," without social purpose (Kelly, "Pound's Joyce" 22). Although Pound's argument is debatable (a Shavian might argue that lumber and fruit have social purposes), Pound tried to make Joyce into the art-for-art's-sake artist as tree, whereas Shaw started out by throwing stones at the establishment. Joyce's night thoughts about Shaw are the "washing" of the *Wake*. Elsewhere the dreamer notes "his washawash tubatubtub and his diagnoser's lampblick" (290.21–22). Thus Joyce continued to associate "washawash" with Shaw, who often spoke in Hyde Park on an overturned washtub. The tubthumping speaker in the middle of "washawash" is Shaun the Post, who carries a lamp in the *Wake*.

Another code word for Shaw, the lamp, is related to Shavian diagnoses of society—made, Shaw insisted, under the light of critical intelligence. Early in his "gropesarching" Joyce's narrator gives a clue to his method: "The piece was this: look at the lamps" (33.10). Joyce's narrator admits, "I had it from Lamppost Shawe"—alias Shaun the Post—who got it "from the Mullah" (193.17–18), the Islamic interpreter of sacred law, comparable to Moses, the supposed source of the divinely inspired first five books of the Bible, to which *Back to Methuselah*'s subtitle "Metabiological Pentateuch" brashly refers. Shaw had considered writing a play about Mahomet after *Methuselah* but wrote

Saint Joan instead. G. B. S.'s Elderly Gentleman, a parallel to H. C. E., admires Mahomet as "a truly wise man, for he founded a religion without a church" (BM 237). Shaw intended to found such a religion through his dramatic scriptures. In the preface to *Man and Superman,* which Shaw insisted was his first version of the new religion, the dramatist compared himself to a lamp, admonishing readers to "study the electric light with which I supply you." He prided himself on bringing to his readers "those two vital qualities of literature, light and heat . . . [as] no mere copper wire amateur but a luminous author . . . with incendiary possibilities" (CP 166). Burrus, a Shavian avatar, speaks to explain his sanguine outlook: "If I were to speak my ohole mouthful to arinam about it you should call me the Ormuzd aliment" (162.36–163.2). Shaw argued, "If you study the electric light which I supply you in that Bumbledonian public capacity of mine over which you make merry from time to time" (CP 166), you will be illuminated. Joyce alludes to Shaw by comparing Burrus to the Zoroastrian Ormazd, Babylonian ("Bumbledonian") son of light. Burrus will speak his mind ("my ohole mouthful") to Erin/Ireland and Ahriman, son of darkness, the Shemian enemy and opposite of the solar deity. It will be recalled that the Prologue of *Caesar and Cleopatra* is spoken by the sun-god Ra, a variant of Ormazd, for Shaw repeatedly associated himself with sun-heroes and the solar element (in Joyce's paradoxical portmanteau, ailment/aliment). Joyce's Shaun/Shaw is a comic Apollo whereas Shem/Jim is a sly Dionysian in the "siamixed twoatalk" (66.20–21) dialectic.

In the *Wake,* as Clive Hart observes, " 'luminosity' is provided by Shaun's symbolic lamp" (100). Shaun has a "beamish brow" as well as "jehovial oyeglances" (405.16, 20), like the jovial jehovah who created Shaw's gospels. Shaw's Elderly Gentleman in *Back to Methuselah* argues that man's creative passion is an "ever burning torch. . . . [T]he individual perishes but the race is immortal" (212). Zoo answers, "But every time that torch is handed on, it dies down to the tiniest spark, and the man who gets it can rekindle it only by his own light." She also speaks of the human "hunger for new lights" (213). When ALP needs a light, she borrows "a loan of the light of his lampion, off one of her swapsons, Shaun the Post" (206.10–11). Shaun is "an eddistoon amid the lampless" (127.15), like the young expatriate who worked briefly in London for the Edison Telephone Company and as councilman in St. Pancras focused his attention on the Committee for Electricity and

Public Lighting. As late as 1934 in *Village Wooing*, the Shavian male announces, "We shall light up for one another a lamp in the holy of holies in the temple of life," which, like "the lightning flash" (of Giambattista Vico?) will turn "the black night into infinite radiance" (*Selected One Act Plays* 173). Having argued that life is a "splendid" torch, not "a brief candle" (GBS 512), Lamppost Shaw lit the "arclight" for his Luciferous disciple and provided, as post, the phallic symbol for canine Joyce to make his mark on.

G. B. S. had, it seems, posted ways into the "Vico Road" (452.21), which is in "Allkey dallkey"—the village south of Dublin where, it will be recalled, Shaw spent the happiest times of his childhood above the Vico Road. The similarities between Shaw's ideas of historical process and Giambattista Vico's *New Science* could not have escaped the clever penman. Yet he steered his surrogate mother, Harriet Shaw Weaver, away from the famed Anglo-Irishman with whom she shared a name (no doubt significantly to Joyce). In 1926 he wrote her that he was studying Vico, using Vico's theories "for all they are worth" because "they have gradually forced themselves on me through circumstances of my own life" (JJL 1:241). The circumstances were, I think, his awareness that *Methuselah*'s cyclical history approximates Vico's, his covert competition with Shaw that included his need to disguise his appropriations, and his cunning determination to rewrite Shaw's cycle of dramas in his own language and, ostensibly, with his own frame of reference. Joyce admitted to Padraic Colum, "I don't take Vico's speculations literally. I use his cycles as a trellis" (Colum and Colum 123). Apparently he was using the vines on his latticework to obscure the archway to Shavian property.

Vico's cyclical history involves three phases and a *ricorso*. It ranges from the Divine (which is in both G. B. S. and Joyce always located in the human) to the Heroic (represented in Shaw by Cain and his avatars, who, as Joyce put it, "sack, sock, stab and slaughter"; 87.16) to the Human cycle (which botches up life and human history, as parts 2, 3, and 4 of *Methuselah* illustrate). After the end of human experience as we know it, there is a regrouping, preceded by a giant thunderclap. In Shaw the end of human experience before the reprise is embodied in the Elderly Gentleman, who dies shortly after ominous thunder heralds the female Oracle of western Ireland. In Shaw's *ricorso* the Ancients reappear, followed by the Life Force and the first parents. In the new, higher cycle of life, Joyce's Biddy the Hen would be at home with people born, like "Haroun Childeric Eggeberth" (4.32), from eggs. Thus the utopian socialist's cycles parallel Vico's, and Joyce—more attuned to the iconoclastic "socianist, commoniser" (132.19–20), a socialist, Socinian heretic who rejected the doctrines of original sin and Christ's divinity, than to Vico's orthodox supernaturalism—perhaps used Vico to disguise, displace, and enrich his annexations.

Nor does Joyce's admitted use of Giordano Bruno's dialectic of interpenetrating opposites obviate the fact that Joyce found similar dualities in Shaw, whose binary poles are, like Joyce's, often slippery. In a letter to Harriet Weaver, Joyce wrote that, according to Bruno, "every power in nature must evolve an opposite in order to realize itself and opposition brings reunion" (JJL 1.224). The chief opposite that Joyce evolved in order to realize himself and his nightbook was his unwitting mentor and kinsman, waked as literary "adversarian" (535.14) and addressed as "my popular endphthisis" (305.21–22), who organized his discussion plays to expose many sides of a given debate while centering on shifting polarities that anticipate the conflicts of the *Wake*. In a typical Shaw play a female, prefiguring Anna Livia, is mediatrix, like Candida. In *Candida* Shaw contrasts the socialist preacher and the artist; in *Arms and the Man,* the practical warrior and the supposedly romantic hero; in *The Devil's Disciple,* the self-realizing apostate and the preacher activist; in *The Shewing up of Blanco Posnet,* the hypocritical "good" brother and the good samaritan reprobate; in *John Bull's Other Island,* the pragmatic English usurper and the visionary Irishman; in "Don Juan in Hell" in *Man and Superman,* Juan, advocate of the "advanced" Shavian philosophy, and the Devil, like Shem champion of art and fleshly pleasures. Like the *Wake,* John Tanner's dream suspends logic and clock time for a lengthy conflation on conflicting values. In *Back to Methuselah* the dialectical process continues, with Adam the digger as the archetypal opposite of Cain the killer, with their future variations overlapping the originals. Eve and her adumbrations are the conciliators, and the contraries are finally reconciled in Eve's favorites—the "creative" ones, artists like Shaw and Joyce. In attempting to have a dialogue with "Fadher" Keegan in *John Bull's Other Island,* the poor, marginalized worker Patsy, who is an awed would-be disciple of the defrocked priest, calls him "your riverence" (Plays 417). This suggests the "riverrun" of line 1 of the *Wake,* which is full of dialogues between the impoverished, marginalized Shem and his brother, the sometimes saintly Shaun. The Shavian dialectic anticipates the couplings and conflicts of the *Wake*.

"One to Do and One to Dare, Par by Par, a Peerless Pair"

The primeval and paranoic antagonisms expressing sibling rivalry in the *Wake* are reiterated in many pairings superimposed upon the twin rivals Shaun and Shem. Their "cycles always intersect in the first place in Dublin" (Hart 117), where Shaw and Joyce were born and had their first clash—or so Joyce must have construed it—over a play that features rival brothers, *The Shewing up of Blanco Posnet*. Since Shaw was known as Sonny and Joyce was known as Sunny when they were boys, it is not surprising that the dreamer's voice announces that "sonnies had a scrap" (194.24). Archibald Henderson's 1911 *George Bernard Shaw* would have assured Joyce that Shaw approved the theme of feuding brothers. According to Henderson, a favorite thesis of Shaw's was "the natural antipathy of blood relations" (69)—sons defying fathers and children in conflict over hegemony. But Shaw also assured his audiences that his characters were modeled on stand-up comics, for "the clown is sometimes the best part of the circus" (*Bernard Shaw: Selection of His Wit and Wisdom* 71). Joyce's twins are often such comics, perhaps in sly reference to Shaw's reputation and Joyce's aspirations. Confused and confusing at times over who is the clown and who Pantaloon (especially considering that Stella Campbell had in her 1922 memoirs divulged her pet name for Shaw, "Joey the Clown"), Joyce—always concerned over who would be top banana—made the older comic the allegedly serious fool. Of the sons of the *Wake,* "Primus [Shaw, the first] was a santryman [sandy man, who as a "Vestray" man worked for better sanitation] and drilled all decent people [that is, incessantly taught them]. Caddy [the cad, Jim] went to Winehouse [to drink] and wrote o peace a farce [the *Wake*, a farce of peace and reconciliation]" (14.13–14). Shaun variants of the *Wake*'s "peerless pair" are the straight men of Joyce's music hall skits.

When Chuff and Glugg face each other in book 2, chapter 1, "Patch Whyte passed O'Sheen ascowl" (223.17–18). Joyce associated white-bearded Shaw with the color white and with his female extension, secretary Blanche Patch. Glugg/Joyce is Oisin/O'Sheen, the legendary wanderer and a Gaelic spelling for Joyce. As noisy, chafing, huffing advocate in the skit of Chuff and Glugg, Shaw/Shaun/John Tanner/Don Juan plays the role of Chuff, the "evangelion . . . from St. Joan's wood" (223.19-20)—the evangelical literary lion, author of *Saint Joan,* "the fine frank fairhaired fellow of the fairytales" (220.12-13)—probably a snide allusion to the implausibly happy ending of *Methuselah*. In Joyce's dreamworld, Chuff "wrestles for tophole with the bold bad bleak boy" (220.13), the drinker Glugg, played by Seumas. Even the setting for the skit, in which Shaun and Shem are cast as Chuff and Glugg, the "Feenichts Playhouse," admission to which is free for the dreamer, suggests Shaw's drama cycle based on the phoenix myth of dying into life. It also calls up the playwright who had fulfilled his desire to be a man of the theater, a wish thwarted for Joyce, one of whose earliest ambitions was to be a dramatist. With *Exiles* (which failed to get a London showing before 1926) and with his English Players, Joyce had tried to rival Shaw's accomplishment at the Court Theatre in London, where G. B. S. acted as writer-manager and, at times, actor-director. Joyce's playhouse for children, like his dream, entails "nightly redistribution of parts and players by the puppetry producer" (219.7-8), himself as well perhaps as Shaw, whose critics repeatedly asserted that his characters were puppets, controlled by Shavian ideas. The producer of Joyce's theatrical has "the benediction" not, I submit, of God but of the creator of *Back to Methuselah*—"the Holy Genesius Archimimus" (219.8-9), the holy archmime, in Joyce's time considered the saintly monarch of drama and the Genesis/genius and archmime because he had mimicked the first book of the Bible in *Methuselah*.

The random and repeated references to drama in the *Wake* suggest that Shem/Glugg's rival is a man of the theater. There is "the prompter's voice" (435.20), "Curtain up. Juice, please! [the electricity that comes from Shaun/Shaw] Foots!" (501.7). The book is "a command performance . . . of the problem passion play of the millentury, running strong since creation" (32.30-33)—a description that could apply equally to Shaw's biblical dramas. Indeed, Shaw is no doubt "our worldstage's practical jokepiece and retired cecelticommediant . . . in . . . tuxedo . . . on every point far outstarching the laundered clawhammers and marble-topped highboys of the pit stalls and early amphitheatre. The piece was this: look at the lamps [associated with Lamppost Shaw throughout]. . . . Ladies circles. . . . Pit . . . standing room only" (33.2-12). Famed for teaching actresses elocution, Shaw is "a noted stagey elocutioner"

(58.34–35). Actresses Florence Farr and Janet Achurch, Shaw's elocution pupils, may be compacted in "Mrs. F . . . A . . . ," who speaks "in a stage whisper" (59.4–5). At "the old vic" (62.6), many Shaw plays were performed.

Joyce's theater also has the "distinguished patronage of their Elderships the Oldens" (219.9–10), who sound suspiciously like Shaw's old ones, the Ancients of *Methuselah,* though other patriarchal oldsters like Mamalujo, the four gospellers, may be included in Joyce's reference. The playbill calls the production *The Mime of Mick, Nick and the Maggies,* the story line of which concerns the rivalry of Mick—the archangel Michael, with whom as Michael-angel Shaw's artist identifies in "As Far as Thought Can Reach"—and Nick, Old Nick, the Mephistopheles of the vaguely Faustian conflict. The Maggies are perhaps multiples of Marguerite in *Faust* in which the higher and lower natures of man vie for possession of the female soul. In the game of Angels and Devils, the two boys compete for female attention, and the Shaun boy triumphs. The Floras who are "Girl Scouts from St. Bride's Finishing Establishment" (220.3–4) seem to be from St. Bride's Church in Dublin, where Shaw's uncle was vicar. Like Shaun a favorite of females, Shaw lectured schoolchildren, Girl Scouts, Salvation Army "Girls," and the "Intelligent Woman" for whom he wrote a guide to socialism—all receptive audiences like the St. Bride's girls, who adore the Shaun/Shaw figure in "heliolatry" (237.1), thus associating Chuff with the solar deities related to G. B. S. throughout the *Wake*.

The setting, "with futurist onehorse balletbattle pictures and the Pageant of Past History" (221.18–19), debunks, decenters, and evokes *Methuselah,* which treats the procession of past history beginning with Adam and Eve and ends, somewhat anticlimactically, in a "onehorse" way in a peaceful sci-fi future where dancing and a festival of the arts have taken the place of battles. Apparently among the props for the play are "Phenecian blends and Sourdanian doofpoosts by Shauveourishe" (221.32–33), so that Shaw is not only an actor and a character but a local establishment—Shavian-Irish—providing what might be Phoenician blends (the inseparable mixture of Joyce's tapestry with the Phoenician script about the phoenix rising?) and sourdine, musically muted, sourdanish, jourdanian doorposts—seemingly unidentifiable props vaguely related to Shaun the Post, the Shaw whose music is muted in the *Wake*. With such obscurantism Joyce makes fun of the advertising credits that prop providers used to get in playbills, but perhaps the important point is that Irish Shaw seems to have provided some of the stage properties for the performance.

Although much of the show seems untranslatable, certain asides evoke the playwright. Some of the mandates of the entertainment randomly suggest him: "And send Jarge for Mary Inklenders" (229.3–4). If he is a gofer, George is to go for merry Englanders and merry inklenders. "Go in for scribenery [a packed reference to scenery, to writing, and to playwright Augustin Eugène Scribe] with the satiety of arthurs" (229.7). The most famous member of the Society of Authors in London was Shaw. When Joyce produced Shaw's plays illegally in Zurich, it was the Society's secretary who chastised him. Shaw began writing plays in the Scribean format but despised the "empty aestheticism" (Valency 54) of Scribe. The surfeit of "arthurs" suggests the Arthurs who were prominent in the organization—Arthur Henry Jones and Arthur Wing Pinero, Shaw's chief dramatic rivals—and perhaps also snidely alludes to the proper Tennysonian, *Idylls of the King* members of the Stage Society and thus to the philosopher kings of Shaw's Camelot-utopia in *Methuselah*.

Once Joyce's entertainment begins, the adoring girls sing the praises of Chuff/Shaun, who for a moment seems to be Joyce's brother "Stainusless" (237.11), but their admiration of the "pure," "sainted youngling" (237.25, 29) seems to take its cue from Frank Harris's assessment of Shaw's popularity with women: Shaw "was more pursued than pursuing. . . . no ascetic," even if "disciples . . . would fain make a plaster saint of him" (109–10). Their adulation becomes a description of Shaw, "our unschoold, pageantmaster, deliverer of softmissives, round the world in forty mails . . . chief celtech chappy" (237.13–20). In spite of the temptation to identify the chief self-taught Celt as Yeats, Shaw was the internationally famous autodidact whose paradoxically soft "missives" appearing in papers around the world often advocated nonviolence. His Christmas pantomime *Androcles and the Lion* and the Malvern Festival over which he presided qualified him as a "pageant master." Like his Elderly Gentleman in *Methuselah*, who has been everywhere as a member of the Travellers' Club, Shaw traveled extensively in later life, emulating Jules Verne's intrepid tourist. In 1932–33, while Joyce was hard at work on his "Work in Progress," Shaw was circumnavigating the globe. The playwright pageant master was, to

Joyce's consternation, the "chief celtech chappy," steeped in scientific technology.

Although the "twain" brothers are "not on terms," the girls who are their audience "knowell their Vico's Road" in Dalkey where Shaw lived as a boy. Shaw links are sprinkled at random, as are seemingly irrelevant allusions to characters in his plays—for example, "Blanche de Blanche" (248.33) of *Widowers' Houses,* as well as Shaw's secretary: Blanche Patch, named earlier in the text ("blanche patch"; 83.26), was, as the press made clear, Shaw's secretary from 1920 until his death. "Sunny, my gander, he's coming to land her" (249.18–19) will to Joyceans seem to be a reference to young Joyce, but it must be remembered that young Shaw was also Sonny. The scrapping twins are both "sonnies" (194.24) to their parents.

Amid the conflict of angels and devils, the abrupt insertion of "For all of these have been thisworlders, time liquescing into state, pitiless age grows angelhood" (251.9–10) is clear derision of old Shaw, once a thisworlder but in his age growing angelhood like the Ancients in their platonic space/state in part 5 of *Methuselah,* and like *Saint Joan.* Toward the end of the dislocating and dislocated entertainment, "the producer (Mr John Baptister Vickar) caused a deep abuliousness to descend upon the Father of Truants" (255.27–28). This abulia seems reflected in the whole mentally disordered episode, but at the conclusion it apparently brings the play to a stop because the dreamer's volition is impaired. It seems that the producer caused a deep sleep to descend upon H. C. E. The distorted dream name of the theatrical producer, a John the Baptist and vicar, refers to the Shaw type in relationship to the truant Nick, for like Shaw as John Tanner, who initiated Joyce into the mysteries of the new religion, his name, "John Baptister Vickar" (while also adumbrating Giambattista Vico), indicates that he is the Baptist who immersed the savior—in this case ironically the Luciferian artist—in his spiritually cleansing waters. In point of fact, Shaw's uncle, vicar of St. Bride's Church in Dublin, baptized him (PP 49). The clergyman in "The Gospel of the Brothers Barnabas" is in "The Thing Happens" a vicar who later becomes an archbishop, having died into life through immersion in water.

The Father of Truants, however, is H. C. E., including both Shem and Shaw, for in his preface to *Misalliance* the devil's disciple advocated truancy because of his disdain for the school system. Harris noted that to Shaw school was "a hated prison" (51) that used corporal punishment and tried to put mental straitjackets on young minds. Shaw's argument may have made him the Father of Truants to the author of "An Encounter" and *Portrait*. Much in the entertainment featuring Chuff (the angel who was once a truant who characterized himself as "mephistophelean" and "diabolonian") and Glugg (the renegade disciple) may create truant readers, for it is not amusing except to the most diligent and patient Joyceans (like Patrick McCarthy, who finds "The Mime" to be "a particularly enjoyable chapter"; 605); but Joyce scatters the section with clues as to the identity of Chuff and the presence, even in the wings, of Shaw.

When the obscure play is about to end, "your wildeshawshowe moves swiftly sterneward!" (256.13), preceded by Sheridan and Goldsmith ("sherrigoldies") and Yeats and Synge ("yeassymgnays") in a catalogue of Irish writers. The show—the "wilde shaw show" in which Oscar Wilde/Joyce is the bad boy antagonist pitted against Shaw the heroic angel—moves swiftly through Jonathan Swift toward its rear-end comic debacle in Laurence Sterne. Although the St. Bride's girls prefer the popular Shaun, "Izzy most unhappy is. Fair Essie fie onhapje?" (257.1-2)—a question that Dick Dudgeon addressed to Essie, the illegitimate daughter of his uncle in *The Devil's Disciple*. In the end, young Essie is indeed unhappy because she is about to lose her cousin, the devil's disciple who has been kind to her. Apparently, some of Joyce's fictional females are not unhappy, for one "laughs her stellas vispirine" (257.2). Because the game is not turning out so that Izzy/Isolde/sister and her illicit (incestuous?) boyfriend can get together, "angellland"—Shaw's angel-land in *Methuselah* and England—is weeping for Isolde, while, it seems, Stella by starlight laughs. The outcome hints that Stella Campbell, whom Shaw addressed in love letters as "Stella Stellarum"—his own vesperine evening star, whom Joyce mixes with Swift's—is laughing through tears. For Shaw had written to her, "Never did a man paint his infatuation across the heavens as I painted mine for you, rapturously and shamelessly" (quoted in Harris 121). The scandalous news revealed in letters published in New York newspapers and implied in her 1922 memoirs was that the actress loved G. B. S., who led her on, but he returned to his St. Bride's girl, his Anglo-Irish wife Charlotte, acting finally more like "Skowood Shaws . . . auld Daddy Deacon" (257.12-14) than the Tristram he had set himself up to be. The Perfect Wagnerite delighted in Tristram and Isolde love triangles with Izzies of his own if they did not entail his drinking a love potion that would make the love irrevocable.

As the play disintegrates with a thunderclap heralding a new cycle, as in *Heartbreak House,* "The Tragedy of an Elderly Gentleman," and Vico, Shakespeare gets the blame that Shaw gave him in "Blaming the Bard"—"You're well held now, Missy Cheekspeer" (257.19–20). The show master demands, "Upploud! / The play thou schouwburgst [Shaw/show burst?], Game, here endeth" (257.29–30). Still thinking of the Shaw who renounced love for mental activity, the narrator interjects, "To Mezouzalem with the Dephilim, diditsdinkun's dud?" which is probably a reference to *Methuselah* and means, Did you think it and/or the "play" just witnessed was a dud? "Mezouzalem with the Dephilim" (258.8–9) suggests Methuselah as well as the oracle at Delphi who appears in the west of Shaw's Ireland, dispensing wisdom to the Elderly Gentleman. Mezuzah, Jerusalem, and Salem are compacted in *Mezouzalem,* the first reminding the reader of the container for the parchment on which are inscribed passages from Deuteronomy, the last book of the *Torah,* which enjoins Jews to love God. The passages also ask Jews to write the verses on the "posts" of their houses. Joyce's Shaun the Post as Shaw had taken on the role of the writer of the *Torah* in his own Pentateuch, in which he preached trust in the Life Force manifest in oracles like himself. "Dephilim" alludes to the "tephilim" of Judaism, the phylactery compacting (like *Methuselah* and the *Wake*) four parts of the Pentateuch. Old Methuselah Shaw, who thought himself Delphic, was growing deaf and also had the devil in him ("Dephilim") as the advocate of the iconoclastic "diabolonian ethics" of *The Devil's Disciple.* "Dephilim" may also hide "the film," for while Joyce was revising the *Wake,* Shaw was making headlines over his negotiations with Gabriel Pascal, who wanted to turn G. B. S.'s plays into films. Because Joyce freely associated everything and dumped all sorts of suggestions into his portmanteaus, it may not be stretching the baggage to remind readers that Shaw's London address was Adelphi Terrace.

If, however, Shaw's Pentateuch was a dud, Joyce's murky theatrical is no better. As the curtain drops on the blurry event, the narrator analyzes the action of the "Mime" as Shaw sometimes did in postscripts to his plays. The *Wake* narrator rewards the Shaun character, who, like Shaw in his temptation to an illicit affair, remained virtuous, and predicts punishment for Nick: "If Nekulon shall be havonfalled surely Makel haven hevens" (258.13–14). If Luciferian Nick shall fall from heaven, as the low content of Shem's book suggests that he does, Michael surely shall have haven/heavens such as Shaw imagined in the finale of *Methuselah*. In "As Far as Thought Can Reach" (part 5), the "Archangel Michael," once a "mighty sculptor and painter" (268), has become a legendary archetype for the great artist who creates beautiful "newly born" surrounded by ancients, the sybils and prophets on the ceiling of the Sistine Chapel. Even in Joyce's extremely obscure skit (the houselights seem to be out in the theater), the basic struggle between Shaun as angel and Shem as devil persists.

The struggle appears again in the fractured dialogue of Butt and Taff (introduced earlier as Mutt and Jute; 16.10), which is so disjointed that only suggestions of the binary pattern surface in the midst of epithets strung together. Taff (Shaun/Shaw) is "looking through the roof towards a relevution of the karma life" (338.5–6), and even though Conan Doyle, another Irishman, gets into the act, he is annoyed at Butt, of Jesuitical "clergical appealance," whom Taff accuses of "roudery" (340.2)—rude robbery, or plagiarism, implying Joyce's imagination of Shaw's response to his thefts: "joyclid, son of a Butt" (Joyce/Euclid) is juxtaposed to "sweet tart of Whiteness" (302.12–14)—Taff/Shaw, encoded with the color white. Throughout the *Wake* Shaw is associated with the tub he upturned so that he could stand on it to preach socialism in Hyde Park. Joyclid acknowledges his literary parenthood as "son of a Butt" in his inverted relationship to Shaw. Indeed, the *Wake* operates on the assumption of Stephen Dedalus's theory about paternity—that father and son are consubstantial. That Taff is "fat" inverted and Butt "tub" is part of Joyce's shamantic word play, associating Shaw with fat, not because he (or his sometimes interchangeable disciple) was obese, but probably because G. B. S. had a fat bankroll, was living off the fat of the land, and was, to his oedipal rival, often a fathead.

In the midst of spouting seemingly obscure nonsense, Butt refers to *Back to Methuselah*—"Mousoumeselles buckwoulds look" (339.16), which he seems to be hiding, for Taff—the Shaun figure—chastises him for "insects appalling, low hum clang sin! A cheap decoy!" (339.22). The incest and insects, like the Earwig, Ondt, and Gracehoper and the low sexual sin of the *Wake,* seem to Taff to be Butt's cheap way of detouring the reader from his real subject, his "walshbrushup" (340.3)—welsher's brushup of wash/Shaw. Shaun calls Shem a "welsher" (322.8; 480.12; 590.13) who "escapa sansa pagar" (464.11) (escaped without paying), as Joyce had escaped in Zurich without paying royalty fees for Shaw's plays and had escaped detection of his literary thefts in the *Wake* and elsewhere. Apparently Butt "immingled" his "Irmenial hairmaierians ammongled his Gospolis fomiliours till . . . I adn't the arts to" (345.1–3). Butt mingled his menial Irish Homerians (characters in *Ulysses* who reappear in the pubkeeper's family) among Taff's familiar gospels and in his polis, the new society modeled on the Greek state that emerges at the end of Shaw's gospels. But at times, despite his "pujealousties" (350.15), the jealous pugilist lacked the arts or heart to go on with the merger, despite his ties to Shaw.

In a typical role reversal, however, Butt forgives Taff, who takes on the role of the priest in offering communion to his double: he does so as pontifex maximus, probably Shaw as Caesar and as the supreme pontiff, whom Shaw imagined himself to be (and Joyce ridiculed). Butt *"takecups the communion of sense at the hands of the foregiver of trosstpassers"* (345.27–28). Noted for not holding grudges, Shaw seemed to have forgiven Joyce's sensuality and shameful trespass against him in coveting his plays. When Shaw defended *Exiles* in London in 1926, the act must have seemed to Joyce to be an offer of communion. Taff's double, now confused with him, is *"that potifex miximhost with haruspical hospedariaty"*—the priest, who practices divination, writes maxims (like Shaw's "Maxims for Revolutionaries"), and offers hospitality as well as the communion host, stupidly happy that Taff now acts like a bosom friend/fiend ("boesen fiennd"; 345.33). Joyce's 1926 letter of congratulation to Shaw for winning the Nobel Prize was an offer of reconciliation that may also have been the act of a bosom fiend, who still secretly envied and resented the world-famous, self-designated seer. In *The Quintessence of Ibsenism* Shaw associated himself with the mystic Maximus ("miximhost") who rejects the rotten past's "pagan sensualism" as well as "Christ or self-abnegatory idealism" to opt for the God in man who will build [Ibsen's] Brand's bridge between flesh and spirit" (MCE 76–77). Thus the seer disdains both empire and Christianity in favor of synthesizing the Emperor and Galilean (of Ibsen's play) in (Shavian) man (79). His message is the same as the dialectic of the *Wake* in which opposites like Butt and Taff are reconciled.

Having received the divine message, Butt takes Taff's place, studying and showing "day's reasons" such as G. B. S. had shown him—how to shake death: "So I begin to study and I soon show them day's reasons how to give the cold shake to they blighty perishers" (347.23–25).

"Horrasure" and "orussheying" happily in fractured Russian, Butt (now practically indistinguishable from Taff) wants to become reassociated with the post-Eden past. "I now with platoonic leave recoil in . . . me misenary post for all them old boyars that's now boomaringing in waulholler" (348.8–10). At the end of *Methuselah* the author of *The Perfect Wagnerite* took Platonic leave in his post as missionary, proclaiming for the old boyos—his Ancients—that men will boomerang into Valhalla, moving into another, higher cycle of Creative Evolution. Later, after Butt admits that "*he codant steal no lunger*" (349.36), Taff is upset over the "dirtiment" of Butt's work, when it is "Notshoh?" (353.4–5)—when it is not Shaw—just as Shaw was upset over the "dirt" of *Ulysses* when it did not have a Shavian purpose. In the end of their obscure debate, however, the great "*Immensipater*" (342.26) is united with his brother/son. According to C. E. M. Joad, Shaw was the great emancipator of his and thus Joyce's generation (28). In Joyce's literary family romance the immense father and twin unites with Butt to become "one and the same person." Though one "lobed the sex of his head" (Shaw) and the other "ates the seep of his traublers" (354.28–29) (eats/hates the semen of his troubles and troublers, perhaps), both were "playing lancifer lucifug" (354.32)—Lucifers who were at times Lancelots. Together in Swift's "toil of his tubb" (354.36), they had conducted the battle of the books—*Methuselah* as against the *Wake*—quarreling over the relative merits of Ancients (Shaw) and Moderns (Joyce). Butt ("*desprot slave wager*") derides Taff's religious enthusiasm, and Taff ("*foeman feodal*") repudiates Butt's skepticism as well as his modernism. The "*stark daniel*" whom Butt pulls (354.3) is probably the hypocritical "good" brother, Elder Daniel of *The Shewing up of Blanco Posnet*—an identification further suggested when Butt, the reprobate brother, lapses into the cowboy drawl that Shaw imitated in his brother play: "Shurenoff" (354.5) suggests Shaw's cowboys. Daniel turns up later as "Daniel in Leonden" (541.16): Shaw, transformed into the sanctimonious religious brother in London and perhaps, like Androcles, in the lion's den.

As Saint Mick to Joyce's Old Nick, one "censor" and the other "miscreant" (JJ1 562), Shawn (Shaw) maintains his role as the voice of morality and conscience. He is "St. Kevin Hydrophilos" (606.4–5)—a lover of water because of his publicized exploits as a swimmer, his advocacy of washing up Dublin after discerning dirt in *Ulysses,* and his

Long Livers who undergo faked drownings in order to be resurrected in this life. St. Kevin, who settled in the sixth century at the Glen of the Two Lakes (Glendalough) in County Wicklow, was a hermit comparable to Shaw's Ancients in the coda of *Methuselah,* but the monk did not like water as well as Shaw did. Nevertheless, Joyce's Kevin invents "celibate matrimony" (605.9), like the eccentric Shaw, whose marriage agreement precluded sex. If literary gossip did not provide such information, Harris's biography, which airs G. B. S.'s views on sex, did. One of Shaw's waggish, apocryphal roles was that of cleric. Probably Joyce's passing assertion "Every monk his own Cashel" (228.269) is a sly allusion to the author of *Cashel Byron's Profession*'s posing as a monk (see PP, facing 181). Like Shaw, Kevin will "wend him to Amorica to quest a cashy job" (562.31). When Shaw visited America in 1933, his interview with Samuel Goldwyn in Hollywood was publicized. When Goldwyn "tried to flatter him into signing a contract for screen rights" to his plays, the witty Irish rejoinder was, "The trouble is, Mr Goldwyn, you are interested in art, whereas I am interested in money" (quoted in H3 307–8). For his spectacular New York lecture at the Metropolitan Opera House Shaw was charged with seeking a "cashy job." Such accusations of Shaw clones pepper Joyce's text, attesting to Shem's jealousy of his hugely successful fantasy "frother."

As Dublin booksellers Brown Nolan, Shaun and Shem are two Dubliners, one Protestant and the other once Catholic, who, like Bruno, sell heretical books. Both are victims of censorship. Another pair are in the last book of the *Wake* "transformed into Muta (the mutant) and Juva (the rejuvenated), the Java Man" (Benstock, *Joyce Again's* 250). In the coda of *Back to Methuselah,* Shaw's rarified, asexual Ancients are mutations, and the first man, Adam, reappears with the message of rejuvenation. Joyce's comic pair change into Tunc and Punc—a druidic Bishop Berkeley and a punk Patrick—a lapsed "petty padre" (612.16), like Shem/Jim, more interested in physical pleasures than the exalted philosophical system of "Balkelly, archdruid" (611.5), who seems to be a permutation of the druid Zosim in "The Tragedy of an Elderly Gentleman." In that play the druid leads the Envoy, the Envoy's wife and daughter, and the Elderly Gentleman to the Pythoness Oracle. She is the spokesperson for Shaw's mystical rejection of the flesh and symbolizes a retreat into what Joyce must have considered the solipsistic subjectivity of Berkeley. Balkelly, Bishop Berkeley, is called *"Burkeley's*

Show's" (Berkeley's Shaw) in the Butt and Taff episode (346.11). In his syncretic portmanteau Joyce superimposes Shaw upon the Protestant bishop and subjective idealist, with good reason, for Ancients of the last play of Shaw's Pentateuch deny the flesh and believe that the ultimate reality is subjective and mental.

Although Campbell and Robinson, Tindall, Begnal, and Eckley argue that Patrick seems to be Shaun and the archdruid Shem, Glasheen (*Third Census*.lix, 29) and McHugh (*Annotations* 86) reverse the roles. By the Shavian arc light, it makes sense to identify "punc Patrick" with the lapsed Catholic and the subjective idealist bishop with late Shaw. Balkelly/Shaun/Shaw is pitted against the "petty padre" (612.16), Punc Patrick, one side of the "crisscouple" who are "crosscomplimentary" (613.10–11). "Paddrock" debates "bookley," who is a paradoxical "puraduxed seer" (611.19–20), like Shaw a paradoxical, pure, and puritan seer. Joyce alludes to his own essay "Ireland, Island of Saints and Sages" and to Shaw, "the sager and the probably eruberuption of the saint" (612.23–24). In mock humility, Punc kneels to the "Great Balenoarch" (612.27), whose initials are G. B., like those of Shaw and George Berkeley. Baal, the Canaanite fertility god dedicated to the Great Mother, is compacted with the patriarch who built Noah's ark for the survival of the human race, even though as Shaw he didn't bail out the ark. He is the "Good safe firelamp" (613.1) of Lamppost Shaw, who is "the laud of laurense"—the praise/bard/lord of Ayot St. Lawrence, "saint and sage" (613.15–16). In Shaw's last book of his optimistic Pentateuch, the Ancients opt for pure mind in a paradise washed clean of the dirt that Shaw found in *Ulysses*. Although in his wish fulfillment "monologuy of the interiors" (119.32–33) Joyce had tried to keep the creator of Ann Whitefield, the Life Force, anonymous, Shaw is the "Annone Wishwashwhose" (614.2–3) "fittest surviva. . . . Clean" (614.11–12).

Perhaps significantly, Wyndham Lewis had written that Shaw's characters in *Methuselah* and *Saint Joan* were like Anglican clergy (49), suggesting "sunday school" and "the rhetoric of the anglican pulpit" (51). He was not the first to comment on the clerical qualities of the *Methuselah* cast, one of whom is an ex-clergyman and another of whom begins as a rector only to become, after repeated rebirths, an archbishop "three times" (BM 165). Indeed, Archbishop Haslam, who has "had several careers" since beginning "this routine of life and death" (165) is a *doppelgänger* of the many-faceted Shaw. Like the Grand Old Man of theater who turned to Platonism in his old age, the Anglican bishop of Cloyne, the solipsist Berkeley, was a utopian and immaterialist. In the "panepiphanal world" of the *Wake* he is a "puraduxed seer in seventh degree of wisdom" (611.13, 19–20), like Shaw's alter ego the "supernatural old man" Shotover in *Heartbreak House*. Shotover desires "to attain the seventh degree of concentration" (Plays 759). Like the rest of the literary world, Joyce knew that in *Methuselah* Shaw had proclaimed himself a saint and visionary. Furthermore, Joyce admitted that the Balkelly-Patrick dialogue is a "defense and indictment of the book itself" (JJL 1:406), perhaps because it stops just short of revealing his main source in late Shaw. In *Methuselah* the Ancient, sounding like Berkeley, insists that "thought is the life" (288); "it was to myself I turned as to the final reality" (295). In reading in Seumus MacManus's *Story of the Irish Race* (first published in 1921) that Bishop Berkeley's pamphlet *The Querist* "is often quoted as Nationalist propaganda" but is actually a narrowly "colonial or ascendancy vision" (678), Joyce would have perceived yet another parallel between his Anglo-Irish mentor and Berkeley and a soft spot in his armor as a Protestant. "The evils he inveighed against did not touch the Gaelic masses, for their trouble was not uneven distribution of wealth, but political and economic annihilation" (679). The Fabian socialist who insisted on arguing for the equal distribution of wealth may have looked to Joyce like the reincarnation of Berkeley in spite of his awareness of political and economic oppression in Ireland. MacManus's comparison of Berkeley to the druids as "on the Platonic side" of the bipolar division of all men (679) may also have influenced Joyce's superimposition of Shaw upon Berkeley and the druid, for one of the characters in *Methuselah* is the druid Zosim.

Joyce's druidic Balkelly is described by an Oriental voice that sounds like Confucius of part 3 of *Methuselah,* "The Thing Happens": "he savvy inside true inwardness of reality . . . Rumnant Patholic, stareotypopticus, no catch all that preachybook, utpiam" (611.20–25). An avatar of the Shaw/Shaun character, the archdruid Balkelly is not a Roman Catholic but a pathetic and pathological contemplative ("Rumnant patholic") all too like the remnant Catholic who thought of Shaw as a twin, because Joyce too had contemplated a religious life, one very different from the one he simultaneously approved and disdained in

Shaw's Methuselan vision. Joyce's Protestant bishop is a "stareotypopticus"—a starry-type pop, a stereotype and stereopticon maker of a "preachybook," a three-dimensional utopian ("utpiam") vision about how to atone, from the Latin *ut* plus *piamen*. It is a vision that not everyone "caught." The "preachybook" is simultaneously *Methuselah* and the *Wake,* Joyce's at-one-ment with himself and Shaw regarding his sins against the old playwright. The stereopticon, which projects through two lanterns arranged so that one picture appears to dissolve while the next is forming, is *Methuselah* dissolving into the *Wake.* Shaun/Shaw holds one lantern while Shem/Joyce subsumes Shaw's vision and thus his Pentateuch.

Shaw is the "Bigseer" whom Punc Patrick "refrects" (reflects, refracts) (612.16). In contrasting Punc Patrick and Belkelly, Joyce deconstructs the traditional view that Saint Patrick brought the new writing of the Roman Empire to Ireland, which had before his arrival only the primitive Ogham alphabet of the druids. This alphabet is no doubt associated with Shaw's simplified alphabet or even his prose as "pidgin" (611.5) English of a "pidginfella" (611.27) compared to Punc's more complex alphabet; for, transforming the verbal to the visual medium of art, he criticizes Balkelly's "pore shiroskuro blackinwhitepaddynger" (612.18)—which is the poor, hence primitive, chiaroscuro of *Methuselah,* a black and white paddy-humdinger book. Compared to the advanced *Wake,* it is the black and white product of a paddy who padded his plays with too much talk. The multiplex and multicolored shadings of Joyce, on the other hand, supersede Shaw by bringing together "principalest of Iro's Irismans ruinboon pot before"—the principal visionary Irish man and men reborn and bringing a boon, as "sager and . . . saint" (612.20–24). Throughout the Berkeley/Patrick "debate" are sprinkled references to "High ober King Leary" (612.4) that suggest King Lear but also Shaw, who had declared that in *Heartbreak House* he had rewritten Shakespeare's tragedy of old age. Under the aegis of Lamppost Shaw's "good safe firelamp" (613.1), "saint and sage have said their say" (613.16). The *Wake* confuses and melds saint and sage, for Shaw was considered to be a saint, but comparison to Berkeley makes him a sage. The envious Shem, of course, aspires to become one with the saint and sage, even though in the Berkeley/Patrick "dialogue" Shem/Jim is the Punc Patrick, who is hardly a saint, but he represents an advanced form of writing that he hopes will supplant the primitive, druidic Ogham of the simplified speller, Shaw. The confrontation between druid and "paddrock" is yet another variation on the literary rivalry which Joyce imagined between himself and his precursor. (Like Patrick's writing which colonized Ireland, Joyce's has taken precedence over Shaw's, at least with literary critics. Posthumously, the punman's wish has come true.)

It will be recalled that Shaw had hoped for a younger artist or one hundred apter hands to replace *Methuselah*. With false modesty, he claimed that *Back to Methuselah* was, as the first major work of the new religion, medieval. But in the revisionist *Wake* pairings, sometimes the venerable character, like Patrick associated with Joyce, is ironically medieval. The two authors are often a confusing and confused duo. The Catholic Saint Patrick is at once a patriarch and, as Punc, modern, whereas Protestant Berkeley is a relatively modern (eighteenth-century) sage. The "peerless pair"—stand-up comic and his slippery straight man—usually splits between the man of action and prevaricating provoker: "One to do and One to Dare"—Chuff and Glugg, Taff and Butt, Mutt and Jute, Balkelly and Patrick, Muta and Juva—the rejuvenated man, like Adam, who reappears in Shaw's coda. All of the couples remind us of the conflict between the Shavian mutations who hope to live the life of pure mind and the more primitive Java man who represents the Shemside of Joyce's dialectic. In the debates of his Dublin doubles, Shem conflicts with Shaun, Joyce with Shaw—the "olympically optimoninous" (613.28–29) (Olympically optimistic) "Dear. . . . Dirtdump Reverend" (615.12)—who is his Other self.

Burrus and Caseous: "Unbeaten Risicide" and "Puir Tyron"

In triangulating male antagonisms, the Burrus-Caseous episode (book 1, 6.161–68) peregrinates over both Oedipal and sibling rivalry—the Brutus-Cassius plot against Caesar and the criticisms by Cassius, "puir tyron" (163.9)—the poor boy tyro who is a Joycean "arrivaliste" "zealous" of his fellow "risicide" (161.17, 21), the nobler Brutus—a laughable killer of laughter—who is Shavian. According to Adaline Glasheen, the episode is a burlesque of a Shaw preface (*Second Census*.236). Part of the answer to question 11 of chapter 6, this disquisition of Butter and Cheese over Caesar reduces to an absurdity the Shaw preface that shadowboxes with its subject and circles around the theme of the play to follow. It ridicules the infamous Shavian digressiveness. So "off the toptic" is the episode that the speaker alludes only once (and then parenthetically) to the subject, which, after Shakespeare's *Julius Caesar,* should be regicide.

Each paragraph starts with a typical Shavian introductory sentence but immediately fractures the familiar. "My readers will recall . . . " becomes "My heeders will recoil . . . " (160.35); "Burrus, let us like to imagine, is a genuine prime . . . " (161.15) (with the interrupting element after the subject, Burrus); "The older sisars (Tyrants, regicide is too good for you!) . . ." (162.1), promising to be a straightforward declarative sentence, is interrupted by parenthetical material such as Shaw often interpolated. In the construction "This in fact, just to show you, is Caseous . . . " (163.8) there is the familiar approach to "you" the reader and the implication that the author, like Shaw, is giving his readers "fact." "Thus we cannot escape our likes and mislikes . . . " (163.12) begins a paragraph with a coordinating adverb, a typical Shavian locution repeated in the next paragraph, which starts with a Shaw favorite, "Now . . . " (163.29). The following paragraph announces a change of subject away from Caesar and the minions who plot against him to music criticism, an early Shaw specialty: "We now romp through a period of pure lyricism of shamebred music . . . " (164.15–16), a digression that continues into the next paragraph, which announces, with Shaw-like directness, "I shall have a word to say in a few yards about the acoustic and orchidectural management of the tonehall" but turns back instead "to pursue Burrus and Caseous" (165.8–12). "Now there can be no question . . . " (166.3) simulates Shaw's reasonable, self-assured style and his tendency in the prefaces to overuse *Now* to introduce a paragraph: "Now most laws are . . . " (CP 1); "Now if England had been governed . . . " (13); "Now the right to bear children . . . " (18); "Now death is not . . . " (45); "Now let us ask . . . " (62); "Now what happened to me . . . " (89); "Now there is no such impulse . . . " (91); "Now children must be taught . . . " (97); "Now if all this can be done . . . " (112); "Now what does this . . . " (119); "Now it is all very well . . . " (152). Joyce's final paragraph gets our attention, however, by starting with an uncharacteristic "No!" (167.18).

The speaker thus parodies Shaw the preface writer, deflating his language, his sententious content, and the way—as H. G. Wells put it—that he dances around fact "and weaves a willful veil of confident assurances about her" (I&R 27). His tendency to illustrate through references to familiar poetry or unascribed biblical quotes gets short shrift from Joyce, who ridicules clichés by deconstructing familiar quotations like Pope's "Fools rush in where angels fear to tread," which becomes "where even michangelines [related to Shaw/Shaun] have fooled to dread . . . " (160.36; 161.1). "There's many a split pretext between bowl and jowl" (161.31–32) distorts the proverbial "There's many a slip twixt the cup and the lip." Burrus is "a king off duty and a jaw for ever" (162.35)—a talker with political ambitions like Shaw's Caesar, who is "off duty" at the opening of *Caesar and Cleopatra,* and like King Magnus, who is in the notorious scene with his mistress Orinthia "off duty." All of Shaw's off-duty kings are, like himself, great talkers, "jaws for ever." In Shaw's prologue to *Caesar and Cleopatra* we are told that Caesar "was a great talker and politician: he bought men with words and with gold . . . " (Plays 251). If Burrus were "a thing of beauty and a joy forever," he would, like Keats, Caesar's foil Apollodorus, and Joyce be a supporter of art for art's sake. Despite his disclaimer that those who can't do, teach, Shaw cast himself in the role of a teacher, one like Professor Jones, who narrates the Burrus-Caseous episode. An adumbration of Professor Cusins in *Major Barbara* and Professor Higgins in *Pygmalion,* he has a Shavian source. In 1922 the playwright sent his American protégé Molly Tompkins for elocution lessons to a professor of phonetics, Daniel Jones—one of Shaw's models for Higgins.

The food references that give the section its impressionistic focus on Butter and Cheese lead the professor, who seems ready to talk about Margareen, "the appetising entry," to suggest that bringing the female mediatrix into the meandering discourse is "plumply pudding the carp before doevre hors" (164.17–18)—plainly putting "the cart before the horse" and bringing the desert and main course before the hors d'oeuvres. But "one plant's breaf is a lunger planner's byscent" (165.10)—one man's meat is another man's poison. When the almighty Caesarian (simultaneously the professor) implies that the gods are dead and "Olymp" stormed, he adds with Shakespearean and Shavian distrust of the mob, "[L]et Demoncracy take the highmost!" (167.25)—a distortion of the expression "Let the devil take the hin' most," from Shaw's inspiration Samuel Butler. Like Shaw's Caesar, who is a writer, not a lover of Cleopatra, the speaker is married to the sacred word "till Breath us depart!" (167.30–31)—till death us do part. Digressing to reveal the missionary zeal that informs *Methuselah,* and preferring prophecy to patriotism, the preacher derides "That mon that hoth no moses in his sole [no music/Moses in his soul—two qualities indispensable to the aging Shaw] nor is not awed by conquests of word's law, who never with humself was fed and leaves his soil to lave his head, when his hope's in his highlows" (167.35-36; 168.1-2). This parodies Sir Walter Scott's *Lay of the Last Minstrel*'s sentimental patriotism: "Breathes there a man, with soul so dead, / Who never to himself hath said / This is my own, my native land!" as well as Robert Burns's "My heart's in the highlands." Carried away with his zeal, the preacher never gets through his final qualifying subordinate clause to a main clause. Thus he creates one long, fragmentary "sentence" with poetic clichés alluding to sentimental patriotism and romantic nationalism—Shavian *bêtes noires.*

Decentering the logocentric prose of Shaw with loaded language that plays on familiar writing patterns, the narrator begins by addressing his readers: "My heeders will recoil . . . how at the outbreak before trespassing on the space question where even michelangelines have fooled to dread I proved to mindself as to your sotisfiction how his abject all through . . . is nothing so much more than a mere cashdime however genteel he may want ours" (160.35-36; 161.1-5). When Shaw wrote *Caesar and Cleopatra* in 1898, before he ventured on the subject of *Back to Methuselah,* in which the angelic artist identifies with "Archangel" Michelangelo, he had reduced everything to "cashdime" considerations, the economic motives in politics and society. Following Theodor Mommsen's interpretation of Caesar (see Weintraub, *Unexpected Shaw,* 110-23), Shaw viewed the fall of the Roman republic in terms of nineteenth-century politics. In a letter to Hesketh Pearson, he wrote that "originality gives a man an air of frankness, generosity, and magnanimity by enabling him to estimate the value of truth, money, or success in any particular instance quite independently of convention and moral generalization" (Weintraub, *Unexpected Shaw* 113). Joyce's misprision of *Caesar and Cleopatra* relates to his own skepticism regarding Shaw's financial interests (as well as his own). Hence he must have noted that in Shaw's play Caesar stops off in Egypt to get money: Caesar's first and repeated declaration in the Egyptian palace is, "I want some money"; "I am badly in want of money" (Plays 263). Cleopatra says she will "steal" Ftatateeta's jewels and give them to Caesar if he will not eat her (259). Balzanor accuses Ftatateeta of hiding Cleopatra in order to sell her "to Caesar or her brother" (256). The Egyptians are in financial trouble; Cleopatra's "guard cannot live on its pay" (255). To alleviate the "cashdime" problem (as Joyce calls it), the cynical, pragmatic Persian in Shaw's play advises selling Cleopatra "secretly to Ptolemy" and then volunteering to Caesar to rescue her (255). Pothinus asks Caesar, "Is it possible that Caesar, the conqueror of the world, has time to occupy himself with such a trifle as our taxes?" Caesar replies, "My friend, taxes are the chief business of a conqueror of the world" (264). In a letter to Harriet Weaver, Joyce had denigrated Shaw's opportunism in writing his plays for money (JJL 1:221). In his Burrus-Caseous "preface" he reduces to an absurdity (and to greed) Shaw's argument that economics are the basis of all social problems. Digressing to attack Shaw's supposed socialist reformism, which seems to his rival to be based, like Caesar's behavior, on pragmatic free enterprise, the narrator (thinking of dairy products) debunks the principle of "selldear to soldthere, once in the dairy days of buy and buy" (161.13–14).

Joyce's narrator nevertheless intends to go onto the private property of his rival's "space question"—Wyndham Lewis's bailiwick, the Egyptian territory of Cleopatra, and the outer-space Platonic garden of part 5 of *Methuselah,* where Shaw as Mick/ Angel/Michelangelo had not feared to tread. In "As Far as Thought Can Reach" in A.D. 31,920, Michelangelo is in the distant future only a mythic memory. Apparently freely associating the desire for perfection in "the hearts of the greatest artists" (268) with his own agenda, Joyce refers to the author of "Professor Ciondolone's too frequently hypothecated *Bettlermensch*" (161.2–3)—that is, to Professor Shaun-alone's insistently promoted Better Man, like Michelangelo and Caesar, creatively evolving into the superman of Shaw and Nietzsche's *Übermensch.*

Joyce's "preface," like Shaw's and like the *Wake* itself, superimposes erudite examples from many writers and ages upon one another. The Burrus-Caseous text overlaps sly allusions to Shakespeare's *Julius Caesar* and *Anthony and Cleopatra* and Shaw's *Caesar and Cleopatra* and *Methuselah.* Brutus and Cassius share the strobe light with Caesar. In ironic admiration of Brutus, Shaw wrote in his preface to *Three Plays for Puritans,* "It cost Shakespeare no pangs to write Caesar down for the more technical purpose of writing Brutus up. And what a Brutus! A perfect Girondon" (CP 749), a sometime moderate republican like Shaw, who was not, however, living during the time of the French

Revolution. Shaw's Caesar vows, "Were Rome a true republic, then were Caesar the first of Republicans" (Plays 267). As a gradualist supporter of the Russian Revolution, Joyce's Burrus/Brutus/Shaw may have earned the role of butter in this episode because of one of Shaw's infamous capers. After his triumphant return from Russia during the depths of the Depression, a *Punch* cartoon in August 1931 displayed Shaw bringing home Russian butter, a surplus product of the Soviet Union. Living in Paris, Joyce no doubt associated himself with the French product, cheese.

After debunking the foodstuffs by stressing the obverse of the alimentary process, the "split pretext bowl and jowl" and "the coarse use of stools" (161.32, 35), the narrator moves on to a paragraph ostensibly about "the older sisars" (162.1). Although the older Caesars "become unbeurrable from age (the compositor of the farce of dustiny however makes a thunpledrum mistake by letting off this pienofarte effect as his furst act as that is where the juke comes in)" (162.1–5). Whereas older Caesars like Shaw and his self-admiring self-portrait as Caesar are unbearable, not malleable like butter, Shaw is denigrated for composing a "farce" about Caesar (and another about Napoleon, the *Man of Destiny*), thus making a "thunpledrum," nonsensical error, concerning "Old Saint mumpledum" (Plays 1005). In a letter (JJL 1.221), Joyce revealed that *thunpledrum* refers to the nonsense word *trumpledum* in a song in the epilogue of *Saint Joan*. Shaw's Caesar establishes himself as a man of destiny by announcing to the Sphinx, "My way hither was the way of destiny" (257). His play let Caesar off in its "furst act" by characterizing him as magnanimous and clement, to Joyce a "pienofarte" instead of a phallic tyrant. G. B. S.'s character is, to Joyce, pianoforte, loud. He is a loud fart and a joke to the derisive Joyce, who recognized Shaw in Caesar's *Commentaries,* his "Commontoryism" as commentator whose politics in *Caesar and Cleopatra* might, with its policy of permeating, be confused with Toryism. An asexual failure (peno-fart) who does not in Shaw's play beget Cleopatra's child, Caesar/Shaw "never quite got the sandhurst out of his eyes so that the champaign he draws for us is a flop as a plankrieg" (162.7–9). The champion/champagne/campaign that Caesar/Shaw draws for us in his plot is a flop as flat as a pancake and a failed warplan. At this point the pretend preface sounds like a theatrical review in which Joyce criticizes Shaw's upper-class ambitions and creation of Caesar as a military gentleman who might have aspired to attend Sandhurst—a modern Englishman instead of an antique Roman. Shaw admittedly set Caesar forth in a "modern light" (CP 46). Anticipating the methods of literary modernism by projecting the "pastness of the past and its presence" (as Eliot put it in "Tradition and the Individual Talent"), Shaw made Caesar a modern, unheroic hero, a practical man who prefers "a good talker—one with an imagination enough to live without continually doing something" (GBS 193). He thus prefigured the mode of *Finnegans Wake* long before Eliot and Joyce blended contemporary idiom with historical and literary allusions. Freely mixing past and present, Shaw purposely made his empire builder (like Leopold Bloom) a modern man in order to establish the relevance of the past to the present.

Shaw may also have unwittingly engaged Joyce in his dialogue by creating in *Caesar and Cleopatra* a foil for the practical politician and teacher in Apollodorus, a "worshipper of beauty" and defender of pure art, whom Caesar calls "son" as he leaves to him the artistic fate of Alexandria, just as he leaves to his other, ruffian "son," Ruffio, the affairs of state. Shaw's treatment of a patriarch who grants power to antithetical surrogate sons would not have escaped the author of the *Wake,* who borrows his theme. Perhaps significantly, after the first professional performance of *Caesar and Cleopatra* in England in 1907, Joyce was writing "The Dead," in which Gabriel "thinks of defending the autonomy of art and its indifference to politics" (JJ1 254). Extremely sensitive to the artistic milieu of his time, Joyce almost invariably found his issues highlighted by Shaw. When, like Shaw's Apollodorus, Joyce declared in 1918, "TOUT POUR L'ART" (JJ1 454), he was in the midst of stealing two Shaw plays with distinct social messages. His choice of *The Dark Lady of the Sonnets* and *Mrs. Warren's Profession* suggests that he was as much attracted to the positions of Caesar and Ruffio as to the aesthetics of Apollodorus.

When Joyce's speaker in the Burrus-Caseous "dialogue" returns to criticism of Caesar's modern, upper-middle-class military aspirations, as a practical man of affairs with no time for art, Caesar denies—"I dannoy the fact of wanton to weste point." He would, however, "paint [point] you to that butter (cheese it!) if you had some wash" (162.16–18). If the reader had some Shaw/cash, Caesar could point him to Burrus, who is the opposite of the "caviller" (caviler, cavalier, opponent of Cromwell's troops in their overthrow of Charles I) Caseous. As cavalier, Caseous may be related to Shakespeare's "mere *preux chevalier*" whom Shaw derides. His "fanatical personal honor, gallantry, and self-sacrifice are founded on a passion for death born of his inability to bear the weight of a life that will not grant ideal conditions to the liver" (CP 752). Although Shaw rejected such romantic heroism, Joyce calls his Burrus/Shaw figure a "reachly roundered head that goes best with thofthinkinq defensive fideism" (162.22–23).

As early as the preface to *John Bull's Other Island* Shaw admitted that his ancestors were Cromwellian roundheads. Burrus is a Shaw figure, whom Joyce accuses of being a soft-thinking, defensive fideist, a doubter who believes in a supreme being but has rejected theological and rational proofs. Shaw's preface to *Back to Methuselah* examines and rejects proofs of theology, of revealed religion, and of the science of Darwin but lauds biologist Lamarck (who leaves a place "for free will") and makes the leap of faith in the "New Vitalism" of Creative Evolution, for the vitalist "metaphysical as well as physical overcomes inertia" (537). In the spirit of open-minded inquiry, of skepticism regarding rational proofs of God's existence, and of a will to believe, Shaw defended the Life Force as the divinity in man that will in time facilitate progress. In labeling him a soft-thinking fideist, Joyce apparently accepted Wyndham Lewis's assessment of Shaw's kindly, genial, ineffectual belief: "He laughs, twinkles, and cackles to hide his incompetence" and the "poor prosaic" "humanitarianism" of his "new religion" (50–51). Joyce may also have read H. G. Wells's 1934 verdict that "Shaw makes Evolution something brighter and softer, by endowing it with an ultimately benevolent Life Force" (quoted in I&R 27). Skeptical regarding orthodox religion and scientific determinism, Shaw made a leap of faith to the god within, having argued that religious truths are not probable, plausible, or rational and that Blake's "Nobodaddy," the God of orthodox Christianity, is a tyrant. But "When a man tells you that you are a product of Circumstantial Selection solely, you cannot finally disprove it. You can only tell him out of the depths of your inner conviction that he is a fool and a liar" (CP 524). Such rejection of Darwinian determinism based on "inner conviction"—faith—is Shaw's fideism. He believed in Creative Evolution because he wanted to.

Like Shaw, who personalized his prefaces and digressed at will, the commercial narrator of the Burrus-Caseous section promises confidentially to "sell you the fulltroth of Burrus when he wore a younker"

(162.33). "And what a cheery ripe outlook" indicates Shaw's cheery, ripe optimism. Suddenly, however, the Joycean voice seems to become Burrus, for he speaks, like a Shaw preface, in the first person to explain his sunny outlook as "the Ormuzd aliment" (163.2). Throughout the *Wake* Lamppost Shaw is, we should recall, associated with light, for he had argued that if the reader were to "study the electric light" which he supplies (CP 166), he would find that Shaw brings light and heat, truth and challenge. As self-appointed light-bringer, G. B. S., the talker, usually spoke his "ohole mouthful" (163.1) on the evils to be found in "THE INFIDEL HALF CENTURY," which he attacked in the preface to *Back to Methuselah* (CP 501).

When Caseous takes over the fractured dialogue as Burrus's "brutherscutch" and "tyron" (tyro/tyrant) Swiss cheese, he parodies, for both, the Shavian Caesar's message of tolerance. "Thus we cannot escape our likes and mislikes . . . let us be tolerant of antipathies" (163.12–15). Even Wyndham Lewis admitted that Shaw, whom he criticized almost as severely as he criticized Joyce, "especially would give an air of fairness to almost anything" (56). Like a good fideist, the speaker (perhaps Burrus and Caseous lumped together) suspends judgment: "I am not hereby giving my final endorsement to the learned ignorants of the Cusanus philosophism" (163.15–17) of old Nick. Whereas Joyce's esoteric references to Church fathers like Nicholas of Cusa derive from his Jesuit education, Shaw peppered his prefaces with references to figures like Aquinas, Roger Bacon, and Savonarola but displayed his Protestant preferences and catholic tastes by referring to Luther, Calvin, and Mahomet.

Joyce's reference to "Cusanus" seems to accuse the fifteenth-century philosopher Nicholas of Cusa of sophism. Cusa, who accepted papal supremacy but argued for general councils over which the emperor would preside in temporal affairs and the pope would preside in spiritual ones, prefigures republican Shaw in arguing that we need to understand that we are ignorant, in order to attain " 'Learned' or 'instructed ignorance' " (Copleston 236)—the learned ignorance of which Joyce seems to accuse Shaw as a parallel to Nicholas of Cusa and twin of Old Nick, Shem/Jim. Nicholas of Cusa argued that "reason cannot bring us anything more than an approximate knowledge of God" (Copleston 237). Like Shaw with his "inner conviction," Nicholas of Cusa went on from doubt to the importance of faith, for, wrote Nicholas, the face of the divine appears "in different ways in a number of mirrors" (Copleston 238). Shaw's Neoplatonic Pentateuch (like the *Wake*) was a modern version of such mirrors, icon, and riddle, one which affirms Cusa's belief that "all things spontaneously desire a higher mode of existence than their own nature will permit. . . . When we have reached one stage in the attainment of truth we can always look forward to a further stage" (Curtis 251). Thus Cusa anticipates the Shavian belief in Creative Evolution. Joyce transforms Nicholas of Cusa's attempt to define and defend Christian orthodoxy into the Shavio-Joycean admission of life eternal without Christianity or belief in an afterlife. Joyce's bumblingly fair-minded academic speaker concludes, however, that he must "find space to look into it myself a little more closely" (163.32), thus needling Shavian gradualism and the meandering personalist style that makes us wonder whether Burrus, surely not the revolutionary republican that we thought he was, will ever decide to become a regicide. As a laughable, laughing "risicide," he talks so much that it becomes doubtful that he will act.

In a digression on "shamebred" chamber music, parodying Shaw's vagrant style and his music criticism, the narrator seems to parallel the Faust triangle of Margaret, Faust, and Mephisto to Cleopatra, Caesar, and Anthony, combined with Burrus and Caseous as part of a "grouptriad" (167.4) "equivalent" to the older "Caesar" just as all of the male characters are subsumed in H. C. E., the patriarch whose rebellious sons want to displace, overthrow, and hence become the father. In his preface to *Three Plays for Puritans,* Shaw compared Shakespeare to Goethe, whose Faust is patterned on a family romance parallel to the triangles of the *Wake*. Goethe adumbrates the theme of rebellion against the patriarchal father (God) and competition between opposites for the female, Margaret. Joyce burlesques her as Margareen, whose interests in fashion link her to Gerty MacDowell, the young temptress of *Ulysses*. Since Margareen appears in a paragraph about Shaw's music criticism, we can safely assume that Joyce alludes to Gounod's *Faust,* which appeared in the late nineteenth century as *Marguerite*. The preface persona, singing in ecstasy of "*Sweet Margareen*" (164.19), seems to compete with his double for Margarine's attentions. In response to the oleaginous crooning, the critic condemns "The pawnbreaking pathos of the first of these shoddy pieces [which] reveals it as a Caseous effort" (164.23–24), thus satirizing Joyce himself, who dwelt on his poverty and the little money he got from his *Chamber Music* poems and his scrupulous, mean pieces collected in *Dubliners*. On the other hand, "Burrus's bit is often used for a toast" (164.24); butter on toast, Shaw's plays (his music) get toasted because of their public celebrity, or they are no more than a condiment. The critic avers that "the unskilled singer continues to pervert our wiser ears by subordinating the space element, that is to sing, the *aria,* to the time-factor, which ought to be killed, *ill tempor*" (164.32–35). Shaw, regularly associated with ears, seems to complain, like the ill-tempered Wyndham Lewis, of Joyce's subordination of space to tempo in his musical time book. The critic's advice to "any unborn singer . . . to forget her temporal diaphragm" (164.35–36), suggests the singing method that Shaw had learned from George Vandeleur Lee, his mother's voice teacher. It simultaneously hints that a woman who is not a born singer might as well not use a birth control device (thus possibly motherhood will be her vocation).

In the middle of a sentence about "the acoustic and orchidectural management of the tonehall" (165.8–9)—the acoustic and architectural/orchestral management of the town hall—which sounds like Shaw's music criticism, the critic seems to return to his theme, Burrus and Caseous, whom he manipulates into a "climactogram up which B and C may fondly be imagined ascending" because they are examples of Creative Evolution, in hatboxes of the latest "spring modes . . . carrying us back to the superimposed claylayers of eocene and pleastoseen formation and the gradual morphological change in our body politic" (165.23–27). This refers satirically to *Back to Methuselah*'s structure, which superimposes, like the *Wake,* clay (that is, human characters) upon the theme of Creative Evolution. *Eocene* combines the serious reference to the earliest epoch in which mammals became dominant with the ridiculous reference to eosin, the red color of the hatboxes (and possibly of the "Red" Shaw) in which surreal evolution seems to be taking place. *Pleastoseen* combines the serious reference to the Pleistocene glacial era, which occurred about a million years ago, before man appeared, and the reference to the material out of which the hatboxes are made. *Methuselah* begins with the appearance of man at the end of the Pleistocene era and with the legendary first family. It stresses "the gradual morphological changes in our body politic"—the political changes that Shaw observed in his own time and predicted for the future.

A parenthetic non sequitur paragraph, the narrator's aside, debates androgyny, which Shaw promoted. He argued that "androgynous heroes" on the stage are a "reaction" to the falsification of Romanticism (CP 744). Late in the Jaun section Joyce called Caesar "cesarella"—a Shaw persona who was "looking on" when "in the beginning [the title of the overture to *Methuselah*] was the gest he jousstly says, for the end is with woman" (468.4–5). Thus he makes fun of Shaw's "womanly woman" while alluding to Shaw's Caesar play and to the end of both G. B. S.'s Pentateuch and the *Wake*. He also refers to Shaw's dictum that all great art begins in a jest or a joke. Like Shaw in *Press Cuttings* and *The Music-Cure,* Joyce was fascinated by the kinky and comic sexual possibilities of the "manly woman" (as we saw in Bella Cohen in *Ulysses*). In the Burrus-Caseous digression on gender crossing, Joyce's speaker perhaps combines Shaw, Joyce, and Wyndham Lewis, who associated homosexuality with feminism, fascinated and repulsed by the "inverted fashion" of "Nancy boys" (69). As a purity-snooper, the professor has "regions to suspect from my post" that "Master Pules . . . her 'little man' is a secondary schoolteacher" (166.20–21) devoted to child seduction, concealing "her own more masculine personality by flaunting frivolish finery over men's inside clothes, for the femininny of that totamulier will always lack the musculink of a verumvirum" (166.24–26). Although his last assertion that the total woman will always lack the muscularity of the true man is not Shavian and is, indeed, a response to Shaw's arguments for gender parity, the speaker's ridicule of wearing frivolous finery to mask a masculine personality, expressed in men's inside clothes, sounds like Shaw, who pressed for clothes that were not designed specifically for one sex or the other. He created the Bolshevik Empress Annajanska, yet another male impersonator, like Julia Craven in *The Philanderer,* who wears a disposable skirt over breeches as a sign that she is a manly woman, and the female lead in *Man of Destiny,* who reveals herself in the end in a uniform identical to Napoleon's. The woman in Joyce's digression must look a bulky mess, not even a successful cross-dresser, but, like Shavian gender crossers, she is female and dressed like a woman to hide her masculine undergarments. Joyce's narrator ridicules such a manly woman as a "femininny"—a ninny because such a total woman will always lack "true" masculinity. As usual, Joyce puts into a sexual context what Shaw treats in a social context, ridiculing Shaw's New Woman and her adumbrations.

Wandering onward after still another digression to take up a leitmotif already mentioned, the mock preface turns to the eternal triangle in which Burrus and Caseous, like Faust and Mephisto, both want the soul of "Margareena," margarine suitable for the company of butter and cheese. Margaret, the eternal femme of *Faust,* is also "A cleopatrician" for whose "misstery" (mystery/mastery, for she is the Life Force muse) Burrus and Caseous "are contending" (166.34–36) when the "wop" Antonius enters the scene, tempting Burrus and Caseous to turn to "phatrisight" (167.1, 10) to eliminate the brotherly competition. His sibling rivalry roused, the speaker thus decides to salute death, but it is unclear whether Caesar or Anthony is to be the victim of the play that should come after this rambling preface. Although suspicious of the demonic mob, like Shaw, Shaw's Caesar, and Shakespeare, Caesar/Brutus declares, "Let Demoncracy take the high most!" (167.25), for he is married to language. Like Shaw and his Caesar, a writer about conquests, Caesar is too busy to get involved with Cleopatra. "The word is my Wife. . . . Till Breath us depart! Wamen. Beware would you change with my years" (167.29–31). Apparently, after saying amen to his "marriage," Caesar/Shaw warns the younger Anthony/Caseous/Burrus not to change places with him.

Shifting abruptly from writing of temporal power, from Caesar's "commontories," to the spiritual message of *Methuselah,* the lecturer, now preacher, begins to sermonize, warning that "that mon that hoth no moses in his sole nor is not awed by conquests of word's law. . . . were he my own breastbrother, my doubled withd love and my singlebiassed hate . . . still I'd fear I'd hate to say!" (167.36; 168.1–12)—and the peroration trails off. Who is the breastbrother? The answer seems to be Shem (as well as Shaun), for the speaker is Shaun as Moses, married to the scriptural word just as G. B. S.'s Caesar (and Shaw himself) is married to work (Plays 269). The narrator is writing a sacred book, the Pentateuch that put "moses in his sole" and made him the apostle of the new gospel; it is also the linguistic "law" of Joyce's new language. Burrus/Shaun does not know what he would say to the man lacking his missionary zeal (one shared by the breastbrother obsessed with language), even if he were the loved/hated brother, "proud purse broken ranger" (Shem), who believes that he shares with Shaw's Caesar the financial embarrassment of being broke when he turns up in Egypt.

Shaw's prefaces, the work of a ranger who is not purse-poor, meander like Montaigne's essays (the work of another fideist). Although his prose is lucid and his paradoxes glittering, Shaw's essays are not models of orderly argument. Like his plays and the works of his secret disciple, Shaw deals in *"unresolved* paradox" (Fergusson 203). Like his plotless plays, Shaw's prefaces expose ideas from several perspectives and sometimes shift with alacrity from one pet peeve to another. Joyce makes fun of the prefaces, through emulating and exaggerating the disorder; he combines seemingly rational locutions with the lawless "Word law" of Shem's anarchic puns and portmanteaus, themselves even more paradoxical than Shavian argument. Nevertheless, the Burrus-Caseous preface discloses the basic pattern of fraternal polarity and Oedipal insurrection that surfaces in all of the episodes featuring the twins, for Joyce borrowed a basic from Shaw, who wrote in his preface to *Three Plays for Puritans* (one of which is *Caesar and Cleopatra*): "My characters are the familiar harlequin and columbine, clown and pantaloon" (CP 467)—like Joyce's stand-up comics, Shaun and Shem.

The antagonistic brothers also find their way into the trial of Festy King (book 1, chapter 4). It seems to collide in the dreamer's unconscious with two of Shaw's plays—*The Shewing up of Blanco Posnet* and, to a lesser extent, *John Bull's Other Island*. The theme of Shaw's brother play, which features a trial and a battle of brothers, floats around the courtroom episode. Shaw's play, set in the American Wild West, concerns litigation against the reprobate Blanco, alleged to be a horse thief. His chief accuser is his sanctimonious brother, Elder Daniel, abetted by a harridan named Feemy and punctuated by a chorus of heckling females and frequenters of the local saloon. A lady of ill repute, Feemy bears false witness against Blanco. When "Show'm the Posed"—both Shaw and Posnet—is tried, "maidies of the bar . . . fluttered and flattered around the willingly pressed, nominating him for the swiney prize" (92.13–15). They are, of course, similar to Shaw's many female admirers (and detractors) who turn up in various guises in the *Wake*. "Willingly pressed" may suggest willingness to be put upon, as well as Shaw's willingness to be the press's favorite. The "swiney prize" for which "Show'm" is nominated may be the Nobel, which the envious punman now denigrates. When "Show'm the Posed" is tried, the "one among all her deputised to defeme him" (92.23–24) seems to be "Feemy," who almost gets Blanco lynched. As Shaw/Shaun he is, however, the lionized favorite of females, to whom he is "their masculine

Oirisher Rose" (92.18). In Joyce, Blanco is apparently "showing off the blink patch to his britgits to prove himself . . . a rael genteel" (93.4–5). In real life, Blanche Patch was the secretary whose faithful service Shaw showed off, making himself seem "rael genteel" to the Brits/brigids. Even the spelling of "rael genteel" implies the western American pronunciation that Shaw tried to copy in his oater.

In G. B. S.'s melodrama, Blanco is a rascal who reforms because of the intercession of the "Rainbow woman" (Plays 599)—who may in the plural be the "Rainbow girls" of the *Wake*. Joyce's Rainbow girls may refract Shaw's play about redemption through altruism, though they also suggest Wagner's Rhine Maidens and the arc leading to Valhalla, appropriate for a dream that drifts into utopianism. If Shem/Jim is imitating the self-styled Perfect Wagnerite Shaw, who got the pot of gold at the rainbow's end, it is all the better. Like Shaw (mercilessly tried in the court of public opinion over his *Common Sense about the War*) and H. C. E., Blanco is eventually acquitted, exonerated because of the appearance of the woman to whom he gave the stolen horse in an effort to help her save her son's life. Like the envious brother Daniel in Shaw's play, "Shun the Punman" is not pleased with the courtroom proceedings. He smugly recalls that he "safely and soundly soccered that fenemine Parish poser" (93.13–14), no doubt in his review of *The Shewing up of Blanco Posnet*. Joyce attacked the play of the female impersonator, Shaw, for being what the playwright said it was—"a sermon in crude melodrama" (CW 207), one that anticipates the sermonizing of Shaun/Jaun later in the *Wake*. Joyce's review was sent to Shaw with a note urging him to help the young writer, a fellow Irishman, but Shaw did not respond. Thus perhaps G. B. S. provided Joyce with another motive for the Oedipal and sibling assaults that lace the *Wake*. Joyce's review indicates his ambivalence about his mentor, for it reveals his early enthusiasm for Shaw's "lively and talkative spirit [which] cannot stand to be subjected to the noble and bare style appropriate to modern playwriting"; at the same time, Joyce's verdict was that "the art is too poor to make it convincing as drama" (CW 208). Perhaps most important, Joyce's review defines Shaw as he portrays the sermonizing Jaun and "Show'm the Posed," the "fenemine Parish Poser": Joyce wrote that "Shaw is a born preacher" (CW 208). Moreover, he seems to have been fascinated by Shaw's valorization of the feminine. In the muddled trial scene of the *Wake*, Shem congratulates himself for having "soccered" Shaun "soundly" in his review, which said in effect that Shaw (and Posnet) was posing as a preacher. The "fenemine" adjective suggests Feemy, Posnet's betrayer, with whom he is eventually reconciled (they go off to the saloon together); the androgyny that Shaw advocated and that Joyce ambiguously mocked; and the intermixing of the brothers: Show'm's feminine character is also "mine." Nevertheless, the Punman believes that he has scored with Shaun, socking and beating the sports enthusiast in a literary soccer game.

Shortly after the Punman's self-congratulation, Shaw's plot surfaces again as "the solid man saved by his sillied woman" (94.3), for Blanco is saved by testimony of the sullied, perhaps silly, mother. The letter retrieved by Biddy the Hen also suggests the play: "It was folded with cunning, sealed with crime, uptied by a harlot, undone by a child. It was life but was it fair? It was free but was it art?" (94.8–10). Blanco's crime was horse theft. Feemy the harlot tied him up at his trial. The death of the child whom Blanco tried to save by giving his mother the stolen horse turned out to be the undoing of the action of the play as well as that of the trumped-up trial of Blanco. The child's death was not fair, even though Blanco was redeemed by trying to save him. Joyce's ticket to the play as reviewer for the Trieste newspaper *Il Piccolo della Sera* was free, but, as his review clarified, he did not think the play was art.

No doubt the play was distasteful to Joyce, whose enthusiasm for Shaw began to cool as the playwright began to "get religion" and as Joyce began to project onto Shaw the disapproval that he thought he himself deserved for betraying his mentor with the unfavorable review. Because Shaw had helped to facilitate Joyce's conversion away from Catholicism in his late teens, Joyce was shocked to discover religion in the writer with "a profane and unruly past. Fabianism, vegetarianism, prohibitionism, music, painting, drama—all the progressive movements in art and politics—have had him as champion. And now, perhaps some divine finger has touched his brain, and he, in the guise of Blanco Posnet, is shewn up" (CW 208). The review clearly indicates that Joyce had followed Shaw's career and writings closely and that he was surprised that the hero had gotten the religion of altruism, though it was contrary to the conventional, conformist religion of Blanco's self-righteous brother. In the *Wake* Joyce's early description of Shaw carries over into his montage portrait of H. C. E. as Shaun. If Shaw was the Devil's

Disciple who encouraged Joyce's apostasy, it must have been hard for his devilish apostle to assimilate what seemed to be a sentimental turn toward salvationism. However, in his portrayal of Shaun he vents his dissatisfaction through mockery. And although the trial of Festy King alludes to many other trials (like Parnell's and Christ's), *The Shewing up of Blanco Posnet* is probably the basis for the confrontation between "Show'm the Posed" and "Shun the Punman."

Early in the trial a central incident in *John Bull's Other Island* seems to lurk in the courtroom evidence. The to-do over "a pedigree pig" (86.14) may allude to the farcical incident in Shaw's Irish play in which Broadbent gets into an automobile accident that greatly amuses the Irish farmers. "The gathering, convened by the Irish Angricultural and Prepostoral Ouraganisations, to help the Irish muck to look his brother dane in the face and attended thanks to Larry by large numbers" (86.20–23), sounds like the preposterous meeting of angry Irish farmers agonizing over their land problems. The locals attend "in large numbers" because of Larry Doyle; it is organized so that the Irish micks/muck (in Irish, *muck* means pig) can meet the good-natured and helpful usurper (Dane), Broadbent.

In Festy's trial, Shaw is apparently among "the litigants" representing "dalkeys" (87.24–26). There is only a hint of John Bull's presence, but it does surface with other reminders of Shaw. The twelve pub customers who are the jury—"doyles when they deliberate" (574.32) are Doyles—the Dail Eireann of the Irish legislature; detective writer Conan Doyle; but also Shaw's judicious, judgmental Irishman Larry Doyle, who might have been reluctant to exonerate the old sod. Among the male jurors is "an absolete turfwoman . . . with . . . sexname of Ann Doyle" (575.4–6) who combines Ann Whitefield, Anna Livia, and Larry Doyle, suggesting—as Joyce so often does—the Shavio-Joycean fascination with androgyny. Joycean males are "sister misters" (393.17), "shehusbands" (390.20), "manowoman. . . . Candidately" (396.5) like Shaw's phallic mother Candida. H. C. E./Shaw is a "tiresome old milkless a ram" (396.15). "Messrs or Missrs Earwicker, Seir, his feminisible name of multitude" (73.4–5) suggests the feminine man whom Shaw advocated.

"Funferal" Fables: "Grimm Gests of Jacko and Esaup"

A fabulist, Joyce used his "music hall pair" (408.26–27) to parody many fables at the "funferal" funeral of the wake, which is both fun for all and feral. He also creates a few fables of his own, variations on existing folktales. The brothers Grimm in these fractured fairy tales are Jacob/Jack/John (as in John Tanner, whom Shaw called "Jack the giant killer") and Esau/Aesop/Shem, perhaps "easing up" on his insults to his brother, who is sometimes his indistinguishable twin. Most disclose the basic struggle between authority or father figures and insurgent sons, the rivalrous fraternal conflict, or Shem and Shaun's slippery brotherhood. The anecdotes about the Norwegian sea captain and the tailor and about how Buckley shot the Russian general (book 2, chapter 3), the myth of the Prankquean (book 1, chapter 1), and the fables of the Mookse and the Gripes (book 1, chapter 6) and of the Ondt and the Gracehoper (book 2, chapter 3) all subscript the conflicts that preoccupy Joyce's dreamer.

According to Bernard Benstock, "the Tale of the Norwegian Captain and Kersse the Tailor presents another set of opposing forces, most often identified with Earwicker confronted by his 'Cadversary'" ("Quiddity" 21). Shaw had touted his Scandinavian ancestry and written of an ancient mariner, Captain Shotover. Shem/Joyce may therefore be the cursed, cursing tailor doing alterations on *Heartbreak House* and *Methuselah.* If the pair merge, as Benstock avers, as Buckley, "to shoot the Earwickean Russian general" (31), they may represent the antiauthoritarian fantasy shared by the two Irishmen. Both opposed the imperialism symbolized by tsarist Russia at the time of the Crimean War. As David Hayman notes, the story is Irish because "the battle of Sevastopol . . . took place in the supposed original homeland of the Gaelic peoples" (40). As a socialist in 1896, Shaw led a demonstration opposing the tsar's visit to England. His 1917 "bravura piece" (CP 851), *Annajanska, The Bolshevik Empress,* is almost as silly and slight as Joyce's tale, which is also a story about a Russian general. The play's antitsarist politics anticipate Joyce's, but the upshot is Shaw's idea of a joke about androgyny. Annajanska, formerly a grand duchess who has defected to the Bolshevik cause, shoots up the general's office and reveals herself dressed as a male officer of the revolution—as the manly woman whose heroism Shaw admired, especially when its target was a corrupt regime. Because both Shaw and Joyce were nonviolent opponents of tyranny, Joyce's story of an Irishman's revenge replicates both Shaw's attitude and his own except in its risqué reliance upon the Russian general's having his pants down and his anal method of desecrating the old sod. The references that regaled Joyce's father's barroom cronies would have offended Joyce's prudish surrogate father, even as Shaw's repeated displays of manly women intended *épater le bourgeois* surprised the bourgeois Joyce and provided canon fodder—not cannon fodder—for his satire.

Whereas the tale of how Buckley shot the Russian general has some Shavian nuances, even more germane to Shavian appearances in the *Wake* is the story of the strong-willed Prankquean (21.5–23.15). A parable of complementary seduction by the same muse, it adds to the Janus profile of the subversive politics that Shaw innocently shared with Joyce. Michael Begnal indicates that the Prankquean is pirate Grace O'Malley, Grania of the Dermot-Grania elopement myth, and Queen Medb, symbol of "the sovereignty of Ireland" (17). Alternatively and additionally, the Prankquean represents another sort of Irish sovereignty, the triumph of the imagination through alliance with the ancient matriarchate. As Suzette Henke notes, the Prankquean is "an archetypal image of folkoric witch—a fiercely independent and willful woman who poses a genuine threat to male domination" (168). She is not, however, the Shan van Vocht or Cathleen ni Houlihan, who require blood sacrifice from Ireland's sons. Instead she is the Life Force and muse of comedy who inspired Joyce and his "frother" to leave Ireland and to attack romantic nationalism. Through the mediation of the naughty, mutinous Prankquean, the twins thwart the aggressively patriarchal Scandinavian invader, Jarl van Hoother, symbol of masculine phallocentric rule as well as a transliteration of Jehovah, the old "Nobodaddy" of Blake whom Shaw predated Joyce in repudiating (CP 533).

The Prankquean stole the brothers in order to take them to their pagan and ancient matriarchal origins, apparently replicated in what Joyce called the "mamafesta." The Prankquean from western Ireland kidnapped Shaun/Shaw, who returned to his Irish origins in *Methuselah*'s "The Death of an Elderly Gentleman," set in the west of Ireland. Joyce too had been seduced by western Ireland in the form of Nora Barnacle as ALP, the life-giver and his belief that his ancestors came from that part of Ireland. The seductress of the *Wake* carried off melancholy Tristopher to the "westerness" of Ireland, where she "washed" him with "soap" in a Shavian baptism related to Shaw's advice regarding *Ulysses*: "go for soap and water." This cleansing ritual converted Tristopher into a "luderman," a play(ful) man devoted to the comic muse, and, like Synge's hero, a playboy of the western world. Significantly, Archibald Henderson's second biography of Shaw, *Bernard Shaw, Playboy and Prophet* (1932), underscored Shaw's dual roles as playboy and John the Baptist—prophet. Laurence Sterne, another Anglo-Irishman, whose playful satire dominates *Tristram Shandy,* is included in Tristopher and "westerness," thus enlarging the archetype for satiric writers, one that includes humorist Mark Twain. His name embodies the trinity of King Mark (Jarl, the father and authority figure) and Tristan/Hilary, the young, sad, soon to be hilarious rival whose love for Irish Isolde steals him away from his allegiance to Mark. The "twin" references mark the two brothers. The Mark Twain allusions may be Joyce's clever way of referring to Shaw and at the same time diverting the reader, for Twain and Shaw, "the greatest living humorist and the greatest living wit" (PP 737), met as early as 1907 and admired one another. The International Mark Twain society honored Shaw as a "Knight of Mark Twain." In 1937 Shaw received the Mark Twain Gold Medal (BSL 3:64).

Having marked the "Wans" (Shaw), the Prankquean said, "Mark the Twy" (21.18; 22.5), upon which she made off with "jimminy hilary" (21.36) and ran "all the lilipath ways to Woeman's Land" (22.8)—on the Lilith path to Woman's land, which is woe to male patriarchy in the utopia of Shaw's androgynous She and He Ancients, for in *Methuselah* he made Lilith creator (instead of the demoness of Jewish folklore), thus stressing his heretical matrifocal values. During the second kidnapping, the Prankquean "provorted" hilary into a "tristian" (22.16–17), thus converting the comic Shaw into a sad variant of Christian. Joyce, it will be remembered, believed that Shaw had undergone a perversion/conversion to something like Christianity that was evident in *The Shewing up of Blanco Posnet* (CW 208). Shaw, the hilarious jester, had betrayed his own tendencies to be sad in *Methuselah,* in which his Elderly Gentleman dies of "discouragement." The religion that had touched G. B. S. was, far from orthodox Christianity, the one of which he appointed himself saint and prophet and the one of which the author of the *Wake* is a "provorted" disciple. Indeed, on the Prankquean's third visit to Jarl van Hoother's, the twins are "belove" and spliced "like knavepaltry and naivebride and in their second infancy" (22.24–26). This union foreshadows the fantasized reconciliations of opposites and their recycling in the *Wake*'s *ricorso,* as well as the late works in which both writers seemed to critics to have entered a second childhood.

For the two comic Irishmen, the Prankquean is a fitting muse who inspires them to defy the spiritual and temporal power that would bind them to the father instead of the motherland, to destructive phallocentric nationalism and religion instead of playful, creative, nurturing art celebrating Ireland. A variant of the "supernatural (white) cow" who carries "children across to an island realm where they are relieved of the petty restraints and dependencies of childhood and magically schooled as heroes before they are returned to their astonished parents and community" (Gifford 123–24), the Prankquean is like the MooCow, Mother Ireland coming down the road to Baby Tuckoo in *Portrait*. "Like Grace O'Malley, her historical prototype, the Prankquean opposes lawless and creative energy to the established order" (O'Sullivan 132)—the sort of lawless energy that Shaw's early writing validated for young Joyce. As Shaw's vitalist Life Force and Joyce's ALP, taking the children to tour the world—"Tourlemonde" (in Irish, Tir na mBan, "Woman's land") and "Woeman's Land," she "actively subverts the father's authority with the upcoming generation" (O'Sullivan 132–33). Something like Candida, a supernatural female who saves Marchbanks for art, ALP's avatar is a threatening, inspirational, energy which inspires Eve's favorite sons, the expatriated creative ones. Joyce, aware of the feminism of his great "*Immensipater*" (342.26) and *Back to Methuselah*'s rejection of power figures like Cain and Napoleon, describes Jarl, "the old terror of the dames" (22.32), as an "orangeman" dressed like the Irish mixed with the British flag in red yellow (orange) and blue-green, in a purple rage—"a rudd yellan grueblean orangeman in his violet indigonation" (23.1–2)—attacking (or raping?) the Life Force, who has stolen his nonviolent, antipatriarchal, artistic jokester sons—sons whose works were defiled by Irish censorship. Although the tale of the Prankquean also adverts to some of Joyce's perverse and fetishistic eroticism, as O'Sullivan argues—to female urination and drink ("porter p[l]ease") as well as Jarl's onanism and anality—it dreams the escape and expatriation of the Dublin twins. They are spirited off by a muse of Irish pranks who is entirely suitable for the two Hibernian pranksters.

As Shaw told Mark Twain, "I am persuaded that the future historian of America will find your work as indispensable to him as a french historian finds the political tracts of Voltaire. I tell you so because I am the author of a play in which a priest says, 'Telling the truth's the funniest joke in the world,' a piece of wisdom which you helped to teach me" (PP 738). Shaw seems to have taught Joyce similar wisdom, for the Prankquean story is about Shem's convoluted but honest conversion to comedy.

The Mookse and the Gripes: "Corked Father" and "Dubville Brooder-on-Low"

Whereas the affinities of Shaun and Shem are the subtext of the Prankquean story caper, the two fight over their differences in other fables, in which Shaw is the heavyweight and Joyce the sparring partner. In the "Fable of the Mookse and the Gripes," part of the eleventh section of the question-and-answer chapter (book 1, chapter 6), the tristian and hilarious twins reveal further aspects of their antagonism. In this fractured fable the "gripe" is paradoxically both Mookse-fox who covets grapes and the griping fox who identifies them as the communion and fruit that, in Aesop's fable, he misses because of his own pride. In *The Quintessence of Ibsenism* Shaw unwittingly provided a gloss for the theme of Joyce's tale: "For the fox not only declares that the grapes he cannot get are sour: he also insists that the sloes he can get are sweet" (MCE 49). Thus as Mookse, Shaun expatiates on the sour-grapes envy of a rival. Joyce's fable is a monologue by Shaun, who is, according to Matthew Hodgart, "polemical . . . and holds forth in the style of George Bernard Shaw's prefaces to the plays" (146–47).

John Garvin writes that the parable is "primarily devoted to a confrontation between Ireland and the Irish Church . . . and . . . the Church of Rome, represented in 'The Mookse' by Pope Adrian (Nicholas Breakspear), the only English pope and author of the papal bull *Laudabiliter* that authorized Henry II's occupation of Ireland" (171). The text supports his evidence, but as usual in the *Wake,* Joyce superimposes autobiographical upon historical allusions. Another conflict runs concurrently in the fable. It concerns the quarrel between the usurpers of Ireland and the native Irish, often associated in Joyce's mind with Shaw as Anglo-Irishman of Protestant descent and himself, the lapsed Catholic Irishman. Readers may object to the coupling of a pope with the lapsed Anglican and opponent of Christianity, whose criticism of the Vatican ("In Ireland England is nothing but the Pope's policeman"; CP 455) anticipated Joyce's; but Joyce's papish allusions in no way interfere with a Shavian correspondence to the Mookse. Despite G. B. S.'s analysis of English and Roman Catholic oppression of the Irish under the pretext of paternalism, Shaw had papal pretensions. His ancestors, like those whom Adrian's bull gave access to Ireland, were admittedly the invaders who co-opted the little green place. With mock solemnity, the aging Shaw had informed his public that he was "prophet" himself (BSL 3:283) and that he aspired to be chief spiritual adviser of the world.

Like Pope Adrian, the patriarch of Creative Evolution worked strenuously to maintain his moral authority. In ridiculing his delusions of papal power, Joyce no doubt perceived, as Maurice Valency does, that in *Back to Methuselah* the bishop of Burrin Pier on the south shore of Galway Bay set himself up as something like a papal authority, "the divine apostolate" for the revelations of his new religion. "In preaching his sermon," Valency writes, "Shaw did not relinquish his customary role as socialist, economist, and statesman. He simply vested himself with his new priesthood, under which all these callings were subsumed" (354). A photo of Neville Lytton's notorious painting *The Modern Pope of Wit and Wisdom,* a blatant copy of Velázquez's painting of Pope Innocent, was reproduced in Henderson's 1911 biography of Shaw (facing 269). Although the prelate is garbed in the papal vestments, his face and hands are Shaw's. Clearly the blasphemous clown who worked closely with Henderson on the so-called biography was willing to jest about his spiritual sovereignty long before he wrote *Methuselah*. After his "Pentateuch," in *Saint Joan* (1925), the warrior maid who "thinks she has God in her pocket" is Shaw's *doppelgänger,* "Pope Joan" (Plays 988). While posing as Frank Harris in his 1913 response to Harris's "Contemporary Portrait," "Pope Bernard" wrote in "How Frank Ought to Have Done It" that Lytton's "picture shews what Shaw would be like in the papal chair" (SSS 125). When Saint Joan was acclaimed by Catholics, Shaw assured them, with mock humility, "There's no room for two Popes in the Roman Catholic Church" (quoted in Pearson 399). Like the Mookse, Shaw seemed to be bragging, "I am superbly in my supremest poncif!" (154.11–12). Joyce's allusions to popes and the reference to "Concionata" (preacher)—a motto of Pope Innocent V—may therefore be, in the *Wake*'s duplicitous writing, snide allusions to Shaw's pontifical pretensions. A Shaw sleuth like Joyce, furthermore, would have known that in the late 1930s the patriarchal octogenarian incongruously, ambiguously, probably ironically identified himself with symbols of logocentric power such as Stalin and the rising fascist dictators Mussolini and Hitler.

Adrian as "our once in only Bragspear . . . every inch an immortal" (152.33–34) is probably also the playful playwright from "Ludstown" (the Latin *ludus* means "play"; the town is London) in "Albo" (England). This suggests the color white which Joyce coded as Shaw, who bragged that he was "better than Shakespear," thus inspiring a *Punch* cartoon captioned "John Bull's Other Playwright" and showing the tall Shaw in Elizabethan garb leaning heavily on a statue of the indignant Shakespeare, the pedestal of which is inscribed, "All the World's a Stage-Society" (GBS, facing 268). As the embodiment of his own Ancients in *Methuselah,* Shaw was "an immortal." Although the questions of the Gripes concerning "the time" (154.16) may refer to "the ancient controversy of the mode of calculating the date for observing the festival of Easter" (Garvin, 171), it may also allude to the Gripes's belief that it is time for the Mookse to step down so that his competitor, the Gripes, can be put on the literary pedestal that he deserves. Because the Mookse does not want to consult his watch, it may also be the season that the Mookse fears, as his own last passion—the Easter time of death and resurrection for the redeemer but also the time of the Gripes's ascension as the new literary savior who will replace him. In his preface to *Methuselah* Shaw stressed his worries about his age, and the plays, despite their fanciful dates, take place in a timeless now.

As Garvin notes, the Gripes's question regarding time reiterates the Cad's question to H. C. E., "A Cad (or Cadet), being a young man aspiring to promotion," to which H. C. E. reacts with "fear of displacement on the ground that his time was up" (174). Joyce's Cad resembles Shaw's obstreperous Cain, who threatens to kill his father in Shaw's Eden Park. Significantly, Joyce wrote that H. C. E.'s encounter with the Cad and their heroic agon is "the basis of my book" (JJL 1:396). Joyce had, of course, been a cad to Shaw by stealing his plays in Zurich. Exposing himself in Phoenix Park is, in part, what Joyce was doing in writing the *Wake*. His distorted dream fixates on the sin of which Shaw had accused *Ulysses*—exposing forbidden sexuality and "incontinence." Furthermore, by attacking Max Nordau's assault on artists as degenerates, Shaw had established himself as an infamous defender of artistic freedom in *The Sanity of Art* (1895), but in his comments on *Ulysses* he had inconsistently admitted his own old-maidish prudery, revealing himself as a puritan "hurt" by Joyce's ribaldry. Modeling Shaun's rejoinder on his own response to what he considered injustice, the real culprit no doubt concluded that Shaw was deeply offended by the Cad's theft of his plays. Nevertheless, while recognizing his guilt for cozening the older man, Joyce no doubt considered the libertarian's response to *Ulysses* treasonous and comparable to Adrian's betrayal of the Irish. Joyce's conflicted feelings toward his mentor collide in the ambiguities of the tale of the Mookse and the Gripes.

Like old H. C. E. and the Mookse, Shaw was worried about time. His fears were, like his every public word, "regularly discussed in literary monthlies and drama columns in newspapers in the early twentieth century" (Mencken xxx). Joyce could not avoid concluding that Shaw wanted secular power in much the same way as Pope Adrian did. The Buffalo Notebooks make this desire clear: identified, like H. C. E., with the siglum ⊓, "Mookse wants temporal power" (McHugh, *Sigla* 34). For the 1917 convention on Home Rule in Ireland, Shaw had volunteered his services (they were denied), just as later he offered himself for a place in Eamon De Valera's government (which was also denied, probably to the detriment of the Free State: the new state would have found it harder to combine the church and state censorship and repression that the Mookse, as Adrian, stands for had the old Fabian been on hand). Because he did not advocate putting *Ulysses* on the Index, however, and in fact took it as a document showing up social problems in need of correction, Shaw cannot be identified with all of the Mookse's qualities. (His puritanical defense of censorship, if little else about him, smacks of the attitudes of William Stead, whom Grace Eckley identifies as H. C. E.) But in his devious writing Joyce combined the Church with the dramatic patriarch. When the Gripes asks the time, the Mookse answers, "Ask my index"—the list of books forbidden by Church authority but also the index to *Methuselah,* which gives the imagined dates of Shaw's plays. The Mookse (who turns rapidly into various popes) asks the Gripes, "Is this space of our couple of hours too dimensional for you, temporiser?" (154.25–26), thus identifying himself simultaneously with Wyndham Lewis, who accused Joyce of being a writer preoccupied with time instead of space, and with activist Shaw, who disapproved of temporizing. His *Methuselah* seems, in comparison to Joyce's many-dimensional book, "too [two] dimensional." In admonishing the toady Gripes to "woshup my nase serene" (154.18–19), the proud Mookse seems to tell the Gripes to wash up his nose so that he won't have to share the "dirt" that Shaw found objectionable in *Ulysses.*

No doubt remembering Shaw's attitude toward his Dublin novel, Joyce let his moralistic Mookse anathematize the Gripes because of his obsession with "inferior" anatomy: "Blast yourself and your anathomy infairioriboos!" (154.10–11); he deems the griping Irishman, who is at the same time the lewd Shem/Joyce, "an animal rurale" like Swift's Yahoos. "In all his specious heavings, as be lived by Optimus Maximus, the Mookse had never seen his Dubville brooder-on-low [the Gripes] in such a pickle" (153.17–19), not only because he is the victim of legalized English tyranny but also because the impoverished Gripes, beleaguered by censorship (like Joyce over *Ulysses*), is a poor mouth. Joyce persisted in thinking of himself as the poverty-stricken Irishman marginalized by the Anglo-Irishman from England, to whom he was, in his imagination, "Dubville brooder-on-low"—Dublin double/brother brooding on low subjects—in the less than "specious heavings"— heavenly, if specious, regions of the great optimist Shaw (and, of course, the pope, who believed in a different sort of specious/spacious heaven). Shaw/Shaun/Adrian is in Joyce's "on-low" (scurrilous) thoughts. The pope, in his "unfallable encyclicling" (153.26), is Adrian with his infallible encyclical *Laudabiliter,* giving the English power in Ireland; but the "unfallable encyclical" may also allude to bicyclist Shaw and to *Methuselah,* in which "unfallable" Adam falls down a flight of stairs but is not depraved in the orthodox Christian sense. "Unfallable," he is not innately evil, and because his sin is not transmitted to his descendants as a consequence of his fall, he is capable of cycling into a better future. As Shaw wrote to Harris, "I am entirely free from the neurosis (as it seems to me) of Original Sin. I never associated sexual intercourse with delinquency" (241).

Adrian, however, deems the "little sowsieved subsquashed Gripes" (155.13)—the poor Irish already strained and squashed by the "old sow who eats her farrow" (P 203)—"barbarousse" (154.23); like Emperor Frederick Barbarossa, Adrian's enemy (Garvin 173), he also takes the stance that Joyce read into Shaw's response to the "dirt" and implied barbarity of *Ulysses*. Part of the Mookse's diatribe concerns rivalry with the Gripes in the royal plural imperative: "Let you be Beeton [*bête,* beaten, beat on, and Beeton, a town absorbed into Los Angeles]. And let me be Los Angeles" (the angels) (154.23–24)—a cross reference to the polarities of "The Ondt and the Gracehoper" (see pp. 337–47) as well as an allusion to Joyce's perception of Shem as beast and to Shaw's perception of himself as the saintly angel to whom he is often compared in Joyce's binary fantasies. Although the Mookse seems to refer also to the beaten, defeated land of Swift's Yahoos, the Gripes will not submit or "give you up"; for the Irish would not give up papal authority, nor would Joyce give up his dialectical relationship with "Methuselah." If the *Laudabiliter* is the Mookse's, the "loudy bullocker" of *John Bull's Other Island* (for which the bull was an ancient symbol) is the Gripes's, for the Mookse says the same thing as the Gripes: "thoutoosezit." His "spetial [special, spatial] inexshellsis" (*in excelsias,* but the inside out of his shell, like the eggshell from which Shaw's higher humans are born) is summoning up the phallic, uterine, and anal orifices: the "belowing of things ab ove" (154.33–35), from the egg. The Griper's excelsior is, like Joyce's, in moving upward from below, evoking the "lower" sexual anatomy, unlike the Shavian pontiff, who prefers mind to body.

Intruding into the stream of his consciousness his awareness of kinship with the Mookse, the Gripes says he will never be "abler to tell Your Honoriousness. . . . [that] my corked father was bott a pseudowaiter whose o'cloak you ware" (154.36, 155.2). This implies that Joyce, the Gripes whose real father John Joyce was a phony "corker" from Cork, will never be able to tell his pseudofather Shaw that he wears (and sells as a "ware") the cloak of his sire (and the emphasis on time—"o'cloak"—that Wyndham Lewis noted in both Irishmen), except by covering him up in his text. In never being "abler"—Abel/Esau, whose birthright he is stealing—the Gripes takes on the role of Cain/Jacob and Joseph's brothers. Like Cain in Shaw's "In the Beginning," Joyce deviously attacked his able brother writer in his sibicidal imagination while borrowing his cloak and his attitude toward time. When in pontifical "consistorous allocution" (155.7–8) the Mookse tells the Gripes that "it is out of my temporal to help you from being killed by inchies" (155.10–11), he is reiterating Shaw's refusal to give money for *Ulysses,* a rebuff that appears to have galled Joyce and, if the obsessive paroxysms of language in the *Wake* are evidence, to have been, at the very least, unsettling.

Beginning to feel the contempt for the lowly Gripes that Joyce seems to have read into Shaw's behavior, the Mookse decrees putting him under the yoke of the "Unionjok" (155.16), joining Ireland to England and also to himself. In 1914, before the Easter Rising raised his patriotic hackles, Shaw's solution to the Home Rule problem was advocacy of

Irish freedom in a federation of the British Isles, giving Ireland, Scotland, and Wales federal status under the union jack. Moreover, Shaw is joined to Joyce in the unionjoke of Joyce's Irish book, which itself repeatedly reenacts the 1800 Act of Union, parallel to Adrian's, joining Anglo and Irish under the English-language yoke. The sly penman reacts, as the Irish did to the English intruders, by co-opting the invader, making him in his Shavian incarnations an indispensable part of the textuality of his multilayered dream of Ireland. The dream ends in union: the Unionjoke/union jack foreshadows the reconciliation of jokesters Shaun/Juan/Jack with Shem.

At the end of their parable, both the Mookse and his adversary intimate their dubious faith in Creative Evolution. After one thousand years they will be, according to "Mookse the pius," "belined" (maligned, bee-lined, blind, perhaps believed) or "botheared" (bothered, both-eared, both heard), says the Gripes (156.19–23). A leitmotif that often surfaces in the monologue of the subconscious is the Shem-blindness of Joyce, who was going blind while writing the *Wake*, coupled with the "Ear weaker"/Shaun deafness of Shaw, who was going deaf at the same time. Nuvoletta, the female temptress and Life Force muse, hearing the quarrel between the "farseeing" Mookse, whose final play in *Methuselah* is "As Far as Thought Can Reach," tries to get the attention of the debaters. The Mookse, however, will not look at her, and the Gripes will not hear her, for they are busy with their "papyrs and buchstubs. . . . As if that was their spiration!" instead of the inspiration of her "queendim!" (157.28–29). Shaw's use of women for inspiration was almost as notorious as his use of the papers and books of others; his alter ego John Tanner was famed for asserting that women arouse the artist's most profound inventive energies. Joyce aped his mentor in using Nora Barnacle and, in the *Wake*, his daughter Lucia as well for inspiration, but he also took ideas from papers (no doubt containing news of Shaw) and books.

Although the subtext throughout Joyce's fable concerns his view of Shaw, the comparison of Nuvoletta to "Mrs Cornwallis-West" (157.33–34), Shaw's beloved Stella Campbell, brings the Shaw link to the surface. Stella was Shaw's archetypal temptress, model for Orinthia in *On the Rocks* (1933), who tries to divert King Magnus from affairs of state. In *Village Wooing* (1934), the female Z won't "stop talking" and "interrupting" the writer who is her prey (*Selected One Act Plays* 171).

An emanation of the vitalist Z and of Ann Whitefield, who pursues the superman, distracting him from his intellectual interests, Nuvoletta is in part the diminutive "Novel" New Woman whom Shaw championed. A femme fatale Isolde, Nuvoletta tries to tempt the writers, but "the Mookse, a dogmad Accanite [dogmatic Canaanite of the promised land of his Pentateuch and a descendant of the theatrical Ham], were not amoosed and the Gripes, a dubliboused [doubly boozing Dublin] Catalick, wis pinefully obliviscent" (158.3–4). "The Mookse had a sound eyes right but he could not all hear," like Ear Weaker Shaw, whereas the Gripes, like Joyce, could "but ill see" (158.12–13). Whereas the Mookse thought on the "deeps of the undths" (the depths and the ends) of "tomorrow," the Gripes felt of "the scripes he would escipe if by grice he had luck enoupes" (158.15–18). The Gripes, like the "gracehoper" (in the fable of "The Ondt and the Gracehoper"), is still guilty and hoping for unmerited love to escape the scrapes in which he has become involved—one of which was appropriating Shaw's plays, another borrowing Shaw as his Dublin double.

At the end of the fable "a woman of no appearance (I believe she was a Black) . . . gathered up his hoariness the Mookse motamourfully" (158.25–27)—metamorphically, metaphorically, mournfully, amorously, like Shaw's Black Girl in search of God, who finds him in a red-headed Irishman (blatant and witty wish fulfillment for the hoaryheaded old Shaw, who reincarnated himself as a young digger cultivating Candide's garden). In *Heartbreak House* (1917), old Shotover announces that his first wife was a "Jamaican: a black one" (CP, 790). Shotover's "negress redeemed" him (769). When he began writing *The Adventures of the Black Girl in Her Search for God* (1932), Shaw declared that he was writing "a gospel of Shawianity" (BSL 3:283), one no doubt suitable for the papal Mookse. Joyce's seeming black woman carried "his hoariness" to Aquila Rapax, which, Garvin notes, was the term assigned to the pontificate of Pius VII, who presided at Napoleon's coronation (173–74). Thus, like the playwright who crowned Napoleon in two plays about him and in *The Adventures of the Black Girl* virtually becomes God, the Mookse succeeds, whereas "the poor Gripes [Joyce and Catholic Ireland] got wrong" (159.1).

If the *Wake* began as a joke on Shaw, the parable of the fox and the grapes began as a reinterpretation of Aesop by Shawlight. Whereas the Fox is Adrian as well as G. B. S. and the grapes represent Ireland, the

Irish, and Joyce's Shem-side, the subject of the fable leads nevertheless to the same moral. The fox covets the grapes as the English pope coveted Ireland for the English king, but he cannot quite succeed in reaching the Irish. The wily Joyce seems to imply that although Rome and England took over Ireland, they could never really eat her; her old sow does that without help. Alternatively, the criticism of *Ulysses* by Shaw (and Wyndham Lewis) was sour grapes. The Mookse, who fails really to achieve his purpose, slyly belittles what he cannot fully possess (like Shaw, rejected by the Irish Free State). In censuring Joyce, Shaw walked away from fruitful communion that the grapes represent, pretending—as Joyce's misprision suggests—that he does not want the grapes. He thus uses the ruse to cover up his own ineptitude. As Joyce's fable interfaces with Aesop, it projects Joyce's envy of Shaw upon the powerful patriarch and rationalizes the disapproval of his critic(s) in a literary act of delusionary fulfillment. The fable about a shrewd fox and grapes, appropriate for sly Shaw and wine imbiber Joyce, has a postscript that makes the Mookse a griping "darling smallfox," adumbrating the small pox of "Major A. Shaw, who had the miner smellpex" (263.7–8). "Horoeshoew!" [hoary Shaw] admits in fractured Russian his admiration for good show/Shaw. Horus the sun god (who as Ra speaks the prologue of *Caesar and Cleopatra*) is packed into Joyce's pun, for "Lamppost Shawe" is the light-bringer throughout the *Wake*. He turns up later as "old sexton, red-Fox Good man" (511.8–9) in questions about the "right reverence" (511.1) involved in "the hoax that joke bilked" (511.34). The sharp-eyed smallfox is, it seems, the wily Shaw (singled out by William Archer for his "keen eye" in the *World* in 1905; quoted in Evans 117), whom the griping Shem "could love ... for being so baileycliaver though he's a nawful curillass [very Baile Atha Claith, Dublin clever, an awful cure-all, cure-ill ass] and I must slav to methodiousness" (159.28–31). Despite admiring the Mookse's cleverness, Sham/Joyce is a slav/slave to the method and system of *Finnegans Wake*.

The Ondt and the Gracehoper: "Veripatetic Imago" and "Artaloner"

The system of the *Wake* is to create a subterranean conduit stuffed with sewage and debris, snippets of evidence, often leading us circuitously to the identity of Joyce's unascribed mentor. The pattern reappears in the "Fable of the Ondt and the Gracehoper" (chapter 3, part 13), in which Joyce's "skillfilledfelon" (355.27) continues to dream obsessively of guilt and envy of his rival. In the mock Aesop/La Fontaine fable of the Ant and the Grasshopper, Joyce's Grand Ondt, whose name, Glasheen helpfully points out, plays on *don't* (*Second Census*.68), represents the repressive superego in whose role Joyce cast Shaw. The Ondt is also a partial reflection of Shaw's defrocked priest Keegan in *John Bull's Other Island*. When this incarnation of Shavian wisdom appears, he is talking to his disciple, a penitent Grasshopper, "Mishter Unworldly Wiseman." Keegan asks the Grasshopper (an avatar of Ireland without the work ethic) "what wickedness" he has done to bring a "curse on him." When the Grasshopper chirps, Keegan accepts his apology (Plays, 416).

Joyce's Ondt is, unlike his Gracehoper, the embodiment of a worldly wise man, "Behailed as His Gross the Ondt" (417.10–11)—an ironic montage of Shaw, who boasted, "I shall be a panjandrum of literature for the next three hundred years" (Harris, 413). Joyce's conception of the Ondt no doubt owes something to the Harris biography, which devotes a chapter to G. B. S.'s "Summer of Success," emphasizing the wealth that "poured in on him; honors . . . heaped on his shoulders" (392). Like the Ondt, a "true and perfect host" (417.24), Shaw was noted for entertaining all sorts of celebrities, although his guest list never included James Joyce. The blind Gracehoper, who knew "entymology" (entomology and etymology), ignoring "lous" and "licens" (law and license) as he had in pirating Shaw's plays in Zurich and by appropriating *Methuselah* in the *Wake*, plunged into "vico," wondering whether the Ondt, when they met, would behold the similarity of their "mouschical [musical cyclical] unsummables" (417.3–9); "it shall be motylucky if he will beheld not a world of differents" (417.9–10). The sentence establishes the Gracehoper's ambivalence: it will be lucky if the Ondt does not behold (that is, see) the *Wake*—a world very different from that created by Shaw; or it will be lucky if the Ondt does behold the similarities of the world according to Vico, Joyce, and himself. The technique of the *Wake* indicates that Joyce both feared that Shaw would recognize the connections between the *Wake* and *Methuselah* and wanted Shaw to recognize his heterodox discipleship. Early in his text, Joyce introduced the motif of the narrator's ambivalent desire that his opposite read his book: "(Stoop) if you are abcdeminded, to this claybook, what curios of signs (please stoop), in this allaphbed!" (18.17–19). The narrator commands, then pleads for the alphabetically absent-minded to read his alphabet, which is simultaneously a laugh whose setting is often in bed. The "you" addressed may be the reluctant reader, but probably is also Shaw, the advocate of the simplified alphabet denigrated by Joyce's punmanship. (Shaw never stooped to read the *Wake*. In 1948 the nonagenarian tried, but like many others he could make nothing of it. Of course, we cannot assume that he would have made anything of it even at a younger age, for G. B. S. preferred logocentric language.)

In Joyce's parable when the parasitic locust comes to the Shavian ant pleading hunger, the "chairmanlooking" (416.5) Ondt, who, like Shaw, seems to have a vocation for chairing committees, disapproves of "the sillybilly of a Gracehoper who had jingled through a jungle of love and debts and ... drikking ... and horing after ladybirdies" (416.8–12). Like Joyce looking for Shavian approval and support, the grasshopper is "heartily hungry" (416.20) for sustenance. Hoping that the Ondt will appreciate his artistic achievements, he petitions him for help, paralleling Joyce's petition to Shaw through Sylvia Beach and Ezra Pound. The "conformed asceticist" (417.16) is superimposed upon famous patriarchs of religion—"aquintance" (Aquinas, whose rationalism old Shaw shared)—and of philosophy—"aristotaller" (Aristotle, whose empirical method and acceptance of a prime mover Shaw shared, while having developed aristocratic leanings and remaining a teetotaler). The Ondt is like the abstemious Shaw and the ascetic Ancients of *Methuselah*. Like the male Ancient who criticizes young Strephon's amoral preoccupations with art and the opposite sex, the asceticist disapproves of the Gracehoper, whereas the successful Ondt is the object of the Gracehoper's envy: immensely successful and "ameising himself hugely" chasing "houris" (417.28)—amazing and amusing himself chasing beautiful virgins of a Muslin paradise instead of whores. In *transition* in 1928, the first version of the Ondt and the Gracehoper fable describes the "blissfilled [Ond] in an allallah bath of houris" ("Continuation" 18). In 1931 Harris confirmed this comparison by writing of "Shaw's talk about the houris of the paradise of Art and the disadvantage of real women ... " (109). In *Methuselah*'s fourth play, "The Tragedy of an Elderly Gentleman," Baghdad is the capital of the world. Thus perhaps the old papa who comes from Babylon and (having visited Russia as Shaw) favors androgynous Russian headgear wears "Papylonian babooshkees" (417.12). Moreover, Shaw's Black Girl searching for

God encounters the Muslim prophet who praises the male pleasures of polygamy. In spite of prudish protestations regarding bodily functions, the elderly Shaw amazed and amused himself, as well as his public, with infamous flirtations. The 1931 biography that Shaw called "my autobiography by Frank Harris" reported that Shaw "was a philanderer—a male flirt" (192) and that Stella Campbell averred, "If he eats beefsteak no woman in London will be safe" (193).

Joyce's Ondt, the "veripatetic imago" (417.32) of the Gracehoper, is, like world tourist Shaw, the completest traveler and, like Aristotle, a peripatetic who teaches while walking, as well as the adult insect and idealized image of the father (nevertheless, possibly very pathetic). An adept at "deviltry" (417.32), the Ondt resembles the G. B. S. who rejected Joyce's appeal, through his literary promoters Beach and Pound, to subscribe for the forthcoming publication of *Ulysses* and hence to help finance it. The Harris-Shaw "autobiography" quotes a 1923 letter to Harris (which is not, however, included in Dan Laurence's *Collected Letters*), which explains the wealthy playwright's attitude toward handouts to less fortunate writers. In response to the plea of a mysterious writer whom he identifies as "X"—the Grasshopper's "word" in *John Bull's Other Island*— Shaw wrote, "I can't afford it"—the five hundred pounds that "X must have . . . on Sunday or perish." If Grant Wood would promote the mystery man's book, Shaw promised to "throw in" his contribution "as in America." Otherwise, "X . . . must drive a taxi; for he has come to Europe where men of high academic and literary distinction are trying to keep body and soul together by writing the most piteous begging letters, and mostly failing. . . . Meanwhile I am a multi-millionaire. . . . I am personally comfortable and keep two cars but I have not a penny to spare" (398–99).

Shaw continued, "There is only one chance for me: to give nothing. So X starves; . . . while I overeat and deplore the shocking condition of others." The letter would have been of considerable interest to Joyce, for it fitted his case. It could, indeed, account for the portrayal of the Ondt as well as the Gracehoper. The letter's reference to contributing money in America indicates what Joyce must have known—that Shaw was privately generous, but, to protect himself from literary parasites, he presented himself publicly as Scrooge. No doubt, like all of G. B. S.'s public pronouncements, his treatment of artistic "beggars" was notorious. Moreover, Joyce had motives for his fable long before the publication of the letter. Although the fable was first published in *transition* in 1928 in an abbreviated version and thus antedates the publication of the letter in the Harris biography, Joyce divined Shaw's attitude, perhaps even knew of the letter, or extrapolated his fable from his umbrage over Shaw's seeming rejection of his Dublin novel. Whether prefiguring Shaw's letter or, in Joycean accretions, postdating it, the disgusted Ondt spurns the Gracehoper, patronizing him by talking in the third person (as Shaw had done in his correspondence with Pound concerning Joyce): "Let him be Artalone the Weeps with his parisites peeling off him I'll be Highfee the Crackasider" (418.1–2). Shem, the Artalone art-for-art's-saker bemoaning his poverty and surrounded by Parisian parasites, is Joyce, and the high-paid crusader—author of *Saint Joan* who makes wisecracking asides and drinks cider—is Shaw. He wrote that "for art's sake alone I would not face the toil of writing a single sentence" (CP 165).

While Joyce's partisans pressed Shaw to buy a copy of *Ulysses,* Joyce wrote Harriet Weaver, complaining that Shaw, who pretended to grumble over the cost, got high fees as a crusading dramatist. He believed that G. B. S. "made £10,000 out of St. Joan or was it out of old saint Mumpledum" (JJL 1:221)—no doubt Methuselah, a double for the Mumpledum that Weintraub finds in the *Wake,* a "ruffian soldier" in *Saint Joan* ("Respectful Distance" 73). Saint Shaw had sent a postcard to Ezra Pound making fun of Joyce's self-pity and of his self-proclaimed identification with "Melancholy Jesus" (JJ1 504). It should be recalled that Shaw annotated the postcard of Ribera's *The Dead Christ,* which depicts Mary weeping over her crucified son, with the caption "Miss Shakespear consoling James Joyce who has fainted on hearing of the refusal of his countryman to subscribe for Ulysses. Isn't it like him?" (BSL 2:766). Memory of such gallows humor no doubt prompted Joyce to let his wisecracking Ondt call the Artaloner "Weeps." The conflict between the Ondt and the Gracehoper mirrors, therefore, in a cracked looking glass, Joyce's revisionist ridicule of Shaw. The fable reflects Joyce's resentment over Shaw's response to *Ulysses;* Shaw's dismissal of the art-for-art's-sake aesthetic that made his countryman a "coterie" author, whereas "serious" Irish talent should belong "to the big world" (BSL 2:767); his refusal in late 1926 to sign Joyce's petition deploring the piracy of *Ulysses* in America; and Joyce's jealousy of the literary success, wealth, and female adulation that his fellow exiled Dubliner and literary parent enjoyed.

Nevertheless, the Gracehoper forgives the Ondt. As the guilty Gracehoper, Joyce knew that he had "sinned" against Shaw in 1918 in Zurich. He also knew that Shaw had magnanimously given him unmerited love by admiring the fidelity of *Ulysses* to Dublin facts and by acknowledging his genius, even while objecting to its cloacal effusions. Such unearned love was a form of grace because Shaw had not taken Joyce to task or to court for the theft of his plays and had not noticed the love-hate libels of the *Wake* (or his presence in *Ulysses*). Though his own play must have reminded Shaw of Joyce's caddish behavior, when *Mrs. Warren's Profession* had its first uncensored production in London in 1926 and Joyce's only play was performed for the first time there, Shaw generously defended *Exiles* even though he may have suspected that it was a covert copy of *Candida* (see pp. 88–108). Perhaps Joyce's congratulatory note to his "distinguished fellow townsman" for winning the Nobel Prize (JJL 3:146) appealed to Shaw's sense of kinship with Joyce, for the letter was the only congratulation for winning the prize that G. B. S. kept. Knowing, however, that he was guilty of piracy (for which the *Wake* is secret vindication and atonement), when "The Ondt and the Gracehoper" was published, Joyce, like the Gracehoper, had ironically forgiven the rival and source whom he had wronged.

In the "constant search for likenesses" (JJ1 634), Joyce asserted that he found them in Irish tenor John Sullivan and Irish writer James Stephens (whose name and birth date Joyce believed to be the same as his own), but he avoided mentioning his likenesses to Shaw—whose last name in Gaelic was, it must be remembered, the same as his own—a fact that the linguist author could not have missed. He had, it seems, privately long recognized the fundamental kinship between himself and Shaw as well as the radical divergences in their aims, styles, and statuses as artists—differences upon which he could rely to keep his secret from his partisans who were not, as a rule, fans of Shaw. Pound, upon whom Joyce depended to promote his works, was downright hostile. In the *Dial* in June 1922 he sneered that Joyce's picture of his native city was "so veridic that a ninth-rate coward like Shaw (Geo. B.) dare not even look it in the face" (quoted in BSL 2:766). Such name-calling must have aroused conflicts in Joyce, who wanted Pound's support but privately felt a kinship with Shaw, about whom he knew Pound's verdict was an outrageous lie. As Joyce's dreamer knows, "bigtree are all against gravstone. . . . Garnd ond mand" (146.34–35), but unlike Pound (who associated pure art with trees; see Kelly, "Pound's Joyce" 22), Joyce secretly admired the Grand Old Man, even while in his text he tried to confuse readers by superimposing the identity of Gladstone upon the gravestone.

Always alert to comments about his own work, Joyce must have read the 1930 preface to Shaw's belatedly published novel of his nonage, *Immaturity* (written in 1879), in which Shaw, still telling the truth as he read it, referred to the "ruthless fidelity" of *Ulysses* (CP 673). The preface would have apprised Joyce of a consanguinity even deeper than what he found in Shaw's biographies and in newspapers and periodicals, one that Shaw himself seems to have noticed. Shaw's description of himself as a young man sounds like an outline of the character of Stephen Dedalus: "I was outside society, outside politics, outside sport, outside the Church. If the term had been invented then I should have been called the Complete Outsider" (680). It seems that Shaw, who admitted reading *A Portrait of the Artist as a Young Man,* reciprocated the awareness of kinship, though he was unaware of his importance to Joyce's anxiety of influence.

When Joyce encouraged his daughter Lucia, who was creating decorative alphabetical letters, to send the lettrines G. B. S. to Shaw on their common birthday in 1932, he might have urged her to send the letters H. C. E. had he been less devious. In proposing that Lucia send her lettrines to Shaw, the father, desperately seeking to avert recognition of Lucia's schizophrenia, hoped that Shaw might like his daughter's "talent" (JJL 3:259). Stanley Weintraub writes that Joyce's "strategy—about as insane as anything which Lucia might have thought of—was to suggest inferentially to the one-time music critic and drama critic that Lucia, who had received dance and voice training, might be worth having her career promoted by G. B. S." ("Respectful Distance" 72). The strategy was not insane, however, if Joyce thought of Shaw as his surrogate father. Fact and Joycean fantasy almost met in the incident, for in a waking dream of wish fulfillment, Joyce seemed to consider Shaw to be Lucia's grandfather and hence benefactor to whom she should send a present on their shared birthday. Assuming that Lucia sent the lettrines, we can only infer that Shaw, unlike Joyce who believed in the special significance of birthdays, did not respond to Lucia's present. And if she sent them, we can also assume that in retaliation for Shaw's indifference, Joyce busied himself anew with berating the chosen and unwitting model for H. C. E./Shaun as father and twin, deepening his objurgations in his textural accretions. Nevertheless, later in 1932 Joyce was vindicated for having "forgiven" Shaw or at least was given cause to feel absolved as well as completely successful in his *Wake* and *Ulysses* cover-ups. Shaw, newly elected president of the Irish Academy of Letters, and Yeats nominated Joyce for membership in their recently organized society for Irish authors (JJL 3:259). Such absolution gave Joyce the occasion for a proud refusal foreshadowed in his fable, in which the Gracehoper asserts aesthetic superiority over the Ondt by deriding his style.

In spite of seeming to mollify the "grondt Ondt" by forgiving him, the Gracehoper picks up his *"reproof, the horsegift of a friend"* (418.20), it seems, from Ezra Pound, who reported to Joyce Shaw's disapproval of his wasting his time as an elitist artist. The Gracehoper defines the Ondt and himself by alluding to Shaw's protestations to Pound that the price of subscribing for *Ulysses* "was too high for me" (JJL 2:765) and to his own claims of poverty: *"We are Wastenot with Want"* (418.30), condemned by Joyce's vengeful imagination to be coupled in his *"risible universe"* (419.3), even though the Ondt *"mocks"* his *"gropes"* (418.32) (as Shaw had in ridiculing Joyce on his postcard to Pound), giving telling evidence of the parallel identities of the Mookse and the Gripes. The Gracehoper, however, gets even. He ends his poem in arrogant if admiring reprisal by scorning the craftsmanship of the Ondt:

> *Your feats end enormous, your volumes immense,*
> *(May the Graces I hoped for sing your Ondtship song sense!),*
> *Your genus its worldwide, your spacest sublime!*
> *But, Holy Saltmartin, why can't you beat time?* (419.5–8)

The only other competing Irish genius whose feats were enormous was Yeats, but no one, not even Joyce, would accuse him of lacking rhythm. Also, apparently Joyce did not think enough of the poet to send him a letter congratulating him when he received the Nobel Prize for literature, even though a few years later he sent such a letter to his spiritual progenitor. Although the Ondt blends, according to Richard Ellmann (JJ1 609) and his followers, into Wyndham Lewis, hostile critic of *Ulysses* and author of *Time and Western Man,* which contains an analysis of Joyce's mind, the most salient Ondt in Joyce's interior literary life was the hard-working social insect, G. B. S. As William York

Tindall notes, "References to Soviet Russia, implying a society of ants or bees, establish Shaun's [and hence the Ondt's] ideal" (289). Like other early commentators on the *Wake,* Tindall did not think of the Ondt's community ideal as related to the most famous Irish admirer of Soviet Russia, but it seems certain that Joyce did.

Whereas Lewis criticized *Ulysses* as a "time book" (195), he also related Joyce to the "philosophy of the space-timest" (197), as an advocate, like Bergson and his famed popularizer Shaw, of Creative Evolution. Significantly, in his analysis, Lewis compared Joyce to Shaw: "Joyce resembles him in some striking particulars," but Joyce "is remote from what must have been the strapping, dashing George Bernard Shaw of the shavian heyday"—a Shaun-like persona. Like the Ondt, *"his genus worldwide,"* Shaw "is much more a world-figure" than Joyce (192). Rousing Joyce's envy of Shaw and reminding him of his kinship, Lewis also set himself up for the attack of Joyce's poisonous pen. He facilitated Joyce, who swatted two vexatious rivals in one, suggesting that Lewis could not beat (that is, win out against) Joyce's time-oriented art and that Shaw, like himself, is a "space-timest" whose *"spacest* [space is] *sublime,"* especially in part 5 of *Methuselah.* Joyce simultaneously asserted his superiority over the painter interested in space and asked Shaw a rhetorical question about longevity—his forte—and poetic rhythm, his self-admitted bogy: *"Why can't you beat time?"*

The Harris biography, from which Shaw expurgated only the most outrageous inaccuracies, confirmed Joyce's criticism of Shaw's musical judgment by reporting that the acting editor of the *World,* for which Shaw had been music critic, "firmly believed that Shaw's musical knowledge was a huge joke—a comic fake by a humorist who did not know B flat from a bull's foot" (111). Already predisposed to believe that his rival lacked the musical skills for which he was known, Joyce's Gracehoper asserts that, despite the genius's enormous accomplishments (a *"genus worldwide"* that cannot be attributed to Wyndham Lewis), worldwide fame, and sublime subject matter—a good résumé of Shaw's reputation at the time of *Methuselah* and *Saint Joan*—his "Ontship," his Ear Weaker, lacks "song sense." The Ondt could not, according to the cynically respectful Gracehoper, *"beat time."* The final *double entente* is, of course, on key, for the aging Shaw's aim in his New Testament was to teach people that they could *"beat"* time, but he admitted in his preface that his own time was running out. Both

346   Chapter 6

profanity and term of address, the "*Holy Saltmartin,*" which punctuates the rhetorical question, appropriately derides the holy Ancients of *Methuselah*'s finale and Old Mumbledum himself, more Protestant, like Martin Luther, than Catholic and as sexless as saltpeter could make him. Always attuned to ironies, Joyce may even have been alluding to Shaw's marriage, like Luther's, to a "nun"—in Shaw's case Charlotte Townshend, who, after her wedding, insisted on keeping the vows of chastity.

After the fable Shem and Shaun have an obscure literary discussion (also a "disarssion") in which Shem compliments Shaun on his "good . . . explosition," "farflung . . . fokloire and . . . velktingeling . . . volupkabulary!" (419.11–12). Shem asks Shaun to "read the strangewrote anaglyptics of those shemletters patent for His Christian's Em" (419.18–19). Joyce's collection of miscellaneous information (as in "ana"), his low relief ornament (as in "anaglyph") is an anagogical interpretation of Shaw's scriptures in something like hieroglyphics, hard to decipher—a strange rote/wrote rendering of "His Christian's Em"—*Methuselah*. As John Gordon observes, ALP "begets . . . a figure whose obscurity is at the heart of the book, a corpse whose last initial is definitely M" (61). My reading of the *Wake* is facilitated by identifying M and the siglum ⋒ with Methuselah as well as with Finn MacCool. When Joyce wrote of "Mezouzalem with the Dephilim" (158.8–9), he was probably referring, as noted earlier, to Shaw's Methuselah as well as to the mezuzah of the *Torah*. In his Pentateuch, "Mr. Moses Shaw," as St. John Ervine called him in the *Observer* (March 11, 1929), enjoined people to love the god inside them and manifest in seers like himself. As Joyce wrote, "The end of aldest mosest ist the beginning of all thisorder" (540.18–19), the Dublinese disorder and method of Joyce's deconstructed copy of old Shaw's Pentateuch, "the tale of the evangelical bussybozzy" (40.7).

When Shem asks the "decent Lettrechaun" (419.17)—mischievous letter-writing, impish Irish man of letters—to read his "shemletters" (419.19), Shaun vaingloriously asserts that he is, like Shaw's Julius Caesar, "afterdusk nobly Roman" (419.21–22). He brags about his own ability, boasting that he can play a scene "sem backwards like Oscan wild" (Oscar Wilde) or "off the Toptic" (419.24–25), like Shaw, whose digressive prefaces Joyce singled out in a 1921 letter to Harriet Weaver (JJL 1:167). Upon looking at the Shemscript, Shaun declares that it "is not a nice production. . . . Overdrawn! Puffedly offal tosh. Besides its auctionable, all about crime and libel!" (419.31–33)—the actionable plagiarism that Joyce feared (and possibly hoped) Shaw would find in his sham and shameful words. In Shaun's response, Joyce imagines with masochistic pleasure Shaw's reaction were he to read *Finnegans Wake* and find the obscenity and plunder hidden under its nearly impenetrable surface. Shaun's criticism applies equally to the *Wake* and to the theatrical productions of *Methuselah,* so "overdrawn" that Arnold Bennett reported that he slept through the performance that he attended, and so "offal" that St. John Ervine argued publicly with Shaw about *Methuselah* in 1921, 1923, and 1928 (BSL 2:731). If Joyce were reading the *Observer* in 1921 he would have seen Ervine's "Mr. Shaw in Despair" (BSL 2: 743), a notice in which Ervine also criticized the pace and casting of *Heartbreak House*. Like his disciple, Shaw was suffering the slings and arrows of outrageous critics. The detractor who might find *Methuselah* long-winded and awful, however, would not find the offal excrement of its deconstructed copy, which contains the same waste material that Shaw found objectionable in *Ulysses*. The "fuellest filth" of Shem's book distinguishes it from "the blarneyed blather" of the "decent Lettrechaun," but in this exercise in self-mockery and Shaw mockery, Joyce begins to blend the two writers and their two "overdrawn" masterworks.

Groundbroken Irishmen and "Anonymoses": The Rann of Persse O'Reilly

Hosty's "Ballad of Persse O'Reilly" (book 1, chapter 2) is a drunken, disoriented tragicomic lampoon-lament for Ireland, which seems to well up from the collective unconscious of Joyce's Irish narrator. It dislocates and decenters archetypes and historical and familial allusions to fallen Irish patriarchs and patriots, condensing into the poem a whole history of factionalism, failure, betrayal, and blood sacrifice. If Hosty is the host of the eucharist, his name is a deflation of the ideal of religious communion as well as an ironic comment on traditional Irish hospitality. His name suggests, indeed, that as archetypal Irishman, he is the host to foreign and native parasites. A reply to the ineffectual, nostalgic patriotism of "Ivy Day in the Committee Room," its voice vacillates between the impotent loyalism of Joe Hynes's romantic belief that things would be better if Charles Stewart Parnell were alive and ridicule of Hynes's sentimental poem predicting that Parnell's spirit will rise "like the Phoenix" (D 107). Although Joyce bitterly averred in his 1911 lecture in Trieste that Irishmen had "honored" Parnell's petition not to "throw him to the wolves" by tearing him "to pieces themselves" and wrote in "Gas from a Burner" that "Twas Irish humor, wet or dry / Flung quicklime into Parnell's eye" (CW 228, 243), in Hosty's ballad, Joyce is less sympathetic with the martyr. Whereas in the Christmas dinner scene of *Portrait* Dante's crucifying Catholic morality seems bigoted and the Parnellism of Casey and Stephen's father seems to win the argument, Hosty's ballad mocks vainglorious nationalism, paralleling it to the Guinness patriotism of the citizen in the Cyclops episode of *Ulysses* in Barney Kiernan's pub as well as to his chorus of bibulous barflies. The rann exposes the absurdity of ethnocentricity and patriotic gore.

One of the denizens of the pub in *Ulysses* says, "Our greatest living phonetic expert" has tried "to delucidate" verse that strikingly resembles "the ranns of ancient Celtic bards" (12.719–23). Shaw, of course, prided himself on being a phonetician, but in linguistic matters Joyce easily outdid him: in "delucidating" he was an expert. An elucidator of the cryptic rann must read through the alcoholic fumes a prophesy of the futility of heroic bloodshed and disdain for the perfidy of the "rabblement." As a rann, reading like a mysterious runic omen, the mean-spirited ballad also mocks traditional Gaelic satirical poetry and hence the Celtic revival that both Shaw and Joyce disowned. It imitates, as Robert Adams explains, " 'the Wren, the wren, the king of all birds' . . . a little folk-poem sung in many parts of Europe and in many languages as part of a festival to celebrate the downfall and sacrifice of a mythical bird-king" (178).

But Hosty's ballad also satirizes and at the same time imitates the bad political verse that flooded Irish newspapers in the mid-nineteenth century and sentimentalized patriotism. It is like the crude broadsides that Thomas Davis found on sale in Dublin Streets in 1842. The *Nation* published many solicited ballads, crude and mawkish; in an 1845 anthology they were accompanied, like Hosty's ballad, by musical scores. James Stephens's rival paper, the *Irish People,* was deluged with a flood of unsolicited martial verse. Yeats's mentor, the famed Fenian John O'Leary, remarked that "patriotism seems to take a peculiar delight in the manufacture of bad verse" (quoted in Malcolm Brown 181). Joyce's bad verse burlesques the maudlin nationalism of the Fenian newspapers and reverses the implications of such patriotic fervor by rejecting physical force. Instead of romanticizing Ireland, in spiteful glee Hosty's rann celebrates the disasters of fallen Irishmen.

The title "The Ballad of Persse O'Reilly" condenses in a name the irreconcilable conflicts that have characterized Ireland's violent history. Like Humpty Dumpty in the ballad, making words work overtime, Joyce calls the composite scapegoat Persse O'Reilly to identify him as Earwicker, the Irish patriarch whose name derives from *perce-orielle,* French for earwig. Whether Joyce was aware of it or not, Lady Augusta Gregory was a descendant of both the Persses of Roxborough, who came over to Ireland with Cromwell, and the O'Gradys. Her work in the Irish literary revival derived from her patriotism, even though she was the widow of a unionist Member of Parliament. The name Persse also refers to Padraic Pearse, leader of the abortive 1916 Easter Rising, who was executed by the British at Kilmainham Gaol with fifteen other rebel leaders, separately put before the firing squad. In the failed revolt, The O'Rahilly, who took his name from the fact that he was head of his Kerry clan, was a leader of the Irish Volunteers and another casualty of the insurrection—a variation on the theme that deepens the implications of infighting and betrayal. The divided loyalties that often led to miscarried bloodshed are implicit even in the genealogy of Pearse—with an English father and an Irish mother—and in O'Rahilly, the descendant of "native" Irish. Their differences adumbrate the conflict between Protestant Shaun and lapsed Catholic Shem that often informs the *Wake*. O'Rahilly did not at first support the badly coordinated bid for independence but threw himself and his men into the street-fighting against the British, only to be shot down on April 28, the fourth day of the uprising.

Combining the two—Pearse, the fanatical advocate of the necessity of sacrifice to free Ireland, and The O'Rahilly, who hesitated but became a blood sacrifice himself—reminds us of the feuds and confusion that typified clannish Irish patriots—a disorientation that the ballad simulates. Another leitmotif of the poem, evoked in the surname in the title, concerns political, artistic, and domestic victimization. Egan O'Rahilly, whose name is a variant of the name O'Reilly, was an eighteenth-century Gaelic bard evicted, so to speak, from the patronage that poets had in Kerry before the English came and took away their lands as well as their livings; he was reduced to begging for help from a usurping English planter. Furthermore, the name O'Reilly has been traced back to Celtic origins in Connacht in the fourth century A.D.

In the title Joyce also compacts allusions to Shaw's two Irish plays, both of which anticipate the thrust of Hosty's rann. Apparently Shaw, like Joyce, was aware of the layered associations of the name Reilly and added one of his own in *John Bull's Other Island,* whose heroine, Nora Reilly, is a symbol for Ireland's reluctant marriage to the usurping English. Yet another version of the capitulation of Ireland to her invaders, Nora has a first name that is especially ironic, for it is borrowed from Ibsen's Nora Helmer and Synge's Nora Burke (of *In The Shadow of the Glen,* 1903), who developed the courage to declare independence from masculine domination. In Shaw's other Irish play, *O'Flaherty V.C.,* Sir Pearce is the name of the Irish estate owner, the Anglo-Irish landlord, complacent and wealthy keeper of the "purse" (as Shaun/Shaw often is in the *Wake*) and foil to O'Flaherty, the Irishman whose family have been Pearce's unwilling tenants. O'Flaherty has returned to Ireland only to be frightened off by his mother (Ireland)'s possessive and rabid nationalism, in reversal of the implications of Yeats's patriotic play *Cathleen ni Hoolihan,* which supports the romantic nationalist plea for revolutionary action and blood sacrifice for Mother Ireland. Supposedly a "recruitment" play to encourage Irishmen to join the army of Great Britain in World War I, *O'Flaherty V.C.* was rejected by Yeats for performance at the Abbey Theatre (no doubt because of its political slant), although he had requested it.

Shaw's play is yet another story about betrayal of Ireland, the one in which Shaw and Joyce participated—the flight of the heroes, the "Wild Geese" who left the country. Ironically, in Shaw's play O'Flaherty is an ordinary peasant who has shed blood for England; he has won the Victoria Cross for heroism. His abandonment of Ireland parallels that of Shaw and Joyce—Joyce's even more than his mentor's, because the figure who tries to hold him in Ireland is his mother. Echoing the words of expatriate Larry Doyle in *John Bull's Other Island,* Shaw's preface to that play argues that "an Irishman's hopes and ambitions turn on his opportunities of getting out of Ireland!" (CP 475). O'Flaherty flees his native land after repeating to Pearce his mother's assertion that "all the English generals is Irish. She says all the English poets and great men was Irish." He anticipates Joyce's poem by saying, "You'll never have a quiet world til you knock the patriotism out of the human race" (Plays 823). Nevertheless, exile from Ireland is another form of disloyalty, of which both Shaw and Joyce were keenly aware.

Joyce's ballad in *Finnegans Wake* is, like *O'Flaherty V.C.*, a dark comedy, made farcical in Joyce through the looking glass of nursery rhyme and Lewis Carroll, for Humpty Dumpty's fall begins and closes the poem, which presents distorted images of many fallen and betrayed Irishmen who cannot be put together again. Joyce's sly innuendos may even include a reference to Isaac Butt, the lawyer who spent his life trying to keep Fenians out of jail only to be defeated as leader in Home Rule agitation by Charles Stewart Parnell: Humpty Dumpty fell "by the butt of the Magazine Wall" (45.4) at the fort in Phoenix Park, where the newly installed chief secretary of Dublin Castle, Lord Frederick Cavendish, and undersecretary Thomas Burke were assassinated in 1882, the year of Joyce's birth. Chief among the deposed, however, is Parnell, to whom the second stanza seems to be a definite reference, though it is undercut and skewed by the remainder of the stanza, which broadens the archetype of the fallen leader, who is also H. C. E., once the king of the family castle. "He was one time our King of the Castle / Now he's kicked about like a rotten old parsnip" (45.7–8). At first the allusion seems surely to be to Parnell, the "dead King" of Mr. Casey in *Portrait* and martyred leader to many patriotic Dubliners who looked to him as a political savior who would achieve Home Rule. When he was a hero to the Irish people, the M.P. from Meath (and Wicklow) was king of Dublin Castle, because he had the allegiance of the Irish people who were ruled from Dublin Castle by the British. When his lieutenants turned on him (inspiring young James Joyce to write his first poem, "Et tu Healy," to excoriate the Judas who betrayed the king/Caesar), Parnell vowed that he would not resign his position even "if the people of Galway kicked him through the streets" (Haslip 300), perhaps like a rotten old parsnip. Parnell ruled, not from Dublin Castle, but in spite of it.

Nevertheless, the Dublin Castle reference evoking Parnell melds with evocation of another victim of prejudice, Oscar Wilde, also once a king at Dublin Castle—a well-known figure at events there with his family, who were, like Parnell's and Shaw's, part of the Anglo-Irish ruling class. "His Worship" orders the hero to jail—from the Criminal Courts on Green Street in Dublin (near Barney Kiernan's pub, scene of Joyce's satire of Irish politics in *Ulysses*); the judge represents the law of the state, but the title His Worship hints also at the part played by the Catholic Church hierarchy, which led the assault on Parnell for his adulterous relationship with

Kitty O'Shea. Because of the dream condensations of the poem, however, His Worship could also be the judge who sentenced Wilde to jail for his homosexual affair with Alfred Lord Douglas.

The pattern becomes further disoriented when the hero is sent "from Green street . . . / To the penal jail of Mountjoy" (45.9–10). This is not where Parnell was incarcerated for seven months in 1881–82 for activities that the English deemed seditious. It is, of course, also not Reading Gaol, where Wilde masochistically lamented his miserable martyrdom, killed by the thing he loved, just as Parnell was "killed" by Kitty O'Shea in the eyes of his turncoat constituency. Parnell had been imprisoned in the infamous Kilmainham Gaol in Dublin, whereas Mountjoy was a Dublin prison to which many Irish "political" prisoners were sent. Probably the Irish rebel whose death made Mountjoy a symbol of British infamy was Trinity College student Kevin Barry, hanged on November 1, 1920, at Mountjoy Prison for his part in an attack on British troops. As the famous ballad about his heroic sacrifice indicates, he was "another martyr for old Ireland, / Another murder for the crown." A year after the execution Shaw described visiting Mountjoy Prison as a Dublin teenager (CP 283). In free-speech conflicts in London, he volunteered to go to prison but escaped the martyrdom he courted. Moreover, Mountjoy Prison suggests two of the Joyce family's brief residences near Mountjoy Square while James Joyce was a boy. In the adult stream-of-consciousness poem, the vindictive and fickle "rabblement" delight in the sufferings of the fallen, no matter who he is. The malicious pub crawlers who become the chorus of Hosty's ballad (and hence the Irish public) sound like the prejudiced philistines who condemned Wilde and turned on their great "Leader": "Jail him and joy" (45.12). Joyce's critique of the standard patriotic prejudices becomes bitterly comic carnival in Hosty's rann.

The stuttering Hosty is, however, aware of the importance of the fallen king: "He was fafafather of all schemes for to bother us" (45.13). In this paternal capacity he is closer to Joyce's assessment of Shaw than to his feelings about Parnell. In his 1909 review of *The Shewing up of Blanco Posnet,* Joyce noted Shaw's provocative role as gadfly-champion of "all the progressive movements in art and politics" (CW 208). The schemes that Hosty's ballad lists make fun of reforms that Shaw projected in Fabian tracts Joyce had in his library. One was better transportation, ironically in "slow coaches," a reference that suggests also John

Mitchell's militant mid-nineteenth-century "railway article," which advised slowing down trains that were facilitating British troop transportation by ambushing them (Malcolm Brown 87). Also listed is birth control through celibacy, which Shaw practiced in his own marriage: "immaculate contraceptives." (In the preface to *Man and Superman* he advocated "modern devices for combining pleasure with sterility"; 174.) Another proposal ridiculed in the ballad is "mare's milk for the sick"; the Fabian wanted socialized milk delivery for all. As a notorious teetotaler, Shaw was, as Joyce noted in the *Blanco Posnet* review, in favor of "prohibitionism" (CW 208)—"seven dry Sundays a week." *The Philanderer,* the preface to *Man and Superman,* and *Getting Married* seem to preach "Openair love," and Shaw's missionary zeal in *Methuselah* seems to be, in Joyce's take-off, "religious reform / Hideous in form" (45.14–18). As G. K. Chesterton pointed out, Shaw was a man who could "argue on the spur of the moment about sewing "machines or sewage, about typhus fever or two-penny tubes" (quoted in PS 9). But, like Parnell, he failed as a reformer. "Arrah, why, says you, couldn't he manage it?" Now, like other fallen Irishmen, he needs "bail, my fine dairyman darling" (45.19–20). Hosty's proposal to bail out the troubled groundbreaking Irishman may refer to the dreamer's inconsistent desire to provide money for a political prisoner or to aid evicted farmers, but it may also refer to Joyce's humorous attempt to redeem the author of *John Bull's Other Island*—a play about Ireland's agrarian troubles—through rewriting *Methuselah* in the *Wake.*

Apparently struck by Shaw's plan to socialize milk delivery, Joyce's balladeer asserts that the aggressiveness of the "dairyman" is, like Shaw's letters and speeches, not really violent: "Like the bumping bull of the Cassidys / All your butter is in your horns" (45.21–22). Although the phallic references may be to Parnell, Wilde, Joyce himself, and/or his father (who sired at least thirteen children; see JJ1 20), butter is associated with Burrus/Shaun and hence with Shaw (see pp. 308). This bullish "butter" with horns is also the lecturer Shaw, who declared for the whole world to hear, "the cart and the trumpet for me" (CP 745). The horn that he tooted was not the goring weapon of the bull as legendary symbol of masculine Irish strength. But in Hosty's randy ballad, before we can find out more about the trumpeter who is the horned (and horny) dairyman, the chorus interrupts to approve of Hosty's rann. They shout, "Hurrah there . . . / Rhyme the rann, the king of all ranns" (45.25–27).

In response, Hosty exclaims, mysteriously, "Balbaccio, balbuccio" (45.28) in an accretional decoy that suggests many languages, none of them Irish or English. The romance languages offer several possible meanings for the intrusive epithets: the Italian "kiss"—*bacio*—is combined with *accio,* an augmentative with a derogatory connotation. In Latin, *balbus* means "stutterer" or "stammerer." Hence the word may refer to Hosty/H. C. E./Finn/Parnell (upon whose stutter Shaw remarked in the preface to *John Bull's Other Island*) and may mean "big ball kisser," "big stammerer," or "oafish stammer" (Giuriceo). In Spanish *bacio* means "chamber pot" and *baltutier* means "to stammer." If the terms are fractured Spanish, they may be related to Kitty O'Shea as Bloom thought of her, "Spanish or half so" (U 13.1408–9), like Molly. The Spanish etymology also works in the distorted pattern of the poem because triumphant over the inferior, legendary Firbolgs of Ireland were the fabled, heroic Milesians, alleged descendants of Noah (who appears later in the rann), said to be from Spain. Nevertheless, whatever the interruption means, it seems to be pejorative and vulgar, perhaps a reference to the stutterer, whose new language may be humorously attributed to a speech impediment; to Parnell; or to Shaw's rhetoric as defective speech.

The rann turns, nevertheless, from this digressive shout (or epithet of address) to the soft-soaping salesman on a soapbox, alliteratively selling the ideal of equal distribution of wealth—"chops, chairs, chewing gum, the chicken pox and china chambers / Universally provided by this soffsoaping salesman" (45.29–31). Incongruously, chicken pox gets into the catalogue of benefits because Shaw argued vociferously (and bullheadedly) against vaccination. As one of the doctors in *The Doctor's Dilemma* says of artist Dudebat, a self-proclaimed "disciple of Bernard Shaw," Shaw was a "notorious and avowed anti-vaccinationist" (Plays 530). In addition to suggesting politician Shaw's lobbying for better lavatories, the china chamber pots offered may be a reform that Joyce, as author of *Chamber Music,* preferred. Because of Shaw's work for social reform, it is ironically "Small wonder . . . our local lads nicknamed him" H. C. E.: "He'll Cheat E'erawan" (46.1). Whereas this may allude to character defamation by Parnell's detractors and Joyce's judgment of his Shemself as cheater of everyone, it blends in with his self-gratifying misreading of Shaw as out to make money, as well as to his being a plagiarist like Shem, for it suggests that Shaw had cheated Samuel Butler by stealing ideas from *Erewhon*. Butler's "Nowhere" was, Shaw admitted, a major source of Methuselan utopianism. When Humphrey "first took the floor" (46.2), he might have been Parnell in Parliament or Joe Biggar, the humpbacked Ulster M.P. who first set the example for Parnell of wielding Irish power in Parliament by obstructing business in the House of Commons. But the reference to taking the floor also alludes to Shaw in the lecture hall or at storefronts in lower-class neighborhoods, "bucketshop store / Down Bargainweg. Lower" (46.3–4).

Whereas Shaw started his career speaking to the ordinary lads (and ladies), later he was, like Parnell, "snug" in his "hotel premises sumptuous / But soon we'll bonfire all his trash, tricks and trumpery" (46.5–6). Parnell was noted for conducting his political business from a hotel suite. The unreliable Hosty, now representing the fickle rabble, determines to trash the hero who had a few stanzas earlier been the "King." The parallel to Shaw also pertains, for both Anglo-Irishmen were pragmatic opportunists for Ireland's sake, speakers who preferred bombast to bombs. In his search for likenesses, Joyce no doubt found many to Parnell in Shaw, who had in Stella Campbell an inamorata comparable to Katherine O'Shea (though not wholly analogous to her). In identifying with Hosty's scorn of the hero, Joyce may be hinting at his betrayal of Shavian "trumpery" (a favorite word of the "cart and trumpet" man) in Dublin in 1909. While Joyce attended *The Shewing up of Blanco Posnet* at the Abbey Theatre, Shaw was, as the newspapers noted, snug in the posh hotel at Parknasilla in County Kerry, making himself aloof from the production of his play, as Parnell often seemed to be from his followers. Had Shaw attended the play, he might have met the envious young rival whose review trashed it as a trumped-up melodrama trumpeting G. B. S.'s newly discovered religion. Because the dream mechanism compresses and the syncretic, *Wake*ian method is to tier allusions upon one another, the bonfires and trashing may also intimate the reprisals of angry tenant farmers in the Irish Land League against their rackrenting Anglo-Irish landlords. Arson became a preferred form of retaliation, which often meant fighting fire with fire.

The appearance of "sheriff Clancy" (46.7) suggests events that made Parnell a traitor to his own principles of nonviolent agitation as the means to achieve Home Rule. Although the parliamentarian wanted to avoid violence, the consummate politician courted Fenian support, Davitt's Land League, American money, and even the priests in trying to create a coalition against British hegemony. When in 1890 Michael Davitt and Tim Healy turned on the "Uncrowned King of Ireland," so did Parnell's incendiary newspaper *United Ireland,* which had a strong influence on Parnell's hero-worshipping public. When his key supporters defected, William O'Brien, formerly his flamboyant editor, became estranged from Parnell because of his disapproval of his fallen hero's part in the O'Shea divorce; he cabled Matthias Bodkin, the new editor, to change the slant of the propaganda sheet in order to undermine his former hero's leadership. Infuriated by this betrayal, Parnell stormed the newspaper offices on Lower Abbey Street in Dublin to expel its new editor and his staff. Although Parnell had been denounced as implicated in the Phoenix Park murders by the militant Invincibles, he was vindicated and, until the newspaper episode, could not be labeled as an advocate of physical force. Sheriff John Clancy, a Parnellite who should have supported law and order, oversaw the proceedings at the newspaper offices. As Bloom recalls in the cabman's shelter in *Ulysses,* "they broke up the type of the *Insuppressible* or was it *United Ireland*" (16.1334–35).

It is tempting to extrapolate on the intrusion of Sheriff Clancy, the watchdog of Bloom's "idol with feet of clay" (*Ulysses* 16.1329–30), into the diffusions of Hosty's crazy-quilt song, for latent content of the dream may be disguised in the historical reference to Clancy. Whereas the manifest content collapses into multiple sly and esoteric references to Irish politics, cultural ethos, and psychology, all coexisting uneasily in Hosty's rann, Joyce, like Clancy, continues the ego identification with Parnell that began when he was a young boy as well as the identification that he recognized in his teens, although covertly, with Shaw. In the synchronic narcissism of Joyce's solipsistic imagination, all of the dream figures are extensions of himself. Thus John Clancy's overseeing the expulsion of the editor of *United Ireland* is comparable to Joyce's bearing witness to Ireland's perfidious internecine warfare. Clancy is a displacement of Joyce's own watchful ego, for whom the incident of Parnell's storming the office of his newspaper may have had special significance. The introduction of subsheriff Clancy, a displaced substitute for the dreamer, evokes the leitmotif of Irish disunity and factionalism that often led to disaster.

With borrowed funds, Clancy's opportunistic hero Parnell purchased printing presses from the bankrupt Richard Piggott, the journalist whose forged letters later aimed to connect Parnell to the Phoenix Park murders. In remotely alluding to Richard Piggott, the rann anticipates a pattern that the *Wake* encodes through various uses of the word *hesitency*—a misspelling of *hesitancy*, for which Joyce provides misspellings of his own, including *heciteny* (119.18), *hisshistenency* (146.34), and *hasateny* (16.26). Shaun "is unhesitent in his unionism and yet a pigotted nationalist" (133.14-15), like the paradoxical Shaw. The word was used to expose Piggott, a forger like Shem, who tried to bring about the fall of Parnell by passing off a letter containing the misspelling as Parnell's. The letter, which implicated Parnell in the Phoenix Park assassinations, would have established that Parnell was an advocate of physical force, but a clever attorney exposed the fraud. Joyce associates Shem as forger with Piggott and Shaun/Shaw with Parnell, the "Moses of the Irish," as Gladstone called him, though Parnell was a Moses who did not write a Pentateuch and who, in desperation, used physical force as Shaw never would.

The fact that the infamous Irish forger tried unsuccessfully to ruin Parnell and then committed suicide may have fitted into Joyce's psychic need to experience guilt and expiation for the "forgeries" of his dreambook. Perhaps significantly, a "family" photograph of the Shaws (see PP, facing 18) taken by Piggott in 1863, before he achieved his ill repute as a forger, may have linked Shaw to Parnell, for the photo blatantly suggests the betrayal of Shaw *père et fils* by George Vandeleur Lee. Seated with his eyes averted from the camera, Lee is in the center of the photo. Shaw's mother stands beside him, with her eyes also averted. George Carr Shaw stands behind Lee and opposite his wife. Piggott had captured the Shaws in the very act of welcoming the usurper. As forger of Shaw's long-winded shorthand and signature, as well as creator of a family portrait featuring Shaws, Joyce is Piggott, but he does not resort to suicide (as Piggott did), even though his detractors thought of the *Wake* as artistic self-destruction. Instead, like Parnell and Shaw, who modeled himself in part on the industrious, talented Lee, he takes advantage of another man's failure and, when he begins to lose control of his sensational and hallucinatory writing, forcibly reassumes command. In Joyce's fantasy of guilt, Shaw was an accuser such as Parnell proved himself to be in repossessing *United Ireland*. The incident in which Parnell denied the newspaper freedom of the press (paralleled by Shaw's nonviolent, verbal inconsistency in deriding the "dirt" of *Ulys-*

ses) may mark the diminished heroism that connects him to other Irish leaders whom Hosty prophesies will not be born again. Like Bloom in the cabman's shelter, the vulgar Hosty has no illusions regarding the hero's return, even though Skin-the-Goat bets that "one morning you would open the paper . . . and read, Return of Parnell" (*Ulysses* 16.1297–98).

Whereas Shaw and Joyce repudiated such patriotism, Yeats endorsed it in "September 1913" and "Easter 1916," although not wholeheartedly. The irrationality of Hosty's poem is commensurate with Joyce's rejection, but in his late poems Yeats was still inviting support for proud Parnell, enjoining his readers, "Come gather round me, Parnellites / And praise our chosen man" (306). Joyce, listening to Shaw's Methuselan sermon even while he mocked it, rejected such reactionary hero-worship and lumped Fenian heroes with Ireland's warrior invaders, merging them as sons of Cain. He assimilated the "old hayheaded philosopher" Shaw into an Irish psyche that disdains the old, demented hostilities by rising above the contraries that give Hosty's paranoid poem its random pattern. Like *O'Flaherty V.C.*, the rann makes a mockery of nationalism and patriotism.

Thus Hosty's ballad, like all of the *Wake*, exemplifies in form and content the psychological displacement that channels the disillusioned dreamer's energy from one ego object to another. If Shaw, the living heroic rival, is the major object of the dream poem, Parnell, Wilde, Pearse, Joyce, John Joyce, and others are distributed in the valences of the poem. In the ballad, despite the intrusion of Joyce's real father as unheroic betrayer and victim, the only figure besides Wilde who is not associated with the violence that the poem finally rejects, is the "old hay-headed philosopher" for whom Joyce felt resentful admiration. Identifying with him was a part of Joyce's daring to overcome the cultural prohibitions of his Irish Catholic upbringing. Even after young Stephen is punished in *Portrait* for his interest in Eileen Vance and after Joyce became disillusioned with Parnell, the Anglo-Irishman whom he admired as a boy, Joyce chose, albeit ambivalently (as he did in Leopold Bloom) another forbidden ego ideal—as he calls him in the fable featuring the ondt, a "veripatetic imago."

Shaw's preface to *John Bull's Other Island* may have persuaded Joyce to take another look at Parnell, for in discussing Irish leadership, Shaw wrote, "Blockheads are of no use to us: we were compelled to follow a supercilious, unpopular, tongue-tied, aristocratic Protestant Parnell . . . with majestic presence and oceans of dignity and sentiment" (CP 447). The master of projection, however, envied his secret mentor and translated his "pujealousties" into Shavian disapproval of himself, transforming his guilty conscience (over his negative review, his piracy of Shaw's plays, his bad-mouthing, and his "stolentelling") into Shavian retaliation in all of the imagined brother battles of *Finnegans Wake,* which are condensed in the conflicts of Hosty's ballad. The regressive and irrational poem transforms anxieties over the Irish troubles into a denial of the death wish symbolized by Cain and thus into implicit affirmation of the nonviolent integration of personality that recurs in the *ricorso.* In rejecting, like Shaw, the collective death instinct of Western civilization symbolized by the Irish "Troubles," the ballad offers a hallucinatory vision of Ireland as a microcosm of the envy, greed, disloyalties, and territoriality that have thus far characterized humankind. It evokes the faults on both sides of the struggle between British imperialism and Irish nationalism. Cain/Cromwell (of stanza 1), with an admixture of Scandinavian Olaf ("Olafa Crumple"), represents the ineffectuality of murderous hate and religious persecution—as the redundant Bloom puts it, the mistake of "perpetuating national hatred between nations" (U 12.1417–18). Pearse/O'Rahilly represents the ineffectuality of blood sacrifice, for inviting martyrdom is passive aggression and masochistic glorification of victimization. To underscore the chaos caused by hatred, the rest of the poem ranges over victims and victimizers, usurping invaders, and capricious public opinion that collaborates with officialdom to destroy men like Parnell and Wilde, both of whom, however, participated in their own downfalls.

Eviction too is relative, good or bad depending upon whether one is evictor or evicted. Hence Parnell expelled the editor who betrayed him. John Joyce and tenants like him were evicted, as was Adam from Eden, by victimizing landlords, but they were also implicated in their own tragedies. When Clancy's presence at the political ejection dissolves into the bailiff who has come to throw the "bum" out, the eviction becomes a conflict between landlord and tenant. The displaced tenant is no doubt John Joyce. The merciless pub customers who form the chorus of the ballad, as changeable as irrational self-interest, demand, "With his rent in his rears, Give him six years!" (47.11–12). With the bailiff's bond—"bailiff's bom at the door" (46.9)—the Irishman is in danger of being thrown out (Joyce's father shamelessly escaped actual eviction by moving his family to new quarters in the middle of the night, leaving no forwarding address). Entering with the "bailiff's bom" is John Joyce, who has been lurking in the shadows with the process-server, who is knocking "Bimbam at the door. / Then he'll bum no more" (46.10–11). The bum is H. C. E. as John Joyce, who turns up later in an allusion to the story of how Buckley shot the Russian general, a tale that Joyce's father told him.

Joyce set the action of the *Wake* near the Wellington monument in Phoenix Park for another Irishman who betrayed his homeland through expatriation and became the hero of the Battle of Waterloo, thus ironically making the Irish proud of him, even though he was fighting in the interests of their oppressors, the British. In the distorted dream, allusion to him occurs adjacent to reference to the father because his mysterious sin in Phoenix Park haunts the dreamer. As the general in Phoenix Park, H. C. E., like other warriors, "caught his death of fusiliers" (47.10), but even more important, as father John Joyce, he is about to be evicted, as Adam and Eve were from Eden and as the Joyces often were because of John's unaccountability. Even the tense inconsistencies, juxtaposing past, present, and future willy-nilly, communicate the futile pattern and parallels of personal, mythic, and Irish history. Comparable in some respects to many of the Irish poor who suffered eviction from their homes, the father is, nevertheless, like Parnell and Wilde, excoriated by the chorus. The fickle crowd's answer to all of Ireland's social problems seems to be prison for the miscreant who has not followed their rules, rules ironically established by their oppressors. H. C. E.'s family, like Joyce's, is victimized because of his irresponsible behavior. "Tis sore pity for his innocent poor children / But look out for his missus legitimate!" (47.13–14).

Thus the ballad about ejections by various landlords includes Joyce's father, who, as a feckless alcoholic raconteur, represented from the unionist point of view the stereotypical Irishman. Like tenant farmers, the city man was a Guinness patriot, noisily favoring Parnell. Like other Parnellites, he lost political patronage after the death of Ireland's "King," whose ancestors were among the invaders of Ireland. They came, paradoxically, by "sweet bad luck," "washed to our island" on the waves (46.12). In this line we should note Joyce's code for Shaw—"washed"—for Shaw's ancestors shared the heritage of Parnell's, who were welcomed, it seems, by "the hooker of that hammerfast viking" (46.13). This last description is an inebriated publican's aspersion of Kitty O'Shea and an allusion to Dergovilla, whose abduction by Dermot MacMurrough led to his appeal to Plantagenet Henry II to come to Ireland as his ally; perhaps to Shaw's Nora Reilly; and to all Irish women like the one Davin describes in *Portrait* standing in her doorway to lure the stranger in. For Hosty's ballad derides heroism, but it degrades women. Insofar as they appear at all, women are dismissed as whores or as sacrificial wives and mothers, or they are spoofed as bisexual combinations of power and sexuality. In the rann there is no "Dark Rosaleen" because, like Shaw, Joyce deplored romantic patriotism, though he admired J. C. Mangan, who translated the anonymous "Roiseen Dubh," a poem admiring the female who inspires Irishmen to give themselves to blood and flames.

The line "The general lost her maidenloo!" (46.33) alludes to Napoleon, hero of Shaw's *Man of Destiny* and a major comic representative of violent power in *Methuselah*. In both Shaw plays he is foiled by females and thus made into a womanly man, like Bloom in Barney Kiernan's pub, accused of being "half and half" (U 12.1052–53). The cross-dressing and sexual crossing that tempted Joyce in *Ulysses* and the *Wake* are in Hosty's poem summarized in the general who "lost her maidenloo." The line may refer obliquely to Kevin Egan, the Fenian exile and dynamitard whom Joyce sought out in 1902, during his first trip to Paris, for he is the patriot type that "The Ballad of Persse O'Reilly" rejects—a demented and compulsively jingoistic fanatic over "lost leaders, the betrayed, wild escapes" (Malcolm Brown 224). As Brown writes, Egan's "patristic and sexual fantasies interchange with each other as forms of death" (225). They prefigure Hosty's poem. In Phoenix Park, H. C. E. is apparently tempted by an androgynous Eve comparable to the one in Shaw's Eden. The "hooker" (which is also a boat) who waits for the invaders is derogated by masculine stereotyping, the sort in which the citizen indulges in *Ulysses*. He blames "the strangers" for Ireland's troubles. "The adulteress and her paramour brought the Saxon robbers here" (12.1156–58). And in the cabman's shelter, the proprietor, like Deasy in the Nestor section, blames the femme fatale: "That bitch, that English whore [Kitty O'Shea] did for him.... She put the first nail in his coffin" (16.1352–53). In *Ulysses* too, Mina Purefoy, the womanly woman whose faith is pure, is comparable to the pitiable legitimate mother and wife of the evictee in Hosty's rann. Here the females, the occasions or victims of male "sin," are in the mind of the dreamer as fragmented as the males. The "missus legitimate" with the "innocent poor children" represents all victimized wives and mothers on the May Joyce model.

Whereas the mother woman is a victim, the female betrayers in Joyce's deconstruction of Irish history fraternized with the usurpers, whom Hosty, as a good "Gall," curses on the day "when Eblana bay / Saw his black and tan man-o'-war" (46.14–15). Because of "Eblana," Ptolemy's name for Dublin, Hosty's line condenses past and present allusions to invaders of Ireland who arrived by water—like the man-of-war that came up the Liffey to shell Dublin during the Easter Rising, the Black and Tan auxiliaries sent to Ireland in 1920 to suppress the revolutionary activity that followed the uprising, or Cromwell in the seventeenth century. All represented power and co-optation through carnage. As an example of the strongman bent on the destruction and domination of Ireland—like Cain, the murderous brother who vanishes at the end of *Back to Methuselah*—Cromwell appears in the ballad at the beginning and at the end. Humpty Dumpty, in the first stanza, "fell . . . / And curled up like Lord Olofa Crumple," whose theocratic efforts to decimate Ireland collapsed when he died. Such carnage cannot, Hosty optimistically avers in the last stanza of the poem, be resurrected, "For there's no true spell in Connacht or hell / That's able to raise a Cain" (47.28–29). This ending plays, ironically, on Cromwell's battle cry while he was ravaging Ireland and driving the Catholic Gaels west—"To hell or Connacht," the desolate part of Ireland to which the lord protector condemned the Irish if he failed to massacre them. It also evokes the part of Ireland where some of the worst skirmishes in the Land War occurred. In *John Bull's Other Island,* set in the west of Ireland, Keegan—ex-priest and seer—writes his own rann about his country, pronouncing it to be the "place of horror and torment known . . . [as] hell" (Plays 449). Shaw's play treats as farcical the "invasion" of Erin by the bumptiously efficient Englishman Broadbent, a comic parallel to others who seized power in Hibernia. G. B. S. prefigured Joyce in ridiculing such usurpation and in rejecting the physical-force movement. The preface to *Man and Superman* decries "the Fenian who collects money from thoughtless Irish Americans to blow up Dublin Castle" (CP 178).

Nevertheless, the invaders have Shavian blood. Shaw wrote, "I have no trace in me of the commercially imported North Spanish strain which passes for aboriginal Irish"—which perhaps exempts him from the strain and stigma revealed in "Balbaccio, balbuccio"—but he admitted to being an amalgam of the invaders of Ireland (CP 442). In Joyce's ballad the Protestant invaders all become one in H. C. E., whose ancestors are Saxon, Norman French, and Scandinavian, sighted from Poolbeg Lighthouse in Dublin—"Poolbeg. . . . Donnez-moi" (46.18–19) for the Normans came saying "Give me," while marauding Norsemen came with "Norveegickers moniker" and as "a Norwegian camel old cod" (46.21–23), like the fishy Shaw. This stanza also compacts Oscar Wilde and Finn MacCool with Shaw's O'Flaherty, and Shaw with Pope Boniface, in "Fingal Mac Oscar Onesine Bargearse Boniface" (46.20). Oscar Fingal O'Flahertie Wilde, the Anglo-Irishman who shared a name with Shaw's proletarian Catholic hero and shared the dubious distinction of being brought down, like Parnell, by "sin," "onesine," is adjacent to "Bargearse," which may allude to the rude, pushy Joe Biggar and the "arse" Shaw, who masqueraded as pope. The pope is present in his own right, however, in another example of the betrayers of Ireland, for to both Shaw and Joyce, Roman Catholicism was more part of the Irish problem than of its solution.

But in Ireland, as Shaw's preface to *John Bull's Other Island* makes clear, many among the Protestant minority were proud of being Irish and were even, like Parnell, Anglophobes. Compressed in H. C. E. are many protties, like the "Norwegian camel old cod" (46.23), whose name implies a camel hump and thus perhaps Joe Biggar, the hunchback M.P. who at first supported Parnell but then turned on him. His hump may also be the burden of sin that John Bunyan's Pilgrim carries on his back, for Shaw was a devotee of *Pilgrim's Progress* even though he rejected its brand of Protestantism. The cod connotes Ireland's victimization as one cheated as well as the mythical salmon of wisdom of the hero Finn and "Old Parr" Shaw, who is related to fish throughout the *Wake* and hence to ICTHUS, symbolizing Christ. From his first "Passion Play" to the end of his career as a dramatist, Shaw had boldly identified himself as a redeemer. In retort to such outrageous pride, Joyce seems to mock the "old cod" as a variant of the scapegoat Christ whose sign was ICTHUS. He is related to Bloom, called a "cod" in *Ulysses,* whose Bloomusalem fantasies match Shaw's paradisiacal vision in *Methuselah.*

G. B. S. courted comparison to Christ (and the Irish also made the comparison with regard to the lost messiah Parnell), though he despised the "Crosstianity" whose symbol for redemption through suffering was to him an offensive and heinously inhuman sign of torture—the human tendency toward cruelty that he hoped individual will and Creative Evolution would obviate. Pearse's morality of blood sacrifice was as much anathema to Shaw as Cromwell's brutality in the name of the Christian God. Shaw's favored dramatic characters court crucifixion but, except for Saint Joan, escape it to go on living in the world, continuing to do good as inverted Christ figures, devil's advocates, thorns in the side of official culture, but also scapegoat redeemers. Plays like *The Devil's Disciple, Major Barbara, Androcles and the Lion,* and *Saint Joan* all support Joyce's association of Shaw with fish, even as the scapegoat of Joycean hostility and the object of a cannibalistic communion in which Joyce devours and transforms his spiritual father. The *Wake* admittedly concerns "that samesake sibsubstitute of a hooky salmon" (28.35) who is at times "too funny for a fish" (127.2). Throughout the *Wake* Shem seems to be eating the substance of the old fish in an ironic communion with the "Gee [who] . . . smells fish. That's U" (299 n.3). The U with whom Joyce's dreamer dialogues in his night thoughts is identified with a Shavian persona, "Selvertunes O'Haggans" (299.23)—Shaw as his phonetics expert Professor Higgins of *Pygmalion*.

Character assassination, political martyrdom, and war were not, however, part of Shaw's program for saving the world. Like Parnell, he tried to educate his audiences to seek nonviolent, parliamentarian solutions, despite characters like Undershaft and Caesar, who makes the devastating concession that Ruffio has done right in killing Cleopatra's dangerous maid. Nevertheless, the author of *Common Sense about the War* preferred to be the prince of peace. In his essay "Shaw and the Uncrucifying of Christ," Richard Dietrich points out a pattern in Shavian dramas that the astute Joyce must also have noted: Shaw repeatedly revealed that "the Cross is no place to rest, unless one is fond of 'deadends.' The purpose of the disillusionment and alienation [of Shaw's heroes and heroines] is to carry one through to enlightenment, rebirth, growth, and social integration" (35). Joyce's rann prophesies the Shavian vision: fallen "heroes of warhorror" will not be born again when humankind has evolved beyond raising Cain. Subtextually,

Hosty's ballad scorns, as Shaw did, what the playwright called "Bardicide" and Joyce called "sibicidal" rivalry, implying that, when hostilities are rejected, rebirth and personality integration will be concomitants of the enlightening reconciliations of a *ricorso.*

In any case, in the ballad, the "heavyweight heathen," while at the Phoenix Park Zoo, "made bold a maiden to woo" (46.29–30), as Adam did in Eden and in the prelude to *Methuselah.* As a "heavyweight heathen," he may be related to Shaw's pugilist lover Cashel Byron in *Cashel Byron's Profession.* After the wooing, however, when "the general lost her maidenloo!" Napoleon slips into the dream-poem because Joyce had become aware that Parnell's ideal was probably Bonapartism, a plebiscite monarchy, or perhaps because Napoleon was Shaw's symbol for the legendary strongman, who was ultimately unsuccessful. In Hosty's ballad his sex change—a subject that fascinated both Irishmen—may ridicule Shaw's insistence upon presenting womanly men and masculine women. Joyce omits reference to strong Irish women like Constance Markievitz and Maud Gonne. In making fun of the sexual role reversal, he implies the Shavian theme of woman as pursuer in sex. Like the general in Shaw's *Press Cuttings,* Napoleon becomes passive in Hosty's sexual stereotyping, female in the "heroticism" of Joyce's imagination. Whether or not Joyce was thinking of Shaw, he let Hosty take the view of hackneyed Irish prejudice by saying, "He ought to blush for himself, the old hayheaded philosopher / For to go and shove himself that way on top of her" (47.1–2). Besides indicating that H. C. E.'s sin is sexual, the lines refer to one of Shaw's favorite ploys—superimposing himself as male upon his female characters, "ventriloquist's puppets," according to William Archer. H. C. E. is a "ventriloquent Agitator" (56.5–6). To Max Beerbohm, "all of Shaw's characters are but so many incarnations of himself" (quoted in Evans 151, 155).

Most significantly, "the old hayheaded philosopher," among whose adumbrations are Adam and Methuselah, is "the crux of the catalogue / Of our antediluvial zoo" (47.1–4). In *Man and Superman*'s "Don Juan in Hell," Juan chooses to be "the philosophic man" because other sorts are "tedious failures" (Plays 379–80). G. K. Chesterton's study of Shaw emphasized the playwright's reputation as a philosopher. In correcting his "Biographer's Blunders," Shaw noted with reference to "The MacManus Biography in Winsten's G. B. S. 90" that "my auburn hair was never really Highland red like my sister Agnes'. But I was a 'blonde beast' of Danish type unmistakably" (SSS 15). Shaw was flaxenhaired in his youth, despite his red beard, but in old age his ideas made him seem "hayheaded"—lightweight, airy, even harebrained, despite being irresistible to his adroit plagiarist. In *Back to Methuselah* all of the avatars of Adam could be catalogued as resembling their creator, just as Joyce's kaleidoscopic archetype of H. C. E. often shapes itself as Shaw.

Titillated by sexual sin (in Parnell, Wilde, Shaw, and Joyce—the principals of the poem), Hosty's bawdy voyeuristic chorus inconsistently relishes the thought of a sentimental but alternatively homosexual liaison, like Wilde's, with "Messrs. Billing and Coo. / Noah's larks, good as noo" (47.5–6) suggests that old larking Noah, like Methuselah, survives disaster, as do Shaw's Ancients in his Pentateuch and H. C. E., rising to begin again, whereas erring sons of violence do not. Thus the ballad deals with the two antennae of the Earwig, both of the parts of Earwicker in conflict. "When that frew gets a grip" on him (whether "frew" be the flu or the crew / few of his tormentors), there will "be earwigs on the green" (47.15–16)—in College Green—representing divided selves, the insect earwig, which, torn apart, fights itself as the Irish do. The reductive insect image augurs Ireland's Civil War in 1922–23. Earwig also means to fill the mind with prejudice by insinuation, which is just what the clerical and conforming Catholic enemies of Ireland's potential redeemers did. In Joyce's absurdist nightmare ballad, insinuating, divisive prejudice causes the fall of Parnell, the failure of the 1916 uprising, and the condemnation in Ireland of writers like himself, Wilde, and Shaw.

Shaw, however, surmounted difficulties with censorship to become a hero in Ireland. His plays dominated the Abbey Theatre in 1917 after he had begun to prove himself to be an Irish patriot, despite Yeats's censorship of both *John Bull's Other Island* and *O'Flaherty V.C.* The vainglorious, self-advertising playwright thought of himself, Joyce imagined, as "Suffoclose! Shikespower! Seudodanto! Anonymoses!" (47.19). The fractured list of literary masters and visionaries—set off in a one-line stanza—is comparable to Shaw's comic condensations in *Back to Methuselah*: "Shakespeare, Shelley, Sheridan, and Shoddy" (211), "spiritual leaders . . . Blitherinjam, Tosh, and Spiffkins" (214), and historians "Thycyderodotus Macollybuckell" (239). The introduction of Joyce's catalogue creates the tension of the rann, for the works of Sophocles, Shakespeare, Dante, and Moses represent the inversion of

Hosty's malevolent skepticism, the triumph over death through the word. According to the tragedians, catastrophe can be ennobling; according to Dante's dream vision, a pilgrimage through hell may lead through purgatory to a heavenly vision; according to the Pentateuch ascribed to Moses, a people can escape bondage and go to the promised land, even though the seer himself does not enter it. All four suggest the progress of Shaw's Pentateuch and Joyce's aspirations, implicit in the pattern of the *Wake*. The presence of the masters corroborates Shaw's theme—that only Cains, heroes of "warhorror," deadend, whereas the creative sons of Eve begin again. In the *Wake* Shaw is a Virgil to Joyce's Dante. Hosty's rann ends in "Connacht or hell," from which Cain cannot be raised, but the cycles of the *Wake* emulate the pilgrim's progress of *Methuselah*.

"Anonymoses" compacts Parnell and the patriarch of Shaw's Pentateuch. Although Gladstone called Parnell the Moses of the Irish, Michael Davitt suspected the "Moses of the Irish race" to be the idol of a cult of hero-worship because he "had counseled militance and victorious militance carried him on its shoulders for its emblem" (Malcolm Brown 304). Therefore, in Hosty's rann, unlike "the old hayheaded philosopher," he is one of the sons of Cain. Like Moses, he did not live to see the promised land any more than the aged Shaw would, even though he posited a new Eden in *Back to Methuselah*. Thus "Suffoclose! Shikespower! Seudodanto! Anonymoses!" simultaneously suggest the affirmations of *Methuselah* and the *Wake* and twit Shaw—and Joyce himself, a twin in ambition—for his prideful aspiration to surpass the Greek and Elizabethan masters of drama as well as the spiritual guides of Christianity and Judaism. In the introduction to *Our Theatre in the Nineties* Shaw wrote, with straight-faced bravado, that "the apostolic succession from Aeschylus to myself is as serious and as continually inspired as that younger institution, the apostolic succession of the Christian church" (CP 779). Indeed, the audacious dramatist compared himself favorably to the Greek masters Aeschylus, Sophocles, and Euripides and dared to consider his discussion dramas "better than Shakespeare" (CP 748), anticipating Joyce. According to James Atherton, Joyce "saw himself as Shakespeare's rival—possibly as his greatest rival" (162), even though he and his contemporaries knew that Shaw was, as foremost dramatist of his time, a stronger competitor.

Identifying with Shaw, Joyce no doubt chose Sophocles because the

Greek writer's *Oedipus Rex* acts out a struggle like the one Joyce experienced with his literary father. Also, he no doubt chose Shakespeare because both he and Shaw had publicized their challenges to the Bard. In *Stephen Hero* Joyce had argued that "the classical drama . . . was dead and so was Shakespeare" (see 41). Davis comments that "peculiarly Bernard Shaw, who was Joyce's elder and in many ways his opposite, had similarly denounced Shakespeare and embraced Ibsen" (45). The oddity disappears, however, when one realizes how often Joyce plundered Shaw for instigation and corroboration of his apocryphal ideas. In Hosty's ballad, the references to Dante and Moses underscore Joyce's attempt to co-opt in the *Wake* the optimistic "religious" message of *Methuselah*. As spiritual guide and writer of the Pentateuch of the new religion, Shaw consciously compared himself to Dante and Moses. Even though Joyce mocks Shaw and himself as "Seudodanto" and "Anonymoses," reference to Dante suggests that lost violent souls will not be reborn, while also vouchsafing the believer entrance to the promised land. A pseudoguide to spiritual life, Shaw was anonymous Moses in the *Wake* because Joyce assiduously covered up his identity.

In Hosty's rann, the archetypal writer and philosopher is distinguished from the archetypal hero of Ireland's political history, for when the hero is to be waked, Hosty proposes that the funeral be the sort of vulgar public brouhaha associated with the interment of a political figure—Parnell, perhaps the socialist sides of Shaw and Wilde, or John Joyce as a Parnell supporter. At Parnell's death the Irish Republican Brotherhood claimed him, appropriating him as a Fenian hero of physical force. *United Ireland* made him a martyr and demanded that he be avenged. A hundred thousand to a hundred fifty thousand people, "depending on the political bias of the witness," marched in the funeral procession (Malcolm Brown 346–47). Hosty declares, "Then we'll have a free trade Gaels' band and mass meeting / For to sod the brave son of Scandiknavery" (47.20–21). Free trade was the desideratum of which union with Great Britain had deprived the Irish. On this, as on every political issue, Shaw had an opinion. As a borough councillor, he gave an address on free trade in 1903 in which he argued that "preference be given 'to goods that are produced under humane and decent conditions' and a handicap be put on 'goods that are produced by slavery'" (PP 235). Hence his support of free trade was qualified. For the Irish, however, free trade bands symbolized the thwarted economic freedom of the Irish while they were marginalized by British colonialism, whose economic policies deprived the Irish of free markets. Brass bands were often assembled to lead the funeral corteges of slain Irish patriots. Although laissez-faire capitalism and Celtic music suggest the inconsistencies of Shaw and Joyce as partially fictionalized in Leopold Bloom, to Anglo-Irish like G. B. S., Parnell, and Wilde, such a funeral would no doubt have been a vulgar incongruity. All three, however, had the necessary Scandinavian ancestry and, in the popular mind, the knavery to finagle such a funeral. The Joyce clan, although Catholic, might have inspired the dreamer to include his own roistering father at such a wake.

Significantly, however, the composite patriarch will not be buried in Glasnevin Cemetery, where Parnell lies near Daniel O'Connell (whose monster meetings featured Gaels' bands) and Joyce's parents are buried. Instead, "we'll bury him down in Oxmanstown / Along with the devil and Danes" (47.22–23). Besides evoking the fact that the corpses of both Robert Emmet and Parnell had briefly lain in St. Michans, Oxmanstown suggests yet another brave defender of Ireland, Jonathan Swift, who is buried in St. Patrick's Cathedral in Oxmanstown, the old Danish section of Dublin. Seumas MacManus's 1921 *The Story of the Irish Race* calls Swift a "true Irish type of the line Shane O'Neill [proud resister of Elizabeth I], Parnell, G. B. Shaw" (697), all of whom Joyce combines in Shaun, whose Scandinavian ancestors might be buried in St. Michans, where the Sheares brothers, executed as insurgents in the 1798 rebellion against the English, are coffined. Perhaps more important, they share the crypt with five mummies that are nearly five hundred years old, one of which is an eight-foot Crusader, who must have reminded Joyce of Finn MacCool.

Thus in St. Michan's the tiering of Irish heroes is a visible reminder of the fact that one cannot "raise a Cain" (although tourists can shake hands with the giant), for although the heroes of Ireland are everywhere superimposed upon each other in a history of betrayal, dispossession, and blood sacrifice, Hosty's garbled barroom ballad, like *Methuselah*, ends by denying the resurrection of the archetypal strongman. Like Yeats's late, gloomy poem "Parnell's Funeral," Joyce's comic incongruities end in impasse. Both celebrate rites of passage that do not lead to rebirth of the hero redeemer, but the difference is between a Shavian and a Yeatsian outlook. Yeats bitterly lamented the loss of the aristocratic cultural ideal, whereas *Back to Methuselah* rejects such reactionary disillusionment. Although all three Irishmen distrusted the "rabblement" and were disillusioned with Irish politics, the two expatriates rejected heroic violence without rejecting Ireland. Yeats's belief that "all that was sung, all that was said in Ireland is a lie" (275) prompted the aged poet to despise political solutions and to escape into art, the only source of yea-saying, even though as late as 1937 he was still sentimentalizing Parnell, who, in his description, "loved his country / And . . . loved his lass" (307).

Shaw was tougher and more optimistic. Although Irish leaders like O'Connell, Parnell, and Pearse had failed to lead Ireland to the promised land, *Methuselah* showed the way over the long haul of history. The "Tragedy of an Elderly Gentleman" makes the Ireland of saints and sages the center of the spiritual life of a brave new world: its capital (perhaps prophetically) is Baghdad, which continues the old internecine backstabbing politics of betrayal. At Burrin Pier in Galway, however, wisdom prevails, and to the wise Irish sybil the Elderly Gentleman has made his hegira. At her touch he dies of discouragement, but centuries later he has become a wise Ancient, a "hayheaded philosopher." Joyce's linguistic and comic tour de force resolves its dialectic with Shaw/Shaun and Shaw/H. C. E. in affirmation of the integrated selfhood, which has expunged the aspects of personality that relate to the archetypal strongman; for, with Shaw, Joyce recognized that the cycles of senseless violence would not end while the blood lust for power reigned. Without resorting to violence, *John Bull's Other Island* demonstrates that throughout Irish history "the same attitudes and values are perpetuated: As much as things change, they remain the same" (Swarzlander 86). Like the men of Parnell who were disunited after his death, "not all the king's men nor his horses / Will resurrect his corpus" (47.26–27)—the corpus of violent men who died for rival causes as betrayers betrayed. A pacifistic artist who prefigured Joyce's own revulsion from violence, the Methuselan Shaw whose weakness was his delusion of being the equal of Sophocles, Shakespeare, Dante, and Moses was not a Cain figure any more than Joyce was, despite the younger Irishman's fratricidal fantasies. Things change in the *Wake* only for the sons of Eve whose creative work of progress leads to reconciliation of contraries and hence to a higher form of personality integration.

In "Don Juan in Hell" Shaw set up the dichotomy upon one side of which Joyce's ballad focuses: the Devil argues that "the power that governs earth is not the power of Life but of Death" (Plays 376), but the philosophical proponent of the Life Force rejects human violence as well as hell, the realm of pleasure and art. Joyce's ballad focuses on the Irish death wish but repudiates the lost leaders fixed in the Irish hell. The end of the ballad foreshadows the *ricorso* in which Shem no longer raises the Cain in himself to attack his "hoary frother." Emulating the Shavian paradigm for the eventual peaceable kingdom, Joyce dismissed centuries of intolerance by unifying the battling brothers and the superannuated father. In *Methuselah* the power figure who glorifies bloodshed turns up in each play with Cain as his bloodthirsty model, followed prominently by Napoleon and Shelley's Ozymandius, symbols of Shaw's disapproval of arrogant power brokers as betrayers of the human enterprise. The optimist Shaw believed that, given long life in which to learn from mistakes, humankind would, through strenuous creativity, evolve through cyclical time an ideal republic in which Cain would disappear, because violence is never a resolution of human problems. At the end of "As Far as Thought Can Reach" and hence of Shaw's gospel, Cain reappears momentarily only to be ousted, no longer needed and thus never to reappear. While disdaining Irish betrayal and usurpation, Joyce's disorienting ballad ends on the Shavian note, consonant with Shaw's hopeful prediction of a future in which political and artistic martyrdom will disappear.

The hallucinatory poem denounces the disunity and degradation of Irish politics and the treacherous mob's fickle loyalties in favor of the Bloomo-Shavian interpretation of history while at the same time laying a hero of Shavian lineage in the grave. The obscurity of the poem, like that of the *Wake,* is in part the result of Joyce's simulation of the dreamwork of the unconscious, in which repressed materials well up into dream, discretely unrepressed and dispersed into substitutions for the self, releasing the instincts of aggression while revealing the dreamer's ambivalence toward Parnell and toward his literary progenitor as well as hostility toward his father and English tyranny. The anxiety dream rejects Freudian adjustment to the internalized demands of society even though it evokes them. The Irish do not get even. They get destroyed or humiliated. Wish fulfillment emerges, however, in the overall pattern that buries the dead.

As early as 1905 Joyce echoed his mentor by insisting that he was not "prepared to be crucified to attest to the perfection" of his art, and even then he disdained "stray heroics" (JJL 2:83). A dream of the psychology, cultural ethos, and politics of the marginalized Irish, Joyce's ballad nevertheless concludes with Shavian sublimation of the killer instinct that paralyzes personal growth and political progress. It is prefigured by the ending of *Methuselah,* in which the creative intelligence facing death turns to the self "as to the final reality" (295). A culmination of centuries of Irish pain, the rann ends in a prophetic breakthrough, not a breakdown, of the ego ideal, thus ending with tragicomic resolution, like a Shaw play, which foreshadows the overall structure of the *Wake.* In *Methuselah* all of the philosopher king's horses would not try to reassemble the dangerous automata produced by the inventor Pygmalion. As products of deterministic cause and effect instead of the creatively evolving Life Force, they perpetuate the cycles of destruction and death.

In *The Quintessence of Ibsenism,* at the conclusion of the account of Ibsen's *When We Dead Awaken,* Shaw wrote that he hoped the last of Ibsen's plays would mean the end of "idols, domestic, moral, religious, and political, in whose name we have been twaddled into misery and confusion and hypocrisy unspeakable. For Ibsen's dead hand still keeps the grip he laid on their masks when he first tore them off: and whilst that grip holds, all the king's horses and all the king's men will find it hard to set Humpty-Dumpties up again" (MCE 140). Decades later, Shaw's disciple and fellow Ibsenite, whose first published review was of *When We Dead Awaken,* was still tearing the masks off of Irish political idols. The Shavian lesson had taken hold. The false ideals of romantic nationalism will not, Hosty asserts, awaken when Finn again awakes. In Joyce's ballad, all of the king's men, seemingly trained by Swift's Houyhnhnms and Shaw's Ancients, will not "raise a Cain."

"Jaunty Jaun": The "Brave Footsore" "Unfrillfrocked Quackfriar"

In the most significant casting of one side of the *Wake*'s shifty dialectic, Joyce transforms Shaun into Jaun, a variant of Don Juan, Shaw's alter ego John Tanner in *Man and Superman.* The assertion of the playwright who put Tanner in hell that "a funeral was always a festivity in black, especially the funeral of a relative" (CP 370), must have been an incitement to the author of the "funferal" *Wake.* When Shem places the "initial T" on Shaun/Jaun/Yawn's temple (486.15), he may be marking him as Tanner. A representative of the iconoclastic puritanism of Shaw's

Don Juan, Jaun is, like Shaun, a "Slavocrates" (328.12) because Shaw had proclaimed that his plays were "Shavo-Socratic dialogues," the symposium in "Don Juan in Hell" being among the most notable. In "Slavocrates" is also compacted the Shavian enthusiasm for the Slavs of Bolshevik Russia. Shaw is also "Paud the Roosky" (335.24) because of his honorary Russian citizenship and because, in Joyce's skewed dream, he is a moneygrubbing paudeen (huckster), who "half for the laugh of the bliss" created "sint barbaras" (335.24-27)—Saint Joan and Major Barbara. Unlike the libertine popularized by Tirso de Molina, Mozart, and Byron, Joyce's Jaun is, like Shaw, a dapper preacher and workaholic. "Jaunty Jaun" is a theatrical favorite who doffs his hat and bows to a "chorus of praise of goodwill girls" (430.18-19), Salvation Army "girls" like Major Barbara. Based on Shaw's reputation, Jaun, "just the killingest ladykiller all by kindness" (430.32-33), was a "lover of lithury, bekant or besant" (432.32)—a lover of literature/liturgy, Kant, and Annie Besant, the freethinker who joined the Fabian Society and fell in love with Shaw (only later to become a famed spiritualist). As Shaun the postman, Jaun seems to be a lover. The "throsands" of letters "for my darling Typette" (478.2-3) may be from Shaw. Iseult's lover is addressed as "Jaunick" (457.36) (thus blurring the identity of the writer between Jaun and Nick), "Joke" (458.13), and "joey" (460.36), Stella Campbell's pet name for Shaw.

In the so-called "Second Watch of Shaun" (book 3, chapter 2), Jaun, an adumbration of Shaun the Post, is, like elocutionist Shaw, concerned with his method of delivery: "Jaun delivered himself with express cordiality, marked by clearance of diction and general delivery" (431.21-22), because he maintains his role as mailman. His sermon reveals some of the inconsistencies that Joyce noted in his mentor, who boldly mated the socialist and capitalist superman. The speech, as Cheryl Herr points out, has an "economic matrix" (271). Hence Jaun's "brokerly advice" (439.27) exaggerates to an absurdity the sort of prudent advice that the millionaire Shaw, a meticulous financial manager, might give. His student and critic could not forgive him for his Marxist analysis of the economic basis of social problems while in his private life he was a good businessman, investor, and hard bargainer, and proud of it. Furthermore, as Herr notes, "For Jaun, virtue is a matter of correct upper class (British) behavior" (273). His "virtues" and manners replicate Shaw's, especially those of the aging Nobel laureate, though Fabian socialism was always a gentlemanly, middle-class association of well-bred men and women dissatisfied with social conditions and pressuring for reform. Nevertheless, in the role of fancy man that may have shocked his Fabian friends, young Shaw identified himself as an Irish Don Juan. His cohorts called him Don Giovanni "in recognition of his love of Mozart's opera as well as his supposedly incorrigible philandering. In 1887 he had written a little story 'Don Giovanni Explains' " (Silver 130). Marriage was, however, birdlime for such flights of fancy. His disciple, whom Nora Barnacle called a "Woman Killer" (JJ New 294) must have identified with Shaw's portrait of the Shavian artist as a young man.

Thus Jaun's sermon is an "*Egg Laid by Former Cock*" (440.20): in *Methuselah*, it will be remembered, reproduction is oviparous in the land of the Ancients, whereas Shaw had made himself well-known as a young writer for championing free love, in which he was an active participant until his marriage to Charlotte Townshend. Jaun's lecture on sexual purity distorts Shaw's postmarriage stance on celibacy to make it look foolish: "Lust, thou shalt not commix idolatry" (433.23). The "former cock" who now advocates female virginity is parodied as an ecclesiastic. He admonishes St. Bride's girls (Shaw's uncle having been vicar of St. Bride's Church), "Remember, maid, thou dust art powder but Cinderella thou must return" (440.26–27). Sounding a bit like Saint Joan, who lectures Bertrand de Poulengey while insisting on calling him Polly, Jaun admonishes "Polly" to pull in her tongue (440.28). He disapproves of "Mr Smuth" (434.36), the scurrilous smut peddlar Shem, and salacious "college swankies" (438.32) like Joyce and Oliver Gogarty. Jaun opposes "secret satieties and onanymous letters" (435.31) such as Shem's masturbatory fantasies, which are comparable to his interest in secret societies like the Freemasons. When Jaun advises "pious fiction . . . licensed and censered" (440.8–11), he is unlike Shaw and more like Grace Eckley's candidate for the H. C. E./Shaun identity—William Stead, sexist lust-sleuth seeking to establish the ideal of sexual purity, whom Shaw deemed "pestiferous" (MCE 55–57). Unquestionably some of Shaw's plays, such as *Androcles, Methuselah,* and *Saint Joan,* could be called pious fictions, but when Jaun advises, "Burn the books" (439.34), Joyce is throwing us off the Shavian scent, for G. B. S. was throughout life an opponent of censorship and, despite his own prudishness, a defender of free choice in sexual matters.

The changeable Jaun seems to represent the Shaw who made a virtue of necessity because he married a frigid woman. To the girls, he advises, "Keep cool your fresh chastity" (440.31–32). Perhaps G. B. S.'s Eve in "In the Beginning" is to Jaun "a colleen coy, [but] a blush on a bush turned first man's laughter into wailful moither" (433.28–30). When Shaw's Snake whispers to Eve what she must do to propagate the species, she is at first intensely amused and interested, but then "an expression of overwhelming repugnance" comes on her face (BM 79). Replicating the biblical Genesis, Eve's coupling with Adam produces their violent son Cain, who brings willful murder into the world and who is satirized by Shaw as a sexist bully. Herr notes that Joyce considers the Fall merely "a result of misfortune or sheer chance" (273), a point that Shaw was at pains to make in the opening play of the Pentateuch, where accident and the discovery of language to describe it (not sin) bring death into the world. Whereas Jaun's sermon, as a "demystifying challenge of the church's transcendence of the everyday" (Herr 258), is Shavian, its satire of Jaun as a pretentious preacher ridicules Shaw, who had throughout his career used the platform as a pulpit from which to propagate his subversive morality. Shaw proclaimed that the "cart and the trumpet" were his media. Jaun "blew his own trumpet" (470.28) with Shavian gusto.

From his platform-pulpit Shaw delivered sermons peppered with the wit of the music hall, such as he put into his plays. Joyce seems to have been an especially astute critic of the preacher's form, for, as Herr notes, "Jaun's sermon becomes as much a revolt against religion's assumptions of authority as a music-hall sermon was" (259). As such, the sermon unmasks the Shavian inconsistency of combining a saintly moral tone with concerns for money—a willful misinterpretation on the part of the jealous Joyce, for it was common knowledge that Shaw refused payment for his soapbox oratory (he got rich from his plays), whether he was attacking Christianity or advocating exercise and vegetarianism. Nevertheless, "He prophets most who bilks the best" (305.1–2) is part of the lesson Shaun, later to be Jaun, is teaching Shem. Like a priestly Shavian health addict, Jaun advises "healthy physicking exorcise" (437.12) and clean living. Among his imperatives are these: "Deal with Nature the great greengrocer" (437.16–17) and "Stamp out bad eggs" (437.21). Late in life, Shaw had with peevishly Swiftian irony advocated stamping out bad eggs—exterminating useless people (see "Extermination," his preface to *On the Rocks*, 1933, in CP). When Jaun announces, "I am, I do, and I suffer" (445.18), he alludes to Caesar's "I came, I saw, I conquered" and thus to activist Shaw, who identified with the Caesarian stance, for the amateur pugilist G. B. S. believed he had, like Jaun, "arrams that carry a wallop" (445.24–25). Like the superman reformer and gradualist Fabian, Jaun inconsistently declares that "the race is to the rashest" (441.3) but preaches, "Clean out the hogshole and generally ginger things up. Meliorism in massquantities" (447.2–3). It will be remembered that Shaw's comments on *Ulysses* concluded that in revealing Dublin's dirt, Joyce's novel was an admonition to clean up Ireland, the household, hog's hole, that *Portrait* denotes as the "old sow who eats her farrow" (203). Shaw's Fabianism was, of course, massively meliorist. It was, admittedly, like Shaun/Jaun's reformism, influenced by Charles Dickens, whom, according to Hodgart, Jaun advocates as "suitable reading" (175). Shaw admitted pilfering from Dickens. In a biography with Shaw's imprimatur, Archibald Henderson concluded that Shaw was "a singular composition of Barnum and Bunyan, of Butler and Blake, of Dickens and Jeremiah" (PP 691)—a combination of circus showman and puritan preacher, utopian reformer and antiauthoritarian mystic, exposer of social ills through writing and Hebrew prophet lamenting the woes of the world—in other words, a character like Joyce's Jaun. "*Burnham and Bailey*" (71.21) was a "*Hoary Hairy Hoax*" (71.15) when Joyce felt like libeling him. In the montage of Jaun, Joyce captures the contradictory Shavian personality.

Jaun is, like Shaw, a hardworking public speaker—"hardworking Jaun . . . braying aloud like Brahmaan's ass" (441.24–25). Joyce's portmanteau simultaneously suggests Balaam's reproving ass, Brahms (whom Shaw called a "sentimental voluptuary"), Brahma (the Hindu creator in dialectic with Shiva, the Shemian destroyer), and Brahmin. It compacts the moralist, music critic, self-styled Vishnu, member of a priestly caste, and intellectual guru whose "arse" Joyce had advised Stanislaus to kick (JJL 2:203). In fact, the leitmotif of Shaun as ass is related to Joyce's assessment of Shaw, abetted by *John Bull's Other Island,* in which G. B. S.'s Anglo avatar and self-parody, Tom Broadbent, is compared to a serviceable ass. Tom may be "Treacle Tom" (39.28), who "had stimulants in the shape of gee and gees" (42.5). Keegan, who calls Broadbent an ass, has a vision of Ireland as a utopian heaven. In the *Wake*, "Jaun the Boast's last fireless words of postludium of his soapbox speech ending in 'sheaven" (469.29–30) refer to the self-laudatory Shaw's preachy discussion plays in *Methuselah,* which end, ironically, in a fireless Shavian heaven ("sheaven")—fireless because it lacks the wit and verve of earlier plays and, "postludium" (beyond play), rules out passion for anything except thought. In the concluding church music, prior to his benediction, Jaun, like Shaw's Don Juan in Hell electing heaven, opts for the icy intellectual calm of G. B. S.'s ideal future.

Like Shaw's Elderly Gentleman having come from Baghdad on a pilgrimage to Galway, on a "salve a tour," Shaun/Jaun goes off "Solo, solone, solong!" (469.21). Joyce's foolhardy fellow goes off in a barrel into the Liffey after the "Redhead . . . meccamaniac" with the "stock of his sermons" (471.14, 19), leaving behind his role as the "wiseabelness of the friarylayman in the pulpitbarrel" (472.3–4). As David Hayman notes, book 3 evokes "Shaun as the Word enveloped in an empty Guinness barrel floating on and gradually filled by the river Liffey." The barrel may be Joycean deflation of Shaw in the character of his own Elderly Gentleman in part 4 of *Methuselah.* Shaun's progress, as Hayman outlines it, follows the development of the Elderly Gentleman, for Shaw's old man "defends his function (iii.1), flourishes and magnifies his presence (iii.2), yields to his underlying spiritual vacuity (iii.3), and finally vanishes" (12).

Joyce's sending Jaun to his fate in a barrel is, however, either prescient or an accretion, for by 1931 Joyce would have had comic reason for specifying a barrel, not merely the upturned tub upon which Shaw, the street-corner lecturer, was famous for standing. Bernard Partrich's *Punch* cartoon of August 12, 1931, heralds Shaw's return from Russia during the Depression with a triumphant G. B. S. pictured midair on a lading crane atop barrels labeled with the word *Butter* and communist slogans—the "goods" that Shaw brought back from Moscow. The caper of bringing barrels of butter home may have earned Shaw the right to travel by barrel in the *Wake* (as well as the dubious honor of being Burrus in the butter-cheese episode; pp 308–21). G. K. Chesterton told his readers that Shaw actually stood on a tub while delivering political sermons. In *On the Rocks* (1933) Shaw called inflammatory public speakers like himself tub-thumpers, perhaps adding to Joyce's incentive for sending the open-air speaker into the Liffey in a tub that is simultaneously a Guinness barrel (suggesting "guinnesses"—the "Genesis" of *Methuselah* as well as an incongruous and comic vehicle for the prohibitionist preacher). Jaun undergoes death by water and subsequent rejuvenation, thus emulating the pattern that Joyce's unwitting collaborator used in *Back to Methuselah* for Long Livers who begin again. Joyce translated this as "the regeneration of all man by affusion of water" (606.12), with "Saint Kevin Hydrophilos" with his "tubbathalter" (tub/bath as altar) (606.2–5) presiding.

In his youth a fiery redhead, the Fabian Shaw, Abel to Joyce's fratricidal imagination, had taken on the role of incendiary lay preacher. As the fanatical apostle of Creative Evolution, he made Baghdad the Mecca and capital of Western civilization in "The Tragedy of an Elderly Gentleman." In that play, however, the penultimate of his Pentateuch, the old man has made a pilgrimage to the spiritually advanced island that has been the scene of the "tragic effacement of a race of heroes and poets" (BM 206–7). *Finnegans Wake* revisits the same Ireland, a microcosm of which is Dublin, where the dreamer begrudgingly admires the "meccamaniac" he fears has drowned. Submerged in water, Jaun is heartened by the sight of silver fish—"gillybrighteners" lighted "by yon socialist sun" (524.25–28)—the kind that the old fish, socialist Shaw, created in his sunlit, ideal commonwealth in *Methuselah*. After Jaun's departure into the Liffey, the narrator keens for him: "Gone is Haun! My grief, my ruin . . . receding on your photophoric pilgrimage to your antipodes in the past" (472.14–18). Shaw's pilgrim, the Elderly Gentleman, dies upon contact with the luminous, phosphoric Oracle from whom he seeks illumination. Delighted with the camera as a tool of both art and documentation, the light-bearing Shaw, like Shaun "smoiling . . . up his lampsleeve" (411.25–26), was himself often photographed in his world travels. His good news gospels are themselves something like a picture pilgrimage between antipodes—polar opposites in time. In 1934 the Shaws visited the Antipodes of New Zealand. Between 1931 and 1936 Shaw traveled by sea around the world as ambassador at large. After all of his lectures and sermonizing, Jaun goes off as "Embrassador-at-Large!" (471.10). That he was carrying a teeming packet of "fanmail" (471.26) suggests that he is, indeed, an avatar of Shaw, whose fan mail was prodigious.

Nevertheless, the old reformer and optimist was honest in his belief that his powers were fading. Even while still criticizing Jaun as a tightwad—"pennyatimer"—the dreamer laments the "now paling light lucerne" of Jaun, the "lampaddyfair"—the waning of the light-bringing

Lucifer who had provided the "glow of a zeal of soul of service such as rarely if ever have I met with single men" (472.21–27). The Lucifer identification with Shaw persisted from *The Devil's Disciple,* Shaw's repeated assertion of his Satanic purpose to depose the ruling powers, and cartoons such as Max Beerbohm's drawing of a spade-bearded "G. B. Shaw in his element"—in flames (PP facing 213). The amazingly prolific socialist epitomized the zeal for reform that Joyce described. Even though the "devil era" of De Valera has begun, the "fun Juhn"— fun Don Juan—rates a prayerful farewell. With only a touch of ironic exaggeration, Shaun (for whom humility is not a virtue) praises the incredibly energetic Jaun/Shaw, in whose honor the Russians had staged a horse race, the "Bernard Shaw Handicap," during his 1931 Moscow visit: Jaun did his two "strong nine furlong mile in slick and slapstick record time . . . with . . . high bouncing gait of going and your feat of passage [which] will be contested with you and through you, for centuries to come" (473.12–16). While Joyce was writing, St. John Ervine was busy contesting Shaw's feat in *Methuselah,* and Shaw defended himself with his usual hyperbole. The *Wake* reader confused by Shaun's praising Jaun should not, therefore, be surprised, for Joyce was making fun of Shaw's notorious, overweening displays of self-love and self-approval. The tribute to Jaun's "feat of passage" no doubt refers to the controversial rites of passage dramatized in *Methuselah* as well as to the comic playwright himself, whose rites of passage G. B. S. seemed to celebrate in his late plays, just as Joyce celebrated them in the *Wake.*

As the dreamer admits, it is the "novel ideas" of the "cantanberous" "queer fish" who is "the poisoner of his word" that preoccupy him. "I'm enormously full of that foreigner [that is, Shaw, the Irish Englishman]. . . . Got by the one goat, suckled by the same nanna" (463.12–16), Mother Ireland. The cantankerous London-based Irishman who was a prisoner and poisoner of language was both corroboration and source of the *Wake*'s ideas—the same Shavian issues got Joyce's goat, and the same Dublin muse (the Prankquean) nurtured him. Although Shem hates Shaun, he is "amorist. I love him" (463.18–19) because nobody else holds a "chef's cankle to the darling at all for sheer dare" (463.33–34). Like his heroine, Saint Joan, Shaw promised to "dare, and dare, and dare" until he died (Plays 975). Joyce admired the daring because he identified with it, even though his Shem projection differed from Shaun's. In Joyce's Irish stew, Shaw, perhaps sharing an allusion to

Stanislaus in the early days when Joyce shared his ideas with his brother, is the "very thoughtful and sympatrico . . . Brother Intelligentius" (464.16–17) whose politics, religious concerns, time philosophy, and comedic sense were far more congenial to Joyce than the conservative, right-wing sympathies of supporters like Pound and Eliot. *The Quintessence of Ibsenism,* now tainted by Joyce's obscenity and dubbed "ibscenest nansense" (535.19), had deeply influenced Joyce when he was a young man. The "long farewell . . . , fair dream of sport and game and always something new!" (472.13–14) eulogizes the brother who seems, like a Shavian Ancient, to be receding on the horizon. Even the references to athletics are apropos for the game playwright who was a boxing aficionado and author of a novel about a fighter. At the end of the Shaun section, Shem addresses him almost prayerfully with "Brave footsore Haun! Work your progress! Hold to! Now! Win out, ye divil ye!" (473.20–21), urging the devilish apostle of progress on. Thus, whether it is called parody or plagiarism, Joyce's artistic appropriation is an act of admiration. Indeed, Linda Hutcheon writes, "parody is normative in its identification with the Other, but it is contesting in its Oedipal need to distinguish itself from the prior Other." For "the very act of parodying invests the Other with . . . authority" (77). In his sanguine well-wishing, Shem cheers on his "polar andthisishis" (177.33) toward the "DIAGONISTIC CONCILIANCE" (275.R1) anticipated throughout the *Wake.*

H. C. E.: "Poppypap's a Passport Out"

The "most omportant" man—portentous, important yet impotent—begins to meld with the father H. C. E., the "gronde old mand" (332.20). In the *Bookman,* December 1924, Robert Lynd wrote, indeed, that "Mr. Bernard Shaw is at the present in danger of becoming the Grand Old Man of European literature" (quoted in Evans 304). During the 1920s and 1930s he was by common consent the patriarch of world theater. He was also world-famed as pest, polemicist, and peacemaker. During the 1930s, while traveling all over the world, the Shaws were accompanied by news reports and photographs by the paparazzi. As H. C. E. (not the "Pappie" that John Joyce was to his children), Shaw was the "Poppypap" who was "a passport out" (25.5). His "fame is spreading like Basilico's ointment" (25.9). But his "heart is in the system of the Shewolf" (26.11–12), the last word suggesting show-off Shaw, whose idiosyncratic spelling of *show* was *shew;* whose awe and sometimes trepidation regarding woman as the Life Force, a predator in sexual pursuit, was well known; and who connected himself through Caesar to Rome and its founder Romulus (implicitly, Joyce would thus be Remus), suckled by a she-wolf ("Shewolf"). His "mate of the Sheawolving class"(49.28–29) is Shem, in Gaelic a Shea like Shaw. Before "the laps of goddesses" he "showed our labourlasses how to free was easy" (25.20–21). For the feminist author of *The Intelligent Woman's Guide to Socialism* (1929) is Joyce's "faunayman at the funeral to compass our cause" (25.32–33).

As has been noted, Shaw's attitude toward funerals was, like that of Irishmen like the adult Joyce, unorthodox. Finally Joyce gave his "Work in Progress" a name after Frank Harris's 1931 biographical conjecture: "Whether the funerals of Dublin Shaws set up an early association in Bernard's imagination between death and humour, or his Irish blood carries in it that delight in mischief . . . , certain it is that death seems to exhilarate Shaw . . . [who] tends to regard himself and us his poor fellow-creatures as provisional makeshifts and our deaths as clearances of scrapped material" (309–10). Harris disapproved of Shaw's black humor regarding funerals as a "hereditary defect" from his father (115), a hereditary defect that Joyce shared with his literary sire. As in so many other attitudes, Shaw's "macabre pleasantries" anticipate those of the younger Irishman who suspected that they shared the same heredity. Even though the ballad about the fake death of a construction worker is the source of Joyce's title, in the *Wake*'s "funeral games" (515.23), Finn/H. C. E. is the "secontonone myther rector and maximost bridgesmaker" (126.10–11), unlike Shem, the "masterbilker" (111.21), a master builder like Ibsen and mythic architect like Vico. That Finn in Celtic means fair or bright associates him with the white-bearded G. B. S. who provides brightness at the Wake.

In debating the merits of socialism in *Socialism and Superior Brains* (1894), a copy of which Joyce owned, Shaw wrote, "I am usually willing to build a bridge of silver for a flying foe" (CP 839). Shaw was famed as a special sort of bridge maker. In a grand celebration of the playwright's seventy-fifth birthday in Moscow, Anatoly Lunacharsky concluded that Shaw "started to build a great bridge from the old world to the new. . . . He is now in his old age completing the last arches of this bridge and entering the new world. In this lies the worldwide historical significance of this occasion" (BSL 3:253). He was, in the punman's mind, also a "myther rector"—like the mythic Anglican rector of "The Gospel of the Brothers Barnabas" who reappears centuries after his first entrance in *Back to Methuselah*. Hugh Kenner observes that "the city-builder/dreamer was named Earwicker" (284). In *Major Barbara*, as Undershaft, Shaw was a city-builder. In *Methuselah* he dreamed of building a new society.

One of Joyce's voices inquires regarding H. C. E., "Have you ever thought, wepowtew, that sheew gweatness was his twadgedy?" (61.6–7). "Shew" is Shaw's spelling for show and "sheewgreatness" (Shaw-greatness) may have been his tragedy. In the "discussion" of Taff and Butt, the Joycean Butt seems to dismiss H. C. E. as "of all the quirasses and all the qwhrmin in the tragedoes of those antiants" (343.22–23). The queer ass who wrote "The Tragedy of an Elderly Gentleman" and a play featuring "antiants" (Ancients) was Shaw. According to Mary and Padraic Colum, Joyce associated "Vico's historical cycles in some way with the Vico Road that follows the bend of Dublin Bay between Dalkey and Killiney—in Joyce's mind they did anyway" (221). After completing *Methuselah*, the man who lived on Vico Road as a child wrote, "Civilization has collapsed over and over again . . . but . . . life will presently begin afresh" (I&R 414). On "The Vico road . . . unappalled by the recoursers," the dream narrator is elated "to be going to meet a king . . . the overking of Hither-on-Thither Erin himself"—the archetypal high king of primeval Ireland, Finn, who came "Before there was patch at all on Ireland" (452.21–29). As H. C. E., Shaw is comparable to the old king. Henderson's 1911 biography calls him "the quintessence of vital energy. He rushes hither and thither" (GBS 503). He called Ireland the "little green patch," and eventually his secretary Blanche Patch was "on Ireland." A follower of Shaw, the cyclical historian optimistic about Creative Evolution, the dreamer goes to the Vico Road to meet the precursor, who also lived at the Rectory at Ayot St. Lawrence—"the Rectory? Vicarage Road?" (291.18).

Significantly, although he had at his command the same intellectual tradition as T. S. Eliot and other moderns, Joyce ruminated on his Irish origins, choosing as his mythical ancestor from Celtic myth Finn the fighter instead of Fergus the dreamer, Ossian, or Cuchulain—heroes of the aristocratic tradition that Yeats preferred. The giant, unaristocratic Finn best symbolized Joyce's own ambitions as well as his reading of those of the combative literary giant Shaw. The meaning of Finn's name in Irish—"fair" or "white" (O'Sullivan 68)—fits in with the pattern of colors Joyce associates with the white-bearded Shaw, whose brave and sometimes comically exaggerated battles for causes were a correlative to Finn's mythic feats. In "The Tragedy of an Elderly Gentleman," the old man has turned to "the mystery and beauty of these haunted islands, thronged with spectres [like Finn and his avatars in the *Wake*] from a magic past" (BM 205). After having "kissed the soil of Ireland" (206), he dies. *Finnegans Wake* celebrates the symbolic passing of Shaw, a modern Finn, for in the real world of the 1930s the famed Irishman was a fallen culture hero.

Nevertheless, "To anyone who knew and loved the christlikeness of the big cleanminded giant H. C. Earwicker throughout his excellence long vicefreegal existence the mere suggestion of him as a lustsleuth nosing for trouble in a boobytrap rings particularly preposterous. Truth, beard on prophet, compels me to add that there is said to have been . . . a quidam" (33.28–35). This could be a fan letter for the bearded prophet Shaw, even though it embraces the larger archetype. The pagan giant on the Vico Road, however, is less like Finn than like Shaw, for that great heroic slaughterer was not vice-free and, of course, not christlike. Although Joyce feared that Shaw had played lust-sleuth with *Ulysses,* the "truth, beard on prophet," about "a quidam"—a certain person—intimates Shaw's affair with Stella Campbell, sensational news in 1922, when Stella's memoirs, including love letters from "Joey," were published. Although he was not a "lustsleuth," there was said to have been one case of lust in Shaw's life. The "quidam" hints also at parallels, however incomplete, between Shaw, Swift, Shakespeare, Wilde, and Parnell, all of whom had affairs with "a certain person" (and in Swift's case perhaps with two, Stella and Vanessa). Joyce detours us from the quidam, however, by suggesting Earwicker's "ongentilmensky" behavior in the park, behavior that hints of Shaw because of the Russianization of the portmanteau. But H. C. E. defends himself from the accusation that he misbehaved with girls, declaring, "I their covin guardient." Like Shaw, whose plays were performed at Covent Garden, H. C. E. claims himself, like the Fabian feminist, to be the guardian of women, even witches in a coven, like Lilith in *Methuselah* or Strega in *The Music Cure*. Old Shotover, suspected to have "sold himself to the devil in Zanzibar" (Plays 760), seems to be presiding over a coven in *Heartbreak House.* "The devil gave [Shotover] ... a black witch for a wife; and these two demon daughters are their mystical progeny" (703).

Finn/H. C. E. is associated with Adam and with all of Shaw's literary ancestors. In widening the paternal archetype, Joyce collapses past and present, making H. C. E. at once Shaw and Swift, both of whom had notorious affairs with Stellas. H. C. E., indistinguishable from Shaun/Shem, has a "blackguard eye and the goatsbeard in his buttinghole of Shemuel Tulliver, my grandsourd, the old cruxader" (12–14). The bearded, satiric Shaw, who had accused Joyce of using "blackguardly" language, is also Swift's Gulliver (although portraits of Swift do not show a beard). In the final book of *Gulliver's Travels,* Gulliver's disgust with bodily functions and his intransigent utopianism parallel Shaw's; as a fanatical convert to belief in a rational utopia, Gulliver is Shavian. But the anal imagination of the sour grandfather Swift parallels Joyce's. Swift was, moreover, like Shaw, a crusader ("cruxader") for Irish causes. Shaun, as usual an adumbration of Shem, urges H. C. E., now recognized as a brother, to admit their common ancestry: "Be bloodysibby. Be Irish. Be Inish" (465.31–32), a sibling by virtue of their Irish blood, even though both had been "Wrestless in the womb" (both Shaw and Joyce were restless in Dublin but not to be wrested from their Irish identity). In beseeching H. C. E. to be a "bloody" sibling, the dreamer relates himself to his "frother," for Joyce, who believed himself (with cause) to be hated by conservative moralists, could identify with Shaw, always the enemy of conservatives, whose Eliza Doolittle was attacked for using the world *bloody* in *Pygmalion.*

Nevertheless, the father, the Adam in "In the Beginning," realizes on "fundamental liberal principles the supreme importance ... of physical life" (35.22–23). "Old Everybody's Father" in *Methuselah* proclaims, "Mine is the Voice of Life," and, before him, Eve asserts that "life is the most beautiful of all the new words" (BM 89, 88, 68). While loving life, the old man also shares Shavian politics: he is "anarchistically respectsful of the liberties of the noninvasive individual" (72.16–17). He proclaims, with Shavian immodesty, his own heroic accomplishments: "respected and respectable" (545.11), he "revoluconized [society] by ... [his] eructions" (545.33)—his Shaun-side erections of social edifices and his Shem-side penal and revolutionary projections in prose. "Irewaker is just a plain pink joint reformee in private life but folks all have it be brehemons laws he has parliamentary honors" (59.27–29). There were rumors while Joyce was writing the *Wake* that pinko Shaw, who awakened Joyce's ire, would get a Parliamentary appointment. Of course, although the Brehon Laws might say that H. C. E. was entitled to honors by virtue of his tribal (that is, Irish) associations, such honors would give the recipient no power, for the distinguishing feature of the old Irish laws was that there was no central government to enforce them. Many thought that Shaw deserved a government appointment in Ireland, but it would take official clout to enforce any Brehon's Law; the conservative De Valera regime did not want the old Fabian. He was, however, offered a knighthood, which he refused because he thought accepting it would be hypocritical for an Irishman who, as Harris noted in a chapter title, saw "Red" (127).

Among the chief colors associated with H. C. E. (see O'Sullivan) are red and white. Red denotes Shaw's communist sympathies as well as his beard as a young man. H. C. E. is "Collosul rhodomantic" (241.8). That Finn MacCool is the hero of the Red Branch cycle of Irish epic material probably amused Joyce, who superimposed Redbarn Shaw upon the legendary hero. Part of the "red raddled . . . cayennepeppercast over the text" (120.14-15), the "Jawjohn Redhead" (471.14) in later life made his massive white beard and white hair his trademark. H. C. E. is "Alderman Whitebeaver" (160.15-16), "Ashe and Whitehead" (311.24), "Whitehed," "Old Whitehowth" (535.22, 26): "(whitesides do his beard!)" (352.4). Shotover, Shaw's alter ego in *Heartbreak House,* has "an immense white beard" (CP 759). "And old Whiteman self, the blighty blotchy [who had "the miner smellpex"] beyond the bays, hope of ostrogothic and ottomanic faith converters, despair of Pandemia's postwartem plastic surgeons" (263.8-12), is the old fideist Shaw, whose new religion was hopefully ecumenical and who disapproved of postwar attempts to carve up Europe—in the pandemonium after World War I, when Shaw was fighting for the League of Nations. The old whitebeard is associated with Finn, Blanco Posnet, and Blanche Patch, all of whose names suggest the color white. While Shaw was young and impecunious, he and his mother survived because of a legacy from a relative named Whitechurch. In 1928 Whitehall Court became his London address. Earwicker, "whitening under restraint in the sititout corner of his conservatory," mourned "the flight of his wild guineese" (71.1-4), as at times Shaw, sitting it out at Ayot St. Lawrence, "Shaw's Corner," must have mourned the transient reputation of his "guineese," his Genesis, in *Methuselah*. As father Ireland he bemoaned the flight of the wild geese, heroes of the old Gaelic order, who like himself fled from Ireland. Joyce included himself in the packed paradigm by letting the old man bemoan the loss of Guinness—simultaneously the drink and Genesis, Paradise lost. A rhetorical question suggests the confused and confusing superimposed doublings: "Will whatever will be written in lappish language with bursts of Maggyer always seem semposed, black looking white and white guarding black, in that siamixed twoatalk?" (66.18–21). Shaw is a Siamese twin of blackguard Shem.

Revealing his Joycean paranoia, the old man keeps a list of his "abusive" names, among them several that hint at a Shavian identity. "*First nighter*" (71.10) points to the drama critic and dramatist. "*Ireland's Eighth Wonderful Wonder*" suggests what fans thought of the self-congratulatory Shaw. "*Cainanabler*" (71.13) alludes to his creation of Adam's family as well as to his coupling with Shem. "*Artist, Unworthy of the Homely Protestant Religion . . . Loose Luther, Hatches Cock's Eggs . . . Luck before Wedlock, I Divorce Thee Husband, Tanner and his Make*" (71.21–28) all have Shavian resonances. The polemical playwright's detractors thought him unworthy of the homely Protestant religion even while he kept calling himself a Protestant and continued to criticize Christianity, but his champions often noted that he was a great, protesting preacher, a heresiarch Protestant in the larger sense—hence a "Loose Luther" sermonizing for a religious reformation. In his youth a free-loving "Cock," in the finale of his *Methuselah* people hatch from eggs. Because Shaw's sexual life supposedly took place before marriage and his marriage was, in the conjugal sense, a divorce, the paradoxical "*Luck before Wedlock*" and "*I Divorce Thee Husband*" seem to apply to Shaw's infamous and eccentric sex life, philandering before wedlock and divorce after. After marrying Shaw, Charlotte divorced herself from the sexual obligations that usually define marriage. "*Tanner and his Make*" is, of course, a reference to John Tanner and Ann Whitefield, who apparently loomed large in Joyce's night thoughts as parallels to the male and female principals of his dream. In his notes for the *Wake* he related Tanner (Shaw) to Noah and Christ by indicating that "Tanner sleeps for forty nights" (Connolly 98).

As the boring, sleepy Yawn, Shaun seems to melt into the Father whom Joyce calls "et sitaraw etcicero": (152.10), thus deflating Shaw's phenomenal abilities as a public speaker by combining *et cetera* and Cicero, who hardly seems related to the publican whom Joyce identifies with H. C. E. In accepting Hugh Kenner's argument that the "alternative self" in the *Wake* is Joyce's pub-crawling father, John Gordon discusses the controversial interview with Brian O'Nolan that may or may not establish that John Joyce stayed at the Mullingar Hotel, which is supposedly the scene of *Finnegans Wake*. One of the facts that Gordon uncovers is that the man who owned the hotel in Chapelizod was named Broadbent (91). Even if the Flann O'Brien interview with Joyce's father (which Gordon believes to be authentic) is a spoof dreamed up by Myles na Gapoleen, who was (as his having three pen names attests) undergoing his own identity crisis and anxiety over the influence of Joyce, a man named Broadbent apparently owned the Mullingar Hotel—a coincidence that may have motivated Joyce's choice of setting, putting two fathers (John Joyce and John Tanner—Tom Broadbent Shaw) in the same bed, so to speak, thus alluding simultaneously to his biological and bookish sires. The actual ownership of H. C. E.'s pub by a man with the name of Shaw's bumptious, utilitarian Protestant double and usurper of Ireland links the setting to Joyce's Anglo-Irish alter ego. Perhaps he was inspired in part by Hotchkiss in *Getting Married* (1908): he asks Mrs. George (Shaw as femme fatale), "What was your father?" She replies, "A licensed victualler who married his barmaid. You would call him a publican, most likely" (Plays 576). Furthermore, Gordon determines that the numbers associated with Shem in book 1, chapter 7, add up to eighty-two (159). Hence, he concludes, they refer to the year 1882, when Joyce was born. Gordon further postulates, however, that the year of the "action" of the *Wake* is 1938 (37). If this is so, the wily penman who seriously solemnized dates (Burgess 17) brings together the year of his birth and Shaw's age, for in 1938 Shaw was eighty-two. When the *Wake* was in its planning stages, Joyce was interested in the ages of other famous Irishmen. An entry in his "Scribbledehobble" Notebooks (571), along with the ages of A. E., George Moore, and Yeats, lists "G. B. S. 67" (Connolly 103). Thus the reader can establish the date of his deliberation as 1923.

Furthermore, for "crossroads puzzlers" like Gordon and myself, Joyce's interest in the mysterious date "1132" (119.26) may be connected to the dates of the "books" of Shaw's Pentateuch. Considering Joyce's arcane clues and subterfuges, 1132 may be a parody of Shaw's arbitrary dating of his four plays after the timeless "In the Beginning." "The Gospel of the Brothers Barnabas" is dated 1914 to place the action at the start of World War I. "The Thing Happens" supposedly occurs in 2170, "The Tragedy of an Elderly Gentleman" in 3000, and "As Far as Thought Can Reach" in A.D.31920. Joyce's 1132 could be borrowed by playing with the digits fourth from the right in Shaw's dates—1, 2, 3, 1. While perhaps ridiculing Shaw's capricious selections of future times, Joyce is equally arbitrary in emphasizing 1132, a medieval date for the relatively old-fashioned family revelations of the *Wake*. After "The Gospel of the Brothers Barnabas" Shaw moves into outer time and space in what Joyce calls a "Gospolis" (345.2), a Greek polis and gospel city of the future.

The initials of the father figure are, as has been noted, also significant—H. C. is one step ahead of G. B. to suggest wryly that the *Wake* is ahead of *Methuselah*. That the father figure is delineated by his monogram suggests the G. B. S. connection too, for Shaw had made the monogram world-famous. As Everybody, however, H. C. E. is a divided self combining a Shavian superego with a Joycean id. Shaun, who represents the puritanical side of the formidable father, moralistically warns St. Bride's Girls to avoid H. C. E., one side of whom is, like the fathers of Shaw and Joyce and like Joyce himself, a dirty old man about "fifty six or so" (443.22) "seeking relief in alcohol" (444.1–2). H. C. E.'s tirades against drunkenness reflect, however, the Protestant virtue of "a teetotum abstainer" (489.17) like Shaw. The simian "flatulence" that Shaw abhorred is, however, also an important part of Chimpden's subconscious.

The Chimp in Humphrey Chimpden Earwicker's name is corroborated by Teddy Roosevelt's epithet for Shaw when he decried World War I—a "blue rumped chimp" (H2 354). It is further justified by an infamous letter that Shaw wrote to defend apes, maligned, according to G. B. S., in the 1928 controversy over Dr. Serge Voronoff's monkey gland operation. In reply to a doctor who had attacked the rejuvenation treatment for possibly introducing apish qualities into its recipients (Yeats displayed none), Shaw attacked Voronoff for tearing glands from apes. Arguing that simians are far less cruel than human beings, he signed his letter to the *Daily News* "Consul Junior"—the name of a famous performing ape—and listed his return address as "the Monkey House, Regent's Park" (quoted in Joad 79). When *The Simpleton of the*

Unexpected Isles was performed in New York in 1935, the reviewer for the *New York Herald-Tribune* wrote, "Like a dignified monkey, he climbs a tree and pelts us with edifying coconuts" (quoted in BSL 3:405). Never afraid to contradict himself, however, in his preface to *Heartbreak House,* Shaw had accepted Shakespeare's evaluation of man as an "angry ape" and Swift's description of him as a Yahoo. Depressed over the war and over being scapegoated for disapproving of it, Shaw wrote his Chekhovian wasteland play while convinced of man's tendencies toward degeneracy—a susceptibility to drift that he would work out of his system in *Back to Methuselah*. Moreover, although Shaw's assumed simian identity may be a source of Chimpden's middle name, the primate sexuality over which Shaw was squeamish is an important part of H. C. E.'s ruminations. Like Everybody's unrepressed unconscious, H. C. E.'s dream world is full of the chimp "incontinence" that Shaw disdained. Nevertheless, in *Too True to Be Good* (1931), the seventy-five-year-old playwright recognized the "lower centres" (*Plays Extravagant* 83) of sexual attraction and desire, but a Shaw spokesperson says that the lower centres "don't talk. Speech belongs to the higher centres." He thinks that great art voices more important issues than sex and that it would be shocking "if anyone's lower centres began to talk" (78). In the *Wake* his cheeky disciple had persistently made the lower centres talk, perhaps to talk back to the paternal Shaw whom he imagines as a senile superego.

Upon considering the unfavorable press notices of *Back to Methuselah,* Shaw wrote St. John Ervine in 1928 that "the religion of the Englishman today, as the reviews of Methuselah show, is simple Phallus" (BSL 3:733); clearly Shaw rejected the "phallicism" that Joyce felt compelled to explore. The younger man preferred to stress the binary opposition of lustful Shem and saintly Shaun, brought together in H. C. E., and with good reason. To the wise Ancients of Shaw's "As Far as Thought Can Reach," to whom the body is a "bore" (*Back to Methuselah* 298), Joyce replied with cloacal glorification and fetishistic scrutiny of the body's systems—the quotidian life cycle as aliment and waste, reproduction and onanism. Finn/H. C. E./Shem drinks, relieves himself, dreams of sexual frustration, guilt, or surfeit—all subjects that would affront a Victorian father, no matter how liberal and avant-garde he pretended to be. Joyce's sexualization of experience is what Harold Bloom in *The Anxiety of Influence* calls Daemonization—in the *Wake*, mutinous interjection of his "Counter-Sublime" to his "precursor's Sublime" (18), which is in *Methuselah* ultimately Neoplatonic. Through this demonization, Joyce anticipates Bloom's theory by creating what Bloom labels "Kenosis" or "movement towards discontinuity with the precursor" (14) that manifests itself in the salaciousness that deflates angelic, Shavian pretensions while also rejecting Shaw's discursive, logocentric language. Perhaps while indulging his scatological imagination, Joyce conjectured that the loved and despised literary parent would be scandalized by his lewd subject matter and his disdain for public communication.

In the "contest between license (drinker, gourmand, lover, rebel, writer) and control (abstainer, belt-tightener, impotent celibate, conqueror, censor)" that Gordon finds at the heart of H. C. E.'s character (50) is the conflict that Joyce imagined between himself and Shaw, even though Joyce's making the older man a censor was the misprision of sour grapes. In Joyce's psyche, G. B. S. is at times a formidable foe, larger than life, but trailing off into senile incoherencies. By emphasizing the weight of H. C. E., Joyce deviously deters and detours readers from his link to Shaw, but H. C. E.'s size is no doubt symbolic. None of the principal male relatives in Joyce's life—his blood sire, brother, or surrogate literary father—was obese. Weight implies, however, the importance, significance, and intellectual appetite of the omnivorous Joyce appointed rival and alter ego. Joyce's father had the wit, garrulousness, and drinking habits but none of the success that Shem envies. At best James Joyce's brother John Stanislaus was "more a comrade and even accomplice than a father" (Cixous 35). Stannie was a retiring university teacher who admittedly did not talk politics and was often in fear of losing his job.

This is not to assert that the Joyce family does not overlap the Shavian portrait, but it is also to argue that Joyce disguised the living source of his dualistic persona's conflicted feelings and hence his debt to him by disorienting the reader with the displacements of dream and the dislocations of the subconscious. Partly in denial, partly tantalized by the wish to reveal himself, H. C. E./Shem confronts the Other, H. C. E./Shaun, in the house of mirrors of his free-flowing, nocturnal meditations. They are, despite synchronous allusions to family, mythic and historical referents, a secreted dialogue with G. B. S., "our worldstage's practical jokepiece and retired cecelticommediant" (33.2–3). At his "general address rehearsal that was antepropreviousday's ... with the memories of the past and the hicnuncs of the present embellicating the musics of the futures," the playwright of *Methuselah* (and his deconstructing imitator) is addressing himself to a "houseful of deadheads" (407.28–36). Even when there was standing room only, performances of *Methuselah* were, like Joyce's unappreciated "funnanimal world" (244.13), often addressed to "deadheads." For, as Desmond MacCarthy concluded in the *New Statesman* (July 9, 1921), *Back to Methuselah* "is an extraordinary, imaginative effort, but not an artistic success" (BSL 3:728).

Nevertheless, in his role as the chosen sire, Joyce's Earwicker/Adam ruminates on "the sameold gamebold adomic structure of our Finnius the old One" (615.6–7), like Shaw and his copier reworking Genesis. The Old Man "daydreamsed we had a lovelyt face for a pulltomine. Back we were by the jerk of a beamstark, backed in paladys last, on the brinks of the wobblish, the man what never put a dramn in the swags but milk from a national cowse. That was the prick of the spindle to me that gave me the keys to dreamland" (615.24–28). Not since Milton's *Paradise Lost* had a writer rewritten the biblical Genesis until Shaw tried it. The giant, paternal playwright's daydream of human perfectibility pulled Joyce's persona into miming its optimism and appropriating it, making it "mine." The nondrinking dramatist who beamed us back to Genesis is the giant of Jack and the Beanstalk. In *Man and Superman* Ann Whitefield compares Tanner to "Jack the Giant Killer" (Plays 339), thus suggesting Shaun, the double whose turn it is to be pulled down. The boy protagonist, Shem/Joyce, stole literary treasure while toppling the gigantic father figure, who became noted in late life for drinking nothing but milk. The fairy tale dialogues with the whole *Wake;* the giant is H. C. E./Shaw and Jack is Shem/Joyce. When their cow won't give milk, Jack's poor old mother (Ireland?) commands him to sell it, but he trades it for seemingly useless beans. However, from the discarded beans, the beanstalk of imagination grows. The hungry boy climbs it three times, stealing gold from the giant, taking his hen (the Life Force/golden egg-source of *Methuselah?*), and then seizing his golden harp (Irish music?). The ogre's wife (a Prankquean/Mother Ireland) feeds Jack and twice hides him in her oven, nurturing and symbolically twice giving birth to him. In searching for Jack, the ogre (like H. C. E.) falls asleep. When finally he pursues the boy, Jack chops the beanstalk down, and the giant (an oedipal father/Finnegan) falls to his death. His wife (Life Force/ALP) survives, but Jack has appropriated the wealth and power of the patriarch. A ricorso celebrates his victory and the giant's death.

Through *Methuselah* the literary giant had lured his secret rival to deconstruct his version of human origins—the "last," latest Paradise lost. However, in a diversionary tactic, Joyce superimposed a freely associated allusion to a nostalgic song by Paul Dresser, Theodore Dreiser's brother, "On the Banks of the Wabash," upon Wobblies, Industrial Workers of the World, whose bid for better wages corresponded to Shaw's socialist agenda. The prepositional phrases ("on the brinks of the wobblish") are an accretion to decoy the reader from the main clause, which offers a skeleton key, the "Allkey dallkey," to Joyce's closet. Joyce knew that the teetotaler who had proved himself to be a dauntless supporter of Ireland ("the national cowse") and socialized milk delivery never put a dram of anything but milk into his personal provisions ("swags") that did not help the Irish cows/cause. Whether inspired by his plays, politics, patriotism, or personality—"the man"—(the pronoun reference, like so much else in Joyce's "meandertale" [18.22], is unclear), Joyce's dreamer was jabbed once and for all into finding the "keys to dreamland." Being spurred by the "spindle" effect of *Methuselah*'s backward look—the effect of impaling papers in layers (a metaphor for Shaw's tiering of time and characters in his "day" dream)—gave entry to Joyce's nocturnal "dreamland." Shaw's Pentateuch apparently opened the door to the imaginary sleep of Joyce's "Mousoumeselles buckwould's look" (339.16). One key on the spindle must have been Shaw's "Maxim for Revolutionists": "The unconscious self is the real genius" (CP 193).

The character of the old night/daydreamer derives in part from another Shaw play, produced in Paris in 1928, *Heartbreak House*. Because, like Shaw's Socratic Ancients in *Methuselah* and "madman" Keegan in *John Bull's Other Island,* H. C. E. experiences trances and talks to himself, he resembles Captain Shotover, Shaw's rum-drinking Ancient Mariner and his version of King Lear. Unwittingly foreshadowing the subject of *Finnegans Wake,* Shotover tells Ellie that she should see for herself "the horror of an old man drinking" (Plays 790). Furthermore, Shaw admitted that Captain Shotover "prophesies like a Druid" (BSL 2:743), a fact that the astute Joyce seems to have observed in creating his "Balkelly, archdruid" (611.5). Like Shotover, on whose door Ellie Dunn knocks, H. C. E. is approached by "youngdammers . . . heartpocking on their betters' doornoggers" (572.2–3). Shotover hopes for apocalyptic change into a new cycle of history, in the Viconian mode. He asks, "Is there no thunder in heaven?" (Plays 775). Like the thunder that presages a new cycle in "The Tragedy of an Elderly Gentleman," in Vico, and in the *Wake,* there is in *Heartbreak House* "a splendid drumming in the sky. . . . Heavens threatening" (794) and the resultant "terrific explosion" of bombs (802). A drinker like the Shemside of H. C. E., Shotover is an old man whose "mind wanders" (760). Like the Shavian side of H. C. E., he dreads drunkenness because "to be drunk means to have dreams. . . . But when you are old: very, very old like me, the dreams come of themselves" with the dubious "happiness of yielding and dreaming instead of resisting and doing" (790). "Many men would be offended" by Shotover's "style of talking" (769), just as they would be by Earwicker's. The aged sea captain states the motive for writing that Shaw shared with Joyce: "A man's interest in the world is only the overflow from his interest in himself" (790).

In his preface to *Heartbreak House,* Shaw himself provided a rationale for Joyce's subject matter: "Nature, abhorring the vacuum" of uncommitted people, "immediately filled it up with sex" (CP 378). Whereas Shaw externalizes the "disorder in ideas, in talk, in feelings" in his heartbreaking, "idle . . . hypochondriacal house" (CP 381), Joyce interiorizes the disorder, superimposing the tragic affirmation of *Back to Methuselah* upon the disillusionment of *Heartbreak House.* One path of Joyce's maze arrives at the pessimism of Shaw's Chekhovian play, which he contemplated naming "Horseback Hall": "in one stable . . . the providential warring of heartshaker with housebreaker and of dramdrinker against freethinker our social something bowls along bumpily, experiencing a jolting series of prearranged disappointments, down the long lane of . . . generations" (107.30–35). This passage vaguely evokes the world of Horseback Hall, which seems to jolt along, with unmotivated, absurd conflicts over sex, a burglar and dramdrinking Shotover pitted against the free-thinking Hector Hushabye, who is all talk and no action. But Joyce reconciles his persona with Shotover: "Under the closed eyes of the inspectors the traits featuring the *chiaroscuro* coalesce, their contraries eliminated, in one stable somebody similarly as by the providential warring of heartshaker with housebreaker" (107.28–31), for the heartshaker is the author of *Heart-*

break House, and the intruder in his house who wants to profit from his thefts or to get a handout is Joyce. Setting the "dramdrinker" against the "freethinker," however, reverses the equation, so that in the allusions to Shaw's play Shaun and Shem confuse their parts and coalesce. But, the hollow people of *Heartbreak House* are the "gloompourers" whom Shaw and the *Wake* reject. Indeed, Matthew Hodgart is convinced that "Shem's house is Shaw's *Heartbreak House*" (150), but the tenant is squatting on Shavian property in an eminent domain which both nonpaying occupant and owner redecorate in *Methuselah* and the *Wake.*

Scholars like John Bishop have considered at length the etymology and significance of the name Earwicker, but it is clear that at least half of H. C. E. is Shem's rival. Shaw's quip in *Music in London* (February 15, 1893) anticipates the Shaun-side of Earwicker. The music critic wrote, "I do not mind confessing that I do not know half as much as you suppose from my articles, but in the kingdom of the deaf the one-eared is king" (2.258). Joyce's criticism of "Ear! Ear! Weakear," a cockney version of "hear," hints at the connection between Earwicker and the "phonemanon" (258.22) Shaw, who not only worked for the phone company when he first went to London but also was a phenomenal phonetician, one of whose alter egos is the professor of phonetics Henry Higgins. Indeed, Joyce's narrator seems to recommend him as a scholarly source: "Read Higgins" (604.6), whose ear is weaker than that of his student Eliza. She tells him, "You said I had a finer ear than you" (Plays 751). Furthermore, as the oracular author of *Back to Methuselah,* G. B. S. thought of himself as "the Clearer of the Air [speaking] from on high" (258.20). In *Methuselah* Shaw seemed, however, to be a "dullaphone" (485.22). Bishop writes that "as a deft practitioner of both 'acounstrick[s] and funantics,' Earwicker becomes 'a layteacher of . . . orthopenethics . . . [who] overheard in his secondary personality . . . [an] undereared poul soul, by accident' (38.27-36)" (301). This Earwicker sounds like "layteacher" (laypreacher) Shaw's secondary personality, Professor Higgins, who overhears the "undereared," (under-reared) Eliza Doolittle "by accident" before making her a student of phonetics. Like Shaw, Earwicker is a man of many talents—interested in both accounting and acoustics—"acounstrick"—and a master of "funantics"—phonetics and fun-antics. His "gossiple [is] so delivered in his epistolear, [that it is] buried teatoastally in their Irish stew" (38.23-24). The epistolary gospel of the aged teetotaler-Lear is (almost) totally submerged in the Irish dish whose main ingredients are Shaw and Joyce.

"Annas" and the "Crisscouple... Crosscomplimentary" "Jined"

In the coda of *Methuselah* the Ancient bored with his body is a mutant, and Cain, the prehistoric man, is rejuvenated. Near the end of the *Wake* Joyce introduces Muta and Juva, commenting obscurely on "wolk in process" (609.30) like that of Shaw and Joyce. Muta and Juva are adumbrations of the two Irishmen, although their gibberish is a far cry from the deconstructed dialogue of Bishop "burkeley" (610.12) and Punc Patrick. Patrick congratulates himself and his opposite: "Shamwork, be in our scheining! And let every crisscouple be so crosscomplimentary" (613.10–11). Both crosscomplimentary saint Shaw and sage Joyce, with whom he is crisscoupled in Joyce's crosswords "puzzler," end their works of progress in recirculating water, even though Shaw's Lilith insists that Man and Woman must "press on" to the "vortex freed from matter, to the whirlpool in pure intelligence" (BM 305). Believing that Adam and Eve will "ford" the "last stream that lies between flesh and spirit," Lilith says that the "horrors" of the past are "but an evil dream"—one whose underside and inner psyche Joyce fathoms in the *Wake*'s steam of consciousness. At the end of "The Tragedy of an Elderly Gentleman," the old man about to die on Galway Bay is like Finnegan/H. C. E. at the "site of Salvocean" (623.29). When the Pythoness, avatar of Lilith, appears, *"Her outline flows and waves—she is almost distinct at moments, and again vague and shadowy. . . . larger than life"* (BM 243). With more sound-sense, Joyce reincarnates her as the sinuous sacred river Liffey, Anna Livia Plurabelle, a duplication of Lilith, whom Shaw prefigured with Ann Whitefield, the beautiful bearer of the élan vital. As Shaw wrote, "Every woman is not Ann but Ann is Everywoman" (CP 161)—a suitable mate for "Here Comes Everybody." She should, however, be in a balance of power with man. The proponent of women, was also for equal rights for everybody. In *The Intelligent Woman's Guide to Socialism,* he lauded the Women's Property Act for correcting "monstrous abuses" of women, but admitted that at times it bordered on impropriety because, in trying to protect women, it "overshot the mark and produced a good deal of injustice for men" (219). Joyce apes his political father by referring to "the Married Woman's Impropriety Act" (617.34–35).

Nevertheless, Annas—Shaw's Life Force and Joyce's version of it—inspired both exiled writers. Both Irishmen were devotees of Annas, adumbrations of the pre-celtic earth goddess Danu, spindled with Anu—mother of the Irish gods—as well as the pre-Olympian Greek fertility goddess Diana and the Vedic Danu who represents the waters of life and of heaven. Like the Tuatha de Danaan—children of Dana—Joyce imagines that he and Shaw have entered into kinship as followers of the goddess: the Life Force whom Shaw identified with Ann Whitefield and Dona Ana in *Man and Superman* and whom Joyce identified with Anna Livia. Shaun wonders for himself and Shem "would we go back there now [to "the dawn of protohistory" and to Ireland] . . . for annas and annas?" (169.24–170.1). Other Shaw heroines surface in the *Wake*'s flow as variations of the Life Force: "katya" and "lavinias" (40.11) of *Great Catherine* and *Androcles and the Lion:* "Vivi vienne, little Annchen" (209.34), Mrs. Warren's daughter as a diminutive of Ann Whitefield/Anna Livia; "jenny" (97.35), the artist's wife in The *Doctor's Dilemma* (and also Jenny Patterson, Shaw's first lover); "Essie Shanahan" (27.14), like Essie in *The Devil's Disciple;* the "presainted maid to majesty," Saint Joan (304.22). "Annushka Lutetiavitch" (207.8) derives from Shaw's 1917 play *Annajanska, The Bolshivek Empress* (as does "anni . . . slowjaneska"; 333.4–5) and Mrs. Lutestring of "The Thing Happens," variations of the primal female energy that Shaw celebrated. Issy, her emanation as a young temptress in the *Wake,* interplays with Shaw's Ellie in *Heartbreak House,* who boldly chooses the oldest, wisest, maddest man available in the aging playwright's act of wish fulfillment. A "Goldylocks" like Joyce's "goldylocks" (615.23), Issy, Ellie acts out desires of which the incestuous H. C. E. only dreams. In Joyce's "mamafesta," the "callback mother Guadyanna that was daughter to a Tanner" (294.28–30) is the gaudy, joyful, reauditioning offspring of tenor Joyce (perhaps with John McCormick in the wings) and Shaw's superman Tanner and Ann—a double for Joyce's life-affirming "annyma" (426.3), and "grannyma" (195.4), the soul of creation. "Humperfelt and Anunska, wedded now evermore in annastomoses" (585.22–23), are Shaw's Ann/Annajanska and Joyce's Anna Livia forever united in the triune Shaw as Moses, writer of the Pentateuch, with whom Shem identifies. While Shaw is her "foostherfather" (215.14), he is also Anna Livia, "the queer old skeowsha" (215.12) who includes father, son, and holy Earth Mother. Thus "white stripe, red stripe, washes his fleet in annacrwatter" (135.6). As "Amnisty Ann" she or he "electrifies man" (207.28) in fighting for peace. As "Fanny Urinia" (171.28), she is the muse Urania (Milton's in *Paradise Lost*, hence Shaw's in rewriting it), related to the heroine of *Fanny's First Play*.

Among the names of the great goddess, "Annah the Allmaziful, the Everliving, the Bringer of Plurabilities, haloed be her eve" (104.1–2), are many Shaw heroines: *"Zoo"* of "The Tragedy of an Elderly Gentleman"; *"Barbaras Done to a Barrel Organ"* of *Major Barbara;* "*La Belle Sauvage,*" a name that Shaw gave to Savvy of "The Gospel of the Brothers Barnabas" and to Sweetie of *Too True to be Good* (1932); *"Cleopater,"* the androgynous pater-creator of *Caesar and Cleopatra* and "As Far as Thought Can Reach," as well as of history and Shakespeare's *Anthony and Cleopatra;* and "Eve" and "Snake" (Lilith) of "In the Beginning" (104.20; 105.15–16; 106.16, 29; 107.3) and, of course, the Bible that Shaw wanted to outmode. After listing *"Airy Ann"* (related to Ann Whitefield), the catalogue alludes to the Eternal Female washerwoman—suggesting with its "wash" the Shaw anagram and Shem's nighttime washup. In the wash, women who figured in Shaw's life also surface—"Charlotte" (his wife) as one of "his sole admirers" (51.35); "blanche patch" (83.26) (his secretary), which gives way to "Patche's blank face" (63.5) and "blink patch" (93.4); and "Stella" Campbell (his beloved), regularly adding a dimension to allusions to Swift's Stella. In his peregrinations on Biddy Doran (related to Biddy Undershaft of *Major Barbara,* Chickabiddy Tarleton of *Misalliance,* and possibly Barney Doran of *John Bull's Other Island*), Joyce's narrator seems to allude to Shaw's preposterous prediction that in the distant future human beings will be egg-born. Joyce's "kindly fowl" (112.9), "As a strow will shaw . . . does the wind blague, recting to show the rudess of a robur curling and shewing the fansaties of a frizette" (112.34–36). Biddy apparently, as a straw will show (Shaw), talks "blague"—humbug—in the wind, trying to show the rudeness of a robber (Shem/Joyce) and displaying (in Shaw's idiosyncratic spelling *shew*) the fantasies of a frizzly-haired dimwit. So much for a hen's laying human-sized eggs in the life to come!

The dream debate in *Man and Superman* ends with Ana's declaration "I believe in the Life to come" (Plays 389). Lilith ends *Methuselah* proclaiming that "of Life only is there no end" (BM 305). In Joyce's *ricorso* ALP echoes Shaw's Life Force, thinking "always" that "if I go all goes" (627.14). If she departs, there will be, as Shaw's Lilith believes regarding herself, an end to existence, but while she is perpetually metamorphosed as the life-giver, "all" will continue to "go." In what Joyce called the "Hearasay in paradox lust" (263.L4) of both heretical Irishmen, Anna/Lilith/Anna Livia Plurabelle, not God the father, is the primary creator and sustainer of life—as Shaw wrote, the incarnation of life's "fecundity" (CP 157). Under the aegis of the primordial mother, the cyclical work of progress will go on, sponsored, G. B. S. avers, by Eve's favorite sons, "swapsons" like Shaun and Shem, who are "stolentellers," who "borrow and never pay. . . . They can remember their dreams. They can dream without sleeping. . . . [T]he serpent said that every dream could be willed into creation by those strong enough to believe in it" (BM 91).

Just as the clash of ideas in Shaw's visionary daydream goes back to "Motometusolum" (378.15), as Joyce put it, the nightdream that Joyce willed into creation ends in affirmative synthesis. It promises, "Lo, improving ages wait ye." "Some time very presently now when yon clouds are dissipated . . . the odds are, we shall be hooked and happy, communionistically, among the fieldnights eliceam *elite* of the elect in the land of lost of time" (453.29–33). In the communistic communion of Shaw's elitist Elysian fields of the distant future, the odds are that we shall be happy. The 31, 920 A.D. setting of "As Far as Thought Can Reach" is, indeed, a sunlit glade replete with classic Greek temple—a blissful pagan paradise "of lost of time." There will be "ecumenecal conciliabulum" (496.10), the ecumenical conciliation to which Shaw was committed. In Joyce's *ricorso* ALP is optimistic, willing that "besoms be bosuns" (621.1) because her brooms or bosoms will provide the rigging for the continued watery journey. Bygones will be bygones in "tobecontinued's tale" (626.18), even though "the lausafire has lost" (621.3). The Lucifer who stormed the heavens is, as Benstock observes, "both the louse-of-fire and praise-of-fire (Prometheus providing fire for mankind)." For *laud* is German for louse and Latin for praise (*Joyce Again's* 250). Louse—a bug like the ant, grasshopper, and earwig who frequent the dream—is both the Dedalus whom Joyce identified with Lucifer and Shaw's Devil's Disciple, the self-proclaimed preacher of "Diabolonian Ethics" (CP 744), who lit the way for Joyce.

In the "lausafire," Lamppost Shaw is absorbed in his disciple in a paradigm for the resolution of the anxiety of influence. Having swerved away from his precursor, Joyce anticipates the "Tessera" that, in Harold Bloom's theory expounded in *The Anxiety of Influence,* is "completion and antithesis"—a "token of recognition" that involves "reading the parent-poem as to retain its terms but to mean them in another sense" (14). Joyce coopted Shaw's *Methuselah* but added his own emphasis on quotidian existence, resolving his dreambook without the ascetic Platonism to which the aging Shaw turned. By eating and digesting the father (although Joyce's acidic writing suggests that he got heartburn) in an act of ritual cannibalism, the narrator of the *Wake* takes on the father's vitality and makes him a son and self (reiterating Shaw's belief in self-creation and Stephen's theory of self-generated paternity in *Ulysses*). Throughout the *Wake* Joyce was competing with Shaw while completing him. In Shem's "haunted inkpot" Shaw mixes thoroughly with Joyce, whose self-realization illustrates Harold Bloom's thesis about poetic influence. According to Bloom, the strong poet transforms himself "into a fouled version of himself" and then confounds "the consequence with the figure of the precursor" (62). As Bloom might read him, Joyce is in the state of Satan in "a constant consciousness of dualism, of being trapped in the finite, not just in space (in the body) but in clock-time as well" (32). Envious of Shaw's assertion that eventually we can lose the shackles of the body, Joyce ridiculed the old man's Neoplatonism by emphasizing the flesh as perceived from inside of the prison house of the psyche.

The "*apophrades*, or return of the dead," of which Bloom writes seems to be central to Joyce's haunting, for he playfully confuses the reader, as Bloom notes other anxious writers do, by hinting that, as later writer, he has "himself written the precursor's characteristic work" (16). The complications of the *Wake* arose partly as Joyce's stratagem to co-opt his elected "Poppypap" without getting caught by him. In rebellion against being a clone (except in *Exiles,* where only the subject matter was intended to affront the paternal figure), Shaw's virtuoso pupil created the language of one hundred apter hands that the older writer had wished for, while regressing to childish images—games, fairy tales, evocations of early childhood—in his effort at appropriation without ascription. At least with himself, despite his concluding fear of failure, Joyce achieved what Bloom concludes to be the goal of all "quest romances"—rebegetting himself and becoming his own "Great Original" (64). Bloom writes that where poetic influence is concerned the "movement toward self-realization" is crystallized in Soren Kierkegaard's maxim "He who is willing to work gives birth to his own father" (26)—a maxim that Shaw, like Joyce, propounded and illustrated in his lifework. The fruitful poetic influence derives from "anxiety and self-saving caricature . . . distortion . . . [and] perverse, willful revisionism . . . " (39), of which the *Wake* is a ripe example.

Whereas Bloom stresses that the poet "confronting his Great Original must find the fault that is not there" (31), Joyce found the faults that are there—the digressions, the interminable talk, the delusions of grandeur, the clowning that undercuts seriousness of purpose—and a flaw that Joyce misinterpreted from Shaw's public persona and out of his own psychic need, one that cannot be accurately applied to the private Shaw: a censorious, miserly puritanism. Joyce swerves away from Shaw by satirizing him while loving him, being of two minds about him and packing his ambivalence in his portmanteaus. He loves in Shaw what is missing in himself as well as his mirror image, blurry as it may often be. Shaw and Joyce are a twosome, "twiminds . . . anarch, egoarch, hiresiarch" (188.14–16). Despite his socialism, Shaw affirmed that privately every man, including himself, is an "anarch." His self-inflated public image was that of an "egoarch," and he had always been a self-admitted "hiresiarch" (for hire, late in life, for "cashy" honorariums). *Finnegans Wake* is therefore an ambiguous and ambivalent portrait of Shaw, who, like his covert disciple, created himself against the odds. In the Joycean subconscious, Shaw is very real despite the fact that Joyce tantalizingly obscures his identity. Perhaps the *Wake* is meant to defy the Shaw who wrote, "No man is real until he has been transmuted into a work of art" (Winsten, *Days with Bernard Shaw* 187).

Whatever anxieties Shaw felt, he sublimated them in the rigorous public life and persona that Joyce evokes in Shaun. Richard Dietrich reminded me in a letter that Shaw usually made his anxieties visible. Even his "swerve away from Shakespeare" was "among the most visible swerves of all time." Whereas the socialist playwright and media personality exorcised his devils and paradoxical inconsistencies by putting them on public view and making them into characters in his plays, Joyce sublimated the anxiety of influence by internalizing the Shavian portrait that was public domain and superimposing himself and all of Irish history and myth upon it. In the dreamwork of his nightbook Joyce worked out the literary family romance, redeeming himself while attacking and, ironically, preserving his "Precurser" and finally coming to terms with his psychic imprint. Even though Joyce was more successful in persuading himself that he had completed Shaw than in persuading the public to read his book, in resurrecting the older and opposite Dublin expatriate, he also redeemed himself. As Bloom avers of the pattern of psychological influence that he finds in "the strong poet," "the poetic father has been absorbed into the id, rather than into the superego" (*The Anxiety of Influence* 80), deviating into his own sense of reconciling and happy appropriation, which is in Joyce "At-onement" with the wronged "Precurser."

Wyndham Lewis's description of the self divided against the self no doubt influenced Joyce's conception of the bipolarities of his book: "You can divide a person against himself . . . as the two halves of a severed earwig become estranged and fight with each other when they meet" (68). Bruno, Yeats with his doctrine of the search for the self through one's masks, and Shaw corroborated Joyce's belief that thesis and antithesis can end in psychological synthesis. Although such a dialectic can be found in Bruno and Hegel and in the dialectical materialism of Marx, perhaps the most important dialectic for Joyce filtered through William Blake into Shaw and on to the younger writer. For, like Yeats, Shaw was an admirer of Blake a generation before Joyce discovered him. In rejecting "Nobodaddy," Shaw affirmed the dynamic philosophy of Blake's "Marriage of Heaven and Hell," which is repeatedly illustrated in the *Wake:* "Without contraries is no progression. Attraction and Repulsion, Reason and Energy, Love and Hate, are necessary to Human existence" (*Poems and Prophesies* 43). In Joyce's binary system, Shaw is a major antinomy. His imagination (like Shaw's) rooted in the romantics, Joyce incorporated into his overall structure the Coleridgean strategy of reconciling opposites through the great synthesizing power of imagination, even while creating a language that contains and does not always balance the contraries that it privileges.

Often foreshadowed in the *Wake,* Joyce's assimilation of self and Shaw, Shem and Shaun, is anticipated in the declaration of Shaw's Lilith that she will see "the enemy reconciled" (305) and in the disappearance of Cain, the prototype of fratricidal violence, in the conclusion of *Methuselah.* A marginal note in the geometry lesson of the *Wake* summarizes the movement of both Shaw's Pentateuch and Joyce's Nightletter: "FROM CENOGENETIC DICHOTOMY THROUGH DIAGNOSTIC

CONCILIANCE TO DYNASTIC CONTINUITY" (275.R1). In Joyce's recirculating coda, the self-castigation and Shaw ridicule that often surface in "the last word in stolentelling" (424.35) dissolve, no longer at issue; for like Butt and Taff, who become *"one and the same"* (354.8), the artful dodger becomes one with his "Bigseer" (612.16) "bredder" (620.16), of whom he wrote, "We were in one class of age like to two clots of egg. I am most beholding to him, my namesick" (489.19–20). One "Doblinganger" realizes that the other is "the sneaking likeness of us, faith, me altar's ego . . . for ever cracking quips on himself, that merry, the jeenjakes" (463.6–9). The comic "lausafire" is the "one stable somebody" (107.29) of the secular trinity: *"Three in one, one and three. / Shem and Shaun and the shame that sunders em. / Wisdom's son, folly's brother"* (526.13–15). In *The Adventures of the Black Girl in Her Search for God,* the heroine's trinity is "three in one and one in three"; her trinity is glossed by an Arab whom she meets in her search as "I am the son of my father and the father of my sons and myself to boot" (CP 669). The trinitarian phrase and implications of Joyce's lines are borrowed from Keegan's vision of Ireland in *John Bull's Other Island*—a vision of secular At-one-ment: "In my dreams it is a country where the State is the Church and the Church the people: three in one and one in three. It is a commonwealth in which work is play and play is life: three in one and one in three. It is a temple in which the priest is the worshipper and the worshipper the worshipped: three in one and one in three. It is a godhead in which all life is human and all humanity divine: three in one and one in three. It is, in short, the dream of a madman" (CP 452).

Joyce's mad dream concerns the shame that sundered Shaun/Shaw and Shem/himself, representatives of the two Irelands of the ascendancy Protestants and Irish Catholics—a shame generated when Joyce stole Shaw's plays in Zurich. Joyce's nightmare resolves itself, however, as dawn comes because he has worked through the antagonisms over church, state, and the bipolar humanity that tormented him as a Cartesian mind and body split, a split that Shaw resolved by accepting humankind as divinely androgynous and creatively evolving into higher humanity. In the bifurcations that Joyce finally reconciled through sublimating the shame and folly of his behavior toward his secret "hoary frother," Shaw is throughout his dream, even in its displacements and conversions, probably Joyce's most important father/brother figure, consubstantial Irish father, twin and son/brother. In completing *Finnegans Wake,* Joyce made saint and sage one. In his "suspensive exanimation" "one once meets melts in tother." Joyce's "earsighted view of old hopeinhaven," Shaw, fuses with the vision of the "fargazer" (143.8–26) who looked "As Far as Thought Can Reach." H. C. E.'s sons, "twinminsters, the pro and the con"—one a professional lay minister, the other a con artist, one representing theatrical "Hams," the other the "Shemites" (552.3, 8–9)—melt into the father. In the last cycle of the tour de farce that began in earnest jest to deride and "crib" from the old "fumbledum" "mumbledum" Methuselah of Creative Evolution, the "dielectrick" (322.31) ends in "reunion by the symphysis of their antipathies" (92.10–11) that was foreshadowed early in the text. In *Back to Methuselah* Conrad Barnabas speaks of "an antipathetic symbiosis between thee and the female" (135), and Joyce, his narrator admitting an inordinate desire for the substance of the old, androgynous one from "Dulkey" with whom he agrees "upon the committee of amusance" (616.11, 18), dreams that "contraries reamalgamerge" (49.36).

When the "pujealousties" (350.15) of jealous Shem, tied to his sparring partner, are over, Joyce can accept and empathize with his "doblinganger ... with a sandy whiskers" (490.17–18) like Shaw's. A letter in the *New York Times* (April 19, 1933) corroborated that in 1907 Shaw's hair "was still streaked with enough red to look washed-out sandy" (I&R 276). But the bearded "Pepep . . . in his last tryon to march through the grand tryomphial arch. His reignbolt's shot" (590.9–10). Although the lines suggest sexual failure, they also point to the sense of literary defeat that assailed both aging Irishmen. The reigning Irish playwright wrote Frank Harris that in *Methuselah* he had "shot his last bolt" (September 15, 1920; British Museum Add., ms. 50562, folio 211). While Joyce's admirers—unable to penetrate the *Wake*'s obscurities—began to express skepticism regarding his "Work in Progress," Shaw's admirers began to lose their enthusiasm for the old man's plays. Both the bottomless book of the depth and the deep dramatic cycle had been condemned by their audiences. Joyce shared what he believed was Shaw's private awareness of death, one confirmed by critics such as Arnold Bennett and St. John Ervine. According to Arnold Silver, Shaw's reputation was eclipsed in the early 1930s by his "ostentatious personality," by "his anti-democratic views and by the overweening vanity of

G. B. S.'s public figure" (3), even though in the first decades of the century he was an undisputed "culture hero" (4). Although Silver misses Shaw's Swiftian ironies, the avid press-clipper Joyce could have found evidence for the view that old Shaw was, like H. C. E./ Shaun, "so warried by his bulb of persecussion. . . . [that] To all's much relief one's half hypothesis of that jabberjaw ape . . . was hotly dropped and his room taken up by that odious and still insufficiently malestimated notesnatcher . . . Shem the Penman" (125.16–23). After *Back to Methuselah*, Shaw was dropped (briefly, for *Saint Joan* picked up the torch for him, at least in the 1920s)—persecuted, worried, warred upon for trying to light the way with his drummer's bulb; but the cribbing Shem, aware that his plagiarism was not accurately estimated, had taken up his other half's theory. He hoped that he had superseded his rival in literary fame. In doing so, he tried to pass himself off as prophet instead of disciple. The compensation for his failed ambition, however, seems to have been humbling self-acceptance and reconciliation with the paternal rival in whom Joyce recognized a consanguinity that he felt with no other writer.

Joyce's acceptance of Shaw was well under way by 1932 when he wrote Padraic Colum that he had "received a couple of letters from Yeats and Shaw" (even though there is no evidence of a letter from Shaw). Colum was "surprised to hear he had made a friendly reference to Shaw in his reply—he was no admirer of G. B. S." (Colum and Colum 220). Although "he feels he ought to be asamed of me as me to be ashunned of him," Shem admits, "I am most beholding to him, my namesick" (489.18–20). Unfortunately, however, Joyce could not bring himself to tell his namesake how beholden he was. Although Joyce had criticized Shaw for needing to write prefaces to explain his work and downgraded him for his "absurd" response to *Ulysses* (Colum and Colum 221), Jim/Shem finally identifies, albeit it privately, protected by the *Wake*'s obscurities, with the "farfamed fine Popp amore" (173.22) whom he had ridiculed. Identified as father of "foxold conningnesses" (590.14) like the Mookse, the father becomes both Shaw and Joyce, a "chameleon" "covenanter . . . in his true false heaven colours" (590.7–8). Shem becomes one with his "Grand Precursor" and "frother," spliced with the "jabberjaw" prophet, in whom penman and propagandist meet.

In declaring that Shem's own faulty masterwork is closed, Anna Livia calls upon the composite Lausafire to "Come! Step out of your shell" (621.3–4), apparently in a new egg-birth such as Shaw described in "As Far as Thought Can Reach." ALP also considers, "We might call on the Old Lord, what do you say? . . . His door is always open. For a newera's day. Much as your own is" (623.4–7). If the Old Lord is the creator of "the Platonic garlens" (622.36) like those of the finale of *Methuselah,* he is probably not the Christian God, even though Anna reassures H. C. E. by reminding him that "You invoiced him last Eatster so he ought to give us hot cockles and everything" (623.7–9). There is no evidence that Joyce and Shaw ever exchanged invitations, but perhaps Anna is feeding her husband's imagination. More conventional than H. C. E., she seems to believe that naming and billing the Old Lord will assure rewards, but she (a surrogate for Joyce) may be fantasizing that the Earwickers should visit Shaw or might get an invitation to dine with him at the time when Christians celebrate the resurrection. For the Old Lord who promised "a newera's day" without any last judgment—an open-door policy like the indeterminacy of *Finnegans Wake*—is probably the author of Shaw's book of back to the future—*Back to Methuselah.*

Interested, like the music critic, in Handel and art with a message, Shaun/Shaw had told the *Kunstler* Shem (obsessed also with cunt)— contrary of a "pair of accomplasses"—that, although "You, allus for the kunst and me for omething with a handel to it," their "twain of doubling bicirculars . . . dunloop into eath the ocher! Lucihere!" (295.28–33). When all is done and about to "redoform again" (624.20), the intertextual, Dublin/double, circular histories of Shaun and Shem hereby loop into each other, like one Dunlop tire. Joyce's cyclical text resolves its internal and spiraling dialogues with his diabolonian double by absorbing his dramatic cycle. Although the *Wake,* like the Life Force that it celebrates, resists closure, shadow self and his dialogic antinomy, both "piractical [practical, piratical] jukersmen" (337.23–24), coalesce. Thus *Finnegans Wake* affirms its maker and perhaps the most significant source of its stolentelling, the fellow literary pickpocket whom Joyce loved to hate. As the "phoenix culprit" foreshadowed at the start of his nocturnal ruminations, his "Shamwork" (613.10) "in process" (609.31)—"corrosive sublimation" (185.36), "sibicidal" rivalry (40.31), literary "eatapus complex" (128.36)—interfaces with the work of progress of his chosen Dublin Other, comic genius and fraternal father, their "Doublends [Dublins, double aims and double ends] Jined" (20.16).

A Shaun the Postscript:
"A Commodius Vicus of Recirculation"

IN TEACHING Joyce's *A Portrait of the Artist as a Young Man* in a modern literature class, I warn students that it is the last positive novel that we will read. It makes estrangement into a success story. What comes after is genuine alienation, nihilism, despair, and a criticism to reflect these states. But, as *"The Last Word in Stolentelling"* has illustrated, Shaw and Joyce made fractious family romances and exile from Ireland into success stories as writers. They were not alienated in the same way as the "gloompourers" of their generation and after. Both offered the belief that life is a jest but that telling the truth is the funniest joke of all, especially while Joyce was telling it slant. Even in such behavior, he had the imprimatur of the roguish side of Shaw, who confessed that he belonged to the group of blarney experts "who lie for the sheer love of lying, who forsake everything else for it, who put into it laborious extra touches of art for which there is no extra pay" (GBS 60). Thus the two literary liars were also supreme paradoxists, for in the disguises of jest they told the truth. And in the comic spirit, both were yea-sayers, life affirmers—a tonic in troubled times that were a lot like ours. Like Molly Bloom, both said "yes" in spite of failure.

By the middle of the twentieth century, when Eric Bentley wrote his reassessment of Shaw, the literary giant's reputation had been tarnished.

In musing on Shaw's unpopularity (when the "have been thisworlder" was over ninety), Bentley noted that even his friend William Archer, like D. H. Lawrence, had snidely rejected him in the 1920s, conferring the title of "Grand Old Man" on him before he was seventy. Edmund Wilson—a literary tastemaker—ridiculed him in the 1930s, and later W. H. Auden rejected him because he distrusted his humor as "an admission that his ideas aren't true" (Bentley 193, 191, 202, 218). Shaw got a "bad literary reputation" (191), one that has continued because he became revered by some as a "patriarch" and despised by others as a "senile prodigy" (192). In arguing that "to gain a hearing" he had to act the "privileged lunatic with the license of a jester" (188), Shaw lost his audience in much the same way as Joyce did in the privileged lunacies of the *Wake*'s language. "In order to be influential" Shaw "consented to be notorious" (194), but he failed, Bentley noted, and "precisely because he was so unusually immune to the common frailties of vulgar ambition and rapacious egoism that he could adopt the manner of the literary exhibitionist without risk to his integrity" (193.)

His student and secret surrogate son, who had become a literary exhibitionist in the *Wake,* recognized the "sheer dare" of this rare "zeal of soul of service" and its harlequin mask long before Bentley did. And he identified with Shaw and his failure, for like him, Methuselah had put up the good if quixotic fight, devoting himself unstintingly to his role as writer and gadfly as Joyce devoted himself obsessively to his experiment with language, a deconstructed portrait of himself and the literary father whom he ambivalently admired and subsumed in the *Wake*ian comedy of litters. Through the hoaxes that jokes built, both Irishmen, one always on stage and the other in the closet whose door Joyceans love to open, defended themselves from pain while telling their often socially unacceptable truths in a disguised but amusing form. For the jokesters' pleasure no doubt derived from the admiration that funferal antics gained for the piractical publicman and the envious punman. But when their audiences doubted them, their frustrations erupted in Shaw's public, and Joyce's privately disruptive pronouncements. For both, literary activity was sublimation: Shaw's verbal jousts with society's villains and Joyce's assault on language were cures for self and phallocentric society. For despite his ostensible rejection of Freud (see JJ1 393, 486), Joyce's wily, displaced introjections are an abreaction and cathexis of his chosen imago, and the *Wake* is the reverend redux, redivivus as himself and his rival alter ego. Thus in his late work he deconstructs the primal myth of killing and eating the father to win and merge with the anima, the Life Force which both Irishmen recognized as the female, creative principle. The latent content of Joyce's mad dream of self-and-Shaw analysis is fulfillment of the wish to bash the womanly man in order to consume his substance and thus to reamalgemerge with him. Astutely aware that G. B. S. was his true progenitor, instead of the drunken one in the pub, Joyce admitted his indebtedness in many cunning, devious, and witty jibes in the *Wake*. Although Shaw failed to make a political and philosophical difference in society, he made a difference in his Dublin double, who also fought the sense of failure with sham-antics. Emulating his androgynous precursor, Joyce miscarried in the *Wake,* but not without making a monumental, at times brilliantly comedic, effort to make his mark on literature.

Like the fashionable literary intelligentsia of our time, the literary and critical smart set of the 1920s and 1930s suspected Shaw's saucy, sanguine optimism. Most of Shaw's work, even though a play like *Too True to Be Good* is not hopeful, may not have seemed sufficiently serious, subtle, gloomy, complex, or, in the 1930s, politically correct. Even though it was subversive, his moral earnestness, undercut by his irrepressible humor, was not then and is not now, despite the persistence of dedicated Shavians, de rigueur. Harold Bloom's hostile assessment as editor of an essay collection on Shaw exemplifies the trend by dismissing Shaw as a popularizer (*Modern Critical Views* 1). Yet if we are not inflexibly proud of a negative cultural relativism and a glum distrust of texts, Shaw's ideas are as relevant today as they were to the avant-garde Joyce, who pretended to agree with his admirers in the literary vanguard by sneering at G. B. S. while he was actually pilfering his pronouncements and his public persona. In presenting evidence for thefts from Shaw in *"The Last Word in Stolentelling,"* I have assumed that the lengthy brief can be read fruitfully by "jurors" who are not biased, abstruse theorists who assume that the author, like God, is dead and thus irrelevant to the reading of his texts. For Joyce is very much alive, as Shaw is, in his words, words that cannot disguise the fact that Joyce created a defensive illusion of dislike when, in fact, he was deeply engaged with Shaw but careful to cover up his compulsive concern about the older writer's influence. By midlife the darling of literary modernism was probably a little embarrassed by Shaw's unpopularity with his partisans, his popularity as a diversion for the hoi polloi, and his own guilty secret. The "Red Theatrocrat" seemed like a passé pinko to jaded, elitist, right-wing moderns who turned on modern civilization and relapsed into the self, with Joyce leading the way in his final modernist novels. Shaw's cheerful insouciance was laughter in the dark that appealed to his fellow Irishman, but was to his detractors no doubt as maddening as his vulgar popular appeal and enough to inspire Joyce's pose of public scorn; his private envy; and his cunning recycling of the Shavian message, of which, at bottom, he approved and from which he indeed derived.

Unavoidably, the problem of derivation brings up the literary looting examined in my book as well as the fine line between theft and eminent domain (as Ellmann calls it in his book with that title). Amid the flotsam and jetsam meant to hide while revealing it, the motif of plagiarism surfaces often in the *Wake*. Indeed, Joyce's dreamer fits the profile of the plagiarist, but he is not so careless with other people's property as Joyce's father, who escaped without paying his landlords. The *Wake* narrator torments himself, while he congratulates himself for escaping without paying: he "escapa sansa pagar" (464.11). In surreptitiously rewriting Shaw, Joyce paid him handsomely for the use of his ideas and his persona, but he did not admit that he had burglarized the Shavian household, perhaps because he was aware that his elected relative was as much a thief as he was and perhaps because he feared the consequences of admission of guilt. For literary plagiarism involves the anxiety of influence, as well (usually) as a groundless fear of inadequacy, sometimes brought on by self-destructive behavior like Samuel Taylor Coleridge's drug addiction or Joyce's alcoholism. Indeed, in his study of *Stolen Words*, Thomas Mallon and his informants associate plagiarism with the death wish, as well as with the Oedipal rivalry that informs the *Wake*. But "pelagiarist" punmanship is a mark of respect for its sources, even if they become, as in *Ulysses* and the *Wake*, objects of parody. Mallon observes that the plagiarist may convince himself that the object of theft is guilty of wronging him (31–32); such behavior marks Joyce's relationship to Shaw, in which he blamed the playwright for failing to give him support when he needed it.

Furthermore, because the plagiarist is "both prolific and blocked," like Coleridge, he may resort to using notebooks (Mallon 29), like Joyce's *Scribbledehobble*. Shem's inspiration in the *Wake* is so low that he covets his neighbor's word. Moreover, the plagiarist may feel guilty and invite shame (121): Joyce's dreamer is "aslimed of himself" (506.7) for using his "pelagiarist pen" (182.3) and on nearly every page dares the reader to penetrate his coverup. Shaun accuses him by insisting that "Every dimmed letter of it is a copy." Aware of his "walshbrushup" (340.3), like other literary plagiarists, Shem feels guilt and self-hatred, abhorring himself "vastly" (539.15) for his "stolentelling" (424.35). And no wonder: Shaw often warned against such fraud. His 1913 preface to *The Quintessence of Ibsenism* declared, "Any attempt to alter ... [another writer's work] is simply fraud and forgery" (MCE 27). Such words no doubt prompted the clever forger of *Back to Methuselah* to obscure his alterations. *Stolen Words* reveals, however, that the plagiarist wants to be caught, a fact that keeps rising to the top of the muddy waters of Joyce's stream-of-consciousness. Mallon's observation that the plagiarist is compulsive (128) is corroborated by the fact that the "skill-filled felon" of the *Wake* spent seventeen years grilling himself about his guilt and inventing a language to disguise it. But, according to Mallon, the plagiarist steals what he admires in order to promote his own fame; although the need to appropriate derives from feelings of inadequacy and uncertainty, the most successful plagiarist—an "insufficiently malestimated notesnatcher" (125.21–22) like Joyce—makes the pirated loot his own. Thus, besides being a sourcebook for all sorts of interests—linguistic, historical, and mythic, *Finnegans Wake* is a paradigmatic study of triumphant "stolentelling."

Although Joyce learned the value of heterodoxy from Shaw, he also learned from his "Shavo-Socratic dialogues" not to privilege a single authoritarian voice, aware that no single, univocal system can genuinely assimilate the valences of subjective experience. The indeterminacy of Joyce's fiction, from the impasse structures of his short stories to the circularity of the *Wake,* attests that Joyce also shared what J. L. Wisenthal calls Shaw's "distaste for finality" (9). Furthermore, G. B. S. believed that usable (but not absolute) truth could derive from the clash of opinions. The preface to *The Shewing Up of Blanco Posnet* argues that, instead of being subjected to censorship, everybody should be forced to "read two newspapers, each violently opposed to the other" (CP 435). His secret sharer used such a dialectic (ostensibly borrowed from Bruno) in his tales of Shaun and Shem. In writing out his intertextual relationship to Shaw, *the* media personality of popular culture in his time, Joyce anticipated Mikhail Bakhtin's thesis that consciousness and art are dialogical communications with social context. Moreover, in Joyce's lifelong dialogue with his Irish cultural milieu, he located himself, just as G. B. S. did, left of center. Whereas in the earlier works—*Stephen Hero, Dubliners, Portrait,* and *Exiles*—Shaw unwittingly provided a stabilizing but iconoclastic subtext, in *Ulysses* and *Finnegans Wake* Joyce tiered his Irish experience on the "spindle" of the cumulative past, as Shaw did as early as *Caesar and Cleopatra* and as late as *Back to Methuselah.* Joyce's last two novels dialogue with his polar antithesis, his "popular endphthisis," and his spiritual father, who unwittingly provided a destabilizing, decentering voice essential to Joyce, for whom he presented a challenge and a subject—the anxiety of influence, which at bottom concerns the question of literary parenthood and hence of personal identity. While Joyce's last two novels dare critics to discover internal coherence or to accept their indeterminacy, both reveal to a "factferreter" a Janus face behind and Shavian ideas buried in their texts, which end in reconciliation of the conflicting voices of the "Grand Precurser" and his "discipular" son in the Anna-anima that both found in the female and in themselves. *Ulysses* and the *Wake,* as "my heeders will recoil," sublimate the guilty secret of the Shavian presence and turn it into parody or submerge it in literary debris. Although Joyce seemed supercilious and contemptuous regarding Shaw, when Pound disappeared from his purview, no longer interested in his work because it was too obscure even for him, Joyce was free to let his imagination of his chosen "frother" range anarchically in his wildly duplistic, linguistic night thoughts and to engage him in clever ways to hide the identity of his private parent while simultaneously supplying hints that could lead the reader to the old jester who provided a focus, a target, an "Adversarian" against whom Joyce could measure his own values and skills and against whose wry "saintliness" he did not measure up.

Shaw was the flamboyant, controversial, but unrevengeful cultural commentator of his time, always out on a limb taking potshots at the establishment, and willing to cut off the limb while he perched on it. Shaw's peashooter target practice seemed to delight his less pugnacious admirer, who parodied and poached his politics, sexual and otherwise, in his prose. Unlike his ambivalent disciple, Shaw was a defender of women because, in the view from Dalkey, they seemed so like men. Perhaps because he aimed his barbs at the misogynistic patriarchy (as

Joyce did at phallocentric prose), the reasserted dominance of the masculinist credo of gender polarity in the middle of our century correlated with diminished esteem for Shaw. The assertion of A, the male in *Village Wooing,* that "I am a woman: and you are a man, with a slight difference that doesn't matter except on special occasions" (*Selected One Act Plays* 150) is still a challenge to our concepts of gender. G. B. S.'s idea that the best sort of man is a "womanly man," tested by Joyce in *Ulysses,* remains provocative and instructive. Surely it animated Joyce, for instead of fighting and fearing the female Life Force, Shaw and later Joyce joined it to themselves, recognizing not difference but likeness, even while at times spoofing the idea of androgyny. Despite his intellectual assent on the "woman question," however, Joyce's sexual politics remain paradoxical, for he ambivalently resisted the lessons of the "femininny" master. Despite all of the polarities in the works of both Irishmen, dualities that are typically masculinist, they honor the unifying Life Force who is also the Prankquean. They cross over the duality of gender to understand that all men and women share characteristics and may in one person—especially a sensitive, creative person—effectively consecrate both supposedly masculine and feminine qualities.

Although feminists may object to my conclusion, I believe that the two Irishmen privileged males because they *were* male and because both recognized that patriarchal society valorizes masculinity, thus giving a womanly man more recognition than a manly woman, even though, like Bella Cohen, she may inspire fear and fascination in a sexual context. Shaw's women want to be more like men because men have the power of self-realization that has often been denied to females. Joyce's women, totally conditioned to accept the female role foisted upon them, are, like Molly and ALP, social and psychological constructs—a fact that Joyce exploits in his fictions. Both polymorphous writers seem to champion gender roles which refuse to rank one sex or group over another. Their outlook anticipates Riane Eisler's proposal in *The Chalice and the Blade* that "domination power" should be translated into "actualization power" (28), which is associated with the chalice and hence with woman. Because both Irishmen located the animating creative force in the female, they could be, like other males in the European literary tradition, accused of isolating and using the female as muse, but unlike their predecessors (and many of their successors like Norman Mailer) they located woman in themselves. Without fixing the female in a binary system as the Other and labeling her as either Madonna or whore, Shaw explicitly and Joyce implicitly championed androgyny as the most realistic, the most engaging, and the most creative form of humanity.

As advocates and sometimes parodists of breaking down gender codes, Shaw and Joyce do not fit into the dead white European male mode of the politically correct. But as products (à la French philosopher Hippolyte Taine's mid-nineteenth-century argument) of race, moment, and milieu—an Irish cultural milieu that shares many of the aspects of our own—they illustrate that what we choose in our environment can break or make us. In demoralized Dublin—a microcosm of modern malaise—Joyce chose Shaw, whose *Quintessence of Ibsenism* opened up a whole new way of looking at life. After reading the subversive tract, he became intertextually involved with Shaw, as we all are in the scripts of significant Others. In order to escape the casting he got from family, education, religion, nationality, and ethnicity, he chose his progenitor and mentor. Coming from a family the current self-help movement would call dysfunctional, the young Catholic must have been heartened by his recognition of a model (even a forbidden, notorious one whom he chose in proud defiance and whom his pride forbade naming) who had escaped the constraining ideals that might have acted as nets to prevent his freedom. For, as Joyce's appropriations of Shaw clarify, a surrogate parent can mean all of the difference to a potential victim like Joyce, with a hunger for meaning and ambition to succeed. Shaw often wrote about role modeling—the older, fatherly male teaching the young who is in his plays often a female like Cleopatra, Ellie (in the *Devil's Disciple*), or Eliza Doolittle, but his males often teach parallel males, as Tanner teaches Octavius in *Man and Superman,* as Dick Dudgeon teaches the Reverend Anderson in *The Devil's Disciple,* and as Doyle teaches Broadbent in *John Bull's Other Island,* in which "Father" Keegan preaches to everyone. Joyce seems to have found the Shavian lessons indispensable. Reading *The Quintessence of Ibsenism* must have been as important to the teenager as learning to read was to Frederick Douglass, for in the printed word both found their half-formed ideas—those forbidden by cultural colonization—articulated. If you did not find this process of discovery in *"The Last Word in Stolentelling,"* I suggest that you, like Anna Livia and Finn, begin again, for its subtext concerns the search for meaning when the old verities no longer satisfy and the old institutions have failed us.

Joyce's "silence, exile and cunning" take on new meaning by Shawlight. The younger writer was, except in "washing" his dirty linen by night, silent about perhaps the most significant literary and endogamous, spiritually incestuous psychological relationship of his life. He was probably convinced that the kinship tie was real, that "Seogh" and Joyce were related and were, in all their jests and verbal feats of genius, discarnate kin. But his pride, his literary connections, his need for acceptance (until he threw that need to the whirlwind in the *Wake*), and even perhaps his shyness condemned him to silence while he warily circled the older man, at first by approaching cohorts like William Archer and Grant Richards, then by encouraging others to contact Shaw—Pound, Beach, and finally his daughter Lucia—and by writing to congratulate him for winning the Nobel Prize. For Shaw, the other infamous Dublin exile, was the one man who might have understood him—and perhaps the one man who did, considering that he kept Joyce's congratulatory letter and, in his preface to *Immaturity*, virtually admitted the similarity of their personalities and experiences in Dublin. The reclusive Joyce, who had more time to brood over their kinship than his activist Other self, perceived that they were basically coincident and, in his nocturnal linguistic puzzlings, coalescent.

Surely their ideas were similar, because Joyce reiterated nearly every one that he learned from Shaw and incorporated them in his fiction, where he ambivalently admired them. But his reluctance to reveal the big secret of his indebtedness and his need to cover it up must have made him feel alienated from those around him, who were not Shaw fans or even Shaw readers. While G. B. S. was in the 1920s and 1930s, as he is today, in critical disfavor with the cognoscenti (despite faithful theatergoers and certain loyal readers who reject critical fashions), Joyce privately paddled his canoe against the mainstream. That he held his tongue regarding perhaps the most pervasive and absorbing influence on his work reveals the cunning powerlessness of the secret son who could not reveal his thefts from the strong—and later in Joyce's life, seemingly senile—father's substance because of pride in his own uniqueness; fear that the chosen father would turn his witty but poisoned pen (and perhaps the law) on him if he had an inkling of plagiarism; and duplicity with his supporters, whose disdain nevertheless served Joyce because he could be reasonably certain that they would not have accorded Shaw serious attention. Hence, as secret sharer Joyce was condemned to loneliness and a guilty secret that ate at him, as nightly the "reverend" put the insomniac on trial in his thoughts. Like his secret kinsman he saved himself through laughter, turned upon both himself and his paternal quarry and finally redeeming both through parodic reconciliation.

What Shaw had to say is still worth hearing, despite the image of a whitebearded leprechaun in his dotage that some of us have seen on television, and the way that Joyce said it is still remarkable, provocative, and worth enjoying, with a little help (which I hope this book has provided). When Eric Bentley came to his defense in the 1950s, it was clear that many disparaged Shaw's politics and worldviews because they had been put off from real study of them by Shaw's antic disposition, but Joyce took the trouble to research G. B. S., who was perhaps the ideal subject for an Irishman who, although going blind, was fascinated by the media in which Shaw's antics and opinions were always news. While registering the details of Shaviana, Jim the punman parodied them, recognizing, as Linda Hutcheon does in her *Theory of Parody,* that parody is two-pronged and ambivalent, both ridicule and admiration. Even as he spoofs Shaw, Joyce grudgingly admires him. For both Irishmen realized that only the examined life is worth living, and that the overexamined life is unbearable without humor. Both Irishmen were, as Bentley writes of Shaw, "compelled" to such examination, not just because one wanted to revolutionize the world and the other wanted to revolutionize the word but because their genius required it and their intelligence made them laugh at themselves while urging their audiences to laugh with them.

In this book I have read Joyce through Shaw. My work is about both self-redeeming laughter and self-realization through role modeling, a Shavian theme and the subtext of all of Joyce's appropriations from his literary father. Although skeptics regarding Shaw and those with vested interests in Joyce as an isolated genius primarily interested in language may have read it in preparation to scoff, I hope that the evidence has taken some of the sting out of their bites. I also hope that the book has been read by lay readers, like young Joyce when he first came upon Shaw, who may profit from the example of reading literature for message as well as medium and who seem more and more to need to choose their parent figures in nonbiological models that can be found in literature as well as life. Joyce chose his fugleman well and spent his mental life debating the choice while writing it out in his confessional fictions. As "crosscomplimentary" closet apostle of the Reverend Shaw, he ineluctably recirculated Shavian ideas. My reevaluation of G. B. S. by Joycelight offers readers the opportunity to "learn in time not to despise even the mask, much less Bernard Shaw" (Bentley 219). For this book has tried to show how Joyce preserved, pickled, and recycled Shaw while continually reassessing his adopted twin in critiques that were also rave notices. Indeed, he assimilated Shaw and Shavian ideas in a "commodius vicus of recirculation."

At the end/beginning of the *Wake,* Anna Livia praises "wash" (that is, Shaw)—"Avelaval" (628:6). She sinks to "die down over his feet . . . only to washup" (628:11)—to worship and wash up, to begin again as Shaw/wash insisted we could, with "Finn again!" (628:14). By the Shavian "arclight" (1:13), the one bearing down on her "under whitespread wings like he'd come from Arkangels" seems to be the whitebearded, angelic, and paternal Shaw. Like the "INTELLIGENT WOMAN" imploring the archangellic G. B. S. to guide her toward happiness in an indefinite, utopian future, in her final "washup"-worship ALP seems to interface with the beautiful female of a *Punch* cartoon, "GRADUS AD MILLENIUM" (H3 opposite 85) (although ALP's role is that of a cosmic Lilith, not just a flapper worshiping the angel of "equal incomes"), moving a step toward the millenium courtesy of a benevolent Shavian angel. Such an angel gave the younger Irishman the keys to his intellectual domain and to his fiction: "The keys to. Given!" (628:15). In the subterranean sewage system of Shem's psychic abode, the ample and valuable contents (commodities) of his commode have been flushed and recirculated "by a commodius vicus of recirculation" through the cyclical conduit of Vico ("vicus"). As "quashed" Anglo-Latin, "commodius" goes beyond the idea of recirculating cloacal effusions, for in Latin, as an adjective, it means "fit for a particular purpose" or "appropriate"; and as a noun, it indicates remuneration for services. Thus "commodius" implies Joyce's method and purpose of disguise, appropriate to the coverup of his Shavian source as well as to the paradoxical payback to his paternal mentor framed in the *Wake*'s cubistic portraiture. Furthermore, in multilayered Anglo-Latin, "vicus" suggests "vici," meaning "I conquered" (as Shaw's Caesar had), altered by the English third-person, objective pronoun into "us" and thus a triune triumph. For in Joyce's Desperanto, "vicus" implies the victory of Shem/Shaun and ALP, the "three in one and one in three" trinity that stands for Ireland in *John Bull's Other Island* and for unity of personality—father, son, and anima—in the *Wake*. For Joyce had kept Shaw in his linguistic domain (the Latin *vicus* means "estate" or "country seat") as both the "riverence," the saintly madman whom Patsy (perhaps a Punc Patrick) addresses in Shaw's great Irish comedy, and as the Life Force, both of whom are recycled into the first word of the *Wake*.

The book's incomplete, recirculating last sentence is addressed, it seems, to "riverrun," reverend Shaw and the Liffey—Life Force—both united in the steam of consciousness of Shem the Penman. Shavio-Viconian cyclical theories lead the *Wake*ian voice back to "riverrun," in which the dreck of the water closet has been sanitized, made madly sane, washed up by Shaw, in one of the paradoxes in which both Seoghs delighted. As the keeper of the "Allkey dallkey" wrote, "Whether it be that I was born mad or a little too sane, my kingdom was not of this world: I was at home only in the realm of my imagination" (CP 680). In the demesne of Shem the Penman's imagination, the redeemer of the *Wake* is also a bit mad. On the last page of the *ricorso*, ALP, like Ellie Dunn turning to the old, mad father figure Shotover, turns to "my cold father, my cold mad father" (628:1–2), the chosen father of James Joyce—George Bernard Shaw. "A way a long a last a loved a long the" (628:15–16).

WORKS CITED

Primary Sources

Joyce

"Continuation of a Work in Progress." *transition* 14 (August 1928): 7–27.
The Critical Writings of James Joyce. Edited by Ellsworth Mason and Richard Ellmann. New York: Viking, 1959.
Dubliners. New York: Viking, 1976.
Exiles. Edited by Padriac Colum. New York: Viking, 1951.
Finnegans Wake. New York: Viking, 1959.
The James Joyce Archive: "Ulysses," "Circe," "Eumaeus." Edited by Michael Groden. New York: Garland, 1978.
Letters of James Joyce. Vol. 1. Edited by Stuart Gilbert. New York: Viking, 1957. Vols. 2 and 3. Edited by Richard Ellmann. New York: Viking, 1966.
"Opening Pages of a Work in Progress." *transition* 1 (April 1927): 9–30.
A Portrait of the Artist as a Young Man. New York: Viking, 1964.
Scribbledehobble: The Ur-Workbook for "Finnegans Wake." Edited by Thomas Connolly. Evanston: Northwestern University Press, 1961.
Stephen Hero. New York: New Directions, 1963.
Ulysses. Edited by Hans Gabler et al. New York: Random House, 1986.

Shaw

Back to Methuslah. London: Penguin, 1987.
Bernard Shaw: Collected Letters. 3 vols. Edited by Dan Laurence. New York: Viking, 1985.
Bernard Shaw: Selection of His Wit and Wisdom. Edited by Caroline T. Harnsberger. Chicago: Follett, 1965.
Bernard Shaw: The Diaries. Edited by Stanley Weintraub. University Park: Pennsylvania State University Press, 1986.
The Complete Plays. London: Constable, 1931.
The Complete Prefaces. Includes *The Adventures of the Black Girl in Her Search for God.* London: Paul Hamlyn, 1965.
Essays in Fabian Socialism. Vol. 30 of *Collected Works*. New York: W. H. Wise, 1932.
Everybody's Political What's What. Vol. 21 of *Collected Works*. New York: W. H. Wise, 1932.
Immaturity. Vol. 1 of *Collected Works*. New York: W. H. Wise, 1930.
The Intelligent Woman's Guide to Socialism. Harmondsworth: Penguin, 1982.
The Irrational Knot. Vol. 5 of *Collected Works*. New York: W. H. Wise, 1931.
Love among the Artists. Vol. 3 of *Collected Works*. New York: W. H. Wise, 1930.
Major Critical Essays. London: Penguin, 1986.
The Matter with Ireland. Edited by David H. Greene and Dan Laurence. London: Rupert Hart-Davis, 1962.
Music in London. 3 vols. Vols. 26, 27, and 28 of *Collected Works*. New York: W. H. Wise, 1931.
Our Theatre in the Nineties. Vol. 11 of *Collected Works*. New York: W. H. Wise, 1932.
Platform and Pulpit. Edited by Dan Laurence. New York: Hill and Wang, 1961.
Plays Extravagant. Middlesex: Penguin, 1981.
The Portable Shaw. Edited by Stanley Weintraub. New York: Penguin, 1986.
Selected One Act Plays. Middlesex: Penguin, 1965.
Shaw: Interviews and Recollections. Edited by A. M. Gibbs. Iowa City: University of Iowa Press, 1990.
Sixteen Self Sketches. London: Constable, 1949.
An Unsocial Socialist. Vol. 5 of *Collected Works*. New York: W. H. Wise, 1930.
What I Really Wrote about the War. Vol. 17 of *Collected Works*. New York: W. H. Wise, 1931.

Secondary Sources

Adams, Robert M. *James Joyce: Common Sense and Beyond.* New York: Random House, 1967.

Atherton, James S. *The Books of the Wake.* New York: Viking, 1960.
Attridge, Derek. "Joyce, Jameson, and the Text of History." In *James Joyce 1: "Scribble" 1 genèsedes Textes.* Paris: Minard, 1988.
Beerbohm, Max. *Around Theatres.* New York: Knopf, 1930.
Begnal, Michael H. "The Prankquean in *Finnegans Wake.*" *James Joyce Quarterly* 1 (Spring 1964): 14–18.
Benstock, Bernard. "*Exiles.*" In *A Companion to Joyce Studies,* edited by Zack Bowen and James F. Carens. Westport, Conn.: Greenwood Press, 1984.
———. *Joyce Again's Wake.* Seattle: University of Washington Press, 1965.
———. "The Quiddity of Shem and the Whatness of Shaun." *James Joyce Quarterly* 1 (Fall 1963): 6–33.
Bentley, Eric. *Bernard Shaw.* New York: New Directions, 1957.
Bishop, John. *Joyce's Book of the Dark: "Finnegans Wake."* Madison: University of Wisconsin Press, 1986.
Bloom, Harold. *The Anxiety of Influence.* New York: Oxford University Press, 1973.
———, ed. *Modern Critical Views: George Bernard Shaw.* New York: Chelsea House, 1987.
Bowen, Zack. *"Ulysses" as a Comic Novel.* Syracuse: Syracuse University Press, 1989.
Brown, Malcolm. *The Politics of Irish Literature.* Seattle: University of Washington Press, 1972.
Brown, Richard. *Joyce and Sexuality.* Cambridge: Cambridge University Press, 1985.
Brown, Terence. *Ireland: A Social and Cultural History.* Ithaca: Cornell University Press, 1985.
Burgess, Anthony. *A Shorter "Finnegans Wake."* London: Faber and Faber, 1985.
Butler, Christopher. "Joyce, Modernism, and Postmodernism." In *The Cambridge Companion to James Joyce,* edited by Derek Attridge, 258–82. Cambridge: Cambridge University Press, 1990.
Cahill, Susan, and Thomas Cahill. *A Literary Guide to Ireland.* New York: Scribners, 1973.
Campbell, Joseph, and Henry Morton Robinson. *A Skeleton Key to "Finnegans Wake."* New York: Harcourt, Brace, 1944.
Campbell, Stella (Mrs. Patrick). *My Life and Some Letters.* New York: Dodd, Mead, 1922.
Carpenter, Charles A. *Bernard Shaw and the Art of Destroying Ideals.* Madison: University of Wisconsin Press, 1965.
Chesterton, G. K. *George Bernard Shaw.* New York: Hill and Wang, 1956.
Cheyette, Bryan. " 'Jewgreek is Greekjew': The Disturbing Ambivalence of Joyce's Semitic Discourse in *Ulysses.*" In *Joyce Studies Annual 1992,* edited by Thomas Staley, 32–56. Austin: University of Texas Press, 1992.

Cixous, Helene. *The Exile of James Joyce.* New York: David Lewis, 1972.
Colbourne, Maurice D. *The Real Bernard Shaw.* Toronto: Dent, 1930.
Collins, Ben. "Joyce's Use of Yeats and of Irish History: A Reading of 'A Mother.' " *Eire Ireland* 5 (1970): 45–66.
Colum, Mary, and Padraic Colum. *Our Friend James Joyce.* Garden City, N.Y.: Doubleday, 1958.
Copleston, Frederick. *A History of Philosophy.* Vol. 3. Garden City, N.Y.: Doubleday, 1985.
Costello, Peter. *Leopold Bloom: A Biography.* Dublin: Gill and Macmillan, 1981.
Curtis, S. J. "Nicholas of Cusa." In *A Short History of Western Philosophy in the Middle Ages,* 245–53. Westminster, Md.: Newman Press, 1950.
Davis, Stan Gebler. *James Joyce: A Portrait of the Artist.* London: Davis Poynter, 1975.
Deane, Seamus. *Celtic Revivals.* London: Faber and Faber, 1985.
———. "Joyce the Irishman." In *The Cambridge Companion to James Joyce,* edited by Derek Attridge, 31–54. Cambridge: Cambridge University Press, 1990.
Dietrich, Richard F. *Portrait of the Artist as a Young Superman.* Gainesville: University of Florida Press, 1969.
———. "Shavian Psychology." *Annual of Bernard Shaw Studies* 4 (1984): 149–71.
———. "Shaw and the Uncrucifying of Christ." *Annual of Bernard Shaw Studies* 8 (1988): 13–38.
DuCann, C. G. L. *The Loves of George Bernard Shaw.* New York: Funk and Wagnalls, 1963.
Eckley, Grace. *Children's Lore in "Finnegans Wake."* Syracuse: Syracuse University Press, 1985.
Eisler, Riane. *The Chalice and the Blade.* Cambridge, Mass.: Harper and Row, 1987.
Ellmann, Richard. *The Consciousness of Joyce.* New York: Oxford University Press, 1977.
———. *Eminent Domain.* New York: Oxford University Press, 1967.
———. *James Joyce.* New York: Oxford University Press, 1959.
———. *James Joyce.* New and revised edition. New York: Oxford University Press, 1982.
Evans, T. F., ed. *Shaw: The Critical Heritage.* London: Routledge and Kegan Paul, 1976.
Fergusson, Francis. *The Idea of a Theatre.* Garden City, N.Y. Doubleday, 1953.
Figes, Eva. *Patriarchal Attitudes.* Greenwich, Conn: Fawcett, 1970.
Gainor, J. Ellen. *Shaw's Daughters.* Ann Arbor: University of Michigan Press, 1991.

Gallop, Jame. *The Daughter's Seduction*. London: Macmillan, 1982.
Ganz, Arthur. *George Bernard Shaw*. New York: St. Martin's Press, 1983.
Garvin, John. *Joyce's Disunited Kingdom and the Irish Dimension*. London: Gill and Macmillan, 1976.
Gibbs, A. M. *The Art and the Mind of Shaw*. Dublin: Gill and Macmillan, 1983.
Gifford, Don. *Joyce Annotated*. Berkeley: University of California Press, 1982.
———, with Robert J. Seidman. *"Ulysses" Annotated*. Berkeley: University of California Press, 1988.
Gilbert, Sandra, and Susan Gubar. *The Madwoman in the Attic*. New Haven: Yale University Press, 1979.
———. *No Man's Land*. Vol. 2 of *Sexchanges*. New Haven: Yale University Press, 1989.
Gillespie, Michael Patrick. *Reading the Book of Himself*. Columbus: Ohio State University Press, 1989.
Giuriceo, Marie. Letter commenting on "Balbaccio Balbuccio." From Comparative Literature Department, Brooklyn College, CUNY, 1990.
Glasheen, Adaline. *A Second Census of "Finnegans Wake."* Evanston: Northwestern University Press, 1963.
———. *A Third Census of "Finnegans Wake."* Berkeley: University of California Press, 1977.
Gordon, John. *"Finnegans Wake": A Plot Summary*. Syracuse: Syracuse University Press, 1986.
Gorman, Herbert. *James Joyce*. New York: Farrar & Rinehart, 1948.
Groden, Michael, ed. *The James Joyce Archive: "Ulysses," "Circe," "Eumaeus."* New York: Garland, 1978.
Harris, Frank. *Bernard Shaw: An Unauthorized Biography Based on Firsthand Information*. London: Gollancz, 1931.
Hart, Clive. *Structure and Motif in "Finnegans Wake."* Evanston: Northwestern University Press, 1962.
Haslip, Joan. *Parnell*. New York: Frederick A. Stokes, 1937.
Hayman, David. *The Wake in Transit*. Ithaca: Cornell University Press, 1990.
Heilbrun, Carolyn. *Toward A Recognition of Androgyny*. New York: Knopf, 1973.
Henderson, Archibald. *George Bernard Shaw: Man of the Century*. New York: Appleton-Century-Crofts, 1956.
———. *Bernard Shaw: Playboy and Prophet*. New York: D. Appleton, 1932.
———. *George Bernard Shaw*. Cincinnati: Steward and Kidd, 1911.
Henke, Suzette. *James Joyce and the Politics of Desire*. London: Routledge, 1990.
———, and Elaine Unkeless, eds. *Women in Joyce*. Urbana: University of Illinois Press, 1982.

Herr, Cheryl. *Joyce's Anatomy of Culture*. Urbana: University of Illinois Press, 1986.

Hodgart, Matthew. *James Joyce*. London: Routledge and Kegan Paul, 1978.

Hoffmeister, Adolf. "James Joyce." In *Portraits of the Artist in Exile: Recollections of James Joyce by Europeans*, edited by Willard Potts, 119–36. New York: Harcourt Brace Jovanovich, 1979.

Holroyd, Michael. *Bernard Shaw: The Lure of Fantasy*. New York: Random House, 1990.

———. *Bernard Shaw: The Pursuit of Power*. New York: Random House, 1989.

———. *Bernard Shaw: The Search for Love*. New York: Random House, 1988.

———, ed. *The Genius of Shaw*. New York: Holt, Rinehart, and Winston, 1979.

Howard, Herbert. *The Irish Writers and Nationalism: 1880–1950*. New York: Hill and Wang, 1959.

Hutcheon, Linda. *A Theory of Parody*. New York: Methuen, 1985.

Ibsen, Henrik. *Letters and Speeches*. New York: Hill and Wang, 1964.

Joad, C. E. M. *Shaw*. London: Gollancz, 1949.

Joyce, Stanislaus. *My Brother's Keeper*. New York: Viking, 1958.

Keane, Patrick J. *Yeats, Joyce, Ireland and the Myth of the Devouring Female*. Columbia: University of Missouri Press, 1988.

Kelly, Joseph. "Pound's Joyce." *James Joyce Literary Supplement* (Spring 1993): 21–33.

———. "Stanislaus Joyce, Ellsworth Mason, and Richard Ellmann: The Making of James Joyce." In *James Joyce Studies Annual 1992*, edited by Thomas Staley, 98–140. Austin: University of Texas Press, 1992.

Kenner, Hugh. *Dublin's Joyce*. Bloomington: Indiana University Press, 1956.

Kershner, R. B. *Joyce, Bakhtin, and Popular Culture*. Chapel Hill: University of North Carolina Press, 1989.

Krause, David. *The Profane Book of Irish Comedy*. Ithaca: Cornell University Press, 1982.

Kristeva, Julia. *Desire in Language*. New York: Columbia University Press, 1980.

Lawrence, Karen. *The Odyssey of Style in "Ulysses."* Princeton: Princeton University Press, 1981.

Levin, Harry. *James Joyce: A Critical Introduction*. Norfolk, Conn.: New Directions, 1941.

Lévi-Strauss, Claude. *The Elementary Structures of Family Kinship*, translated by J. H. Bell and J. R. von Sturmer. Boston: Beacon, 1969.

Lewis, Wyndham. *The Essential Wyndham Lewis*, edited by Julian Symons. London: Andre Deutsch, 1984.

Lyons, John Benignus. *James Joyce and Medicine.* Dublin: Dolmen Press, 1973.
MacManus, Seumas. *The Story of the Irish Race.* Old Greenwich, Conn.: Devin-Adair, 1980.
McCarthy, Patrick. "The Structure and Meanings of *Finnegans Wake.*" In *A Companion to Joyce Studies,* edited by Zack Bowen and James F. Carens, 559–632. Westport, Conn.: Greenwood Press, 1984.
McHugh, Roland. *Annotations to "Finnegans Wake."* Austin: University of Texas Press, 1976.
——. *The Sigla of "Finnegans Wake."* Baltimore: Johns Hopkins University Press, 1980.
Maddox, Brenda. *Nora.* Boston: Houghton Mifflin, 1988.
Magalaner, Marvin, and Richard M. Kain. *Joyce: The Man, the Work, and the Reputation.* New York: Collier Books, 1962.
Manganiello, Dominic. *Joyce's Politics.* London: Routledge and Kegan Paul, 1980.
——. "The Politics of the Unpolitical in Joyce's Fictions." *James Joyce Quarterly* 29 (Winter 1992): 241–58.
Meisel, Martin. *Shaw and the Nineteenth Century.* New York: Limelight Editions, 1984.
Mencken, H. L. *George Bernard Shaw: His Plays.* Boston: W. Luce, 1905.
Millett, Kate. *Sexual Politics.* Garden City, N.Y.: Doubleday, 1970.
Moreiras, Alberto. "Pharmaconomy: Stephen and the Daedalids." In *Joyce: The Return of the Repressed,* edited by Susan Stanford Friedman, 58–86. Ithaca: Cornell University Press, 1993.
Morgan, Margery M. *The Shavian Playground.* London: Methuen, 1972.
Nadel, Ira. *Joyce and the Jews: Culture and Texts.* London: Macmillan, 1989.
Nathan, Rhoda B. "Candida and Exiles: The Shaw-Joyce Connection." *Independent Shavian* 29 (1991): 3–11.
Norris, Margot. *The Decentralized Universe of "Finnegans Wake."* Baltimore: Johns Hopkins University Press, 1974.
O'Sullivan, J. Colm. *Joyce's Use of Colors: "Finnegans Wake" and the Earlier Works.* Ann Arbor: University of Michigan Press, 1987.
Paglia, Camille. *Sexual Personae.* New York: Random House, 1991.
Parrinder, Patrick. *James Joyce.* Cambridge: Cambridge University Press, 1980.
Patch, Blanche. *30 Years with G. B. S.* London: Gollancz, 1951.
Pearson, Hesketh. *Bernard Shaw: His Life and Personality.* London: Collins, 1942.
Peters, Margot. *Mrs. Pat: The Life of Mrs. Patrick Campbell.* New York: Knopf, 1984.
Potts, Willard, ed. *Portraits of the Artist in Exile: Recollections of James Joyce by Europeans.* New York: Harcourt Brace Jovanovich, 1979.

Power, Arthur. *Conversations with James Joyce.* Edited by Clive Hart. New York: Harper and Row, 1974.
Restuccia, Frances L. *Joyce and the Law of the Father.* New Haven: Yale University Press, 1989.
Reynolds, Mary T. *Joyce and Dante.* Princeton: Princeton University Press, 1981.
Rodgers, W. R. *Irish Literary Portraits.* New York: Taplinger, 1973.
Rossett, B. C. *Shaw of Dublin.* University Park: Pennsylvania State University Press, 1964.
Sandulescu, C. George. *The Language of the Devil.* Gerrards Cross, Eng.: Colin Smythe, 1987.
Scholes, Robert. "Joyce and Modern Ideology." In *Coping With Joyce,* edited by Morris Beja and Shari Benstock, 91–107. Columbus: Ohio State University Press, 1989.
Scott, Bonnie Kime. *Joyce and Feminism.* Bloomington: Indiana University Press, 1984.
Shechner, Mark. *Joyce in Nighttown: A Psychoanalytic Inquiry into "Ulysses."* Berkeley: University of California Press, 1974.
Showalter, Elaine. *Sexual Anarchy: Gender and Culture at the Fin de Siècle.* New York: Viking, 1990.
Silver, Arnold. *Bernard Shaw: The Darker Side.* Stanford: Stanford University Press, 1982.
Steinberg, Erwin R. "Reading Leopold Bloom/1904 in 1989." *James Joyce Quarterly* 26 (Spring 1989): 397–416.
———. "The Religion of Ellen Higgins Bloom." *James Joyce Quarterly* 23 (Spring 1986): 350–55.
Swarzlander, Susan. "To Learn to Respect Reality: Bernard Shaw's *John Bull's Other Island.*" In *Shaw: The Annual of Bernard Shaw Studies* 8 (1988): 85–96.
Terry, Ellen. *Ellen Terry and Bernard Shaw: A Correspondence.* Edited by Christopher St. John. New York: Putnam's, 1931.
Tindall, William York. *A Reader's Guide to "Finnegans Wake."* New York: Farrar, Straus, and Giroux, 1969.
Ussher, Arland. *Three Great Irishmen: Shaw, Yeats, and Joyce.* London: Gollancz, 1952.
Valency, Maurice. *The Cart and the Trumpet.* New York: Oxford University Press, 1973.
Vico, Giambattista. *The New Science.* Ithaca: Cornell University Press, 1965.
Walzl, Florence. "Dubliners." In *A Companion to Joyce Studies,* edited by Zack Bowen and James F. Carens, 157–228. Westport, Conn: Greenwood Press, 1984.
———. "Dubliners: Women in Irish Society." In *Women in Joyce:* 31–56.

Wardle, Irving. "The Plays." In *The Genius of Shaw*, edited by Michael Holroyd, 143–65. New York: Holt, Rinehart, and Winston, 1979.

Watson, Barbara Bellow. *A Shavian Guide to the Intelligent Woman*. New York: Norton, 1972.

Watson, George. *Politics and Literature in Modern Britain*. Totowa, N.J.: Rowan and Littlefield, 1977.

Weintraub, Stanley. *Journey to Heartbreak House*. New York: Weybright and Talley, 1971.

———. "A Respectful Distance: James Joyce and His Dublin Townsman Bernard Shaw." *Journal of Modern Literature* 13 (March 1986): 61–75.

———. *The Unexpected Shaw*. New York: Frederick Ungar, 1982.

Winsten, Stephen. *Days with Bernard Shaw*. New York: Vanguard Press, 1949.

———, ed. *G. B. S. 90: Aspects of Bernard Shaw's Life and Work*. London: Hutchinson, 1946.

Wisenthal, J. L. *The Marriage of Contraries: Bernard Shaw's Middle Plays*. Cambridge, Mass.: Harvard University Press, 1977.

Woolf, Virginia. *Diaries*. Vol. 2. New York: Harcourt Brace Jovanovich, 1977.

Yeats, William Butler. *The Collected Poems*. New York: Macmillan, 1951.

Zipes, Jack, ed. *Arabian Nights*. New York: Penguin, 1991.

Index

Abbey Theatre, 42, 48, 169, 215, 350, 355, 366
Academy of Irish Letters, 20, 51, 344
Achurch, Janet, 296
Act of Union, 334–35
Adams, Robert, 181, 348
Adrian, Pope (Nicholas Breakspear), 278, 329–36; *Laudabiliter,* 329, 333–34
Adventures of the Black Girl in Her Search for God, The. See Shaw, George Bernard—works
A. E. (George Russell), 22, 132, 250, 253, 255, 387
Aeneid, The (Virgil), 218
Aeschylus, 367; *Oresteaid, The,* 145
Aesop, 329, 336–38
"After the Race." *See* Joyce, James—works
Alacoque, Blessed Margaret Mary, 160
alcoholism, 25–26, 69, 172–87, 213, 388, 390, 392
ALP (Anna Livia Plurabelle; character in *Finnegans Wake*), 89, 95, 274, 284, 291, 293, 324, 328, 346, 395–98, 404, 411–13, 416–17
anarchism, 16, 37–38, 73, 222–25, 227, 400. *See also* Fabian socialism; politics
Androcles and the Lion. See Shaw, George Bernard—works
androgyny, 7, 171, 201–6, 209, 214, 230, 235–36, 258–59, 280, 283, 319, 325, 327, 361, 408, 412–13. *See also* gender
Annajanska, The Bolshevik Empress. See Shaw, George Bernard—works
Anna Karenina (Tolstoy), 135
Anna Livia Plurabelle. *See* ALP
Anthony and Cleopatra (Shakespeare), 312, 397
Anxiety of Influence, The (Harold Bloom), 5, 389–90, 398–400
Apollo, 291. *See also* Ra
Apple Cart, The. See Shaw, George Bernard—works
Aquinas, Saint Thomas. *See* Thomas Aquinas, Saint
Arabian Nights, 126, 128
"Araby." *See* Joyce, James—works

Archer, William, 11, 35, 41, 48, 58, 337, 365, 407, 414
Aristotle, 9, 79, 110, 339–40
Arius, 255
Arms and the Man. See Shaw, George Bernard—works
Arrah-na-Pogue (Boucicault), 270
Art: for art's sake, 13, 49, 62, 64, 66, 79, 283, 290, 310, 314, 342, 405; as religion, 27, 64; as social propaganda, 2–3, 5–6, 8, 13, 38, 41–42, 60, 62–64, 110–13, 283, 405
Asquith, Herbert Henry, 200
Assumption of the Virgin (Titian), 81, 89, 95, 128, 160, 191
Atherton, James, 20, 273, 367
Attridge, Derek, 196
Auden, W. H., 407
autobiography, 22, 56, 265, 269, 274, 340
Aveling, Edward, 106

Back to Methuselah. See Shaw, George Bernard—works
Bacon, Roger, 316
Bakhtin, Mikhail, 17, 411
Bakunin, Mikhail, 37, 73, 222. *See also* anarchism
Balfour, Arthur James, 200
Balzac, Honoré de, 109
Barbarossa, Emperor Frederick, 333
Barnacle, Nora. *See* Joyce, Nora
Barnum, P. T., 64, 376
Barry, Kevin, 352
Bashkirtseff, Marie, 203
Battle of the Boyne, 3
Beach, Sylvia, 50, 272, 339, 414
Beerbohm, Max, 18, 198, 268, 365, 379
Begnal, Michael, 305, 326
Belvedere College, 24
Bennett, Arnold, 347, 403
Benstock, Bernard, 20–21, 92, 271, 273–74, 325, 398
Bentley, Eric, 406–7, 415
Bergson, Henri, 8, 231; *Creative Evolution,* 44

Berkeley, Bishop George, 22, 285, 304–8, 394
Berlitz School, 39
Bernard of Clairvaux, Saint, 216, 350
Bernard Shaw (Frank Harris), 269–71, 273, 284–85, 289, 298, 304, 330, 333, 338–41, 345, 381
Bernard Shaw: Playboy and Prophet (Henderson), 249, 268, 276, 285, 289, 327, 376
"Bernard Shaw's Battle with the Censor." *See* Joyce, James—works
Bernhardt, Sara, 145–46
Besant, Annie, 106, 202, 373; *Our Corner,* 56; *To-Day,* 32, 56
Besant, Reverend Frank, 106
betrayal, 40–41, 43, 47, 90, 99, 105–8, 117, 124, 155, 187, 212, 215, 332, 347–51, 356, 358, 363, 370–71
"Better Than Shakespear?" *See* Shaw, George Bernard—works
Biggar, Joseph, 355, 363
Bishop, John, 393–94
Blake, William, 55, 72, 87–88, 315, 326, 376; "The Marriage of Heaven and Hell," 72, 401
"Blaming the Bard." *See* Shaw, George Bernard—works
Bland, Hubert, 106
"Blarney Castle," 27
"Blessed Damozel, The" (Rossetti), 128
Bloom, Harold, 9, 266, 408; *The Anxiety of Influence,* 5, 389–90, 398–400
Bloom, Leopold (character in *Ulysses*), 7, 46–47, 196–98, 200–201, 203–38, 242, 245, 248–55, 257–59, 314, 356, 358, 361, 363, 369, 371
Bloom, Molly (character in *Ulysses*), 27, 50, 198, 201–4, 207–8, 230, 236–37, 239–49, 251, 253–55, 258–59, 274, 406, 412
"Boarding House, The." *See* Joyce, James—works
Bodkin, Matthias, 356
Bodkin, Michael, 106

Bohemian Girl, The (Michael William Balfe), 164–65, 186
Boswell, James, 267
Boucicault, Dion, 22, 63; *Arrah-na-Pogue*, 270; *The Colleen Bawn*, 2, 7
Bowen, Zack, 17, 196
Brahms, Johannes, 376
Brand (Ibsen), 302
Brandes, Georg, 57
Brehon Laws, 385
British imperialism. *See* Irish nationalism
Broadbent, Tom (character in *John Bull's Other Island*), 39, 148–54, 175, 197, 252, 324, 362, 376, 387, 413
Brown, Richard, 17, 203
Brown, Terence, 123
Browne, Sir Thomas, 18
Browning, Robert, 188
Bruno, Giordono, 9, 289, 293, 304, 401, 410
Bulwar-Lytton, Edward, 123–24
Bunyan, John, 376; *Pilgrim's Progress*, 363
Burke, Edmund, 22, 142, 286
Burke, Thomas, 351
Burns, Robert, 311
Butler, Christopher, 17
Butler, Samuel, 8, 310, 376; *Erewhon*, 354–55
Butt, Isaac, 351
Byatt, A. S., 23
Byron, George Gordon, 30, 77–78, 134; *Don Juan*, 373

Caesar, Julius (character in *Caesar and Cleopatra*), 85, 207–8, 210, 252, 254, 257, 302, 308–14, 316, 320, 346, 364, 376, 381, 416
Caesar and Cleopatra. *See* Shaw, George Bernard—works
Cain (character in *Back to Methuselah*), 266, 275–76, 293, 358–59, 362, 364, 367, 369, 370–72, 375, 386, 401
Calvin, John, 316
Campbell, Joseph, 129; and Joseph Robinson, 305

Campbell, Stella (Mrs. Patrick Campbell; Mrs. Cornwallis-West), 145–46, 202, 271, 288, 294, 299, 335, 340, 355, 373, 383–84, 397; *My Life and Some Letters*, 209
Candida (character in *Candida*), 68, 78, 80–83, 89–100, 102–6, 190–91, 247–48, 293, 324
Candida. *See* Shaw, George Bernard—works
Candide (Voltaire), 80, 273, 276, 289
Captain Brassbound's Conversion. *See* Shaw, George Bernard—works
Carmen (Bizet), 88–92, 104, 107–8
Carpenter, Edward, 203, 251
Carpentier, Georges, 262, 284
Carr, Henry, 260
Carroll, Lewis, 351
Casement, Roger, 215, 271
Cashel Byron's Profession. *See* Shaw, George Bernard—works
Cathleen ni Houlihan (Shan van Vocht). *See* Mother Ireland
Cathleen ni Houlihan (Yeats), 6, 10, 105, 141–42, 144, 191, 213–14
Catholicism. *See* religion
Cavendish, Frederick, 351
Celtic Revival. *See* Celtic Twilight
Celtic Twilight (Celtic Revival; Gaelicism), 7, 38, 41, 66, 78–79, 132–34, 187, 214
censorship, 42–44, 49–50
Chamberlain, Joseph, 227
Chamber Music. *See* Joyce, James—works
Charlemagne, 265
Charles I, 314
Charrington, Charles, 106
Chekhov, Anton, 37, 111, 389, 393
Chesterton, G. K., 13, 87, 224–26, 254, 353, 365, 377
Cheyette, Bryan, 206
Chocolate Soldier, The (Oscar Strauss), 219
Christian Brothers, 154
Christianity. *See* religion
Cicero, 386–87

Circe episode (in *Ulysses*), 198, 207, 222–32, 235–39
Cixous, Hélène, 12, 14–15
Clancy, Sheriff John, 355–56, 359
"Clay." *See* Joyce, James—works
Clongowes Wood, 76
Cohen, Bella (character in *Ulysses*), 200, 222, 231, 235–39, 241, 249, 319, 412
Coleridge, Samuel Taylor, 401, 409
Colleen Bawn, The (Boucicault), 2, 7
Collins, Benjamin, 143

Colum, Mary: and Padraic Colum, 382
Colum, Padraic, 93, 100, 107, 292, 404; and Mary Colum, 382
comedy, 2, 19, 21, 33, 41, 194, 196, 198, 219–20, 266, 317, 326–29, 407
"Come Gather Round Me, Parnellites" (in *The Countess Cathleen*) (Yeats), 61, 144
Confessions (Augustine), 55
Confessions (Rousseau), 55
Connolly, James, 205
Conrad, Joseph, 162
Cornwallis-West, Mrs. *See* Campbell, Stella
corporal punishment, 74–76, 199–200
Cosgrave, Vincent, 106
Costello, Peter, 207
"Counterparts." *See* Joyce, James—works
Count of Monte Cristo, The (Dumas père), 81, 85, 141
creative evolution, 262, 274–75, 281, 303, 315, 317–18, 330, 335, 378, 402–3
Creative Evolution (Bergson), 44
"Crib for Home Rulers, A." *See* Shaw, George Bernard—works: *The Matter with Ireland*
Cromwell, Oliver, 267, 314–15, 349, 359, 362, 364
"Croppy Boy, The," 27
Cuchulain, 213, 382
Culture and Anarchy (Arnold), 34
Curran, J. P., 199
Cyclops episode (in *Ulysses*), 147, 166, 199, 206, 210–15, 222, 348, 351, 361

Daedalus. *See* Icarus
Dana, 141, 251, 395
Dante, 264, 366–68, 370; *The Divine Comedy*, 65, 74, 77, 181, 192–93, 367
Darwinism, 231, 315
Davis, Stan Gebler, 368
Davis, Thomas, 348
Davitt, Michael, 355–56, 367
"Day of the Rabblement, The." *See* Joyce, James—works
"Dead, The." *See* Joyce, James—works
Dead Christ, The (Ribera), 197, 341
Deane, Seamus, 7, 13, 17, 32
Dedalus, Stephen (Joyce character), 6, 9, 11, 26, 28, 30, 32, 47, 55, 69, 71–83, 85–88, 109, 132, 140, 162, 192, 196–98, 201, 204, 206, 209, 231, 240, 247, 251–58, 301, 343, 358, 398
Degeneration (Max Nordau), 13, 267, 275, 331
Deirdre, 83
Dempsey, Jack, 262
De Quincy, Thomas, 96
Dergovilla, 361
Descartes, René, 402
De Valera, Eamon, 21, 279, 332, 385
Devil's Disciple, The. See Shaw, George Bernard—works
Dickens, Charles, 376; *Oliver Twist*, 177
Dietrich, Richard, 30, 50, 82–83, 138, 208, 230, 342, 364
Divine Comedy, The (Dante), 65, 74, 77, 181, 192–93, 367
Doctor's Dilemma, The. See Shaw, George Bernard—works
Doll's House, A (Ibsen), 92, 97, 102, 270
Don Giovanni (Mozart), 27, 231, 256, 374
"Don Giovanni Explains." *See* Shaw, George Bernard—works
Don Juan (John Tanner; character in *Man and Superman*), 31, 60, 64–66, 74, 87, 136, 168–70, 183, 191–92, 197, 204,

229, 236, 241, 242–43, 252–53, 256–57, 270, 273, 287, 289, 293, 298, 325, 335, 365, 372–74, 379, 386–87, 396, 413
Don Juan (Byron), 373
"Don Juan in Hell." *See* Shaw, George Bernard—works: *Man and Superman*
Don Quixote (Cervantes), 198
"Dooleyprudence." *See* Joyce, James—works
Doolittle, Eliza (character in *Pygmalion*), 239, 252, 286, 384, 394, 413
Douglas, Alfred Lord, 352
Douglass, Frederick, 413
Doyle, Sir Arthur Conan, 301, 324
Doyle, Larry (character in *John Bull's Other Island*), 39–40, 68–69, 132–34, 148–49, 151–55, 173–74, 197, 204, 211–13, 252, 324, 350, 413
Dreiser, Theodore, 392
Dresser, Paul, 392
Dubliners. *See* Joyce, James—works
Dudgeon, Dick (Devil's Disciple; Shaw character), 39, 57, 60, 72, 74, 85, 87, 204, 252, 299, 413
Dujardin, Edouard, 9

Earwicker, Humphrey Chimpden (character in *Finnegans Wake*). *See* H. C. E.
"Easter 1916" (Yeats), 215
Easter Rising, 138, 205, 213, 215, 334
Eckley, Grace, 21, 305, 332, 374
Edward VII, 43, 148, 187
Egan, Kevin, 361
Eisler, Riane, 127, 412
Elderly Gentleman (character in *Back to Methuselah*), 278, 280, 291–92, 297, 304, 326–27, 339, 370, 377–78, 383, 395
Eliot, T. S., 4, 18, 132–33, 314, 380, 382
Ellen Terry and Bernard Shaw (Terry), 288
Ellis, Havelock, 17, 251
Ellmann, Richard, 10, 11, 14–17, 21, 38, 45, 49, 195–96, 201, 344, 409

Emmet, Robert, 369
Emperor and Galilean (Ibsen), 161, 302
"Encounter, An." *See* Joyce, James—works
Engels, Friedrich, 67, 238
Epstein, Jacob, 18, 265
Erewhon (Butler), 354–55
Ernani (Verdi), 220
Eros-Thanatos. *See* Romanticism
Ervine, St. John, 18, 267, 346–47, 379, 389, 403
"Et Tu, Healy." *See* Joyce, James—works
Eumaeus episode (in *Ulysses*), 200, 233–35, 356, 358, 361
Euripides, 367
"Eveline." *See* Joyce, James—works
Everybody's Political What's What. *See* Shaw, George Bernard—works
Exiles. *See* Joyce, James—works

Fabian socialism, 16, 37, 44, 47, 61–62, 67, 178–79, 224–29, 232–35, 306, 373–74, 376. *See also* politics; socialism
family, 6, 68–70, 168–69
Fanny's First Play. *See* Shaw, George Bernard—works
Farr, Florence, 296
Faust (Goethe), 236, 266, 296, 317, 320
Faust (Gounod), 317, 320
Feilbogen, Sigmund, 45
Fergus, 132, 382
Ferrero, Guglielmo, 203
Figes, Eva, 136
Finn (Finnegan) MacCool (character in *Finnegans Wake*), 213–14, 265, 275–76, 287, 354, 363, 369, 381–85, 389, 413, 416
Finnegans Wake. *See* Joyce, James—works
Firbolgs, 354
Fitton, Mary, 201
Flaubert, Gustave, 37, 111; *Madam Bovary*, 159; "A Simple Heart," 161
Fortnightly Review, 35, 59
free love. *See* marriage and free love

Freeman's Journal, 66
Freud, Sigmund, 244, 253, 371, 407

Gaelicism. *See* Celtic Twilight
Gainor, J. Ellen, 236, 248
Ganz, Arthur, 252, 254, 257
Garvin, John, 329, 331, 336
"Gas from a Burner." *See* Joyce, James—works
gender, 124, 202, 238, 259, 281, 319, 412. *See also* androgyny; manly man; manly woman (phallic female); mother-right; new woman; patriarchy; woman as victim; womanly man; womanly woman
George, Lloyd, 226
George, Saint, 73, 287
George Bernard Shaw (Henderson), 10, 208, 216, 249, 286, 294, 330, 382
George Bernard Shaw: Man of the Century (Henderson), 233, 258
Geshlect und Charakter (Otto Weininger), 201
Getting Married. See Shaw, George Bernard—works
Ghosts (Ibsen), 11, 18
Gifford, Don, 182; and Robert J. Seidman, 199, 229
Gilbert, Sandra: and Susan Gubar, 237, 248, 259
Gilbert and Sullivan, 281
Gillespie, Michael Patrick, 17
Gladstone, William Ewart, 343, 367
Glasheen, Adeline, 20, 276, 282, 286, 289, 305, 308, 338
Goethe, Johann Wolfgang von, 58, 258, 264; *Faust,* 236, 266, 296, 317, 320
Gogarty, Oliver, 197, 374
Goldman, Emma, 231
Goldsmith, Oliver, 2, 22, 299
Goldwyn, Samuel, 304
Gonne, Maud, 365
Gordon, John, 21, 36, 287–88, 346, 387, 390
Gorman, Herbert, 15, 52, 251, 264–65
"Grace." *See* Joyce, James—works

Grania, 83, 326
Great Catherine. See Shaw, George Bernard—works
Gregory, Lady Augusta, 349
Grigson, Geoffrey, 51–52
Grimm brothers, 325
Gubar, Susan: and Sandra Gilbert, 237, 248, 259
Gulliver's Travels (Swift), 281, 288–89, 333–34, 372, 384, 389
Gurly, Walter (uncle of George Bernard Shaw), 25, 42

Hail and Farewell (George Moore), 112, 214
Hamlet (Shakespeare), 107, 201, 253, 257–58
Handel, George Frideric, 263, 405
Harris, Frank, 18–19, 59, 201, 287, 330, 403; *Bernard Shaw,* 269–71, 273, 284–85, 289, 298, 304, 330, 333, 338–41, 345, 381; *My Life and Loves,* 19, 52
Hart, Clive, 268, 291
Harte, Bret, 190
Hathaway, Ann, 253
Hauptmann, Gerhart, 7; *Michael Kramer,* 135–36
Hayman, David, 325, 377
H. C. E. (Humphrey Chimpden Earweaker; character in *Finnegans Wake*), 18, 21, 261, 268, 270, 276, 278, 280–81, 286, 291, 298, 324–25, 331–32, 336, 343–44, 349, 351, 354, 360–61, 363, 366, 370, 374, 380–94, 403–5
Healy, Timothy M., 141, 356
Heartbreak House. See Shaw, George Bernard—works
Hedda Gabler (Ibsen), 89, 92–93, 160
Hegel, Georg Wilhelm Fredrich, 401
Heilbrun, Caroline, 202
Henderson, Archibald, 18–19, 283; *Bernard Shaw: Playboy and Prophet,* 249, 268, 276, 285, 289, 327, 376; *George Bernard Shaw,* 10, 208, 216, 249, 286, 294, 330, 382; *George*

Bernard Shaw: Man of the Century, 233, 258
Henke, Suzette, 80, 82–83, 141, 143, 146, 159, 217, 326
Henry II, 329, 361
Herr, Cheryl, 17, 373, 375
Higgins, Henry (character in *Pygmalion*), 100, 206–7, 252, 310, 364, 394
Hitler, Adolph, 285, 330
Hodgart, Matthew, 20, 329, 376, 393
Hoffmeister, Adolph, 18
Holroyd, Michael, 31, 78, 106, 235
"Holy Office, The." *See* Joyce, James—works
Homer, 9, 246; *The Odyssey*, 22, 206–8, 218, 220
Home Rule. *See* Irish nationalism
Horus. *See* Lucifer; Ormazd; Ra
Howarth, Herbert, 215–16
How He Lied to Her Husband. See Shaw, George Bernard—works
Hutcheon, Linda, 250, 380, 415

Ibsen, Henrik, 11, 17, 32–37, 57–58, 64, 87, 96–98, 143, 230, 258, 381; *Brand*, 302; *A Doll's House*, 92, 97, 102, 270; *Emperor and Galilean*, 161, 302; *Ghosts*, 11, 18; *Hedda Gabler*, 89, 92–93, 160; *When We Dead Awaken*, 11, 35, 58, 92, 372; *The Wild Duck*, 92
Icarus, 77, 79, 85–88
idealists. *See* tripartite society
"I Dreamt That I Drelt in Marble Halls" (Michael William Balfe), 165, 186
Il Piccolo della Sera, 40, 42
Immaturity. See Shaw, George Bernard—works
Innocent V, Pope, 330
In the Shadow of the Glen (Synge), 350
I Puritani (Vincenzio Bellini), 186
Ireland, 329, 332–37
"Ireland, Island of Saints and Sages." *See* Joyce, James—works
"Ireland at the Bar." *See* Joyce, James—works
Irish cultural revival, 6–7, 132, 138–39, 143–44, 187–88. *See also* Celtic Twilight
Irish Free State, 337
Irish literary revival. *See* Celtic Twilight; Irish cultural revival
Irish nationalism (romantic nationalism), 6–7, 38, 40–41, 46, 65–66, 78–79, 138, 143–45, 147–66, 174, 185, 198–200, 206, 210–16, 306, 334, 361; Home Rule, 78, 149, 153, 271, 287, 332, 334–35, 351, 355. *See also* Celtic Twilight; Cultural revival
Irish People, The (James Stephens), 348
Irrational Knot, The. See Shaw, George Bernard—works
Isolde, 93, 135, 288, 299
"Ivy Day in the Committee Room." *See* Joyce, James—works

"Jack and the Beanstalk" ("Jack the Giant Killer"), 325, 391–92
Jane Eyre (Charlotte Brontë), 55
Jesuits, 25, 54, 75, 154
Jesus Christ, 155, 160, 180–81, 198, 215, 231, 241, 268, 281, 286, 302, 324, 341, 363–64
Jews, 199, 201, 204, 206, 213–15, 277
Joad, C. E. M., 9, 14, 303
Job, 181
John, Augustus, 18
John Bull's Other Island. See Shaw, George Bernard—works
Johnson, Esther (Stella), 383–84
Johnson, Samuel, 267
Jones, Arthur Henry, 198, 297
Jones, Daniel, 310
Jong, Erica, 242
Joyce, George (brother of James Joyce), 10
Joyce, Giorgio (George, son of Nora and James Joyce), 10, 14, 287
Joyce, James: and art for art's sake, 49; and the idea of art as socially redeeming, 42, 110, 112, 113; and Ibsen, 33, 35–36; and Ireland, 40–41; and Shakespeare, 368; on Shaw, 2, 13,

436   Index

Joyce, James—continued
  19, 41–43, 48–50, 52, 64–65, 209, 260, 312, 322–23, 341, 343, 346, 352–53, 404; to Shaw, 50, 342; and his theft of *Dark Lady of the Sonnets* and *Mrs. Warren's Profession,* 314; and World War I, 45–48; and Yeats, 38–39, 41
  —works: "After the Race," 115, 173–75, 187; "Araby," 32, 95, 115, 124–31, 156, 174, 188–89; "Bernard Shaw's Battle with the Censor," 42, 71; "The Boarding House," 114, 155, 165–70, 186; *Chamber Music,* 41, 80, 318, 354, 383; "Clay," 114, 148, 156, 162–65, 186, 190; "Counterparts," 115, 133, 141, 155–56, 175–180, 187; "The Day of the Rabblement," 7, 11; "The Dead," 81, 114–15, 143, 156–57, 185–93, 314; "Dooleyprudence," 44–48; "Drama and Life," 33; *Dubliners,* 1, 6, 8, 17–18, 29, 32, 36, 38–42, 57, 93, 109–193, 260, 289, 318, 411; "An Encounter," 32, 75, 114–15, 120–25, 188, 299; "Et Tu, Healy," 351; "Eveline," 69, 114, 156–62, 186; *Exiles,* 1, 7–8, 17, 19–20, 48–49, 51, 88–108, 197, 206, 252–53, 260, 269, 295, 302, 342, 411; *Finnegans Wake,* 1, 3–4, 8, 14, 18, 19–23, 46–47, 50–53, 78, 89, 95, 202, 209, 228, 252, 261–405, 407–10, 411; "Gas from a Burner," 43, 289, 348; "Grace," 115, 155–56, 161, 180–87; "The Holy Office," 38–39; "Ireland at the Bar," 40; "Ireland, Island of Saints and Sages," 40–41, 67–69, 274, 305; "Ivy Day in the Committee Room," 114–15, 147–55, 187, 347–48; "A Little Cloud," 114, 132–35, 187; "A Mother," 114–15, 138–47, 187; "A Painful Case," 114, 135–38, 187–88; *A Portrait of the Artist as a Young Man,* 1, 6, 18, 28, 30–31, 38, 44, 54–57, 59, 67, 69–88, 148, 162, 192, 240, 343, 348, 351, 358, 361, 406, 411; *Scribbledehobble,* 409; "The Sisters," 115–20, 125, 186, 188; *Stephen Hero,* 1, 6, 13, 18, 30, 37–38, 54–70, 75, 79–80, 159, 368, 411; "Two Gallants," 116, 155–56, 170–72, 186; *Ulysses,* 1, 4, 7, 9, 14, 17–19, 26, 28–29, 38, 46–47, 50–52, 66, 72, 105, 108, 112, 132, 147, 166, 170, 194–259, 261, 270, 272, 276, 281, 287, 289, 290, 302–3, 305, 317, 326, 331–34, 337, 341–43, 347–48, 351, 356, 358, 361, 376, 383, 398–99, 404, 409, 411
Joyce, John Stanislaus (father of James Joyce), 19, 25–26, 334, 353, 358–60, 368, 380, 387, 390
Joyce, Lucia (daughter of Nora and James Joyce), 10, 14, 51, 53, 335, 343, 414
Joyce, May (mother of James Joyce), 25–29, 246, 252, 362
Joyce, Michael, 51
Joyce, Nora (Nora Barnacle; wife of James Joyce), 14, 21, 29–30, 32, 37, 67, 98–99, 106, 161, 189, 191, 207, 209, 243, 253–54, 335, 374
Joyce, Stanislaus (brother of James Joyce), 12–14, 19, 113, 195, 278, 297, 376, 380, 390; *My Brother's Keeper,* 13–14, 24, 32, 270
Julius Caesar (Shakespeare), 309, 312

Kain, Richard. *See* Magalaner, Marvin
Kant, Emmanuel, 373
Keane, Patrick, 143
Keats, John, 96; *Endymion,* 80; "Ode on a Grecian Urn," 310
Keegan (character in *John Bull's Other Island*), 40–41, 65, 152–54, 225–26, 229, 293, 338, 362, 376, 382, 392, 402, 413
Kelly, Joseph, 13
Kenner, Hugh, 141, 267, 382, 387
Kershner, Brandon, 17, 80, 124, 127–28, 142, 162
Kevin, Saint, 304, 378
Kierkegaard, Sren, 399
"Killing for Sport." *See* Shaw, George Bernard—works

King Lear (Shakespeare), 307, 394
Kristeva, Julia, 251

La Fontaine, Jean de, 338
Lalor, Peter, 386
Lamarck, Chevalier de, 315
Larbaud, Valery, 10
Lassalle, Ferdinand, 204
"Lass of Aughrim, The," 189
Laudabiliter (Pope Adrian), 329, 333–34
Laurence, Dan, 3, 262, 340
Lawrence, D. H., 407
Lawrence, Karen, 199, 235, 257
Lee, George Vandeleur, 25–27, 105–6, 239, 254, 256, 318, 357
LeFanu, Sheridan, 22
Leon, Paul Leopold, 52
Leopold the Good, 216
Leslie, Shane, 194
Levin, Harry, 273
Lewis, Wyndham, 21, 305, 312, 318–19, 334, 337, 344, 401; on Shaw, 315–16; on Shaw and Joyce, 334, 345; *Time and Western Man,* 332, 344–45
Liebes tod. See Romanticism
Life Force, 33, 62–63, 85, 92, 95, 136, 161, 163, 185, 188–89, 232, 246–47, 251, 258, 268, 274, 284, 292, 300, 305, 315, 326, 328, 335, 405, 412, 417
Lilith (character in *Back to Methuselah*), 274, 279, 284, 286, 327, 383, 395, 397, 416
Linati, Carlo, 48
Lynd, Robert, 380
"Little Cloud, A." *See* Joyce, James—works
Little Review, 50
London Programme. See Shaw, George Bernard—works
Love among the Artists. See Shaw, George Bernard—works
Lucifer (Satan), 6, 11–12, 31, 61, 64, 71–73, 76, 85, 87, 95, 181, 192, 196, 215, 298, 300, 379, 398, 401, 404
Lunacharsky, Anatoly, 381
Luther, Martin, 316, 346, 386

Lyons, John Benignus, 17
Lytton, Neville, 330

MacDowell, Gerty (character in *Ulysses*), 198, 200, 211, 217–21, 241, 244, 249, 317
MacMurrough, Dermot, 361
Madam Bovary (Flaubert), 159
Maddox, Brenda, 243
Madonna. *See* Virgin Mary
Magalaner, Marvin: and Richard M. Kain, 17, 164, 194
Magna Mater, 206, 246
Mahomet (Mohammed), 290–91, 316
Mailer, Norman, 412
Major Barbara (Shaw character), 87, 183, 239, 254, 281, 283, 373, 396
Major Barbara. See Shaw, George Bernard—works
"Making of the Irish Nation." *See* Shaw, George Bernard—works: *The Matter with Ireland*
Mallon, Thomas, 19, 32, 409–10
Malvern Festival, 286
Man and Superman. See Shaw, George Bernard—works
Mangan, James Clarence, 126–28, 132, 189, 361
Manganiello, Dominic, 16, 21, 64, 195, 222–24, 321, 366–69
Manly Man, 122, 131, 177, 200. *See also* gender
Manly Woman, 102, 124, 171, 198, 200, 203–4, 237–39, 249, 319, 325–26, 412. *See also* gender
Man of Destiny. See Shaw, George Bernard—works
Marchbanks (character in *Candida*), 16, 37, 41, 56, 65, 80–83, 89–90, 93–107, 132–33, 190, 257, 283, 287, 328
Marcus, Steven, 242
Markievitz, Constance (Gore Booth), 365
marriage and free love, 8, 12, 32, 67–69, 80, 165, 170, 228, 238, 386
"Marriage of Heaven and Hell, The" (Blake), 72, 401

Married Woman's Property Act, 395
Mary Magdalen, 95–96, 168
Marx, Eleanor, 106
Marx, Karl, 35, 37, 106, 204, 401
Marxism, 61, 179, 224, 373
Massingham, H. W., 200
Maturin, Charles Robert, 22
Maupassant, Guy de, 109, 111
Maynooth Catechism, 135, 137, 182
"Maxims for Revolutionists." *See* Shaw, George Bernard—works: *Man and Superman*
McAlmon, Robert, 17–18
McCarthy, Desmond, 211, 391
McCarthy, Patrick, 299, 304, 307–8
McCormick, John, 21, 27, 396
McHugh, Roland, 20, 305
McNulty, Edward, 240
Meisel, Martin, 1, 168
Merchant of Venice, The (Shakespeare), 255
Michael Kramer (Hauptmann), 135–36
Michelangelo, 301, 311–12
Milesians, 354
Mill, John Stuart, 67, 238
Millett, Kate, 239
Misalliance. *See* Shaw, George Bernard—works
Mitchell, John, 352–53
Molière, 6, 111, 263
Mommsen, Theodore, 311
Montaigne, Michel Eyquem de, 321
Moore, George, 18, 41, 269, 387; *Hail and Farewell*, 112, 214; *The Untilled Field*, 111–12
Moore, Thomas, 22, 123–25, 199, 327
Moreiras, Albert, 85
Morris, May, 106
Morris, William, 56, 106
Moses, 46, 204, 216, 231, 273, 290, 310, 320, 346, 366–68, 370
"Mother, A." *See* Joyce, James—works
Mother Ireland (Cathleen ni Houlihan; Shan van Vocht), 86, 108, 144–46, 155, 191, 212–13, 326, 328, 379
mother-right, 139. *See also* gender

Mrs. Warren (Shaw character), 231, 239, 245–46
Mrs. Warren's Profession. *See* Shaw, George Bernard—works
Music-Cure, The. *See* Shaw, George Bernard—works
Mussolini, Benito, 285, 330
My Brother's Keeper (Stanislaus Joyce), 13–14, 24, 32, 270
My Heart Laid Bare (Baudelaire), 55
My Life and Loves (Frank Harris), 19, 52

Nadel, Ira, 206
Na Gapoleen, Myles. *See* O'Brien, Flann
Napoleon (Shaw character), 210, 263–65, 279, 313, 319, 328, 361, 365, 371
Nathan, Rhoda, 17, 107
nationalism. *see* Irish nationalism
Nausicaa episode (in *Ulysses*), 200, 209, 217–22
Nesbit, Edith, 106
New Magdalen, The (Collins), 168
New Statesman, 44
New Woman, 95, 140–44, 147, 171, 187, 198, 202–3, 237, 241, 287, 319, 336. *See also* gender
New York Times, 44
Nicholas of Cusa, 316–17
Nietzsche, Frederick, 11, 64, 72–73, 103, 136–37, 197, 284, 312
Nobel Prize, 50, 108, 262, 302, 342, 344, 414
Norris, Margot, 267, 275

O'Bolger, Demetrius, 26
O'Brien, Flann (Brian O'Nolan; Myles Na Gapoleen), 387
O'Brien, William, 356
O'Connell, Daniel, 369–70
Odyssey, The (Homer), 22, 206–8, 218, 220
Oedipal rivalry, 243, 264, 266–67, 275, 368, 405
Oedipus Rex (Sophocles), 368
O'Flaherty, V. C. *See* Shaw, George Bernard—works

Ogham (druidic "alphabet"), 307–8
O'Leary, John, 348
Oliver Twist (Dickens), 177
O'Malley, Grace, 326, 328
"On Diabolonian Ethics." *See* Shaw, George Bernard—works
Oneida community, 228
O'Neill, Shane, 369
O'Noland, Brian. *See* O'Brien, Flann
On the Rocks. *See* Shaw, George Bernard—works
O'Rahilly, Egan, 349
O'Rahilly, The, 349, 359
Orangeman, 3, 328
Oresteaid, The (Aeschylus), 145
Ormazd, 291. *See also* Ra
O'Shea, Kitty, 74, 288, 352, 354–55, 361
Ossian, 382
O'Sullivan, Colm, 328
Othello (Shakespeare), 94
O'Toole, Lawrence, 287
Our Corner (Annie Besant), 56
Our Theatre in the Nineties. *See* Shaw, George Bernard—works
Overruled. *See* Shaw, George Bernard—works
"Ozymandius" (Shelley), 371

Paglia, Camille, 4
Paine, Thomas, 44
"Painful Case, A." *See* Joyce, James—works
Pankhurst, Christabel, 198
Paradise Lost (Milton), 391, 396
"Pardoner's Tale, The" (Chaucer), 182
Parnell, Charles Stewart, 21, 28, 74, 78–79, 141, 147, 150, 155, 198, 215–16, 225, 234, 287, 289, 324, 347–48, 351–61, 363–71, 383
"Parnell Forger, The." *See* Shaw, George Bernard—works: *The Matter with Ireland*
"Parnell's Funeral" (Yeats), 369–70
Parrinder, Patrick, 17
Pascal, Gabriel, 300
Patch, Blanche, 271, 294, 298, 322, 382, 385, 397
paternity, 5–6, 19, 22, 25, 32–33, 52, 55, 66, 68–70, 77, 80, 86–88, 198, 201, 251, 253, 255–59, 301, 325, 398, 402, 404–5, 408, 414–17
patriarchy, 138–42, 145, 161, 177, 195, 412. *See also* gender
Patrich, Bernard, 377
Patrick, Saint, 304–8, 394
Pearse, Padraic, 349, 358–59, 364, 370
Pearson, Hesketh, 45
Peel, Robert, 3
Pélleas et Mélisande (Maurice Maeterlinck), 145–46
Penitent Magdelan, The (Georges de la Tour), 96
Peregrine Pickle (Smollett), 8
Phillips, Stephen, 14
Piggott, Richard, 356–57
Pilgrim's Progress (Bunyan), 363
Pinero, Arthur Wing, 14, 297
plagiarism, 8, 11, 15, 19, 49–50, 229, 263, 272–73, 285, 301–2, 354–55, 359, 405, 408–10
Plato, 110, 306, 398; *The Republic*, 177
Playboy of the Western World (Synge), 169, 326
Plays Pleasant. *See* Shaw, George Bernard—works
Plays Unpleasant. *See* Shaw, George Bernard—works
politics, 16, 195, 222–30, 232–35, 325, 347. *See also* anarchism; Celtic Twilight; Fabian socialism; Irish nationalism; socialism
Portrait of the Artist as a Young Man, A. *See* Joyce, James—works
Pound, Ezra, 4, 9, 12–13, 18, 49–50, 197, 280–82, 290, 330, 339, 341–44, 380, 411, 414
Power, Arthur, 131
Press Cuttings. *See* Shaw, George Bernard—works
Prezioso, Robert, 106

problem play, 36, 94–95
Prometheus, 71–72, 74, 87, 398
Protestantism. *See* religion
Proudhon, Pierre-Joseph, 38, 222, 227. *See also* anarchism

Quest for the Holy Grail, The (Weston), 127
Quinn, John, 49, 262
Quintessence of Ibsen, The. See Shaw, George Bernard—works

Ra, 85–86, 256, 337. *See also* Apollo; Horus; Lucifer; Ormazd
Raina (character in *Arms and the Man*), 36–37, 217–22, 252
Reisman, David, 159
religion, 6, 61, 69; Catholicism and the British Empire, 7, 12, 28, 32, 39–41, 43, 63–65, 75–78, 120, 161, 179–81, 183, 197, 204–5, 209, 211, 229, 327, 364, 375, 386, 404–5; Catholics and Catholicism, 3, 27–28, 32, 40–41, 64–65, 71, 115–20, 161, 180–81, 183–85, 204, 219, 329–30, 363; Protestantism, 3, 70–71, 73, 233; Salvation Army, 180–81, 183, 209
Republic, The (Plato), 177
Restuccia, Frances, 251
"Revolutionist's Handbook." *See* Shaw, George Bernard—works: *Man and Superman*
Reynolds, Mary, 21
Richards, Grant, 13, 41–42, 49, 110, 120, 260, 414
Riders to the Sea (Synge), 49
Roberts, George, 43, 260, 289
Robinson, Joseph: and Joseph Campbell, 305
Rodin, Auguste, 18, 265
Romanticism, 55–60, 68, 90, 109, 125, 134, 185, 191–92, 217, 221, 236, 319; *liebes tod*, 83, 92, 96, 115, 189; romantic love (worship of woman), 6, 65–66, 80, 82, 90–92, 94, 96, 98, 101, 107–8, 191, 196, 218–19

Romeo and Juliet (Shakespeare), 189, 256
Roosevelt, Theodore, 388
Rossett, B. C., 26
Rousseau, Jean-Jacques, 121; *Confessions,* 55
Royce, Edward, 17
Russell, Bertrand, 233, 271
Russell, George. *See* A. E.

Sabellius, 255, 258
Sacher-Masoch, Leopold von, 239
Sacred Allegory, The (Jacopo Bellini), 251
Saint Joan. *See* Shaw, George Bernard—works
Sanity of Art, The. See Shaw, George Bernard—works
Satan. *See* Lucifer
Savonarola, Girolamo, 316
Scholes, Robert, 17, 111
Schopenhauer, Arthur, 136
Scott, Bonnie Kime, 12, 143
Scott, Dixon, 211
Scott, Sir Walter, 123–24, 127, 311
Scribe, Augustin Eugene, 297
Seidman, Robert J., 199, 229; and Don Gifford, 182
"September 1913" (Yeats), 212
Shakespeare, William, 8, 58, 62, 201, 252–53, 255–56, 258, 264, 286, 296, 300, 310, 314, 320, 331, 366–68, 370, 383, 389, 400; *Anthony and Cleopatra,* 312, 397; *Hamlet,* 107, 201, 253, 257–58; *Julius Caesar,* 309, 312; *King Lear,* 307, 394; *The Merchant of Venice,* 255; *Othello,* 94; *Romeo and Juliet,* 189, 256
"Shall Parnell Go?" *See* Shaw, George Bernard—works
Shan van Vocht (Cathleen ni Houlihan). *See* Mother Ireland
Shaun, the Post (character in *Finnegans Wake*), 18–19, 21, 33, 47, 52, 267–68, 270–72, 277–78, 285, 287, 291, 294–97, 299–301, 305–8, 310, 312, 321–

24, 326, 331–32, 335, 344–46, 349, 353, 357, 370, 372–75, 377–78, 384, 389–90, 393, 395, 401–3, 405, 410, 416–17
Shaw, Agnes (sister of George Bernard Shaw), 365
Shaw, Charlotte Townshend (wife of George Bernard Shaw), 52, 67, 202, 288, 299, 346, 374, 386, 397
Shaw, George Bernard (pseudonyms: Cornetto di Bassetto, 256; Don Giovanni, 374; Pshaw, 286; Redbarn Wash, 289; Redburn Wash, 289): and anarchism, 16, 222; and animal slaughter, 122, 206, 250; and anti-idealism, 34, 113, 118, 131, 185; and anti-philistinism, 32, 34, 185; and anti-romanticism (and worship of woman), 34, 57–60, 88, 94, 123, 125–26, 129, 191–92, 219, 221; and art (drama) as religion, 75, 82; and art as socially redeeming, 2–3, 30, 34, 62, 110–11, 113; and autobiography, 21–22, 56, 265; and capitalism (and poverty), 44, 177–78, 225, 228; and Catholicism and the British Empire, 40, 65; and Catholics, 70–71, 223; and corporal punishment, 121, 199–200; and creative evolution, 273, 275, 315; and the "credible hero," 207–8; and "Crosstianity," 64, 118, 179–83, 229, 264; and "Diabolonian ethics," 6, 57, 72; as Don Juan, 31, 374; and drama (problem plays, 34–45, 111; well-made plays, 33, 36); and the Easter Rising, 215; and *Exiles*, 51, 302, 342; and Fabian socialism, 228, 233; and funerals, 372, 381; and Gaelicism, 7, 38, 78, 132, 214; and gender, 201–3, 230, 319, 412–13; and God, 6, 27, 61, 63–64, 76–77; and Home Rule, 2, 45, 78, 153; and the Irish betrayal, 40, 43; and Irish (romantic) nationalism, 6–7, 38, 40, 78, 154–55, 169, 212; and Jesus Christ, 215; and Jews, 199, 204; on Joyce, 50–52, 105, 269, 282, 341; and the Life Force (*see* Life Force); and marriage, 8, 12, 80, 100–101, 106, 165, 228; and parents and children, 75–76, 254–55; and Parnell, 78, 358–59; and plagiarism, 8, 263, 410; and Protestantism, 26–27, 70–71, 223, 269; and realism (facing fact), 34, 74, 114; and school, 121, 298; and Shakespeare, 38, 58, 258; and the "slave" woman as Circe, 243; as a socialist superman, 11, 37, 73, 83, 137, 224; and tripartite society, 113; and *Ulysses*, 28–29, 50–51, 194, 261, 272, 290, 326; and vegetarianism, 250; and the victimization of women, 67, 156, 238; and woman, 249; and womanly man, 200–201, 230; and womanly woman, 80, 141, 161, 183–84, 218; and World War I, 44–45; and Yeats, 7, 38
—works: *The Adventures of the Black Girl in Her Search for God*, 2, 227, 336, 339–40; *Androcles and the Lion*, 207, 210–11, 216, 228, 230, 281, 286, 297, 364, 374, 396; *Annajanksa, The Bolshevik Empress*, 204, 319, 325, 396; *The Apple Cart*, 283, 310, 335; *Arms and the Man*, 36–37, 100, 129, 166, 217–21, 252, 282, 293; *Back to Methuselah*, 20, 46, 216, 227, 262–66, 269–70, 272–74, 284, 288–90, 292, 295–96, 298–301, 303–8, 311, 316, 318–20, 328, 330–33, 338–39, 345–47, 353, 361–63, 366–72, 374, 377–78, 382, 384, 386, 388–92, 394, 398, 401, 403–5, 411 ("In the Beginning" (part 1), 270, 274–77, 375, 384, 388; "The Gospel of the Brothers Barnabas" (part 2), 275–77, 298, 382, 388, 396, 403; "The Thing Happens" (part 3), 227, 277, 298, 388, 396; "The Tragedy of an Elderly Gentleman" (part 4), 2, 198–99, 229, 272, 277–80, 291, 300, 326–27, 339, 370, 377–78, 382, 388, 392, 396; "As Far as Thought Can Reach" (part 5), 268, 273, 280–82, 296, 298, 301, 304, 335, 345, 371–72,

Shaw, George Bernard—*continued*
388–89, 397–98, 402, 404); "Better than Shakespear?" 58; "Blaming the Bard," 258; *Caesar and Cleopatra*, 58, 85, 108, 207–8, 252, 254, 291, 311–12, 314, 321, 337, 396, 411; *Candida*, 7, 16–17, 19, 30, 37–38, 41, 48, 51, 54, 56, 65, 68, 80, 86, 89–108, 132, 160, 190, 206, 252, 257, 260, 287, 293; *Captain Brassbound's Conversion*, 35, 37, 85, 108, 146, 208; *Cashel Byron's Profession*, 16, 30–31, 56, 266, 284, 304, 365; *Common Sense about the War*, 44–47, 226, 364; "A Crib for Home Rulers," 2; *The Dark Lady of the Sonnets*, 15–16, 49, 196, 201, 253, 260–61, 314; *The Devil's Disciple*, 11, 16, 37, 44, 57, 60–61, 63–64, 72, 74, 85, 108, 196, 208, 252, 287, 293, 299–300, 364, 379, 396, 413; "On Diabolonian Ethics" (preface to *Three Plays for Puritans*), 6, 15, 61, 72 (*see also* Lucifer); *The Doctor's Dilemma*, 244, 250, 252, 257, 354, 396; "Don Giovanni Explains," 374; *Essays in Fabian Socialism*, 228, 232; *Everybody's Political What's What*, 235; *Fanny's First Play*, 16, 84, 112, 396; *Getting Married*, 12, 16, 67, 69, 146, 169, 182, 228, 237–38, 353, 387; *Great Catherine*, 279, 283, 396; *Heartbreak House*, 20, 233, 279, 283, 300, 306–7, 336, 347, 383–85, 389, 392–94, 398, 401, 404–5, 417; *How He Lied to Her Husband*, 94, 100–102, 105–7; *Immaturity*, 28, 30, 343; *The Intelligent Woman's Guide to Socialism*, 381, 395; *The Irrational Knot*, 30, 88, 92, 161; *John Bull's Other Island*, 7, 16, 38–41, 43, 63–65, 70, 77–78, 86, 115, 132–33, 143, 147–49, 151–55, 171, 175, 178, 200, 204, 210–13, 223, 225–27, 229, 252, 270, 293, 315, 321, 324, 334, 338, 340, 350, 353–54, 358–59, 362–63, 366, 370, 376, 392, 397, 402, 413, 417; "Killing for Sport," 122, 206; *The London Programme*, 224; *Love among the Artists*, 16, 30, 56; "The Making of the Irish Nation," 2; *Major Barbara*, 16, 44, 74, 100, 118, 171, 173, 176–83, 209, 222–23, 225, 234, 254, 283, 310, 364, 382, 396–97; *Man and Superman*, 2–3, 11–12, 20, 37, 60–61, 74, 168, 173–74, 192, 197, 205, 228, 241–43, 252–53, 256, 269–70, 284, 287–88, 293, 353, 362, 365, 372, 395, 397 ("Don Juan in Hell," 60, 79, 169, 183, 192, 229, 236, 293, 365, 370–71, 373, 413; "Maxims for Revolutionists," 117, 312, 392; "Revolutionist's Handbook," 61, 72–73); *Man of Destiny*, 203, 279, 313, 319, 361; *Misalliance*, 16, 69, 75, 203–4, 254–55, 257, 298; *Mrs. Warren's Profession*, 15–16, 36, 43–44, 49, 67, 146, 165–67, 169, 203, 232, 260–61, 342; *The Music Cure*, 198, 236, 238–39, 242, 319, 383; *O'Flaherty V. C.*, 2, 7, 11, 350–51, 358, 363, 366; *On the Rocks*, 335, 375, 377; *Our Theatre in the Nineties*, 256, 367; *Overruled*, 243; *The Perfect Wagnerite*, 13, 33, 71, 73, 283–84; *The Philanderer*, 12, 67, 100, 170–71, 200–201, 203, 228, 230, 256, 319, 353; *Plays Pleasant*, 41, 110; *Plays Unpleasant*, 41, 110, 113, 131; *Press Cuttings*, 198, 200, 236–39, 242, 319, 365; *Pygmalion*, 8, 21, 97, 100, 146, 202, 207, 252, 310, 364, 384, 394; *The Quintessence of Ibsenism*, 5, 10–11, 13, 16, 28, 34–36, 54, 58, 65, 67–70, 78, 113–15, 120, 156, 161, 167, 170, 183–85, 198, 203, 216–17, 230, 238–41, 287, 302, 329, 372, 380, 410, 413; *Saint Joan*, 20, 291, 298, 305, 330, 341, 345, 364, 374, 403; *The Sanity of Art*, 13, 16, 34, 60–62, 265, 331; *The Shewing Up of Blanco Posnet*, 15–16, 19–21, 42–44, 210, 231, 271, 293–94, 303, 321–24, 327, 352, 355, 385, 410; *The Simpleton of the Unexpected Isles*,

388–89; *Sixteen Self-Sketches*, 24, 56, 252; *Socialism and Superior Brains*, 233–34, 381; *Three Plays for Puritans*, 15, 58, 64, 125–26, 317, 321; *Too True to be Good*, 389, 396, 408; "The Tories and Ireland," 2; *An Unsocial Socialist*, 26, 31–32, 56, 60, 76; *Village Wooing*, 271, 292, 335–36, 412; *Widowers' Houses*, 16, 60, 67, 110–11, 157, 167, 284, 298; *You Never Can Tell*, 254
Shaw, George Carr (father of George Bernard Shaw), 25, 256, 260, 357
Shaw, Lucinda (mother of George Bernard Shaw), 10, 25, 27–29, 169, 239–40, 251–52, 357
Shaw, Lucy (sister of George Bernard Shaw), 10, 69, 225–26
Sheares brothers, 169
Shechner, Mark, 21, 207, 256
Sheehy, Hannah. *See* Sheehy-Skeffington, Hannah
Sheehy-Skeffington, Hannah, 147
Sheela na Gig, 141
Shelley, Percy Bysshe, 55, 60, 78, 96, 229, 264, 366; "Ozymandius," 371
Shem (character in *Finnegans Wake*), 19–22, 47, 52, 264, 267, 273, 281, 283, 285, 289–91, 294–95, 304–5, 307–8, 320, 325, 329, 333, 335, 346–48, 372, 375, 386, 389–90, 393, 396–97, 401–5, 409–10, 416–17
Sheridan, Richard Brinsley, 2, 299, 366
Shewing up of Blanco Posnet, The. See Shaw, George Bernard—works
Shotover (character in *Heartbreak House*), 257, 306, 325, 336, 383–85, 392–93, 417
Showalter, Elaine, 23, 171, 202–3, 333
Siegfried (Wagner), 37, 72–74, 87
Silver, Arnold, 302, 403
"Simple Heart, A" (Flaubert), 161
Simpleton of the Unexpected Isles, The. See Shaw, George Bernard—works
Sirr, Major, 150

"Sisters, The." *See* Joyce, James—works
Sixteen Self-Sketches. See Shaw, George Bernard—works
Skeffington, Francis Sheehy-, 32, 37, 66–68, 147, 233, 271
socialism, 11–12, 31–32, 67, 194–96, 203, 232. *See also* Fabian socialism; politics
Society of Authors, 49, 261, 297
Socrates, 79
Sophocles, 264, 366–68, 370; *Oedipus Rex,* 368
Soul of Man under Socialism, The (Wilde), 196
Sparling, Henry, 106
Stage Society, 48
Stead, William, 21, 203, 332, 374
Steele, Richard, 286
Steinberg, Erwin, 206
Stendhal, 111
Stephen Hero. See Joyce, James—works
Stephens, James, 9, 215, 342; *The Irish People,* 348
Sterne, Laurence, 22, 286, 299, 327
Stirner, Max, 64, 222–23
Story of the Irish Race, The (Seumas MacManus), 306, 369
Sullivan, John, 342
Sutro, Alfred, 14
Svevo, Italo, 9
Swift, Jonathan, 20, 45, 286, 299, 369, 383; epitaph of, 108; *Gulliver's Travels,* 281, 288–89, 333–34, 372, 384, 389; *A Tale of a Tub,* 303
Sykes, Claud W., 14
Synge, John Millington, 299; *In the Shadow of the Glen,* 350; *Playboy of the Western World,* 169, 326; *Riders to the Sea,* 49

Taine, Hippolyte, 413
Tale of a Tub, A (Swift), 303
Tannhäuser (Wagner), 103–4, 120–21
Tennyson, Alfred, 77–78, 297
Terry, Ellen, 202, 209, 214, 271; *Ellen Terry and Bernard Shaw,* 288

Thomas Aquinas, Saint, 9, 79, 250, 316, 339
Three Plays for Puritans. See Shaw, George Bernard—works
Thring, G. Herbert, 261
Time and Western Man (Lewis), 332, 344–45
Times (London), 3
Tindall, William York, 17, 107, 305, 345
Tirso de Molina, 373
To-Day (Annie Besant), 32, 56
Tolstoy, Leo, 7, 87; *Anna Karenina,* 135
Tompkins, Molly, 310
Tone, Wolfe, 6
Tonio Kröger (Mann), 56
Too True to be Good. See Shaw, George Bernard—works
Torah, 265, 300, 346
"Tories in Ireland, The." *See* Shaw, George Bernard—works: *The Matter with Ireland*
Townshend, Charlotte. *See* Shaw, Charlotte
tripartite society: idealists, 6, 13, 32, 34, 37, 65, 70–80, 109, 113–14, 131–33, 135–38, 196 (*see also* Romanticism); philistines, 6, 32, 37, 57–58, 73, 84, 101, 113–14, 119–20, 130, 133, 150, 167–70, 172, 183–86, 204; "realists," 6, 34, 70, 78, 87, 113–14, 131, 185
Tristram, 82, 93, 285, 287, 299
Troubetzkoy, Prince, 265
Tucker, Benjamin, 16, 222–23. *See also* anarchism
Twain, Mark, 18, 328–29
Twelve-Pound Look, The (J. M. Barrie), 48

Ulysses. *See* Joyce, James—works
Undershaft (character in *Major Barbara*), 100, 172, 179, 183, 257, 262, 283, 364
University College, Dublin, 24
Unsocial Socialist, An. See Shaw, George Bernard—works
Untilled Field, The (George Moore), 111–12
Ussher, Arland, 9, 123

Vaertine, Mathilde and Matthias, 203
Valency, Maurice, 330
Vanessa (Esther Vanhomrigh), 383
Velázquez, Diego, 330
Verne, Jules, 297
Vico, Giambattista, 9, 14, 292–93, 298, 300, 338, 381–82, 392, 416
Victoria, Queen, 6
Village Wooing. See Shaw, George Bernard—works
Virgil, 77, 367; *The Aeneid,* 218
Virgin Mary (Madonna), 68, 75, 81–82, 86, 95, 98, 105, 130, 163–64, 176, 191, 218–19, 241, 247, 413. *See also* religion
Voltaire, 328; *Candide,* 80, 273, 276, 289

Wagner, Richard, 11, 27, 33, 35, 83, 103, 253, 322; *Siegfried,* 37, 72–74, 87; *Tannhäuser,* 103–4, 120–21
Walzl, Florence, 143, 146–47
Wardle, Irving, 202
Warren, Vivie (character in *Mrs. Warren's Profession*), 36, 231, 240, 396
Watson, George, 2, 33
Weaver, Harriet, 10, 49, 198, 261, 263–64, 270, 292, 312, 341
Webb, Beatrice, 61, 106, 202
Webb, Sydney, 61, 106
Weintraub, Stanley, 19–20, 32, 51, 56, 282, 341, 343
Wells, H. G., 12, 47, 51, 211, 300, 309, 315
West, Rebecca, 45
When We Dead Awaken (Ibsen), 11, 35, 58, 92, 372
Whitefield, Ann (Dona Ana) (character in *Man and Superman*), 78, 89, 168, 241, 247, 253, 284, 305, 324, 336, 386, 391, 395, 397
"Who Goes with Fergus" (Yeats), 132
Widowers' Houses. See Shaw, George Bernard—works

Wild Duck, The (Ibsen), 92
Wilde, Oscar, 2, 17, 22, 41, 196, 271, 286, 299, 346, 351–53, 358–60, 363, 366, 368–69, 383; *The Soul of Man Under Socialism,* 196
William of Orange, 3
Wilson, Edmund, 407
Winsten, Stephen, 365
Wisenthal, J. L., 150, 410
Wollstonecraft, Mary, 67, 142
woman as victim, 156–59, 162–65, 171, 186. *See also* gender
womanly man, 124, 171, 200–201, 205–8, 230–31, 235, 249, 259, 412. *See also* gender
womanly woman, 80, 82, 131, 138–39, 141, 158–59, 161–63, 165, 183–85, 198, 200, 202, 217–21, 230, 238, 241, 245, 319. *See also* gender
woman suffrage, 198, 239

Wood, Grant, 349
Woolf, Virginia, 18
Wordsworth, William, 78, 135–36, 234
Wyndham's Land Act, 149, 227–28

Yeats, William Butler, 6, 9, 22, 34, 38–39, 41, 48, 51, 60, 64, 82, 87, 205, 221, 286, 344, 348, 366, 382, 387–88, 401, 404; *Cathleen ni Houlihan,* 6, 10, 105, 141–42, 144, 191, 213–14; "Come Gather Round Me, Parnellites" (in *The Countess Cathleen*), 61, 144; "Easter 1916," 215; "Parnell's Funeral," 369–70; "September 1913," 212; and Swift's epitaph, 108; "Who Goes With Fergus," 132
You Never Can Tell. See Shaw, George Bernard—works

Zola, Émile, 111

OHIO UNIVERSITY LIBRARY

Please return this book as soon as you have finished with it. In order to avoid a fine it must be returned by the latest date stamped below. All books are subject to recall after two weeks or immediately if needed for reserve.

JUN 1 3 2008
RECEIVED

JUN 1 8 2008

CF